T0188907

Lecture Notes in Artificial Intelligence   12678

Subseries of Lecture Notes in Computer Science

Series Editors

Randy Goebel
University of Alberta, Edmonton, Canada
Yuzuru Tanaka
Hokkaido University, Sapporo, Japan
Wolfgang Wahlster
DFKI and Saarland University, Saarbrücken, Germany

Founding Editor

Jörg Siekmann
DFKI and Saarland University, Saarbrücken, Germany

More information about this subseries at http://www.springer.com/series/1244

Wolfgang Faber · Gerhard Friedrich ·
Martin Gebser · Michael Morak (Eds.)

Logics in Artificial Intelligence

17th European Conference, JELIA 2021
Virtual Event, May 17–20, 2021
Proceedings

 Springer

Editors
Wolfgang Faber ⓘ
University of Klagenfurt
Klagenfurt, Austria

Gerhard Friedrich ⓘ
University of Klagenfurt
Klagenfurt, Austria

Martin Gebser ⓘ
University of Klagenfurt
Klagenfurt, Austria

Michael Morak ⓘ
University of Klagenfurt
Klagenfurt, Austria

ISSN 0302-9743   ISSN 1611-3349 (electronic)
Lecture Notes in Artificial Intelligence
ISBN 978-3-030-75774-8   ISBN 978-3-030-75775-5 (eBook)
https://doi.org/10.1007/978-3-030-75775-5

LNCS Sublibrary: SL7 – Artificial Intelligence

This Springer imprint is published by the registered company Springer Nature Switzerland AG
The registered company address is: Gewerbestrasse 11, 6330 Cham, Switzerland

Preface

This volume contains the proceedings of the 17th European Conference on Logics in Artificial Intelligence, which was to take place at the University of Klagenfurt, Austria, but due to the COVID-19 pandemic was held as an online event during May 17–20, 2021.

The European Conference on Logics in Artificial Intelligence (or Journées Européennes sur la Logique en Intelligence Artificielle—JELIA) began back in 1988, as a workshop, in response to the need for a European forum for the discussion of emerging work in this field. Since then, JELIA has been organized biennially, with proceedings published in the Springer series *Lecture Notes in Artificial Intelligence*. Previous meetings took place in Roscoff, France (1988), Amsterdam, The Netherlands (1990), Berlin, Germany (1992), York, UK (1994), Évora, Portugal (1996), Dagstuhl, Germany (1998), Málaga, Spain (2000), Cosenza, Italy (2002), Lisbon, Portugal (2004), Liverpool, UK (2006), Dresden, Germany (2008), Helsinki, Finland (2010), Toulouse, France (2012), Madeira, Portugal (2014), Larnaca, Cyprus (2016), and Rende, Italy (2019).

The aim of JELIA is to bring together active researchers interested in all aspects concerning the use of logics in artificial intelligence to discuss current research, results, problems, and applications of both theoretical and practical nature. JELIA strives to foster links and facilitate cross-fertilization of ideas among researchers from various disciplines, among researchers from academia and industry, and between theoreticians and practitioners. The scientific community has been increasingly showing interest in JELIA, which during the years featured the growing participation of researchers from outside Europe and a very high overall technical quality of contributions; hence, the conference turned into a major biennial forum and a reference for the discussion of approaches, especially logic-based, to artificial intelligence.

JELIA 2021 received 68 submissions in two different formats (long and short papers). Throughout the reviewing process, at least three Program Committee members took care of each work. Out of the 68 submissions, 27 long and 3 short papers were accepted, amounting to an acceptance rate of 44%, which is comparable to previous JELIA conferences. Of the accepted papers, 13 were declared to be student papers (21 submitted), 5 to be system papers (6 submitted), and 1 to be an application paper (4 submitted) by the authors upon submission.

We would like to thank the members of the Program Committee and the additional reviewers for their efforts to produce fair and thorough evaluations of the submitted papers, the local organization committee, and of course the authors of the scientific papers, including those not accepted for publication. The quality of the contributions was very high, which is the essential ingredient for a successful scientific conference.

The conference program included invited talks by Thomas Eiter, Esra Erdem, and Alessandra Russo, and had prizes for the Best Paper and Best Student Paper, each received a prize money of EUR 500, kindly offered by Springer. We are grateful to all sponsors for their generous support: Förderverein Technische Fakultät, Springer, and of course the University of Klagenfurt. Last, but not least, we thank the people of EasyChair for providing resources and a marvellous conference management system.

March 2021   Wolfgang Faber
                                                                          Gerhard Friedrich
                                                                          Martin Gebser
                                                                          Michael Morak

Organization

Program Chairs

Wolfgang Faber   University of Klagenfurt, Austria
Gerhard Friedrich   University of Klagenfurt, Austria
Martin Gebser   University of Klagenfurt, Austria and TU Graz, Austria

Program Committee

Jose Julio Alferes	Universidade NOVA de Lisboa, Portugal
Mario Alviano	University of Calabria, Italy
Grigoris Antoniou	University of Huddersfield, UK
Carlos Areces	Universidad Nacional de Córdoba, Spain
Franz Baader	TU Dresden, Germany
Peter Baumgartner	CSIRO, Australia
Leopoldo Bertossi	Universidad Adolfo Ibáñez, Chile
Armin Biere	Johannes Kepler University Linz, Austria
Alexander Bochman	Holon Institute of Technology, Israel
Bart Bogaerts	Vrije Universiteit Brussel, Belgium
Gerhard Brewka	Leipzig University, Germany
Pedro Cabalar	University of A Coruña, Spain
Marco Calautti	University of Trento, Italy
Francesco Calimeri	University of Calabria, Italy
Giovanni Casini	ISTI-CNR, Italy
Lukas Chrpa	Czech Technical University in Prague, Czech Republic
Mehdi Dastani	Utrecht University, The Netherlands
Thomas Eiter	Vienna University of Technology, Austria
Esra Erdem	Sabanci University, Turkey
Eduardo Fermé	Universidade da Madeira, Portugal
Michael Fisher	University of Manchester, UK
Sarah Alice Gaggl	TU Dresden, Germany
Michael Gelfond	Texas Tech University, USA
Laura Giordano	Università del Piemonte Orientale, Italy
Lluis Godo	IIIA-CSIC, Spain
Markus Hecher	Vienna University of Technology, Austria
Tomi Janhunen	Tampere University, Finland
Gabriele Kern-Isberner	Technische Universität Dortmund, Germany
Sébastien Konieczny	CRIL-CNRS, France
Roman Kontchakov	Birkbeck, University of London, UK
Jérôme Lang	Université Paris-Dauphine, France
Joao Leite	Universidade NOVA de Lisboa, Portugal
Vladimir Lifschitz	University of Texas at Austin, USA

Emiliano Lorini	IRIT, France
Thomas Lukasiewicz	University of Oxford, UK
Ines Lynce	Universidade de Lisboa, Portugal
Marco Maratea	University of Genoa, Italy
Pierre Marquis	Institut Universitaire de France, France
Loizos Michael	Open University of Cyprus, Cyprus
Angelo Montanari	University of Udine, Italy
Michael Morak	University of Klagenfurt, Austria
Manuel Ojeda-Aciego	University of Malaga, Spain
Magdalena Ortiz	Vienna University of Technology, Austria
David Pearce	Universidad Politécnica de Madrid, Spain
Luís Moniz Pereira	Universidade NOVA de Lisboa, Portugal
Rafael Peñaloza	University of Milano-Bicocca, Italy
Andreas Pieris	University of Edinburgh, UK
Henri Prade	IRIT-CNRS, France
Francesco Ricca	University of Calabria, Italy
Chiaki Sakama	Wakayama University, Japan
Torsten Schaub	University of Potsdam, Germany
Michael Thielscher	University of New South Wales, Australia
Mirek Truszczynski	University of Kentucky, USA
Mauro Vallati	University of Huddersfield, UK
Ivan Varzinczak	Artois University and CNRS, France
Carlos Viegas Damásio	Universidade NOVA de Lisboa, Portugal
Joost Vennekens	Katholieke Universiteit Leuven, Belgium
Toby Walsh	University of New South Wales, Australia
Antonius Weinzierl	Vienna University of Technology, Austria
Frank Wolter	University of Liverpool, UK
Stefan Woltran	Vienna University of Technology, Austria
Leon van der Torre	University of Luxembourg, Luxembourg

Additional Reviewers

Stefan Borgwardt	Elena Mastria
Johannes K. Fichte	Seemran Mishra
Pietro Galliani	Anna Rapberger
John Goulermas	Javier Romero
Xiaowei Huang	Amanda Vidal Wandelmer
Rafael Kiesel	Philipp Wanko
Patrick Koopmann	Prudence Wong
Jan Maly	Jessica Zangari

Organizing Committee

Markus Blauensteiner

Mohammed El-Kholany

Michael Morak

Anna Otti

Philipp Pobaschnig

Haya Majid Qureshi

Konstantin Schekotihin

Christine Seger

Alice Tarzariol

Pierre Tassel

Erich Teppan

Petra Wiesner

Contents

Argumentation

Belief Revision

Reasoning about Actions, Causality, and Change

Constraint Satisfaction

Description Logics and Ontological Reasoning

Non-classical Logics

Logic Programming and Answer Set Programming

Argumentation

Graph-Classes of Argumentation Frameworks with Collective Attacks

Wolfgang Dvořák[iD], Matthias König[(✉)][iD], and Stefan Woltran[iD]

Institute of Logic and Computation, TU Wien, Vienna, Austria
{dvorak,mkoenig,woltran}@dbai.tuwien.ac.at

Abstract. Argumentation frameworks with collective attacks (SETAFs) have gained increasing attention in recent years as they provide a natural extension of the well-known abstract argumentation frameworks (AFs) due to Dung. Concerning complexity, it is known that for the standard reasoning tasks in abstract argumentation, SETAFs show the same behavior as AFs, i.e. they are mainly located on the first or second level of the polynomial hierarchy. However, while for AFs there is a rich literature on easier fragments, complexity analyses in this direction are still missing for SETAFs. In particular, the well-known graph-classes of acyclic AFs, even-cycle-free AFs, symmetric AFs, and bipartite AFs have been shown tractable. In this paper, we aim to extend these results to the more general notion of SETAFs. In particular, we provide various syntactic notions on SETAFs that naturally generalize the graph properties for directed hypergraphs, and perform a complexity analysis of the prominent credulous and skeptical acceptance problems for several different widely used semantics.

Keywords: Abstract argumentation · Complexity · SETAF · Collective attacks

1 Introduction

Formal argumentation provides formalisms to resolve conflicts in potentially inconsistent or incomplete knowledge, which is essential to draw conclusions of any kind in such a setting. In this context, argumentation frameworks (AFs), introduced in the influential paper by Dung [5], turned out to be a versatile system for reasoning tasks in an intuitive setting. In AFs we view arguments just as abstract entities, represented by nodes in a directed graph, independent from their internal structure. Conflicts are modeled in form of attacks between these arguments, constituting the edges of said graph representation. Different semantics have been defined for AFs and deliver sets of arguments that are jointly acceptable given the topology of attacks in the AF at hand. However, by their limited syntax it is hard to formalize certain naturally occurring statements in AFs, which is why various generalizations of the standard formalism have been proposed, see, e.g. [1]. One such generalization extends the syntax by *collective attacks*, i.e. a construction where a set T of arguments attacks an

© Springer Nature Switzerland AG 2021
W. Faber et al. (Eds.): JELIA 2021, LNAI 12678, pp. 3–17, 2021.
https://doi.org/10.1007/978-3-030-75775-5_1

argument h, but no proper subset of T does; the resulting class of frameworks is often referred to as *SETAFs*. The underlying structure of SETAFs then is a *directed hypergraph*. When they introduced SETAFs [23], Nielsen and Parsons argued that collective attacks naturally appear in various contexts, e.g. when languages are not closed under conjunction. In fact, in certain settings standard AFs require artificial additional arguments and attacks, while the same setting can be natively represented in SETAFs. These observations have been backed up by recent practically driven investigations [25]. Moreover, SETAFs have been proven to be strictly more expressive than AFs, as shown in [11] by means of signatures. In spite of these advantages, there has not yet been much work on computational aspects of SETAFs. The general complexity of the most common reasoning tasks has been investigated in [12], where also an implementation of a solver for SETAFs with answer-set programming has been introduced. Moreover, algorithmic approaches for SETAFs have been studied in [16,22].

The main aim of this paper is to deepen the complexity analysis of [12] which has shown that the complexity of SETAFs coincides with the results for classical AFs in general. In particular, this means that reasoning in many popular semantics is on the first or second level of the polynomial hierarchy. To still achieve manageable runtimes with large instances, the approach we shall take in this paper is to restrict the syntax of SETAFs. We propose certain constraints on the hypergraph structure such that the induced class of frameworks is easy to reason on (i.e. the problems in question are computable in *polynomial time*). On AFs this approach turned out to be fruitful: we say an AF is acyclic, symmetric, or bipartite, if its attack relation is, respectively. The thereby obtained graph classes are *tractable fragments* of AFs [2,6,7,10]. Even though there exist translations from SETAFs to AFs [20,24], it is not at all clear whether tractability results for AFs carry over to SETAFs. This is due to the fact that these translations can lead to an exponential blowup in the number of arguments; moreover certain structural properties are lost in the translation.

In what follows, we thus focus on defining graph properties for SETAFs "from scratch" - these can then be checked and exploited without a detour via AFs. Our main contributions can be summarized as follows:

- Novel definitions for graph classes of directed hypergraphs: these notions are conservative generalizations (i.e. in the special case of AFs they coincide with the respective classical notions) of well known properties of directed graphs such as acyclicity, symmetry, bipartiteness and 2-colorability. As a byproduct of the detailed analysis we state certain syntactical and semantical properties of SETAFs within these classes.
- We pinpoint the complexity of credulous and skeptical reasoning in the respective graph classes w.r.t. seven widely used argumentation semantics, that is admissible, grounded, complete, preferred, stable, stage, and semi-stable [12,20,23]. We provide (efficient) algorithms to reason on these computationally easy frameworks, and give negative results by providing hardness results for classes that yield no computational speedup.

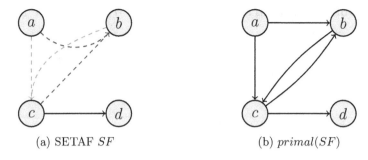

(a) SETAF *SF*   (b) *primal(SF)*

Fig. 1. An example SETAF and its primal graph.

– We establish the status of *tractable fragments* for the classes acyclicity, even-cycle-freeness, primal-bipartiteness, and self-attack-free full-symmetry. In fact, we not only show that these classes are easy to reason in, but the respective properties can also be recognized efficiently. This result allows one to perform such a check as a subroutine of a general-purpose SETAF-solver such that the overall asymptotic runtime is polynomial in case the input framework belongs to such a class.

Note that some proofs are not given in full length, they are available in a technical report [13].

2 Preliminaries

2.1 Argumentation Frameworks

Throughout the paper, we assume a countably infinite domain $\mathfrak{A}$ of possible arguments.

Definition 1. *A SETAF is a pair $SF = (A, R)$ where $A \subseteq \mathfrak{A}$ is finite, and $R \subseteq (2^A \setminus \{\emptyset\}) \times A$ is the attack relation. For an attack $(T, h) \in R$ we call T the* tail *and h the* head *of the attack. SETAFs (A, R), where for all $(T, h) \in R$ it holds that $|T| = 1$, amount to (standard Dung) AFs. In that case, we usually write (t, h) to denote the set-attack $(\{t\}, h)$.*

Given a SETAF (A, R), we write $S \mapsto_R a$ if there is a set $T \subseteq S$ with $(T, a) \in R$. Moreover, we write $S' \mapsto_R S$ if $S' \mapsto_R a$ for some $a \in S$. We drop subscript R in $\mapsto_R$ if there is no ambiguity. For $S \subseteq A$, we use S_R^+ to denote the set $\{a \mid S \mapsto_R a\}$ and define the range *of S (w.r.t. R), denoted $S_R^\oplus$, as the set $S \cup S_R^+$.*

Example 1. Consider the SETAF $SF = (A, R)$ with $A = \{a, b, c, d\}$ and $R = \{(\{a, b\}, c), (\{a, c\}, b), (\{c\}, d)\}$. For an illustration see Fig. 1a - the dashed attacks are collective attacks.

Table 1. Extensions of the example SETAF SF from Example 1.

σ	$\sigma(SF)$
cf	$\{\emptyset, \{a\}, \{b\}, \{c\}, \{d\}, \{a,b\}, \{a,c\}, \{a,d\}, \{b,c\}, \{b,d\}, \{a,b,d\}\}$
adm	$\{\emptyset, \{a\}, \{a,b\}, \{a,c\}, \{a,b,d\}\}$
com	$\{\{a\}, \{a,c\}, \{a,b,d\}\}$
grd	$\{\{a\}\}$
$pref/stb/stage/sem$	$\{\{a,c\}, \{a,b,d\}\}$

We will now define special 'kinds' of attacks and fix the notions of redundancy-free and self-attack-free SETAFs.

Definition 2. *Given a SETAF $SF = (A, R)$, an attack $(T, h) \in R$ is redundant if there is an attack $(T', h) \in R$ with $T' \subset T$. A SETAF without redundant attacks is redundancy-free. An attack $(T, h) \in R$ is a self-attack if $h \in T$. A SETAF without self-attacks attacks is self-attack-free.*

Redundant attacks can be efficiently detected and then be omitted without changing the standard semantics [17,24]. In the following we always assume redundancy-freeness for all SETAFs, unless stated otherwise. The well-known notions of conflict and defense from classical Dung-style-AFs naturally generalize to SETAFs.

Definition 3. *Given a SETAF $SF = (A, R)$, a set $S \subseteq A$ is conflicting in SF if $S \mapsto_R a$ for some $a \in S$. A set $S \subseteq A$ is conflict-free in SF, if S is not conflicting in SF, i.e. if $T \cup \{h\} \not\subseteq S$ for each $(T, h) \in R$. $cf(SF)$ denotes the set of all conflict-free sets in SF.*

Definition 4. *Given a SETAF $SF = (A, R)$, an argument $a \in A$ is defended (in SF) by a set $S \subseteq A$ if for each $B \subseteq A$, such that $B \mapsto_R a$, also $S \mapsto_R B$. A set $T \subseteq A$ is defended (in SF) by S if each $a \in T$ is defended by S (in SF).*

The semantics we study in this work are the grounded, admissible, complete, preferred, stable, stage and semi-stable semantics, which we will abbreviate by *grd, adm, com, pref, stb, stage* and *sem* respectively [12,20,23].

Definition 5. *Given a SETAF $SF = (A, R)$ and a conflict-free set $S \in cf(SF)$. Then,*

- $S \in adm(SF)$, *if S defends itself in SF,*
- $S \in com(SF)$, *if $S \in adm(SF)$ and $a \in S$ for all $a \in A$ defended by S,*
- $S \in grd(SF)$, *if $S = \bigcap_{T \in com(SF)} T$,*
- $S \in pref(SF)$, *if $S \in adm(SF)$ and there is no $T \in adm(SF)$ s.t. $T \supset S$,*
- $S \in stb(SF)$, *if $S \mapsto a$ for all $a \in A \setminus S$,*
- $S \in stage(SF)$, *if $\nexists T \in cf(SF)$ with $T_R^{\oplus} \supset S_R^{\oplus}$, and*
- $S \in sem(SF)$, *if $S \in adm(SF)$ and $\nexists T \in adm(SF)$ s.t. $T_R^{\oplus} \supset S_R^{\oplus}$.*

Table 2. Complexity for AFs and SETAFs (C-c denotes completeness for C).

	grd	*adm*	*com*	*pref*	*stb*	*stage*	*sem*
$Cred_\sigma$	P-c	NP-c	NP-c	NP-c	NP-c	Σ_2^P-c	Σ_2^P-c
$Skept_\sigma$	P-c	trivial	P-c	Π_2^P-c	coNP-c	Π_2^P-c	Π_2^P-c

For an example of the extensions of a SETAF see Table 1. The relationship between the semantics has been clarified in [12,20,23] and matches with the relations between the semantics for Dung AFs, i.e. for any SETAF SF:

$$stb(SF) \subseteq sem(SF) \subseteq pref(SF) \subseteq com(SF) \subseteq adm(SF) \subseteq cf(SF) \quad (1)$$
$$stb(SF) \subseteq stage(SF) \subseteq cf(SF). \quad (2)$$

The following property also carries over from Dung AFs: For any SETAF SF, if $stb(SF) \neq \emptyset$ then $stb(SF) = sem(SF) = stage(SF)$.

2.2 Complexity

We assume the reader to have basic knowledge in computational complexity theory[1], in particular we make use of the complexity classes L (logarithmic space), P (polynomial time), NP (non-deterministic polynomial time), coNP, Σ_2^P and Π_2^P. For a given SETAF $SF = (A, R)$ and an argument $a \in A$, we consider the standard reasoning problems (under semantics σ) in formal argumentation:

- Credulous acceptance $Cred_\sigma$: Is the argument a contained in at least one σ extension of SF?, and
- Skeptical acceptance $Skept_\sigma$: Is the argument a contained in all σ extensions of SF?

The complexity landscape of SETAFs coincides with that of Dung AFs and is depicted in Table 2. As SETAFs generalize Dung AFs the hardness results for Dung AFs [2,4,8,9,18,19] (for a survey see [10]) carry over to SETAFs. Also the same upper bounds hold for SETAFs [12]. However, while the complexity results for AFs can be interpreted as complexity w.r.t. the number of arguments $|A|$, the complexity results for SETAFs should be understood as complexity w.r.t. $|A| + |R|$ (as $|R|$ might be exponentially larger than $|A|$).

3 Graph Classes

The directed hypergraph-structure of SETAFs is rather specific and to the best of the authors' knowledge the hypergraph literature does not provide generalizations of common graph classes to this kind of directed hypergraphs. Thus we first

---

[1] For a gentle introduction to complexity theory in the context of formal argumentation, see [10].

identify such generalizations for SETAFs for the graph classes of interest. Then, we show the tractability of acyclicity and even-cycle-freeness (the latter does not hold for stage semantics) in SETAFs, and that odd-cycle-freeness lowers the complexity to the first level of the polynomial hierarchy as for AFs. Then, we adapt the notion of symmetry in different natural ways, only one of which will turn out to lower the complexity of reasoning as with symmetric AFs. Finally, we will adapt and analyze the notions of bipartiteness and 2-colorability. Again we will see a drop in complexity only for a particular definition of this property on hypergraphs. All of the classes generalize classical properties of directed graphs in a way for SETAFs such that in the special case of AFs (i.e. for SETAFs where for each attack (T, h) the tail T consists of exactly one argument) they coincide with said classical notions, respectively. Finally, we will argue that these classes are not only efficient to reason on, but are also efficiently recognizable. Hence, we can call them *tractable fragments of argumentation frameworks with collective attacks*.

When defining these classes we will use the notion of the *primal graph*, an implementation of the hypergraph structure of a SETAF into a directed graph. An illustration is given in Fig. 1.

Definition 6. *Given a SETAF $SF = (A, R)$. Then its* primal graph *is defined as* $primal(SF) = (A', R')$, *where* $A' = A$, *and* $R' = \{(t, h) \mid (T, h) \in R, t \in T\}$.

3.1 Acyclicity

Akin to cycles in AFs, we define cycles on SETAFs as a sequence of arguments such that there is an attack between each consecutive argument.

Definition 7. *A cycle C of length $|C| = n$ is a sequence of pairwise distinct arguments $C = (a_1, a_2, \ldots, a_n, a_1)$ such that for each a_i there is an attack (A_i, a_{i+1}) with $a_i \in A_i$, and there is an attack (A_n, a_1) with $a_n \in A_n$. A SETAF is* cyclic *if it contains a cycle (otherwise it is* acyclic*),* even-cycle-free *if it contains no cycles of even length, and* odd-cycle-free *if it contains no cycles of odd length.*

Note that a SETAF SF is acyclic if and only if its primal graph $primal(SF)$ is acyclic. It can easily be seen that acyclic SETAFs are well founded [23], i.e. there is no infinite sequence of sets $B_1, B_2, \ldots$, such that for all i, B_i is the tail of an attack towards an argument in B_{i-1}. As shown in [23], this means grounded, complete, preferred, and stable semantics coincide. Moreover, as therefore there always is at least one stable extension, stable, semi-stable and stage semantics coincide as well, and the lower complexity of $Cred_{grd}$ and $Skept_{grd}$ carries over to the other semantics. Together with the hardness from AFs, we immediately obtain our first result.

Theorem 1. *For acyclic SETAFs the problems $Cred_\sigma$ and $Skept_\sigma$ for $\sigma \in \{grd, com, pref, stb, stage, sem\}$ are* P-complete. *Moreover $Cred_{adm}$ is* P-complete.

For AFs we have that the absence of even-length cycles forms a tractable fragment for all semantics under our consideration but stage. The key lemma is that every AF with more than one complete extension has to have a cycle of even length [9]. This property also holds for SETAFs, which in turn means even-cycle-free SETAFs have exactly one complete extension, namely the grounded extension, which is then also the only preferred and semi-stable extension. Our proof of this property follows along the lines of the respective known proof for AFs. Moreover, the grounded extension is the only candidate for a stable extension, and thus for reasoning with stable semantics it suffices to check whether the grounded extension is stable. Finally, note that the hardness of $Cred_{stage}$ and $Skept_{stage}$ carries over from AFs (cf. [10]) to SETAFs.

Theorem 2. *For even-cycle-free SETAFs the problems $Cred_\sigma$ and $Skept_\sigma$ for $\sigma \in \{com, pref, stb, sem\}$ are P-complete. Moreover the problem $Cred_{adm}$ is P-complete, the problem $Cred_{stage}$ is Σ_2^P-complete, and the problem $Skept_{stage}$ is Π_2^P-complete.*

For odd-cycle free SETAFs the situation is just like with odd-cycle-free AFs [8]. If there is a sequence of arguments $(a_1, a_2, \dots)$, we say a_1 *indirectly attacks* the arguments a_{2*i-1} and *indirectly defends* the arguments a_{2*i} for $i \geq 1$ (cf. [23]). As odd-cycle-free SETAFs are *limited controversial* [23], i.e. there is no infinite sequence of arguments such that each argument indirectly attacks and defends the next, they are coherent, i.e. stable and preferred semantics coincide, and therefore we experience a drop of the complexity to the first level of the polynomial hierarchy.

Theorem 3. *For odd-cycle-free SETAFs the problems $Cred_\sigma$ for $\sigma \in \{adm, stb, pref, com, stage, sem\}$ are NP-complete, problems $Skept_\sigma$ for $\sigma \in \{stb, pref, stage, sem\}$ are coNP-complete, and the problems $Cred_{grd}$, $Skept_{grd}$, and $Skept_{com}$ are P-complete.*

3.2 Symmetry

In the following we provide two generalizations of symmetry[2] for SETAFs. The first definition via the primal graph is inspired by the notion of counter-attacks: an AF $F = (A, R)$ is symmetric if for every attack $(a, b) \in R$ there is a counter-attack $(b, a) \in R$. As we will show, the corresponding definition for SETAFs is not sufficiently restrictive to lower the complexity of the reasoning problems in questions, except for a fast way to decide whether an argument is in the grounded extension or not. For an illustration of the following definitions see Fig. 2.

Definition 8. *A SETAF $SF = (A, R)$ is* primal-symmetric *iff for every attack $(T, h) \in R$ and $t \in T$ there is an attack $(H, t) \in R$ with $h \in H$.*

As expected, a SETAF is primal-symmetric iff its primal graph is symmetric. Notice that the notion of primal-symmetry coincides with the definition of symmetry of Abstract Dialectical Frameworks in [3]. The next notion intuitively captures the "omnidirectionality" of symmetric attacks: for every attack all involved arguments have to attack each other. In the definition of fully-symmetry we distinguish between self-attacks and attacks which are not self-attacks.

---

[2] Further symmetry-notions for SETAFs have been investigated in [21].

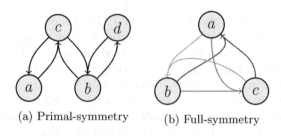

(a) Primal-symmetry   (b) Full-symmetry

Fig. 2. Different notions of symmetry.

Definition 9. *A SETAF $SF = (A, R)$ is* fully-symmetric *iff for every attack $(T, h) \in R$ we either have*

- *if $h \in T$, then $\forall x \in T$ it holds $(T, x) \in R$, or*
- *if $h \notin T$, then $\forall x \in S$ it holds $(S \setminus \{x\}, x) \in R$ with $S = T \cup \{h\}$.*

We have that every fully-symmetric SETAF is primal-symmetric, the converse does not hold. In symmetric AFs every argument defends itself against all incoming attacks, hence, admissible sets coincide with conflict-free sets, and it becomes computationally easy to reason on admissible, complete, and preferred extensions. However, this is not the case with our notions of symmetry for SETAFs. Consider the fully-symmetric (and thus also primal-symmetric) SETAF from Fig. 2b: we have that for example the singleton set $\{a\}$ is conflict-free, but $\{a\}$ cannot defend itself against the attacks towards a. That is, the argument for tractability from AFs does not transfer to SETAFs. This corresponds to the the fact that we will obtain full hardness for the admissibility-based semantics in question, when making no further restrictions on the graph structure.

For both notions of symmetry we have that an argument is in the grounded extension iff it is not in the head of any attack, which can easily be checked in logarithmic space. This is by the characterization of the grounded extension as least fixed point of the *characteristic function* [23], i.e. the grounded extension can be computed by starting from the empty set and iteratively adding all defended arguments. For primal-symmetric SETAFs with and without self-attacks, as well as fully-symmetric SETAFs (allowing self-attacks) this is the only computational speedup we can get, the remaining semantics maintain their full complexity.

In order to show the hardness for primal-symmetric SETAFs we provide a translation that transforms each SETAF $SF = (A, R)$ in a primal-symmetric SETAF SF': we construct SF' from SF by adding, for each attack $r = (T, h)$ and $t \in T$, mutually attacking arguments $a_{r,t}^1, a_{r,t}^2$, the (ineffective) counterattack $(\{a_{r,t}^1, a_{r,t}^2, h\}, t)$, and attacks $(t, a_{r,t}^1), (t, a_{r,t}^2)$. It can be verified that the resulting SETAF SF' is primal-symmetric, does not introduce self-attacks and preserves the acceptance status of the original arguments.

Theorem 4. *For primal-symmetric SETAFs (with or without self-attacks) the problems $Cred_{grd}$, $Skept_{grd}$ and $Skept_{com}$ are in L, the complexity of the other problems under our consideration coincides with the complexity for the general problems (see Table 2).*

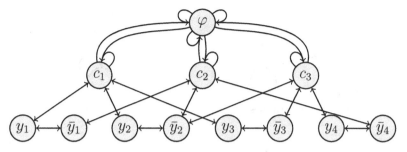

Fig. 3. Illustration of SF_φ^1 for a formula φ with atoms $Y = \{y_1, y_2, y_3, y_4\}$, and clauses $C = \{\{y_1, y_2, y_3\}, \{\bar{y}_1, \bar{y}_2, \bar{y}_4\}\}, \{\bar{y}_2, \bar{y}_3, y_4\}\}$.

We will see the same hardness results for fully-symmetric SETAFs, but here the hardness relies on the use of self-attacks. Stable, stage, and semi-stable semantics have already their full complexity in symmetric AFs allowing self-attacks [10]. For the admissible, complete and preferred semantics, hardness can be shown with adjustments to the standard reductions. That is, we substitute some of the occurring directed attacks (a, b) by classical symmetric attacks $(a, b), (b, a)$, and others by symmetric self-attacks $(\{a, b\}, a), (\{a, b\}, b)$. For instance, for admissible semantics, given a CNF-formula φ with clauses C over atoms Y we define $SF_\varphi^1 = (A', R')$ (cf. Fig. 3), with $A' = \{\varphi\} \cup C \cup Y \cup \bar{Y}$ and R' given by (a) the usual attacks $\{(y, \bar{y}), (\bar{y}, y) \mid y \in Y\}$, (b) symmetric attacks from literals to clauses $\{(y, c), (c, y) \mid y \in c, c \in C\} \cup \{(\bar{y}, c), (c, \bar{y}) \mid \bar{y} \in c, c \in C\}$, and (c) the symmetric self-attacks $\{(\{c, \varphi\}, \varphi), (\{c, \varphi\}, c) \mid c \in C\}$. The attacks (c) ensure that all c have to be attacked in order to accept φ and that all c are unacceptable.

Theorem 5. *For fully-symmetric SETAFs (allowing self-attacks) the problems $Cred_{grd}$, $Skept_{grd}$ and $Skept_{com}$ are in L, the complexity of credulous and skeptical acceptance for the other semantics under our consideration coincides with the complexity for the general problems (see Table 2).*

Investigations on symmetric AFs often distinguish between AFs with and without self-attacks [10]. Indeed, also for *self-attack-free* fully-symmetric SETAFs we have that all naive extensions (i.e. ⊆-maximal conflict-free sets) are stable, hence, one can construct a stable extension containing an arbitrary argument a by starting with the conflict-free set $\{a\}$ and expanding it to a maximal conflict-free set. As stable extensions are admissible, complete, preferred, stage, and semi-stable, an argument is trivially credulously accepted w.r.t. these semantics. Similarly, it is easy to decide whether an argument is in all extensions.

Theorem 6. *For self-attack-free fully-symmetric SETAFs the problems $Cred_\sigma$ are trivially true for $\sigma \in \{adm, com, pref, stb, stage, sem\}$. The problems $Skept_\sigma$ are in L for $\sigma \in \{grd, com, pref, stb, stage, sem\}$. Moreover, $Cred_{grd}$ is in L.*

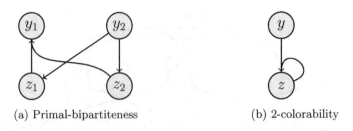

(a) Primal-bipartiteness   (b) 2-colorability

Fig. 4. Different notions of bipartiteness.

3.3   Bipartiteness

In the following we will provide two generalizations of bipartiteness; the first - primal-bipartiteness - extends the idea of partitioning for directed hypergraphs, the second is a generalization of the notion of 2-colorability. In directed graphs bipartiteness and 2-colorability coincide. However, this is not the case in SETAFs with their directed hypergraph-structure. As it will turn out, 2-colorability is not a sufficient condition for tractable reasoning, whereas primal-bipartiteness makes credulous and skeptical reasoning P-easy. For an illustration of the respective definitions see Fig. 4.

Definition 10. *Let $SF = (A, R)$ be a SETAF. Then SF is primal-bipartite iff its primal graph $primal(SF)$ is bipartite, i.e. iff there is a partitioning of A into two sets (Y, Z), such that*

– *$Y \cup Z = A$, $Y \cap Z = \emptyset$, and*
– *for every $(T, h) \in R$ either $h \in Y$ and $T \subseteq Z$, or $h \in Z$ and $T \subseteq Y$.*

For bipartite AFs, Dunne provided an algorithm to enumerate the arguments that appear in admissible sets [6]; this algorithm can be adapted for SETAFs (see Algorithm 1). Intuitively, the algorithm considers the two sets of the partition separately. For each partition it iteratively removes arguments that cannot be defended, and eventually ends up with an admissible set. The union of the two admissible sets then forms a superset of every admissible set in the SETAF. As primal-bipartite SETAFs are odd-cycle-free, they are coherent [23], which means preferred and stable extensions coincide. This necessarily implies the existence of stable extensions, which means they also coincide with stage and semi-stable extensions. These results suffice to pin down the complexity of credulous and skeptical reasoning for the semantics under our consideration.

Theorem 7. *For primal-bipartite SETAFs the problems $Cred_\sigma$ and $Skept_\sigma$ for $\sigma \in \{com, pref, stb, stage, sem\}$ are P-complete. Moreover the problem $Cred_{adm}$ is P-complete.*

It is noteworthy that the complexity of deciding whether a set S of arguments is *jointly* credulously accepted w.r.t. preferred semantics in primal-bipartite SETAFs was already shown to be NP-complete for bipartite AFs (and, hence,

---

Algorithm 1: Compute the set of credulously accepted arguments w.r.t. *pref* semantics

---

Input : A primal-bipartite SETAF $SF = (A, R)$ with a partitioning (Y, Z)
Output: The admissible set Y_i of credulously accepted arguments in Y
1 $i := 0$
2 $Y_0 := Y$
3 $R_0 := R$
4 **repeat**
5     $i := i + 1$
6     $Y_i := Y_{i-1} \setminus \{y \mid y \in Y_{i-1}$, there is some $(Z', y) \in R_{i-1}$ with $Z' \subseteq$ Z such that $\forall z \in Z'\ |\{(Y', z) \mid (Y', z) \in R_{i-1}\}| = 0\}$
7     $R_i := R_{i-1} \setminus \{(Y', z) \mid Y' \subseteq Y, z \in Z, Y' \not\subseteq Y_i\}$
8 **until** $Y_i = Y_{i-1}$;

---

for SETAFs) in [6]; however, this only holds if the arguments in question distribute over both partitions - for arguments that are all within one partition this problem is in P, which directly follows from the fact that Algorithm 1 returns the set Y_i of credulously accepted arguments - which is itself an admissible set.

It is natural to ask whether the more general notion of 2-colorability also yields a computational speedup. We capture this property for SETAFs by the following definition:

Definition 11. *Let $SF = (A, R)$ be a SETAF. Then SF is 2-colorable iff there is a partitioning of A into two sets (Y, Z), such that*

- $Y \cup Z = A$, $Y \cap Z = \emptyset$, *and*
- *for every attack $(T, h) \in R$ we have $(T \cup \{h\}) \cap Y \neq \emptyset$ and $(T \cup \{h\}) \cap Z \neq \emptyset$.*

Note that both primal-bipartiteness and 2-colorability do not allow self-loops (a, a) with a single argument in the tail, but 2-colorable SETAFs may contain self-attacks (T, h) with $|T| \geq 2$.

For admissibility-based semantics that preserve the grounded extension (such as *grd, com, pref, stb, sem*) it is easy to see that the problems remain hard in 2-colorable SETAFs: intuitively, one can add two fresh arguments to any SETAF and add them to the tail T of every attack (T, h) - they will be in each extension of the semantics in question, and other than that the extensions will coincide with the original SETAF (this translation is *faithful*, cf. [19]). To establish hardness for stage semantics we can adapt the existing reductions by replacing self-attacking arguments by a construction with additional arguments such that 2-colorability is ensured, and replace certain classical AF-attacks by collective attacks.

Theorem 8. *For 2-colorable SETAFs the complexity of $Cred_\sigma$ and $Skept_\sigma$ for all semantics under our consideration coincides with the complexity of the general problem (see Table 2).*

Table 3. Tractable fragments in SETAFs.

		grd	adm	com	pref	stb	stage	sem
General	$Cred_\sigma$	P-c	NP-c	NP-c	NP-c	NP-c	Σ_2^P-c	Σ_2^P-c
	$Skept_\sigma$	P-c	trivial	P-c	Π_2^P-c	coNP-c	Π_2^P-c	Π_2^P-c
Acyclicty	$Cred_\sigma$	P-c	P-c	P-c	P-c	P-c	P-c	P-c
	$Skept_\sigma$	P-c	trivial	P-c	P-c	P-c	P-c	P-c
Even-cycle-freeness	$Cred_\sigma$	P-c	P-c	P-c	P-c	P-c	Σ_2^P-c	P-c
	$Skept_\sigma$	P-c	trivial	P-c	P-c	P-c	Π_2^P-c	P-c
self-attack-free full-symmetry	$Cred_\sigma$	in L	trivial	trivial	trivial	trivial	trivial	trivial
	$Skept_\sigma$	in L	trivial	in L	in L	in L	in L	in L
Primal-bipartiteness	$Cred_\sigma$	P-c	P-c	P-c	P-c	P-c	P-c	P-c
	$Skept_\sigma$	P-c	trivial	P-c	P-c	P-c	P-c	P-c

3.4 Tractable Fragments

The (relatively speaking) low complexity of reasoning in SETAFs with the above described features on its own is convenient, but to be able to fully exploit this fact we also show that these classes are easily *recognizable*. As mentioned in [14], the respective AF-classes can be efficiently decided by graph algorithms. As for acyclicity, even-cycle-freeness, and primal-bipartiteness it suffices to analyze the primal graph, these results carry over to SETAFs. Moreover, for primal-bipartite SETAFs we can efficiently compute a partitioning, which is needed as input for Algorithm 1. Finally, we can test for full-symmetry efficiently as well: one (naive) approach is to just loop over all attacks and check whether there are corresponding attacks towards each involved argument. Likewise, a test for self-attack-freeness can be performed efficiently. Summarizing the results of this work, we get the following theorem.

Theorem 9. *Acyclicity, even-cycle-freeness, self-attack-free full-symmetry, and primal-bipartiteness are* tractable fragments *for SETAFs.*

In particular, for credulous and skeptical reasoning in the semantics under our consideration the complexity landscape including tractable fragments in SETAFs is depicted in Table 3.

4   Conclusion

In this work, we introduced and analyzed various different syntactic classes for SETAFs. These new notions are conservative generalizations of properties of directed graphs, namely acyclicity, even/odd-cycle-freeness, symmetry, and bipartiteness, which have been shown to lower the complexity for acceptance problems of AFs. The starting point for our definitions is the *primal graph* of the SETAF, a structural embedding of directed hypergraph into a directed graph.

Other than establishing basic properties, we performed a complete complexity analysis for credulous and skeptical reasoning in classes of SETAFs with these generalized properties. For the notions regarding cycles, we established the same properties for acyclicity, even-cycle-freeness, and odd-cycle-freeness for SETAFs that also hold for AFs. This includes the fact that the same upper and lower bounds on the complexity holds as in AFs, namely reasoning in acyclicity becomes tractable for all semantics under our consideration, even-cycle-freeness becomes tractable for all semantics but stage, and in odd-cycle-free SETAFs the complexity drops to the first level of the polynomial hierarchy. The symmetry notions we introduced generalize the concept of counter-attacks. We have established that a symmetric primal graph is not a sufficient condition for a SETAF to lower the complexity. The more restricting notion of full-symmetry yields a drop in complexity, but only if one also requires the SETAFs to be self-attack-free. Allowing self-attacks, even this notion does not yield a drop in the complexity for the semantics in question, which is the case for admissible, preferred, and complete semantics in AFs. We also investigated notions of bipartiteness. While in directed graphs bipartiteness and 2-colorability coincide, this in not the case in directed hypergraphs. We provided an algorithm that allows one to reason efficiently on primal-bipartite SETAFs, a result that does not apply for the more general notion of 2-colorable SETAFs. Finally, we argued that these classes can also be efficiently recognized, which is a crucial condition if one wants to implement the more efficient algorithms as a sub-routine of a general SETAF-solver.

In the future, tractability for SETAFs could be established by performing parametrized complexity analysis, as it has been done for AFs [10,15]. In particular, we understand these results as a starting point for investigations in terms of backdoors (i.e. measuring and exploiting a bounded *distance* of a given SETAF to a certain tractable class), along the lines of similar investigations for AFs [14]. Moreover, it is important to analyze whether SETAFs that occur in applications belong to any of the graph-classes introduced in this work. For example, it can be checked that the frameworks generated for a particular application in [25]— even though they do not belong to one of our tractable fragments—enjoy a (weak) symmetry-property, which allows one to reason in L on the grounded extension. This can be shown using the same proof as for our primal-symmetry result. Finally, as the purpose of the algorithms featured in this work was solely to illustrate the membership to the respective complexity classes, undoubtedly they yield a potential for improvement and optimization.

Acknowledgments. This research has been supported by the Vienna Science and Technology Fund (WWTF) through project ICT19-065, and by the Austrian Science Fund (FWF) through projects P30168 and P32830.

References

1. Brewka, G., Polberg, S., Woltran, S.: Generalizations of Dung frameworks and their role in formal argumentation. IEEE Intell. Syst. **29**(1), 30–38 (2014). https://doi.org/10.1109/MIS.2013.122
2. Coste-Marquis, S., Devred, C., Marquis, P.: Symmetric argumentation frameworks. In: Godo, L. (ed.) ECSQARU 2005. LNCS (LNAI), vol. 3571, pp. 317–328. Springer, Heidelberg (2005). https://doi.org/10.1007/11518655_28
3. Diller, M., Keshavarzi Zafarghandi, A., Linsbichler, T., Woltran, S.: Investigating subclasses of abstract dialectical frameworks. Argument Comput. **11**, 191–219 (2020). https://doi.org/10.3233/AAC-190481
4. Dimopoulos, Y., Torres, A.: Graph theoretical structures in logic programs and default theories. Theor. Comput. Sci. **170**(1–2), 209–244 (1996). https://doi.org/10.1016/S0304-3975(96)80707-9
5. Dung, P.M.: On the acceptability of arguments and its fundamental role in nonmonotonic reasoning, logic programming and n-person games. Artif. Intell. **77**(2), 321–358 (1995). https://doi.org/10.1016/0004-3702(94)00041-X
6. Dunne, P.E.: Computational properties of argument systems satisfying graph-theoretic constraints. Artif. Intell. **171**(10–15), 701–729 (2007). https://doi.org/10.1016/j.artint.2007.03.006
7. Dunne, P.E., Bench-Capon, T.J.M.: Complexity and combinatorial properties of argument systems. Department of Computer Science, University of Liverpool, Technical Report (2001)
8. Dunne, P.E., Bench-Capon, T.J.M.: Coherence in finite argument systems. Artif. Intell. **141**(1/2), 187–203 (2002). https://doi.org/10.1016/S0004-3702(02)00261-8
9. Dvořák, W.: Computational Aspects of Abstract Argumentation. Ph.D. thesis, Vienna University of Technology, Institute of Information Systems (2012). http://permalink.obvsg.at/AC07812708
10. Dvořák, W., Dunne, P.E.: Computational problems in formal argumentation and their complexity. FLAP **4**(8) (2017). http://www.collegepublications.co.uk/downloads/ifcolog00017.pdf
11. Dvořák, W., Fandinno, J., Woltran, S.: On the expressive power of collective attacks. Argument Comput. **10**(2), 191–230 (2019). https://doi.org/10.3233/AAC-190457
12. Dvořák, W., Greßler, A., Woltran, S.: Evaluating SETAFs via answer-set programming. In: Thimm, M., Cerutti, F., Vallati, M. (eds.) Proceedings of the Second International Workshop on Systems and Algorithms for Formal Argumentation (SAFA 2018) co-located with the 7th International Conference on Computational Models of Argument (COMMA 2018), Warsaw, Poland, vol. 2171, pp. 10–21. CEUR Workshop Proceedings CEUR-WS.org (2018). http://ceur-ws.org/Vol-2171/paper_2.pdf
13. Dvořák, W., König, M., Woltran, S.: Graph-classes of argumentation frameworks with collective attacks. Technical Report DBAI-TR-2021-120, Technische Universität Wien (2021). http://www.dbai.tuwien.ac.at/research/report/dbai-tr-2021-120.pdf
14. Dvořák, W., Ordyniak, S., Szeider, S.: Augmenting tractable fragments of abstract argumentation. Artif. Intell. **186**, 157–173 (2012). https://doi.org/10.1016/j.artint.2012.03.002
15. Dvořák, W., Pichler, R., Woltran, S.: Towards fixed-parameter tractable algorithms for abstract argumentation. Artif. Intell. **186**, 1–37 (2012). https://doi.org/10.1016/j.artint.2012.03.005

16. Dvořák, W., Rapberger, A., Wallner, J.P.: Labelling-based algorithms for SETAFs. In: Gaggl, S.A., Thimm, M., Vallati, M. (eds.) Proceedings of the Third International Workshop on Systems and Algorithms for Formal Argumentation co-located with the 8th International Conference on Computational Models of Argument (COMMA 2020), vol. 2672, pp. 34–46. CEUR Workshop Proceedings. CEUR-WS.org (2020). http://ceur-ws.org/Vol-2672/paper_4.pdf

17. Dvořák, W., Rapberger, A., Woltran, S.: On the different types of collective attacks in abstract argumentation: equivalence results for SETAFs. J. Logic Comput. 30(5), 1063–1107 (2020). https://doi.org/10.1093/logcom/exaa033

18. Dvořák, W., Woltran, S.: Complexity of semi-stable and stage semantics in argumentation frameworks. Inf. Process. Lett. 110(11), 425–430 (2010). https://doi.org/10.1016/j.ipl.2010.04.005

19. Dvořák, W., Woltran, S.: On the intertranslatability of argumentation semantics. J. Artif. Intell. Res. (JAIR) 41, 445–475 (2011)

20. Flouris, G., Bikakis, A.: A comprehensive study of argumentation frameworks with sets of attacking arguments. Int. J. Approx. Reason. 109, 55–86 (2019). https://doi.org/10.1016/j.ijar.2019.03.006

21. König, M.: Graph-Classes of Argumentation Frameworks with Collective Attacks. Master's thesis, TU Wien (2020). http://permalink.obvsg.at/AC15750327

22. Nielsen, S.H., Parsons, S.: Computing preferred extensions for argumentation systems with sets of attacking arguments. In: Dunne, P.E., Bench-Capon, T.J.M. (eds.) Computational Models of Argument: Proceedings of COMMA 2006, 11–12 September 2006, Liverpool, UK. Frontiers in Artificial Intelligence and Applications, vol. 144, pp. 97–108. IOS Press (2006). http://www.booksonline.iospress.nl/Content/View.aspx?piid=1930

23. Nielsen, S.H., Parsons, S.: A generalization of dung's abstract framework for argumentation: arguing with sets of attacking arguments. In: Maudet, N., Parsons, S., Rahwan, I. (eds.) ArgMAS 2006. LNCS (LNAI), vol. 4766, pp. 54–73. Springer, Heidelberg (2007). https://doi.org/10.1007/978-3-540-75526-5_4

24. Polberg, S.: Developing the Abstract Dialectical Framework. Ph.D. thesis, Vienna University of Technology, Institute of Information Systems (2017). https://permalink.obvsg.at/AC13773888

25. Yun, B., Vesic, S., Croitoru, M.: Toward a more efficient generation of structured argumentation graphs. In: Modgil, S., Budzynska, K., Lawrence, J. (eds.) Computational Models of Argument - Proceedings of COMMA 2018, Warsaw, Poland. Frontiers in Artificial Intelligence and Applications, vol. 305, pp. 205–212. IOS Press (2018). https://doi.org/10.3233/978-1-61499-906-5-205

Introducing a Tool for Concurrent Argumentation

Stefano Bistarelli[1] and Carlo Taticchi[2]([⊠])

[1] University of Perugia, Perugia, Italy
stefano.bistarelli@unipg.it
[2] Gran Sasso Science Institute, L'Aquila, Italy
carlo.taticchi@gssi.it

Abstract. Agent-based modelling languages naturally implement concurrency for handling complex interactions between communicating agents. On the other hand, the field of Argumentation Theory lacks of instruments to explicitly model concurrent behaviours. In this paper we introduce a tool for dealing with concurrent argumentation processes and that can be used, for instance, to model agents debating, negotiating and persuading. The tool implements operations as expansion, contraction and revision. We also provide a web interface exposing the functionalities of the tool and allowing for a more careful study of concurrent processes.

Keywords: Argumentation Theory · Concurrency · Programming languages

1 Preliminaries

Many applications in the field of artificial intelligence aim to reproduce the human behaviour and reasoning in order to allow machines to think and act accordingly. One of the main challenges in this sense is to provide tools for expressing a certain kind of knowledge in a formal way so that the machines can use it for reasoning and infer new information. Argumentation Theory provides formal models for representing and evaluating arguments that interact with each other. In his seminal work [7], Dung introduces a representation for Argumentation Frameworks in which arguments are abstract, that is their internal structure, as well as their origin, is left unspecified. An Abstract Argumentation Framework (AF) consists of a couple $\langle Arg, R \rangle$ where Arg is a set of arguments and R a binary attack relation between them. Given an AF, it is possible to examine the question on which set(s) of arguments can be accepted by, using criteria called argumentation semantics. Several authors have investigated the dynamics of AFs [2,5,11]. The works in this direction take into account different kinds of modification (addition or removal of arguments and attacks [6]) and borrow concepts from belief revision with different purposes, for example updating an AF [13] or enforcing arguments [2].

W. Faber et al. (Eds.): JELIA 2021, LNAI 12678, pp. 18–24, 2021.
https://doi.org/10.1007/978-3-030-75775-5_2

Although some of these approaches could be exploited to implement applications based on argumentation, for instance to model debates among political opponents, none of them considers the possibility of having concurrent interactions. This lack represents a significant gap between the reasoning capacities of AFs and their possible use in real life tools. Consider, for example, the situation in which two debating agents share a knowledge base, represented by an AF, and both of them want to update it with new information in such a way that the new beliefs are consistent with the previous ones. The agents can act independently and simultaneously. Similarly to what happens in concurrent programming, if no synchronization mechanism is taken into account, the result of the revision can be unpredictable and can also lead to the introduction of inconsistencies.

Motivated by the above considerations, we defined a concurrent argumentation language [4] for modelling negotiations and debates. Such language allows for modelling concurrent processes, inspired by notions such as the *Ask-and-Tell constraint system* [14]. Besides specifying a logic for argument interaction, our language can model debating agents (e.g., chatbots) that take part in a conversation and provide arguments. AGM [1] and KM [9] theories give operations (like expansion, contraction, revision, extraction, consolidation and merging) for updating and revising beliefs on a knowledge base. Looking at such operations, the language is endowed with primitives for the specification of interaction between agents through the fundamental operations of adding (or removing) arguments and attacks. The aim is to define a core calculus with a small collection of constructs that allow for the simple modelling of more complex operations that can be used for representing debating agents in a natural way.

Starting from the CC syntax, we enrich the ask and tell operators in order to handle the interaction with an AF used as knowledge base for the agents. We replace the aks with three decisional operations: a syntactic *check* that verifies if a given set of arguments and attacks is contained in the knowledge base, and two semantic *test* operations that we use to retrieve information about the acceptability of arguments in an AF. The tell operation (that we call **add**) augments the store with additional arguments and attack relations. We can also remove parts of the knowledge base through a specifically designed removal operation. Finally, a guarded parallel composition $\|_G$ allows for executing all the operations that satisfy some given conditions, and a prioritised operator $+_P$ is used to implement if-then-else constructs. The remaining operators are classical concurrency compositions: an agent in a parallel composition obtained through $\|$ succeeds if all the agents succeeds; any agent composed through $+$ is chosen if its guards succeeds; the existential quantifier $\exists_x A$ behaves like agent A where variables in x are local to A. The parallel composition operator enables the specification of complex concurrent processes. For example, a debate involving many agents that asynchronously provide arguments can be modelled as a parallel composition of add operations performed on the knowledge base.

With this work, we take a further step towards an argumentation-based system able to handle concurrent interactions between intelligent agents: we present ConArg_lang, a tool implementing the concurrent language of [4] and exposing its functionalities through a web interface. In the following section, we provide a detailed description of the tool, focusing on implementation choices and definition of the core functions. We also show how the interface works giving two examples of program executions.

2   Implementation

We develop a working implementation for ConArg_lang. We use python and ANTLR[1] (ANother Tool for Language Recognition), a parser generator for reading, processing, executing, and translating structured text. ANTLR provides two ways of traversing the parse tree: either trough a listener (the default option) or a visitor. The biggest difference between the listener and visitor mechanisms is that listener methods are called independently, whereas visitor methods must walk their children with explicit visit calls. Not invoking visitor methods on the children of a node means those subtrees are not visited. Since we want to implement guards in our language, we need the possibility to decide which part of the tree will be visited, making our choice fall on the visitor approach.

Our project consists of a grammar file and seven python classes, the most interesting being the *CustomVisitor*, in which we define the behaviour of the parser, and the class *ArgFun* containing all the auxiliary argumentation-related functions used to process the knowledge base of the agents (that is, indeed, an AF). The visit of the parse tree always starts with the execution of the function *visitPrg*, which recursively visits all its children. The parser recognises twenty types of node (the non terminal elements in the grammar) for which the desired behaviour is specified. Below, we provide details on the implementation of visiting functions.

- *visitPrg*: calls the visit on its children, collects the results and, in case of termination, returns the output of the whole program.
- *visitPar*: starts two separated threads to execute (visit) two actions in parallel, returning true if both succeeds, false if at least one action fails, and suspends if an action is waiting for its guard to become true.
- *visitAdd* and *visitRmv*: modify the AF by either adding or removing part of the AF, respectively. Always succeeds and continues on the children. Note that *visitRmv* succeeds also if the specified arguments and/or attacks are not in the AF. In that case, the AF is left unchanged.
- *visitSuc* and *visitFlr*: correspond to visits to terminal nodes and return true (success) and false (failure), respectively.
- *visitNdt*: implements a concatenation of + operators, inspecting the guards of all its children and randomly selecting a branch to execute among the possible ones. A guard can be a waiting check or either of the waiting tests. If no guards are found with satisfiable conditions, *visitNdt* waits for changes in the AF until some child can be executed.

---

[1] ANTLR website: https://www.antlr.org/.

- *visitGpa*: implements a concatenation of $\|_G$ operators. Execute all its children in separated threads. Contrary to *visitNdt*, *visitGpa* only works with expressions that can fail (and do not suspend), thus allowing for two possible outcomes, that is success if at least one expression succeeds, and failure if all expressions fail.
- *visitIte*: behaves like an if-then-else construct. The first child must be an expression with guaranteed termination (either success or failure). The children are executed in the same order in which they are specified and as soon as a satisfiable guard is found, the corresponding branch is executed. Since some of the children can be waiting expression, *visitIte* is not guaranteed to terminate.
- *visitCkw* and *visitCkf*: check if a given set of arguments and/or attacks is present in the knowledge base. In case of success, both nodes proceed visiting the consequent action. On the other hand, when the knowledge base does not contain the specified parts of AF, *visitCkw* waits for the condition to become true, while *visitCkf* immediately returns false and leads to branch failure.
- *visitTcw*, *visitTcf*, *visitTsw* and *visitTsf*: call the ConArg [3] solver to execute credulous and sceptical tests on the acceptability of a given set of arguments. As with the checks, the test functions are also available in two versions, one that always terminates (with either a success or a failure) and the other that possibly suspends and waits for the condition to become true.

In addition to the visiting functions, we have a set of core functions responsible for managing auxiliary tasks, like starting new threads when a parallel composition is detected, making changes to the shared AF and computing the semantics for the test operations. All the components are put together in the *Main* class, which takes in input and runs the user-defined program.

2.1 Web Interface

To facilitate the use of the tool we develop a web interface exposing the functionalities of our language. The interface consists of a web page[2] divided into three main areas: an input form, one text box for the program output and one for the shared AF (shown in Fig. 1). The output of our tool shows, for each step, the executed operation and the remaining part of the program, together with the results of check and test operations.

The user can either manually input a program in the designated area or select a sample program from those available a the drop down menu. Two buttons below the input area run the program and display the result in different ways. Clicking the button "Run all", the result of the whole program is immediately displayed in the area below and the AF shown on the right represent the final state of the shared store. On the other hand, the button "Run 1 step" shows, as the name suggests, one step at time: each click on the button makes another step of the execution appear in the output area. The AF on the right side is

---

[2] Web interface available at http://dmi.unipg.it/conarg/lang/.

Program Output:

```
 1 prg: checkw({c},{})->add({a,b},{(a,c)})->success||add({c},{})->success;
 2 par: checkw({c},{})->add({a,b},{(a,c)})->success||add({c},{})->success
 3 ckw: checkw({c},{})->add({a,b},{(a,c)})->success
 4 Check failed
 5 Repeat visit
 6 add: add({c},{})->success
 7 suc: success
 8 ckw: checkw({c},{})->add({a,b},{(a,c)})->success
 9 Check succeeded
10 add: add({a,b},{(a,c)})->success
11 suc: success
12 SUCCESS
```

AF:

```
arg(c).
arg(a).
arg(b).
att(a,c).
```

Fig. 1. Execution of the program in Example 1.

updated after each **add** or **rmv** operation, showing the evolution of the underlying knowledge base. Note that the difference between the two usable modes is only in the visualisation, since both compute the whole result beforehand. Regardless of the chosen method, the executed operation is highlighted in yellow in each line of the output.

Example 1 (Parallel actions). Consider the program below.

```
checkw({c},{}) -> add({a,b},{(a,c)}) -> success ||
add({c},{}) -> success;
```

Running the program produces the results in Fig. 1. Note that the AF representing the knowledge base is always empty at the beginning. In line 1 of the output, the parser recognises a valid program. Two threads (one for each action) are started. In this example, the action that occurred first in the program is also executed first, but in general it can happen in any order. In line 3, the program executes a waiting **checkw**: if the AF contains an argument c then the visit on that branch can continue (and the add operation is executed). Otherwise, the **checkw** is repeated until it (possibly) becomes true. Since the AF is empty by default and no other action has modified it yet, the check on the AF return a negative answer (line 4). In the meanwhile, the **add** operation of the second thread is executed in line 6. The AF is modified accordingly, introducing an argument c. AF $= \langle\{c\}, \{\}\rangle$. This branch of the execution terminates in line 7 with a success. At this point, the check of the first thread (which had previously given negative results) is repeated, this time giving an affirmative answer (lines 8 and 9). The execution then continues in line 10 with the **add** operation which produces further modifications on the AF. At this point, AF $= \langle\{c, a, b\}, \{(a, c)\}\rangle$. This branch successfully terminates in line 11 and since both the parallel actions of our program succeed, the whole program terminates with a success (line 12).

Example 2 (If-then-else). We run the following program, whose result is shown in Fig. 2.

Program Output: AF:

```
1 prg: add({a,b},{(a,b)})->checkf({c},{})->add({d},{})-
  >success+Ptestcf({b},in,complete)->add({e},{})->success;
2 par: add({a,b},{(a,b)})->checkf({c},{})->add({d},{})-
  >success+Ptestcf({b},in,complete)->add({e},{})->success
3 add: add({a,b},{(a,b)})->checkf({c},{})->add({d},{})-
  >success+Ptestcf({b},in,complete)->add({e},{})->success
4 ite: checkf({c},{})->add({d},{})->success+Ptestcf({b},in,complete)->add({e},{})-
  >success
5 ckf: checkf({c},{})->add({d},{})->success
6 Check failed
7 tcf: testcf({b},in,complete)->add({e},{})->success
8 Test failed
9 FAILURE
```

```
arg(a).
arg(b).
att(a,b).
```

Fig. 2. Execution of the program in Example 2.

```
add({a,b},{(a,b)}) ->
    checkf({c},{}) -> add({d},{}) -> success +P
    testcf({b},in,complete) -> add({e},{}) -> success;
```

After initialising the AF with two arguments and an attack between them in line 3 (AF = $\langle\{a,b\}, \{(a,b)\}\rangle$.), the program executes an if-then-else construct (line 4). The first condition consists of a checkf operation, which immediately fails (lines 5 and 6). The program proceed with the second condition, this time a testcf, that also fails (lines 7 and 8). Since both conditions fail, also the program terminates with a failure in line 9. We remark that more than two conditions can be declared by the use of +P and only the last one can be a waiting expression.

3 Conclusion and Future Work

We present ConArg_lang, a tool for modelling concurrent argumentation processes. We give insights on the implementation choices and we describe the main components of the tool, i.e., the parser and the web interface. The parser recognises up to twenty syntactic elements from an input program and produces a parse tree that is visited to obtain the execution result. The web interface, then, allows the user to enter a program (written with ConArg_lang syntax) and to execute it either all at once or one step at a time, showing the evolution of the shared AF as well.

For the future, we plan to extend this work in many directions. First of all, given the known issues of abstract argumentation [12], we want to consider structured AFs and provide an implementation for our expansion, contraction and revision operators, for which a different store (structured and not abstract, indeed) need to be considered. The concurrent primitives are already general enough and do not require substantial changes. To obtain a spendable implementation, we will consider operations that can be done in polynomial time [8]. As a final consideration, whereas in real-life cases it is always clear which part involved in a debate is stating a particular argument, AFs do not hold any notion of "ownership" for arguments or attacks, that is, any bond with the one making the assertion is lost. To overcome this problem, we want to implement the possibility of attaching labels on (groups of) arguments and attacks of AFs, in order to preserve the information related to whom added a certain argument or attack, extending and taking into account the work in [10]. Consequently, we can also obtain a notion of locality (or scope) of the belief in the knowledge base: arguments owned by a given agent can be placed into a local store and used in the implementation of specific operators through hidden variables.

References

1. Alchourrón, C.E., Gärdenfors, P., Makinson, D.: On the logic of theory change: partial meet contraction and revision functions. J. Symb. Log. **50**(2), 510–530 (1985)
2. Baumann, R.: What does it take to enforce an argument? Minimal change in abstract argumentation. In: ECAI. Frontiers in Artificial Intelligence and Applications, vol. 242, pp. 127–132. IOS Press (2012)
3. Bistarelli, S., Santini, F.: Conarg: a constraint-based computational framework for argumentation systems. In: ICTAI, pp. 605–612. IEEE Computer Society (2011)
4. Bistarelli, S., Taticchi, C.: A concurrent language for argumentation. In: AI^3@AI*IA. CEUR Workshop Proceedings, vol. 2777, pp. 75–89. CEUR-WS.org (2020)
5. Boella, G., Kaci, S., van der Torre, L.: Dynamics in argumentation with single extensions: attack refinement and the grounded extension (extended version). In: McBurney, P., Rahwan, I., Parsons, S., Maudet, N. (eds.) ArgMAS 2009. LNCS (LNAI), vol. 6057, pp. 150–159. Springer, Heidelberg (2010). https://doi.org/10.1007/978-3-642-12805-9_9
6. Cayrol, C., de Saint-Cyr, F.D., Lagasquie-Schiex, M.: Revision of an argumentation system. In: KR, pp. 124–134. AAAI Press (2008)
7. Dung, P.M.: On the acceptability of arguments and its fundamental role in non-monotonic reasoning, logic programming and n-person games. Artif. Intell. **77**(2), 321–358 (1995)
8. Dvořák, W., Dunne, P.E.: Computational problems in formal argumentation and their complexity. FLAP **4**(8) (2017)
9. Katsuno, H., Mendelzon, A.O.: On the difference between updating a knowledge base and revising it. In: KR, pp. 387–394. Morgan Kaufmann (1991)
10. Maudet, N., Parsons, S., Rahwan, I.: Argumentation in multi-agent systems: context and recent developments. In: Maudet, N., Parsons, S., Rahwan, I. (eds.) ArgMAS 2006. LNCS (LNAI), vol. 4766, pp. 1–16. Springer, Heidelberg (2007). https://doi.org/10.1007/978-3-540-75526-5_1
11. Moguillansky, M.O., Rotstein, N.D., Falappa, M.A., García, A.J., Simari, G.R.: Dynamics of knowledge in DeLP through argument theory change. Theory Pract. Log. Program. **13**(6), 893–957 (2013)
12. Prakken, H., Winter, M.D.: Abstraction in argumentation: necessary but dangerous. In: COMMA. Frontiers in Artificial Intelligence and Applications, vol. 305, pp. 85–96. IOS Press (2018)
13. de Saint-Cyr, F.D., Bisquert, P., Cayrol, C., Lagasquie-Schiex, M.: Argumentation update in YALLA (yet another logic language for argumentation). Int. J. Approx. Reason. **75**, 57–92 (2016)
14. Saraswat, V.A., Rinard, M.C.: Concurrent constraint programming. In: POPL, pp. 232–245. ACM Press (1990)

Probabilistic Argumentation: An Approach Based on Conditional Probability –A Preliminary Report–

Pilar Dellunde[1,2(✉)], Lluís Godo[2], and Amanda Vidal[2]

[1] Universitat Autònoma de Barcelona and Barcelona Graduate School of Mathematics,
Bellaterra, Spain
Pilar.Dellunde@uab.cat
[2] Artificial Intelligence Research Institute (IIIA-CSIC), Campus de la UAB, 08193 Bellaterra,
Barcelona, Spain
{godo,amanda}@iiia.csic.es

Abstract. A basic form of an instantiated argument is as a pair (support, conclusion) standing for a conditional relation 'if support then conclusion'. When this relation is not fully conclusive, a natural choice is to model the argument strength with the conditional probability of the conclusion given the support. In this paper, using a very simple language with conditionals, we explore a framework for probabilistic logic-based argumentation based on an extensive use of conditional probability, where uncertain and possibly inconsistent domain knowledge about a given scenario is represented as a set of defeasible rules quantified with conditional probabilities. We then discuss corresponding notions of attack and defeat relations between arguments, providing a basis for appropriate acceptability semantics, e.g. based on extensions or on DeLP-style dialogical trees.

1 Introduction

In the literature, there have been a number of approaches [3,5,10–13,15,19,21,25] to combine different theories of argumentation with probability theory, and other uncertainty models, in order to allow for a more fine-grained reasoning when arguments involve uncertain information. Since the earliest works of Pollock [17,18], where he introduced the notion of strength of an argument in terms of numerical degrees of belief, one main open problem has been to determine how the strength of arguments can be related to probability theory, see e.g. [19].

In [23], arguments are generated in ASPIC+ and their rebutting attacks are resolved with probabilistic strengths of arguments. However, some difficulties are encountered when assigning probabilities to arguments in an abstract framework. In a natural way, probabilities can be assigned to the truth of statements or to outcomes of events, but an argument is neither a statement nor an event. Thus, there is a need for a meaningful definition of what the probability of an argument is, and this has to be done at the level of structured argumentation, for instance along the line of the epistemic approach to probabilistic argumentation [10,19,20]. In particular, in the setting of classical-logic based argumentation, Hunter considers in [10] the probability of an argument to be the

© Springer Nature Switzerland AG 2021
W. Faber et al. (Eds.): JELIA 2021, LNAI 12678, pp. 25–32, 2021.
https://doi.org/10.1007/978-3-030-75775-5_3

probability of its premises according to a fixed, and a priori given, probability distribution on the set of interpretations of the language. Similarly, in [19], Prakken discusses the application of the ASPIC+ framework to default reasoning with probabilistic generalisations, taking the probability of an argument to be the probability of the conjunction of all its premises and conclusions.

In contrast to [10] but similarly to [19], in this paper we consider logic-based arguments $A = (support; conclusion)$ pervaded with uncertainty due a non-conclusive conditional link between their supports and their conclusions. In such a case, it is very reasonable to supplement the argument representation with a quantification α of how certain *conclusion* can be claimed to hold whenever *support* is known to hold, leading to represent arguments as triples $A = (support; conclusion : \alpha)$. A very natural choice is to interpret α as a conditional probability, namely the probability $P(conclusion \mid support)$. As we frame our proposal in logic-based argumentation, where arguments rely on the notion of proof in some underlying logic, we internalise the conditional link specified by an argument in the logic as a conditional formula or a set of conditional formulas in the general case, so that our basic probabilistic arguments will be of the form

$$A = (\{\psi\}, \{\psi \rightsquigarrow \varphi : \alpha\}; \varphi : \alpha),$$

where ψ and φ are classical propositions, $\psi \rightsquigarrow \varphi$ is a conditional formula and α is interpreted as a lower bound for the conditional probability $P(\varphi \mid \psi)$. When arguments get more complex and need several uncertain conditionals to link the support with the conclusion, conditional probabilities are attached to each of the involved conditionals, so arguments become of the form

$$A = (\Pi, \Delta = \{(\psi_1 \rightsquigarrow \varphi_1 : p_1), \ldots, (\psi_n \rightsquigarrow \varphi_n : p_n)\}; \varphi : \alpha),$$

where Π is a finite set of factual (i.e. non conditional) premises and α the probability with which φ can be logically entailed from Π and Δ. In fact, this type of arguments can be seen as a probabilistic generalization of those at work in the Defeasible Logic Programming argumentation framework (DeLP) [7]. This is a formalism combining logic programming and defeasible argumentation, that provides the possibility of representing information in the form of weak rules and a defeasible argumentation inference mechanism for warranting the entailed conclusions, see [8] for more details.

Our proposal can be cast in the above mentioned epistemic approach that assigns probabilities to arguments. However, in contrast to many works in the literature, we do not assign probabilities to the arguments a priori, but rather use smaller pieces of probabilistic information that govern the universe of study, and use these to compute the probability of a complex argument built from the more basic information items it contains. Moreover, our approach also notably differs from previous schemes in that, to compute the probability for an argument, we consider the whole family of probability distributions compatible with the support, and not fixing only one distribution.

This paper is structured as follows. Section 2 is devoted to introduce notions about logic and probability necessary for the rest of the paper; in Sect. 3 we introduce and explore the framework of probabilistic argumentation based on conditional probabilities. We conclude the paper commenting on promising future work and open questions.

2 Logic and Probability

When aiming towards the definition of a formal argumentation framework, a first step is the selection of a underlying purely propositional language and the logical system that will govern the derivation of new knowledge from a given set of information. In this paper, our logical formalism will be inspired in DeLP [7].

Let $\mathcal{V}$ be the set of *propositional variables*, simply a countable set of symbols. A *literal* is any propositional variable $x \in \mathcal{V}$ or a negated variable $\neg x$ for $x \in \mathcal{V}$. If ℓ is a literal, we will use the notation $\neg \ell$ to refer to x if $\ell = \neg x$ and to $\neg x$ if $\ell = x$. A *conjunction* of literals is a formula of the form $\ell_1 \wedge \ldots \wedge \ell_n$ with $n \geq 1$, where each ℓ_i is a literal. A *conditional* is a formula of the form $\ell_1 \wedge \ldots \wedge \ell_n \rightsquigarrow \ell$. Finally, we call *formula* any conjunction or conditional, and denote the set of formulas by Fm. Given a set of formulas $\Psi \subseteq Fm$, we will denote by $lit(\Psi)$ the set of literals appearing in Ψ.

Definition 1 (c.f. Def. 2.5 from [7]). *Let Σ be a finite set of conditionals, Φ a finite set of literals and ℓ a literal. A DeLP derivation of ℓ from Σ and Φ, denoted $\Sigma, \Phi \vdash \ell$, is a finite sequence $\ell_1, \ldots, \ell_n = \ell$ of literals, such that, for each $1 \leq i \leq n$:*

a) either $\ell_i \in \Phi$, or
b) there is a conditional $p_1 \wedge \ldots \wedge p_k \rightsquigarrow p \in \Sigma$ such that $p = \ell_i$ and for each $1 \leq j \leq k$, $p_j \in \{l_1, \ldots \ell_{i-1}\}$.

A pair $\{\Sigma, \Phi\}$ is *consistent* if it is not the case that there exists a literal ℓ such that both $\Sigma, \Phi \vdash \ell$ and $\Sigma, \Phi \vdash \neg\ell$. Let Ω stand for the set of truth-evaluations of variables $e : \mathcal{V} \rightarrow \{0, 1\}$, that extend to literals and conjunctions of literals following the rules of classical logic. Probabilities on the set of formulas Fm are defined in the standard way, as it is done in probability logics: defining a probability distribution on Ω and extending it to all formulas by adding up the probabilities of their models. More precisely, let $P : \Omega \rightarrow [0, 1]$ be a probability distribution on Ω. Then P induces a probability[1] $P : Fm \rightarrow [0, 1]$ by letting:

- $P(C) = \Sigma_{e \in \Omega, e(C)=1} P(e)$, if C is a conjunction of literals,
- $P(\ell_1 \wedge \ldots \wedge \ell_n \rightsquigarrow \ell) = P(\ell \wedge \ell_1 \wedge \ldots \wedge \ell_n)/P(\ell_1 \wedge \ldots \wedge \ell_n)$, whenever $P(\ell_1 \wedge \ldots \wedge \ell_n) > 0$ and undefined otherwise. Namely, the probability of ℓ conditioned to $\ell_1 \wedge \ldots \wedge \ell_n$.

Notice that the probability of a conditional $C \rightsquigarrow \ell$ is interpreted as the conditional probability $P(\ell \mid C)$, not as a probability of the material implication $\neg C \vee \ell$, understood as the implication in classical logic. Nevertheless, these two notions do coincide when the probability equals to 1. Namely, for $P(C) > 0$ for a conjunction of literals C, then

$$P(C \rightsquigarrow \ell) = 1 \text{ if and only if } P(\neg C \vee \ell) = 1.$$

We will call *probabilistic-valued formulas* (and denote this set of formulas by Fm_{Pr}) to all pairs of the form $\varphi : \alpha$, where $\varphi \in Fm$ and $\alpha \in [0, 1]$. A probability $P : \Omega \rightarrow [0, 1]$ satisfies $\varphi : \alpha$, written $P \models \varphi : \alpha$, whenever $P(\varphi) \geq \alpha$. Similarly, P satisfies a finite set

---

[1] Since there is no place to confusion, we will use the same symbol P to denote the probability distribution over Ω and its associated probability over Fm.

of valued formulas $\Sigma = \{\varphi_i : \alpha_i\}_{i \in I}$ if it satisfies each pair in Σ. We will denote the set of probabilities that satisfy Σ by $PMod(\Sigma)$.

Given a set of literals Π representing observations on the domain, one can define two probabilistic consequence relations, depending on how the set of observations Π is interpreted: either as facts holding with probability 1, or as assumptions over which to condition the consequence. These two definitions are intrinsically related to the two types of arguments we will introduce in the next section.

Definition 2 (Factual probabilistic entailment). *Let Π be a set of literals, Σ a set of valued formulas, ℓ a literal and $\alpha \in [0, 1]$. We write $\Pi, \Sigma \models_{Pr}^{f} \ell : \alpha$ whenever for each probability $P \in PMod(\Sigma)$, if $P(c) = 1$ for each $c \in \Pi$ then $P(\ell) \geq \alpha$.*

Definition 3 (Conditioned probabilistic entailment). *Let Π be a set of literals, Σ a set of valued formulas, ℓ a literal and $\alpha \in [0, 1]$. We write $\Pi, \Sigma \models_{Pr}^{c} \ell : \alpha$ whenever for each probability $P \in PMod(\Sigma)$, it holds that $P(\bigwedge_{c \in \Pi} c \leadsto \ell) \geq \alpha$.*

These two notions of entailment do not coincide. First observe that the conditioned probabilistic entailment is **stronger** than the unconditioned one, namely $\Pi, \Sigma \models_{Pr}^{c} \ell : \alpha$ implies $\Pi, \Sigma \models_{Pr}^{f} \ell : \alpha$. However, the converse does not hold, i.e. the conditioned probabilistic entailment is **strictly stronger** than the factual one. For instance, if we take the observation $\Pi = \{a\}$ and the valued formulas $\Sigma = \{a \leadsto b : 0.7, b \leadsto c : 0.5\}$, it t is easy to check that $\Pi, \Sigma \models_{Pr}^{f} c : 7/20$, but $\Pi, \Sigma \not\models_{Pr}^{c} c : 7/20$.

3 Using Conditional Probability in Arguments

Our approach is inspired by DeLP, ASPIC+ and other systems that differentiates knowledge that is certain and consistent (strict) from other that is tentative and possibly uncertain and inconsistent (defeasible). Probabilities offer a finer classification of the uncertain knowledge and so increase the trustworthiness and accurateness of arguments. In this paper, we assume the strict domain knowledge to come attached with probability 1, but other values could be used (e.g. if precise statistical data is possessed).

Definition 4. $\mathcal{K} = \langle \Pi, \Delta \rangle$ *is a probabilistic conditional knowledge base (KB) whenever*

- $\Pi = \Pi_F \cup \Pi_D \subseteq Fm$ *is a consistent^2 set of formulas encompassing the strict knowledge in $\mathcal{K}$, divided in factual knowledge (Π_F) under the form of literals, and domain knowledge (Π_D) under the form of strict rules.*
- $\Delta \subseteq Fm_{Pr}$ *encompasses uncertain probabilistic knowledge.*

Example 1. The following KB is a probabilistic refinement of Example 2.1 in [7], a variant of the famous Tweety example. Chickens usually do not fly (even if they are birds), but they may if they are scared, for instance if a fox is near. However, if a chicken has nestling babies, most likely it will not abandon them in any case.

---

^{2} According to $\vdash$.

$$\Pi_F = \left\{ \begin{array}{l} chicken \\ fox \\ nestlings \end{array} \right\}$$

$$\Pi_D = \left\{ chicken \rightsquigarrow bird \right\}$$

$$\Delta = \left\{ \begin{array}{l} bird \rightsquigarrow flies : 0.85 \\ chicken \rightsquigarrow \neg flies : 0.9 \\ chicken \wedge nestlings \rightsquigarrow \neg flies : 0.95 \\ chicken \wedge fox \rightsquigarrow scared : 0.8 \\ chicken \wedge scared \rightsquigarrow flies : 0.6 \end{array} \right\}$$

To specify an argument, we needed to specify which observations and which (consistent) part of the uncertain probabilistic knowledge it is based upon. We propose two main definitions for a probabilistic argument, each one following relying in one of the definitions of probabilistic entailment from the previous section. In what follows, for a set of formulas $\Gamma \subseteq Fm$ we let $\Gamma^+ = \{\gamma : 1\}_{\gamma \in \Gamma} \subseteq Fm_{Pr}$. Conversely, for a set of valued formulas $\Sigma \subseteq Fm_{Pr}$, we let $\Sigma^- = \{\sigma \mid \sigma : \alpha \in \Sigma$ for some $\alpha \in [0, 1]\} \subseteq Fm$.

Definition 5 (Argument). *Let* $\star \in \{f, c\}^3$, *and a* $KB = \langle \Pi, \Delta \rangle$. *A* $\star$-*probabilistic argument* $\mathcal{A}$ *for a literal* ℓ *in* KB *is a structure* $A = \langle \Phi, \Gamma; \ell : \alpha \rangle$, *where* $\Phi \subseteq \Pi_F$, $\Gamma = \{(\varphi_1 \rightsquigarrow l_1 : \alpha_1), \ldots, (\varphi_n \rightsquigarrow l_n : \alpha_n)\} \subseteq \Delta$ *and* $\alpha > 0$ *such that:*

(1) $PMod(\Gamma \cup \Pi^+) \neq \emptyset$ (3) $\alpha = \max\{ \beta \in [0, 1] : \Phi, \Pi_D^+ \cup \Gamma \models_{Pr}^{\star} \ell : \beta \}$

(2) $\Pi, \Gamma^- \vdash \ell$ (4) Φ *and* Γ *are minimal satisfying* (1), (2) *and* (3).

Thus, an argument for a literal provides for both a logical and an optimal probabilistic derivation of its conclusion (in any of the two variants) from its premises.

Some simple examples of probabilistic arguments over the KB from Example 1 are:

$\mathcal{A}_1 = (\{chicken\}, \{bird \rightsquigarrow flies : 0.85\}; flies : 0.85)$

$\mathcal{A}_2 = (\{chicken\}, \{chicken \rightsquigarrow \neg flies : 0.9\}; \neg flies : 0.9)$

$\mathcal{A}_3 = (\{chicken, fox\}, \{chicken \wedge fox \rightsquigarrow scared : 0.8, chicken \wedge scared \rightsquigarrow flies : 0.6\};$
$\quad flies : 0.54)$

$\mathcal{A}_4 = (\{chicken, nestlings\}, \{chicken \wedge nestlings \rightsquigarrow \neg flies : 0.95\}; \neg flies : 0.95)$

$\mathcal{A}_1$, $\mathcal{A}_2$ and $\mathcal{A}_4$ are both f- and c-arguments, while $\mathcal{A}_3$ is a f-argument but not a c-argument. This occurs because $\models_{Pr}^c$ becomes non-informative (its degree equals 0) when its logical derivation involves the chaining of more than one conditional, due to the well-known failure of transitivity on conditional probabilities [9], unless some additional assumptions are made. For instance, in [19] arguments implicitly make probabilistic independence assumptions and it is shown that the independence assumptions, that justify the use a version of the chain rule for probabilities, is useful in certain cases, but it is clearly invalid in general.

In order to define an attack relation between probabilistic arguments, we need the notions of subargument and of disagreement between probabilistic-valued literals.

Definition 6 (Subargument, Disagreement and Attack).
1) Let $\mathcal{A} = (\Phi, \Gamma; \ell : \alpha)$ *be an* $\star$-*argument for* ℓ. *A subargument of* $\mathcal{A}$ *is an* $\star$-*argument* $\mathcal{B} = (\Phi', \Gamma'; \ell' : \beta)$ *where* $\Phi' \subseteq \Phi$ *and* $\Gamma' \subseteq \Gamma$.

---

[3] Standing for factual or conditioned arguments.

2) Let $KB = (\Pi, \Delta)$ be a knowledge base. We say that the valued-literals $\ell : \alpha$ and $h : \beta$ disagree whenever they are probabilistically inconsistent with the strict knowledge, i.e. when $PMod(\Pi^+ \cup \{l{:}\alpha, h{:}\beta\}) = \emptyset$.
3) A $\star$-argument $\mathcal{A} = (\Phi_1, \Gamma_1; \ell, \alpha)$ attacks another $\star$-argument $\mathcal{B} = (\Phi_2, \Gamma_2; p : \beta)$ at a literal h if there is a $\star$-subargument $\mathcal{B}' = (\Phi_2', \Gamma_2'; h : \gamma)$ of $\mathcal{B}$ such that $\ell : \alpha$ and $h : \gamma$ disagree.

Using only the probabilities to determine when an attack can be deemed as effective may be counterintuitive in some cases (see e.g. arguments $\mathcal{A}_2$ and $\mathcal{A}_3$), thus we combine them with the use of specificity criterion (gaining inspiration in [1,2,7]).

Definition 7 (Activation sets and Specificity). *Given a knowledge base KB, an activation set of an argument $\mathcal{A} = (\Phi, \Gamma; \ell, \alpha)$ is a set of literals $H \subseteq lit(KB)$ such that $H \cup \Pi_D \cup \Gamma^- \vdash \ell$. We denote by $Act(\mathcal{A})$ the set of activation sets for the argument $\mathcal{A}$.*
An argument $\mathcal{A}$ is more specific *than another argument $\mathcal{B}$ when $Act(\mathcal{A}) \subsetneq Act(\mathcal{B})$. $\mathcal{A}$ and $\mathcal{B}$ are* equi-specific *if $Act(\mathcal{A}) = Act(\mathcal{B})$, and* incomparable *whenever $Act(\mathcal{A}) \not\subseteq Act(\mathcal{B})$ and $Act(\mathcal{A}) \not\supseteq Act(\mathcal{B})$.*

In our running example, we can easily check that $\mathcal{A}_3$ and $\mathcal{A}_4$ are incomparable, and both are more specific than $\mathcal{A}_2$, which is itself more specific than $\mathcal{A}_1$.

Definition 8 (Strength and Defeat). *An argument $\mathcal{A} = (\Phi_1, \Gamma_1; \ell : \alpha)$ is* stronger *than another argument $\mathcal{B} = (\Phi_2, \Gamma_2; p : \beta)$ when $\mathcal{A}$ is more specific than $\mathcal{B}$, or when $\mathcal{A}$ and $\mathcal{B}$ are equi-specific or incomparable and $\alpha > \beta$.*
An argument $\mathcal{A} = (\Phi_1, \Gamma_1; \ell : \alpha)$ defeats *another argument $\mathcal{B} = (\Phi_2, \Gamma_2; p : \beta)$ when $\mathcal{A}$ attacks $\mathcal{B}$ on a subargument $\mathcal{B}' = (\Phi_2', \Gamma_2'; h : \gamma)$ and $\mathcal{A}$ is stronger than $\mathcal{B}'$.*

Following with the running example, we have that $\mathcal{A}_2$ defeats $\mathcal{A}_1$, and $\mathcal{A}_3$ defeats $\mathcal{A}_2$ based on the specificity criterion. On the other hand $\mathcal{A}_4$ defeats $\mathcal{A}_3$ on the basis of probability degree criterion, while it defeats $\mathcal{A}_2$ due to specificity.

The proposed setting serves to define an argumentation semantics by considering an argumentation theory and substituting the notions of argument, attack and defeat from the original theory by the ones we propose here. In this fashion, it is natural how to produce argumentation systems with different high-level semantics: from Dung's abstract argumentation systems [4], or other relevant weighted argumentation systems based on it (e.g. [10]), to the rule-based DeLP argumentation framework and its dialectical-tree based semantics [7], or other systems like ASPIC+ [16] or ABA [24]. The definition of the systems is rather immediate and we do not detail them here due to a lack of space. However, the exploration of the resulting systems and the differences with the original ones will involve more work, and we leave it for future work.

4   Future Work

Plenty of issues could be worked out and studied in future works. First, it seems likely that in certain situations, a richer language of conditionals would be useful, e.g. considering conditional logics in the style of Kern-Isberner's three-valued conditionals [14] or the logic of Boolean conditionals [6]. Secondly, other interpretations of the probability entailment can be explored: for instance, to allow for interpreting the weights in valued formulas not only as a lower bound but with other constraints like an equality or a strict lower bound, or to compute the probability of the conclusion of an argument by means of the Maximum Entropy distribution underlying the premises [22,26]. Lastly, a finer gradual notion of attack could be introduced so to allow an attacker argument to debilitate the attacked argument, instead of an all-or-nothing attack.

Acknowledgments. The authors acknowledge partial support by the Spanish projects TIN2015-71799-C2-1-P and PID2019-111544GB-C21.

References

1. Bamber, D., Goodman, I.R., Nguyen, H.T.: Robust reasoning with rules that have exceptions: from second-order probability to argumentation via upper envelopes of probability and possibility plus directed graphs. Ann. Math. Artif. Intell. **45**, 83–171 (2005)
2. Bodanza, G.A., Alessio, C.A.: Rethinking specificity in defeasible reasoning and its effect in argument reinstatement. Inf. Comput. **255**, 287–310 (2017)
3. Cerutti, F., Thimm, M.: A general approach to reasoning with probabilities. Int. J. Approximate Reasoning **111**, 35–50 (2019)
4. Dung, P.M.: On the acceptability of arguments and its fundamental role in nonmonotonic reasoning, logic programming, and n-person games. Artif. Intell. **77**(2), 321–357 (1995)
5. P. M. Dung and P. M. Thang. Towards probabilistic argumentation for jury-based dispute resolution. In: Baroni, P., Cerutti, F., Giacomin, M., Simari, G.R. (eds.) Proceedings of COMMA 2010, volume 216 of Frontiers in Artificial Intelligence and Applications, pp. 171–182. IOS Press Inc. (2010)
6. Flaminio, T., Godo, L., Hosni, H.: Boolean algebras of conditionals, probability and logic. Artif. Intell. **286**, 103347 (2020)
7. Garcia, A., Simari, G.: Defeasible logic programming: an argumentative approach. Theory Pract. Logic Program. **4**(1–2), 95–138 (2004)
8. Garcia, A., Simari, G.: Argumentation based on logic programming. In: Baroni, P., Gabbay, D.M., Giacomin, M., van der Torre, L. (eds.) Handbook of Formal Argumentation, pp. 409–437. College Publications (2018)
9. Gilio, A., Pfeifer, N., Sanfilippo, G.: Transitivity in coherence-based probability logic. J. Appl. Logic **14**, 46–64 (2016)
10. Hunter, A.: A probabilistic approach to modelling uncertain logical arguments. Int. J. Approximate Reasoning **54**(1), 47–81 (2013)
11. Hunter, A.: Probabilistic qualification of attack in abstract argumentation. IJAR **55**(2), 607–638 (2014)
12. Hunter, A., Thimm, M.: On partial information and contradictions in probabilistic abstract argumentation. In: Baral, C., et al. (eds.) Proceedings of KR 2016, pp. 53–62. AAAI Press (2016)
13. Hunter, A., Thimm, M.: Probabilistic reasoning with abstract argumentation frameworks. J. Artif. Intell. Res. **59**, 565–611 (2017)
14. Kern-Isberner, G. (ed.): Conditionals in Nonmonotonic Reasoning and Belief Revision. LNCS (LNAI), vol. 2087. Springer, Heidelberg (2001). https://doi.org/10.1007/3-540-44600-1
15. Li, H., Oren, N., Norman, T.J.: Probabilistic argumentation frameworks. In: Modgil, S., Oren, N., Toni, F. (eds.) TAFA 2011. LNCS (LNAI), vol. 7132, pp. 1–16. Springer, Heidelberg (2012). https://doi.org/10.1007/978-3-642-29184-5_1

16. Modgil, S., Prakken, H.: Abstract rule-based argumentation. In: Baroni, P., Gabbay, D.M., Giacomin, M., van der Torre, L. (eds.) Handbook of Formal Argumentation, pp. 409–437. College Publications (2018)
17. Pollock, J.L.: Justification and defeat. Artif. Intell. **67**, 377–408 (1994)
18. Pollock, J.L.: Cognitive Carpentry. A Blueprint for How to Build a Person. MIT Press, Cambridge (1995)
19. Prakken, H.: Historical overview of formal argumentation. In: Baroni, P., Gabbay, D., Giacomin, M., van der Torre, L. (eds.) Handbook of Formal Argumentation, vol. 1, pp. 73–141. College Publications (2018)
20. Prakken, H.: Probabilistic strength of arguments with structure. In: Thielscher, M., Toni, F., Wolter, F. et al. (eds.) Proceedings of KR 2018, pp. 158–167. AAAI Press (2018)
21. Talbott, W.: Bayesian epistemology. In: Zalta, E.N. (eds.) The Stanford Encyclopedia of Philosophy. Metaphysics Research Lab, Stanford University (2016)
22. Thimm, M., Kern-Isberner, G., Fisseler, J.: Relational probabilistic conditional reasoning at maximum entropy. In: Liu, W. (ed.) ECSQARU 2011. LNCS (LNAI), vol. 6717, pp. 447–458. Springer, Heidelberg (2011). https://doi.org/10.1007/978-3-642-22152-1_38
23. Timmer, S., Meyer, J.J.C., Prakken, H., Renooij, S., Verheij, B.: A two-phase method for extracting explanatory arguments from Bayesian networks. Int. J. Approximate Reasoning **80**, 475–494 (2017)
24. Toni, F.: A tutorial on assumption-based argumentation. Argument Comput. **5**(1), 89–117 (2014)
25. Verheij, B.: Jumping to conclusions: a logico-probabilistic foundation for defeasible rule-based arguments. In: del Cerro, L.F., Herzig, A., Mengin, J. (eds.) JELIA 2012. LNCS (LNAI), vol. 7519, pp. 411–423. Springer, Heidelberg (2012). https://doi.org/10.1007/978-3-642-33353-8_32
26. Wilhelm, M., Kern-Isberner, G., Ecke, A.: Propositional probabilistic reasoning at maximum entropy modulo theories. In: Markov, Z., Russell, I. (eds.) Proceedings of the 29th International Florida Artificial Intelligence Research Society Conference, FLAIRS 2016, pp. 690–694. AAAI Press (2016)

Belief Revision

Conditional Descriptor Revision and Its Modelling by a CSP

Jonas Haldimann[1]([✉]) [ID], Kai Sauerwald[1] [ID], Martin von Berg[1],
Gabriele Kern-Isberner[2] [ID], and Christoph Beierle[1]

[1] FernUniversität in Hagen, 58084 Hagen, Germany
{jonas.haldimann,kai.sauerwald,christoph.beierle}@fernuni-hagen.de
[2] TU Dortmund University, 44227 Dortmund, Germany
gabriele.kern-isberner@cs.tu-dortmund.de

Abstract. Descriptor revision is a belief change framework that was introduced by Hansson as an alternative to the currently prevailing AGM paradigm. One central idea of descriptor revision is to describe the desired outcome of a belief change. Thus, descriptor revision allows expressing different kinds of belief change operations like revision or contraction in a structured and combined way. In this paper, we investigate the framework of conditional descriptor revision. Conditional descriptor revision is a variation of descriptor revision aimed at the revision of ranking functions in the context of conditional logic. It is obtained by applying descriptor revision to conditional logic and additionally requiring the belief changes to fulfil the principle of conditional preservation. We show how conditional descriptor revision can be characterized by a constraint satisfaction problem (CSP). In contrast to previous work, we cover the full descriptor language over conditionals closed under conjunction, disjunction, and negation. We also line out an implementation of conditional descriptor revision based on its CSP representation. Since propositional logic can be embedded into conditional logic, our approach also provides descriptor revision for propositional logic.

1 Introduction

In knowledge representation and reasoning, conditionals play a central role, in particular in belief change [8,10,20,25,27]. Having a simple and intuitive structure, a large part of human knowledge is typically given in the form of '*If A then usually B*' rules, often formally written as $(B|A)$. Let us give a small (artificial and simplified) example from the medical domain dealing with bacterial infections.

Example 1. Let s indicate that a person is sick, b that she has a serious bacterial infection, w that she is in a weakened condition, and h that she should be hospitalized. We can model "A person with a bacterial infection and a weakened condition is usually sick" by $(s|bw)$. Likewise, "A sick and weakened person usually should be hospitalized" can be modelled by $(h|sw)$ and "a person who is not sick usually should not be hospitalized" can be modelled by $(\overline{h}|\overline{s})$.

© Springer Nature Switzerland AG 2021
W. Faber et al. (Eds.): JELIA 2021, LNAI 12678, pp. 35–49, 2021.
https://doi.org/10.1007/978-3-030-75775-5_4

Conditionals are three-valued entities [11] and can be evaluated in epistemic states. Usually, a given set of conditionals can be accepted by various epistemic states. If an agent lives in a dynamic world, she must change her epistemic state in order to account for incoming information. The work by Alchourrón, Gärdenfors, and Makinson [1] (AGM) and its successors have shaped the currently dominating paradigm for such belief changes. By AGM, mainly three kinds of belief changes are subject of interest: *revision*, *contraction* and *expansion*. The core difference between these kinds of changes is their success condition: The aim of revision is to incorporate new beliefs into an agent's belief state while maintaining consistency, contraction is the process of removing some belief from the agent's belief state, and expansion is the process of adding a new belief to an agent's belief state, possibly without maintaining consistency.

Descriptor revision is another framework for belief change proposed by Hansson [13]. Motivation for the design of descriptor revision was the requirement of epistemic states for iterative belief change [10] and problems like the non-finite representability of the result of a contraction [17] or concerns about the 'select-and-intersect' approach of AGM [19]. In contrast to the AGM paradigm, in descriptor revision, different kinds of changes are expressible in one joint framework. This is achieved by employing a full language for success conditions, called belief descriptors, allowing to express and analyse change processes that go beyond the classical AGM operations; a related approach is presented in [2]. While properties of descriptor revision have been investigated intensively [14–19,29], a first approach to the realization and implementation of descriptor revision has been developed only recently, albeit just for basic literal descriptors [26]; a rudimentary suggestion how it could be extended to disjunctive descriptors has been made in the short paper [12]. In this paper, we largely extend the work presented in [12,26], specifically, by providing, realizing, and implementing the full descriptor language, including in particular descriptors containing disjunctions, over a conditional logic. Note that disjunctions allow us to express descriptors requiring to make up one's mind on a specific topic, e.g., in Example 1, whether a person should be hospitalized or not. As semantic models of conditionals, we use ordinal conditional functions [28], also called ranking functions, as representations for epistemic states. We adapt the sophisticated principle of conditional preservation by Kern-Isberner [20,21] for employment in our descriptor revision approach. Its realization and implementation extend the characterization of c-representations and c-revisions via solutions of a constraint satisfaction problem (CSP) [5]. In summary, the main contributions of this article are:

- Instantiation of the descriptor revision framework by conditional logic, yielding conditional descriptor revision (CDR).
- Employment of the principle of conditional preservation (PCP) for the complete descriptor language over conditionals, including descriptors with disjunctions.
- Generalization of descriptor revision and of PCP with respect to a set of conditionals as contextual information.
- A sound and complete characterization of CDR by a CSP.
- Implementation of CDR using constraint logic programming.

2   Logical Preliminaries

Let Σ be a propositional signature (non-empty finite set of propositional variables) and $\mathcal{L}^{\text{prop}}$ the propositional language over Σ. We denote the propositional variables in Σ with lower case letters $a, b, c, \ldots$ and formulas in $\mathcal{L}^{\text{prop}}$ with upper case letters $A, B, C, \ldots$. We may write $A \to B$ for $\neg A \vee B$ as well as AB for $A \wedge B$ and $\overline{A}$ for $\neg A$. With $\top$, we denote a propositional tautology and with $\bot$ a propositional falsum. The set of propositional interpretations $\Omega = \mathcal{P}(\Sigma)$, also called set of worlds, is identified with the set of corresponding complete conjunctions over Σ, where $\mathcal{P}(\cdot)$ is the powerset operator. Propositional entailment is denoted by $\models$, the set of models of A with $Mod(A)$, and $Cn(A) = \{B \mid A \models B\}$ is the deductive closure of A. For a set X, we define $Cn(X) = \{B \mid X \models B\}$ and say X is a *belief set* if it is deductively closed, i.e. if $X = Cn(X)$.

A function $\kappa : \Omega \to \mathbb{N}$ such that $\kappa^{-1}(0) \neq \emptyset$ is a called an *ordinal conditional function (OCF)* or *ranking function* [28]. It expresses degrees of implausibility of interpretations. This is lifted to propositional formulas A by defining $\kappa(A) := \min\{\kappa(\omega) \mid \omega \models A\}$, where $\min \emptyset = \infty$, yielding a function $\kappa : \mathcal{L}^{\text{prop}} \to \mathbb{N} \cup \{\infty\}$ which specifies a degree of implausibility for every formula. With $Mod(\kappa) = \{\omega \mid \kappa(\omega) = 0\}$ we denote the minimal interpretations with respect to κ, and $Bel(\kappa)$ denotes the set of propositional formulas that hold in every $\omega \in Mod(\kappa)$.

Over Σ and $\mathcal{L}^{\text{prop}}$, we define the set of conditionals $\mathcal{L}^{\text{cond}} = \{(B|A) \mid A, B \in \mathcal{L}^{\text{prop}}\}$. A conditional $(B|A)$ formalizes *"if A then usually B"* and establishes a plausible connection between the *antecedent* A and the *consequent* B. Conditionals $(A|\top)$ with tautological antecedents are taken as plausible statements about the world. Because conditionals go well beyond classical logic, they require a richer setting for their semantics than classical logic. Following De Finetti [11], a conditional $(B|A)$ can be *verified (falsified)* by a possible world ω iff $\omega \models AB$ $(\omega \models A\overline{B})$. If $\omega \not\models A$, then we say the conditional is *not applicable* to ω.

Here, ranking functions serve as interpretations in a model theory for the conditional logic $\mathcal{L}^{\text{cond}}$. We say a conditional $(B|A)$ is accepted by an OCF κ, written as $\kappa \models (B|A)$, iff $\kappa(AB) < \kappa(A\overline{B})$, i.e., iff the verification AB of the conditional is more plausible than its falsification $A\overline{B}$. For a propositional formula A, we define $\kappa \models A$ iff $\kappa \models (A|\top)$, i.e., iff $\kappa(A) < \kappa(\overline{A})$ or equivalently iff $\kappa(\overline{A}) > 0$, since at least one of $\kappa(A), \kappa(\overline{A})$ must be 0 due to $\kappa^{-1}(0) \neq \emptyset$. The models of a conditional $(B|A)$ are the set of all ranking functions accepting $(B|A)$, i.e. $Mod((B|A)) = \{\kappa \mid \kappa \models (B|A)\}$. A conditional $(B_1|A_1)$ entails $(B_2|A_2)$, written $(B_1|A_1) \models (B_2|A_2)$, if $Mod((B_1|A_1)) \subseteq Mod((B_2|A_2))$ holds. Furthermore, we define the set of consequences for $X \subseteq \mathcal{L}^{\text{cond}}$ by $Cn(X) = \{(B|A) \mid X \models (B|A)\}$. Again, $X \subseteq \mathcal{L}^{\text{cond}}$ is called deductively closed if $X = Cn(X)$. This ranking function based semantics can be mapped to, and can also be obtained from, other semantics of conditionals [4].

Example 2 (continued). Let $\Sigma = \{s, b, w, h, v\}$ be the signature containing the propositional variables from Example 1 and additionally v denoting that a person is vaccinated. The ranking function κ for worlds over Σ from Table 1 satisfies the conditionals $(s|bw)$, $(h|sw)$, and $(\overline{h}|\overline{s})$ from Example 1.

Table 1. κ is a ranking function accepting the conditionals $\{(s|bw), (h|sw), (\overline{h}|\overline{s})\}$. The ranking function κ' is a descriptor revision of κ by $\Psi_{\mathrm{prop}} = \{\mathfrak{B}(v), \mathfrak{B}(s) \vee \mathfrak{B}(\overline{s})\}$, and $\kappa_1^\circ, \kappa_2^\circ$ are possible results of a conditional descriptor revision of κ by $\Psi = \{\mathfrak{B}((\overline{s}|v)), \mathfrak{B}((s|b)) \vee \mathfrak{B}((\overline{s}|b))\}$. All four ranking functions are c-representations of the corresponding conditionals.

ω	κ	κ'	κ_1°	κ_2°	ω	κ	κ'	κ_1°	κ_2°	ω	κ	κ'	κ_1°	κ_2°	ω	κ	κ'	κ_1°	κ_2°
$sbwhv$	0	0	3	3	$s\bar{b}whv$	0	0	5	1	$\bar{s}bwhv$	2	3	3	4	$\bar{s}\bar{b}whv$	1	2	1	1
$sbwh\bar{v}$	0	1	0	3	$s\bar{b}wh\bar{v}$	0	1	2	1	$\bar{s}bwh\bar{v}$	2	4	5	5	$\bar{s}\bar{b}wh\bar{v}$	1	3	3	2
$sbw\bar{h}v$	2	2	5	5	$s\bar{b}w\bar{h}v$	2	2	7	3	$\bar{s}bw\bar{h}v$	1	2	2	3	$\bar{s}\bar{b}w\bar{h}v$	0	1	0	0
$sbw\bar{h}\bar{v}$	2	3	2	5	$s\bar{b}w\bar{h}\bar{v}$	2	3	4	3	$\bar{s}bw\bar{h}\bar{v}$	1	3	4	4	$\bar{s}\bar{b}w\bar{h}\bar{v}$	0	2	2	1
$sb\bar{w}hv$	0	0	3	3	$s\bar{b}\bar{w}hv$	0	0	5	1	$\bar{s}b\bar{w}hv$	1	2	2	3	$\bar{s}\bar{b}\bar{w}hv$	1	2	1	1
$sb\bar{w}h\bar{v}$	0	1	0	3	$s\bar{b}\bar{w}h\bar{v}$	0	1	2	1	$\bar{s}b\bar{w}h\bar{v}$	1	3	4	4	$\bar{s}\bar{b}\bar{w}h\bar{v}$	1	3	3	2
$sb\bar{w}\bar{h}v$	0	0	3	3	$s\bar{b}\bar{w}\bar{h}v$	0	0	5	1	$\bar{s}b\bar{w}\bar{h}v$	0	1	1	2	$\bar{s}\bar{b}\bar{w}\bar{h}v$	0	1	0	0
$sb\bar{w}\bar{h}\bar{v}$	0	1	0	3	$s\bar{b}\bar{w}\bar{h}\bar{v}$	0	1	2	1	$\bar{s}b\bar{w}\bar{h}\bar{v}$	0	2	3	3	$\bar{s}\bar{b}\bar{w}\bar{h}\bar{v}$	0	2	2	1

3   Descriptors and Descriptor Revision

The main building blocks of descriptor revision are belief descriptors, which provide a language for expressing membership constraints for a belief set.

Definition 1 (atomic/molecular/composite descriptor [18]). *Let $\mathcal{L}$ be a logical language. For any sentence $\varphi \in \mathcal{L}$ the expression $\mathfrak{B}\varphi$ is an atomic descriptor (over $\mathcal{L}$). Any connection of atomic descriptors with disjunction, conjunction and negation is called a molecular descriptor (over $\mathcal{L}$). A composite descriptor (over $\mathcal{L}$) is a set of molecular descriptors (over $\mathcal{L}$).*

Differing from Hansson [18], we use *descriptor* as umbrella term for atomic, molecular and composite descriptors. A molecular descriptor of the form $\mathfrak{B}\varphi$ or $\neg\mathfrak{B}\varphi$ is called a *literal descriptor*. An *elementary descriptor* is a set of literal descriptors (and therefore a composite descriptor).

Definition 2 (Descriptor semantics [18]). *An atomic descriptor $\mathfrak{B}\varphi$ holds in a belief set X, written $X \Vdash \mathfrak{B}\varphi$, if $\varphi \in X$. This is lifted to molecular descriptors truth-functionally. A composite descriptor Ψ holds in X, likewise written $X \Vdash \Psi$, if $X \Vdash \alpha$ holds for every molecular descriptor $\alpha \in \Psi$.*

Example 3. Assume that $\mathcal{L}_{ab}$ is the propositional language over $\Sigma = \{a, b\}$ and $X = Cn(a \vee b)$. Then, $\neg\mathfrak{B}a$ expresses that a is not part of the belief set, whereas $\mathfrak{B}\neg a$ states that the formula $\neg a$ is part of the belief set, e.g. $X \Vdash \neg\mathfrak{B}a$ and $X \not\Vdash \mathfrak{B}\neg a$. Likewise, $\mathfrak{B}a \vee \mathfrak{B}b$ expresses that a or b is believed, whereas $\mathfrak{B}(a \vee b)$ states that the formula $a \vee b$ is believed, e.g. $X \Vdash \mathfrak{B}(a \vee b)$ in the former case and $X \not\Vdash \mathfrak{B}a \vee \mathfrak{B}b$ in the latter.

For the setting of belief change, we assume that every agent is equipped with a belief state, also called epistemic state, which contains all information necessary for performing belief change operations. We denote belief states by $K, K_1, K_2, \ldots$ following the notion of Hansson [18]. General descriptor revision does not specify what a belief state is, but assumes that a belief set $\text{Bel}(K)$ is immanent for every epistemic state K. To make descriptors compatible with belief states, we naturally lift the semantics to belief states, i.e. $K \Vdash \Psi$ if $\text{Bel}(K) \Vdash \Psi$.

Example 4 (continued). Assume ranking functions as representations of belief states. Let κ be the belief state as given in Table 1 and let $\Psi = \{\mathfrak{B}(h \to s)\}$ be a descriptor. Ψ expresses the belief that everyone who is hospitalized is sick. Then Ψ holds in κ, as $h \to s \in \text{Bel}(\kappa)$, i.e., every world with rank 0 fulfils $h \to s$.

AGM theory [1] focuses on properties of revision (or contraction) operations by examining the interconnections between prior belief state, new information and posterior belief state of a change. In contrast, descriptor revision examines the interconnection between prior belief state and posterior belief states that satisfy a particular descriptor. Let $\mathbb{K}_K$ denote the set of all reasonably conceivable successor belief states for a belief state K. A descriptor revision by a descriptor Ψ is the process of choosing a state K' from $\mathbb{K}_K$ such that $K' \Vdash \Psi$. We abstract from how $\mathbb{K}_K$ is obtained and define descriptor revision[1] as follows.

Definition 3 (Descriptor Revision, adapted from [18]). *Let K be a belief state, $\mathbb{K}_K$ a set of belief states and $C : \mathcal{P}(\mathbb{K}_K) \to \mathbb{K}_K$ be a choice function. Then the change from K to $K^\circ = K \circ \Psi$ is called a descriptor revision by Ψ realised by C over $\mathbb{K}_K$ if the following holds:*

$$K \circ \Psi = C(\{K' \in \mathbb{K}_K \mid K' \Vdash \Psi\}) \tag{1}$$

We say that the change from K to K° is a descriptor revision (by Ψ), if C and $\mathbb{K}_K$ (and Ψ) exist such that the change from K to K° is realised by C over $\mathbb{K}_K$. We also say K° is the result of the descriptor revision of K (by Ψ under $\mathbb{K}_K$). Note that descriptors allow us to express a variety of different success conditions, e.g., $\{\mathfrak{B}\varphi\}$ – revision by φ, $\{\neg\mathfrak{B}\varphi\}$ – contraction by φ (also called revocation [19]), $\{\neg\mathfrak{B}\varphi, \neg\mathfrak{B}\neg\varphi\}$ – giving up the judgement on φ (also called ignoration [6]). Additionally, Hansson provides the following examples [19]: $\{\mathfrak{B}\varphi_1, \ldots, \mathfrak{B}\varphi_n\}$ – package revision by $\{\varphi_1, \ldots, \varphi_n\}$, $\{\neg\mathfrak{B}\varphi, \mathfrak{B}\psi\}$ – replacement of φ by ψ, $\{\mathfrak{B}\varphi_1 \vee \ldots \vee \mathfrak{B}\varphi_n\}$ – choice revision by $\{\varphi_1, \ldots, \varphi_n\}$, $\{\mathfrak{B}\varphi \vee \mathfrak{B}\neg\varphi\}$ – making up one's mind about φ.

Example 5 (cont.). Let κ and κ' be as given in Table 1, let $\mathbb{K}_\kappa$ be the set of all ranking functions, let C be a choice function such that if $\kappa' \in X$ then $C(X) = \kappa'$, and let $\Psi_{\text{prop}} = \{\mathfrak{B}(v), \mathfrak{B}(s) \vee \mathfrak{B}(\bar{s})\}$ be a descriptor. The descriptor Ψ_{prop} expresses posterior belief in v and either belief or disbelief in s. In particular, $\mathfrak{B}(s) \vee \mathfrak{B}(\bar{s})$ forces the agent to make up his mind on whether she believes s or

---

[1] In the original framework by Hansson this is much more elaborated. Following the terminology of Hansson, here we present a form of local deterministic monoselective descriptor revision [18]. Moreover, we primarily focus on one change, while Hansson designs the framework for change operators.

not. For this, there is no direct counterpart in the AGM framework. Note that we have $s, v \in \mathrm{Bel}(\kappa')$, and therefore, the descriptor Ψ_{prop} holds in κ'. Thus, the change from κ to κ' is a descriptor revision by Ψ_{prop} realised by C over $\mathbb{K}_\kappa$.

4   Conditional Descriptor Revision

We instantiate descriptor revision for the case in which the underlying logic is the conditional logic $\mathcal{L}^{\mathrm{cond}}$ and ranking functions serve as a representation for epistemic states. Furthermore, we adapt the principle of conditional preservation by Kern-Isberner [21] to the requirements of descriptor revision.

Instantiation for Conditional Logic. In the formal framework of descriptor revision by Hansson, as recalled in Sect. 3, semantics of a descriptor refer to a belief set, containing formulas of the underlying logic. Thus, when using the logic $\mathcal{L}^{\mathrm{cond}}$, we need to refer to the set of conditionals accepted by a ranking function κ when choosing ranking functions as representations for epistemic states. Note that the belief set $\mathrm{Bel}(\kappa)$ of a ranking function κ is a set of propositional beliefs, i.e. $\mathrm{Bel}(\kappa) \subseteq \mathcal{L}^{\mathrm{prop}}$, and thus, we define the set of conditional beliefs for a ranking function κ as $\mathrm{Bel}^{cond}(\kappa) = \{ (B|A) \mid \kappa \models (B|A) \}$. Clearly, the set $\mathrm{Bel}^{cond}(\kappa)$ is deductively closed for every ranking function κ and therefore a belief set. Descriptors and descriptor revision for $\mathcal{L}^{\mathrm{cond}}$ then refer to the set of conditional beliefs $\mathrm{Bel}^{cond}(\kappa)$, and their formal definition can be easily obtained by correspondingly modifying Definitions 1 to 3.

Example 6. Consider the signature $\Sigma = \{s, b, w, h, v\}$ from our running example. $\Psi = \{\mathfrak{B}((\overline{s}|v)), \mathfrak{B}((s|b)) \vee \mathfrak{B}((\overline{s}|b))\}$ is an example for a descriptor over $\mathcal{L}^{\mathrm{cond}}$. Note that the logical junctors for disjunction, conjunction, and negation are not used on the level of conditionals, but only on the level of atomic descriptors over the conditionals (cf. Definition 1).

The conditional logic $\mathcal{L}^{\mathrm{cond}}$ embeds the propositional logic $\mathcal{L}^{\mathrm{prop}}$, because every proposition $A \in \mathcal{L}^{\mathrm{prop}}$ can be represented by $(A|\top)$. Moreover, the definition of $\mathrm{Bel}^{cond}(\kappa)$ ensures compatibility of propositional beliefs with the conditional beliefs, i.e. $\{(A|\top) \mid A \in \mathrm{Bel}(K)\} \subseteq \mathrm{Bel}^{cond}(K)$. Thus, our approach to descriptor revision by conditionals, presented in the following, subsumes descriptor revision for propositions.

For a fixed signature, there are only finitely many conditionals in $\mathcal{L}^{\mathrm{cond}}$ up to equivalence, where $(B|A)$ and $(B'|A')$ are equivalent according to de Finettis's semantics [11] if $AB \equiv A'B'$ and $A\overline{B} \equiv A'\overline{B'}$. Thus, for every descriptor over $\mathcal{L}^{\mathrm{cond}}$ it is possible to find a finite descriptor that is equivalent, i.e. that describes the same ranking functions. For this reason, we will only consider finite descriptors from now on.

Conditional Preservation. When an agent performs a belief change, the change might not only affect explicit beliefs, but also implicit beliefs. Boutilier proposed that belief change should also minimize the effect on conditional beliefs [8]. However, Darwiche and Pearl [10] showed that a strict minimization may lead to counterintuitive results. Instead, they proposed axioms specifying a principle of conditional preservation (PCP) for specific cases in more detail. Kern-Isberner [21] proposed a general and thorough axiomatization of such a principle in her (PCP) principles that deal with different change operators in a uniform way. Moreover, these principles strictly separate conditional preservation from the respective success condition. Implicitly, these (PCP) axioms not even make use of the input to the change process but allow for considering general sets of conditionals with respect to which the change process should obey (PCP). We make this explicit for conditional descriptor revision in the following. For this, we extract from the descriptor Ψ the involved set of conditionals $cond(\Psi)$ and we use $cond(\alpha)$ as shorthand for $cond(\{\alpha\})$:

- for $\Psi = \emptyset$ let $cond(\Psi) = \emptyset$,
- for $\Psi = \{\mathfrak{B}(B|A)\}$ let $cond(\Psi) = \{(B|A)\}$,
- for $\Psi = \{\alpha, \beta, \ldots\}$ let $cond(\Psi) = cond(\{\alpha\}) \cup cond(\{\beta, \ldots\})$,
- for $\Psi = \{\alpha \vee \beta\}$ let $cond(\Psi) = cond(\{\alpha\}) \cup cond(\{\beta\})$,
- for $\Psi = \{\alpha \wedge \beta\}$ let $cond(\Psi) = cond(\{\alpha\}) \cup cond(\{\beta\})$, and
- for $\Psi = \{\neg\alpha\}$ let $cond(\Psi) = cond(\{\alpha\})$.

Definition 4 (PCP for OCF changes, adapted from [22]). *A change of an OCF κ to an OCF κ° fulfils the principle of conditional preservation with respect to the conditionals $\mathcal{R} = \{(B_1|A_1), \ldots, (B_n|A_n)\}$, if for every two multisets of propositional interpretations $\Omega_1 = \{\omega_1, \ldots, \omega_m\}$ and $\Omega_2 = \{\omega'_1, \ldots, \omega'_m\}$ with the same cardinality m such that the multisets Ω_1 and Ω_2 contain the same number of interpretations which verify, respectively falsify, each conditional $(B_i|A_i)$ in $\mathcal{R}$, the OCFs κ and κ° are balanced in the following way:*

$$\sum_{i=1}^{m} \kappa(\omega_i) - \sum_{i=1}^{m} \kappa(\omega'_i) = \sum_{i=1}^{m} \kappa^\circ(\omega_i) - \sum_{i=1}^{m} \kappa^\circ(\omega'_i) \tag{2}$$

In the following, we use a central characterisation [20,22] of the principle of conditional preservation to obtain a characterisation of the principle of conditional preservation for descriptor revisions.

Definition 5 ($\kappa_{\vec{\gamma}}$). *Let κ be an OCF over Σ and $\mathcal{R} = \{(B_1|A_1), \ldots, (B_n|A_n)\}$ be a set of conditionals. For $\vec{\gamma} = (\gamma_1^-, \gamma_1^+, \ldots, \gamma_n^-, \gamma_n^+) \in \mathbb{Z}^{2n}$ we define $\kappa_{\vec{\gamma}}$ by*

$$\kappa_{\vec{\gamma}}(\omega) = \kappa_0 + \kappa(\omega) + \sum_{\substack{1 \leqslant i \leqslant n \\ \omega \models A_i B_i}} \gamma_i^+ + \sum_{\substack{1 \leqslant i \leqslant n \\ \omega \models A_i \wedge \neg B_i}} \gamma_i^- \tag{3}$$

where κ_0 is chosen such that $\kappa_{\vec{\gamma}}$ is a ranking function, i.e., $\kappa_{\vec{\gamma}}(\omega) \geqslant 0$ for all $\omega \in \Omega$ and $\kappa_{\vec{\gamma}}(\omega') = 0$ for at least one $\omega' \in \Omega$.

The idea underlying Definition 5 is that interpretations that are verifying and falsifying the same conditionals are treated in the same way. Thus, for every conditional $(B_i|A_i) \in cond(\Psi)$, the two constants γ_i^+ and γ_i^- handle how interpretations that verify or falsify $(B_i|A_i)$ are shifted over the change process. The constant κ_0 is used to ensure that κ° is indeed a ranking function, i.e. κ° is non-negative and there is at least one world ω such that $\kappa^\circ(\omega) = 0$.

Proposition 1 (PCP characterization, adapted from [22]). *Let* $\mathcal{R} = \{(B_1|A_1), \dots, (B_n|A_n)\}$ *be a set of conditionals and let* κ° *be the result of a belief change of* κ. *Then this change satisfies the* principle of conditional preservation *with respect to the conditionals in* $\mathcal{R}$ *if and only if there is a vector of numbers[2]* $\vec{\gamma} \in \mathbb{Q}^{2n}$ *such that* $\kappa^\circ = \kappa_{\vec{\gamma}}$.

The proof of Proposition 1 is directly obtainable from a proof given by Kern-Isberner [20, Theorem 4.6.1], since no specific information on the success condition for the conditionals in the descriptor was used in Proposition 1.

Example 7 (cont.). Consider the change from κ to κ_1°, both as given in Table 1. This change satisfies the principle of conditional preservation with respect to the conditionals in $\mathcal{R} = \{(\overline{s}|v), (s|b), (\overline{s}|b)\}$. We can obtain κ_1° from κ via Equation (3) by choosing $\kappa_0 = 1$, $\gamma_1^+ = -1$, $\gamma_1^- = 0$, $\gamma_2^+ = 2$, $\gamma_2^- = 2$, $\gamma_3^+ = 0$, and $\gamma_3^- = 0$.

Descriptor Revision with Conditional Preservation. The principle of conditional preservation is a powerful basic principle of belief change and it is natural to demand satisfaction of this principle. The principle demands a specific relation between the conditionals in the prior belief state K, the conditionals in the posterior state K° and the conditionals in the descriptor Ψ. Remember that by Definition 3, a descriptor revision from K to K° is determined by a choice function C, the descriptor Ψ and the set $\mathbb{K}_K$ such that Equation (1) holds, but none of these components allow us to express a direct relation between K, K° and Ψ. Thus, there is no possibility to express conditional preservation by the means of descriptor revision. The principle of conditional preservation is somewhat orthogonal to descriptor revision, which gives rationale to the following definition of conditional descriptor revision.

Definition 6 (Conditional Descriptor Revision). *Let* κ *be a ranking function. A descriptor revision of* κ *to* κ° *by a descriptor* Ψ *over* $\mathcal{L}^{cond}$ *(realised by* C *over* $\mathbb{K}_\kappa$*) is called a* conditional descriptor revision *of* κ *to* κ° *by* Ψ *(realised by* C *over* $\mathbb{K}_\kappa$*) if the change from* κ *to* κ° *satisfies the principle of conditional preservation with respect to* $cond(\Psi)$.

In Definition 6, we choose ranking functions as representations for belief states, but note that the principle of conditional preservation also applies to

---

[2] All $\kappa_0, \gamma_i^+, \gamma_i^-$ can be rational [22], but κ° has to satisfy the requirements for an OCF, in particular, all $\kappa^\circ(\omega)$ must be non-negative integers. In this paper, it suffices to assume $\kappa_0, \gamma_i^+, \gamma_i^-$ to be integers and we will thus focus on the case $\vec{\gamma} \in \mathbb{Z}^{2n}$.

other representations [20]. Thus, for other kinds of representations of belief states one might give a definition of conditional descriptor revision similar to the one given here. However, for the rest of the article, we focus on ranking functions. Moreover, we assume $\mathbb{K}_\kappa$ to be the set of all ranking functions, i.e. when revising by a descriptor over Ψ, we choose from the set of all ranking functions.

Example 8 (cont.). Consider κ and κ_1° as given in Table 1 and the descriptor $\Psi = \{\mathfrak{B}((\overline{s}|v)), \mathfrak{B}((s|b)) \vee \mathfrak{B}((\overline{s}|b))\}$. This descriptor requires the revision with $(\overline{s}|v)$ and making up one's mind about $(\overline{s}|b)$. The change from κ to κ_1° fulfils the principle of conditional preservation with respect to the conditionals in $cond(\Psi) = \{(\overline{s}|v), (s|b), (\overline{s}|b)\}$ (see Example 7). Ψ holds in κ_1°. Hence, this change is a conditional descriptor revision by Ψ.

5 Modelling Conditional Descriptor Revision by a CSP

C-changes can be characterized as solutions of a constraint satisfaction problem. Similarly, this holds for conditional descriptor revision as it fulfils the PCP.

Definition 7 ($\mathrm{CR}_D(\kappa, \Psi, \mathcal{R})$, **constraints for a descriptor with respect to** $\mathcal{R}$). *Let κ be an OCF, $\mathcal{R} = \{(B_1|A_1), \ldots, (B_n|A_n)\}$ a set of conditionals, and Ψ a descriptor with $cond(\Psi) \subseteq \mathcal{R}$. The CSP for Ψ in κ under $\mathcal{R}$, denoted by $\mathrm{CR}_D(\kappa, \Psi, \mathcal{R})$, on the constraint variables $\gamma_1^-, \gamma_1^+, \ldots, \gamma_n^-, \gamma_n^+$ is given by:*

1. If $\Psi = \mathfrak{B}(B_i|A_i)$ is atomic, $\mathrm{CR}_D(\kappa, \Psi, \mathcal{R})$ is given by, for $i = 1, \ldots, n$:

$$
\gamma_i^- - \gamma_i^+ > \min_{\omega \models A_i B_i} \left(\kappa(\omega) + \sum_{\substack{j \neq i \\ \omega \models A_j B_j}} \gamma_j^+ + \sum_{\substack{j \neq i \\ \omega \models A_j \bar{B}_j}} \gamma_j^- \right)
$$
$$
- \min_{\omega \models A_i \bar{B}_i} \left(\kappa(\omega) + \sum_{\substack{j \neq i \\ \omega \models A_j B_j}} \gamma_j^+ + \sum_{\substack{j \neq i \\ \omega \models A_j \bar{B}_j}} \gamma_j^- \right)
$$

(4)

2. If $\Psi = \neg\alpha_1$, then $\mathrm{CR}_D(\kappa, \Psi, \mathcal{R})$ is $\neg\big(\mathrm{CR}_D(\kappa, \alpha_1, \mathcal{R})\big)$.
3. If $\Psi = \alpha_1 \vee \alpha_2$, then $\mathrm{CR}_D(\kappa, \Psi, \mathcal{R})$ is $\big(\mathrm{CR}_D(\kappa, \alpha_1, \mathcal{R})\big) \vee \big(\mathrm{CR}_D(\kappa, \alpha_2, \mathcal{R})\big)$.
4. If $\Psi = \alpha_1 \wedge \alpha_2$, then $\mathrm{CR}_D(\kappa, \Psi, \mathcal{R})$ is $\big(\mathrm{CR}_D(\kappa, \alpha_1, \mathcal{R})\big) \wedge \big(\mathrm{CR}_D(\kappa, \alpha_2, \mathcal{R})\big)$.
5. If $\Psi = \{\alpha_1, \ldots, \alpha_m\}$, then $\mathrm{CR}_D(\kappa, \Psi, \mathcal{R})$ is $\mathrm{CR}_D(\kappa, \alpha_1 \wedge \cdots \wedge \alpha_m, \mathcal{R}) = \big(\mathrm{CR}_D(\kappa, \alpha_1, \mathcal{R})\big) \wedge \cdots \wedge \big(\mathrm{CR}_D(\kappa, \alpha_m, \mathcal{R})\big)$.

The logic combinators of the constraint systems are interpreted truth-functionally. A vector $\vec{\gamma}$ fulfils a constraint $A \vee B$ if $\vec{\gamma}$ fulfils either A or B or both. Analogously, $\vec{\gamma}$ fulfils $A \wedge B$ if it fulfils both A and B. $\vec{\gamma}$ fulfils $\neg A$ if it does not fulfil A. This is equivalent to $Sol(A \vee B) = Sol(A) \cup Sol(B)$, $Sol(A \wedge B) = Sol(A) \cap Sol(B)$ and $Sol(\neg A) = \mathbb{Z}^{2n} \setminus Sol(A)$.

Definition 8 ($\mathrm{CR}_D(\kappa, \Psi)$). *Let κ be a OCF and Ψ a descriptor. The constraint system for Ψ in κ, denoted by $\mathrm{CR}_D(\kappa, \Psi)$, is given by $\mathrm{CR}_D(\kappa, \Psi, cond(\Psi))$.*

Proposition 2 (Soundness and Completeness of $CR_D(\kappa, \Psi, \mathcal{R})$). *Let κ be a ranking function, $\mathcal{R} = \{(B_1|A_1), \ldots, (B_n|A_n)\}$ a set of conditionals, and Ψ a descriptor with $cond(\Psi) \subseteq \mathcal{R}$. Then $\kappa_{\vec{\gamma}} \models \Psi$ iff $\vec{\gamma} \in Sol(CR_D(\kappa, \Psi, \mathcal{R}))$.*

Proof. We show this proposition by structural induction.

1. If $\Psi = \mathfrak{B}(B_i|A_i)$ is atomic, $CR_D(\kappa, \Psi, \mathcal{R})$ is given by (4). It can be shown [5,20,26] that $\vec{\gamma} \in Sol(CR_D(\kappa, \Psi, \mathcal{R}))$ iff $\kappa_{\vec{\gamma}} \models (B_i|A_i)$ which is equivalent to $\kappa \models \Psi$.
2. If $\Psi = \neg\alpha_1$, then $CR_D(\kappa, \Psi, \mathcal{R})$ is $\neg(CR_D(\kappa, \alpha_1, \mathcal{R}))$. We have $\vec{\gamma} \in Sol(\neg(CR_D(\kappa, \Psi, \mathcal{R})))$ iff $\vec{\gamma} \notin Sol(CR_D(\kappa, \alpha_1, \mathcal{R}))$ which is equivalent to $\kappa \models \Psi \Leftrightarrow \kappa \not\models \alpha_1$ due to the induction hypothesis.
3. If $\Psi = \alpha_1 \vee \alpha_2$, then $CR_D(\kappa, \Psi, \mathcal{R})$ is $(CR_D(\kappa, \alpha_1, \mathcal{R})) \vee (CR_D(\kappa, \alpha_2, \mathcal{R}))$. We have $\vec{\gamma} \in Sol(CR_D(\kappa, \alpha_1, \mathcal{R}) \vee CR_D(\kappa, \alpha_2, \mathcal{R}))$ iff $\vec{\gamma} \in Sol(CR_D(\kappa, \alpha_1, \mathcal{R}))$ or $\vec{\gamma} \in Sol(CR_D(\kappa, \alpha_2, \mathcal{R}))$. This is equivalent to $\kappa \models \alpha_1$ or $\kappa \models \alpha_2$ due to the induction hypothesis. This is in turn equivalent to $\kappa \models \alpha_1 \vee \alpha_2$.
4. If $\Psi = \alpha_1 \wedge \alpha_2$, then $CR_D(\kappa, \Psi, \mathcal{R})$ is $(CR_D(\kappa, \alpha_1, \mathcal{R})) \wedge (CR_D(\kappa, \alpha_2, \mathcal{R}))$. We have $\vec{\gamma} \in Sol(CR_D(\kappa, \alpha_1, \mathcal{R}) \wedge CR_D(\kappa, \alpha_2, \mathcal{R}))$ iff $\vec{\gamma} \in Sol(CR_D(\kappa, \alpha_1, \mathcal{R}))$ and $\vec{\gamma} \in Sol(CR_D(\kappa, \alpha_2, \mathcal{R}))$. This is equivalent to $\kappa \models \alpha_1$ and $\kappa \models \alpha_2$ due to the induction hypothesis. This is in turn equivalent to $\kappa \models \alpha_1 \wedge \alpha_2$.
5. If $\Psi = \{\alpha_1, \ldots, \alpha_m\}$, then $CR_D(\kappa, \Psi, \mathcal{R})$ is $CR_D(\kappa, \alpha_1 \wedge \cdots \wedge \alpha_m, \mathcal{R}) = (CR_D(\kappa, \alpha_1, \mathcal{R})) \wedge \cdots \wedge (CR_D(\kappa, \alpha_m, \mathcal{R}))$. As $\Psi = \{\alpha_1, \ldots, \alpha_m\}$ is equivalent to $\alpha_1 \wedge \cdots \wedge \alpha_m$, (4) implies that $\vec{\gamma} \in Sol(\Psi)$ iff $\kappa_{\vec{\gamma}} \models \Psi$. □

Definition 9 ($OCF(CR_D(\kappa, \Psi, \mathcal{R}))$). *Let κ be a ranking function, Ψ be a descriptor, and $\mathcal{R}$ be a set of conditionals such that $cond(\Psi) \subseteq \mathcal{R}$. We define $OCF(CR_D(\kappa, \Psi, \mathcal{R})) := \{\kappa_{\vec{\gamma}} \mid \vec{\gamma} \in Sol(CR_D(\kappa, \Psi, \mathcal{R}))\}$.*

Proposition 3 (Soundness and Completeness of $CR_D(\kappa, \Psi)$). *Let κ be a ranking function and Ψ a descriptor. $\kappa_{\vec{\gamma}}$ is a conditional descriptor revision of κ by Ψ iff $\kappa_{\vec{\gamma}} \in OCF(CR_D(\kappa, \Psi))$.*

Proof. The proposition is equivalent to the conjunction of:

1. For $\vec{\gamma} \in Sol(CR_D(\kappa, \Psi))$, $\kappa_{\vec{\gamma}}$ is a conditional descriptor revision of κ by Ψ.
2. If κ° is a conditional descriptor revision of κ by Ψ, then there is a solution $\vec{\gamma} \in Sol(CR_D(\kappa, \Psi))$ such that $\kappa^\circ = \kappa_{\vec{\gamma}}$.

We show both parts of the conjunction.

(1) Let $\vec{\gamma} \in Sol(CR_D(\kappa, \Psi))$. By construction, the change from κ to $\kappa_{\vec{\gamma}}$ fulfils the principle of conditional preservation with respect to $cond(\Psi)$ (Proposition 1). Proposition 2 shows, that $\kappa_{\vec{\gamma}} \models \Psi$. Let $\mathbb{K}_\kappa = \{\kappa' : \Omega \rightarrow \mathbb{N}_0\}$ and $C : \mathcal{P}(\mathbb{K}_\kappa) \rightarrow \mathbb{K}_\kappa$ such that $C(\{\kappa_{\vec{\gamma'}} \mid \vec{\gamma'} \in Sol(CR_D(\kappa, \Psi))\}) = \kappa_{\vec{\gamma}}$. The change from κ to $\kappa_{\vec{\gamma}}$ is a conditional descriptor revision of κ by Ψ (realised by C over $\mathbb{K}_\kappa$).

(2) Let κ° be a conditional descriptor revision of κ by Ψ (realised by C over $\mathbb{K}_K$). Because the change fulfils the principle of conditional preservation with respect to $cond(\Psi)$, there is a vector $\vec{\gamma}$ such that $\kappa^\circ = \kappa_{\vec{\gamma}}$ (see Proposition 1). Because $\kappa_{\vec{\gamma}} \models \Psi$, we have that $\vec{\gamma} \in Sol(CR_D(\kappa, \Psi))$ (see Proposition 2). □

Example 9 (cont.). Consider the conditional descriptor revision of κ (as given in Table 1) with $\Psi = \{\mathfrak{B}((\overline{s}|v)), \mathfrak{B}((s|b)) \vee \mathfrak{B}((\overline{s}|b))\}$ described in Example 8. Let $\mathcal{R} = cond(\Psi)$. The constraint system corresponding to this descriptor is

$$\mathrm{CR_D}(\kappa, \mathfrak{B}(\overline{s}|v), \mathcal{R}) \wedge \big(\mathrm{CR_D}(\kappa, \mathfrak{B}(s|b), \mathcal{R}) \vee \mathrm{CR_D}(\kappa, \mathfrak{B}(\overline{s}|b), \mathcal{R})\big).$$

The result of the revision is selected from the set

$$S = OCF(\mathrm{CR_D}(\kappa, \mathfrak{B}(\overline{s}|v), \mathcal{R})) \cap$$
$$\big(OCF(\mathrm{CR_D}(\kappa, \mathfrak{B}(s|b), \mathcal{R})) \cup OCF(\mathrm{CR_D}(\kappa, \mathfrak{B}(\overline{s}|b), \mathcal{R}))\big)$$

The set $OCF(\mathrm{CR_D}(\kappa, \mathfrak{B}(\overline{s}|v), \mathcal{R}))$ contains both ranking functions κ_1° and κ_2° as given in Table 1. κ_1° is also an element of $OCF(\mathrm{CR_D}(\kappa, \mathfrak{B}(s|b), \mathcal{R}))$ while κ_2° is an element of $OCF(\mathrm{CR_D}(\kappa, \mathfrak{B}(\overline{s}|b), \mathcal{R}))$. Hence, κ_1° and κ_2° are two possible outcomes of the conditional descriptor revision of κ by Ψ.

The set $\mathcal{R}$ in $\mathrm{CR_D}(\kappa, \Psi, \mathcal{R})$ governs the possible solutions of the constraint satisfaction problem. The next two propositions state that adding conditionals to $\mathcal{R}$ will not remove possible revisions and that expanding $\mathcal{R}$ can indeed lead to more possible outcomes of the revision.

Proposition 4. *Let κ be an OCF, $\mathcal{R} \subseteq \mathcal{R}'$ sets of conditionals, and Ψ a descriptor with $cond(\Psi) \subseteq \mathcal{R}$. Then $OCF(\mathrm{CR_D}(\kappa, \Psi, \mathcal{R})) \subseteq OCF(\mathrm{CR_D}(\kappa, \Psi, \mathcal{R}'))$.*

Proof. Let $\kappa_{\vec{\gamma}} \in OCF(\mathrm{CR_D}(\kappa, \Psi, \mathcal{R}))$. Proposition 2 implies that $\kappa_{\vec{\gamma}} \models \Psi$. Let $\vec{\gamma}' \in \mathbb{Z}^{2 \cdot |\mathcal{R}'|}$ be a vector that assigns the same impacts to the conditionals in $\mathcal{R}$ as $\vec{\gamma}$ and impacts $\gamma_i^- = \gamma_i^+ = 0$ to all other conditionals. Then we have $\kappa_{\vec{\gamma}'} = \kappa_{\vec{\gamma}}$ and hence $\kappa_{\vec{\gamma}'} \models \Psi$. Proposition 2 implies that $\gamma' \in Sol(\mathrm{CR_D}(\kappa, \Psi, \mathcal{R}'))$. ☐

Proposition 5. *There is an OCF κ, sets of conditionals $\mathcal{R}, \mathcal{R}'$ with $\mathcal{R} \subseteq \mathcal{R}'$, and a descriptor Ψ with $cond(\Psi) \subseteq \mathcal{R}$ such that $OCF(\mathrm{CR_D}(\kappa, \Psi, \mathcal{R})) \not\supseteq OCF(\mathrm{CR_D}(\kappa, \Psi, \mathcal{R}'))$.*

Proof. Consider the ranking function $\kappa : \{ab \mapsto 0, \overline{a}b \mapsto 1, a\overline{b} \mapsto 1, \overline{a}\overline{b} \mapsto 2\}$ over the signature $\Sigma = \{a, b\}$. Let $\mathcal{R} = \{(\overline{a}|\top)\}$ and $\mathcal{R}' = \{(\overline{a}|\top), (\overline{b}|\top)\}$. Furthermore, let $\Psi = \{\mathfrak{B}(\overline{a}|\top)\}$. Then we have $\vec{\gamma}' = (0, 2, 0, 1) \in Sol(\mathrm{CR_D}(\kappa, \Psi, \mathcal{R}'))$ with $\kappa_{\vec{\gamma}'} : \{ab \mapsto 1, \overline{a}b \mapsto 0, a\overline{b} \mapsto 1, \overline{a}\overline{b} \mapsto 0\} \in OCF(\mathrm{CR_D}(\kappa, \Psi, \mathcal{R}'))$. However, since the change from κ to $\kappa_{\vec{\gamma}'}$ violates the principle of conditional preservation with respect to $\mathcal{R}$, there is no $\vec{\gamma} \in Sol(\mathrm{CR_D}(\kappa, \Psi, \mathcal{R}))$ such that $\kappa_{\vec{\gamma}} = \kappa_{\vec{\gamma}'}$. ☐

Interestingly, the revision with the conjunction (or disjunction) of two descriptors can have additional outcomes compared with the intersection (or union) of the possible outcomes of each of the revisions. This is because only the revision with the conjunction (or disjunction) allows to assign non-negative impacts to conditionals from both descriptors.

Proposition 6. *Let κ be a ranking function and α_1, α_2 molecular descriptors.*

$$OCF(\mathrm{CR_D}(\kappa, \alpha_1)) \cap OCF(\mathrm{CR_D}(\kappa, \alpha_2)) \subseteq OCF(\mathrm{CR_D}(\kappa, \alpha_1 \wedge \alpha_2)) \quad (5)$$
$$OCF(\mathrm{CR_D}(\kappa, \alpha_1)) \cup OCF(\mathrm{CR_D}(\kappa, \alpha_2)) \subseteq OCF(\mathrm{CR_D}(\kappa, \alpha_1 \vee \alpha_2)) \quad (6)$$

Proof. We show the subset relation (6) first. Let $\mathcal{R} = cond(\{\alpha_1 \vee \alpha_2\})$. We have $Sol(\mathrm{CR_D}(\kappa, \alpha_1, \mathcal{R})) \cup Sol(\mathrm{CR_D}(\kappa, \alpha_2, \mathcal{R})) = Sol(\mathrm{CR_D}(\kappa, \alpha_1 \vee \alpha_2, \mathcal{R})) = Sol(\mathrm{CR_D}(\kappa, \alpha_1 \vee \alpha_2))$ and thus $OCF(\mathrm{CR_D}(\kappa, \alpha_1, \mathcal{R})) \cup OCF(\mathrm{CR_D}(\kappa, \alpha_2, \mathcal{R})) = OCF(\mathrm{CR_D}(\kappa, \alpha_1 \vee \alpha_2))$. Because $cond(\alpha_1), cond(\alpha_2) \subseteq \mathcal{R}$ we have $OCF(\mathrm{CR_D}(\kappa, \alpha_1)) \subseteq OCF(\mathrm{CR_D}(\kappa, \alpha_1, \mathcal{R}))$ and $OCF(\mathrm{CR_D}(\kappa, \alpha_2)) \subseteq OCF(\mathrm{CR_D}(\kappa, \alpha_2, \mathcal{R}))$ (Proposition 4). Therefore, (6) holds. This analogously applies to descriptors with conjunction, yielding (5). □

In general, the inverse of the inclusions in Proposition 6 does not hold.

Proposition 7. *There is an OCF κ and molecular descriptors α_1, α_2, such that*

$$OCF(\mathrm{CR_D}(\kappa, \alpha_1)) \cap OCF(\mathrm{CR_D}(\kappa, \alpha_2)) \nsupseteq OCF(\mathrm{CR_D}(\kappa, \alpha_1 \wedge \alpha_2)) \quad (7)$$

$$OCF(\mathrm{CR_D}(\kappa, \alpha_1)) \cup OCF(\mathrm{CR_D}(\kappa, \alpha_2)) \nsupseteq OCF(\mathrm{CR_D}(\kappa, \alpha_1 \vee \alpha_2)) \quad (8)$$

Proof. We can show both not-subset-relations with one example. Consider the OCF $\kappa : \{ab \mapsto 0, \bar{a}b \mapsto 1, a\bar{b} \mapsto 1, \bar{a}\bar{b} \mapsto 2\}$ over the signature $\Sigma = \{a, b\}$. Let $\alpha_1 = \{\mathfrak{B}(\bar{a}|\top)\}$ and $\alpha_2 = \{\mathfrak{B}(\bar{b}|\top)\}$. Every ranking function $\kappa_1' \in S_1 = OCF(\mathrm{CR_D}(\kappa, \alpha_1))$ has the form $\kappa_1' : \{ab \mapsto \gamma_1^-, \bar{a}b \mapsto 1 + \gamma_1^+, a\bar{b} \mapsto 1 + \gamma_1^-, \bar{a}\bar{b} \mapsto 2 + \gamma_1^+\}$ and every ranking function $\kappa_2' \in S_2 = OCF(\mathrm{CR_D}(\kappa, \alpha_2))$ has the form $\kappa_2' : \{ab \mapsto \gamma_2^-, \bar{a}b \mapsto 1 + \gamma_2^-, a\bar{b} \mapsto 1 + \gamma_2^+, \bar{a}\bar{b} \mapsto 2 + \gamma_2^+\}$. Now $\vec{\gamma}' = (0, 2, 0, 1) \in Sol(\mathrm{CR_D}(\kappa, \alpha_1 \wedge \alpha_2))$ and $\vec{\gamma}' \in Sol(\mathrm{CR_D}(\kappa, \alpha_1 \wedge \alpha_2))$ with $\kappa_{\vec{\gamma}'} : \{ab \mapsto 1, \bar{a}b \mapsto 0, a\bar{b} \mapsto 1, \bar{a}\bar{b} \mapsto 0\} = \{ab \mapsto 1, \bar{a}b \mapsto 1 + (-1), a\bar{b} \mapsto 1 + 0, \bar{a}\bar{b} \mapsto 2 + (-2)\}$. $\kappa_{\vec{\gamma}'}$ is neither in S_1 or S_2. Hence, relations (7) and (8) hold. □

6   Implementation

We implemented conditional descriptor revision for all finite descriptors. Given a ranking function κ and an descriptor Ψ, our system, called ChangeOCF, calculates a list of possible outcomes of a conditional descriptor revision of κ with Ψ. To calculate the possible outcomes of the revision, ChangeOCF uses a constraint system based on $\mathrm{CR_D}(\kappa, \Psi)$ introduced in Sect. 5. Following Proposition 2, the solutions of this constraint system correspond to the outcomes of a conditional descriptor revision. I.e., the set $OCF(\mathrm{CR_D}(\kappa, \Psi))$ is the desired output of our implementation. In general, $Sol(\mathrm{CR_D}(\kappa, \Psi))$ and $OCF(\mathrm{CR_D}(\kappa, \Psi))$ may contain infinitely many elements, but there is only a finite number of equivalence classes with respect to the acceptance of conditionals. Therefore, it is possible to restrict the set of solutions to finitely many without losing interesting results. To do this, we used an approach inspired by *maximal impacts* for c-representations [5,7] that addresses a similar problem for the enumeration of c-representations. The idea of maximal impacts is to add explicit bounds for the value of each γ_i^+, γ_i^-. This reduces the set of possible solutions to a finite set. If the bounds are chosen appropriately, no solutions that are not equivalent to a solution within the bounds are lost. ChangeOCF limits the value of $\gamma_1^+, \gamma_1^-, \ldots, \gamma_n^+, \gamma_n^-$ to an individual finite domain by extending the constraint system $\mathrm{CR_D}(\kappa, \Psi)$ with constraints $u_i^{\min -} \leqslant \gamma_i^- \leqslant u_i^{\max -}$ and $u_i^{\min +} \leqslant \gamma_i^+ \leqslant u_i^{\max +}$ for $1 \leqslant i \leqslant n$. We denote this extended CSP by $CR_D^{\vec{u}}(\kappa, \Psi)$ with $\vec{u} = \langle u_1^{\min -}, u_1^{\max -}, u_1^{\min +}, u_1^{\max +},$ $\ldots, u_n^{\max +}\rangle$. Like for c-representations [23], it is an open problem which values for $\vec{u}$ guarantee that a representative for each equivalence class of solutions with respect to the acceptance of conditionals is found for a given κ and Ψ.

To simplify the construction of $CR_D^{\vec{u}}(\kappa, \Psi)$, we require the descriptor to be converted to a disjunction of elementary descriptors. This form resembles the disjunctive normal form for propositional formulae. As the atomic descriptors are combined like atoms in a formula and descriptors are evaluated truth-functionally, every descriptor has an equivalent descriptor in this normal form. Here, equivalency means that two descriptors accept the same ranking functions.

The implementation of ChangeOCF employs InfOCF-Lib [24], a Java library for reasoning with conditionals and ranking functions. InfOCF-Lib calculates the c-representations of a conditional knowledge base by solving a constraint system similar to $CR_D^{\vec{u}}(\kappa, \Psi)$. The interface of ChangeOCF is implemented in Java. To solve $CR_D^{\vec{u}}(\kappa, \Psi)$, we use SICStus Prolog and its constraint logic programming library for finite domains [9]. The Prolog implementation is an adaption of the implementation of InfOCF [3] to the more general case of belief change.

7   Summary and Future Work

In this work, we investigated conditional descriptor revision and its realisation. Conditional descriptor revision is an extension of descriptor revision for conditionals, obeying the principle of conditional preservation. We developed a characterization of conditional descriptor revision by a constraint satisfaction problem that allows us to express arbitrary descriptors, covering the complete descriptor language over conditionals closed under conjunction, disjunction, and negation. Additionally, we presented an implementation of conditional descriptor revision using its CSP characterization and employing constraint logic programming.

So far, we focussed on calculating the complete set of admissible outcomes of conditional descriptor revision. In our current work, we are developing criteria which of the possible solutions should be selected. We will also address the open problem of determining maximal impacts for the CSP such that all solutions up to equivalence with respect to acceptance of conditionals are captured.

Acknowledgements. We thank the anonymous reviewers for their valuable hints and comments that helped us to improve the paper. This work was supported by DFG Grant BE 1700/9-1 awarded to Christoph Beierle and DFG Grant KE 1413/10-1 awarded to Gabriele Kern-Isberner as part of the priority program "Intentional Forgetting in Organizations" (SPP 1921). Kai Sauerwald is supported by the grant BE 1700/9-1.

References

1. Alchourrón, C.E., Gärdenfors, P., Makinson, D.: On the logic of theory change: partial meet contraction and revision functions. J. Symb. Log. **50**(2), 510–530 (1985)

2. Banerjee, M., Dubois, D.: A simple logic for reasoning about incomplete knowledge. Int. J. Approx. Reason. **55**(2), 639–653 (2014). https://doi.org/10.1016/j.ijar.2013.11.003
3. Beierle, C., Eichhorn, C., Kutsch, S.: A practical comparison of qualitative inferences with preferred ranking models. KI - Künstliche Intelligenz **31**(1), 41–52 (2017)
4. Beierle, C., Kern-Isberner, G.: Semantical investigations into nonmonotonic and probabilistic logics. Ann. Math. Artif. Intell. **65**(2–3), 123–158 (2012)
5. Beierle, C., Eichhorn, C., Kern-Isberner, G., Kutsch, S.: Properties of skeptical c-inference for conditional knowledge bases and its realization as a constraint satisfaction problem. Ann. Math. Artif. Intell. **83**(3-4), 247–275 (2018)
6. Beierle, C., Kern-Isberner, G., Sauerwald, K., Bock, T., Ragni, M.: Towards a general framework for kinds of forgetting in common-sense belief management. KI **33**(1), 57–68 (2019)
7. Beierle, C., Kutsch, S.: Computation and comparison of nonmonotonic skeptical inference relations induced by sets of ranking models for the realization of intelligent agents. Appl. Intell. **49**(1), 28–43 (2018). https://doi.org/10.1007/s10489-018-1203-5
8. Boutilier, C.: Iterated revision and minimal change of conditional beliefs. J. Philos. Logic **25**(3), 263–305 (1996)
9. Carlsson, M., Ottosson, G., Carlson, B.: An open-ended finite domain constraint solver. In: Glaser, H., Hartel, P., Kuchen, H. (eds.) PLILP 1997. LNCS, vol. 1292, pp. 191–206. Springer, Heidelberg (1997). https://doi.org/10.1007/BFb0033845
10. Darwiche, A., Pearl, J.: On the logic of iterated belief revision. Artif. Intell. **89**, 1–29 (1997)
11. de Finetti, B.: La prévision, ses lois logiques et ses sources subjectives. Ann. Inst. H. Poincaré 7(1), 1–68 (1937). English translation in Studies in Subjective Probability, Kyburg, H., Smokler, H.E. (eds.) pp. 93–158. Wiley, New York (1974)
12. Haldimann, J., Sauerwald, K., von Berg, M., Kern-Isberner, G., Beierle, C.: Towards a framework of Hansson's descriptor revision for conditionals. In: The 36th ACM/SIGAPP Symposium on Applied Computing (SAC 2021), 22–26 March 2021, Virtual Event, Republic of Korea, pp. 889–891. ACM, New York (2021)
13. Hansson, S.O.: Descriptor revision. Studia Logica **102**(5), 955–980 (2014)
14. Hansson, S.O.: A monoselective presentation of AGM revision. Studia Logica **103**(5), 1019–1033 (2015). https://doi.org/10.1007/s11225-015-9604-5
15. Hansson, S.O.: Blockage revision. J. Logic Lang. Inf. **25**(1), 37–50 (2015). https://doi.org/10.1007/s10849-015-9223-6
16. Hansson, S.O.: Iterated descriptor revision and the logic of ramsey test conditionals. J. Philos. Logic **45**(4), 429–450 (2015). https://doi.org/10.1007/s10992-015-9381-7
17. Hansson, S.O.: AGM contraction is not reconstructible as a descriptor operation. J. Log. Comput. **27**(4), 1133–1141 (2017). https://doi.org/10.1093/logcom/exv076
18. Hansson, S.O.: Descriptor Revision. TL, vol. 46. Springer, Cham (2017). https://doi.org/10.1007/978-3-319-53061-1
19. Hansson, S.O.: Back to basics: belief revision through direct selection. Studia Logica **107**(5), 887–915 (2018). https://doi.org/10.1007/s11225-018-9807-7
20. Kern-Isberner, G.: Conditionals in Nonmonotonic Reasoning and Belief Revision. LNCS (LNAI), vol. 2087. Springer, Heidelberg (2001). https://doi.org/10.1007/3-540-44600-1
21. Kern-Isberner, G.: A thorough axiomatization of a principle of conditional preservation in belief revision. Ann. Math. Artif. Intell. **40**(1–2), 127–164 (2004)

22. Kern-Isberner, G., Bock, T., Sauerwald, K., Beierle, C.: Iterated contraction of propositions and conditionals under the principle of conditional preservation. In: Benzmüller, C., Lisetti, C., Theobald, M. (eds.) GCAI 2017. 3nd Global Conference on Artificial Intelligence, Miami, USA, 20–22 October 2017. EPiC Series in Computing, vol. 50. EasyChair, October 2017. https://easychair.org/publications/volume/GCAI_2017

23. Komo, C., Beierle, C.: Upper and lower bounds for finite domain constraints to realize skeptical c-inference over conditional knowledge bases. In: International Symposium on Artificial Intelligence and Mathematics (ISAIM 2020), Fort Lauderdale, FL, USA, 6–8 January (2020)

24. Kutsch, S.: InfOCF-Lib: A Java library for OCF-based conditional inference. In: Beierle, C., Ragni, M., Stolzenburg, F., Thimm, M. (eds.) Proceedings of the 8th Workshop on Dynamics of Knowledge and Belief (DKB-2019) and the 7th Workshop KI & Kognition (KIK-2019) Co-Located with 44nd German Conference on Artificial Intelligence (KI 2019), Kassel, Germany, 23 September 2019. CEUR Workshop Proceedings, vol. 2445, pp. 47–58. (2019)

25. Makinson, D., Gärdenfors, P.: Relations between the logic of theory change and nonmonotonic logic. In: Fuhrmann, A., Morreau, M. (eds.) The Logic of Theory Change. LNCS, vol. 465, pp. 183–205. Springer, Heidelberg (1991). https://doi.org/10.1007/BFb0018421

26. Sauerwald, K., Haldimann, J., von Berg, M., Beierle, C.: Descriptor revision for conditionals: literal descriptors and conditional preservation. In: Schmid, U., Klügl, F., Wolter, D. (eds.) KI 2020. LNCS (LNAI), vol. 12325, pp. 204–218. Springer, Cham (2020). https://doi.org/10.1007/978-3-030-58285-2_15

27. Sauerwald, K., Kern-Isberner, G., Beierle, C.: A conditional perspective for iterated belief contraction. In: Giacomo, G.D., Catalá, A., Dilkina, B., Milano, M., Barro, S., Bugarín, A., Lang, J. (eds.) ECAI 2020–24th European Conference on Artificial Intelligence. Frontiers in Artificial Intelligence and Applications, vol. 325, pp. 889–896. IOS Press (2020). https://doi.org/10.3233/FAIA200180

28. Spohn, W.: Ordinal Conditional Functions: A Dynamic Theory of Epistemic States, pp. 105–134. Springer, Dordrecht (1988). https://doi.org/10.1007/978-94-009-2865-7_6

29. Zhang, L.: Believability relations for select-direct sentential revision. Studia Logica **105**(1), 37–63 (2017)

Trust Is All You Need: From Belief Revision to Information Revision

Ammar Yasser[1](✉) and Haythem O. Ismail[1,2]

[1] German University in Cairo, New Cairo, Egypt
{ammar.abbas,haythem.ismail}@guc.edu.eg
[2] Cairo University, Giza, Egypt

Abstract. Belief revision is a hallmark of knowledge representation, logic, and philosophy. However, despite the extensive research in the area, we believe a fresh take on belief revision is needed. To that end, it is our conviction that believing a piece of information depends on trust in information sources that conveyed said piece and that trust in information sources is affected by changes in beliefs. Trust is also an impress of philosophy and all time favorite of psychology and multi-agent systems. Hence, many approaches were developed for trust representation, yet, in isolation from belief revision. While admittedly crucial to a realistic treatment of belief revision, trust revision, to our dismay, did not receive the same level of attention. In this paper, we argue that a formal treatment for the joint interdependent revision of belief and trust is called for. Moreover, we propose a new framework called information revision that captures the joint revision of belief and trust. Further, we provide postulates that govern such process of revision. Finally, we provide a class of operators called relevant change propagation operators and provide their representation theorem.

Keywords: Information revision · Belief revision · Trust · Trust revision

1 Introduction

Belief revision is a hallmark of knowledge representation, databases, logic and philosophy. Theory change and belief revision have been thoroughly investigated during the last two decades of the previous century [7,12,20, for example]. That was, to a large degree, due the seminal work of Alchourrón, Gärdenfors, and Makinson [1,2,9] which sparked discussion and discourse in the field for four decades despite the extensive criticism [10,13,23,25, for instance]. However, we believe that a fresh and more realistic take on belief revision is needed. To that end, we propose the incorporation, and revision, of trust.[1]

There is no shortage of research on trust within multi-agent systems [5,6,8,16,24], and philosophy [14,15,22]. Nevertheless, research on the relation

---

[1] This work builds on foundations proposed in [29,30].

© Springer Nature Switzerland AG 2021
W. Faber et al. (Eds.): JELIA 2021, LNAI 12678, pp. 50–65, 2021.
https://doi.org/10.1007/978-3-030-75775-5_5

between trust in information sources and belief revision is relatively slim despite recent contributions [3,4,21,27]. Trust revision did not receive the same level of attention as belief revision. Yet, there are notable contributions [17,26] specially in the field of information fusion [18,19]. In this paper, we argue that a systematic study of the *joint* revision of belief and trust, which is (to the best of our knowledge) currently missing, is called for. We propose a new framework called *information revision* that captures the joint revision of the two attitudes, provide postulates that govern this process, and present a representation theorem characterizing rational information revision operators.

This paper is structured as follows. In Sect. 2 we motivate why belief and trust revision should not be separated. Section 3 presents formal preliminaries that will be needed throughout the paper. In Sect. 4 we provide AGM-style postulates for the joint belief-trust revision, highlighting the intuitions behind formulating them, and prove a representation theorem in Sect. 5. Finally, in Sect. 6 we conclude our work and point towards future directions.

2 Motivation

In this paper, we take trust to be a measure of the credibility of an information source, which need not be a cognitive agent. To show how belief and trust are intertwined in nature, affect each other, and why it is important to incorporate both when considering a more realistic approach to belief revision, consider the following examples.

Example 1. The army of the dead is marching towards Winterfell, the largest castle on their way to total domination. *Jon*, the lord of Winterfell who is very trusted by his people, is preparing his army for battle. Before the battle, the children and the elderly were sent to a secret location for safety. *Jon* has two advisors. *Peter* who is his oldest advisor and *Sam* the most recent one. After some time, *Peter* hurries to the safe place and says "Jon won" (*JWon*). People rushed out of the safe place to celebrate. Then, to their surprise, they found *Jon* who said, in dismay, "we lost" ($\neg JWon$).

This is a classic example of belief revision where the people of Winterfell already believing *JWon* are confronted with a conflicting pieces of information $\neg JWon$. Which piece of information should the people of Winterfell believe? Clearly, *Jon* is more trusted than *Peter* specially when it comes to whether or not *Jon* won the battle. Hence, the people of Winterfell will stop believing *JWon* and start believing $\neg JWon$. This example shows the effect of trust in information sources on belief revision.

Example 2. The living decided to flee Winterfell and escape to Casterly Rock. *Peter* said "Casterly Rock is to the east" (*CEast*), *Sam* said that "the way to Casterly rock is to the west" (*CWest*). The people are confused because they used to trust *Peter* but after he just lied to them they are cautious to accept information from him. Also, they do not fully trust *Sam* yet because he is just a new advisor of *Jon*. Shortly after, they found a map in an old text book clearly showing that "Casterly Rock is to the west".

Sam conveyed a piece of information and the people of Winterfell did not believe it strongly. However, finding the map in the text book *supported Sam*'s claim which in turn could (should) make him more trusted.

Example 3. On their way to Casterly Rock, one of the survivors, *Tyrion*, found a strange looking plant called Frya. The survivors are hungry and hence *Tyrion* decides to harvest some of the plant to feast because he believes that "Frya is edible" (*FEdible*). However, on his way, he remembers that the person who told him that "Frya is edible" was *Peter*.

In the previous example, new information acquisition led to strengthening a belief which in turn affected trust making *Sam* more trusted. In this example, after *Peter*'s misleading of the people of Wintefell twice, it is safe to assume that *Tyrion* does not trust *Peter*. Thus, despite Frya being edible or not is not something logically related to both Jon losing or winning the battle or to Casterly Rock being to the west not to the east, *Tyrion* would give up (or at the very least doubt) his belief that Frya is edible.

These examples show that:

1. Trust acts as an information filter. In Example 1, the people of Winterfell believed what *Jon* conveyed over what *Peter* conveyed because *Jon* is more trusted.
2. We trust someone more if what they conveyed turns out to be true. In Example 2 the book's support of *Sam*'s claim proves *Sam*'s credibility.
3. We trust someone less if what they conveyed is false or if they were misleading us. After the first two examples, trust in *Peter* did (or at least should) decrease.
4. Logically unrelated beliefs may be retracted or weakened in the course of belief revision due to changes in trust. *Tyrion* disbelieving or doubting that Frya is edible in Example 3.
5. Believing a piece of information depends on trust in whoever/whatever is the source.
6. Trusting someone (or something) depends on how much we believe the information they previously conveyed to us.

Hence, it is our conviction that belief revision and trust revision are intertwined and interdependent processes that should be carried out together.

3   Formal Preliminaries

To perform information revision, an agent needs to be able to represent more than just its beliefs which are traditionally represented in a belief set or base. An agent needs to be able to represent its beliefs, trust attribution in sources as well as a record of which information source conveyed which piece of information. Hence, we propose *information states*. Let $\mathcal{L}$ be a logical language with a Tarskian consequence operator Cn [28], $\mathcal{S}$ be a finite non-empty set of information sources, $\mathcal{D}_b$ and $\mathcal{D}_t$ be non-empty, countable sets; with $\prec_b$ and $\prec_t$, respectively, being total orders over $\mathcal{D}_b$ and $\mathcal{D}_t$. $\mathcal{D}_b$ and $\mathcal{D}_t$ represent the "degrees" of belief and trust. In other words, $\mathcal{D}_b$ and $\mathcal{D}_t$, with their total orders, represent the preferences of an agent among beliefs and sources. $\mathcal{D}_b$ and $\mathcal{D}_t$ are not necessarily finite, disjoint, different or identical.[2] Thus, an agent's information state $\mathcal{K}$ is a triple $\langle \mathcal{B}, \mathcal{T}, \mathcal{H} \rangle$ where $\mathcal{B} : \mathcal{L} \hookrightarrow \mathcal{D}_b$ is a partial function referred to as the *belief base*, $\mathcal{T} : \mathcal{S} \hookrightarrow \mathcal{D}_t$ is a partial function referred to as the *trust base*, and $\mathcal{H} \subseteq \mathcal{L} \times \mathcal{S}$, *the history*, is a finite set of pairs (ϕ, σ) that denotes a conveyance of formula ϕ by information source σ.[3] An example to show how the information state of Tyrion could look like after Example 3 is as follows.

Example 4. Let $\mathcal{L}_\mathcal{V}$ be a propositional language with the set $\mathcal{V} = \{JWon, FEdible, CEast, CWest\}$ of propositional variables. Let $\mathcal{D}_b$ and $\mathcal{D}_t$ be the set of natural numbers with their natural order. Let $\mathcal{K} = (\mathcal{B}, \mathcal{T}, \mathcal{H})$ where

- $\mathcal{B} = \{(\neg JWon, 10), (CWest, 9)\}$
- $\mathcal{T} = \{(Peter, 1), (Sam, 5), (Book, 8), (Jon, 10)\}$
- $\mathcal{H} = \{(FEdible, Peter), (JWon, Peter), (\neg JWon, Jon), (CEast, Peter), (CWest, Sam), (CWest, Book)\}$

The following useful abbreviations which we will later use.

- $\sigma(\mathcal{H}(\mathcal{K})) = \{\phi \mid (\phi, \sigma) \in \mathcal{H}(\mathcal{K})\}$. Intuitively, the set of formulas conveyed by a particular source σ.
- $\mathcal{S}_\mathcal{K} = \{\sigma \mid (\phi, \sigma) \in \mathcal{H}(\mathcal{K})\}$. The set of information sources that previously conveyed formulas.
- $For(\mathcal{B}(\mathcal{K})) = \{\phi \mid (\phi, b) \in \mathcal{B}(\mathcal{K})\}$. The set of believed formulas regardless grades.
- $\Phi_\mathcal{K} = \{\phi \mid (\phi, \sigma) \in \mathcal{H}(\mathcal{K})$ *for any* $\sigma\}$. The set of all formulas whether believed or not.

We use the following notations to talk about changes in beliefs and trust.

Definition 1. *Let $\phi \in \mathcal{L}$ and $\sigma \in \mathcal{S}$.*

*1. ϕ is **more entrenched** in state $\mathcal{K}_2$ over state $\mathcal{K}_1$, denoted $\mathcal{K}_1 \prec_\phi \mathcal{K}_2$, if (i) $\phi \notin Cn(For(\mathcal{B}(\mathcal{K}_1)))$ and $\phi \in Cn(For(\mathcal{B}(\mathcal{K}_2)))$; or (ii) $(\phi, b_1) \in \mathcal{B}(\mathcal{K}_1)$, $(\phi, b_2) \in \mathcal{B}(\mathcal{K}_2)$, and $b_1 \prec_b b_2$. If $\mathcal{K}_1 \not\prec_\phi \mathcal{K}_2$ and $\mathcal{K}_2 \not\prec_\phi \mathcal{K}_1$, we write $\mathcal{K}_1 \equiv_\phi \mathcal{K}_2$.*

---

[2] $\mathcal{D}_b$ and $\mathcal{D}_t$ are usually the same; however, a qualitative account of trust and belief might have different sets for grading the two attitudes.

[3] Information states contain trust bases and histories to model languages where trust and conveyance are part of the object language as well as those which do not have trust and conveyance as part of the object language.

2. σ *is* **more trusted** *in state* $\mathcal{K}_2$ *over state* $\mathcal{K}_1$, *denoted* $\mathcal{K}_1 \prec_\sigma \mathcal{K}_2$, *if* $(\sigma, t_1) \in T(\mathcal{K}_1)$, $(\sigma, t_2) \in T(\mathcal{K}_2)$, *and* $t_1 \prec_t t_2$. *If* $\mathcal{K}_1 \not\prec_\sigma \mathcal{K}_2$ *and* $\mathcal{K}_2 \not\prec_\sigma \mathcal{K}_1$, *we write* $\mathcal{K}_1 \equiv_\sigma \mathcal{K}_2$.

As proposed earlier, the degrees of trust in sources depend on the degrees of belief in formulas conveyed by these sources and vice versa. Hence, by changing the degree of belief in some formula ϕ, the degree of trust in a source σ, that previously conveyed ϕ, is likely to change. Moreover, when the degree of trust in σ changes, the degrees of belief in formulas conveyed by σ might change as well. To model such dependence, we need to keep track of which formulas and which sources are "relevant" to each other. First, we recall a piece of terminology due to [11]: $\Gamma \subset \mathcal{L}$ is a ϕ-*kernel* if $\Gamma \models \phi$ and, for every $\Delta \subset \Gamma$, $\Delta \not\models \phi$.

Definition 2. *Let* $\mathcal{K}$ *be an information state. The* **support graph** $\mathfrak{G}(\mathcal{K}) = (\mathcal{S}_\mathcal{K} \cup \Phi_\mathcal{K}, E)$ *is such that* $(u, v) \in E$ *if and only if*

1. $u \in \mathcal{S}_\mathcal{K}$, $v \in \Phi_\mathcal{K}$, *and* $v \in u(\mathcal{H}(\mathcal{K}))$;
2. $u \in \Phi_\mathcal{K}$, $v \in \Phi_\mathcal{K}$, $u \neq v$, *and* $u \in \Gamma \subseteq \Phi_\mathcal{K}$ *where* Γ *is a* v-*kernel; or*
3. $u \in \Phi_\mathcal{K}$, $v \in \mathcal{S}_\mathcal{K}$, *and* $(v, u) \in E$.

A node u **supports** *a node* v, *given information state* $\mathcal{K}$, *denoted* $u \triangleright_\mathcal{K} v$, *if there is a simple path from* u *to* v *that does not contain tautologies. A node* u *is* **relevant** *to a node* v *denoted* $u \bowtie_\mathcal{K} v$ *if* $u = v$, $u \triangleright_\mathcal{K} v$, *or* $v \triangleright_\mathcal{K} u$.[4]

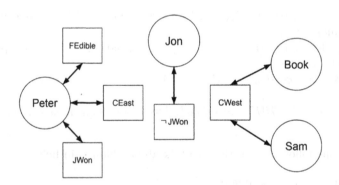

Fig. 1. The support graph capturing the state in Example 4. Sources are depicted with circles and formulas are represented with rectangles.

The support graph allows us to trace back and propagate changes in trust and belief to relevant beliefs and information sources along support paths. The support graph provides the basis for constructing an operator of rational information revision. Figure 1 shows an example of the support graph of the information state shown in Example 4. Every source supports and is supported by

---

[4] Thus, relevance is the reflexive, symmetric, transitive closure of E.

every formula that the source conveyed. Also, we can find that source *Book* supports source *Sam* by virtue of having a tautology free path between them, namely, $\langle Book, CWest, Sam \rangle$. Thus, we can expect that the degree of trust in one of them could affect trust in the other. The strength of the support graph does not stop here though. Traditionally, belief revision is concerned with minimal change. In this paper, we model minimality using relevance. However, our notion of relevance is not restricted to *logical* relevance as with classical belief revision; it also accounts for *source* relevance. This is captured in this example by how *FEdible* is relevant to *JWon* through the common source *Peter* despite them being logically unrelated. Hence, our goal using the support graph is to confine changes in belief and trust when an information state $\mathcal{K}$ is revised with formula ϕ conveyed by source σ to only formulas and sources relevant to ϕ, $\neg\phi$, and σ.

4 Information Revision

We now present the postulates we believe any rational operator of information revision, denoted ($\ltimes$), should observe. In the rest of this paper[5], $\mathcal{K}$ is an information state; $\phi, \psi, \xi \in \mathcal{L}$; and $\sigma, \sigma' \in \mathcal{S}$.

($\ltimes_1$: **Belief Consistency**). $Cn(For(\mathcal{B}(\mathcal{K}\ltimes(\phi,\sigma)))) \neq \mathcal{L}$.

At the core of belief revision, achieving consistency is paramount. Hence, a rational operation of information revision should retain the consistency of the belief base even if the formula of revision is itself a contradiction.

($\ltimes_2$: **Supported Entrenchment**). $\mathcal{K}\ltimes(\phi,\sigma) \prec_\phi \mathcal{K}$ only if $Cn(For(\mathcal{B}(\mathcal{K}))) = \mathcal{L}$.

Starting with a consistent belief base $\mathcal{B}(\mathcal{K})$, it could be that (i) $\phi, \neg\phi \notin Cn(For(\mathcal{B}(\mathcal{K})))$, (ii) $\neg\phi \in Cn(For(\mathcal{B}(\mathcal{K})))$, or (iii) $\phi \in Cn(For(\mathcal{B}(\mathcal{K})))$. On revising the first two cases, ϕ could either succeed or not. In both cases, ϕ could either become more entrenched (because it is now added to the belief base) or not get less entrenched (because it was not already believed). In the last case, because ϕ is already believed, revision with ϕ should either make it more entrenched or leave it as is. Thus, in all cases, starting with a consistent belief base, there is no scenario where ϕ should become less entrenched.

($\ltimes_3$: **Opposed Entrenchment**). $\mathcal{K} \not\prec_{\neg\phi} \mathcal{K}\ltimes(\phi,\sigma)$.

Revising a belief base with ϕ (even if the belief base is inconsistent) does not provide any new support for $\neg\phi$ and hence it should not become more entrenched.

---

[5] Due to space limitations, we were not able to provide most of our results and all proofs in this paper. However, the main proofs could be found in this online appendix: proofs.

The following are examples showcasing supported and opposed entrenchment.

Example 5. *Jon* conveys "the battle is tomorrow" (ϕ). Since we trust *Jon*, we believe that "the battle is tomorrow" ($\mathcal{K} \prec_\phi \mathcal{K} \ltimes (\phi, Jon)$).

Example 6. *Jon* conveys "the battle is tomorrow" (ϕ) and since we trust *Jon* we believe ϕ. Then, any of the following scenarios could occur:

- *Jon* himself repeats ϕ. As this is not a new evidence for ϕ, we decide not to increase ϕ's degree of belief ($\mathcal{K} \equiv_\phi \mathcal{K} \ltimes (\phi, Jon)$).
- *Peter* conveys that "there is no battle tomorrow" ($\neg\phi$). Since we trust *Jon* the most, we decide to discard $\neg\phi$ ($\neg\phi$ is rejected and $\mathcal{K} \equiv_\phi \mathcal{K} \ltimes (\phi, Jon)$).

Example 7. *Varys*, who is not in the military, conveys that "the battle is tomorrow" (ϕ). Since we do not trust *Varys* on military topics, we have no reason to believe him (ϕ is rejected yet it does not become less entrenched because it was not already believed).

Example 8. *Sam* conveys "the battle is tomorrow" (ϕ). We trust *Sam* a bit so we believe ϕ with a degree d_1. Later, *Jon* conveys ϕ. Since there is new support for ϕ, we increase our degree of belief in ϕ to d_2 where $d_2 \succ_b d_1$ ($\mathcal{K} \prec_\phi \mathcal{K} \ltimes (\phi, Jon)$).

Example 9. *Peter* conveys "there is no battle tomorrow" ($\neg\phi$) so we believe $\neg\phi$. Then, any of the following could occur:

- *Jon* conveys ϕ. Because we trust *Jon* more than *Peter*, we revise our beliefs and accept ϕ ($\mathcal{K} \ltimes (\phi, Jon) \prec_{\neg\phi} \mathcal{K}$ and $\mathcal{K} \prec_\phi \mathcal{K} \ltimes (\phi, Jon)$).
- *Tyrion*, who used to be in the military, conveys ϕ. Since *Peter* is an advisor of *Jon*, we trust *Peter* more than *Tyrion*. However, we do not fully trust *Peter* and hence *Tyrion*'s conveyance makes us doubt our beliefs (ϕ is rejected yet $\mathcal{K} \ltimes (\phi, Tyrion) \prec_{\neg\phi} \mathcal{K}$).
- *Sam* conveys ϕ. Since both *Peter* and *Sam* are advisors of *Jon*, we trust them to a similar extent. Hence, as we do not have enough evidence to exclusively believe either formula, we believe neither (ϕ and $\neg\phi$ are rejected).

($\ltimes_4$: **Belief Confirmation**). If $\mathcal{K} \prec_\psi \mathcal{K} \ltimes (\phi, \sigma)$ then $\mathcal{K} \prec_\phi \mathcal{K} \ltimes (\phi, \sigma)$ and $\phi \triangleright_{\mathcal{K} \ltimes (\phi, \sigma)} \psi$.

For an agent to strengthen any of its beliefs (ψ) after revision, it must be provided with a *new support* where a new formula or source supports ψ or a *stronger support* where one of the existing supports of ψ becomes more entrenched (or trusted). Thus, if a conveyance of ϕ by σ makes ϕ more entrenched, this could be a reason for an agent to strengthen its degree of belief in ψ given that ψ is supported by ϕ.

Example 10. *Sam* conveys "the battle is tomorrow" (ψ) so we believe ψ. We also know that "if the army is preparing then the battle is tomorrow" ($\phi \rightarrow \psi$). After some time, *Jon* conveys that "the army is preparing" (ϕ) and we believe ϕ. Now, "the army is preparing" supports "the battle is tomorrow" which makes us strengthen our degree of belief in ψ ($\mathcal{K} \prec_\phi \mathcal{K} \ltimes (\phi, Jon)$, $\phi \triangleright_{\mathcal{K} \ltimes (\phi, \sigma)} \psi$, and $\mathcal{K} \prec_\psi \mathcal{K} \ltimes (\phi, Jon)$).

($\bowtie_5$: **Belief Refutation**). If $\mathcal{K}\bowtie(\phi,\sigma) \prec_\psi \mathcal{K}$, then
1. $\psi \bowtie_\mathcal{K} \xi \in \Gamma \subseteq For(\mathcal{B}(\mathcal{K}))$, with Γ a $\neg\phi$-kernel, and $\mathcal{K}\bowtie(\phi,\sigma) \prec_{\neg\phi} \mathcal{K}$;
2. $\psi \bowtie_{\mathcal{K}\bowtie(\phi,\sigma)} \phi$ and $\mathcal{K}\bowtie(\phi,\sigma) \prec_\phi \mathcal{K}$ or $\mathcal{K}\bowtie(\phi,\sigma) \prec_\sigma \mathcal{K}$.

On revising with ϕ, to achieve consistency, it should be compared to $\neg\phi$ (if it exists). The revision could reject ϕ, $\neg\phi$, or in fact both. Rejecting a formula (or making it less entrenched) could negatively affect other relevant formulas. Hence, if $\neg\phi$ becomes less entrenched, formulas that are relevant to $\neg\phi$ could become less entrenched. However, the postulate was stated in a way to consider formulas relevant to formulas in kernels of $\neg\phi$ and not just formulas relevant to $\neg\phi$ directly. The reason is that in the case where $\neg\phi$ belongs to the consequence of the believed formulas but is not an explicit belief, there will be no formulas relevant to $\neg\phi$ (as it does not belong to the graph). Hence, formulas that could get affected are those relevant to kernels of $\neg\phi$.[6] On the other hand, formulas relevant to ϕ could get affected if ϕ got less entrenched, or if σ (the source of ϕ) got less trusted. Since, relevance is an equivalence relation, any formula ψ such that $\psi \bowtie_\mathcal{K} \sigma$ is also $\psi \bowtie_\mathcal{K} \phi$. Unlike the treatment of $\neg\phi$, the postulate states the relevance relation directly to ϕ because ϕ will always be in the graph.

Example 11. *Peter* conveys "it is not cold outside" (ψ), then he conveys "the army is not preparing" (ξ). We believe both formulas. We also know that "if the army is not preparing then the battle is not tomorrow" ($\xi \to \neg\phi$). Later, *Jon* conveys that "the battle is tomorrow" (ϕ). Since we trust *Jon*, we believe ϕ. To achieve consistency, we reject $\neg\phi$ and ξ (because it is in a kernel of $\neg\phi$). Thus, $\mathcal{K}\bowtie(\phi, Jon) \prec_{\neg\phi} \mathcal{K}$, $\mathcal{K}\bowtie(\phi, Jon) \prec_\xi \mathcal{K}$, and because we now doubt what *Peter* says, also $\mathcal{K}\bowtie(\phi, Jon) \prec_\psi \mathcal{K}$ (Case 1 where $\psi \bowtie_\mathcal{K} \xi \in \Gamma \subseteq For(\mathcal{B}(\mathcal{K}))$, with Γ a $\neg\phi$-kernel, and $\mathcal{K}\bowtie(\phi,\sigma) \prec_{\neg\phi} \mathcal{K}$).

Example 12. *Peter* conveys "it is not cold outside" (ψ) so we believe ψ. Later, *Jon* conveys "the battle is tomorrow" ($\neg\phi$) and we strongly believe it. Afterwards, *Peter* conveys "there is no battle tomorrow" (ϕ). ϕ is discarded and we realize that *Peter* is not credible so we trust him less and start doubting other pieces of information acquired through him (Case 2 where $\psi \bowtie_{\mathcal{K}\bowtie(\phi,\sigma)} \phi$ and $\mathcal{K}\bowtie(\phi,\sigma) \prec_\sigma \mathcal{K}$).

($\bowtie_6$: **Trust Confirmation**). If $\mathcal{K} \prec_{\sigma'} \mathcal{K}\bowtie(\phi,\sigma)$ then, $\mathcal{K} \prec_\phi \mathcal{K}\bowtie(\phi,\sigma)$ and
1. $\phi \rhd_{\mathcal{K}\bowtie(\phi,\sigma)} \sigma' \neq \sigma$; or
2. $\sigma' = \sigma$ and there is $\Gamma \subseteq For(\mathcal{B}(\mathcal{K}))$ where Γ is a σ-independent ϕ-kernel.

Similar to how formulas could become more entrenched, for a source to become more trusted, it must be that the formula of revision provides new support for said source. Further, a σ-independent ϕ-kernel is, intuitively, a ϕ-kernel that would still exist if σ did not exit. More precisely, for every $\psi \in \Gamma$, where Γ is a ϕ-kernel, ψ is supported by some $\sigma'' \neq \sigma$. Thus, if a source σ conveys a formula

---

[6] If a formula is relevant to $\neg\phi$ directly and not just to a formula in a kernel of $\neg\phi$, the postulate still holds because $\{\neg\phi\}$ is trivially a $\neg\phi$-kernel.

ϕ and it is accepted, we should expect that trust might increase in σ. However, what if σ keeps conveying formulas that are only supported by σ itself, should we keep trusting σ more? We believe that the answer is no. Hence, for trust to increase in σ because of the new conveyance of ϕ, there must be evidence (independent of σ) that was already believed before the revision.

Recall what happens to Sam's trust after Example 2 where revision with $(CWest, Book)$ succeeds where $CWest\triangleright_{\mathcal{K}\ltimes(CWest,Book)}Sam \neq Book$. To demonstrate the second case, consider the following example.

Example 13. Jon conveys "the battle is tomorrow" (ϕ) so we believe ϕ. Later, Sam conveys ϕ. Since there is a ϕ-kernel, namely $\{\phi\}$, such that ϕ has a source $Jon \neq Sam$, the existing Sam-independent evidence makes him more trusted ($\mathcal{K} \prec_{Sam} \mathcal{K}\ltimes(\phi, Sam)$).

($\ltimes_7$: **Trust Refutation**). If $\mathcal{K}\ltimes(\phi, \sigma) \prec_{\sigma'} \mathcal{K}$, then
1. $\sigma' \bowtie_{\mathcal{K}} \psi$ with $\mathcal{K}\ltimes(\phi, \sigma) \prec_{\psi} \mathcal{K}$; or
2. $\sigma' = \sigma$ and $\phi \notin Cn(For(\mathcal{B}(\mathcal{K}\ltimes(\phi, \sigma))))$.

A source could become less trusted if it is relevant to some formula which got negatively affected by the revision. That is, trust in a source can change only if belief in a formula relevant to this source changes. Intuitively that is the case because reducing trust in a source depends not on the source themselves but on how much we believe/disbelieve the things a source previously conveyed. Also, if source σ conveys ϕ and it is rejected, that could be a sign of σ's lack of credibility and hence trust in σ could decrease.

For Case 1, recall Example 11 and consider $\mathcal{K}\ltimes(\phi, Jon) \prec_{Peter} \mathcal{K}$. For Case 2, recall the second scenario in Example 6 where $\mathcal{K}\ltimes(\phi, Peter) \prec_{Peter} \mathcal{K}$.

($\ltimes_8$: **History Expansion**). $\mathcal{H}(\mathcal{K}\ltimes(\phi, \sigma)) = \mathcal{H}(\mathcal{K}) \cup \{(\phi, \sigma)\}$.

Information revision should keep track of which information source conveyed which piece of information.

($\ltimes_9$: **Evidential Success**). If $\phi \in Cn(For(\mathcal{B}(\mathcal{K}\ltimes(\phi, \sigma))))$, then $\phi \in For(\mathcal{B}(\mathcal{K}\ltimes(\phi, \sigma)))$.

If after revision with ϕ, ϕ follows from the beliefs, it must be a belief.

Note that, in none of the postulates, do we require that trust *should* change in certain ways, only that it should not. We believe it be unwise to postulate sufficient conditions for trust change in a generic information revision operation. For example, one might be tempted to say that, if after revision with ϕ, $\neg\phi$ is no longer believed, then trust in any source supporting $\neg\phi$ *should* decrease. Things are not that straightforward, though.

Example 14. $Tyrion$ believes that "If we attack we will win" ($Attack \rightarrow Win$) and that "If we retreat we will not attack" ($Retreat \rightarrow \neg Attack$). $Peter$ conveys Win, then conveys $Retreat$. Since $Tyrion$ has no evidence against either, he believes both. Now, *Jon*, who is more trusted than *Peter*, conveys *Attack*. Consequently, *Tyrion* starts believing *Attack* despite having evidence against it. To maintain consistency, *Tyrion* also stops believing *Retreat* (because it supports ¬*Attack*).

What should happen to *Tyrion*'s trust in *Peter*? We might, at first glance, think that trust in *Peter* should decrease as he conveyed *Retreat* which is no longer believed. However, one could also argue that trust in *Peter* should increase because he conveyed *win*, which is now being confirmed by *Jon*. This example shows that setting *general* rules for how trust *must* change is almost impossible, as it depends on several factors. Whether *Tyrion* ends up trusting *Peter* less, more, or without change appears to depend on how the particular revision operators manipulates grades. The situation becomes more complex if the new conveyance by *Jon* supports several formulas supporting *Peter* and refutes several formulas supported by him. In this case, how trust in *Peter* changes (or not) would also depend on how the effects of all these support relations are aggregated. We contend that such issues should not, and cannot, be settled by general constraints on information revision.

5   Relevant Change Propagation

We now consider a class of operators called *relevant change propagation* operators. The operation of a relevant change propagation operator, applied on an information state $\mathcal{K}$ and a formula-source pair (ϕ, σ), is broken down into three steps, called *waves* as follows: 1) revision, 2) refutation, and 3) confirmation.

5.1   Joint Revision Wave

The first wave is a process of belief revision based on *kernel contraction* [11] and conditional trust revision. By conditional we mean that trust is not always revised in this wave, only given a certain condition. On the other hand, belief revision is always carried on in this wave. To that end, let $\mathcal{B} \perp\!\!\!\perp \phi$ denote the set of ϕ-kernels in $For(\mathcal{B})$. Further, let $\mathbb{I}$ be an *incision function* which, given a set of ϕ-kernels, selects from their union some elements to be removed such that $For(\mathcal{B}) \setminus \mathbb{I}(\mathcal{B} \perp\!\!\!\perp \phi) \not\models \phi$. For enhanced readability, we will use the notation $\mathcal{B} \setminus \mathbb{I}(\mathcal{B} \perp\!\!\!\perp \phi)$ to denote the removal of formula-degree pairs from $\mathcal{B}$ such that $For(\mathcal{B}) \setminus \mathbb{I}(\mathcal{B} \perp\!\!\!\perp \phi) \not\models \phi$. Finally, let $\mathfrak{K}$ is the set of all information states induced by $\mathcal{L}$, $\mathcal{S}$, $\mathcal{D}_b$, $\mathcal{D}_t$, $\prec_b$ and $\prec_t$.

Definition 3. *A **joint revision wave** is a function* $\mathbb{W}_{JR} : \mathfrak{K} \times \mathcal{L} \times \mathcal{S} \longrightarrow \mathfrak{K} \times 2^{\mathcal{L} \cup \mathcal{S}} \times 2^{\mathcal{L} \cup \mathcal{S}}$ *such that* $\mathbb{W}_{JR}(\mathcal{K}, \phi, \sigma) = \langle \mathcal{K}^*, \mathcal{R}, \mathcal{C} \rangle$ *where* $\mathcal{K} = \langle \mathcal{B}, \mathcal{T}, \mathcal{H} \rangle$ *and* $\mathcal{K}^* = \langle \mathcal{B}^*, \mathcal{T}^*, \mathcal{H} \cup \{(\phi, \sigma)\} \rangle$. *Moreover,* $\mathcal{B}^*$, $\mathcal{T}^*$, $\mathcal{R}$, *and* $\mathcal{C}$ *are restricted as follows.*

1. $\mathcal{B}^*$, *where* $d, d_1, d_2 \in \mathcal{D}_b$ *and* $\mathbb{I}$ *an incision function, is one of the following if* $Cn(\{\phi\}) \neq \mathcal{L}$:

(a) $\mathcal{B} \setminus \mathbb{I}(\mathcal{B} \perp\!\!\!\perp \neg\phi) \cup \{(\phi, d)\}$, only if $\phi \notin For(\mathcal{B})$;

(b) $\mathcal{B} \setminus (\mathbb{I}(\mathcal{B} \perp\!\!\!\perp \neg\phi) \cup \{(\phi, d_1)\}) \cup \{(\phi, d_2)\}$, where $(\phi, d_1) \in \mathcal{B}$ and $d_2 \prec_b d_1$ only if $\neg\phi \in Cn(For(\mathcal{B}))$;

(c) $\mathcal{B} \setminus (\mathbb{I}(\mathcal{B} \perp\!\!\!\perp \phi) \cup \{(\neg\phi, d_1)\}) \cup \{(\neg\phi, d_2)\}$, only if $(\neg\phi, d_1) \in \mathcal{B}$ and $d_1 \nprec_b d_2$;

(d) $\mathcal{B} \setminus (\mathbb{I}(\mathcal{B} \perp\!\!\!\perp \neg\phi) \cup \mathbb{I}(\mathcal{B} \perp\!\!\!\perp \phi))$, only if $\phi \notin Cn(For(\mathcal{B}))$ or $\neg\phi \in Cn(For(\mathcal{B}))$. and is $\mathcal{B} \setminus \mathbb{I}(\mathcal{B} \perp\!\!\!\perp \phi)$ if $Cn(\{\phi\}) = \mathcal{L}$.

2. $\mathcal{T}^* = \mathcal{T} \setminus \{(\sigma, d_1)\} \cup \{(\sigma, d_2)\}$ where $d_2 = d_1$ or $d_2 \prec d_1$ only if $\phi \notin Cn(For(\mathcal{B}^*))$.

3. $\mathcal{R} = \bigcup_{r \in \Delta \cup \delta} [r]_{\bowtie_{\mathcal{K}}}$ where $\Delta = \{\psi \mid \mathcal{K}^* \prec_\psi \mathcal{K}\}$ and $\delta = \{\sigma' \mid \mathcal{K}^* \prec_{\sigma'} \mathcal{K}\}$.

4.
$$\mathcal{C} = \begin{cases} \{\phi\} \cup \{\sigma' | \phi \rhd \sigma' \neq \sigma\} \cup \{\psi | \phi \rhd \psi\} \cup \Upsilon & \mathcal{K} \prec_\phi \mathcal{K}^*, \\ \varnothing & otherwise \end{cases}$$

with Γ_ϕ^σ being the set of σ-independent ϕ-kernels, if $\Gamma_\phi^\sigma \neq \varnothing$ then $\Upsilon = \{\sigma\}$ else $\Upsilon = \varnothing$.

We illustrate each point in order as follows. Starting with $\mathcal{B}^*$, the goal is to retain consistency. Hence, if ϕ is a contradiction, then it is contracted from the belief base without being added. On the other hand, if ϕ is not a contradiction there are four cases which we will, from now on, refer to as $\mathbb{W}_{JR}$'s choices 1-(a), 1-(b), 1-(c), and 1-(d). In choice 1-(a), ϕ which is not in the formulas is accepted. Choice 1-(b) captures scenarios where ϕ was already believed with degree d_1 and then it becomes believed with degree d_2. It could be that $d_1 \prec_b d_2$ making ϕ more entrenched, d_1 is the same as d_2, or $d_1 \succ_b d_2$ in which case ϕ becomes less entrenched. This last case is only allowed to occur if $\neg\phi$ was also already believed. In choice 1-(c), $\neg\phi$ succeeds over ϕ but that could only occur if $\neg\phi$ was already believed. Moreover, given the restrictions on the grades, $\neg\phi$ can not become more entrenched. Finally, in choice 1-(d), both ϕ and $\neg\phi$ could get contracted (rejected) only if ϕ is not already believed or $\neg\phi$ is already believed.

Moving on to $\mathcal{T}^*$. If $\phi \notin Cn(For(\mathcal{B}^*))$, that means ϕ was rejected. In this case and in this case only, $\mathbb{W}_{JR}$ could decrease trust in σ. Otherwise, $\mathbb{W}_{JR}$ does not change the degree of trust in any source.

To achieve consistency (the main concern of belief revision) some formulas could become less entrenched. Those formulas are recorded in set Δ. Then, the *refuted set* $\mathcal{R}$ is constructed to contain all formulas and sources relevant to formulas in Δ alongside σ, potentially through δ, in the limiting case where ϕ is rejected without becoming less entrenched. $\mathcal{R}$ is crucial for the operation of the second wave.

Finally, the *confirmed set* $\mathcal{C}$ records all formulas and sources that potentially received new (or stronger) evidence only if ϕ gets more entrenched. These formulas include ϕ and any formula supported by ϕ. On the other hand, the sources in $\mathcal{C}$ are those supported by ϕ and σ is only added if there is pre-existing σ-independent kernels of ϕ. However, if ϕ does not get more entrenched, $\mathcal{C}$ will be empty. As we will shortly see, $\mathcal{C}$ is needed in the last wave.

The following lemmas hold where $\mathbb{W}_{JR}(\mathcal{K}, \phi, \sigma) = \langle \mathcal{K}^*, \mathcal{R}, \mathcal{C} \rangle$.

Lemma 1. $Cn(For(\mathcal{B}(\mathcal{K}^*))) \neq \mathcal{L}$.

Lemma 2. $\mathcal{K} \prec_\psi \mathcal{K}^*$ only if $\psi = \phi$.

Lemma 3. There is no σ' such that $\mathcal{K} \prec_{\sigma'} \mathcal{K}^*$

Lemma 4. $\mathcal{K}^* \prec_{\sigma'} \mathcal{K}$ only if $\sigma' = \sigma$.

Lemma 5. $\mathcal{K}^* \prec_\phi \mathcal{K}$ only if $\neg\phi \in Cn(For(\mathcal{B}))$.

Lemma 6. $\mathcal{K} \not\prec_{\neg\phi} \mathcal{K}^*$.

Lemma 7. $(\psi, b_1) \in \mathcal{B}(\mathcal{K})$ and $(\psi, b_2) \in \mathcal{B}(\mathcal{K}^*)$ where $b_2 \prec_b b_1$ only if $\psi = \phi$ or $\psi = \neg\phi$.

Lemma 8. For every $\psi \in \Delta$, $\psi \in \Gamma \subseteq For(\mathcal{B})$ where Γ is a $\neg\phi$-kernel or a ϕ-kernel.

Lemma 9. For every $r \in \mathcal{R}$, $r \bowtie_\mathcal{K} \psi \in \Gamma \subseteq For(\mathcal{B})$ where Γ is a $\neg\phi$-kernel or $r \bowtie_{\mathcal{K}^*} \phi$.

5.2 Refutation Propagation Wave

In this wave, a relevant change propagation operator propagates the negative effects of the revision.

Definition 4. *A **refutation propagation** wave is a function* $\mathbb{W}_{RP} : \mathfrak{K} \times 2^{\mathcal{L} \cup \mathcal{S}} \times 2^{\mathcal{L} \cup \mathcal{S}} \longrightarrow \mathfrak{K} \times 2^{\mathcal{L} \cup \mathcal{S}}$ *such that* $\mathbb{W}_{RP}(\mathcal{K}, \mathcal{R}, \mathcal{C}) = \langle \mathcal{K}^*, \mathcal{C} \rangle$ *with* $\mathcal{K} = \langle \mathcal{B}, \mathcal{T}, \mathcal{H} \rangle$ *and* $\mathcal{K}^* = \langle \mathcal{B}^*, \mathcal{T}^*, \mathcal{H} \rangle$ *where*

- $\mathcal{B}^* = \{(\psi, d) | (\psi, d) \in \mathcal{B}, \psi \notin \mathcal{R}\} \cup \{(\psi, d) | (\psi, d') \in \mathcal{B}, d \not\prec_b d',$ *and* $\psi \in \mathcal{F}_R(\mathcal{R})\}$
- $\mathcal{T}^* = \{(\sigma', d) | (\sigma', d) \in \mathcal{T}, \sigma' \notin \mathcal{R}\} \cup \{(\sigma', d) | (\sigma', d') \in \mathcal{T}, d \not\prec_t d',$ *and* $\sigma' \in \mathcal{R}\}$.

with $\mathcal{F}_R$ *being a refutation selection function where* $\mathcal{F}_R(\mathcal{R}) \subseteq \mathcal{R}$ *and for every* $\psi \in \mathcal{R} \setminus \mathcal{F}_R(\mathcal{R})$, $\psi \notin Cn(For(\mathcal{B}^*))$.

$\mathbb{W}_{RP}$ operates on the belief and trust base of the incoming information state guided by the refuted set. Any formula that is not in the $\mathcal{R}$ is unchanged in $\mathcal{B}^*$. However, where $\mathcal{B}^*$ differs from $\mathcal{B}$ is that the formulas in the refuted set are subject to a change. The refutation selection function $\mathcal{F}_R(\mathcal{R}) \subseteq \mathcal{R}$ selects formulas that will remain. Hence, any formula in $\mathcal{R} \setminus \mathcal{F}_R(\mathcal{R})$ is contracted. Moreover, any formula in $\mathcal{F}_R(\mathcal{R})$ will be added to $\mathcal{B}^*$ without becoming more entrenched. In other words, it will have a belief degree equal to or smaller than its degree of belief in $\mathcal{B}$. Similarly, any source not in $\mathcal{R}$ is unchanged while any source in $\mathcal{R}$ will not get more trusted in $\mathcal{T}^*$ over $\mathcal{T}$.

The following holds where $\mathbb{W}_{RP}(\mathcal{K}, \mathcal{R}, \mathcal{C}) = \langle \mathcal{K}^*, \mathcal{C} \rangle$.

Lemma 10. There is no $\psi \in For(\mathcal{B}(\mathcal{K}^*))$ (or $\sigma' \in \mathcal{S}_{\mathcal{K}^*}$) such that $\mathcal{K} \prec_\psi \mathcal{K}^*$ (or $\mathcal{K} \prec_{\sigma'} \mathcal{K}^*$).

Lemma 11. If $\mathcal{K}^* \prec_\psi \mathcal{K}$ (or $\mathcal{K}^* \prec_{\sigma'} \mathcal{K}$) then $\psi \in \mathcal{R}$ (or $\sigma' \in \mathcal{R}$).

Lemma 12. $For(\mathcal{B}^*) \subseteq For(\mathcal{B})$.

5.3 Confirmation Propagation Wave

In this wave, a relevant change propagation operator propagates the positive effects of the revision.

Definition 5. *A **confirmation propagation** wave is a function* $\mathbb{W}_C : \mathfrak{K} \times 2^{\mathcal{L} \cup \mathcal{S}} \longrightarrow \mathfrak{K}$ *such that* $\mathbb{W}_{CP}(\mathcal{K}, \mathcal{C}) = \mathcal{K}^*$ *with* $\mathcal{K} = \langle \mathcal{B}, \mathcal{T}, \mathcal{H} \rangle$ *and* $\mathcal{K}^* = \langle \mathcal{B}^*, \mathcal{T}^*, \mathcal{H} \rangle$ *where*

- $\mathcal{B}^* = \{(\psi, d) | (\psi, d) \in \mathcal{B}, \psi \notin \mathcal{C}\} \cup \{(\psi, d) | (\psi, d') \in \mathcal{B}, d \nprec_b d' \text{ and } \psi \in \mathcal{C}\}$
- $\mathcal{T}^* = \{(\sigma', d) | (\sigma', d) \in \mathcal{T}, \sigma' \notin \mathcal{C}\} \cup \{(\sigma', d) | (\sigma', d') \in \mathcal{T}, d \nprec_t d' \text{ and } \sigma' \in \mathcal{C}\}$

Similar to the description of the operation of $\mathbb{W}_{RP}$, $\mathbb{W}_{CP}$ operates on the belief and trust base of the incoming information state. However, $\mathbb{W}_{CP}$ is guided by the confirmed set. Hence, any formula that is not in the $\mathcal{C}$ is unchanged in $\mathcal{B}^*$ and any source that is not in $\mathcal{C}$ is unchanged in $\mathcal{T}^*$. Further, any formula in $\mathcal{C}$ will be added to $\mathcal{B}^*$ without becoming less entrenched. In other words, it will have a belief degree equal to or larger than its degree of belief in $\mathcal{B}$. The same goes for sources in $\mathcal{C}$ where any source in $\mathcal{R}$ will not get less trusted in $\mathcal{T}^*$ over $\mathcal{T}$.

The following holds where $\mathbb{W}_{CP}(\mathcal{K}, \mathcal{C}) = \mathcal{K}^*$.

Lemma 13. *There is no* $\psi \in For(\mathcal{B}(\mathcal{K}^*))$ *(or* $\sigma' \in \mathcal{S}_{\mathcal{K}^*}$*) such that* $\mathcal{K}^* \prec_\psi \mathcal{K}$ *(or* $\mathcal{K}^* \prec_{\sigma'} \mathcal{K}$*).*

Lemma 14. *If* $\mathcal{C} = \varnothing$ *then there is no* $\psi \in For(\mathcal{B}(\mathcal{K}^*))$ *(or* $\sigma' \in \mathcal{S}_{\mathcal{K}^*}$*) such that* $\mathcal{K} \prec_\psi \mathcal{K}^*$ *(or* $\mathcal{K} \prec_{\sigma'} \mathcal{K}^*$*).*

Lemma 15. *If* $\mathcal{K} \prec_\psi \mathcal{K}^*$ *(or* $\mathcal{K} \prec_{\sigma'} \mathcal{K}^*$*) then* $\psi \in \mathcal{C}$ *(or* $\sigma' \in \mathcal{C}$*).*

Lemma 16. $For(\mathcal{B}^*) = For(\mathcal{B})$.

Thus, the revision of information state $\mathcal{K}$ with formula ϕ conveyed by source σ, given a relevant change propagation operator, is the composition of the three functions in order as follows: $\mathbb{W}_{CP}(\mathbb{W}_{RP}(\mathbb{W}_{JR}(\mathcal{K}, \phi, \sigma)))$. We believe that the decision made by the joint revision function $\mathbb{W}_{JR}$ *should* be based on a comparison between ϕ and its negation if the negation exists in the consequence. Then, given the weight of evidence and trust in information sources supporting both, one of the choices (1-(a) through 1-(d)) is made. As shown in Example 14, a full explanation of what *must* happen to the degrees of trust in information sources can not be captured by high-level postulates and hence, to avoid loss of generality when describing the operator, we stay silent on how $\mathbb{W}_{JR}$'s choices are made.

In the sequel, let $\mathbb{W}_{JR}(\mathcal{K}, \phi, \sigma) = \langle \mathcal{K}_{JR}, \mathcal{R}, \mathcal{C} \rangle$, $\mathbb{W}_{RP}(\mathcal{K}_{JR}, \mathcal{R}, \mathcal{C}) = \langle \mathcal{K}_{RP}, \mathcal{C} \rangle$, and $\mathbb{W}_{CP}(\mathcal{K}_{RP}, \mathcal{C}) = \mathcal{K}_\varkappa$.

Observation 1. *If* $\neg\phi \in For(\mathcal{B}(\mathcal{K}_\varkappa))$, *then* $\neg\phi \in For(\mathcal{B}(\mathcal{K}_{JR}))$.

Observation 2. *If* $\mathcal{K}_{JR} \prec_\psi \mathcal{K}$, *then* $\mathcal{K}_\varkappa \prec_\psi \mathcal{K}$.

Given the previous results, we can now provide a representation theorem for relevance change propagation operators to fully characterize the process of information revision in terms of postulates and operators.

Theorem 1. *A ⋉ operator is an information revision operator if and only if it is a relevant change propagation operator.*

6 Conclusion and Future Work

In this work, we argued that a new, and more realistic, take on belief revision is needed. Moreover, we provided an argument for why belief and trust revision, as we denote *information revision*, are intertwined processes that should not be separated. A model for representing information, be it beliefs or trust, with minimal assumptions on the modeling language was outlined. Then, we introduced the support graph which is a formal structure that allows for the identification of the relevance relations between not only formulas, but also, information sources. Further, we illustrated the postulates, we believe, any rational information revision operator should observe. Finally, we proposed the *relevant change propagation* operator showing that any information revision operator could be modeled as a relevant change propagation operator. In doing so, we hope to have opened a new direction of research and discourse that further investigates the relationship between belief and trust in the credibility of information sources allowing for building more astute agents similar to the spark first induced by the original AGM-approach.

Future work could go in one or more of the following directions

1. We intend on incorporating trust and conveyance in the object language.
2. We plan on incorporating mistrust as opposed to simply not trusting an agent to a general framework capturing misleading, trust, mistrust, beliefs and their revision.
3. Finally, we would like to add desires, intentions and possibly other mental attitudes and attempt to create a unified revision theory for all mental attitudes. The reason is that there is a direct relationship between trust and other mental attitudes. For example, trusting your friend who told you "Gym X is the best gym" will affect your intention formulation to achieve the goal "get in shape" by choosing to go to gym X in particular. Similarly, by trusting a review online that "Restaurant Y has the best pizza", your desires could get affected by now desiring to go to restaurant Y of all restaurants. Lastly, since the credibility of the source of any piece of information is always subject to revision, what constitutes any mental attitude is also subject to revision given trust change.

References

1. Alchourrón, C.E., Gärdenfors, P., Makinson, D.: On the logic of theory change: partial meet contraction and revision functions. J. Symbol. Logic **50**(2), 510–530 (1985)

2. Alchourrón, C.E., Makinson, D.: On the logic of theory change: contraction functions and their associated revision functions. Theoria **48**(1), 14–37 (1982)
3. Barber, K.S., Kim, J.: Belief revision process based on trust: agents evaluating reputation of information sources. In: Falcone, R., Singh, M., Tan, Y.H. (eds.) Trust Cyber-Soc., pp. 73–82. Springer, Heidelberg (2001)
4. Booth, R., Hunter, A.: Trust as a precursor to belief revision. J. Artif. Intell. Res **61**, 699–722 (2018)
5. Castelfranchi, C., Falcone, R.: Principles of trust for MAS: cognitive anatomy, social importance, and quantification. In: Proceedings International Conference on Multi Agent Systems (Cat. No. 98EX160), pp. 72–79. IEEE (1998)
6. Castelfranchi, C., Falcone, R.: Trust is much more than subjective probability: mental components and sources of trust. In: Proceedings of the 33rd Annual Hawaii International Conference on System Sciences, p. 10. IEEE (2000)
7. Darwiche, A., Pearl, J.: On the logic of iterated belief revision. Artif. Intell. **89**(1–2), 1–29 (1997)
8. Falcone, R., Castelfranchi, C.: Social trust: A cognitive approach. In: Trust and deception in virtual societies, pp. 55–90. Springer (2001)
9. Gärdenfors, P., Makinson, D.: Revisions of knowledge systems using epistemic entrenchment. In: Proceedings of the 2nd Conference on Theoretical Aspects of Reasoning about Knowledge, TARK 1988, pp. 83–95. Morgan Kaufmann Publishers Inc. (1988)
10. Hansson, S.O.: Belief contraction without recovery. Studia logica **50**(2), 251–260 (1991)
11. Hansson, S.O.: Kernel contraction. J. Symb. Logic **59**(3), 845–859 (1994). http://www.jstor.org/stable/2275912
12. Hansson, S.O.: A survey of non-prioritized belief revision. Erkenntnis **50**(2–3), 413–427 (1999)
13. Hansson, S.O.: Ten philosophical problems in belief revision. J. Logic Comput. **13**(1), 37–49 (2003)
14. Hardwig, J.: The role of trust in knowledge. J. Philos. **88**(12), 693–708 (1991)
15. Holton, R.: Deciding to trust, coming to believe. Aust. J. Philos. **72**(1), 63–76 (1994)
16. Huynh, T.D., Jennings, N.R., Shadbolt, N.R.: An integrated trust and reputation model for open multi-agent systems. Auton. Agents Multi-Agent Syst. **13**(2), 119–154 (2006)
17. Jonker, C.M., Treur, J.: Formal analysis of models for the dynamics of trust based on experiences. In: Garijo, F.J., Boman, M. (eds.) MAAMAW 1999. LNCS (LNAI), vol. 1647, pp. 221–231. Springer, Heidelberg (1999). https://doi.org/10.1007/3-540-48437-X_18
18. Jøsang, A., Hayward, R., Pope, S.: Trust network analysis with subjective logic. In: Proceedings of the 29th Australasian Computer Science Conference, vol. 48, pp. 85–94. Australian Computer Society, Inc. (2006)
19. Jøsang, A., Ivanovska, M., Muller, T.: Trust revision for conflicting sources. In: 2015 18th International Conference on Information Fusion (Fusion), pp. 550–557. IEEE (2015)
20. Katsuno, H., Mendelzon, A.O.: Propositional knowledge base revision and minimal change. Artif. Intell. **52**(3), 263–294 (1991)
21. Lorini, E., Jiang, G., Perrussel, L.: Trust-based belief change. In: Schaub, T., Friedrich, G., O'Sullivan, B. (eds.) Proceedings of the 21st European Conference on Artificial Intelligence (ECAI 2014). Frontiers in Artificial Intelligence and Applications, vol. 263, pp. 549–554. IOS Press, Amsterdam (2014)

22. McLeod, C.: Trust. In: Zalta, E.N. (ed.) The Stanford Encyclopedia of Philosophy. Metaphysics Research Lab, Stanford University, fall 2015 edn. (2015)

23. Niederée, R.: Multiple contraction a further case against gärdenfors' principle of recovery. In: Fuhrmann, A., Morreau, M. (eds.) The Logic of Theory Change. LNCS, vol. 465, pp. 322–334. Springer, Heidelberg (1991). https://doi.org/10.1007/BFb0018427

24. Ramchurn, S.D., Huynh, D., Jennings, N.R.: Trust in multi-agent systems. Knowle. Eng. Rev. 19(1), 1–25 (2004)

25. Rott, H.: Preferential belief change using generalized epistemic entrenchment. J. Logic Lang. Inf. 1(1), 45–78 (1992)

26. Tamargo, L.H., García, A.J., Falappa, M.A., Simari, G.R.: On the revision of informant credibility orders. Artif. Intell. 212, 36–58 (2014)

27. Tamargo, L.H., Gottifredi, S., García, A.J., Simari, G.R.: Sharing beliefs among agents with different degrees of credibility. Knowl. Inf. Syst. 50(3), 999–1031 (2016). https://doi.org/10.1007/s10115-016-0964-6

28. Tarski, A.: Logic semantics, metamathematics papers from 1923 to 1938. Translated by JH Woodger (1956)

29. Yasser, A., Ismail, H.O.: On the joint revision of belief and trust. In: Proceedings of the 6th Workshop on Formal and Cognitive Reasoning (FCR) Co-Located with the 43rd German Conference on Artificial Intelligence (KI 2020), Bamberg, Germany, 21–25 September 2020, pp. 55–68. CEUR Workshop Proceedings. http://ceur-ws.org/Vol-2680/paper5.pdf

30. Yasser, A., Ismail, H.O.: Information revision: the joint revision of belief and trust. In: Proceedings of the 18th International Workshop on Non-Monotonic Reasoning (NMR2020), pp. 150–160 (2020). https://nmr2020.dc.uba.ar/WorkshopNotes.pdf

Reasoning about Actions, Causality, and Change

Computing Defeasible Meta-logic

Francesco Olivieri[1], Guido Governatori[2], Matteo Cristani[3]([✉]),
and Abdul Sattar[1]

[1] Institute for Integrated and Intelligent Systems, Griffith University,
Nathan, QLD 4111, Australia
{f.oliveri,a.sattar}@griffith.edu.au
[2] Data61, CSIRO, Dutton Park, QLD 4102, Australia
guido.governatori@data61.csiro.au
[3] University of Verona, 37136 Verona, Italy
matteo.cristani@univr.it

Abstract. The use of meta-rules, i.e., rules whose content includes other rules, has been advocated to model policies and the notion of power in legal reasoning, where an agent has the power to create new norms affecting other agents. The use of Defeasible Logic (DL) to model meta-rules in the application area we just alluded to has been investigated, but not from a computational viewpoint. Our aim is to fill this gap by introducing a variant of DL, Defeasible Meta-Logic, to represent defeasible meta-theories, by proposing efficient algorithms to compute the (meta-)extensions of such theories, and by proving their computational complexity.

1 Introduction

We investigate the issue of efficient computation of meta-rules: rules having rules as their elements. The key idea is that a rule is a (binary) relationship between a set of conditions, and a conclusion. The meaning of such a relationship is to determine under which conditions a conclusion can be generated. Meta-rules generalise such an idea by establishing that, in addition to standard conclusions, rules themselves can be the "conclusion" (and part of the set of conditions), and new rules can hence be generated from other rules. Meta-rules (or rules with nested rules) occur frequently in real life scenarios, such as normative reasoning, policies for security systems. Very often when a set of policies is represented by a set of rules, we have to consider the policy that contains conditions (rules) about itself (or about another set of rules/policies). Consider the example in [27], where a company has a security policy specifying that: (i) a piece of information is deemed confidential when its disclosure would harm the interests of the company, and that (ii) confidential information must be protected (and hence cannot be disclosed). Such a policy can be naturally represented by the meta-rule

$$\big(Disclose(x) \rightarrow HarmInterests\big) \rightarrow Confidential(x).$$

© Springer Nature Switzerland AG 2021
W. Faber et al. (Eds.): JELIA 2021, LNAI 12678, pp. 69–84, 2021.
https://doi.org/10.1007/978-3-030-75775-5_6

Now, in this policy, the condition about harming the interests should be represented by an hypothetical expression: an 'IF (...) THEN (...)' rule is the most natural way to represent such a construct. Furthermore, the hypothetical is part of the conditions to define when a piece of information is confidential (actually, in this case, is the condition itself). Unfortunately, we cannot use classical material implication ($\supset$), given the well-known paradoxes of material implication. Consequently, if we model the policy as

$$(Disclose(x) \supset HarmInterests) \rightarrow Confidential(x),$$

given the equivalence between $Disclose(x) \supset HarmInterests$ and $\neg Disclose(x) \lor HarmInterests$, we have the counter-intuitive scenarios where (1) if x is not disclosed then x is confidential (information that is not confidential, no matter if disclosed or not, it does not need to be protected), and (2) if, for any reason, company interests are harmed, then x is confidential, for any piece of information. The policy can neither be defined as

$$(Disclose(x) \land HarmInterests) \rightarrow Confidential(x)$$

given that a disclosed information (with consequent harm of interest) can no longer be considered confidential. Another situation where meta-rules are useful is when the inclusion of a rule in a set of rules depends upon whether other rules are already in the system. For instance, we can have

$$r_1 \rightarrow r_2,$$

indicating that the existence of rule r_2 in the system depends on the existence in the system of rule r_1. However, typically, such dependencies among rules are stored externally, but if we model them directly into the system using meta-rules, then we can include (or remove) r_2 automatically, depending on the other rules it depends upon (and thus automating the system's maintenance functionalities). In addition, this feature is beneficial to system integration as it supports context dependant rules. The definition of context dependant policies is valuable in many situations; for instance, the defence forces of a country can have different rules of engagement, depending on the environment in which they are situated. One might think that a simple (and somehow naive) way to achieve this would be to partition the rules into independent rule sets, one for each context, and then to use simpler rules (without nested rules). However, as discussed, there could be dependencies among the rules, and the environments themselves can be defined in terms of rules. Thus, a clear partition of the simple rules might not be feasible.

Meta-rules are useful when a set of rules can provide conditions about other conditions in the same policy. This is the case in legal documents, where often there are provisions conferring power, or delegation, to some agents; in the legal domain, the notion of power is when the legal system allows an agent to create, issue, or revoke, norms affecting other agents. Several works (see [10, 18]) tried to model such notions using conditional logics since, similarly to hypothetical conditionals, such notions can be faithfully and efficiently represented as rules.

Another area of legal reasoning, where meta-rules proved to be essential to represent the legal processes at hand, is related to the of field of norm change. As we argued, many legislative instruments contain provisions (norms) about who has the power to create, modify, revoke, or abrogate other norms. If norms can be represented as rules [26], and there are norms 'speaking about' other norms, then it would be natural to have rules whose content consists of other rules.

Different variants of defeasible logic have been proposed [4,16] to incorporate meta-rules in order to describe the logical behaviour of norm changes. An important aspect of norm changes is that some legal systems can specify that specific norms cannot exist (or cannot be in force) in that particular legal system. For example, in the Italian Constitution, Article 27 prescribes that there cannot be norms in the Italian legal system prescribing Capital Punishment. This means that a meta-norm can speak about the positive existence of a rule, as well as preventing a rule to be generated.

To this end, we will distinguish between the content of a rule (which is a binary relationship between a set of premises and a conclusion, both represented as propositions in an underlying, given language), and the name, or identifier, of the rule itself. In this set up, a rule can be understood as a function associating a label to the content of the rule. Similarly, a meta-rule is a function that associates the name, or label, to the content, but in this case the elements of the binary relation corresponding to the content of the meta-rule can contain other rules.

In addition, we will admit negation of rules. If we are able to conclude that a (positive) rule holds, then it means that we can insert the rule (the content of the rule, with a specific name) in the system, and we can use the resulting rule to derive new conclusions. For a negated rule, the meaning is that it is not possible to obtain a rule with that specific content (irrespective of the name).

The paper is structured as follows. In Sect. 2 we introduce a variant of Defeasible Logic able to handle rules and meta-rules and we propose the proof theory of the logic. Then in Sect. 3 we introduce a computationally efficient algorithm to compute the extension of a Defeasible Theory with rules and meta rules and we show that the extension is computable in polynomial time. Finally, we provide some conclusion and a quick discussion on some related work in Sect. 4.

2 Logic

Defeasible Logic [1] is a simple and efficient rule-based non-monotonic formalism that proved to be suitable for the logical modelling of different application areas, specifically agents [5,14,19], legal reasoning [4,16], and workflows from a business process compliance perspective [13,24,25]. Some of these application fields requires the modelling of contexts and the use of rules in the scope of other rules. Accordingly, extensions of the logic have been developed to capture such features by adopting meta-rules. However, the work on meta-rules in Defeasible Logic focused on defining the extensions of the logic, specifically the proof theoretic features, neglecting to investigate the computational aspects. A major strength of the Defeasible Logic approach, that makes it appealing from the application point of view, is its feasible computational complexity. This paper fills the gap. We start by providing the presentation of the logic from the proof theoretic point of view, and then we will see how to create an efficient algorithm to compute the extension of a defeasible meta-theory.

Let PROP be a set of propositional atoms, and Lab be a set of arbitrary labels (the names of the rules). Accordingly, Lit = PROP $\cup$ {$\neg l \,|\, l \in$ PROP} is the set of *literals*. The *complement* of a literal l is denoted by $\sim l$: if l is a positive literal p then $\sim l$ is $\neg p$, and if l is a negative literal $\neg p$ then $\sim l$ is p. If $\alpha \in$ Lab is a rule label, then $\neg\alpha$ is a rule expression as well, and we use the same convention defined for literals for $\sim\alpha$. We use lower-case Latin letters to denote literals, and lower-case Greek letters to denote rule labels and negated rule labels.

The set of rules is made of two sets: standard rules R^S, and meta-rules R^M. A *standard rule* $\beta \in R^S$ is an expression of the type '$\beta : A(\beta) \hookrightarrow C(\beta)$', and consists of: (i) the unique name $\beta \in$ Lab, (ii) the *antecedent* $A(\beta) \subseteq$ Lit, (iii) an *arrow* $\hookrightarrow \in \{\rightarrow, \Rightarrow, \rightsquigarrow\}$ denoting, respectively, a strict rule, a defeasible rule and a defeater, (iv) its *consequent* $C(\beta) \in$ Lit, a single literal. Hence, the statement "All computing scientists are humans" is formulated through a strict rule (as there is no exception to it), whilst "Computing scientists travel to the city of the conference" is instead formalised through a defeasible rule as "During pandemic travels might be prohibited" is a defeater representing an exception to it.

A meta rule is a slightly different concept than a standard rule: (i) standard rules can appear in its antecedent, and (ii) the conclusion itself can be a standard rule. Accordingly, a *meta rule* $\beta \in R^M$ is an expression of the type '$\beta : A(\beta) \hookrightarrow C(\beta)$', and consists of: (i) a unique name $\beta \in$ Lab, (ii) the antecedent $A(\beta)$ is now a finite subset of Lit $\cup R^S$, (iii) the *arrow* $\hookrightarrow$ with the same meaning as for standard rules, and (iv) its *consequent* $C(\beta) \in$ Lit $\cup R^S$, that is either a single literal or a standard rule (meta-rules can be used to derive standard rules).

A *defeasible meta-theory* (or simply theory) D is a tuple $(F, R, >)$, where $R = R^{stand} \cup R^{meta}$ such that $R^{stand} \subseteq R^S$ and $R^{meta} \subseteq R^M$. F is the set of facts, indisputable statements that are considered to be always true, and which can be seen as the inputs for a case. Rules in R can be of three types: *strict rules*, *defeasible rules*, or *defeaters*. Strict rules are rules in classical sense: every time the premises are the case, so is the conclusion. Defeasible rules represent the non-monotonic part of a defeasible meta-theory as they describe pieces of information that are true under some circumstances, while false or undetermined under others. Accordingly, when the premises of a defeasible rules are the case, so *typically* is the conclusion but it can be prevented to be the case by contrary evidence. Defeaters are a special type of rules whose only purpose is to defeat contrary statements, but cannot be used to *directly* draw a certain conclusion. Finally, we have the *superiority* or *preference relation* > among rules, which is binary and irreflexive, and is used to solve conflicts. The notation $\beta > \gamma$ means $(\beta, \gamma) \in >$.

Some abbreviations. The set of strict rules in R is R_s, and the set of strict and defeasible rules is R_{sd}. $R[X]$ is the rule set with head $X \in \{$Lit $\cup R^S\}$. A *conclusion of D* is either a *tagged literal* or a *tagged label* (for a standard rule), and can have one of the following forms with the standard meanings in DL:

- $\pm \Delta l$ means that $l \in$ Lit is *definitely provable* (resp. *refuted*, or *non provable*) in D, i.e. there is a definite proof for l (resp. a definite proof does not exist);
- $\pm \Delta^{meta} \alpha$, $\alpha \in R^{stand}$, with same meaning as above;
- $\pm \partial l$ means that l is *defeasibly provable* (resp. *refuted*) in D;
- $\pm \partial^{meta} \alpha$, $\alpha \in R^{stand}$, with the same meaning as above.

The definition of proof is also the standard in DL. Given a defeasible meta-theory D, a proof P of length n in D is a finite sequence $P(1), P(2), \ldots, P(n)$ of tagged formulas of the type $+\Delta X$, $-\Delta X$, $+\partial X$, $-\partial X$, where the proof conditions defined in the rest of this section hold. $P(1..n)$ denotes the first n steps of P.

Derivations are based on the notions of a rule being *applicable* or *discarded*. Briefly, in Standard DL when antecedents are made only by literals, a rule is applicable when every antecedent's literal has been proved at a previous derivation step. Symmetrically, a rule is discarded when one of such literals has been previously refuted. We need to adapt such concepts to deal so that standard rules may appear both in the antecedent, and as conclusions of meta-rules: we thus say that a meta-rule is applicable when each of the standard rules in its antecedent either is in the initial set of standard rules, or has been proved.

Definition 1 (Applicability). *Given a defeasible meta-theory $D = (F, R, >)$, $R = R^{stand} \cup R^{meta}$, a rule $\beta \in R$ is #-applicable, $\# \in \{\Delta, \partial\}$, at $P(n+1)$ iff*

1. $\forall l \in$ Lit $\cap A(\beta)$. $+ \#l \in P(1..n)$,
2. $\forall \alpha \in R^S \cap A(\beta)$ *either (a)* $\alpha \in R^{stand}$, *or (b)* $+\#^{meta} \alpha \in P(1..n)$.

Notion of discardability is derived by applying the principle of *strong negation*[1].

Definition 2 (Discardability). *Given a defeasible meta-theory $D = (F, R, >)$, $R = R^{stand} \cup R^{meta}$, a rule $\beta \in R$ is #-discarded, $\# \in \{\Delta, \partial\}$, at $P(n+1)$ iff*

1. $\exists l \in$ Lit $\cap A(\beta)$. $- \#l \in P(1..n)$, *or*
2. $\exists \alpha \in R^S \cap A(\beta)$ *such that (a)* $\alpha \notin R^{stand}$ *and (b)* $-\#^{meta} \alpha \in P(1..n)$

When β is a meta-rule and α is not in R^{stand} (hence α is the conclusion of a meta-rule), then β will stay dormant until a decision on α (of being proved/refuted) is made. The following example is to get acquainted with the concepts introduced.

Example 1. Let $D = (F = \{a, b\}, R, \emptyset)$ be a theory such that

$$R = \{\alpha : a \Rightarrow \beta; \quad \beta : b, \beta \Rightarrow \zeta; \quad \gamma : c \Rightarrow d; \quad \varphi : \psi \Rightarrow d\}.$$

Here, both α and β are applicable (we will see right below how to prove $+\partial^{meta} \beta$), whilst γ and φ are discarded as we cannot prove $+\partial c$ nor $\partial^{meta} \psi$.

---

[1] The strong negation principle applies the function that simplifies a formula by moving all negations to an inner most position in the resulting formula, and replaces the positive tags with the respective negative tags, and the other way around see [15].

All proof tags for literals are the standard in DL literature [1], and reported here to make the paper self-contained. For this reason, we will omit the negative counterparts as they are straightforwardly obtained from the positive ones by applying the strong negation principle. The definition of Δ for literals describes forward chaining of strict rules.

$+\Delta l$: If $P(n+1) = +\Delta l$ then
  (1) $l \in F$, or (2) $\exists \beta \in R_s[l]$ s.t. β is Δ-applicable.

We now introduce the proof tag for defeasible provability of a literal.

$+\partial l$: If $P(n+1) = +\partial l$ then
  (1) $+\Delta l \in P(1..n)$, or
  (2) (1) $-\Delta{\sim}l \in P(1..n)$, and
      (2) $\exists \beta \in R_{\text{sd}}[l]$ s.t. β is ∂-applicable, and
      (3) $\forall \gamma \in R[{\sim}l]$ then either
          (1) γ is discarded, or (2) $\exists \varepsilon \in R[l]$ s.t ε is ∂-applicable and $\varepsilon > \gamma$.

We are finally ready to propose the proof tags to prove (standard) rules.

$+\Delta^{meta}\alpha$: If $P(n+1) = +\Delta^{meta}\alpha$ then
  (1) $\alpha \in R^{stand}$, or (2) $\exists \beta \in R_s^{meta}[\alpha]$ s.t. β is Δ-applicable.

A standard rule is strictly proven if either (1) such a rule is in the initial set of standard rules, or (2) there exists an applicale, strict meta-rule for it.

$+\partial^{meta}\alpha$: If $P(n+1) = +\partial^{meta}\alpha$ then
  (1) $+\Delta^{meta}\alpha \in P(1..n)$, or
  (2) (1) $-\Delta^{meta}{\sim}\alpha \in P(1..n)$, and
      (2) $\exists \beta \in R_{\text{sd}}^{meta}[(\alpha : a_1, \ldots, a_n \hookrightarrow c)]$ s.t.
      (3) β is ∂-meta-applicable, and
      (4) $\forall \gamma \in R^{meta}[{\sim}(\zeta : a_1, \ldots, a_n \hookrightarrow c)]$, then either
          (1) γ is ∂-meta-discarded, or
          (2) $\exists \varepsilon \in R^{meta}[(\chi : a_1, \ldots, a_n \hookrightarrow c)]$ s.t.
              (1) $\chi \in \{\alpha, \zeta\}$, (2) ε is ∂-meta-applicable, and (3) $\varepsilon > \gamma$.

A standard rule α is defeasibly proven if it has previously strictly proven (1), or (2.1) the opposite is not strictly proven and (2.2-2.3) there exists an applicable (defeasible or strict) meta-rule β such that every meta-rule γ for ${\sim}\zeta$ ($A(\alpha) = A(\zeta)$ and $C(\alpha) = C(\zeta)$) either (2.4.1) γ is discarded, or defeated (2.4.2.3) by (2.4.2.1–2.4.2.2) an applicable meta-rule for the same conclusion c. Note that in Condition 2.3 we do not impose that $\alpha \equiv \zeta$, whilst for γ-rules we do impose that the label of the rule in $C(\gamma)$ is either α or ζ.

$-\partial^{meta}\alpha$: If $P(n+1) = -\partial^{meta}\alpha$ then
  (1) $-\Delta^{meta}\alpha \in P(1..n)$, and either
  (2) (1) $+\Delta^{meta}{\sim}\alpha \in P(1..n)$, or
      (2) $\forall \beta \in R_{\text{sd}}^{meta}[(\alpha : a_1, \ldots, a_n \hookrightarrow c)]$ then

(3) β is ∂-meta-discarded, or

(4) $\exists \gamma \in R^{meta}[\sim(\zeta : a_1, \ldots, a_n \hookrightarrow c)]$ s.t.

(1) γ is ∂-meta-applicable, and

(2) $\forall \varepsilon \in R^{meta}[(\chi : a_1, \ldots, a_n \hookrightarrow c)]$ then

(1) $\chi \notin \{\alpha, \zeta\}$, or (2) ε is ∂-meta-discarded, or (3) $\varepsilon \not\succ \gamma$.

Given a defeasible meta-theory D, we define the set of positive and negative conclusions of D as its *meta-extension*:

$$E(D) = (+\Delta, -\Delta, +\Delta^{meta}, -\Delta^{meta}, +\partial, -\partial, +\partial^{meta}, -\partial^{meta}),$$

where $\pm\# = \{l \,|\, l$ appears in D and $D \vdash \pm\#l\}$ and $\pm\#^{meta} = \{\alpha \in R^S \,|\, \alpha$ appears as consequent of a meta-rule β and $D \vdash \pm\#^{meta}\alpha\}$, $\# \in \{\Delta, \partial\}$.

Let us propose two theories to explain how the derivation mechanism works.

Example 2. Let $D = (\mathrm{F} = \{a\}, R, >= \{(\zeta, \chi)\})$ be a theory such that

$$R^{stand} = \{\alpha : a \Rightarrow b, \qquad \beta : b \Rightarrow \sim c, \qquad \zeta : \sim c \Rightarrow \sim d, \qquad \chi : a \Rightarrow d\},$$
$$R^{meta} = \{\gamma : (\alpha : a \Rightarrow b) \Rightarrow c\}.$$

As $a \in \mathrm{F}$, we prove $D \vdash +\Delta a$, which in cascade give us $D \vdash +\partial a$ (β is hence ∂-applicable). Since $\alpha \in R^{stand}$, α is ∂-applicable and $D \vdash +\partial b$. Moreover, $D \vdash +\Delta^{meta}\alpha$ and $D \vdash +\partial^{meta}\alpha$, which makes in turn γ being ∂-applicable. We conclude with both $D \vdash -\partial c$ and $D \vdash -\partial \sim c$, as the superiority does not solve the conflict between β and γ. The dormant χ and ζ can now be considered: χ is ∂-applicable whereas ζ is ∂-discarded. Thus, $D \vdash +\partial d$.

Example 3. Let $D = (\mathrm{F} = \{a, c, d, g\}, R, >= \{(\beta, \gamma)(\zeta, \eta)\})$ be a theory where

$$R^{stand} = \{\alpha : a \Rightarrow b, \qquad \zeta : g \Rightarrow \sim b\},$$
$$R^{meta} = \{\beta : c, (\alpha : a \Rightarrow b) \Rightarrow (\eta : d \Rightarrow b), \qquad \gamma : d \Rightarrow \sim(\chi : d \Rightarrow b)\}.$$

As a, c, d and g are facts, we strictly and defeasibly prove all of them. Hence, α, ζ, β and γ are all ∂-applicable. As before, $\alpha \in R^{stand}$, thus $D \vdash +\Delta^{meta}\alpha$ and $D \vdash +\partial c$ make β being ∂-applicable as well. As $\beta > \gamma$, we conclude that $D \vdash +\partial^{meta}\eta$, but we prove also $D \vdash -\partial^{meta}\chi$ (by Conditions 2.4 and 2.4.1 of $-\partial^{meta}$). Again, d being a fact makes η to be ∂-applicable. ζ has been dormant so far, but it can now be confronted with η: since η is weaker than ζ, then $D \vdash +\partial \sim b$ (and naturally $D \vdash -\partial b$).

The logic presented above is coherent and consistent. This means that given a defeasible meta-theory D: (a) it is not possible to establish that a conclusion is, at the same time, proved and refuted, and (b) if we have positive defeasible proofs for a conclusion and its complement, then the inconsistency depends on the strict (monotonic) part of the theory. This is formally stated in next Proposition 1, which follows from the adoption of the strong principle to formulate the definitions of the proof conditions for positive/negative pairs of proof tags [15].

Proposition 1. *Let D be a theory. There is not literal p, or label α, such that*

(a) $D \vdash +\#p$ and $D \vdash -\#p$, for $\# \in \{\Delta, \Delta^{meta}, \partial, \partial^{meta}\}$.

(b) If $D \vdash +\partial p$ and $D \vdash +\partial \sim p$, then $D \vdash +\Delta p$ and $D \vdash +\Delta p$; if $D \vdash +\partial^{meta}\alpha$ and $D \vdash +\partial^{meta}\sim\alpha$, then $D \vdash +\Delta^{meta}\alpha$ and $D \vdash +\Delta^{meta}\alpha$.

3   Algorithms

The algorithms presented in this section compute the meta-extension of a defeasible meta-theory. The main idea being to compute, at each iteration step, a *simpler* theory than the one at the previous step. By simpler, we mean that, by proving and disproving literals and standard rules, we can progressively simplify the rules of the theory itself. We remind the reader that, roughly said, a rule is applicable when everything in its antecedent has been proved. Note that, trivially, a rule with empty antecedent is always applicable, as there is nothing to prove. Symmetrically, a rule is discarded if (at least) one of the antecedent's element has been previously rejected. When a rule is discarded, it can no longer play part in neither supporting its conclusion, nor rejecting the opposite.

Let us consider the theory proposed in Example 2, and let us assume that, at iteration j, the algorithm proves $+\partial b$. At the next iteration $j + 1$, β will be modified according to what discussed above, and will be $\beta : \emptyset \Rightarrow \sim c$ (β is thus applicable). Later on, at iteration k, the algorithms prove $-\partial \sim c$, and then proceed in removing χ from the set of the potentially applicable rules (as χ is ∂-discarded according to Definition 2) and the tuple (ζ, χ) from the superiority, as χ can no longer play any part in supporting $\sim d$.

According to these observations, during the run of the algorithms, every time that a literal or a standard rule is proven, we can remove it from all the antecedents where it appears in. A rule thus becomes applicable when we have removed all the elements from its antecedent. On the contrary, whenever a literal or a standard rule is rejected, we can remove all the rules where such an element appears in the antecedent, as those rules are now discarded. We can also remove all the tuples of the superiority relation containing such discarded rules. The idea of these simplifications is taken from [12,14].

As discussed in Sect. 2, a meta-rule is applicable when each standard rule in its antecedent is either in the initial set of rules (i.e., in R^{stand}), or has been proved later on during the computation and then added to the set of standard rules. This it the reason for the support sets at Lines 1 and 2: R_{appl} is the rule set of the initial standard rules, $R^{\alpha C}$ is the set of standard rules which are not in the initial set but are instead conclusions of meta-rules. As rules in $R^{\alpha C}$ are proved/disproved during the algorithms' execution, both these sets are updated.

At Line 3, we populate the Herbrand Base (HB), which consists of all literals that appear in the antecedent, or as a conclusion of a rule. As literals not in the Herbrand base do not have any standard rule supporting them, such literals are already disproved (Line 4). For every literal in HB, we create the support set of the rules supporting that particular conclusion (Line 6), and we initialise the relative set used later on to manage conflicts and team defeater (Line 7).

Algorithm 1: Existence

Input: Defeasible meta-theory $D = (F, R, >)$, $R = R^{stand} \cup R^{meta}$
Output: The defeasible meta-extension $E(D)$ of D

1   $\pm\partial \leftarrow \emptyset$; $\pm\partial^{meta} \leftarrow \emptyset$; $R_{appl} \leftarrow R^{stand}$;

2   $R^{\alpha C} \leftarrow \{\alpha \in R^S \,|\, \exists\beta \in R^{meta}. C(\beta) = \alpha\}$;

3   $HB = \{l \in \text{Lit} \,|\, \exists\beta \in R^{stand}. l \in A(\beta) \cup C(\beta)\} \cup \{l \in \text{Lit} \,|\, \exists\beta \in R^{meta}.\exists\alpha \in$
    $R^S \,(\alpha \in A(\beta) \cup C(\beta)) \wedge (l \in A(\alpha) \cup C(\alpha))\}$;

4   **for** $l \in \text{Lit} \wedge l \notin HB$ **do** $-\partial \leftarrow -\partial \cup \{l\}$;

5   **for** $l \in HB$ **do**

6     $R[l] = \{\beta \in R^S \,|\, C(\beta) = l \wedge (\beta \in R^{stand} \vee \exists\gamma \in R^{meta}. \beta \in C(\gamma))\}$;

7     $R[l]_{infd} \leftarrow \emptyset$;

8   **for** $\alpha \notin R^{stand} \cup R^{\alpha C}$ **do** $-\partial^{meta} \leftarrow -\partial^{meta} \cup \{\alpha\}$;

9   **for** $\big(\alpha : A(\alpha) \hookrightarrow C(\alpha)\big) \in R^{\alpha C}$ **do**

10     $R[\alpha] \leftarrow \{\beta \in R^{meta} \,|\, \alpha = C(\beta)\}$;

11     $R[\alpha]_{opp} \leftarrow \{\gamma \in R^{meta} \,|\, C(\gamma) = \sim(\zeta : A(\alpha) \hookrightarrow C(\alpha))\}$;

12     $R[\alpha]_{supp} \leftarrow \{\varepsilon \in R^{meta} \,|\, \big(C(\varepsilon) = (\chi : A(\alpha) \hookrightarrow C(\alpha))\big) \wedge \big(\exists\gamma \in R[\alpha]_{opp}. \varepsilon >$
      $\gamma\big) \wedge \big(\chi = \alpha \vee (\exists\gamma \in R[\alpha]_{opp}.C(\gamma) = \sim(\zeta : A(\alpha) \hookrightarrow C(\alpha)) \wedge \chi = \zeta)\big)\}$;

13   **for** $l \in F$ **do**

14     $+\partial \leftarrow +\partial \cup \{l\}$;

15     $R \leftarrow \{A(\beta) \setminus \{l\} \hookrightarrow C(\beta) \,|\, \beta \in R\} \setminus \{\beta \in R \,|\, \sim l \in A(\beta)\}$;

16     $> \leftarrow > \setminus \{(\beta,\gamma),(\gamma,\beta) \in > \,|\, \sim l \in A(\beta)\}$;

17   **for** $\alpha \in R^{stand}$ **do**

18     $+\partial^{meta} \leftarrow +\partial^{meta} \cup \{\alpha\}$;

19     $R^{meta} \leftarrow \{A(\beta) \setminus \{\alpha\} \hookrightarrow C(\beta) \,|\, \beta \in R^{meta}\} \setminus \{\gamma \in R^{meta} \,|\, \{\sim\alpha\} \in A(\gamma)\}$;

20     $> \leftarrow > \setminus \{(\beta,\gamma),(\gamma,\beta) \in > \,|\, \{\sim\alpha\} \in A(\beta)\}$;

21 **repeat**

22   $\partial^{\pm} \leftarrow \emptyset$

23   **for** $l \in HB$ **do**

24   **if** $R[l] = \emptyset$ **then** REFUTE(l);

25   **if** $\exists\beta \in R[l]. A(\beta) = \emptyset$ **then**

26       $R[\sim l]_{infd} \leftarrow R[\sim l]_{infd} \cup \{\gamma \in R[\sim l] \,|\, \beta > \gamma\}$;

27   **if** $\{\gamma \in R[\sim l] \,|\, \gamma > \beta\} = \emptyset$ **then** REFUTE($\sim l$);

28   **if** $R[\sim l] \setminus R[\sim l]_{infd} = \emptyset$ **then**

29   PROVE(l); REFUTE($\sim l$);

30   $\pm\partial \leftarrow \pm\partial \cup \partial^{\pm}$;

31   $\pm\partial_{meta} \leftarrow \emptyset$;

32   **for** $\big(\alpha : A(\alpha) \hookrightarrow C(\alpha)\big) \in R^{\alpha C}$ **do**

33   **if** $R[\alpha] = \emptyset$ **then** REFUTE(α);

34   **if** $\exists\beta \in R[\alpha]. A(\beta) = \emptyset$ **then**

35       $R[\alpha]_{opp} \leftarrow R[\alpha]_{opp} \setminus \{\gamma \in R^{meta} \,|\, \beta > \gamma\}$;

36   **if** $\big(R[\alpha]_{opp} \setminus \{\gamma \in R[\alpha]_{opp} \,|\, \varepsilon \in R[\alpha]_{supp} \wedge A(\varepsilon) = \emptyset \wedge \varepsilon > \gamma\}\big) = \emptyset$
      then

37   PROVE(α);

38   **for** $\gamma \in R[\alpha]_{opp}. C(\gamma) = \sim(\zeta)$ **do** REFUTE($\sim\zeta$);

39   $\pm\partial^{meta} \leftarrow \pm\partial^{meta} \cup \partial^{\pm}_{meta}$

40 **until** $\partial^+ = \emptyset$ **and** $\partial^- = \emptyset$ **and** $\partial^+_{meta} = \emptyset$ **and** $\partial^-_{meta} = \emptyset$;

41 **return** $E(D) = (+\partial, -\partial, +\partial^{meta}, -\partial^{meta})$

We need to do the same for those labels for standard rules that are conclusions of a meta-rule. First, if a label for standard rule is neither in the initial set of standard rules, nor a conclusion of a meta-rules, then such a rule is disproved (Line 8). We assume such sets to have empty intersection, as previously motivated. Second, the following loop at Lines 17–20 initialises three support sets: $R[\alpha]$ contains the meta-rules whose conclusion is α, $R[\alpha]_{opp}$ contains the meta-rules attacking α (γ-like rules in $\pm\partial^{meta}$), while $R[\alpha]_{supp}$ contains the meta-rules supporting α (ε-like rules in $\pm\partial^{meta}$).

The following **for** loop takes care of the factual literals, as they are proved without any further computation. We assume the set of facts to be consistent. Analogously, loop at Lines 17–20 does the same for rules in the initial set of standard rules that may appear in the antecedent of meta-rules.

The algorithm now enters the main cycle (**Repeat-Until**, Lines 21–40). For every literal l in HB (Lines 23–29), we first verify whether there is a rule supporting it, and, if not, we refute l (Line 24). Otherwise, if there exists an applicable rule β supporting it (**if** at Line 25), we update the set of *defeated* rules supporting the opposite conclusion $R[\sim l]_{infd}$ (Line 26). Given that $R[\sim l]$ contains the γ rules supporting $\sim l$, and given that we have just verified that β for l is applicable, we store in $R[\sim l]_{infd}$ all those γs defeated by β. The next step is to check whether there actually exists any rule supporting $\sim l$ stronger than β: if not, $\sim l$ can be refuted (Line 27).

The idea behind the **if** at Lines 28–29 is the following: if $D \vdash +\partial l$, eventually the **repeat-until** cycle will have added to $R[\sim l]_{infd}$ enough rules to defeat all (applicable) supports for $\sim l$. We thus invoke **Prove** on l, and **Refute** on $\sim l$.

Similarly, when we prove a rule instead of a literal, but we now use $R[\alpha]_{opp}$ and $R[\alpha]_{supp}$ in a slightly different way than $R[l]_{infd}$, to reflect the differences between $+\partial$ and $+\partial^{meta}$. Every time, a meta-rule β for α is applicable (**if** at Lines 34–38), we remove from $R[\alpha]_{opp}$ all the γs defeated by β itself (Line 35). If now there are enough applicable ε rules supporting α (**if** check at Line 36), then: (i) we prove α, and (ii) we refute all ζ rules conclusion of γ rules in $R[\alpha]_{opp}$.

Procedure Prove

    Input: X, which is either $l \in$ Lit, or a rule $\alpha : A(\alpha) \hookrightarrow C(\alpha)$

1   **if** X *is* l **then**
2 | $\partial^+ \leftarrow \partial^+ \cup \{l\}$; $HB \leftarrow HB \setminus \{l\}$;
3 | $R_{appl} \leftarrow \{A(\beta) \setminus \{l\} \hookrightarrow C(\beta) \,|\, \beta \in R_{appl}\}$;
4 | $R^{meta} \leftarrow \{A(\beta) \setminus \{l\} \hookrightarrow C(\beta) \,|\, \beta \in R^{meta}\}$;
5   **else**
6 | $\partial^+_{meta} \leftarrow \partial^+_{meta} \cup \{\alpha\}$;
7 | $R^{\alpha C} \leftarrow R^{\alpha C} \setminus \{\alpha\}$;
8 | $R^{meta} \leftarrow \{A(\beta) \setminus \{\alpha\} \hookrightarrow C(\beta) \,|\, \beta \in R^{meta}\}$;
9 | **if** $\exists l \in -\partial \cap A(\alpha)$ **then** $A(\alpha) \leftarrow A(\alpha) \setminus +\partial$; $R_{appl} \leftarrow R_{appl} \cup \{\alpha\}$;

Procedure PROVE is invoked when a literal or a standard rule is proved. In case of a literal, we simplify the rules of the theory following what said at the beginning of this section. In case of a rule, we also need to verify whether any of the literal in its antecedent has been already refuted (**if** check at Line 9). If this is the not case, we can proceed in simplifying α's antecedent, and then in adding α to the set of standard rules to be evaluated to be applicable.

Procedure Refute

Input: X, which is either $l \in$ Lit, or a rule $\alpha : A(\alpha) \hookrightarrow C(\alpha)$

1   **if** X *is* l **then**
2 | $\partial^- \leftarrow \partial^- \cup \{l\}$; $HB \leftarrow HB \setminus \{l\}$;
3 | $R_{appl} \leftarrow R_{appl} \setminus \{\beta \in R_{appl} \mid l \in A(\beta)\}$;
4 | $R^{meta} \leftarrow R^{meta} \setminus \{\beta \in R^{meta} \mid l \in A(\beta)\}$;
5 | $> \leftrightarrow > \setminus \{(\beta, \gamma), (\gamma, \beta) \in > \mid l \in A(\beta)\}$;
6   **else**
7 | $\partial^-_{meta} \leftarrow \partial^-_{meta} \cup \{\alpha\}$;
8 | $R^{\alpha C} \leftarrow R^{\alpha C} \setminus \{\alpha\}$;
9 | $R^{meta} \leftarrow R^{meta} \setminus \{\beta \in R^{meta} \mid \alpha \in A(\beta)\}$;
10 | $> \leftrightarrow > \setminus \{(\beta, \gamma), (\gamma, \beta) \in > \mid \alpha \in A(\beta)\}$;
11 | **for** $\zeta \in R^{\alpha C}. \sim\!\left(\zeta : A(\alpha) \hookrightarrow C(\alpha)\right)$ **do**
12 | | $R[\zeta]_{opp} \leftarrow R[\zeta]_{opp} \setminus \{\beta \in R[\zeta]_{opp} \mid C(\beta) = \alpha\}$;
13 | **for** $\chi \in R^{\alpha C}. \left(\chi : A(\alpha) \hookrightarrow C(\alpha)\right)$ **do**
14 | | $R[\chi]_{supp} \leftarrow R[\chi]_{supp} \setminus \{\varepsilon \in R[\chi]_{supp} \mid C(\varepsilon) = \alpha\}$;

Procedure REFUTE is invoked when a literal or a standard rule is refuted. Again, in case of literals, the simplification operations are the ones detailed in the beginning of this section. In case of rules, the differences are in the two loops at Lines 11–12 and 13–14. The former loop updates $R[\zeta]_{opp}$, as βs for α no longer support the counter-argument; symmetrically, the latter loop updates $R[\chi]_{supp}$.

3.1   Computational Properties

We discuss the computational properties of Algorithm 1 EXISTENCE. Due to space reasons, we only sketch the proofs by providing the motivations of why our algorithms are sound, complete, terminate, and leave out the technical details.

In order to discuss termination and computational complexity, we start by defining the *size* of a meta-theory D as $\Sigma(D)$ to be the number of the occurrences of literals plus the number of occurrences of rules plus 1 for every tuple in the superiority relation. Thus, the theory $D = (F, R, >)$ such that $F = \{a, b, c\}$, $R^{stand} = \{(\alpha : a \Rightarrow d), (\beta : b \Rightarrow \sim d)\}$, $R^{meta} = \{(\gamma : c \Rightarrow (\zeta : a \Rightarrow d))\}$, $>= \{(\zeta, \beta)\}$, has size $3 + 6 + 5 + 1 = 15$.

Note that, by implementing hash tables with pointers to rules where a given literal occurs, each rule can be accessed in constant time. We also implement hash tables for the tuples of the superiority relation where a given rule appears as either of the two element, and even those can be accessed in constant time.

Theorem 1. *Algorithm 1* EXISTENCE *terminates and its complexity is* $O(\Sigma^2)$.

Proof. Termination of Procedures PROVE and REFUTE is straightforward, as the size of the input theory is finite, and we modify finite sets. The complexity of PROVE is $O(\Sigma)$, whereas of REFUTE is $O(\Sigma^2)$ (two inner **for** loops of is $O(\Sigma)$).

Termination of Algorithm 1 EXISTENCE is bound to termination of the **repeat-until** cycle at Lines 21–40, as all other cycles loop over finite sets of elements of the order of $O(\Sigma)$. Given that both HB and $R^{\alpha C}$ are finite, and since every time a literal or a rule is proved/refuted, they are removed from the corresponding set, the algorithm eventually empties such sets, and, at the next iteration, no modification to the extension can be made. This proves the termination of Algorithm 1 EXISTENCE.

Regarding its complexity: (1) all set modifications are in linear time, and (ii) the aforementioned **repeat-until** cycle is iterated at most $O(\Sigma)$ times, and so are the two **for** loops at lines 23–29 and 32–38. This would suggest that the **repeat-until** cycle runs in $O(\Sigma^2)$. A more discerning analysis shows that the complexity is actually $O(\Sigma)$: the complexity of each **for** cannot be considered separately from the complexity of the external loop (they are strictly dependent). Indeed, the overall number of operations made by the sum of all loop iterations cannot outrun the number of occurrences of the literals or rules $(O(\Sigma) + O(\Sigma))$, because the operations in the inner cycles directly decrease, iteration after iteration, the number of the remaining repetitions of the outmost loop, and the other way around. This sets the complexity of Algorithm 1 EXISTENCE to $O(\Sigma^2)$.

Theorem 2. *Algorithm 1* EXISTENCE *is sound and complete, that is*

1. $D \vdash +\partial p$ *iff* $p \in +\partial p$ *of* $E(D)$, $p \in \text{Lit}$
2. $D \vdash +\partial^{meta} \alpha$ *iff* $p \in +\partial \alpha$ *of* $E(D)$, $\alpha \in \text{Lab}$
3. $D \vdash -\partial p$ *iff* $p \in -\partial p$ *of* $E(D)$, $p \in \text{Lit}$
4. $D \vdash -\partial^{meta} \alpha$ *iff* $p \in -\partial^{meta} \alpha$ *of* $E(D)$, $\alpha \in \text{Lab}$.

Proof. The aim of Algorithm 1 EXISTENCE is to compute a defeasible meta-extension of the input theory through successive transformations on the set of facts, rules and the superiority relation. These transformations act in a way to obtain a simpler theory while retaining the same extension. By simpler theory we mean a theory with less symbol in it. Note that if $D \vdash +\partial l$ then $D \vdash -\partial \sim l$, and that if $D \vdash +\partial^{meta} \alpha$ then $D \vdash -\partial^{meta} \gamma$, with $C(\gamma) = \sim C(\alpha)$. Suppose that the algorithm proves $+\partial l$ or $+\partial \alpha$ (meaning that $l \in +\partial$ or $\alpha \in +\partial^{meta}$). Accordingly, we remove l or α from every antecedent where it appears in, as by Definition 1, the applicability of such rules will not depend any longer on l or α, but only on the remaining elements in their antecedents. Moreover, we can eliminate from the set of rules all those rules with $\sim l$ or γ in their antecedent (with $C(\gamma) = \sim C(\alpha)$), as such rules are discarded by Definition 2 (and adjust the superiority relation accordingly). Finally, when we prove $+\partial \alpha$, then α becomes active in supporting its conclusion and rebutting the opposite.

The proof follows the schemata of the ones in [12,14], and consists in proving that the meta-extension of the original theory D and the meta-extension of the simpler theory D' are the same. Formally, suppose that $D \vdash +\partial l$ (symmetrically $D \vdash +\partial^{meta} \alpha$) at $P(n)$. Thus, if R' of D' is obtained from R of D as follows

$$R' = R_{appl} \leftarrow \{A(\beta) \setminus \{l/\alpha\} \hookrightarrow C(\beta) \mid \beta \in R\} \setminus \{\beta \in R \mid \sim l/\sim\gamma \in R\},$$

and if $>'$ of D' is obtained from $>$ of D as follows

$$>' => \setminus \{(\beta,\zeta),(\zeta,\beta) \mid \sim l \in A(\zeta) \text{ or } \sim\gamma \in A(\zeta)\}$$

with $A(\gamma) = A(\alpha)$ and $C(\gamma) = C(\alpha)$, then for every $\in$ Lit and every $\chi \in$ Lab

- $D \vdash \pm\partial p$ iff $D' \vdash \pm\partial p$, and
- $D \vdash \pm\partial^{meta}\chi$ iff $D' \vdash \pm\partial^{meta}\chi$.

The proof that the transformation above produces theories equivalent to the original one is by induction on the length of derivations and contrapositive.

4 Conclusions and Related Work

The topic of this paper is the efficient computation of rules from meta-rules. In general, the topic of how to use (meta-)rules to generate other rules has received little attention. Some exceptions are [4,16] on the use of meta-rules for norm modifications, and [27] which is specifically dedicated to a logic for deriving rules from meta-rules. However, none these works investigate the computationally complexity, nor address the issue of defining algorithms for their logics.

The large majority of the studies that have made use of meta-rules have focused upon the usage of these as a means to determine the *scope* of rule application, or the *result* of the application of the rules. In particular, we can identify two research lines: Logic Programming, and Meta-logic.

Logic programming studies investigated the issue of enhancing the expressivity by allowing nested expressions [20,21]. Nevertheless, these approaches are based on the so called Lloyd-Toper transformation, that transforms nested expressions in (equivalent) logical expressions. Similarly, in [17] disjunctive DAT-ALOG is enriched with nested rules; however, such nested rules, potentially, can be eliminated by using (stratified) negation, but these are kept because they allow for a more natural correspondence with the natural language description of the underlying problem. We have seen in Sect. 1 that this approach suffers from some problems, and it is not appropriate for many uses of meta-rules, in particular when the aim is to represent meta-rules as means to derive rules. Some papers (e.g., [9]) extended logic programming with negation with nested hypothetical implications plus constraints or negation as failure. Specifically, they consider rules with conditional goals in the body, but not implications in the head, and study some goal directed proof procedures.

The notion of meta-rules and close concepts, including meta-logic [3] and meta-reasoning [7], have been employed widely in Logic Programming [2] but also outside it, specifically in *context theory* [11]. In general, we can look at these studies as methodologically coherent with the notion of *hierarchical* reasoning, where it is devised a method to choose which reasoning process is more appropriate for the specific scenario in which the process is employed. A specific line of research (strictly connected with the studies in the semantics of

Logic Programming) is the Answer Set Programming (ASP) and preferences [8]. Further on, many studies on ASP where meta-rules took place. However, these investigations have not focusing upon *nested rules*.

A line of work considering the generation of rules from other rules is the work on Input/Output logic (IOL) [22]. The idea of IOL is to define a set of operations on input/output rules (where an input/output rule is a pair (x, y), where x and y are formulas in a logical language) to derive new input/output pairs. Differently to what we do (1): IOL does not consider nested rules, and (2) the derivation mechanism depends on the properties of the operations on which the variant of IOL is defined, and not on the rules on which the logic operates.

A field of investigation that has strongly employed meta-rules, but in a sense that is indeed similar to the one of the theory of contexts, is *argumentation*. The basic concept derived by the combination of meta-logical structures and argumentation is the metalevel argumentation [23]. Applied metalevel has been investigated in the view of developing a framework where, for instance, admissibility of arguments, and other issues in this field, are dealt with [6].

The problem of nested rules in non-monotonic frameworks from a computational complexity viewpoint deserves a deeper study, and this paper fills this gap. Currently, the focus was on Defeasible Logic without modal operators and temporal expressions (most of the work on meta-rules considers combinations of such features). The basic version of modal and temporal variants of the logic computationally feasible. We plan to extend and combine the algorithm presented in this paper with the algorithms for modal and temporal Defeasible Logic and we expect that the complexity results to carry over to the combination.

References

1. Antoniou, G., Billington, D., Governatori, G., Maher, M.J.: Representation results for defeasible logic. ACM Trans. Comput. Log. **2**(2), 255–287 (2001). https://doi.org/10.1145/371316.371517
2. Azab, K., Habel, A.: High-level programs and program conditions. In: Ehrig, H., Heckel, R., Rozenberg, G., Taentzer, G. (eds.) ICGT 2008. LNCS, vol. 5214, pp. 211–225. Springer, Heidelberg (2008). https://doi.org/10.1007/978-3-540-87405-8_15
3. Basin, D., Clavel, M., Meseguer, J.: Reflective metalogical frameworks. ACM Trans. Comput. Logic **5**(3), 528–576 (2004). https://doi.org/10.1145/1013560.1013566
4. Cristani, M., Olivieri, F., Rotolo, A.: Changes to temporary norms. In: Keppens, J., Governatori, G. (eds.) ICAIL 2017 pp. 39–48. ACM. https://doi.org/10.1145/3086512.3086517
5. Dastani, M., Governatori, G., Rotolo, A., Song, I., van der Torre, L.: Contextual agent deliberation in defeasible logic. In: Ghose, A., Governatori, G., Sadananda, R. (eds.) PRIMA 2007. LNCS (LNAI), vol. 5044, pp. 98–109. Springer, Heidelberg (2009). https://doi.org/10.1007/978-3-642-01639-4_9
6. Dupin De Saint-Cyr, F., Bisquert, P., Cayrol, C., Lagasquie-Schiex, M.C.: Argumentation update in YALLA (yet another logic language for argumentation). Int. J. Approx. Reason. **75**, 57–92 (2016). https://doi.org/10.1016/j.ijar.2016.04.003

7. Dyoub, A., Costantini, S., De Gasperis, G.: Answer set programming and agents. Knowl. Eng. Rev. **33**(1) (2018). https://doi.org/10.1017/S0269888918000164
8. Eiter, T., Faber, W., Leone, N., Pfeifer, G.: Computing preferred answer sets by meta-interpretation in answer set programming. Theory Pract. Logic Program. **3**(4–5), 463–498 (2003). https://doi.org/10.1017/S1471068403001753
9. Gabbay, D.M., Giordano, L., Martelli, A., Olivetti, N.: A language for handling hypothetical updates and inconsistency. Log. J. IGPL **4**(3), 385–416 (1996). https://doi.org/10.1093/jigpal/4.3.385
10. Gelati, J., Governatori, G., Rotolo, A., Sartor, G.: Normative autonomy and normative co-ordination: declarative power, representation, and mandate. Artif. Intell. Law **12**(1–2), 53–81 (2004)
11. Ghidini, C., Giunchiglia, F.: Local models semantics, or contextual reasoning = locality + compatibility. Artif. Intell. **127**(2), 221–259 (2001). https://doi.org/10.1016/S0004-3702(01)00064-9
12. Governatori, G., Olivieri, F., Rotolo, A., Scannapieco, S.: Computing strong and weak permissions in defeasible logic. J. Philos. Logic **42**(6), 799–829 (2013). https://doi.org/10.1007/s10992-013-9295-1
13. Governatori, G., Olivieri, F., Scannapieco, S., Cristani, M.: Designing for compliance: norms and goals. In: Olken, F., Palmirani, M., Sottara, D. (eds.) RuleML 2011. LNCS, vol. 7018, pp. 282–297. Springer, Heidelberg (2011). https://doi.org/10.1007/978-3-642-24908-2_29
14. Governatori, G., Olivieri, F., Scannapieco, S., Rotolo, A., Cristani, M.: The rationale behind the concept of goal. Theory Pract. Log. Program. **16**(3), 296–324 (2016). https://doi.org/10.1017/S1471068416000053
15. Governatori, G., Padmanabhan, V., Rotolo, A., Sattar, A.: A defeasible logic for modelling policy-based intentions and motivational attitudes. Log. J. IGPL **17**(3), 227–265 (2009). https://doi.org/10.1093/jigpal/jzp006
16. Governatori, G., Rotolo, A.: Changing legal systems: legal abrogations and annulments in defeasible logic. Log. J. IGPL **18**(1), 157–194 (2010)
17. Greco, S., Leone, N., Scarcello, F.: Datalog with nested rules. In: Dix, J., Pereira, L.M., Przymusinski, T.C. (eds.) LPKR 1997. LNCS, vol. 1471, pp. 52–65. Springer, Heidelberg (1998). https://doi.org/10.1007/BFb0054789
18. Jones, A.J.I., Sergot, M.J.: A formal characterisation of institutionalised power. Log. J. IGPL **4**(3), 427–443 (1996). https://doi.org/10.1093/jigpal/4.3.427
19. Kravari, K., Bassiliades, N.: A survey of agent platforms. J. Artif. Soc. Soc. Simul. **18**(1), 11 (2015). https://doi.org/10.18564/jasss.2661
20. Lifschitz, V., Tang, L.R., Turner, H.: Nested expressions in logic programs. Ann. Math. Artif. Intell. **25**(3), 369–389 (1999). https://doi.org/10.1023/A:1018978005636
21. Lloyd, J.W., Topor, R.W.: Making prolog more expressive. J. Logic Program. **1**(3), 225–240 (1984). https://doi.org/10.1016/0743-1066(84)90011-6
22. Makinson, D., Van Der Torre, L.: Input/output logics. J. Philos. Logic **29**(4), 383–408 (2000)
23. Modgil, S., Bench-Capon, T.: Metalevel argumentation. J. Logic Comput. **21**(6), 959–1003 (2011). https://doi.org/10.1093/logcom/exq054
24. Olivieri, F., Cristani, M., Governatori, G.: Compliant business processes with exclusive choices from agent specification. In: Chen, Q., Torroni, P., Villata, S., Hsu, J., Omicini, A. (eds.) PRIMA 2015. LNCS (LNAI), vol. 9387, pp. 603–612. Springer, Cham (2015). https://doi.org/10.1007/978-3-319-25524-8_43

25. Olivieri, F., Governatori, G., Scannapieco, S., Cristani, M.: Compliant business process design by declarative specifications. In: Boella, G., Elkind, E., Savarimuthu, B.T.R., Dignum, F., Purvis, M.K. (eds.) PRIMA 2013. LNCS (LNAI), vol. 8291, pp. 213–228. Springer, Heidelberg (2013). https://doi.org/10.1007/978-3-642-44927-7_15
26. Sartor, G.: Legal Reasoning: A Cognitive Approach to the Law. Springer (2005)
27. Song, I., Governatori, G.: Nested rules in defeasible logic. In: Adi, A., Stoutenburg, S., Tabet, S. (eds.) RuleML 2005. LNCS, vol. 3791, pp. 204–208. Springer, Heidelberg (2005). https://doi.org/10.1007/11580072_18

Syntax Splitting for Iterated Contractions, Ignorations, and Revisions on Ranking Functions Using Selection Strategies

Jonas Haldimann[1($\boxtimes$)] ⓘ, Christoph Beierle[1], and Gabriele Kern-Isberner[2] ⓘ

[1] FernUniversität in Hagen, 58084 Hagen, Germany
jonas.haldimann@fernuni-hagen.de
[2] TU Dortmund University, 44227 Dortmund, Germany

Abstract. For characterizing belief sets consisting of independent parts, Parikh introduced the notion of syntax splitting. Corresponding postulates have been developed for the reasoning from and for the revision of belief bases with respect to syntax splitting. Kern-Isberner and Brewka introduced syntax splitting for epistemic states and iterated belief revision. Only recently, syntax splitting has also been studied for contractions and iterated contractions of epistemic states; however, all of the evaluated contractions proposed in the literature failed to fulfil the full syntax splitting postulates. In this paper, we study syntax splitting for iteratively contracting and revising epistemic states, represented by ranking functions, not only with respect to a set of formulas, but with respect to a set of conditionals. Using a framework of belief change governed by the principle of conditional preservation, we employ the concept of selection strategies. We develop axioms for selection strategies ensuring that the induced contractions and revisions fully obey the desired syntax splitting properties. Furthermore, we transfer our approach to ignorations and prove a theorem showing how selection strategies satisfying the axioms can effectively be constructed.

1 Introduction

As intelligent agents live in a dynamic environment they must be able to adapt their state of mind if they receive new information. This process is called belief change and has been investigated intensively in the literature, researchers studied e.g. the revision of belief sets (i.e. sets of formulas, e.g. [1]), preorders (e.g. [8]), and ranking functions (e.g. [14]).

In 1999, Parikh introduced the notion of syntax splitting for belief sets [20]. In the same paper, he developed a postulate (P) for belief revision, the basic idea being that if a belief base splits into separate sub-bases over disjoint sub-signatures, revisions of one of the sub-bases should be independent from the other sub-bases. The concept of syntax splitting has been investigated further, e.g., by Peppas et al. [22]. More recently, the notion of syntax splitting was extended

© Springer Nature Switzerland AG 2021
W. Faber et al. (Eds.): JELIA 2021, LNAI 12678, pp. 85–100, 2021.
https://doi.org/10.1007/978-3-030-75775-5_7

to other representations of epistemic states, total preorders and ranking functions, by Kern-Isberner and Brewka [17]. Again, postulates for belief revision of total preorders and ranking functions in the presence of a syntax splitting were introduced in the same paper [17]. Another major belief change operation besides revision is belief contraction. While already introduced by AGM, contraction of beliefs gained more interest only recently (e.g. [7,18,19,23,25]). In [11], we developed syntax splitting postulates for belief contraction on belief sets, epistemic states with total preorders, and ranking functions, and evaluated different contraction operations with respect to syntax splitting, namely moderate contraction [23], natural contraction [23], lexicographic contraction [23], and c-contractions which are special kinds of operations on ranking functions [6,16] that are based on the principle of conditional preservation [13,14]. It was shown that none of the evaluated contraction operators is fully compatible with syntax splitting; even the (with respect to syntax splitting) well-behaved c-contractions do not fulfil all the syntax splitting postulates in general [11].

In this paper, we refine the notion of c-contraction as used in [11] in such a way that all required syntax splitting properties are ensured. For this, we employ the concept of selection strategies that has been proposed for reasoning with c-representations and c-revisions recently [5,15]. We extend selection strategies to general belief change operations in the c-change framework based on the principle of conditional preservation [6,16]. In this way, our approach covers not only iterated contractions but also iterated revisions both of which are fully compatible with syntax splitting. Furthermore, we will show that this transfers also to iterated ignorations where an ignoration is a specific contraction where the agent gives up the judgement on a belief, see e.g. [6]. Thus, here we will focus on the syntax splitting for the revision, contraction, and ignoration of ranking functions. Since the corresponding postulates with respect to syntax splitting considered here are structurally very similar, we generalize them to postulates for belief changes. We also extend the syntax splitting postulates to cover belief change with sets of conditionals instead of sets of formulas. Note that this extension goes far beyond the classic AGM framework [1]. The most general postulate $(P_\circ^{ocf})$ developed in this paper entails all syntax splitting postulates for revision and contraction in [11,17]. In our general framework, each selection strategy for belief change induces a belief change operator. We develop a very natural postulate (IP^{cc}) for selection strategies for c-changes and show that each change operator fulfils $(P_\circ^{ocf})$ and therefore all considered syntax splitting postulates if it is induced by a selection strategy that fulfils (IP^{cc}). We also prove a theorem yielding an effective method for constructing selection strategies satisfying (IP^{cc}).

In summary, the main contributions of this paper are:

- Introduction of syntax splitting postulates $(P_\circ^{ocf})$, $(MR_\circ^{ocf})$, and $(P_\circ^{it-ocf})$ for belief change on ranking functions that generalize syntax splitting postulates introduced in [17] and [11] and cover changes with sets of conditionals
- Introduction of selection strategies for c-contractions and c-ignorations

- Introduction of a new postulate (IP^{cc}) for selection strategies for contractions, revisions, and ignorations
- Proof that if a selection strategy fulfils (IP^{cc}) then the induced c-change fulfils $(P_\circ^{ocf})$ and therefore $(MR_\circ^{ocf})$ and $(P_\circ^{it-ocf})$
- Effective construction of selection strategies satisfying (IP^{cc})
- Iterative contraction, revision, and ignoration of ranking functions by sets of conditionals fully compatible with syntax splitting.

2 Background

Let Σ be a (propositional) signature. The set of all propositional formulae over Σ is denoted by $\mathrm{Form}(\Sigma)$. We will use $\bar{A}$ as shorthand for $\neg A$ and AB as shorthand for $A \wedge B$ with $A, B \in \mathrm{Form}(\Sigma)$. The set of all interpretations, also called worlds, of Σ will be denoted as $\mathrm{Int}(\Sigma)$ or Ω. An interpretation $\omega \in \mathrm{Int}(\Sigma)$ is a *model* for $A \in \mathrm{Form}(\Sigma)$, denoted as $\omega \models A$, if A holds in ω. The set of models for a formula is $Mod_\Sigma(A) = \{\omega \in \mathrm{Int}(\Sigma) \mid \omega \models A\}$. A formula with at least one model is called *consistent*, otherwise *inconsistent*. For $A, B \in \mathrm{Form}(\Sigma)$ we say A entails B if $Mod_\Sigma(A) \subseteq Mod_\Sigma(B)$. The concepts of models, consistency and entailment are analogously used for sets of formulae. For $M \subseteq \mathrm{Form}(\Sigma)$, the *deductive closure* of M is $\mathrm{Cn}_\Sigma(M) = \{A \in \mathrm{Form}(\Sigma) \mid M \models A\}$. If $M = \mathrm{Cn}_\Sigma(M)$ then M is called *deductively closed*. Based on propositional logic, we define the set of conditionals $\mathrm{Cond}(\Sigma) = \{(B|A) \mid A, B \in \mathrm{Form}(\Sigma)\}$. A conditional $(B|A)$ formalizes that the *antecedent* A plausibly entails the *consequent* B. Propositional logic can be embedded in conditional logic by using conditionals $(A|\top)$ with tautological antecedents. A conditional $(B|A)$ is *verified* by a world $\omega \in \mathrm{Int}(\Sigma)$ if $\omega \models AB$ and is *falsified* by ω if $\omega \models A\bar{B}$. If $\omega \not\models A$, then the conditional is *not applicable* to ω (see [9]). A conditional $(B|A)$ is called *self-fulfilling* if $Mod(A) \subseteq Mod(B)$ and *contradictory* if $Mod(A) \cap Mod(B) = \emptyset$. The *counter-conditional* of a conditional $(B|A)$ is the conditional $(\bar{B}|A)$. The counter-conditional of a self-fulfilling conditional is contradictory and vice versa.

There are many approaches to model the epistemic state of a reasoning agent. In this paper, we consider agents whose epistemic state is completely represented by a ranking function over a fixed signature. A *ranking function* or *ordinal conditional function (OCF)*, introduced (in a more general form) in [26], is a function $\kappa : \Omega \to \mathbb{N}_0$ with $\kappa^{-1}(0) \neq \emptyset$. The rank of $\omega \in \Omega$ is $\kappa(\omega)$. The lower the rank of a world, the more plausible it is. The most plausible worlds are those with rank 0. The rank of a formula A is $\kappa(A) = \min_{\omega \in Mod(A)} \kappa(\omega)$ and A is *accepted* by κ, denoted as $\kappa \models A$, if $\kappa(A) = 0$. An OCF κ *accepts* a conditional $(B|A)$, denoted as $\kappa \models (B|A)$, if $\kappa(AB) < \kappa(A\bar{B})$, i.e., if the verification of the conditional is more plausible than its falsification. If κ models the epistemic state of an agent, she considers the formulas and conditionals accepted by κ to be (plausibly) true. A set $\mathcal{R}$ of conditionals is called *consistent* if there is at least one OCF that accepts every conditional in $\mathcal{R}$. Otherwise, $\mathcal{R}$ is called *inconsistent*.

A reasoning agent is usually not in a static environment and needs to adapt her beliefs in order to account for incoming information. An operation that maps an epistemic state and some given input to an epistemic state is called a *belief change*. While in the AGM framework, the new input is only a formula, we will use c-changes that are a special kind of change operations on ranking functions taking a set of conditionals as new input.

Definition 1 (c-change, $\kappa_{\vec{\gamma}}$ [16]). *Let κ be a ranking function and $\Delta = \{(B_1|A_1), \ldots, (B_n|A_n)\}$ be a set of conditionals. For $\vec{\gamma} = (\gamma_1^+, \gamma_1^-, \ldots, \gamma_n^+, \gamma_n^-) \in \mathbb{Q}^{2n}$ we define $\kappa_{\vec{\gamma}}$ by $\kappa_{\vec{\gamma}}(\omega) = \kappa_0 + \kappa(\omega) + \sum_{\substack{i=1 \\ \omega \models A_i B_i}}^{n} \gamma_i^+ + \sum_{\substack{i=1 \\ \omega \models A\overline{B}_i}}^{n} \gamma_i^-$ where $\kappa_0 \in \mathbb{Q}$ is a normalization factor ensuring that the minimal worlds have rank 0. A change from κ with Δ to κ° is a c-change if there is $\vec{\gamma} \in \mathbb{Q}^{2n}$, called* impact vector, *such that $\kappa^\circ = \kappa_{\vec{\gamma}}$.*

The impacts γ_i^+, γ_i^- are values that are added to the rank of a world ω if ω verifies or falsifies $(B_i|A_i)$, respectively. The idea of c-changes is based on the principle of conditional preservation; a detailed motivation and explanation is given in [13, 14].

3   Contractions, Revisions, and Ignorations

In this section, we will define the belief change operations contraction, revision, and ignoration on ranking functions for sets of conditionals. Furthermore, we will discuss the realization of these belief change operations with c-changes.

Definition 2 (Revision $\kappa * \Delta$). *A belief change operator $*$ is a revision operator if for any ranking function κ and consistent set of conditionals Δ we have $\kappa * \Delta \models (B|A)$ for all $(B|A) \in \Delta$.*

A belief revision introduces new information to the epistemic state and changes the existing knowledge to resolve conflicts. A contraction operator on the other hand removes beliefs from the epistemic state.

Definition 3 (Contraction $\kappa - \Delta$). *A belief change operator $-$ is a contraction operator if for any ranking function κ and set of conditionals Δ that does not contain self-fulfilling conditionals we have $\kappa - \Delta \not\models (B|A)$ for all $(B|A) \in \Delta$.*

Note that there are several approaches to contraction of multiple statements. Definition 3 represents a "package contraction" approach. While c-contractions for single conditionals and c-change for sets of conditionals in general have been investigated before [16], c-contractions for sets of conditionals have not been considered so far. A third kind of belief change is ignoration. While ignoration was introduced for single conditionals in [6, 16], it can be defined in a more general way for sets of conditionals.

Definition 4 (Ignoration $\kappa \div \Delta$). *A belief change operator $\div$ is an ignoration operator if for any ranking function κ and set of conditionals Δ that does not contain self-fulfilling or contradictory conditionals, we have $(\kappa \div \Delta) \not\models (B|A)$ and $(\kappa \div \Delta) \not\models (\overline{B}|A)$ for all $(B|A) \in \Delta$.*

Thus, an ignoration "forgets" both the conditionals and their counter-conditionals. The three operations defined above are called c-revision, c-contraction, and c-ignoration, respectively, if they are c-changes (Definition 1). Similar to c-representations and c-inference they can each be characterized by a constraint satisfaction problem (CSP), cf. [4].

Definition 5 $(CR^*(\kappa, \Delta), CR^-(\kappa, \Delta), CR^\div(\kappa, \Delta))$. *Let κ be a ranking function and $\Delta = \{(B_1|A_1), \ldots, (B_n|A_n)\}$ be a set of conditionals. The constraint satisfaction problem $CR^\circ(\kappa, \Delta)$ with $\circ \in \{*, -, \div\}$ for constraint variables $\gamma_1^+, \gamma_1^-, \ldots, \gamma_n^+, \gamma_n^-$ taking values in $\mathbb{Q}$ is given by the set of constraints*

$$\gamma_i^- - \gamma_i^+ \sim_\circ \min_{\omega \models A_i B_i} \left\{ \kappa(\omega) + \sum_{\substack{j \neq i \\ \omega \models A_j B_j}} \gamma_i^+ + \sum_{\substack{j \neq i \\ \omega \models A_j \overline{B_j}}} \gamma_i^- \right\}$$

$$- \min_{\omega \models A_i \overline{B_i}} \left\{ \kappa(\omega) + \sum_{\substack{j \neq i \\ \omega \models A_j B_j}} \gamma_i^+ + \sum_{\substack{j \neq i \\ \omega \models A_j \overline{B_j}}} \gamma_i^- \right\}$$

for $i = 1, \ldots, n$ where $\sim_\circ$ is $>$ for $\circ = *$, or $\leqslant$ for $\circ = -$, or $=$ for $\circ = \div$.

The CSP for c-revisions is given by $CR^*(\kappa, \Delta)$, the CSP for c-contractions is given by $CR^-(\kappa, \Delta)$, and the CSP for c-ignorations is given by $CR^\div(\kappa, \Delta)$.

The set of solutions of a CSP CR is denoted by $Sol(CR)$.

Proposition 1 (Soundness and completeness of $CR^*(\kappa, \Delta)$, $CR^-(\kappa, \Delta)$ and $CR^\div(\kappa, \Delta)$). *Let κ be a ranking function and $\Delta = \{(B_1|A_1), \ldots, (B_n|A_n)\}$ be a set of conditionals.*

1. *If $\vec{\gamma} \in Sol(CR^*(\kappa, \Delta))$, then the change from κ with Δ to $\kappa_{\vec{\gamma}}$ is a c-revision. Conversely, if Δ is consistent and the change from κ with Δ to κ^* is a c-revision, then there is a $\vec{\gamma} \in Sol(CR^*(\kappa, \Delta))$ such that $\kappa^* = \kappa_{\vec{\gamma}}$.*
2. *If $\vec{\gamma} \in Sol(CR^-(\kappa, \Delta))$, then the change from κ with Δ to $\kappa_{\vec{\gamma}}$ is a c-contraction. If Δ does not contain self-fulfilling conditionals and the change from κ with Δ to κ^- is a c-contraction, there is a $\vec{\gamma} \in Sol(CR^-(\kappa, \Delta))$ such that $\kappa^- = \kappa_{\vec{\gamma}}$.*
3. *If $\vec{\gamma} \in Sol(CR^\div(\kappa, \Delta))$, the change from κ with Δ to $\kappa_{\vec{\gamma}}$ is a c-ignoration. If Δ does not contain self-fulfilling or contradictory conditionals and the change from κ with Δ to $\kappa^\div$ is a c-ignoration, there is a $\vec{\gamma} \in Sol(CR^\div(\kappa, \Delta))$ such that $\kappa^\div = \kappa_{\vec{\gamma}}$.*

Proof. A proof for (1.) is given in [4,14], and (2) and (3.) can be shown by analogous derivations. □

All three mentioned types of c-change exist if not prohibited by Δ.

Proposition 2. *Let κ be a finite ranking function and Δ be a set of conditionals.*

1. $Sol(CR^*(\kappa, \Delta)) \neq \emptyset$ iff Δ is consistent.
2. $Sol(CR^-(\kappa, \Delta)) \neq \emptyset$ iff Δ does not contain self-fulfilling conditionals.
3. $Sol(CR^{\div}(\kappa, \Delta)) \neq \emptyset$ iff Δ does not contain self-fulfilling or contradictory conditionals.

Proof. We first consider the $\Leftarrow$-direction in the three statements. The theorems given in [14] imply (1.). For proving (2.) and (3.) let κ be a ranking function and $\Delta = \{(B_1|A_1), \ldots, (B_n|A_n)\}$ a set of non-self-fulfilling conditionals. The impacts of a c-contraction can be constructed by the following algorithm.

1: $\gamma_1^-, \gamma_1^+, \ldots, \gamma_n^-, \gamma_n^+ \leftarrow 0$
2: $\kappa' \leftarrow \kappa; \quad \Delta' \leftarrow \Delta$
3: **while** $\Delta' \neq \emptyset$ **do**
4: $\quad (A_k|B_k) \leftarrow \arg\min_{(B_i|A_i) \in \Delta} \kappa'(A_i)$ $\qquad\qquad$ ▷ Select a conditional...
5: $\quad$ **if** $\kappa'(A_k B_k) < \kappa'(A_k \bar{B}_k)$ **then** $\qquad\qquad$ ▷ ...and assign impacts for it.
6: $\qquad \gamma_k^- \leftarrow \kappa'(A_k B_k) - \kappa'(A_k \bar{B}_k)$
7: $\quad$ **if** $\kappa'(A_k B_k) > \kappa'(A_k \bar{B}_k)$ **then**
8: $\qquad \gamma_k^+ \leftarrow \kappa'(A_k \bar{B}_k) - \kappa'(A_k B_k)$
9: $\quad \Delta' \leftarrow \Delta' \setminus \{(B_k|A_k)\}$ $\qquad\qquad\qquad\qquad$ ▷ Update Δ', κ'
10: $\quad \kappa'(\omega) \leftarrow \kappa(\omega) + \sum_{\omega \models A_i \bar{B}_i} \gamma_i^- + \sum_{\omega \models A_j B_j} \gamma_j^+$ for all $\omega \in \Omega$
11: **return** $(\gamma_1^+, \gamma_1^-, \ldots, \gamma_n^+, \gamma_n^-)$

If all conditionals in Δ are neither self-fulfilling nor contradictory, then the algorithm yields a c-ignoration. This approach shows that c-contraction and c-ignoration operators exist.

For the $\Rightarrow$-direction, if Δ is not consistent, there is no ranking function accepting all conditionals in Δ. Therefore, (1.) holds. If Δ contains self-fulfilling conditionals, there is no ranking function that contracts all conditionals in Δ. Therefore, (2.) holds. Analogously, (3.) holds because there is no ranking function that can ignore a self-fulfilling or a contradictory conditional. $\qquad\square$

All change operations in this section can be applied to a set of formulas $\{A_1, \ldots, A_n\}$ by representing the formulas with conditionals $(A_1|\top), \ldots, (A_n|\top)$.

4   Syntax Splitting on Ranking Functions

The concept of syntax splitting and corresponding postulates for belief change were originally developed by Parikh [20] for belief revision on belief sets. The basic idea is that for a belief set that contains independent information over different parts of the signature, the revision with a formula that contains only variables from one of such parts should only affect the information about this part of the signature. The notion of syntax splitting was later extended to other representations of epistemic states such as ranking functions [17]. Considering that Parikh's (P) is incompatible with the Darwiche-Pearl-Postulates [8] as stated in [2,21], it might seem problematic to investigate the combination of syntax splitting and frameworks for iterated belief revision. But while (P) only focusses on the belief set, the syntax splitting postulates for ranking functions considered here require syntax splittings on the whole ranking function. Therefore, the mentioned incompatibility results do not apply here.

Definition 6 (syntax splitting for ranking functions [17]**).** *Let Σ be a signature and κ a ranking function over $\Omega = \text{Int}(\Sigma)$. Let ω^j be the variable assignment of the variables in $\Sigma_j \subseteq \Sigma$ as in ω. A partitioning $\Sigma = \Sigma_1 \dot{\cup} \ldots \dot{\cup} \Sigma_n$ is a* syntax splitting *for κ if there are ranking functions $\kappa_i : \Sigma_i \mapsto \mathbb{N}_0$ for $i = 1, \ldots, n$ such that $\kappa(\omega) = \kappa_1(\omega^1) + \cdots + \kappa_n(\omega^n)$, denoted as $\kappa = \kappa_1 \oplus \cdots \oplus \kappa_n$.*

The following proposition shows that syntax splitting for ranking functions respects conditional knowledge.

Proposition 3. *Let $\kappa = \kappa_1 \oplus \cdots \oplus \kappa_n$ be a ranking function with syntax splitting $\Sigma = \Sigma_1 \dot{\cup} \ldots \dot{\cup} \Sigma_n$ and $r = (B|A)$ a conditional with $A, B \in \Sigma_j$ for any $j \in \{1, \ldots, n\}$. Then $\kappa \models (B|A)$ iff $\kappa_j \models (B|A)$.*

Proof. Let κ and $(B|A)$ be as in the proposition. Because of $\kappa(\omega) = \sum_{1 \leqslant i \leqslant n} \kappa_i(\omega_i)$ we have that $\kappa(C) = \kappa_i(C)$ if $C \in \Sigma_i$ for $i = 1, \ldots, n$. Therefore, it holds that $\kappa \models (B|A)$ iff $\kappa(AB) < \kappa(A\overline{B})$ iff $\kappa_j(AB) < \kappa_j(A\overline{B})$ iff $\kappa_j \models (B|A)$. $\square$

For the definition of some syntax splitting postulates for ranking functions, the concept of the marginalisation of a ranking function is important. Marginalisation formalizes the restriction of a ranking function to a sub-signature.

Definition 7 (marginalisation on ranking functions [3,17]**).** *Let Σ be a signature and κ be an OCF over $\Omega = \text{Int}(\Sigma)$. Let $\Theta \subseteq \Sigma$. The* marginalisation *of κ to Θ is the function $\kappa_{|\Theta} : \Theta \mapsto \mathbb{N}_0$ with $\kappa_{|\Theta}(\omega) = \kappa(\omega)$ for $\omega \in \Omega_\Theta$.*

For an OCF $\kappa = \kappa_1 \oplus \cdots \oplus \kappa_n$ with syntax splitting $\Sigma_1 \dot{\cup} \ldots \dot{\cup} \Sigma_n$ it holds that $\kappa_{|\Sigma_i} = \kappa_i$ for $i = 1, \ldots, n$. Note that the marginalization of OCFs presented above is a special case of a general forgetful functor $Mod(\varrho)$ from Σ-models to Σ'-models given in [3] where $\Sigma' \subseteq \Sigma$ and ϱ is the inclusion from Σ' to Σ. Informally, a forgetful functor forgets everything about the interpretation of the symbols in $\Sigma \backslash \Sigma'$ when mapping a Σ-model to a Σ'-model.

All syntax splitting postulates for ranking functions proposed so far can only deal with revision or contraction of a ranking function with a set of formulas. The postulate (MR^{ocf}) describes that a revision of an OCF with syntax splitting should only depend on the relevant part of the OCF and the relevant formula.

Postulate (MR^{ocf}) ([17]**).** *Let $*$ be a revision operator on ranking functions. For every ranking function $\kappa = \kappa_1 \oplus \cdots \oplus \kappa_n$ with syntax splitting $\Sigma = \Sigma_1 \dot{\cup} \ldots \dot{\cup} \Sigma_n$ and $C = \{C_1, \ldots, C_n\}$ such that $C_i \in \text{Form}(\Sigma_i)$ for $i = 1, \ldots, n$ it holds that $(\kappa * C)_{|\Sigma_i} = \kappa_{|\Sigma_i} * C_i = \kappa_i * C_i$ for $i = 1, \ldots, n$.*

Another postulate (P^{it-ocf}) states that a syntax splitting of a ranking function should survive a revision under certain circumstances.

Postulate (P^{it-ocf}) ([11]**).** *Let $*$ be a revision operator on ranking functions. For every ranking function $\kappa = \kappa_1 \oplus \cdots \oplus \kappa_n$ with syntax splitting $\Sigma = \Sigma_1 \dot{\cup} \ldots \dot{\cup} \Sigma_n$ and $C = \{C_1, \ldots, C_n\}$ such that $C_i \in \text{Form}(\Sigma_i)$ for $i = 1, \ldots, n$ the partitioning $\Sigma_1 \dot{\cup} \ldots \dot{\cup} \Sigma_n$ is a syntax splitting for $\kappa * C$.*

Both postulates can be combined into one postulate. It can be shown that (MR^{ocf}) and (P^{it-ocf}) together are equivalent to (P^{ocf}).

Postulate (P^{ocf}) ([17]). *Let $*$ be a revision operator on ranking functions. For every ranking function $\kappa = \kappa_1 \oplus \cdots \oplus \kappa_n$ with syntax splitting $\Sigma = \Sigma_1 \dot{\cup} \ldots \dot{\cup} \Sigma_n$ and $C = \{C_1, \ldots, C_n\}$ such that $C_i \in \text{Form}(\Sigma_i)$ for $i = 1, \ldots, n$ it holds that $\kappa * C = (\kappa_1 * C_1) \oplus \cdots \oplus (\kappa_n * C_n)$.*

These postulates have been transferred to contractions of OCFs [11].

Postulate (P_-^{ocf}) ([11]). *Let $-$ be a contraction operator on ranking functions. For every ranking function $\kappa = \kappa_1 \oplus \cdots \oplus \kappa_n$ with syntax splitting $\Sigma = \Sigma_1 \dot{\cup} \ldots \dot{\cup} \Sigma_n$ and $C = \{C_1, \ldots, C_n\}$ such that $C_i \in \text{Form}(\Sigma_i)$ for $i = 1, \ldots, n$ it holds that $\kappa - C = (\kappa_1 - C_1) \oplus \cdots \oplus (\kappa_n - C_n)$.*

Postulate (P_-^{it-ocf}) ([11]). *Let $-$ be a contraction operator on ranking functions. For every ranking function $\kappa = \kappa_1 \oplus \cdots \oplus \kappa_n$ with syntax splitting $\Sigma = \Sigma_1 \dot{\cup} \ldots \dot{\cup} \Sigma_n$ and $C = \{C_1, \ldots, C_n\}$ such that $C_i \in \text{Form}(\Sigma_i)$ for $i = 1, \ldots, n$ the partition $\Sigma_1 \dot{\cup} \ldots \dot{\cup} \Sigma_n$ is a syntax splitting for $\kappa - C$.*

Postulate (MK^{ocf}) ([11]). *Let $-$ be a contraction operator on ranking functions. For every ranking function $\kappa = \kappa_1 \oplus \cdots \oplus \kappa_n$ with syntax splitting $\Sigma = \Sigma_1 \dot{\cup} \ldots \dot{\cup} \Sigma_n$ and $C = \{C_1, \ldots, C_n\}$ such that $C_i \in \text{Form}(\Sigma_i)$ for $i = 1, \ldots, n$ it holds that $(\kappa - C)_{|\Sigma_i} = \kappa_i - C_i = \kappa_{|\Sigma_i} - C_i$ for $i = 1, \ldots, n$.*

A contraction operator $-$ fulfils (P_-^{ocf}) iff it fulfils (MK^{ocf}) and (P_-^{it-ocf}). As the postulates for revision and contraction are structurally similar, we can generalize these postulates to cover both revisions and contractions with sets of conditionals. Furthermore, the following generalized postulate $(\text{P}_\circ^{ocf})$ also fully covers ignorations by set of conditionals.

Postulate $(\text{P}_\circ^{ocf})$. *Let $\circ$ be a revision, contraction, or ignoration operator on ranking functions with sets of conditionals. For every ranking function $\kappa = \kappa_1 \oplus \cdots \oplus \kappa_n$ with syntax splitting $\Sigma = \Sigma_1 \dot{\cup} \ldots \dot{\cup} \Sigma_n$ and $\Delta = \Delta_1 \cup \cdots \cup \Delta_n$ with $\Delta_i = \{(B_{i,1}|A_{i,1}), \ldots, (B_{i,k_i}|A_{i,k_i})\}$ with $A_{i,j}, B_{i,j} \in \text{Form}(\Sigma_i)$ for $j = 1, \ldots, k_i$ for every $i = 1, \ldots, n$ it holds that $\kappa \circ \Delta = (\kappa_1 \circ \Delta_1) \oplus \cdots \oplus (\kappa_n \circ \Delta_n)$.*

The postulate $(\text{P}_\circ^{ocf})$ is a generalisation of (P^{ocf}) and (P_-^{ocf}) in several ways: First, as mentioned, $(\text{P}_\circ^{ocf})$ covers both revision and contraction, and furthermore, also ignorations. Second, $(\text{P}_\circ^{ocf})$ allows for revision, contraction, and ignorations with respect to conditionals instead of formulas. This is a generalization, as a change with a formula A can be realized by a change with the conditional $(A|\top)$. Third, $(\text{P}_\circ^{ocf})$ covers changes where the number of partitions in the knowledge base does not equal the number of conditionals in the set that the knowledge base is changed with. Similarly, we can generalize (MR^{ocf}) and (MK^{ocf}) to $(\text{MR}_\circ^{ocf})$ as well as (P^{it-ocf}) and (P_-^{it-ocf}) to $(\text{P}_\circ^{it-ocf})$.

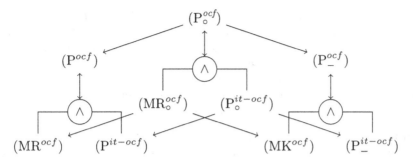

Fig. 1. Overview of the syntax splitting postulates for ranking functions mentioned in this paper. The arrows indicate that a postulate or a combination of postulates implies another postulate.

Postulate ($\mathrm{MR}_\circ^{ocf}$). *Let $\circ$ be a revision, contraction, or ignoration operator on ranking functions. For every ranking function $\kappa = \kappa_1 \oplus \cdots \oplus \kappa_n$ with syntax splitting $\Sigma = \Sigma_1 \dot\cup \ldots \dot\cup \Sigma_n$ and $\Delta = \Delta_1 \cup \cdots \cup \Delta_n$ with $\Delta_i = \{(B_{i,1}|A_{i,1}), \ldots, (B_{i,k_i}|A_{i,k_i})\}$ with $A_{i,j}, B_{i,j} \in \mathrm{Form}(\Sigma_i)$ for $j = 1, \ldots, k_i$ for every $i = 1, \ldots, n$ it holds that $(\kappa \circ \Delta)_{|\Sigma_i} = \kappa_{|\Sigma_i} \circ \Delta_i = \kappa_i \circ \Delta_i$ for $i = 1, \ldots, n$.*

Postulate ($\mathrm{P}_\circ^{it-ocf}$). *Let $\circ$ be a revision, contraction, or ignoration operator on ranking functions. For every ranking function $\kappa = \kappa_1 \oplus \cdots \oplus \kappa_n$ with syntax splitting $\Sigma = \Sigma_1 \dot\cup \ldots \dot\cup \Sigma_n$ and $\Delta = \Delta_1 \cup \cdots \cup \Delta_n$ with $\Delta_i = \{(B_{i,1}|A_{i,1}), \ldots, (B_{i,k_i}|A_{i,k_i})\}$ with $A_{i,j}, B_{i,j} \in \mathrm{Form}(\Sigma_i)$ for $j = 1, \ldots, k_i$ for every $i = 1, \ldots, n$ the partitioning $\Sigma_1 \dot\cup \ldots \dot\cup \Sigma_n$ is a syntax splitting for $\kappa \circ C$.*

Proposition 4. *A revision, contraction, or ignoration operator fulfils ($\mathrm{P}_\circ^{ocf}$) iff it fulfils both ($\mathrm{MR}_\circ^{ocf}$) and ($\mathrm{P}_\circ^{it-ocf}$).*

Proof. The direction $\Rightarrow$ is clear.
Direction $\Leftarrow$: Let $\circ$ be a change operator that fulfils ($\mathrm{MR}_\circ^{ocf}$) and ($\mathrm{P}_\circ^{it-ocf}$). Let $\kappa = \kappa_1 \oplus \cdots \oplus \kappa_n$ be a ranking function with syntax splitting $\Sigma = \Sigma_1 \dot\cup \ldots \dot\cup \Sigma_n$ and $\Delta = \Delta_1 \cup \cdots \cup \Delta_n$ with $\Delta_i = \{(B_{i,1}|A_{i,1}), \ldots, (B_{i,k_i}|A_{i,k_i})\}$ with $A_{i,j}, B_{i,j} \in \mathrm{Form}(\Sigma_i)$ for $j = 1, \ldots, k_i$ for every $i = 1, \ldots, n$. ($\mathrm{P}_\circ^{it-ocf}$) implies that $\Sigma = \Sigma_1 \dot\cup \ldots \dot\cup \Sigma_n$ is a syntax splitting for $\kappa^\circ = \kappa \circ \Delta$, i.e., there are ranking functions $\kappa_1^\circ, \ldots, \kappa_n^\circ$ such that $\kappa^\circ = \kappa_1^\circ \oplus \cdots \oplus \kappa_n^\circ$. ($\mathrm{MR}_\circ^{ocf}$) implies that $\kappa_i^\circ = \kappa^\circ_{|\Sigma_i} = \kappa_i \circ \Delta_i$ for $i = 1, \ldots, n$. Therefore, $\circ$ fulfils ($\mathrm{P}_\circ^{ocf}$). $\square$

An overview of the different conditionals is given in Fig. 1.

5   Selection Strategies for c-Changes

For a given ranking function κ and a set of conditionals Δ, the definition of c-changes does not determine the output of the change. In fact, the constraint systems $CR^*(\kappa, \Delta)$, $CR^-(\kappa, \Delta)$, and $CR^{\div}(\kappa, \Delta)$ may have multiple solutions that lead to different outcomes of the belief change. A c-revision, c-contraction, or c-ignoration operator has to select one of the possible solutions. A similar situation occurs when a c-representation is determined [4]. In [15], the selection of an impact vector for c-representations is formalized by introducing *selection strategies* that select one of the possible solutions of a constraint system as an impact vector. Selection strategies for c-revisions are introduced in [5].

We adapt this idea to the case of c-changes here.

Definition 8 (selection strategy). *A selection strategy for c-revisions (c-contractions, or c-ignorations, respectively) is a function* $\sigma : (\kappa, \Delta) \mapsto \vec{\gamma}$ *mapping an OCF κ and a set of conditionals Δ to an impact vector $\vec{\gamma}$ such that* $\vec{\gamma} \in Sol(CR^*(\kappa, \Delta))$ *($\vec{\gamma} \in Sol(CR^-(\kappa, \Delta))$, or $\vec{\gamma} \in Sol(CR^{\div}(\kappa, \Delta))$, resp.).*

The selection of a solution takes both Δ and κ into account, as the sets $Sol(CR^*(\kappa, \Delta))$, $Sol(CR^-(\kappa, \Delta))$, and $Sol(CR^{\div}(\kappa, \Delta))$ of possible solutions depend on Δ and κ. Each selection strategy induces a change operator.

Definition 9 $(*_\sigma, \; -_\sigma, \; \div_\sigma)$. *The c-revision (c-contraction, or c-ignoration, respectively) of a ranking function κ with a set of conditionals Δ induced by a selection strategy σ, denoted by $\kappa *_\sigma \Delta$ (or $\kappa -_\sigma \Delta$ or $\kappa \div_\sigma \Delta$, respectively) is given by $\kappa_{\vec{\gamma}}$ with $\vec{\gamma} = \sigma(\kappa, \Delta)$.*

Now we can formalize desirable properties of selection strategies. A natural property is that the impacts chosen for two independent subproblems should be preserved when choosing impacts for the combination of the two subproblems.

Definition 10 (impact preserving, (IP^{cc})). *A selection strategy σ for c-revisions, c-contractions, or c-ignorations fulfils (IP^{cc}) and is called impact preserving if for any ranking function $\kappa = \kappa_1 \oplus \kappa_2$ with syntax splitting $\Sigma_1 \dot\cup \Sigma_2$ and set of conditionals $\Delta = \Delta_1 \cup \Delta_2$ such that $A, B \in \text{Form}(\Sigma_i)$ for every $(B|A) \in \Delta_i$, $i = 1, 2$ it holds that $\sigma(\kappa, \Delta) = (\sigma(\kappa_1, \Delta_1), \sigma(\kappa_2, \Delta_2))$.*

While (IP^{cc}) is defined only for syntax splittings with two partitions, it implies the described property also for syntax splittings with more partitions.

Proposition 5. *If a selection strategy σ for c-revisions, c-contractions, or c-ignorations fulfils (IP^{cc}), then for any ranking function $\kappa = \kappa_1 \oplus \cdots \oplus \kappa_n$ with syntax splitting $\Sigma_1 \dot\cup \ldots \dot\cup \Sigma_n$ and set of conditionals $\Delta = \Delta_1 \cup \cdots \cup \Delta_n$ such that $A, B \in \text{Form}(\Sigma_i)$ for every $(B|A) \in \Delta_i$, $i = 1, \ldots, n$ it holds that:*

$$\sigma(\kappa, \Delta) = (\sigma(\kappa_1, \Delta_1), \ldots, \sigma(\kappa_n, \Delta_n)). \tag{1}$$

Proof. Let σ be a selection strategy for c-revisions, c-contractions, or c-ignorations that fulfils (IP^{cc}). Let $\kappa = \kappa_1 \oplus \cdots \oplus \kappa_n$ be a ranking function with a syntax splitting $\Sigma = \Sigma_1 \dot\cup \ldots \dot\cup \Sigma_n$. Let $\Delta = \Delta_1 \cup \cdots \cup \Delta_n$ with $\Delta_i = \{(B_{i,1}|A_{i,1}), \ldots, (B_{i,k_i}|A_{i,k_i})\}$ with $A_{i,j}, B_{i,j} \in \text{Form}(\Sigma_i)$ for $j = 1, \ldots, k_i$ for every $i = 1, \ldots, n$. The proof is by induction over $n \geqslant 2$.

Base case: For $n = 2$ this is (IP^{cc}).

Induction step: For $n > 2$ we have that $\Sigma = \Sigma_1 \dot{\cup} (\bigcup_{2 \leqslant l \leqslant n} \Sigma_l)$ is a syntax splitting for $\kappa = \kappa_1 \oplus (\bigoplus_{2 \leqslant l \leqslant n} \kappa_l)$. The induction hypothesis implies that $\sigma(\bigoplus_{2 \leqslant l \leqslant n} \kappa_l, \bigcup_{2 \leqslant l \leqslant n} \Delta_l) = (\sigma(\kappa_2, \Delta_2), \ldots, \sigma(\kappa_n, \Delta_n))$ because $\bigcup_{2 \leqslant l \leqslant n} \Sigma_l$ is a syntax splitting for $\bigoplus_{2 \leqslant l \leqslant n} \kappa_l$. Because of (IP^{cc}), we know that

$$\sigma(\kappa, \Delta) = \left(\sigma(\kappa_1, \Delta_1), \sigma\left(\bigoplus_{1 \leqslant l \leqslant n} \kappa_l, \bigcup_{1 \leqslant l \leqslant n} \Sigma_l\right)\right)$$

$$\overset{\substack{\text{induction} \\ \text{hypothesis}}}{=} (\sigma(\kappa_1, \Delta_1), \sigma(\kappa_2, \Delta_2), \ldots, \sigma(\kappa_n, \Delta_n)). \qquad \square$$

In the next section, we show how (IP^{cc}) relates to syntax splitting.

6   Selection Strategies and Syntax Splitting

In this section, we will connect property (IP^{cc}) on selection strategies with $(P_\circ^{ocf})$ for belief change.

Proposition 6 ((IP^{cc}) ensures $(P_\circ^{ocf})$). *If a selection strategy σ for revision, contractions, or ignorations, respectively, fulfils (IP^{cc}), then the induced c-revision $*_\sigma$, c-contraction $*_\sigma$, or c-ignoration $*_\sigma$, respectively, fulfils $(P_\circ^{ocf})$.*

Proof. Let σ be a selection strategy for c-revisions that fulfils (IP^{cc}). Let $\kappa = \kappa_1 \oplus \cdots \oplus \kappa_n$ be a ranking function with a syntax splitting $\Sigma = \Sigma_1 \dot{\cup} \ldots \dot{\cup} \Sigma_n$. Let $\Delta = \Delta_1 \cup \cdots \cup \Delta_n$ with $\Delta_i = \{(B_{i,1}|A_{i,1}), \ldots, (B_{i,k_i}|A_{i,k_i})\}$ with $A_{i,j}, B_{i,j} \in \text{Form}(\Sigma_i)$ for $j = 1, \ldots, k_i$ for every $i = 1, \ldots, n$. Let $\gamma = (\gamma_{1,1}^+, \gamma_{1,1}^-, \ldots, \gamma_{n,k_n}^+, \gamma_{n,k_n}^-) = \sigma(\kappa, \Delta)$. Let $\kappa^* = \kappa *_\sigma \Delta$. We have:

$$\kappa^*(\omega) = \kappa_0 + \kappa(\omega) + \sum_{\substack{1 \leqslant i \leqslant n \\ 1 \leqslant j \leqslant k_i \\ \omega \models A_{i,j} B_{i,j}}} \gamma_{i,j}^+ + \sum_{\substack{1 \leqslant i \leqslant n \\ 1 \leqslant j \leqslant k_i \\ \omega \models A_{i,j} \overline{B_{i,j}}}} \gamma_{i,j}^-$$

$$= \kappa_0 + \sum_{1 \leqslant i \leqslant n} \kappa_i(\omega) + \sum_{\substack{1 \leqslant i \leqslant n \\ 1 \leqslant j \leqslant k_i \\ \omega \models A_{i,j} B_{i,j}}} \gamma_{i,j}^+ + \sum_{\substack{1 \leqslant i \leqslant n \\ 1 \leqslant j \leqslant k_i \\ \omega \models A_{i,j} \overline{B_{i,j}}}} \gamma_{i,j}^-$$

$$= \kappa_0 + \sum_{1 \leqslant i \leqslant n} \left(\kappa_i(\omega) + \sum_{\substack{1 \leqslant j \leqslant k_i \\ \omega \models A_{i,j} B_{i,j}}} \gamma_{i,j}^+ + \sum_{\substack{1 \leqslant j \leqslant k_i \\ \omega \models A_{i,j} \overline{B_{i,j}}}} \gamma_{i,j}^-\right) \qquad (2)$$

Now, consider a revision of κ_i with Δ_i. This is revision is properly defined, as κ_i is defined for the signature Σ_i and Δ_i only contains variables from Σ_i. Because of Proposition 5, we know that $\sigma(\kappa_i, \Delta_i) = (\gamma_{i,1}^+, \gamma_{i,1}^-, \ldots, \gamma_{i,k_i}^+, \gamma_{i,k_i}^-)$. Let $\kappa_i^* = \kappa_i *_\sigma \Delta_i$. We have $\kappa_i^*(\omega) = \kappa_{i,0} + \kappa_i(\omega) + \sum_{\substack{1 \leqslant j \leqslant k_i \\ \omega \models A_{i,j} B_{i,j}}} \gamma_{i,j}^+ + \sum_{\substack{1 \leqslant j \leqslant k_i \\ \omega \models A_{i,j} \overline{B_{i,j}}}} \gamma_{i,j}^-$.

The combination of all κ_i^* is

$$\left(\bigoplus_{1 \leqslant i \leqslant n} \kappa_i^* \right)(\omega) = \sum_{1 \leqslant i \leqslant n} \kappa_i^*(\omega_i)$$

$$= \sum_{1 \leqslant i \leqslant n} \left(\kappa_{i,0} + \kappa_i(\omega_i) + \sum_{\substack{1 \leqslant j \leqslant k_i \\ \omega_i \models A_{i,j} B_{i,j}}} \gamma_{i,j}^+ + \sum_{\substack{1 \leqslant j \leqslant k_i \\ \omega_i \models A_{i,j} \overline{B_{i,j}}}} \gamma_{i,j}^- \right)$$

$$\overset{*}{=} \underbrace{\sum_{1 \leqslant i \leqslant n} \kappa_{i,0}}_{\kappa_0} + \sum_{1 \leqslant i \leqslant n} \left(\kappa_i(\omega_i) + \sum_{\substack{1 \leqslant j \leqslant k_i \\ \omega \models A_{i,j} B_{i,j}}} \gamma_{i,j}^+ + \sum_{\substack{1 \leqslant j \leqslant k_i \\ \omega \models A_{i,j} \overline{B_{i,j}}}} \gamma_{i,j}^- \right) \quad (3)$$

with $\omega = \omega_1 \ldots \omega_n$. Equation $*$ holds because $A_{i,j}, B_{i,j} \in \mathrm{Form}(\Sigma_i)$ and therefore $\omega_i \models A_{i,j} B_{i,j}$ iff $\omega \models A_{i,j} B_{i,j}$ for any $i = 1, \ldots, n, j = 1, \ldots, k_n$.

Now, let us compare term (3) with (2). They are identical except for the term κ_0 or $\sum_{1 \leqslant i \leqslant n} \kappa_{i,0}$. We know that (3) is a ranking function, because it is the combination of the ranking functions $\kappa_1^*, \ldots, \kappa_n^*$. As κ_0 is chosen such that (2) is a ranking function, we know that $\kappa_0 = \sum_{1 \leqslant i \leqslant n} \kappa_{i,0}$ and that (2) and (3) are equal. This implies that $*_\sigma$ fulfils $(\mathrm{P}_\circ^{ocf})$. Taking the variations in $CR^-(\kappa, \Delta)$ and $CR^{\div}(\kappa, \Delta)$ into account, the proofs for $-_\sigma$ and $\div_\sigma$ are similar.   □

We illustrate the connection between (IP^{cc}) and $(\mathrm{P}_\circ^{ocf})$.

Example 1. Let κ be the ranking function over $\Sigma = \{a, b\}$ illustrated in Fig. 2. $\kappa = \kappa_1 \oplus \kappa_2$ has a syntax splitting $\{a\} \overset{.}{\cup} \{b\}$. Let $r_1 = (a|\top), r_2 = (b|\top)$ and $\Delta = \{r_1, r_2\}$. Let σ_1, σ_2 be two selection strategies for contraction with

$$\sigma_1(\kappa, \Delta) = (0, -2, 0, -2) \quad \sigma_1(\kappa_1, \{r_1\}) = (0, -2) \quad \sigma_1(\kappa_2, \{r_2\}) = (0, -1)$$
$$\sigma_2(\kappa, \Delta) = (0, -2, 0, -1) \quad \sigma_2(\kappa_1, \{r_1\}) = (0, -2) \quad \sigma_2(\kappa_2, \{r_2\}) = (0, -1).$$

Thus, $\gamma_1^+ = \gamma_2^+ = 0$ in these six impact vectors. The selection strategy σ_2 fulfils (IP^{cc}), the selection strategy σ_1 does not fulfil (IP^{cc}). The contractions induced by σ_1 and σ_2 are displayed in Fig. 2. We can see that $-_{\sigma_1}$ does not fulfil $(\mathrm{MR}_\circ^{ocf})$ while $-_{\sigma_2}$ fulfils $(\mathrm{P}_\circ^{ocf})$.

Finally, it is left to show that selection strategies exists that fulfil (IP^{cc}).

Proposition 7. *There are selection strategies for contraction, ignoration, and revision that fulfil (IP^{cc}).*

Proof. We first prove the statement about revisions by constructing a selection strategy for belief revision. Let κ be a ranking function over Σ and Δ be a set of conditionals in $\mathrm{Cond}(\Sigma)$. We can distinguish two cases.

Case 1: κ *and* Δ *have no common syntax splitting.* In this case we choose $\sigma(\kappa, \Delta)$ arbitrarily from $Sol(CR^*(\kappa, \Delta))$. This is allowed as (IP^{cc}) does not state anything about such situations. Proposition 2 ensures that there is at least one impact vector to choose.

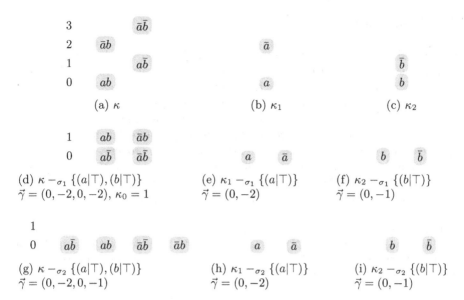

Fig. 2. Comparison of the selection strategies σ_1 and σ_2 from Example 1. The OCFs κ, κ_1, and κ_2 from Example 1 are displayed in the first row (Figs. 2a to 2c). The boxes represent worlds; their vertical alignment corresponds to their rank. The further up a box is placed, the higher its rank is. The second row (Figs. 2d to 2f) illustrates the results of contractions of these OCFs using selection strategy σ_1. All impacts $\vec{\gamma}$ are given in the caption of the Figs. 2d to 2i. Note that for the normalization constant κ_0, in Fig. 2d we have $\kappa_0 = 1$, and $\kappa_0 = 0$ in all other cases. The third row (Figs. 2g to 2i) illustrates contractions of these OCFs using selection strategy σ_2.

Case 2: κ *and* Δ *have a common syntax splitting.*   Let $\Sigma = \Sigma_1 \dot{\cup} \ldots \dot{\cup} \Sigma_n$ be the finest common splitting of κ and Δ, i.e., $\kappa = \kappa_1 \oplus \cdots \oplus \kappa_n$ and $\Delta = \Delta_1 \cup \cdots \cup \Delta_n$ with $\Delta_i = \{(B_{i,1}|A_{i,1}), \ldots, (B_{i,k_i}|A_{i,k_i})\}$ with $A_{i,j}, B_{i,j} \in \text{Form}(\Sigma_i')$ for $j = 1, \ldots, k_i$ for every $i = 1, \ldots, n$. Choose impacts $\sigma(\kappa_i, \Delta_i)$ for each of the revisions $\kappa_i * \Delta_i$ as in Case 1. Let $\sigma(\kappa, \Delta) = (\sigma(\kappa_1, \Delta_1), \ldots, \sigma(\kappa_n, \Delta_n))$ according to (IP^{cc}) and Eq. (1). We have $\kappa -_\sigma \Delta = (\kappa_1 -_\sigma \Delta_1) \oplus \cdots \oplus (\kappa_n -_\sigma \Delta_n)$. The revised ranking function $\kappa -_\sigma \Delta$ accepts Δ because of Proposition 3.

The proofs for contractions and ignorations can be done analogously.   □

An implication of Proposition 7 is that there are revisions, contractions, and ignorations that fulfil $(P_\circ^{ocf})$, and therefore also the specific postulates (P^{ocf}) and (P_-^{ocf}) in the case of revisions and contractions, respectively. Thus, all three belief change operations are fully compatible with syntax splitting, while no such operators having this property have been known before.

7 Conclusion

We generalized syntax splitting postulates from [17] and [11]. Our new generalized postulates cover not only the iterated contraction, ignoration, and revision of ranking functions, representing the epistemic state of an agent, with sets of formulas, but also with sets of conditionals. Using selection strategies for c-changes, we showed that all contractions, ignorations, and revisions fulfil the generalized postulates (and therefore the original postulates) if they are induced by a selection strategy that fulfils the newly developed property (IP^{cc}).

Our current work includes generalizing the concept of selection strategies to further belief changes like, for instance, complex belief change operations based on descriptor revision [12] over a conditional logic [10,24].

Acknowledgements. We thank the anonymous reviewers for their valuable hints. This work was supported by DFG Grant BE 1700/9-1 awarded to Christoph Beierle and DFG Grant KE 1413/10-1 awarded to Gabriele Kern-Isberner as part of the priority program "Intentional Forgetting in Organizations" (SPP 1921).

References

1. Alchourrón, C., Gärdenfors, P., Makinson, D.: On the logic of theory change: partial meet contraction and revision functions. J. Symbolic Logic **50**(2), 510–530 (1985)
2. Aravanis, T.I., Peppas, P., Williams, M.: Incompatibilities between iterated and relevance-sensitive belief revision. J. Artif. Intell. Res. **69**, 85–108 (2020). https://doi.org/10.1613/jair.1.11871
3. Beierle, C., Kern-Isberner, G.: Semantical investigations into nonmonotonic and probabilistic logics. Ann. Math. Artif. Intell. **65**(2–3), 123–158 (2012)
4. Beierle, C., Eichhorn, C., Kern-Isberner, G., Kutsch, S.: Properties of skeptical c-inference for conditional knowledge bases and its realization as a constraint satisfaction problem. Ann. Math. Artif. Intell. **83**(3-4), 247–275 (2018)
5. Beierle, C., Kern-Isberner, G.: Selection strategies for inductive reasoning from conditional belief bases and for belief change respecting the principle of conditional preservation. In: Proceedings of the 34th International Florida Artificial Intelligence Research Society Conference, FLAIRS 2021 (2021)
6. Beierle, C., Kern-Isberner, G., Sauerwald, K., Bock, T., Ragni, M.: Towards a general framework for kinds of forgetting in common-sense belief management. KI **33**(1), 57–68 (2019)
7. Caridroit, T., Konieczny, S., Marquis, P.: Contraction in propositional logic. Int. J. Approx. Reason. **80**, 428–442 (2017). https://doi.org/10.1016/j.ijar.2016.06.010
8. Darwiche, A., Pearl, J.: On the logic of iterated belief revision. Artif. Intell. **89**(1–2), 1–29 (1997)
9. de Finetti, B.: La prévision, ses lois logiques et ses sources subjectives. Ann. Inst. H. Poincaré **7**(1), 1–68 (1937). engl. transl. Theory of Probability, Wiley (1974)
10. Haldimann, J., Sauerwald, K., von Berg, M., Kern-Isberner, G., Beierle: Towards a framework of Hansson's descriptor revision for conditionals. In: The 36th ACM/SIGAPP Symposium on Applied Computing (SAC 2021), 22–26 March 2021, Virtual Event, Republic of Korea, pp. 889–891. ACM, New York (2021)

11. Haldimann, J.P., Kern-Isberner, G., Beierle, C.: Syntax splitting for iterated contractions. In: Calvanese, D., Erdem, E., Thielscher, M. (eds.) Proceedings of the 17th International Conference on Principles of Knowledge Representation and Reasoning, KR 2020, Rhodes, Greece, 12–18 September 2020, pp. 465–475 (2020). https://doi.org/10.24963/kr.2020/47
12. Hansson, S.O.: Descriptor revision. Studia Logica **102**(5), 955–980 (2014)
13. Kern-Isberner, G.: Conditionals in Nonmonotonic Reasoning and Belief Revision. LNCS (LNAI), vol. 2087. Springer, Heidelberg (2001). https://doi.org/10.1007/3-540-44600-1
14. Kern-Isberner, G.: A thorough axiomatization of a principle of conditional preservation in belief revision. Ann. Mathe. Artif. Intell. **40**(1–2), 127–164 (2004)
15. Kern-Isberner, G., Beierle, C., Brewka, G.: Syntax splitting = relevance + independence: New postulates for nonmonotonic reasoning from conditional belief bases. In: KR-2020, pp. 560–571 (2020)
16. Kern-Isberner, G., Bock, T., Sauerwald, K., Beierle, C.: Iterated contraction of propositions and conditionals under the principle of conditional preservation. In: GCAI 2017, 3rd Global Conference on Artificial Intelligence, Miami, FL, USA, 18–22 October 2017, pp. 78–92 (2017)
17. Kern-Isberner, G., Brewka, G.: Strong syntax splitting for iterated belief revision. In: Proceedings of the Twenty-Sixth International Joint Conference on Artificial Intelligence, IJCAI 2017, Melbourne, Australia, 19–25 August 2017, pp. 1131–1137 (2017)
18. Konieczny, S., Pino Pérez, R.: On iterated contraction: syntactic characterization, representation theorem and limitations of the Levi identity. In: Moral, S., Pivert, O., Sánchez, D., Marín, N. (eds.) SUM 2017. LNCS (LNAI), vol. 10564, pp. 348–362. Springer, Cham (2017). https://doi.org/10.1007/978-3-319-67582-4_25
19. Nayak, A., Goebel, R., Orgun, M., Pham, T.: Taking LEVI IDENTITY seriously: a plea for iterated belief contraction. In: Lang, J., Lin, F., Wang, J. (eds.) KSEM 2006. LNCS (LNAI), vol. 4092, pp. 305–317. Springer, Heidelberg (2006). https://doi.org/10.1007/11811220_26
20. Parikh, R.: Beliefs, belief revision, and splitting languages. Logic Lang. Comput. **2**, 266–278 (1999)
21. Peppas, P., Fotinopoulos, A.M., Seremetaki, S.: Conflicts between relevance-sensitive and iterated belief revision. In: Ghallab, M., Spyropoulos, C.D., Fakotakis, N., Avouris, N.M. (eds.) ECAI 2008–18th European Conference on Artificial Intelligence, Patras, Greece, 21–25 July 2008, Proceedings. Frontiers in Artificial Intelligence and Applications, vol. 178, pp. 85–88. IOS Press (2008). https://doi.org/10.3233/978-1-58603-891-5-85
22. Peppas, P., Williams, M., Chopra, S., Foo, N.Y.: Relevance in belief revision. Artif. Intell. **229**, 126–138 (2015)
23. Ramachandran, R., Nayak, A.C., Orgun, M.A.: Three approaches to iterated belief contraction. J. Philos. Logic **41**(1), 115–142 (2012)
24. Sauerwald, K., Haldimann, J., von Berg, M., Beierle, C.: Descriptor revision for conditionals: literal descriptors and conditional preservation. In: Schmid, U., Klügl, F., Wolter, D. (eds.) KI 2020. LNCS (LNAI), vol. 12325, pp. 204–218. Springer, Cham (2020). https://doi.org/10.1007/978-3-030-58285-2_15

25. Sauerwald, K., Kern-Isberner, G., Beierle, C.: A conditional perspective for iterated belief contraction. In: Giacomo, G.D., Catalá, A., Dilkina, B., Milano, M., Barro, S., Bugarín, A., Lang, J. (eds.) ECAI 2020–24th European Conference on Artificial Intelligence, 29 August-8 September 2020, Santiago de Compostela, Spain, 29 August - 8 September 2020 - Including 10th Conference on Prestigious Applications of Artificial Intelligence (PAIS 2020). Frontiers in Artificial Intelligence and Applications, vol. 325, pp. 889–896. IOS Press (2020). https://doi.org/10.3233/FAIA200180
26. Spohn, W.: Ordinal conditional functions: a dynamic theory of epistemic states. In: Harper, W., Skyrms, B. (eds.) Causation in Decision, Belief Change, and Statistics, II, pp. 105–134. Kluwer Academic Publishers (1988)

An Epistemic Logic for Multi-agent Systems with Budget and Costs

Stefania Costantini[1] , Andrea Formisano[2(✉)] , and Valentina Pitoni[1]

[1] DISIM, Università di L'Aquila, L'Aquila, Italy
stefania.costantini@univaq.it,
valentina.pitoni@graduate.univaq.it
[2] DMIF, Università di Udine, Udine, Italy
andrea.formisano@uniud.it

Abstract. In Artificial Intelligence, Multi-Agent Systems are able to model many kinds of collective behavior and have a wide range of application. Logic is often used to model aspects of agents' reasoning process. In this paper, we discuss social aspects of such systems. We propose a logical framework (Logic of "Inferable") which reasons about whether a group of agents can perform an action, highlighting the concepts of action *cost* and *budget* that the group must have available in order to perform actions. The focus is on modeling the group dynamics of cooperative agents: if an agent of a group performs an action, that action to be considered as performed by the whole group, and the group can support a component agent in performing actions not affordable by that agent alone.

Keywords: Multi agents systems · Epistemic logic · Mental actions

1 Introduction

Multi-agent systems are widely employed to model societies whose members are to some extent cooperative towards each other. To achieve better results via cooperation, agents must be able to reason about their own belief states, and those of others. They must also be able to reason about what a group of agents can do, because it is often the case that a group can fulfill objectives that are out of reach for the single agent.

Many kinds of logical frameworks can be found in the literature which try to emulate cognitive aspects of human beings, also from the cooperative point of view. We propose a new logical framework (a new Logic of "Inferable", called *L-DINF*), that draws inspiration from the concepts of Theory of Mind [20] and of Social Intelligence [21]. We consider the notion of executability of inferential actions, that may require resource consumption (and hence involve a *cost*). So, in order to execute an action the agent must possess the necessary *budget*. In our approach however, when an agent belongs to a group, if that agent does not have enough budget to perform an intended action, it may be supported by its group. So, 'our' agents are *aware* of themselves, of the group they belong to, and possibly of other groups. We assume that agents belonging to a group are

Supported by Action COST CA17124 "DigForASP" and by INdAM-GNCS.

W. Faber et al. (Eds.): JELIA 2021, LNAI 12678, pp. 101–115, 2021.
https://doi.org/10.1007/978-3-030-75775-5_8

cooperative. Hence, an action can be executed by the group if at least one agent therein is able to execute it, and the group can bear (in some way) the cost.

Since the seminal work of Fagin and Halpern [19], logics concerning some aspects of awareness, implicit and explicit belief have been proposed. To the best of our knowledge however, such logics make no use of concepts as 'reasoning' or 'inference'. Instead, *L-DINF* provides a constructive theory of explicit beliefs, so it accounts for the perceptive and inferential steps leading from agent's knowledge and beliefs to new beliefs, and possibly to perform physical actions. The main point however is that we consider both "executability" of actions and costs related to their execution.

Epistemic attitudes are modeled similarly to other approaches, among which we mention the dynamic theory of evidence-based beliefs [4] —that uses, as we also do, a neighborhood semantics for the notion of evidence— the sentential approach to explicit beliefs and their dynamics [22], the dynamic theory of explicit and implicit beliefs [26], and the dynamic logic of explicit beliefs and knowledge [3].

Concerning logics of inference, the seminal proposals were Velázquez-Quesada [25] and the logical system $DES4_n$ proposed by Duc [16]. We are indebted to Velázquez-Quesada concerning the idea of modeling inference steps by means of dynamic operators in the style of dynamic epistemic logic (DEL). We however emphasize the concepts of explicit belief and of background knowledge, and we introduce issues related to executability and costs. *L-DINF* is also indebted to [16], concerning the point of view that an agent reaches a certain belief state by performing inferences, and that making inferences takes time (we tackled the issue of time in previous work, discussed in [13,14,24]). Differently from this work however, in *L-DINF* inferential actions are represented both at the syntactic level, via dynamic operators in the DEL style, and at a semantic level as neighborhood-update operations. Moreover, *L-DINF* enables an agent to reason on executability of inferential actions.

The notion of explicit beliefs constitutes a difference between *L-DINF* and *active logics* [17,18], besides other important differences. First, while active logics provide models of reasoning based on long-term memory and short-term memory (or working memory) like in our approach, they do not distinguish –as we do– between the notion of explicit belief and the notion of background knowledge, conceived in our case as a radically different kind of epistemic attitude. Second, *L-DINF* accounts for a variety of inferential actions that have not been explored in the active logic literature, whereas they are in our opinion very useful for inferring new beliefs. Note that these actions are *mental operation*, not physical ones. They correspond to basic operations of "mind-reading" in the sense of Theory of Mind [20]. However, the consequence of a mental operation can entail the execution of physical actions, among which "active sensing" actions, where the agent performs to check (aspects of) the state of its environment.

Section 2 introduces syntax and semantics of *L-DINF* and an example of application of our logic. In Sect. 3 we provide an axiomatization of the proposed logical system and state its soundness. The proof of strong completeness of the logic is also shown. In Sect. 4 we briefly discuss complexity and future work, and then conclude.

2   Logical Framework

L-DINF is a logic which consists of a static component and a dynamic one. The static component, called *L-INF*, is a logic of explicit beliefs and background knowledge. The dynamic component, called *L-DINF*, extends the static one with dynamic operators capturing the consequences of the agents' inferential actions on their explicit beliefs as well as a dynamic operator capturing what an agent can conclude by performing some inferential action in its repertoire.

2.1   Syntax

In this section we provide and illustrate the syntax of the proposed logic. Let $Atm = \{p, q, \ldots\}$ be a countable set of atomic propositions. By $Prop$ we denote the set of all propositional formulas, i.e. the set of all Boolean formulas built out of the set of atomic propositions Atm. A subset Atm_A of the atomic propositions represent the physical actions that an agent can perform, including "active sensing" actions (e.g., "let's check whether it rains", "let's measure the temperature"). Moreover, let Agt be a set of agents. The language of *L-DINF*, denoted by $\mathcal{L}_{L\text{-}DINF}$, is defined by the following grammar:

$$\varphi, \psi ::= p \mid \neg\varphi \mid \varphi \wedge \psi \mid \mathbf{B}_i\,\varphi \mid \mathbf{K}_i\,\varphi \mid do(\phi_A) \mid do^P(\phi_A) \mid exec_G(\alpha) \mid [G : \alpha]\,\varphi$$
$$\alpha \quad ::= \vdash(\varphi,\psi) \mid \cap(\varphi,\psi) \mid \downarrow(\varphi,\psi)$$

where p ranges over Atm and $i \in Agt$. (Other Boolean operators are defined from $\neg$ and $\wedge$ in the standard manner.) The language of *inferential actions* of type α is denoted by $\mathcal{L}_{\mathsf{ACT}}$. Plainly, the static part *L-INF* of *L-DINF*, includes only those formulas not having sub-formulas of type α, namely, no inferential operation is admitted.

Notice the expression $do(\phi_A)$, where it is required that $\phi_A \in Atm_A$. This expression indicates *actual execution* of action ϕ_A, automatically recorded by the new belief $do^P(\phi_A)$ (postfix "P" standing for "past" action). In fact, do and do^P are not axiomatized, as they are realized by what has been called in [27] a *semantic attachment*, i.e., a procedure which connects an agent with its external environment in a way that is unknown at the logical level. As seen below, in general the execution of actions may have a cost. We impose the meta-constraint that a "physical" action is necessarily determined as a consequence of a mental action, thus it is the latter which bears the cost.

Before introducing a formal semantics, let us provide an intuition about the intended meaning of formulas predicating on beliefs and background knowledge. The formula $\mathbf{B}_i\,\varphi$ is read "the agent i explicitly believes that φ is true" or, more shortly, "agent i believes φ". Explicit beliefs are accessible in the working memory and are the basic elements of the agents' reasoning process, according the logic of local reasoning by Fagin and Halpern [19]. In such approach agents cannot distinguish between logically equivalent formulas, i.e., if two facts φ and ψ are logically equivalent and an agent explicitly believes that φ is true, then it believes that ψ is true as well. Unlike explicit beliefs, background knowledge is assumed to satisfy *omniscience* principles, such as closure under conjunction and known implication, closure under logical consequence, and introspection. More specifically, $\mathbf{K}_i$ is nothing but the well-known S5 modal operator often used to model/represent knowledge. The fact that background knowledge is closed under logical consequence is justified by the fact that we conceive it as a kind of deductively closed *belief base*. We assume the background knowledge to include: facts (formulas) known by the agent from the beginning: plus facts the agent has decided to store in its long-term memory (by means of some decision mechanism not treated here) after having processed them in its working memory, as well their logical consequences. We therefore assume that background knowledge is irrevocable in the sense of being stable over time. A formula of the form $[G : \alpha]\,\varphi$, with $G \in 2^{Agt}$, states that "φ holds after the inferential action α has been performed by at least one of the agents in G, and all agents in G have common knowledge about this fact".

Remark 1. If an action is performed by an agent $i \in G$, the others agents belonging to the same group G have full visibility of this action and, therefore, as we suppose agents to be cooperative, it is as if they had performed the action themselves.

Borrowing from and extending [2], we distinguish three types of inferential actions α which allow us to capture some of the dynamic properties of explicit beliefs and background knowledge: $\vdash(\varphi,\psi)$, $\cap(\varphi,\psi)$ and $\downarrow(\varphi, \psi)$. These actions characterize the basic operations of forming explicit beliefs via inference:

- $\downarrow(\varphi, \psi)$ is the inferential action which consists in inferring ψ from φ in case φ is believed and, according to agent's background knowledge, ψ is a logical consequence of φ. In other words, by performing this inferential action, an agent tries to retrieve from its background knowledge in long-term memory the information that φ implies ψ and, if it succeeds, it starts believing ψ;
- $\cap(\varphi,\psi)$ is the inferential action which closes the explicit belief φ and the explicit belief ψ under conjunction. In other words, $\cap(\varphi,\psi)$ characterizes the inferential action of deducing $\varphi \wedge \psi$ from the explicit belief φ and the explicit belief ψ;
- $\vdash(\varphi,\psi)$ is the inferential action which infers ψ from φ in case φ is believed and, according to agent's working memory, ψ is logical consequence of φ. This last action operates directly on the working memory without retrieving anything from the background knowledge.

Remark 2. In the mental actions $\vdash(\varphi,\psi)$ and $\downarrow(\varphi, \psi)$, the formula ψ which is inferred and asserted as a new belief can be $do(\phi_A)$, which denotes the actual execution of physical action ϕ_A, where $do^P(\phi_A)$ is the belief to have done such action in the past. In fact, we assume that when inferring $do(\phi_A)$ the action is actually executed, and the corresponding belief $do^P(\phi_A)$ asserted, possibly augmented with a time-stamp. Actions are supposed to succeed by default, in case of failure a corresponding failure event will be perceived by the agent. The do^P beliefs constitute a *history* of the agent's operation, so they might be useful for the agent to reason about its own past behavior, and/or, importantly, they may be useful to provide *explanations* to human users.

Finally, a formula of the form $exec_G(\alpha)$ expresses executability of inferential actions. It has to be read as: "α is an inferential action that an agent in G can perform".

As said in the Introduction, we intend to model agents which, to execute an action, may have to pay a cost, so they must have a consistent budget available. In our approach, agents belong to groups (where the smallest possible group is the single agent), and agents belonging to a group are by definition cooperative. With respect to action execution, an action can be executed by the group if at least one agent in the group is able to execute it, and the group has the necessary budget available, sharing the cost according to some policy. In order to keep the complexity of the logic reasonable, we have not introduced costs and budget in the language.[1] In fact, by making the assumption that agents are cooperative, we also assume that they are aware of and agree with the cost-sharing policy. So, as seen below, costs and budget are coped with at the semantic level. Variants of the logic can be easily worked out, where the modalities of cost sharing are different from the one shown here, where the group members share an action's cost in equal parts. Below we indicate which are the points that should be modified to change the cost-sharing policy. Moreover, for brevity we introduce a single budget function, and thus, implicitly, a single resource to be spent. Several budget functions, each one concerning a different resource, might be plainly defined.

2.2 Semantics

Definition1 introduces the notion of *L-INF model*, which is then used to introduce semantics of the static fragment of the logic. As before let *Agt* be the set of agents.

Definition 1. *A model is a tuple* $M = (W, N, \mathcal{R}, E, B, C, V)$ *where:*

- W *is a set of objects, called* worlds *(or* situations*);*[2]
- $\mathcal{R} = \{R_i\}_{i \in Agt}$ *is a collection of equivalence relations on* W: $R_i \subseteq W \times W$ *for each* $i \in Agt$;
- $N : Agt \times W \longrightarrow 2^{2^W}$ *is a neighborhood function such that for each* $i \in Agt$, *each* $w, v \in W$, *and each* $X \subseteq W$ *these conditions hold:*
  - **(C1)** *if* $X \in N(i, w)$ *then* $X \subseteq \{v \in W \mid wR_iv\}$,
  - **(C2)** *if* wR_iv *then* $N(i, w) = N(i, v)$;
- $E : Agt \times W \longrightarrow 2^{\mathcal{L}_{\mathsf{ACT}}}$ *is an executability function such that for each* $i \in Agt$ *and* $w, v \in W$, *it holds that:*
  - **(D1)** *if* wR_iv *then* $E(i, w) = E(i, v)$;
- $B : Agt \times W \longrightarrow \mathbb{N}$ *is a budget function such that for each* $i \in Agt$ *and* $w, v \in W$, *the following holds*
  - **(E1)** *if* wR_iv *then* $B(i, w) = B(i, v)$;
- $C : Agt \times \mathcal{L}_{\mathsf{ACT}} \times W \longrightarrow \mathbb{N}$ *is a cost function such that for each* $i \in Agt$, $\alpha \in \mathcal{L}_{\mathsf{ACT}}$, *and* $w, v \in W$, *it holds that:*
  - **(F1)** *if* wR_iv *then* $C(i, \alpha, w) = C(i, \alpha, v)$;
- $V : W \longrightarrow 2^{Atm}$ *is a valuation function.*

---

[1] We intend to use this logic in practice, to formalize memory in DALI agents, where DALI is a logic-based agent-oriented programming language [5,6,15]. So, computational effectiveness was crucial. Assuming that agents share the cost is reasonable when agents share resources, or cooperate to a common goal, as discussed, e.g., in [7,8].

[2] Concerning Definition 1, a world is just an arbitrary object. No "internal structure" is required. In Sect. 3 we will take advantage of this and define worlds as set of formulas.

To simplify the notation, let $R_i(w)$ denote the set $\{v \in W \mid wR_iv\}$, for $w \in W$. The set $R_i(w)$ identifies the situations that agent i considers possible at world w. It is the *epistemic state* of agent i at w. In cognitive terms, $R_i(w)$ can be conceived as the set of all situations that agent i *can* retrieve from its long-term memory and reason about.

While $R_i(w)$ concerns background knowledge, $N(i, w)$ is the set of all facts that agent i explicitly believes at world w, a fact being identified with a set of worlds. Hence, if $X \in N(i, w)$ then, the agent i has the fact X under the focus of its attention and believes it. We say that $N(i, w)$ is the explicit *belief set* of agent i at world w.

The executability of actions is determined by the function E. For an agent i, $E(i, w)$ is the set of inferential actions that agent i can execute at world w. The value $B(i, w)$ is the budget the agent has available to perform actions. Similarly, the value $C(i, \alpha, w)$ is the cost to be paid by agent i to execute the action α in the world w.

Constraint (**C1**) imposes that agent i can have explicit in its mind only facts which are compatible with its current epistemic state. Moreover, according to constraint (**C2**), if a world v is compatible with the epistemic state of agent i at world w, then agent i should have the same explicit beliefs at w and v. In other words, if two situations are equivalent as concerns background knowledge, then they cannot be distinguished through the explicit belief set. Analogous properties are imposed by constraints (**D1**), (**E1**), and (**F1**). Namely, (**D1**) imposes that agent i always knows which actions it can perform and those it cannot. (**E1**) states that agent i always knows the available budget in a world (potentially needed to perform actions). Finally, (**F1**) determines that agent i always knows how much it costs to perform an inferential action.

Truth values for formulas of *L-DINF* are inductively defined. Given a model $M = (W, N, \mathcal{R}, E, B, C, V)$, $i \in Agt$, $G \subseteq Agt$, $w \in W$, and a formula $\varphi \in \mathcal{L}_{L\text{-}INF}$, we introduce a shorthand notation for the set of all words R_i-related to w that satisfy φ:

$$\|\varphi\|_{i,w}^M = \{v \in W : wR_iv \text{ and } M, v \models \varphi\}$$

whenever $M, v \models \varphi$ is well-defined (see below). Then, we set:

- $M, w \models p$ iff $p \in V(w)$
- $M, w \models exec_G(\alpha)$ iff there exists $i \in G$ with $\alpha \in E(i, w)$
- $M, w \models \neg\varphi$ iff $M, w \not\models \varphi$
- $M, w \models \varphi \wedge \psi$ iff $M, w \models \varphi$ and $M, w \models \psi$
- $M, w \models \mathbf{B}_i \varphi$ iff $\|\varphi\|_{i,w}^M \in N(i, w)$
- $M, w \models \mathbf{K}_i \varphi$ iff $M, v \models \varphi$ for all $v \in R_i(w)$

For any inferential action α performed by any agent i, we set:

- $M, w \models [G : \alpha]\varphi$ iff $M^{[G:\alpha]}, w \models \varphi$

where we put $M^{[G:\alpha]} = \langle W; N^{[G:\alpha]}, \mathcal{R}, E, B^{[G:\alpha]}, C, V \rangle$, representing the fact that the execution of an inferential action α affects the sets of beliefs of agent i and modifies the available budget. Such operation can add new beliefs by direct perception, by means of one inference step, or as a conjunction of previous beliefs. Hence, when introducing new beliefs (i.e., performing mental actions), the neighborhood must be extended accordingly.

A key aspect in the definition of the logic is the following, which states under which conditions, and by which agent(s), an action may be performed:

$$enabled_w(G, \alpha) \equiv_{Def} \exists j \in G \left(\alpha \in E(j, w) \land \frac{C(j, \alpha, w)}{|G|} \leq \min_{h \in G} B(h, w) \right).$$

This condition as defined above expresses the fact that an action is enabled when: at least an agent can perform it; and the "payment" due by each agent, obtained by dividing the action's cost equally among all agents of the group, is within each agent's available budget. In case more than one agent in G can execute an action, we implicitly assume the agent j performing the action is the one corresponding to the lowest possible cost. Namely, j is such that $C(j, \alpha, w) = \min_{h \in G} C(h, \alpha, w)$. This definition reflects a parsimony criterion reasonably adoptable by cooperative agents sharing a crucial resource such as, e.g., energy or money.

Remark 3. Notice that the policy we have specified to enable the action, share the costs, and select the executor of the action is just one among many possible options. Other choices might be viable, for example, depending on the specific implementation choices of an agent system or on the characteristics of the concrete real-world application at hand. So variations of this logic can be easily defined by devising some other enabling condition and policy for cost sharing, or even by introducing differences in neighborhood update. The semantics is, in a sense, parametric w.r.t. such choice. Notice, moreover, that the definition of the enabling function basically specifies the **"role"** that agents take while concurring with their own resources to actions' execution. Also, in case of specification of different resources, different corresponding enabling functions should be defined.

The updated neighborhood $N^{[G:\alpha]}$ is as follows.

$$N^{[G:\downarrow(\psi,\chi)]}(i, w) = \begin{cases} N(i, w) \cup \{||\chi||_{i,w}^M\} & \text{if } i \in G \text{ and } enabled_w(G, \downarrow(\psi, \chi)) \text{ and} \\ & M, w \models \mathbf{B}_i\psi \land \mathbf{K}_i(\psi \to \chi) \\ N(i, w) & \text{otherwise} \end{cases}$$

$$N^{[G:\cap(\psi,\chi)]}(i, w) = \begin{cases} N(i, w) \cup \{||\psi \land \chi||_{i,w}^M\} & \text{if } i \in G \text{ and } enabled_w(G, \cap(\psi,\chi)) \text{ and} \\ & M, w \models \mathbf{B}_i\psi \land \mathbf{B}_i\chi \\ N(i, w) & \text{otherwise} \end{cases}$$

$$N^{[G:\vdash(\psi,\chi)]}(i, w) = \begin{cases} N(i, w) \cup \{||\chi||_{i,w}^M\} & \text{if } i \in G \text{ and } enabled_w(G, \vdash (\psi,\chi)) \text{ and} \\ & M, w \models \mathbf{B}_i\psi \land \mathbf{B}_i(\psi \to \chi) \\ N(i, w) & \text{otherwise} \end{cases}$$

Notice that after an action α has been performed by an agent $j \in G$, all agents $i \in G$ see the same update in the neighborhood. Conversely, for any agent $h \notin G$ the neighborhood remains unchanged (i.e., $N^{[G:\alpha]}(h, w) = N(h, w)$). However, even for agents in G, the neighborhood remains unchanged if the required preconditions, on explicit beliefs, knowledge, and budget, do not hold (and hence the action is not executed). Notice also that we might devise variations of the logic by making different decisions about neighborhood update to implement, for instance, partial visibility within a group.

Since each agent in G has to contribute to cover the costs of execution by consuming part of its available budget, an update of the budget function is needed. As before, for an action α, we require $enabled_w(G, \alpha)$ to hold and assume that $j \in G$ executes α. Then, depending on α, we have:

$$B^{[G:\downarrow(\psi,\chi)]}(i,w) = \begin{cases} B(i,w) - \frac{C(j,\downarrow(\psi,\chi),w)}{|G|} & \text{if } i \in G \text{ and } enabled_w(G,\downarrow(\psi,\chi)) \text{ and} \\ & M,w \models \mathbf{B}_i\psi \wedge \mathbf{K}_i(\psi \rightarrow \chi) \\ B(i,w) & \text{otherwise} \end{cases}$$

$$B^{[G:\cap(\psi,\chi)]}(i,w) = \begin{cases} B(i,w) - \frac{C(j,\cap(\psi,\chi),w)}{|G|} & \text{if } i \in G \text{ and } enabled_w(G,\cap(\psi,\chi)) \text{ and} \\ & M,w \models \mathbf{B}_i\psi \wedge \mathbf{B}_i\chi \\ B(i,w) & \text{otherwise} \end{cases}$$

$$B^{[G:\vdash(\psi,\chi)]}(i,w) = \begin{cases} B(i,w) - \frac{C(j,\vdash(\psi,\chi),w)}{|G|} & \text{if } i \in G \text{ and } enabled_w(G,\vdash(\psi,\chi)) \text{ and} \\ & M,w \models \mathbf{B}_i\psi \wedge \mathbf{B}_i(\psi \rightarrow \chi) \\ B(i,w) & \text{otherwise} \end{cases}$$

We write $\models_{L\text{-}DINF} \varphi$ to denote that $M, w \models \varphi$ holds for all worlds w of every model M.

Property 1. As consequence of previous definitions, for any set of agents G and each $i \in G$, we have the following:

- $\models_{L\text{-}INF} (\mathbf{K}_i(\varphi \rightarrow \psi)) \wedge \mathbf{B}_i\varphi) \rightarrow [G : \downarrow(\varphi,\psi)]\mathbf{B}_i\psi$.
  Namely, if an agent has φ among beliefs and $\mathbf{K}_i(\varphi \rightarrow \psi)$ in its background knowledge, then as a consequence of the action $\downarrow(\varphi,\psi)$ the agent starts believing ψ.
- $\models_{L\text{-}INF} (\mathbf{B}_i\varphi \wedge \mathbf{B}_i\psi) \rightarrow [G : \cap(\varphi,\psi)]\mathbf{B}_i(\varphi \wedge \psi)$.
  Namely, if an agent has φ and ψ as beliefs, then as a consequence of the action $\cap(\varphi,\psi)$ the agent starts believing $\varphi \wedge \psi$.
- $\models_{L\text{-}INF} (\mathbf{B}_i(\varphi \rightarrow \psi)) \wedge \mathbf{B}_i\varphi) \rightarrow [G : \vdash(\varphi,\psi)]\mathbf{B}_i,\psi$.
  Namely, if an agent has φ among its beliefs and $\mathbf{B}_i(\varphi \rightarrow \psi)$ in its working memory, then as a consequence of the action $\vdash(\varphi,\psi)$ the agent starts believing ψ.

Proof. Let $i \in G$, $M=\langle W, N, \mathcal{R}, E, B, C, V \rangle$, and $w \in W$.

- Let $M, w \models \mathbf{K}_i(\varphi \rightarrow \psi) \wedge \mathbf{B}_i\varphi$. We have to show that $M, w \models [G:\downarrow(\varphi,\psi)]\mathbf{B}_i\psi$ holds. This holds iff $M^{[G:\downarrow(\varphi,\psi)]}, w \models \mathbf{B}_i\psi$, with $M^{[G:\downarrow(\varphi,\psi)]} = \langle W, N^{[G:\downarrow(\varphi,\psi)]}, \mathcal{R}, E, B^{[G:\downarrow(\varphi,\psi)]}, C, V \rangle$, where $N^{[G:\downarrow(\varphi,\psi)]}(i,w) = N(i,w) \cup \{ \parallel \psi \parallel_{i,w}^M \}$, because $M, w \models (\mathbf{K}_i(\varphi \rightarrow \psi) \wedge \mathbf{B}_i\varphi)$ and $i \in G$, by hypothesis. $M^{[G:\downarrow(\varphi,\psi)]}, w \models \mathbf{B}_i\psi$ holds because $\parallel \psi \parallel_{i,w}^{M^{[G:\downarrow(\varphi,\psi)]}}$ is member of $N^{[G:\downarrow(\varphi,\psi)]}(i,w)$.
- Let $M, w \models \mathbf{B}_i\varphi \wedge \mathbf{B}_i\psi$. We have to show that $M, w \models [G : \cap(\varphi,\psi)]\mathbf{B}_i(\varphi \wedge \psi)$. This holds iff $M^{[G:\cap(\varphi,\psi)]}, w \models \mathbf{B}_i(\varphi \wedge \psi)$, with $M^{[G:\cap(\varphi,\psi)]} = \langle W, N^{[G:\cap(\varphi,\psi)]}, \mathcal{R}, E, B^{[G:\cap(\varphi,\psi)]}, C, V \rangle$ and $N^{[G:\cap(\varphi,\psi)]} = N(i,w) \cup \{ \parallel \varphi \wedge \psi \parallel_{i,w}^M \}$, because $M, w \models \mathbf{B}_i\varphi \wedge \mathbf{B}_i\psi$, by hypothesis. Then, $M^{[G:\cap(\varphi,\psi)]}, w \models \mathbf{B}_i(\varphi \wedge \psi)$ holds.
- Let $M, w \models (\mathbf{B}_i(\varphi \rightarrow \psi) \wedge \mathbf{B}_i\varphi)$. The proof that $M, w \models [G : \vdash(\varphi,\psi)]\mathbf{B}_i\psi$ follows the same line of the proof developed for the case of action $\downarrow(\varphi,\psi)$.

2.3 Problem Specification and Inference: An Example

In this section we propose an example of problem specification and inference in *L-DINF*. Note that an agent performs physical actions to interact with other agents or with the surrounding environment in consequence to some internal inference. Therefore, we consider inferential actions as a prerequisite for physical ones, and so it is inferential actions which bear costs.

Consider a group of n agents, where each agent manages a smart home, which is a prosumer (producer+consumer) of energy. The electricity is produced by solar panels during the day. The budget available for the night is the difference between energy produced and energy consumed. More energy can be bought at high cost from the outside, so agents try to avoid this extra cost. Assume that the agents are available to lend energy to others. Now, assume that an agent i would like to use some appliance (e.g., air conditioning system, washing machine, etc.) during the night, but its own budget is insufficient. Nevertheless, agent i could use the needed appliance if the group as a whole has sufficient budget. To consider a more concrete situation, let $n = 4$ and assume that in world w_1 these four agents have the following budgets to perform actions: $B(1, w_1) = 10$, $B(2, w_1) = 7$, $B(3, w_1) = 8$, and $B(4, w_1) = 20$. The physical actions any agent can perform are, e.g.,: $switch\text{-}on-airconditioning_A$, $switch\text{-}on-washing\text{-}machine_A$, $close-electric\text{-}shutter_A$.

Among the various possible inferential actions that agents might be able to do, let us, for simplicity, consider only the following ones:

$$\alpha_1 : \ \downarrow(temperature-high, \ do(switch\text{-}on-airconditioning_A))$$
$$\alpha_2 : \ \downarrow(dirty-clothes, \ do(switch\text{-}on-washing\text{-}machine_A))$$
$$\alpha_3 : \ \downarrow(night \wedge thieves-fear, \ do(close-electric\text{-}shutter_A))$$
$$\alpha_4 : \ \cap (night, \ thieves-fear)$$

Assume that their costs are $C(i, \alpha_1, w) = 20$, $C(i, \alpha_2, w) = 12$, $C(i, \alpha_3, w) = 8$, $C(i, \alpha_4, w) = 1$; that $\alpha_j \in E(i, w)$ holds for each world w, each agent i, and each action α_j; and that the knowledge base of each agent i contains the following rules:

1. $\mathbf{K}_i(temperature-high \rightarrow do(switch\text{-}on-airconditioning_A))$
   This rule indicates that an agent knows that if the temperature inside the house is high, it can switch on the air conditioner;
2. $\mathbf{K}_i(do^P(switch\text{-}on-airconditioning_A) \rightarrow do(close-electric\text{-}shutter_A))$
   This rule indicates that if an agent knows that someone has switched on the air conditioning (past action, postfix "*P*"), it can close the electric shutter so as not to let the heat in from the outside;
3. $\mathbf{K}_i(dirty-clothes \rightarrow do(switch\text{-}on-washing\text{-}machine_A))$
   This rule indicates that if an agent knows that there are dirty clothes inside the washing machine, it can switch it on;
4. $\mathbf{K}_i(night \wedge thieves-fear \rightarrow do(close-electric\text{-}shutter_A))$
   This rule indicates that if an agent knows that it is night and someone has the fear of thieves, it can close the electric shutter.

Assume also that the agents have the following beliefs:

$\mathbf{B}_1(temperature-high)$ $\mathbf{B}_2(dirty-clothes)$ $\mathbf{B}_3(thieves-fear)$ $\mathbf{B}_3(night)$
$\mathbf{B}_4(temperature-high \rightarrow do(switch\text{-}on-airconditioning_A))$

The latter formula —which states that if the temperature in the house is high, then agent 4 can switch on the air conditioner—, represents an inference that agent 4 may perform by exploiting its working memory (i.e., its own present beliefs). This implication allows agent 4 to infer $\mathbf{B}_4(do(switch\text{-}on\text{-}airconditioning_A))$ depending on the contents of its own working memory. In particular such inference requires the presence of the belief $\mathbf{B}_4(temperature\text{-}high)$. Compare this formula with rule (1) shown earlier, as part of the knowledge base of the agent. There, the implication concerns the agent's long-term memory and the inference would thus exploit background knowledge.

Suppose agent 1 wants to perform α_1. It alone cannot perform α_1, because it does not have enough budget. But, using the inferential action

$$[G : \downarrow(temperature\text{-}high, do(switch\text{-}on\text{-}airconditioning_A))],$$

with $G = \{1, 2, 3, 4\}$, the other agents can lend its part of their budgets to share the cost, so the group can perform α_1, because $\frac{C(1,\alpha_1,w_1)}{|G|} \le \min_{h \in G} B(h, w_1)$. Hence, $\mathbf{B}_1(do(switch\text{-}on\text{-}airconditioning_A))$ can be inferred by agent 1 and this determines the execution of the concrete physical action. Note that each agent $i \in G$ adds $\mathbf{B}_i(do(switch\text{-}on\text{-}airconditioning_A))$ to its beliefs. Indeed, the inferential action is considered as performed by the whole group and each agent of G updates its neighborhood. After the execution of the action the budget of each agent is updated (cf., Sect. 2.2) as follows: $B(1, w_2) = 5$, $B(2, w_2) = 2$, $B(3, w_2) = 3$, and $B(4, w_2) = 15$, where, for simplicity, we name w_2 the situation reached after executing the action.

Let us now consider the case in which, in such situation, agent 2 wants to perform $do(switch\text{-}on\text{-}washing\text{-}machine_A)$, enabled by the inferential action

$$\downarrow(dirty\text{-}clothes, do(switch\text{-}on\text{-}washing\text{-}machine_A)).$$

In this case, the right precondition $\mathbf{B}_2(dirty\text{-}clothes)$ holds, but, even considering the entire group G, the available budgets do not satisfy the constraint $\frac{C(2,\alpha_2,w_2)}{|G|} = 3 \le \min_{h \in G} B(h, w_2)$ (in particular, because the available budget of agent 2 is 2).

Let us, instead, assume that agent 3 wants to perform α_3 (in w_2), to enable the physical action $close\text{-}electric\text{-}shutter_A$ This cannot be done directly, because before executing the inferential action $\downarrow(night \wedge thieves\text{-}fear, do(close\text{-}electric\text{-}shutter_A))$, it has to perform the inferential action $\cap(night, thieves\text{-}fear)$ in order to infer the belief $\mathbf{B}_3(night \wedge thieves\text{-}fear)$. Considering its current budget, the execution of $[\{3\} : \cap(night, thieves\text{-}fear)]$ can be completed (and, after that, the budget for agent 3 becomes 2). So, agent 3 obtains the belief needed as precondition to the execution of $\downarrow(night \wedge thieves\text{-}fear, do(close\text{-}electric\text{-}shutter_A))$. Nonetheless, in order to execute such action it needs the help of other agents (because its budget does not suffice), and the new belief $\mathbf{B}_3(do(close\text{-}electric\text{-}shutter_A))$ will be inferred through $[G : \downarrow(night \wedge thieves\text{-}fear, do(close\text{-}electric\text{-}shutter_A))]$. Again, all agents in G acquire the belief inferred by agent 3 and extend their belief sets, The condition on cost sharing is also satisfied for action α_3, and the budgets after the execution become $3, 0, 0, 13$, for the agents $1, 2, 3, 4$, respectively. At this point, since agents 2 and 3 have exhausted their budgets, they cannot perform any other action.

The non-executability depends on the policy adopted to share action cost among agents. For instance, a policy requiring proportional sharing of costs with respect to agents' budgets, could be adopted. By applying this criterion, the execution of action α_1 in world w_1, by agent 1 as part of G, would have generated the following budgets $6, 4, 4, 11$ for the agents $1, 2, 3, 4$, respectively, because agents would have contributed paying $4, 3, 4, 9$, respectively (where we rounded values to the closest integer). Similarly, with a proportional sharing of costs even in the the last situation of the example, agents of G would collectively have the budget to perform more actions.

3 Axiomatization and Strong Completeness

In this section we present an axiomatization of our logic and discuss the proof of its strong completeness w.r.t. the proposed class of models.

The *L-INF* and *L-DINF* axioms and inference rules are the following:

1. $(\mathbf{K}_i\,\varphi \wedge \mathbf{K}_i(\varphi \rightarrow \psi)) \rightarrow \mathbf{K}_i\,\psi$;
2. $\mathbf{K}_i\,\varphi \rightarrow \varphi$;
3. $\neg\mathbf{K}_i(\varphi \wedge \neg\varphi)$;
4. $\mathbf{K}_i\,\varphi \rightarrow \mathbf{K}_i\,\mathbf{K}_i\,\varphi$;
5. $\neg\mathbf{K}_i\,\varphi \rightarrow \mathbf{K}_i\,\neg\mathbf{K}_i\,\varphi$;
6. $\mathbf{B}_i\,\varphi \wedge \mathbf{K}_i\,(\varphi \leftrightarrow \psi) \rightarrow \mathbf{B}_i\,\psi$;
7. $\mathbf{B}_i\,\varphi \rightarrow \mathbf{K}_i\,\mathbf{B}_i\,\varphi$;
8. $\dfrac{\varphi}{\mathbf{K}_i\,\varphi}$;
9. $[G:\alpha]p \leftrightarrow p$;
10. $[G:\alpha]\neg\varphi \leftrightarrow \neg[G:\alpha]\varphi$;
11. $exec_G(\alpha) \rightarrow \mathbf{K}_i\,(exec_G(\alpha))$;
12. $[G:\alpha](\varphi \wedge \psi) \leftrightarrow [G:\alpha]\varphi \wedge [G:\alpha]\psi$;
13. $[G:\alpha]\mathbf{K}_i\,\varphi \leftrightarrow \mathbf{K}_i\,([G:\alpha]\varphi)$;
14. $[G:\downarrow(\varphi,\psi)]\mathbf{B}_i\,\chi \leftrightarrow \mathbf{B}_i\,([G:\downarrow(\varphi,\psi)]\chi) \vee ((\mathbf{B}_i\,\varphi \wedge \mathbf{K}_i\,(\varphi \rightarrow \psi))$
    $\wedge\mathbf{K}_i\,([G:\downarrow(\varphi,\psi)]\chi \leftrightarrow \psi))$;
15. $[G:\cap(\varphi,\psi)]\mathbf{B}_i\,\chi \leftrightarrow \mathbf{B}_i\,([G:\cap(\varphi,\psi)]\chi) \vee ((\mathbf{B}_i\,\varphi \wedge \mathbf{B}_i\,\psi)$
    $\wedge\mathbf{K}_i\,[G:\cap(\varphi,\psi)]\chi \leftrightarrow (\varphi \wedge \psi))$;
16. $[G:\vdash(\varphi,\psi)]\mathbf{B}_i\,\chi \leftrightarrow \mathbf{B}_i\,([G:\vdash(\varphi,\psi)]\chi) \vee ((\mathbf{B}_i\,\varphi \wedge \mathbf{B}_i\,(\varphi \rightarrow \psi))$
    $\wedge\mathbf{B}_i\,([G:\vdash(\varphi,\psi)]\chi \leftrightarrow \psi))$;
17. $\dfrac{\psi \leftrightarrow \chi}{\varphi \leftrightarrow \varphi[\psi/\chi]}$;

We write *L-DINF*$\vdash \varphi$ to denote that φ is a theorem of *L-DINF*. It is easy to verify that the above axiomatization is sound for the class of *L-INF* models, namely, all axioms are valid and inference rules preserve validity. In particular, soundness of axioms (14)–(16) immediately follows from the semantics of $[G:\alpha]\varphi$, for each inferential action α, as defined in Sect. 2.2. As before let *Agt* be a set of agents. For the proof that *L-INF* is strongly complete we use a standard canonical-model argument.

Definition 2. *The canonical L-INF model is a tuple* $M_c = \langle W_c, N_c, \mathcal{R}_c, E_c, B_c, C_c, V_c \rangle$ *where:*

- W_c *is the set of all maximal consistent subsets of* $\mathcal{L}_{L\text{-}INF}$;

- $\mathcal{R}_c = \{R_{c,i}\}_{i \in Agt}$ *is a collection of equivalence relations on* W_c *such that, for every* $i \in Agt$ *and* $w, v \in W_c$, $wR_{c,i}v$ *if and only if (for all* φ, $\mathbf{K}_i \varphi \in w$ *implies* $\varphi \in v$)
- *For* $w \in W_c$, $\varphi \in \mathcal{L}_{L\text{-}INF}$ *let* $A_\varphi(i, w) = \{v \in R_{c,i}(w) \mid \varphi \in v\}$. *Then, we put* $N_c(i, w) = \{A_\varphi(i, w) \mid \mathbf{B}_i \varphi \in w\}$.
- $E_c : Agt \times W_c \longrightarrow 2^{\mathcal{L}_{\mathsf{ACT}}}$ *is such that for each* $i \in Agt$ *and* $w, v \in W_c$, *if* $wR_{c,i}v$ *then* $E_c(i, w) = E_c(i, v)$;
- $B_c : Agt \times W_c \longrightarrow \mathbb{N}$ *is such that for each* $i \in Agt$ *and* $w, v \in W_c$, *if* $wR_{c,i}v$ *then* $B_c(i, w) = B_c(i, v)$;
- $C_c : Agt \times \mathcal{L}_{\mathsf{ACT}} \times W_c \longrightarrow \mathbb{N}$ *is such that for each* $i \in Agt$, $\alpha \in \mathcal{L}_{\mathsf{ACT}}$, *and* $w, v \in W_c$, *if* $wR_{c,i}v$ *then* $C_c(i, \alpha, w) = C_c(i, \alpha, v)$;
- $V_c : W_c \longrightarrow 2^{Atm}$ *is such that* $V_c(w) = Atm \cap w$.

Note that, analogously to what done before, $R_{c,i}(w)$ denotes the set $\{v \in W_c \mid wR_{c,i}v\}$, for each $i \in Agt$.

It is easy to verify that M_c is an *L-INF* model as defined in Definition 1, since, it satisfies conditions (**C1**),(**C2**),(**D1**),(**E1**),(**F1**). Hence, it models the axioms and the inference rules (1)–(17) introduced before. Consequently, the following properties hold too. Let $w \in W_c$, then

- given $\varphi \in \mathcal{L}_{L\text{-}INF}$, it holds that $\mathbf{K}_i \varphi \in w$ if and only if $\forall v \in W_c$ such that $wR_{c,i}v$ we have $\varphi \in v$;
- for $\varphi \in \mathcal{L}_{L\text{-}INF}$, if $\mathbf{B}_i \varphi \in w$ and $wR_{c,i}v$ then $\mathbf{B}_i \varphi \in v$;

Thus, $R_{c,i}$-related worlds have the same knowledge and N_c-related worlds have the same beliefs. By proceeding similarly to what is done in [2] we obtain the proof of strong completeness. Let us start with some preliminary results:

Lemma 1. *For all* $w \in W_c$ *and* $\mathbf{B}_i \varphi, \mathbf{B}_i \psi \in \mathcal{L}_{L\text{-}INF}$, *if* $\mathbf{B}_i \varphi \in w$ *but* $\mathbf{B}_i \psi \notin w$, *it follows that there exists* $v \in R_{c,i}(w)$ *such that* $\varphi \in v \leftrightarrow \psi \notin v$.

Proof. Let $w \in W_c$ and φ, ψ be such that $\mathbf{B}_i \varphi \in w$ and $\mathbf{B}_i \psi \notin w$. Assume now that for every $v \in R_{c,i}(w)$ we have $\varphi \in v \wedge \psi \in v$ or $\varphi \notin v \wedge \psi \notin v$; then, from previous statements it follows that $\mathbf{K}_i(\varphi \leftrightarrow \psi) \in w$ so that by axiom (6), $\mathbf{B}_i \psi \in w$ which is a contradiction.

Lemma 2. *For all* $\varphi \in \mathcal{L}_{L\text{-}INF}$ *and* $w \in W_c$ *it holds that* $\varphi \in w$ *iff* $M_c, w \models \varphi$.

Proof. We have to prove the statement for all $\varphi \in \mathcal{L}_{L\text{-}INF}$. The proof is by induction on the structure of formulas. For instance, if $\varphi = p$ and $w \in W_c$, then $p \in w$ iff $p \in V_c(w)$ and this means that $M_c, w \models p$ by the semantics defined in Sect. 2.2. The case of formulas of the form $\mathbf{B}_i \varphi$ is the most involved: assume $\mathbf{B}_i \varphi \in w$ for $w \in W_c$. We have that $A_\varphi(i, w) = \{v \in R_{c,i}(w) \mid \varphi \in v\}$. By the definition of W_c and of $\| \cdot \|_{i,w}^M$ in Sect. 2.2, we have $A_\varphi(i, w) = \| \varphi \|_{i,w}^{M_c} \cap R_{c,i}(w)$. Hence, by the definition of $N_c(i, w)$ it follows that $\mathbf{B}_i \varphi \in w$ and then, $M_c, w \models \mathbf{B}_i \varphi$.

Suppose $\mathbf{B}_i \varphi \notin w$, so $\neg \mathbf{B}_i \varphi \in w$ and we have to prove $\| \varphi \|_w^{M_c} \cap R_{c,i}(w) \notin N_c(i, w)$. Choose $A \in N_c(i, w)$: by definition we know that $A = A_\psi(i, w)$ for some ψ with $\mathbf{B}_i \psi \in w$. By Lemma 1 there is some $v \in R_{c,i}(w)$ such that $\varphi \in v \leftrightarrow \psi \notin v$. By induction hypothesis, we obtain that either $v \in (\| \varphi \|_w^{M_c} \cap R_{c,i}(w)) \setminus A_\psi(i, w)$

or $v_I \in A_\psi(i, w) \setminus (\parallel \varphi \parallel_{i,w}^{M_c} \cap R_{c,i}(w))$ holds. Consequently, in both cases, $A_\psi(i, w) \neq \parallel \varphi \parallel_{i,w}^{M_c} \cap R_{c,i}(w)$. Thanks to the arbitrariness in the choice of A in $N_c(i, w)$ we conclude that $\parallel \varphi \parallel_{i,w}^{M_c} \cap R_{c,i}(w) \notin N_c(i, w)$. Hence $M_c, w \not\models \mathbf{B}_i \varphi$.

A crucial result states that each *L-DINF* formula has an equivalent *L-INF* formula:

Lemma 3. *For all $\varphi \in \mathcal{L}_{L\text{-}DINF}$ there exists $\tilde{\varphi} \in \mathcal{L}_{L\text{-}INF}$ such that L-DINF $\vdash \varphi \leftrightarrow \tilde{\varphi}$.*

Proof. We have to prove the statement for all $\varphi \in \mathcal{L}_{L\text{-}DINF}$ but we show the proof only for $\varphi = p$, because the others are proved analogously. By the axiom (9) we have $[G : \alpha]p \leftrightarrow p$, and by rule (3) we have $\dfrac{[G:\alpha]p \leftrightarrow p}{\varphi \leftrightarrow \varphi[[G:\alpha]p/p]}$ which means that we can obtain $\tilde{\varphi}$ by replacing $[G : \alpha]p$ with p in φ.

The previous lemmas allow us to prove the following theorems.

Theorem 1. *L-INF is strongly complete for the class of L-INF models.*

Proof. Any consistent set φ may be extended to a maximal consistent set of formulas $w^\star \in W_c$ and $M_c, w^\star \models \varphi$ by Lemma 2. Then, *L-INF* is strongly complete for the class of *L-INF* models.

Theorem 2. *L-DINF is strongly complete for the class of L-INF models.*

Proof. If K is a consistent set of $\mathcal{L}_{L\text{-}DINF}$ formulas then, by Lemma 3, we can obtain the set $\hat{K} = \{\tilde{\varphi} \mid \varphi \in K\}$, which is a consistent set of $\mathcal{L}_{L\text{-}INF}$ formulas. By Theorem 1 $M_c, w \models \hat{K}$. Since *L-DINF* is sound and for each $\varphi \in K$, *L-DINF* $\vdash \varphi \leftrightarrow \tilde{\varphi}$, and it follows $M_c, w \models K$ then *L-DINF* is strongly complete for the class of *L-INF* models.

4 Discussion and Future Work

In this paper we discussed some cognitive aspects of autonomous systems, concerning executability of actions in a group of agents, depending upon the available budget. To model these aspects we have proposed the new epistemic logic *L-DINF*, that we have shown "at work" via an example, and of which we have proved some useful properties among which strong completeness. The logic is easily extensible to accommodate kinds of resources, and kinds of agents' "roles", meaning capabilities of executing actions, and amounts they are required to spend according to their role.

The complexity of other logics which are based on the same principles as ours (Kripke semantics, canonical models, update of the neighborhood upon performing mental actions, proof of strong completeness via a standard canonical-model argument) has been thoroughly studied, thus, 'mutatis mutandis', we can borrow from there. After re-perusing those proofs we can in fact safely claim that, like in the analogous cases, the satisfiability problem is NP-complete in the single-agent case and it is, instead, PSPACE-complete in the multi-agent case.

Concerning related work, in alternating time temporal logics [23] costs appears explicitly in the language, and it is even possible to ask, e.g., what is the minimal amount of a resource that makes a given goal achievable; but, decision problems are strictly more complex. However, in the present work we did not intend to design a logic to reason about coalitions and strategies like done, e.g., in [23], rather we meant to model the internal mental processes of an agent which is a member of a group, with a certain "role". In this sense the two approaches are orthogonal rather than in competition. There has been a considerable amount of work on logics concerning coalitions' strategic abilities where agents' actions consume resources, or both produce and consume resources. For a review of this work and a discussion of the complexity of this kind of logics, the reader may refer to [1]. We have done ourselves some work on resource consumption/production, with preferences concerning which resources to spend or to save [9–12], for the single-agent case; the add-on is that we have devised a prototypical (freely available) implementation (see http://users.dimi.uniud.it/~andrea.formisano/raspberry/).

In future work, we mean to extend our logic so as to integrate temporal aspects, i.e., in which instant or time interval an action has been or should be performed, and how this may affect resource usage, and agent's and group's functioning.

References

1. Alechina, N., Demri, S., Logan, B.: Parameterised resource-bounded ATL. In: The Thirty-Fourth AAAI Conference on Artificial Intelligence, AAAI 2020, The Thirty-Second Innovative Applications of Artificial Intelligence Conference, IAAI 2020, The Tenth AAAI Symposium on Educational Advances in Artificial Intelligence, EAAI 2020, New York, NY, USA, 7–12 February 2020, pp. 7040–7046. AAAI Press (2020)
2. Balbiani, P., Duque, D.F., Lorini, E.: A logical theory of belief dynamics for resource-bounded agents. In: Proceedings of the 2016 International Conference on Autonomous Agents & Multiagent Systems, AAMAS 2016, pp. 644–652. ACM (2016)
3. Balbiani, P., Fernández-Duque, D., Lorini, E.: The dynamics of epistemic attitudes in resource-bounded agents. Studia Logica 107(3), 457–488 (2019)
4. van Benthem, J., Pacuit, E.: Dynamic logics of evidence-based beliefs. Studia Logica 99(1–3), 61–92 (2011)
5. Costantini, S., Tocchio, A.: A logic programming language for multi-agent systems. In: Flesca, S., Greco, S., Ianni, G., Leone, N. (eds.) JELIA 2002. LNCS (LNAI), vol. 2424, pp. 1–13. Springer, Heidelberg (2002). https://doi.org/10.1007/3-540-45757-7_1
6. Costantini, S., Tocchio, A.: The DALI logic programming agent-oriented language. In: Alferes, J.J., Leite, J. (eds.) JELIA 2004. LNCS (LNAI), vol. 3229, pp. 685–688. Springer, Heidelberg (2004). https://doi.org/10.1007/978-3-540-30227-8_57
7. Costantini, S., De Gasperis, G.: Flexible goal-directed agents' behavior via DALI mass and ASP modules. In: 2018 AAAI Spring Symposia, Stanford University, Palo Alto, California, USA, 26–28 March 2018. AAAI Press (2018)
8. Costantini, S., De Gasperis, G., Nazzicone, G.: DALI for cognitive robotics: principles and prototype implementation. In: Lierler, Y., Taha, W. (eds.) PADL 2017. LNCS, vol. 10137, pp. 152–162. Springer, Cham (2017). https://doi.org/10.1007/978-3-319-51676-9_10
9. Costantini, S., Formisano, A.: Modeling preferences and conditional preferences on resource consumption and production in ASP. J. Algorithms 64(1), 3–15 (2009). https://doi.org/10.1016/j.jalgor.2009.02.002
10. Costantini, S., Formisano, A.: Answer set programming with resources. J. Log. Comput. 20(2), 533–571 (2010). https://doi.org/10.1093/logcom/exp071

11. Costantini, S., Formisano, A.: Weight constraints with preferences in ASP. In: Delgrande, J.P., Faber, W. (eds.) LPNMR 2011. LNCS (LNAI), vol. 6645, pp. 229–235. Springer, Heidelberg (2011). https://doi.org/10.1007/978-3-642-20895-9_24
12. Costantini, S., Formisano, A., Petturiti, D.: Extending and implementing RASP. Fundam. Inform. **105**(1–2), 1–33 (2010)
13. Costantini, S., Formisano, A., Pitoni, V.: Timed memory in resource-bounded agents. In: Ghidini, C., Magnini, B., Passerini, A., Traverso, P. (eds.) AI*IA 2018. LNCS (LNAI), vol. 11298, pp. 15–29. Springer, Cham (2018). https://doi.org/10.1007/978-3-030-03840-3_2
14. Costantini, S., Pitoni, V.: Memory management in resource-bounded agents. In: Alviano, M., Greco, G., Scarcello, F. (eds.) AI*IA 2019. LNCS (LNAI), vol. 11946, pp. 46–58. Springer, Cham (2019). https://doi.org/10.1007/978-3-030-35166-3_4
15. De Gasperis, G., Costantini, S., Nazzicone, G.: Dali multi agent systems framework. DALI GitHub Software Repository, July 2014, DALI. http://github.com/AAAI-DISIM-UnivAQ/DALI. https://doi.org/10.5281/zenodo.11042
16. Duc, H.N.: Reasoning about rational, but not logically omniscient, agents. J. Log. Comput. **7**(5), 633–648 (1997)
17. Elgot-Drapkin, J., Kraus, S., Miller, M., Nirkhe, M., Perlis, D.: Active logics: a unified formal approach to episodic reasoning. Technical report, UMIACS–University of Maryland (1999). cS-TR-4072
18. Elgot-Drapkin, J.J., Miller, M.I., Perlis, D.: Life on a desert island: ongoing work on realtime reasoning. In: Brown, F.M. (ed.) The Frame Problem in Artificial Intelligence, pp. 349–357. Morgan Kaufmann (1987)
19. Fagin, R., Halpern, J.Y.: Belief, awareness, and limited reasoning. Artif. Intell. **34**(1), 39–76 (1987)
20. Goldman, A., et al.: Theory of mind. In: The Oxford Handbook of Philosophy of Cognitive Science, vol. 1. Oxford University Press (2018)
21. Herzig, A., Lorini, E., Pearce, D.: Social intelligence. AI Soc. **34**(4), 689 (2019)
22. Jago, M.: Epistemic logic for rule-based agents. Journal Logic Lang. Inf. **18**(1), 131–158 (2009)
23. Nguyen, H.N., Alechina, N., Logan, B., Rakib, A.: Alternating-time temporal logic with resource bounds. J. Log. Comput. **28**(4), 631–663 (2018)
24. Pitoni, V., Costantini, S.: A temporal module for logical frameworks. In: Bogaerts, B., et al. (eds.) Proceedings of ICLP 2019 (Technical communications). EPTCS, vol. 306, pp. 340–346 (2019)
25. Velázquez-Quesada, F.R.: Explicit and implicit knowledge in neighbourhood models. In: Grossi, D., Roy, O., Huang, H. (eds.) LORI 2013. LNCS, vol. 8196, pp. 239–252. Springer, Heidelberg (2013). https://doi.org/10.1007/978-3-642-40948-6_19
26. Velázquez-Quesada, F.R.: Dynamic epistemic logic for implicit and explicit beliefs. Journal Logic Lang. Inf. **23**(2), 107–140 (2014)
27. Weyhrauch, R.W.: Prolegomena to a theory of mechanized formal reasoning. Artif. Intell. **13**(1–2), 133–170 (1980)

Epistemic Reasoning About Rationality and Bids in Auctions

Munyque Mittelmann[1]([✉]), Andreas Herzig[2], and Laurent Perrussel[1]

[1] Université de Toulouse - IRIT, Toulouse, France
{munyque.mittelmann,andreas.herzig,laurent.perrussel}@irit.fr
[2] Université de Toulouse - IRIT-CNRS, Toulouse, France

Abstract. In this paper, we investigate strategic reasoning in the context of auctions. More precisely, we establish an explicit link between bidding actions and bounded rationality. To do so, we extend the Auction Description Language with an epistemic operator and an action choice operator and use it to represent a classical auction where agents have imperfect information about other agents' valuations. We formalize bounded rationality concepts in iterative protocols and show how to use them to reason about the players' actions. Finally, we provide a model checking algorithm.

Keywords: Logics for multi-agent systems · Game description language · Bounded rationality · Auction-based markets

1 Introduction

Building a General Auction Player is similar to the General Game Playing (GGP) challenge [9], it aims at designing an agent that can participate in an auction while discovering the rules governing it. As for games, there is a wide variety of auction-based markets. Auctions may differ in the participants' type (e.g., only buyers, both buyers and sellers, ...), the kind and amount of goods being auctioned, the bidding protocol, and the allocation and payment rules [13].

Inspired by the Game Description Language (GDL), which is a logic programming language for representing and reasoning about game rules [9], we defined a general language to describe auction-based markets from the auctioneer perspective [15]: *Auction Description Language* (ADL). In this paper, we consider the player's perspective and our goal is to show how an agent may reason about the rules governing an auction and also about their knowledge of other agents' valuations for eliciting her bid. More precisely, we show that computing a rational bid requires to assume that other agents are also bidding rationally. Following [2], we understand 'rational' as 'not playing dominated actions'.

This research is supported by the ANR project AGAPE ANR-18-CE23-0013 and by the EU project TAILOR (EU Horizon 2020 program, GA No 952215).

W. Faber et al. (Eds.): JELIA 2021, LNAI 12678, pp. 116–130, 2021.
https://doi.org/10.1007/978-3-030-75775-5_9

Our contribution is twofold. We first extend ADL with knowledge operators from Epistemic GDL [12] and the action modality from the GDL variant proposed in [21]. This extension aims at providing the ground for the design of General Auction Players. Second, we characterize rationality along two dimensions: (i) the impact of the level of higher-order knowledge about other agents and (ii) the impact of looking-ahead beyond the next action to be executed. We also explore the complexity of model-checking for evaluating rationality.

Related Work. To the best of our knowledge, there is no contribution that focuses on the strategic dimension of auctions through a logical perspective. However, numerous contributions define logical systems for representing games and representing strategic reasoning. GGP uses the Game Description Language (GDL) [9] for representing games. The Auction Description Language (ADL) [15] extends GDL by handling numerical variables, a key feature for representing an auction mechanism with its allocation and payment rules.

Alternating-time Temporal Logic (ATL) [1] provides a logic-based analysis of strategic decisions. Strategy Logic (SL) generalizes ATL with first-order quantifications over strategies [4]. These approaches cannot model the internal structures of strategies, which makes it difficult to easily design strategies aiming to achieve a goal state. A logic for reasoning about composite strategies in turn-based games is introduced in [17], where strategies are treated as programs that are combined by PDL-like connectives. Zhang and Thielscher [22] present a variant of GDL to describe game strategies, where strategies can be understood as moves for a player. However, their work can only model turn-based games.

To incorporate imperfect information games, GDL has been extended to GDL-II [18] and GDL-III [19]. GDL-II and GDL-III aim at describing the rules of an imperfect information game, but do not provide tools for reasoning about how a player infers information based on these rules. All these logics face decidability and tractability issues: their expressive power prevents them from being implemented realistically in an artificial agent. Jiang et al. [12] propose an epistemic extension of GDL (EGDL) to represent and reason about imperfect information games. Their language allows us to represent the rules in the imperfect information setting. A key characteristic of EGDL is that it manages the balance between expressiveness and computational complexity of model checking (Δ_2^P).

Epistemic Game Theory (EGT) considers strategic reasoning with uncertain information and is about the interplay between knowledge, belief and rationality [3,14]. More precisely, EGT shows how dominated strategies may be eliminated in an iterative manner [2]. These contributions however require perfect reasoners, who can reason about higher-order knowledge at arbitrary depth, which is unrealistic. In [5], the authors abandon this hypothesis but do not propose a full logic detailing the impact of bounded rationality.

Structure of the Paper. The remainder of the paper proceeds as follows. In Sect. 2, we define the models of E-ADL in terms of State-Transition structures. In Sect. 3 we present the language and its semantics and illustrate our approach

by describing a Dutch auction. In Sect. 4 we show how to express bounded rationality with higher-order knowledge. In Sect. 5 we present the model-checking
algorithm. Section 6 concludes the paper.

2 Auctions as State-Transition Models

In this section, we introduce a logical framework for reasoning about auction
protocols while considering imperfect information. The framework is based on
ADL [15] and Epistemic GDL [11]. We call the framework *Epistemic Auction
Description Language*, denoted by E-ADL.

Definition 1. *An auction signature $\mathcal{S}$ is a tuple $(N, V, \mathcal{A}, \Phi, Y)$, where: (i)
$N = \{1, 2, \cdots, n\}$ is a nonempty finite set of agents; (ii) $V \subset \mathbb{Z}$ is a finite subset
of integer numbers representing the range of valuations, bids and payments; (iii)
$\mathcal{A} = \bigcup_{r \in N} A^r$, where each A^r consists of a nonempty finite set of actions performed by agent $r \in N$ and $A^r \cap A^s = \emptyset$ if $r \neq s$. For convenience, we may write
a^r for denoting an action in A^r; (iv) $\Phi = \{p, q, \cdots\}$ is a finite set of atomic
propositions for specifying individual features of a state; (v) $Y = \{y_1, y_2, \cdots\}$ is
a finite set of numerical variables for specifying numerical features of a state.*

We assume a total order among the agents in N, denoted by $\prec$, where $r \prec i$
means that agent r precedes agent i in $\prec$; it will be used to break ties in winner
determination. Throughout the rest of the paper, we fix an auction signature
$\mathcal{S}$ and all concepts will be based on this signature, except if stated otherwise.
We adopt a semantics based on state-transition models. This is more suitable
for describing the dynamics than stable models that were initially considered for
GDL and GGP [9].

Definition 2. *A state transition ST-model M is a tuple $(W, I, T, \{R_r\}_{r \in N}$,
$U, \pi_\Phi, \pi_Y)$, where: (i) W is a finite nonempty set of states; (ii) $I \subseteq W$ is a
set of initial states; (iii) $T \subseteq W \setminus I$ is a set of terminal states; (iv) $R_r \subseteq W \times W$
is an equivalence relation for agent r, indicating the states that are indistin-
guishable for r; (v) $U : W \times (\prod_{r \in N} A^r) \to W$ is an update function, specifying
the transitions for each combination of joint actions; (vi) $\pi_\Phi : W \to 2^\Phi$ is the
valuation function for the state propositions; and (vii) $\pi_Y : W \times Y \to V$ is the
valuation function for the numerical variables.*

For a group of agents $G \in 2^N \setminus \{\emptyset\}$, we write $d^G \in \prod_{r \in G} A^r$ to denote a joint
action of the agents in G. We denote by d^r the individual action for agent $r \in G$
in the joint action d^G. When $G = N$ then we omit N and simply write d instead
of d^N. Let $R_r(w)$ denote the set of all states that agent r cannot distinguish from
w, i.e., $R_r(w) = \{u \in W : wR_r u\}$.

For every $w \in W$ and $d \in \prod_{r \in N} A^r$, we call (w, d) a *move*. Given a group of
agents $G \in 2^N \setminus \{\emptyset\}$, we write $(w, \langle d^G, d^{-G} \rangle)$ instead of (w, d) when we want to
talk about G's part in (w, d), where $d^{-G} \in \prod_{s \in N \setminus G} A^s$ denotes the actions of all
the agents except those in G in the joint action d. Our notion of move resembles
the turn-based definition proposed in [21] and [22].

Definition 3. *Two moves (w, d) and (u, e) are equivalent for agent r, written $(w, d) \approx_r (u, e)$, iff $w R_r u$ and $d^r = e^r$.*

Clearly relation $\approx_r$ is reflexive, transitive and symmetric. Differently from standard GDL, our semantics is based on moves instead of paths. This allows the agent to reason about the effects of actions without exploring all ways the game could proceed (i.e., all the reachable states in each complete path where she takes this action). In E-ADL, we define the action execution modality in games with synchronous moves. The idea of move-based semantics and action modalities stems from [21]. Their approach is restricted to turn-based games, where only one action can be performed at a given state.

3 Epistemic Auction Description Language

The *Epistemic Auction Description Language* (E-ADL) is a framework to allow epistemic reasoning for auction players. First, we introduce the syntax.

3.1 Syntax

Let $z \in \mathcal{L}_z$ be a numerical term defined as follows: $z ::= t \mid add(z, z) \mid sub(z, z) \mid min(z, z) \mid max(z, z) \mid times(z, z) \mid y$, where $t \in V$, $y \in Y$. The meaning of numerical terms is the natural one; for instance, the term $min(z_1, z_2)$ specifies the minimum value between z_1 and z_2. Finally, y denotes the value of the variable $y \in Y$ in the current state.

A formula in E-ADL, denoted $\varphi \in \mathcal{L}_{\text{E-ADL}}$, is defined by the following BNF:

$$\varphi ::= p \mid z \otimes z \mid r \prec r \mid initial \mid terminal \mid does(a^r) \mid \neg\varphi \mid \varphi \wedge \varphi \mid \mathsf{K}_r\varphi \mid [d^G]\varphi$$

where $p \in \Phi$, $r \in \mathrm{N}$, $\otimes \in \{>, <, =\}$, $a^r \in \mathcal{A}$, $G \in 2^{\mathrm{N}} \setminus \{\emptyset\}$, $d^G \in \prod_{r \in G} \mathrm{A}^r$ and $z \in \mathcal{L}_z$. Other connectives $\vee, \to, \leftrightarrow, \top$ and $\bot$ are defined by $\neg$ and $\wedge$ in the standard way. The comparison operators $\leq, \geq$ and $\neq$ are defined by $\vee, >$, $<$ and $=$. The extension of the operators $>, <$ and $=$ and numerical terms $max(z_1, z_2), min(z_1, z_2), add(z_1, z_2)$ to multiple arguments is straightforward. The formula $r_1 \prec r_2$ denotes the tie-breaking priority of r_1 over r_2.

Intuitively, *initial* and *terminal* specify the initial and the terminal states, respectively; $does(a^r)$ asserts that agent r takes action a^r at the current move. The epistemic operator K_r is taken from the Epistemic Logic [7]. The formula $\mathsf{K}_r\varphi$ is read as "agent r knows that φ". The action execution operator comes from the GDL variant with action modalities [21] and the formula $[d^G]\varphi$ means that if joint action d^G is executed, φ will be true next. The abbreviation $does(d^G)$ specifies that each agent in G performs her respective action in d^G, that is, $does(d^G) \stackrel{\text{def}}{=} \bigwedge_{r \in G} does(d^r)$. As in [21], we use the action modality to define the temporal operator $\bigcirc$:

$$\bigcirc\varphi =_{def} \bigvee_{d \in \prod_{r \in \mathrm{N}} \mathrm{A}^r} (does(d) \wedge [d]\varphi)$$

The formula $\bigcirc\varphi$ reads "φ will be true next". We also use the following abbreviation from Epistemic Logic: $\widehat{\mathsf{K}}_r\varphi =_{def} \neg\mathsf{K}_r\neg\varphi$ where $\widehat{\mathsf{K}}_r\varphi$ represents that "φ is compatible with agent r's knowledge". Given $j > 0$ and $G \in 2^{\mathrm{N}} \setminus \{\emptyset\}$, we write $\sigma^G = (\prod_{r \in G} \mathrm{A}^r)^j$ for a sequence of joint actions for G. The i-th joint action in σ^G is noted σ_i^G. Finally, define $[\,\sigma^G\,]^j\,\varphi$, for $|\sigma^G| = j$ by induction of j:

$$[\,\sigma^G\,]^1\,\varphi \stackrel{\mathrm{def}}{=} [\,\sigma^G\,]\varphi$$

$$[\,\sigma^G\,]^{j+1}\,\varphi \stackrel{\mathrm{def}}{=} [\,\sigma^G\,][\,\sigma_j^G\,]\varphi$$

The formula $[\,\sigma^G\,]^j\,\varphi$ means that if the group G followed the sequence of joint actions described by σ^G for the next j stages, then φ would hold.

3.2 Semantics

The semantics for E-ADL is given in two steps. First, function f interprets the meaning of numerical terms $z \in \mathcal{L}_z$. Next, a formula $\varphi \in \mathcal{L}_{\text{E-ADL}}$ is interpreted with respect to a move. In Definition 4, we specify function f to evaluate the meaning of any $z \in \mathcal{L}_z$ in a move.

Definition 4. *Let* M *be an ST-Model. Define Function* $f : W \times (\prod_{r \in \mathrm{N}} \mathrm{A}^r) \times \mathcal{L}_z \to \mathbb{Z}$, *assigning any* $w \in W$, $d \in \prod_{r \in \mathrm{N}} \mathrm{A}^r$, *and* $z \in \mathcal{L}_z$ *to a number in* $\mathbb{Z}$:
If z *is on the form* $add(z', z'')$, $sub(z', z'')$, $min(z', z'')$, $max(z', z'')$ *or* $times(z', z'')$, *then* $f(w, d, z)$ *is defined through the application of the corresponding mathematical operators and functions over* $f(w, d, z')$ *and* $f(w, d, z'')$. *Otherwise,* $f(w, d, z) = z$ *if* $z \in V$ *and* $f(w, d, z) = \pi_Y(w, z)$ *if* $z \in Y$.

Definition 5. *Let* M *be an ST-Model. Given a move* (w, d), *where* $w \in W$ *and* $d \in \prod_{r \in \mathrm{N}} \mathrm{A}^r$, *and a formula* $\varphi \in \mathcal{L}_{ADL}$, *we say that* φ *is true in the move* (w, d) *under* M, *denoted by* $M \models_{(w,d)} \varphi$, *according to the following rules:*

$M \models_{(w,d)} p$ *iff* $p \in \pi_\Phi(w)$

$M \models_{(w,d)} \neg\varphi$ *iff* $M \not\models_{(w,d)} \varphi$

$M \models_{(w,d)} \varphi_1 \wedge \varphi_2$ *iff* $M \models_{(w,d)} \varphi_1$ *and* $M \models_{(w,d)} \varphi_2$

$M \models_{(w,d)} initial$ *iff* $w \in I$

$M \models_{(w,d)} terminal$ *iff* $w \in T$

$M \models_{(w,d)} r_1 \prec r_2$ *iff* $r_1 \prec r_2$

$M \models_{(w,d)} does(a^r)$ *iff* $d^r = a^r$

$M \models_{(w,d)} z_1 \otimes z_2$ *iff* $f(w, d, z_1) \otimes f(w, d, z_2)$, *where* $\otimes \in \{>, <, =\}$

$M \models_{(w,d)} \mathsf{K}_r\varphi$ *iff for every* $u \in W$ *and* $e \in \prod_{s \in \mathrm{N}} \mathrm{A}^s$, *if* $(w, d) \approx_r (u, e)$, *then* $M \models_{(u,e)} \varphi$

$M \models_{(w,d)} [b^G]\varphi$ *iff* $M \models_{(U(w,e),c)} \varphi$, *where* $e = \langle b^G, d^{-G}\rangle$, *for every* $c \in \prod_{r \in \mathrm{N}} \mathrm{A}^r$

A formula φ is *globally true* in an ST-Model M, written $M \models \varphi$, if $M \models_{(w,d)} \varphi$ for all $w \in W$ and $d \in \prod_{r \in \mathrm{N}} \mathrm{A}^r$. Finally, let Σ be a set of formulas in $\mathcal{L}_{\text{E-ADL}}$, then M is a *model* of Σ if $M \models \varphi$ for all $\varphi \in \Sigma$.

Each K_r is a normal modal operator. It satisfies that if all r-accessible worlds agree on φ then r knows either φ or $\neg\varphi$. If φ is true then r knows that φ.

Proposition 1. *Let* M *be an ST-Model,* $r \in \mathrm{N}$ *be an agent and* $\varphi \in \mathcal{L}_{E\text{-}ADL}$ *be a formula, then* $\mathrm{M} \models \varphi \rightarrow \mathrm{K}_r \varphi$ *if and only if for all* $w, u \in \mathrm{W}$ *and all* $d, e \in \prod_{r \in \mathrm{N}} \mathrm{A}^r$ *such that* $(w, d) \approx_r (u, e)$, $\mathrm{M} \models_{(w,d)} \varphi$ *iff* $\mathrm{M} \models_{(u,e)} \varphi$.

It follows from the equivalence relation $\approx_r$ that agent r knows the actions she performs. This is similar to the uniform strategies in Alternating-time Temporal Epistemic Logic [10] and Dynamic Epistemic Logic [20].

Proposition 2. *For any agent* $r \in \mathrm{N}$, *action* $a^r \in \mathrm{A}^r$, *formula* $\varphi \in \mathcal{L}_{E\text{-}ADL}$, *number of steps* $j > 0$, *group of agents* $G \in 2^{\mathrm{N}} \setminus \{\emptyset\}$ *and* $\sigma^r \in (\prod_{r \in G} \mathrm{A}^r)^j$:

1. $\mathrm{M} \models does(a^r) \rightarrow \mathrm{K}_r does(a^r)$
2. *If* $\mathrm{M} \models [\sigma^G]^j \varphi$ *then* $\mathrm{M} \models \mathrm{K}_r [\sigma^G]^j \varphi$
3. *If* $\mathrm{M} \models [\sigma^G]^j \mathrm{K}_r \varphi$ *then* $\mathrm{M} \models \mathrm{K}_r [\sigma^G]^j \varphi$

Let us now illustrate how to represent an auction-based protocol in E-ADL, namely, a Dutch auction. First, we show the syntactical representation through E-ADL-formulas. Later, we address the semantical representation.

3.3   Running Example: Dutch Auction

In a Dutch auction, the auctioneer starts by proposing a high asking price. The price is decreased until it reaches a predefined reserve price or some bidder shows interest at purchasing the good. The auction then ends and the object is sold at the given price to the bidder who signaled her interest [13].

Let $\mathcal{S}_{\mathrm{dut}}$ be an auction signature and starting, reserve $\in \mathrm{N}$, dec, n $\in \mathrm{N} \setminus \{0\}$ be constant values. The constants starting, reserve, dec, n represent the starting and reserve prices, the decrement in each round and the number of agents, respectively. The auction signature is defined as follows: $\mathcal{S}_{\mathrm{dut}} = (\mathrm{N}_{\mathrm{dut}}, \mathrm{V}_{\mathrm{dut}}, \mathcal{A}_{\mathrm{dut}}, \Phi_{\mathrm{dut}}, \mathrm{Y}_{\mathrm{dut}})$, where $\mathrm{N}_{\mathrm{dut}} = \{1, \ldots, n\}$, $\mathrm{V}_{\mathrm{dut}} = \{0, \ldots, \mathrm{starting}\}$, $\mathcal{A}_{\mathrm{dut}} = \{\mathrm{bid}_r, \mathrm{wait}_r : r \in \mathrm{N}_{\mathrm{dut}}\}$, $\Phi_{\mathrm{dut}} = \{winner_r : r \in \mathrm{N}\}$ and $\mathrm{Y}_{\mathrm{dut}} = \{\mathrm{payment}_r, \vartheta_r : r \in \mathrm{N}\}$. The numerical variables $\mathrm{payment}_r$ and ϑ_r specify the payment and the private valuation for an agent r.

Syntactical Representation. The rules of the Dutch auction are formulated by E-ADL-formulas as shown in Fig. 1.

In an initial state, the price starts at starting and there is no winner (Rule 1). If an agent is a winner, she pays the current price. Otherwise, she does not pay anything (Rules 2 and 3). The terminal state is reached when it is not possible to decrease the price anymore or there is a winner (Rule 4). While not in the terminal state, the price either decreases if no agent bids or the price is settled if some agent accepted to purchase the good (Rules 5 and 6). If only one agent accepts, she is marked as the winner. In case two or more agents bid, the winner is assigned according to the tie-breaking rule. Rules 7 and 8 ensure no proposition or numerical variable change its value after a terminal state. Finally, Rule 9 specifies that each agent is aware of how much she valuates the good. Let Σ_{dut} be the set of Rules 1–9.

1. *initial* $\leftrightarrow$ price = starting $\wedge \bigwedge_{r \in N_{dut}} \neg winner_r$
2. *winner*$_r$ $\rightarrow$ payment$_r$ = price, for each $r \in N_{dut}$
3. $\neg winner_r$ $\rightarrow$ payment$_r$ = 0, for each $r \in N_{dut}$
4. *terminal* $\leftrightarrow$ sub(price, dec) < reserve $\vee \bigvee_{r \in N_{dut}} winner_r$
5. $\neg terminal \wedge$ price = $x \wedge \bigwedge_{r \in N_{dut}} does(\text{wait}_r) \rightarrow \bigcirc$(price = sub(price, dec) $\wedge$ $\bigwedge_{r \in N_{dut}} \neg winner_r$), for each $x \in V_{dut}$
6. $\neg terminal \wedge$ price = $x \wedge does(\text{bid}_r) \wedge \bigwedge_{s \neq r, s \in N_{dut}} (\neg does(\text{bid}_s) \vee r \prec s) \rightarrow$ $\bigcirc(winner_r \wedge \bigwedge_{s \neq r, s \in N_{dut}} \neg winner_s)$, for each $x \in V_{dut}$ and each $r \in N_{dut}$
7. *terminal* $\wedge y = x \rightarrow \bigcirc y = x$, for each $y \in Y_{dut}$ and each $x \in V_{dut}$
8. *terminal* $\wedge win \rightarrow \bigcirc win$, for each $win \in \{winner_r, \neg winner_r : r \in N_{dut}\}$
9. $K_r(\vartheta_r = x) \vee K_r \neg(\vartheta_r = x)$, for each $x \in V_{dut}$ and $r \in N_{dut}$

Fig. 1. Dutch auction represented by Σ_{dut}

Model Representation. Let us address the model representation of the Dutch auction. Let us define $\mathcal{M}_{dut}$ as the class of models M_{dut} defined for a signature $\mathcal{S}_{dut}$ and the constants starting, reserve, dec and n. Each $M_{dut} =$ $(W_{dut}, I_{dut}, T_{dut}, \{R_{r,dut}\}_{r \in N}, U_{dut}, \pi_{\Phi,dut}, \pi_{Y,dut})$ is defined as follows:

- $W_{dut} = \{\langle pr, buyer, val_1, \ldots, val_n \rangle : 0 \leq pr \leq$ starting & buyer $\in N_{dut} \cup \{none\}$ & $0 \leq val_r \leq$ starting for each $r \in N_{dut}\}$;
- $I_{dut} = \{\langle$starting, $none, val_1, \ldots, val_n \rangle : 0 \leq val_r \leq$ starting for each $r \in N_{dut}\}$;
- $T_{dut} = \{\langle pr, buyer, val_1, \ldots, val_n \rangle : 0 \leq pr \leq$ starting & buyer $\in N_{dut}$ & $0 \leq val_r \leq$ starting for each $r \in N_{dut}\} \cup \{\langle pr, buyer, val_1, \ldots, val_n \rangle : pr - dec <$ reserve & buyer $\in N_{dut} \cup \{none\}$ & $0 \leq val_r \leq$ starting for each $r \in N_{dut}\}$;
- For each agent $r \in N_{dut}$ and for any two states $w = \langle pr, buyer, val_1, \ldots, val_n \rangle$ and $u = \langle pr', buyer', val_1', \ldots, val_n' \rangle$ in W_{dut}, the relation $R_{r,dut}$ is defined as follows: $wR_{r,dut}u$ iff (i) $pr = pr'$; (ii) buyer = buyer$'$; and (iii) $val_r = val_r'$.
- For all states $w = \langle pr, buyer, val_1, \ldots, val_n \rangle$ and all joint actions $d = (a^r)_{r \in N_{dut}}$, such that $w \in W_{dut}$ and $a^r \in \{bid_r, wait_r\}$, we define U_{dut} as follows:
  - If $w \notin T_{dut}$, then $U_{dut}(w, d) = \langle pr', buyer', val_1, \ldots, val_n \rangle$, such that the components pr' and buyer$'$ are defined as follows: (i) $pr' = pr - dec$ if $a^r = wait_r$, for all $r \in N_{dut}$; otherwise $pr' = pr$; (ii) buyer$' = r$ if $a^r = bid_r$ for some $r \in N$ and for all $s \in N_{dut}$ such that $s \neq r$, either $a^s = wait_s$ or $r \prec s$; otherwise, buyer$' = none$;
  - Otherwise, $U_{dut}(w, d) = w$.
- Finally, for each state $w = \langle pr, buyer, val_1, \ldots, val_n \rangle$, such that $w \in W_{dut}$, let $\pi_{\Phi,dut}(w) = \{winner_r : buyer = r \ \& \ r \in N_{dut}\}$; $\pi_{Y,dut}(w, price) = pr$. For each agent $r \in N_{dut}$, let $\pi_{Y,dut}(w, \vartheta_r) = val_r$ and $\pi_{Y,dut}(w, payment_r) = pr$ if buyer = r. Otherwise, $\pi_{Y,dut}(w, payment_r) = 0$.

Let us assume a model $M_{dut} \in \mathcal{M}_{dut}$ and Σ_{dut} for some $\mathcal{S}_{dut}$ and the constants starting, reserve $\in \mathbb{N}$, dec, n $\in \mathbb{N} \setminus \{0\}$.

Proposition 3. M_{dut} *is an ST-Model and* $M_{dut} \models \Sigma_{dut}$, *i.e.,* M_{dut} *is a model of* Σ_{dut}.

That is, M_{dut} is a sound representation of Σ_{dut}. Notice that as M_{dut} is not the unique model for Σ_{dut}, thereby, the completeness does not hold. It follows from Proposition 1 and 3 that each agent knows the auction rules denoted by Σ_{dut}, that is, $M_{dut} \models \bigwedge_{r \in N}(K_r \Sigma_{dut})$. In the next section, we define rationality in E-ADL.

4   Rationality in Auctions

To characterize rationality of auction players, we assume $\{\vartheta_r, payment_r : r \in N\} \subseteq Y$ and $\{winner_r : r \in N\} \subseteq \Phi$, where $\vartheta_r, payment_r$ and $winner_r$ specify the agents valuation, payment and whether she won the auction, resp. Let $ut \in V$, we denote whether the utility of agent $r \in N$ is equal to ut in a single good and unit auction according to the truth value of the following formula:

$$utility_r = ut \overset{\text{def}}{=} (ut = sub(\vartheta_r, payment_r) \wedge winner_r) \vee$$
$$(ut = -payment_r \wedge \neg winner_r)$$

Note that we can extend the notion of utility to multiple units and goods by including numerical variables representing the agents' allocations and their valuations for such allocations. In this work, we focus on epistemic reasoning about action choice and rationality of auction players. For a discussion on expressivity and hierarchy of valuations functions, the reader may refer to Feige et al. [8].

Similar to the strong strategy dominance (see [14]), we say an action a^r of an agent r is a *strongly dominated action* if and only if, there exists another action b^r of r such that, for all actions a^{-r} of the other agents, playing b^r while others play a^{-r} leads to a better utility than playing a^r while others play a^{-r}. In E-ADL, the agents' utility is captured in a move of a model and the action choice operator allows us to compare what would have happened if a group of agents took a given joint action.

4.1   Rationality

We adapt the weak rationality formalization from [14] to E-ADL formulas. Different from his approach, we consider levels of rationality instead of common knowledge. Our notion of k-order rationality is based on [6]: an agent is k-order rational if she is weakly rational and knows all agents are $(k-1)$-order rational.

GDL-based languages explicit the stages of a game execution through paths (or runs). The game starts from an initial state and the succeeding states are defined according to the agents' joint actions. Since GDL agents choose "on-the-fly strategies" during the game, the players should be able to evaluate the current state of the game and to decide which action they will execute.

Adopting these features from GDL in E-ADL allows us to explicitly model information feedback, which is a key feature in the design of iterative auctions [16]. For instance, in E-ADL, we can describe auctions where the agents are assigned to allocations and payments at any stage, which may be different from their final assignments in the terminal state. For this reason, instead of defining utilities as a function to strategy profiles as in ATL [1], we model the agents' utility as being dependent on the current state of the auction.

We refrase the rationality notions from [6,14] by, at first, considering k-order of knowledge and, second, by taking into account state-based utilities and exploring bounded sequences of actions. A rational agent plays according to her utility after performing an action. When reasoning about iterative auctions, the agent considers her utility after playing according to a sequence of j actions. Since most auction-based markets are finite (in the sense that the auction finishes eventually), it is reasonable to assume the agents only need to include in their reasoning which actions may occur in the next j steps. Given a fixed number of steps $j > 0$, we inductively define that an agent is k-order rational, for $k \leq j$. The base case is that any agent is 0-order rational, that is, $\mathrm{Rat}(r, 0, j) \overset{\mathrm{def}}{=} \top$. For all $k > 0$, we define:

$$\mathrm{Rat}(r, k+1, j) \overset{\mathrm{def}}{=} \mathrm{WR}(r, j) \wedge \mathsf{K}_r \big(\bigwedge_{s \in \mathrm{N}} \mathrm{Rat}(s, k, j) \big)$$

That is, an agent is $(k+1)$-order rational if she is weakly rational when looking j stages ahead and knows every other agent is k rational. Weak rationality is defined by:

$$\mathrm{WR}(r, j) \overset{\mathrm{def}}{=} \bigwedge_{a^r \in \mathrm{A}^r} \big(does(a^r) \rightarrow \bigvee_{\rho^r \in (\mathrm{A}^r)^{j-1}} \mathrm{WRAction}(r, (a^r, \rho^r), j) \big)$$

where

$$\mathrm{WRAction}(r, \sigma^r, j) =_{def} \bigwedge_{\chi^r \in (\mathrm{A}^r)^j} \Big(\bigvee_{\sigma^{-r} \in (\prod_{s \neq r} \mathrm{A}^s)^j} (\widehat{\mathsf{K}}_r does(\sigma_1^{-r}) \wedge$$

$$\bigvee_{ut, ut' \in \mathrm{V}} ([\chi^r, \sigma^{-r}]^j \, utility_r = ut' \wedge [\sigma^r, \sigma^{-r}]^j \, utility_r = ut \wedge ut' \leq ut)) \Big)$$

An agent a^r is weakly rational when reasoning j stages ahead if when she performs an action a^r, there exists a sequence of j actions starting by a^r that is weakly rational for her to follow over j stages. Finally, it is weakly rational for agent r to follow a sequence of actions σ^r for j steps, noted $\mathrm{WRAction}(r, \sigma^r, j)$, if for every other sequence of actions χ^r there exists a sequence of joint actions σ^{-r} that r considers possible to be executed such that her utility after following σ^r for j steps is at least as good as her utility after following χ^r.

Notice that if j is large enough to reach terminal states, the state-based utilities represent strategy-based utility functions. Our definition of rationality requires to assume that all agents are rational: as soon as one is known to be non-rational, it is no longer possible to be k-order rational, for $k > 1$. This requirement entails that looking ahead without considering knowledge leads to consider all actions as rational:

Proposition 4. *For every ST-Model* M, *state* $w \in$ W, *joint action* $d \in \prod_{r \in \mathrm{N}} \mathrm{A}^r$, *agent* $r \in \mathrm{N}$ *and* $j > 0$, *it holds that* M $\models_{(w,d)} does(d^r) \wedge \mathrm{Rat}(r, 0, j)$.

Next, considering higher-order knowledge enables us to eliminate strongly dominated actions.

Theorem 1. *For any ST-Model* M, *state* $w \in W$, *joint action* $d \in \prod_{r \in N} A^r$, $k > 0$, $j > 0$, *agent* $r \in N$ *and action* $a^r \in A^r$, *if* $M \models_{(w,d)} does(a^r) \wedge \text{Rat}(r, k, j)$ *then* $M \models_{(w,d)} does(a^r) \wedge \text{Rat}(r, k-1, j)$.

Proof. Assume $M \models_{(w,d)} does(a^r) \wedge \text{Rat}(r, k, j)$. Thus, $M \models_{(w,d)} does(a^r) \wedge \text{WR}(r,j) \wedge K_r(\bigwedge_{s \in N} \text{Rat}(s, k-1, j))$. Since R_r is reflexive, it follows that $M \models_{(w,d)} does(a^r) \wedge \text{Rat}(r, k-1, j)$.

Note that increasing j may not enable the elimination of actions. The larger j, the more stages will be considered. Ideally, j should be large enough to reach terminal states. However, termination may not be ensured in auction protocols and real world players usually have time restrictions to decide their actions.

4.2   Example: Rationality on the Dutch Auction

Let us consider the Dutch auction from Sect. 3.3. Consider a specific instance M_{dut} in $\mathcal{M}_{dut}$, such that there are only two players r and s whose valuation for the good being auctioned is 7 and 4, respectively. The auctioneer starts by proposing the price 10 and in each round the price is decreased by 1. Formally, $N_{dut} = \{r, s\}$, $V_{dut} = \{0, \ldots, 10\}$, $\mathcal{A}_{dut} = \{bid_r, wait_r, bid_s, wait_s\}$, $\Phi_{dut} = \{winner_r, winner_s\}$ and $Y_{dut} = \{payment_r, \vartheta_r, payment_s, \vartheta_s\}$. Let M_{dut} be the model defined by the signature $\mathcal{S}_{dut} = (N_{dut}, V_{dut}, \mathcal{A}_{dut}, \Phi_{dut}, Y_{dut})$ and the constants starting $= 10$, dec $= 1$, reserve $= 0$ and n $= 2$. We consider the initial state $w_0 \in I$, such that $\pi_Y(w_0, \vartheta_r) = 7$ and $\pi_Y(w_0, \vartheta_s) = 4$.

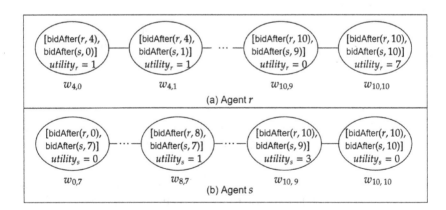

Fig. 2. The utilities agents r and s consider possible to obtain when they are 1st-order rational

Due to the starting price and the decrement, the auction is ensured to end after 10 stages. We therefore focus on the case $j = 10$. If the auction reaches a terminal state before 10 stages, the update function ensures a loop in the terminal state. Since the auction ends at the first bid, we write bidAfter(r, m) as the sequence of actions σ^r, such that $\sigma^r_i = \text{wait}_r$ for $i < m \leq j$ and $\sigma^r_i = \text{bid}_r$ for $m \leq i \leq j$. The sequence is read "r bids after m steps". Let onlywait(r) be the sequence of j actions wait$_r$. We use a similar notation for expressing agent s's sequence of actions. Let d be a joint action, we will examine which sequences of actions are rational for each agent to follow. We assume the Dutch auction protocol Σ_{dut} and the tie-breaking ordering are common knowledge among the agents in N_{dut}.

If the agents are 0-order rational, that is, if $M_{\text{dut}} \models_{(w_0,d)} \text{Rat}(r, 0, j) \wedge \text{Rat}(s, 0, j)$, then both agents consider possible that any sequence of joint actions will be taken. If we now consider 1st-order rationality for r, that is $M_{\text{dut}} \models_{(w_0,d)} \text{Rat}(r, 1, j)$, then r is not going to follow any sequence of actions that are strongly dominated in j steps. The weakly rational sequences of actions for r are those where she waits until the price is below her private valuation (e.g., bidAfter$(r, 4)$, bidAfter$(r, 5)$, and so on). The sequence of actions onlywait(r) is not rational for r. The weakly rational actions for agent s when $M_{\text{dut}} \models_{(w_0,d)} \text{Rat}(s, 1, j)$ are defined similarly. Figure 2 illustrates the utilities each agent considers possible to achieve when playing a weakly rational sequence of actions.

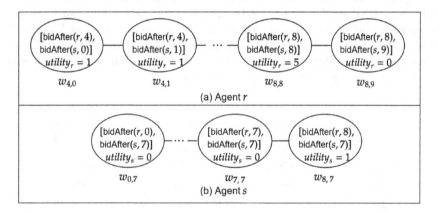

(a) Agent r

(b) Agent s

Fig. 3. The utilities agents r and s consider possible to obtain when they are 7th-order rational and $M_{\text{dut}} \models (2 \leq \vartheta_s \leq \text{starting}) \wedge (2 \leq \vartheta_r \leq \text{starting})$

For $k > 1$, which actions a k-order rational agent considers possible her opponents will take depends on her knowledge about their valuations. For instance, let us consider the case where it is common knowledge that $(2 \leq \vartheta_s \leq \text{starting}) \wedge (2 \leq \vartheta_r \leq \text{starting})$, i.e., we have $M_{\text{dut}} \models (2 \leq \vartheta_s \leq \text{starting}) \wedge (2 \leq \vartheta_r \leq \text{starting})$. By Proposition 1, both agents then know their opponent has a valuation between 2 and the starting price. If the agent s is 2nd-order rational, she will know the sequence of actions onlywait(r) is not weakly rational for r. Due to the tie-breaking rule, if both agents bid at the same stage, agent r wins. Thus, agent s

cannot win by waiting for the price to reach zero and it is not weakly rational to perform bidAfter$(s, 10)$. If r is 3rd-order rational, she knows that s knows onlywait(r) is not rational for her and consequently, that it cannot be the case that s will bidAfter$(s, 10)$. If the agents are 4th-order rational, they will not consider possible that the good is not sold before the price be zero. Thus, a similar reasoning will happen due tie-breaking when the price is 1. Finally, Fig. 3 illustrates the utilities each agent considers possible when she is 7th-order rational. Since agents are uncertain about which value between 2 and starting represents the valuation of their opponents, raising the order of rationality beyond 7 would not modify the actions they consider possible to be taken by their opponent.

5   Model Checking

Now we examine the upper bound of the complexity of deciding whether an E-ADL formula is true with respect to a model and a move. To prove this bound, we provide a model-checking algorithm and analyze its complexity. Let $\varphi \in \mathcal{L}_{\text{E-ADL}}$ be a formula and $M = (W, I, T, \{R_r\}_{r \in N}, U, \pi_\Phi, \pi_Y)$ be an ST-Model over $\mathcal{S}$. We say that ψ is a subformula of φ if either (i) $\psi = \varphi$; (ii) φ is of the form $\neg\phi$, $K_r\phi$ or $[d^G]\phi$ and ψ is a subformula of ϕ; or (iii) φ is of the form $\phi \wedge \phi'$ and ψ is a subformula of either ϕ or ϕ'. Denote $Sub(\varphi)$ as the set of all subformulas of φ.

Algorithm 1. $modelCheck(M, w, d, \varphi)$

Input: an ST-model $M = (W, I, T, \{R_r\}_{r \in N}, U, \pi_\Phi, \pi_Y)$, a state w of W, a joint action $d \in \prod_{r \in N} A^r$ and a formula $\varphi \in \mathcal{L}_{\text{E-ADL}}$.

Output: true if $M \models_{(w,d)} \varphi$, and **false** otherwise

1: $S \leftarrow Sub(\varphi)$ ordered by ascending length
2: Let $isTrue[1, \cdots, |\varphi|]$ be a boolean array initiated with $true$ values
3: **for** $i \leftarrow 1$ to $|\varphi|$ **do**
4:     $\phi \leftarrow S[i]$
5:     **switch** the formula type of ϕ **do**
6:         **case** ϕ is of the form $\phi' \wedge \phi''$
7:             $isTrue[i] \leftarrow isTrue[getIndex(S, \phi')] \wedge isTrue[getIndex(S, \phi'')]$
8:         **case** ϕ is of the form $\neg\phi'$
9:             $isTrue[i] \leftarrow \neg isTrue[getIndex(S, \phi')]$
10:        **case** ϕ is atomic
11:            $isTrue[i] \leftarrow M \models_{(w,d)} \phi$
12:        **case** ϕ is of the form $[b^G]\phi'$
13:            $e^G \leftarrow \langle b^G, d^{-G} \rangle$
14:            **for each** $c \in \prod_{r \in N} A^r$ **do**
15:                $isTrue[i] \leftarrow isTrue[i] \wedge modelCheck(M, U(w, e), c, \phi')$
16:        **case** ϕ is of the form $K_r\phi'$
17:            **for each** $u \in R_r(w)$ and each $e \in \prod_{r \in N} A^r$ with $e^r = d^r$ **do**
18:                $isTrue[i] \leftarrow isTrue[i] \wedge modelCheck(M, u, e, \phi')$
19: **return** $isTrue[|\varphi|]$

Theorem 2. *The following problem is in $\mathcal{O}(|W| \times |\mathcal{A}|^m)$, where $m = |N| \times |\varphi|$: Given an ST-Model M, a state $w \in W$, a joint action $d \in \prod_{r \in N} A^r$ and a formula $\varphi \in \mathcal{L}_{E\text{-}ADL}$, determine whether $M \models_{(w,d)} \varphi$ or not.*

Proof. Algorithm 1, named *modelCheck*, works in the following way: first it gets all subformulas of φ and orders them in a vector S by ascending length. Thus, $S(|\varphi|) = \varphi$, i.e., the position $|\varphi|$ in S corresponds to the formula φ itself, and if ϕ_i is a subformula of ϕ_j then $i < j$. An induction on S labels each subformula ϕ_i depending on whether or not ϕ_i is true in M at the move (w,d). If ϕ_i does not have any subformula, its truth value is obtained directly from the model. Since S is ordered by formulas length, if ϕ_i is either of the form $\phi' \wedge \phi''$ or $\neg\phi'$ the algorithm labels ϕ_i according to the label assigned to ϕ' and/or ϕ''. If ϕ_i is of the form $[b^G]\phi'$ then its label is recursively defined according to ϕ' truth value in the updated state given the joint action $\langle b^G, d^{-G} \rangle$, for any joint action to be taken in the next move. Since we compare with every joint action, this is done in an exponential number of steps, based on the size of the set of agents (i.e., according to $|\mathcal{A}|^n$, where $n = |N|$). Finally, the case where ϕ_i is in the form $K_r\phi'$ is recursively defined according to the truth value of ϕ' in all moves that are equivalent to (w,d). Similar to the previous case, since we compare with all possible moves and all states in $R_r(w) \subseteq W$, this step is done in an exponential number of steps (i.e., according to $|W| \times |\mathcal{A}|^n$, where $n = |N|$). As Algorithm *modelCheck* visits each subformula at most once, and the number of subformulas is not greater than the size of φ, the algorithm can clearly be implemented in $\mathcal{O}(|W| \times |\mathcal{A}|^m)$, where $m = |N| \times |\varphi|$.

It follows that checking agent rationality is exponential in the quantity of agents, the order of rationality and how many rounds are considered.

Corollary 1. *Given an ST-model M, a state $w \in W$, a joint action $d \in \prod_{r \in N} A^r$, an agent r, $j > 0$ and $k > 0$, the problem of checking whether $M \models_{(w,d)} \mathrm{Rat}(r, k+1, j)$ is in $\mathcal{O}(|W| \times |\mathcal{A}|^{nkj})$, where $n = |N|$.*

6   Conclusion

In this paper, we present *Epistemic Auction Description Language* (E-ADL), a language to allow reasoning about knowledge and action choice in auctions. E-ADL extends ADL with epistemic operators and action modalities. Our goal is to provide the ground for the design of General Auction Players and the characterization of their rational behavior. As in the GGP competition, real world players may have time restrictions to decide their actions. For those scenarios, we explore bounded rationality in relation to the level of higher-order knowledge about other agents and bounded looking-ahead beyond the next state. For future work, we intend to investigate the interplay between agents' bounded rationality and the auctioneer revenue and to generalize the definitions to combinatorial auctions.

References

1. Alur, R., Henzinger, T.A., Kupferman, O.: Alternating-time temporal logic. J. ACM (JACM) **49**(5), 672–713 (2002)
2. Aumann, R.: Backward induction and common knowledge of rationality. Games Econ. Behav. **8**, 6–19 (1995)
3. Bonanno, G.: Epistemic foundations of game theory. In: van Ditmarsch, H., Halpern, J.Y., van der Hoek, W., Kooi, B. (eds.) Handbook of Logics for Knowledge and Belief, chap. 9, pp. 411–450. College Publications (2015)
4. Chatterjee, K., Henzinger, T.A., Piterman, N.: Strategy logic. Inf. Comput. **208**(6), 677–693 (2010)
5. Chen, J., Micali, S.: Leveraging possibilistic beliefs in unrestricted combinatorial auctions. Games **7**(32), 83–101 (2016)
6. Chen, J., Micali, S., Pass, R.: Tight revenue bounds with possibilistic beliefs and level-k rationality. Econometrica **83**(4), 1619–1639 (2015)
7. Fagin, R., Moses, Y., Halpern, J.Y., Vardi, M.Y.: Reasoning about Knowledge. MIT Press, Cambridge (2003)
8. Feige, U., Feldman, M., Immorlica, N., Izsak, R., Lucier, B., Syrgkanis, V.: A unifying hierarchy of valuations with complements and substitutes. In: Proceedings of AAAI 2015, pp. 872–878. AAAI Press (2015)
9. Genesereth, M., Thielscher, M.: General Game Playing. Synthesis Lectures on Artificial Intelligence and Machine Learning. Morgan & Claypool Publishers, San Rafael (2014)
10. Jamroga, W., van der Hoek, W.: Agents that know how to play. Fundamenta Informaticae **63**(2–3), 185–219 (2004)
11. Jiang, G., Perrussel, L., Zhang, D.: On axiomatization of epistemic GDL. In: Baltag, A., Seligman, J., Yamada, T. (eds.) LORI 2017. LNCS, vol. 10455, pp. 598–613. Springer, Heidelberg (2017). https://doi.org/10.1007/978-3-662-55665-8_41
12. Jiang, G., Zhang, D., Perrussel, L., Zhang, H.: Epistemic GDL: a logic for representing and reasoning about imperfect information games. In: Procedings of IJCAI-2016 (2016)
13. Krishna, V.: Auction Theory. Academic Press, San Diego (2009)
14. Lorini, E.: A minimal logic for interactive epistemology. Synthese **193**(3), 725–755 (2015). https://doi.org/10.1007/s11229-015-0960-5
15. Mittelmann, M., Perrussel, L.: Auction description language (ADL): a general framework for representing auction-based markets. In: ECAI 2020. IOS Press, Santiago de Compostela (2020)
16. Parkes, D.C.: Iterative Combinatorial Auctions. Combinatorial Auctions. MIT Press, Cambridge (2006). https://doi.org/10.7551/mitpress/9780262033428.003.0003
17. Ramanujam, R., Simon, S.: Dynamic logic on games with structured strategies. In: Proceedings of KR-2008, pp. 49–58. AAAI Press (2008)
18. Thielscher, M.: A general game description language for incomplete information games. In: Proceedings of AAAI 2010, pp. 994–999 (2010)
19. Thielscher, M.: GDL-III: a description language for epistemic general game playing. In: Proceedings of IJCAI-2017, pp. 1276–1282 (2017)

20. Van Benthem, J.: Games in dynamic-epistemic logic. Bull. Econ. Res. **53**(4), 219–248 (2001). https://doi.org/10.1111/1467-8586.00133
21. Zhang, D., Thielscher, M.: A logic for reasoning about game strategies. In: Proceedings of AAAI 2015, pp. 1671–1677. AAAI Press (2015)
22. Zhang, D., Thielscher, M.: Representing and reasoning about game strategies. J. Philos. Logic **44**(2), 203–236 (2014). https://doi.org/10.1007/s10992-014-9334-6

Constraint Satisfaction

Tractable Combinations of Theories via Sampling

Manuel Bodirsky and Johannes Greiner$^{(\boxtimes)}$

Institut für Algebra, Technische Universität Dresden, Dresden, Germany
{manuel.bodirsky,johannes.greiner}@tu-dresden.de

Abstract. For a first-order theory T, the Constraint Satisfaction Problem of T is the computational problem of deciding whether a given conjunction of atomic formulas is satisfiable in some model of T. In this article we develop sufficient conditions for polynomial-time tractability of the constraint satisfaction problem for the union of two theories with disjoint relational signatures. To this end, we introduce the concept of sampling for theories and show that samplings can be applied to examples which are not covered by the seminal result of Nelson and Oppen.

1 Introduction

Reasoning tasks for intelligent agents often require to check whether certain configurations or situations are legitimate or possible. Such decision problems can often be modelled as *Constraint Satisfaction Problems (CSPs)*. The CSP of a first-order theory T with finite relational signature is the computational problem of deciding whether a set of atomic formulas is satisfiable in some model of T. We are interested in theories T where this computational problem can be solved efficiently and would like to understand for which theories T this problem is computationally hard. Many problems of the form $\text{CSP}(T)$ that are relevant in practice are either in the complexity class P, i.e., can be solved in polynomial time, or NP-hard (and thus not expected to be solvable in polynomial time). However, it is also known that every decision problem is polynomial-time Turing equivalent to a CSP [5], and in particular that there are theories T such that $\text{CSP}(T)$ is in NP but neither in P nor NP-hard (unless P = NP).

In reasoning scenarios in artificial intelligence the theory T under consideration is often of the form $T_1 \cup T_2$ where T_1 and T_2 are first-order theories with disjoint relational signatures such that $\text{CSP}(T_1)$ and $\text{CSP}(T_2)$ are both known to be in P. This problem has already been studied by Nelson and Oppen [17] and many others have continued this line of research (see for example Baader and Schulz [1]). CSPs of unions of theories are at the heart of SMT-Solvers (SAT Modulo Theories) and occur frequently in software verification [10]. The results

---

Both authors have received funding from the European Research Council (ERC Grant Agreement no. 681988, CSP-Infinity), and the DFG Graduiertenkolleg 1763 (QuantLA).

W. Faber et al. (Eds.): JELIA 2021, LNAI 12678, pp. 133–146, 2021.
https://doi.org/10.1007/978-3-030-75775-5_10

of Nelson and Oppen [17,18] provide sufficient conditions for the polynomial-time tractability of $\mathrm{CSP}(T_1 \cup T_2)$, covering a great variety of theories. Schulz [19] as well as Bodirsky and Greiner [3] have shown that in many situations, the conditions of Nelson and Oppen are also necessary for polynomial-time tractability (unless $\mathrm{P} = \mathrm{NP}$).

In this article we will present new sufficient conditions for polynomial-time tractability of $\mathrm{CSP}(T_1 \cup T_2)$. To illustrate that our conditions are incomparable to the conditions provided by Nelson and Oppen we consider the following example.

Example 1. Given parts of a huge machine, each of which can be mounted by exactly one of two robots, and precedence constraints on the order in which parts can be mounted, calculate a possible order in which the machine can be assembled. Some parts must be mounted by one robot, some by the other robot, and some parts can be mounted by both robots. The two robots are not allowed to work simultaneously but one robot may mount multiple parts at the same time. This reasoning task can be modelled as $\mathrm{CSP}(T_1 \cup T_2)$ where $T_1 := \mathrm{Th}(\mathfrak{A}_1)$ for a first-order expansion $\mathfrak{A}_1$ of $(\mathbb{Q}; <)$ that allows to model the precedence constraints, and $T_2 := \mathrm{Th}(\mathfrak{A}_2)$ where $\mathfrak{A}_2$ has two disjoint countably infinite unary relations and their union as domain. We choose $\mathfrak{A}_1 := (\mathbb{Q}; <, R)$ where R is the ternary relation defined by $R(x, y, z) \Leftrightarrow x = \min(y, z)$ and we will see at the end of the article that $\mathrm{CSP}(T_1 \cup T_2)$ is polynomial-time tractable using our results but T_1 does not satisfy the conditions of Nelson and Oppen.

For many computational reasoning tasks in artificial intelligence the only known algorithms have an at least exponential worst-case time-complexity, which is why one typically uses heuristic approaches and hopes that in reasoning instances that appear in practise the exponential worst-case behaviour does not show up. However, this is no longer an option in safety-critical systems where one needs a correct result within a reasonably short amount of time for *all* conceivable inputs.

The central idea how to prove polynomial-time tractability of $\mathrm{CSP}(T_1 \cup T_2)$ in this article is to introduce the notion of *sampling* for theories. Intuitively, a sampling for T maps a given instance ϕ of $\mathrm{CSP}(T)$ to a finite set L of finite structures such that ϕ is satisfiable in some model of T if and only it is satisfiable in one of the structures in L. We construct a sampling for $T_1 \cup T_2$ from given samplings for T_1 and T_2 and provide conditions when polynomial-time tractability of $\mathrm{CSP}(T_1)$ and $\mathrm{CSP}(T_2)$ carries over to $\mathrm{CSP}(T_1 \cup T_2)$. Some of the proofs have been omitted due to space restrictions. They can be found in [4].

2   Sampling for a Theory

Let τ be a finite *relational signature*, i.e., a finite set of relation symbols, each of which endowed with a natural number denoting its arity. A τ-*structure* $\mathfrak{A}$ is a tuple starting with a set A, followed by an n-ary relation $R^{\mathfrak{A}} \subseteq A^n$ for each symbol $R \in \tau$ of arity n. We will always denote structures with uppercase fraktur letters and their domain with the corresponding uppercase Latin letter. A *theory* is a set of first-order sentences. A τ-*theory* is a theory where all non-logical symbols are in τ. By $\mathrm{Th}(\mathfrak{A})$ we denote the *theory of* $\mathfrak{A}$, i.e., the set of all first-order sentences which are satisfied in $\mathfrak{A}$. A τ-structure $\mathfrak{A}$ is a *model* of a τ-theory T, if all sentences of T are satisfied in $\mathfrak{A}$. An *atomic* τ-*formula* is either of the form $R(x_1, \ldots, x_n)$ with $R \in \tau$ of arity n and variables $x_1, \ldots, x_n$, of the form $x_1 = x_2$, or of the form $\bot$, indicating the logical "false". We now present the central definitions of this article.

Definition 1. *Let* τ *be a finite relational signature and* T *a* τ-*theory. A sampling for* T *is a sequence* $(L_n)_{n \in \mathbb{N}}$ *of finite sets of finite* τ-*structures such that for all* $n \in \mathbb{N}$ *and all conjunctions of atomic* τ-*formulas* ϕ *with at most* n *variables, there exists a model for* T *in which* ϕ *is satisfiable if and only if there exists* $\mathfrak{B} \in L_n$ *such that* ϕ *is satisfiable in* $\mathfrak{B}$. *An element of* L_n *is called* n-sample, *or simply* sample, *for* T.

In order to talk about efficient computations of samplings we will need a few auxiliary definitions. A sampling $(L_n)_{n \in \mathbb{N}}$ is *computable* if there exists an algorithm that, given n, computes L_n. If this algorithm runs in time polynomial in n, then (L_n) is *computable in polynomial time*. For a sampling $(L_n)_{n \in \mathbb{N}}$ for T we define $|L_n| := \sum_{\mathfrak{B} \in L_n} |B|$. A sampling (L_n) is *polynomial* if there exists a polynomial $p \in \mathbb{Z}[x]$ such that $|L_n| \leq p(n)$ for all $n \in \mathbb{N}$. We will also sample structures. A *sampling* for a structure $\mathfrak{A}$ is a sampling for $\mathrm{Th}(\mathfrak{A})$.

Remark 1. While we are not aware that samplings have been defined for theories before, there is a definition for structures by Bodirsky, Macpherson, and Thapper [6] and we will now compare the two notions. We need the classical notion of a CSP which is defined for structures instead of theories. Let τ be a finite relational signature and $\mathfrak{A}$ a τ-structure. $\mathrm{CSP}(\mathfrak{A})$ is the computational problem of deciding whether a conjunction of atomic τ-formulas is satisfiable in $\mathfrak{A}$. Notice that $\mathrm{CSP}(\mathrm{Th}(\mathfrak{A})) = \mathrm{CSP}(\mathfrak{A})$ holds for all relational structures $\mathfrak{A}$, because $\mathrm{Th}(\mathfrak{A})$ explicitly states which instances are satisfiable. Therefore, the definition of 'sampling for $\mathfrak{A}$' in [6] can be attained from our definition by imposing the additional conditions on (L_n) that for all $n \in \mathbb{N}$ the set L_n may only contain one structure $\mathfrak{B}_n$ and that $\mathfrak{B}_n$ needs to have a homomorphism to $\mathfrak{A}$. Hence, any structure which has "efficient sampling" in the definition of Bodirsky, Macpherson, and Thapper has a sample which is computable in polynomial time in our definition, and is thus polynomial.

We will now prove that samplings for *structures* only require one element in each L_n, just like in the definition of Bodirsky, Macpherson, and Thapper. However, we will see in Example 3 that dropping the requirement that $\mathfrak{B}_n$ is homomorphic to $\mathfrak{A}$ allows smaller samples in some cases and can therefore reduce the runtime of algorithms that run on the samples.

Definition 2. *Let* T *be a theory with finite relational signature.* T *has the* Joint Homomorphism Property *(JHP)* *if for any two models* $\mathfrak{A}$, $\mathfrak{B}$ *of* T *there exists a model* $\mathfrak{C}$ *of* T *such that both* $\mathfrak{A}$ *and* $\mathfrak{B}$ *homomorphically map to* $\mathfrak{C}$.

Proposition 1 (Proposition 2.1 in [3]). *Let T be a theory with finite relational signature. Then there exists a model $\mathfrak{A}$ of T such that $\mathrm{CSP}(\mathfrak{A}) = \mathrm{CSP}(T)$ if and only if T has the* Joint Homomorphism Property (JHP).

Definition 3. *For a set L of τ-structures we define the* disjoint union $\biguplus_{\mathfrak{B} \in L} \mathfrak{B}$ *as the structure with domain $\biguplus_{\mathfrak{B} \in L} B$ and a k-ary relation $R \in \tau$ holds on a tuple t if and only if there exists $\mathfrak{B} \in L$ such that $t \in B^k$ and $R(t)$ holds in $\mathfrak{B}$.*

Proposition 2. *Let T be a theory with JHP and let $(L_n)_{n \in \mathbb{N}}$ be a sampling for T. Then $(L'_n)_{n \in \mathbb{N}}$ with $L'_n := \{\biguplus_{\mathfrak{B} \in L_n} \mathfrak{B}\}$ is also a sampling for T. Moreover, $|L'_n| = |L_n|$ for all $n \in \mathbb{N}$.*

Due to Proposition 2, and the fact that $\biguplus_{\mathfrak{B} \in L_n} \mathfrak{B}$ has size $|L_n|$, we will now often assume that samplings for structures contain only one element $\mathfrak{B}_n$ in L_n (for all $n \in \mathbb{N}$). We will write $(\mathfrak{B}_n)_{n \in \mathbb{N}}$ instead of $(\{\mathfrak{B}_n\})_{n \in \mathbb{N}}$. Motivated by these cases we define, for $n \geq 1$ and any τ-theory T, the set $S_n(T)$ as the class of all finite τ-structures $\mathfrak{B}_n$ such that a conjunction of atomic τ-formulas with at most n variables is satisfiable in $\mathfrak{B}_n$ if and only if it is satisfiable in some model of T. To justify why our definition of 'sampling' allows L_n to contain multiple structures in general, we would like to give an example of a theory T which has a sampling but no sampling (L_n) of T has only one element in L_n for some $n \geq 2$.

Example 2 (Similar to Example 2.2 in [3]). Let τ be a signature consisting of the unary symbols O, P, Q and the binary symbol I. Let T be the set of the following sentences

$$\forall x, y.((O(x) \wedge O(y)) \Rightarrow x = y),$$

$$\forall x.\neg(P(x) \wedge Q(x)), \quad \text{and}$$

$$\forall x, y.(I(x, y) \Leftrightarrow \neg(x = y)).$$

The following is a sampling for T which is computable in polynomial time: For $n \in \mathbb{N}$ let L_n consist of $\mathfrak{B}_1$ and $\mathfrak{B}_2$ defined on $\{1, \ldots, 2n\}$ where $P^{\mathfrak{B}_1} = P^{\mathfrak{B}_2} := \{1, \ldots, n\}$, $Q^{\mathfrak{B}_1} = Q^{\mathfrak{B}_2} := \{n+1, \ldots, 2n\}$, $O^{\mathfrak{B}_1} := \{1\}$ and $O^{\mathfrak{B}_2} := \{n+1\}$. In both structures, the I-relation denotes the inequality relation. While it is easy to check that $(L_n)_{n \in \mathbb{N}}$ is a sampling for T, there is no sampling with only one element in L_n for some $n \geq 2$. To prove this, consider the formulas $\phi_1 :\equiv O(x) \wedge P(x)$, which is satisfiable in $\mathfrak{B}_1$, and $\phi_2 := O(y) \wedge Q(y)$, which is satisfiable in $\mathfrak{B}_2$. Assume that both are satisfiable in some τ-structure $\mathfrak{B}$. Then there exists $a \in O^{\mathfrak{B}} \cap P^{\mathfrak{B}}$ and $b \in O^{\mathfrak{B}} \cap Q^{\mathfrak{B}}$. If $a = b$, then $\psi_1 := P(x) \wedge Q(x)$ is satisfiable in $\mathfrak{B}$. If $a \neq b$, then $\psi_2 := O(x) \wedge O(y) \wedge I(x, y)$ is satisfiable in $\mathfrak{B}$ or $\psi_3 := I(x, y) \wedge x = y$ is satisfiable in $\mathfrak{B}$ (in case $I^{\mathfrak{B}}$ is not the complement of equality). However, none of ψ_1, ψ_2, ψ_3 is satisfiable in some model of T, contradiction.

Proposition 3. *Let T be a theory with finite relational signature. Then, T has a computable sampling if and only if $\mathrm{CSP}(T)$ is decidable.*

To prove Proposition 3, we need the following definition.

Definition 4. *Let τ be a relational signature and let ϕ be a conjunction of atomic τ-formulas with variables $x_1, \ldots, x_n$. The canonical database $D(\phi)$ is defined as the structure with domain $x_1, \ldots, x_n$ such that a tuple t is in a relation $R^{D(\phi)}$ for $R \in \tau$ if and only if $R(t)$ is a conjunct of ϕ.*

Clearly, there is a homomorphism from $D(\phi)$ to $\mathfrak{A}$ iff ϕ is satisfiable in $\mathfrak{A}$.

Proof (Proof of Proposition 3). Let τ be the signature of T. Suppose there exists a computable sampling $(L_n)_{n \in \mathbb{N}}$ for T. Let ϕ be a conjunction of atomic τ-formulas with at most n variables. Then there are only finitely many maps from $D(\phi)$ to structures in L_n and for each of them we can determine whether it is a homomorphism or not. Therefore $\mathrm{CSP}(T)$ is decidable.

Conversely, suppose that $\mathrm{CSP}(T)$ is decidable. There are only finitely many atomic formulas on n variables because τ is finite and the arity of each relation is finite. Hence, there are only finitely many conjunctions of atomic formulas with at most n variables such that no conjunct is repeated. Using the decision procedure for $\mathrm{CSP}(T)$, we may determine which of the conjunctions are satisfiable in some model of T and define L_n as the set of all canonical databases of the satisfiable conjunctions. Then, by construction, (L_n) is a sampling for T.

To determine whether a theory has a polynomial sampling the following general observation is helpful.

Remark 2. Let $\mathfrak{A}$ be a structure with finite relational signature τ. By Proposition 2, $\mathfrak{A}$ has a polynomial sampling iff for all $n \in \mathbb{N}$ there exists $\mathfrak{B}_n \in S_n(\mathrm{Th}(\mathfrak{A}))$ such that $(\mathfrak{B}_n)_{n \in \mathbb{N}}$ is a polynomial sampling. If $\mathfrak{B}_n \in S_n(\mathrm{Th}(\mathfrak{A}))$ and there exists a homomorphism $h \colon \mathfrak{B}_n \to \mathfrak{A}$, then $h(\mathfrak{B}_n) \in S_n(\mathrm{Th}(\mathfrak{A}))$ and $|h(B_n)| \leq |B_n|$. If we can prove that each element of S_n homomorphically maps to $\mathfrak{A}$ we can therefore assume that L_n consists of a single substructure of $\mathfrak{A}$. An element of $S_n(\mathrm{Th}(\mathfrak{A}))$ which is a substructure of $\mathfrak{A}$ is called an *n-universal substructure* of $\mathfrak{A}$. Minimal sizes of n-universal substructures are easier to determine than minimal sizes of L_n in general and have been explored in the past [12,15,16].

In general, $S_n(\mathrm{Th}(\mathfrak{A}))$ may contain structures which are smaller than the smallest n-universal substructure of $\mathfrak{A}$ and Example 3 will provide an example for this case. Remark 2 can be used to prove Lemma 1. The theory T in Lemma 1 is contained in the theory of every undirected, loopless graphs with a binary relation symbol E for the edge relation and a binary relation symbol N for the set of all pairs of distinct elements that are not related by an edge.

Lemma 1. *Let τ consist of the binary relation symbols E and N and let T contain only the sentence*

$$\forall x, y. \big(\neg E(x,x) \wedge \neg(E(x,y) \wedge \neg E(y,x)) \wedge \neg N(x,x) \wedge \neg(E(x,y) \wedge N(x,y))\big).$$

Then there is a sampling for T but not a polynomial sampling.

Theories with polynomial samplings include all theories of finite structures, the theory of successor on the natural numbers, and the theories of the structures in Lemma 2 and Lemma 3 below.

3   Sampling for Unions of Theories

Let T_1, T_2 be two theories with disjoint relational signatures and with polynomial samplings. In this section we will present sufficient conditions on T_1 and T_2 such that $T_1 \cup T_2$ has polynomial sampling. To this end, we will need to construct models for $T_1 \cup T_2$. Let τ_1, τ be relational signatures with $\tau_1 \subseteq \tau$ and $\mathfrak{A}$ a τ-structure. The τ_1-*reduct* of $\mathfrak{A}$, written $\mathfrak{A}^{\tau_1}$, is the structure we get when all relations with symbols not contained in τ_1 are removed from $\mathfrak{A}$. The following definition goes back to Tinelly and Ringeisen [20].

Definition 5. *Let $\mathfrak{A}_1$ and $\mathfrak{A}_2$ be τ_1 and τ_2 structures respectively. A $\tau_1 \cup \tau_2$-structure $\mathfrak{A}$ is a* fusion *of $\mathfrak{A}_1$ and $\mathfrak{A}_2$ if and only if $\mathfrak{A}^{\tau_i}$ is isomorphic to $\mathfrak{A}_i$ for $i = 1$ and $i = 2$.*

Proposition 4 (Proposition 1 and Lemma 1 in [1]). *For $i = 1, 2$, let T_i be a τ_i theory. A $\tau_1 \cup \tau_2$-structure $\mathfrak{A}$ is a model of $T_1 \cup T_2$ if and only if $\mathfrak{A}$ is a fusion of a model for T_1 and a model for T_2. Furthermore, two structures have a fusion if and only if their domains have the same cardinality.*

The proof of Lemma 1 in [1] essentially argues that any bijection between the domains of two structures with disjoint signatures defines a fusion of the two structures, which is a fact we will use later on. As a first consequence, we can observe that an instance $\phi_1 \wedge \phi_2$ of $\mathrm{CSP}(T_1 \cup T_2)$ is satisfiable if and only if for $i = 1$ and $i = 2$ there exist models $\mathfrak{A}_i$ of T_i with $|A_1| = |A_2|$ such that ϕ_i is satisfiable in $\mathfrak{A}_i$ and the satisfying assignments of ϕ_1 and ϕ_2 identify exactly the same variables. The following notion describes a property of a sampling that allows us to transfer identifications of variables between models and samples.

Definition 6. *We call a sampling $(L_n)_{n \in \mathbb{N}}$ for T* equality-matching *if for all $n \in \mathbb{N}$ and all conjunctions of atomic τ-formulas ϕ with variables in $\{x_1, \ldots, x_n\}$ and for any conjunction ψ of equalities and negated equalities on $\{x_1, \ldots, x_n\}$, there exists a model of T in which $\phi \wedge \psi$ is satisfiable if and only if there exists $\mathfrak{B} \in L_n$ such that $\phi \wedge \psi$ is satisfiable in $\mathfrak{B}$. A sampling is* equality-matching *for a structure $\mathfrak{A}$ if it is equality-matching for $\mathrm{Th}(\mathfrak{A})$.*

To be equality-matching will be the property that samplings for T_1 and T_2 must satisfy in order to construct a sampling for $T_1 \cup T_2$ in Theorem 1. An example for an equality-matching sampling is the one constructed in Example 2 because I is the negation of equality in all models of T and the constructed samples and therefore, the instances of $\mathrm{CSP}(T)$ themselves can specify how to identify variables. Also, the sampling constructed in the proof of Proposition 3 is equality-matching if there exists $I \in \tau$ such that in all models of T we have $I(x, y) \Leftrightarrow \neg(x = y)$.

Another class of theories where an equality-matching sampling always exists are ω-categorical theories. A theory is ω-*categorical* if it has only one countable model (up to isomorphism). For a structure $\mathfrak{A}$, the *orbit* of $t \in A^k$ is $\{\alpha(t) \mid \alpha \in \mathrm{Aut}(\mathfrak{A})\}$ where $\mathrm{Aut}(\mathfrak{A})$ is the set of automorphisms of $\mathfrak{A}$ and α is applied componentwise.

Proposition 5. *Let T be an ω-categorical theory with finite relational signature. Then there exists an equality-matching sampling for T.*

It follows from Proposition 3 that there are ω-categorical structures without computable sampling, because some of those structures have an undecidable CSP [7]. There are also theories with a sampling computable in polynomial time, but without polynomial equality-matching sampling. Indeed, let τ contain the binary relations E and N and let T contain only

$$\forall x, y \left(\neg \big(E(x,y) \wedge \neg E(y,x) \big) \wedge \neg \big(E(x,y) \wedge N(x,y) \wedge x \neq y \big) \right)$$

and sentences of the form $\exists x_1, \ldots, x_n \left(\bigwedge_{i<j} x_i \neq x_j \right)$ for all $n \in \mathbb{N}$. Then $L_n :=$ $\{(\{0\}; E, N)\}$ with $E = N := \{(0,0)\}$ for all $n \in \mathbb{N}$ yields a sampling for T. If there exists a polynomial equality-matching sampling for T, then there exists a polynomial sampling for $T' := T \cup \mathrm{Th}(\mathbb{Z}; \neq)$ by Proposition 6. However, with $\neq$ in the signature, instances of $\mathrm{CSP}(T')$ can include $E'(x,y) := E(x,y) \wedge x \neq y$ and $N'(x,y) := N(x,y) \wedge x \neq y$. But E' and N' satisfy the theory from Lemma 1. Therefore, a polynomial equality-matching sampling for T' cannot exist.

It is in general not true that if $(L_n)_{n \in \mathbb{N}}$ is equality-matching then $(L'_n)_{n \in \mathbb{N}} :=$ $(\bigcup_{\mathfrak{B} \in L_n} \mathfrak{B})_{n \in \mathbb{N}}$ is equality-matching as well. An example is $\mathfrak{A} = (\{0,1\}; <)$ with L_4 consisting of two copies of $\mathfrak{A}$. Then $x_1 < x_2 \wedge x_3 < x_4 \wedge \bigwedge_{i<j} x_i \neq x_j$ is not satisfiable in $\mathfrak{A}$ or L_4, but is satisfiable in (L'_4). Even homomorphic images of equality-matching samplings, such as in Remark 2, need not be equality-matching.

For later use, we now present two classes of structures with equality-matching sampling computable in polynomial time. If $\mathfrak{B}$ is a reduct of $\mathfrak{A}$ and all relations in $\mathfrak{A}$ have a first-order definition in $\mathfrak{B}$, then $\mathfrak{A}$ is called a *first-order expansion* of $\mathfrak{B}$.

Lemma 2. *All reducts of first-order expansions of $(\mathbb{Q}; <)$ have an equality-matching sampling computable in polynomial time.*

Lemma 3. *Let $P_1, \ldots, P_m$ be a partition of $\mathbb{Q}$ where all parts are infinite and co-infinite. All reducts of first-order expansions of $(\mathbb{Q}; P_1, \ldots, P_m)$ have an equality-matching sampling computable in polynomial time.*

Another condition we need in order to construct a sampling for the union of two theories is a primitive positive version of the classical concept of *no algebraicity* in model theory (see [13]). A formula is called *primitive positive* *(pp)* if it is a conjunction of atomic formulas where some variables may be existentially quantified.

Definition 7. *A τ-structure $\mathfrak{A}$ has no pp-algebraicity if for any primitive positive τ-formula $\phi(x)$ with parameters $a_1, \ldots, a_n$ the set $\{b \in A \mid \mathfrak{A} \models \phi(b)\}$ is either contained in $\{a_1, \ldots, a_n\}$ or infinite.*

It is easy to check that first-order expansions of $(\mathbb{Q}; <)$ or $(\mathbb{Q}; P_1, \ldots, P_m)$ do not have pp-algebraicity because $a < x < b$ has either no or infinitely many satisfying assignments in $(\mathbb{Q}; <)$ (for all $a, b \in \mathbb{Q}$), and in $(\mathbb{Q}; P_1, \ldots, P_m)$ any two distinct elements in P_i are indistinguishable for first-order definable relations. When it is clear from context that we mean a set, we will use $[n]$ as a shorthand for $\{1, 2, \ldots, n\}$. We are now ready to present the first main result.

Theorem 1. *Let T_1 and T_2 be theories with finite relational and disjoint signatures τ_1, τ_2 respectively. If all models of T_1 and T_2 do not have pp-algebraicity and T_1 and T_2 have equality-matching samplings $(O_n), (P_n)$ respectively, then there exists an equality-matching sampling (L_n) for $T := T_1 \cup T_2$ with $|L_n| = |O_n| \cdot |P_n|$ for all $n \in \mathbb{N}$. If (O_n) and (P_n) are computable in polynomial time, then (L_n) is also computable in polynomial time.*

Proof. Let (O_n) and (P_n) be equality-matching samplings of T_1, T_2, respectively. Fix $n \in \mathbb{N}$ and let $\{\mathfrak{B}_{i,1}, \ldots, \mathfrak{B}_{i,p_i}\}$ be O_n for $i = 1$ and P_n for $i = 2$. For all $i \in [p_1], j \in [p_2]$ we now define a $\tau_1 \cup \tau_2$-structure $\mathfrak{M}_{i,j}$ with domain $M_{i,j} := B_{1,i} \times B_{2,j}$ as follows.

For $R \in \tau_1$ of arity k we define

$$((a_1, b_1), \ldots, (a_k, b_k)) \in R^{\mathfrak{M}_{i,j}} \Leftrightarrow$$
$$(\forall i, j.(a_i = a_j \Leftrightarrow b_i = b_j)) \wedge (a_1, \ldots, a_k) \in R^{\mathfrak{B}_{1,i}}.$$

Analogously, we define for $R \in \tau_2$ of arity k

$$((a_1, b_1), \ldots, (a_k, b_k)) \in R^{\mathfrak{M}_{i,j}} \Leftrightarrow$$
$$(\forall i, j.(a_i = a_j \Leftrightarrow b_i = b_j)) \wedge (b_1, \ldots, b_k) \in R^{\mathfrak{B}_{2,j}}.$$

Let $\phi_i(x_1, \ldots, x_n)$ be a conjunction of atomic τ_i-formulas for $i = 1$ and $i = 2$. Notice that forcing ϕ_1 and ϕ_2 to have the same variables can be done without loss of generality by introduction of dummy constraints like $x = x$. Suppose there exists a homomorphism $g: D(\phi_1(x_1, \ldots, x_n) \wedge \phi_2(x_1, \ldots, x_n)) \to \mathfrak{A}$ where $\mathfrak{A}$ is a model of T. Then $g: D(\phi_i(x_1, \ldots, x_n)) \to \mathfrak{A}^{\tau_i}$ is also a homomorphism for $i = 1$ and $i = 2$. As the chosen samplings are equality-matching, there exists $u_i \in [p_i]$ and homomorphisms $h_i: D(\phi_i(x_1, \ldots, x_n)) \to \mathfrak{B}_{i,u_i}$ for $i = 1$ and $i = 2$ such that h_1 and h_2 both identify variables in the same way that g does. Then, by construction, $x_i \mapsto (h_1(x_i), h_2(x_i))$ defines a homomorphism from $D(\phi_1 \wedge \phi_2)$ to $\mathfrak{M}_{u_1, u_2}$ identifying the same variables as g.

For the reverse direction suppose that h is a homomorphism from $D(\phi_1 \wedge \phi_2)$ to $\mathfrak{M}_{u_1, u_2}$. We want to show the existence of a homomorphism g from $D(\phi_1 \wedge \phi_2)$ to $\mathfrak{A}$, where $\mathfrak{A}$ is a model of T and g and h identify the same variables. To simplify presentation, we would like to assume that h is injective. Suppose there exists x_i, x_j such that $h(x_i) = h(x_j)$. Then we replace all occurrences of x_j in ϕ_1 and ϕ_2 by x_i and iterate until h is injective on the remaining variables. Call the resulting formulas ϕ_1' and ϕ_2'. If there exists an injective homomorphism g from $D(\phi_1' \wedge \phi_2')$ to a model of T, we can extend g to the formerly substituted variables via $g(x_j) := g(x_i)$ to get a homomorphism from $D(\phi_1 \wedge \phi_2)$ to some model of T which has the same identifications as h. Hence, it is sufficient to prove the existence of g under the assumption that h is injective.

Let $h_i := \pi_i^2 \circ h$ for $i \in [2]$, where π_i^2 is the projection to the i-th coordinate out of two coordinates. Now suppose there exists a set $S \subseteq h(D(\phi))$ of size at least two such that any two elements in S are equal in the first coordinate (the case with the second coordinate can be proven analogously). Without loss of generality we will assume $S = \{h(x_1), \ldots, h(x_k)\}$. Furthermore, we may assume that S is maximal, i.e., for all $i > k$ we have $h_1(x_i) \neq h_1(x_1)$. For $i \in [k]$ let $\psi_i(x_i, x_{k+1}, \ldots, x_n)$ be the conjunction of all conjuncts in $\phi_1(x_1, \ldots, x_n)$ which do not contain x_j for all $j \in [k] \setminus \{i\}$. Then ϕ_1 is equivalent to $\bigwedge_{i=1}^k \psi_i(x_i, x_{k+1}, \ldots, x_n)$ because no conjunct of ϕ_1 can contain more than one variable from $x_1, \ldots, x_k$, as this conjunct would not be satisfied in the image of h_1 in $\mathfrak{M}_{u_1, u_2}$. As T_1 has an equality-matching sampling, there exists a homomorphism $g_1 \colon D(\phi_1) \to \mathfrak{A}_1$ for some model $\mathfrak{A}_1$ of T_1, such that g_1 has the same identifications as h_1. By the definition of no pp-algebraicity, the set

$$\{a \in A \mid \mathfrak{A}_1 \models \psi_i(a, g_1(x_{k+1}), \ldots, g_1(x_n))\}$$

is infinite for all $i \in [k]$. Hence, there exists a homomorphism $g_1' \colon D(\phi_1) \to \mathfrak{A}_1$ such that $g_1'(x_i) \neq g_1'(x_j) \neq g_1'(x_l) = g_1(x_l)$ for all $i, j \in [k]$ and $l \in [n] \setminus [k]$. As the sampling for T_1 is equality-matching, there exists $u_1' \in [p_1]$ and a homomorphism $h_1' \colon D(\phi_1) \to \mathfrak{B}_{1,u_1'}$ with the same identifications as g_1'. This yields a homomorphism $x_i \mapsto (h_1'(x_i), h_2(x_i))$ to $\mathfrak{M}_{u_1', u_2}$ where strictly less variables are mapped to the same row or column than by h.

Iterated application of this argument to h_1 and, in an analogous way, to h_2 proves that there exist injective homomorphisms h_1^* and h_2^* such that the map $h^* \colon D(\phi_1(x_1, \ldots, x_n) \wedge \phi_2(x_1, \ldots, x_2)) \to \mathfrak{M}_{u_1^*, u_2^*}$ defined by $x_i \mapsto (h_1^*(x_i), h_2^*(x_i))$ is a homomorphism. As (O_n) and (P_n) are equality-matching samplings there exist injective homomorphisms $g_i^* \colon D(\phi_i(x_1, \ldots, x_n)) \to \mathfrak{A}_i^*$ where $\mathfrak{A}_i^*$ is a model of T_i for $i = 1$ and $i = 2$. Now observe that $\mathfrak{A}_1^*$ and $\mathfrak{A}_2^*$ are both either empty (in which case the theorem becomes trivial) or infinite because no pp-algebraicity implies that $\{x \mid \mathfrak{A}_i^* \models x = x\}$ is infinite or empty. If A_i^* is uncountable, then there exists a $\mathfrak{A}_i'$ with countable domain such that $\mathrm{Th}(\mathfrak{A}_i') = \mathrm{Th}(\mathfrak{A}_i^*)$ due to the Downward Löwenheim-Skolem Theorem (see [13], page 90) and we may substitute $\mathfrak{A}_i^*$ by $\mathfrak{A}_i'$. Hence, we may assume that $|A_1^*| = |A_2^*|$ and therefore, there exists a bijection $f \colon A_1^* \to A_2^*$ such that $f(g_1^*(x_i)) = g_2^*(x_i)$ for all $i \in [n]$. However, any bijection from A_1^* to A_2^* induces a fusion $\mathfrak{A}$ of $\mathfrak{A}_1^*$ and $\mathfrak{A}_2^*$ with domain A_1^* and therefore a model of T by Proposition 4. Clearly, $g \colon D(\phi) \to \mathfrak{A}^*$ defined by $g(x_i) := g_1^*(x_i)$ for all $i \in [n]$ is an injective homomorphism. Hence, (L_n) with $L_n := \{\mathfrak{M}_{1,1}, \ldots, \mathfrak{M}_{p_1, p_2}\}$ is an equality-matching sampling for T.

We have $|L_n| = \sum_{i \in [p_1], j \in [p_2]} |\mathfrak{B}_{1,i}| \cdot |\mathfrak{B}_{2,j}| = |O_n| \cdot |P_n|$ for all $n \in \mathbb{N}$ and to determine whether a relation $R^{\mathfrak{M}_{i,j}}$ holds on an tuple t requires at most n^2 checks for equality and a check if $t \in R^{\mathfrak{B}_{1,i}}$ or $t \in R^{\mathfrak{B}_{2,j}}$. Therefore, if both samplings are computable in polynomial time, (L_n) is computable in polynomial time as well.

Remark 3. Notice that with almost the same construction, an equality-matching sampling for any finite number of theories can be constructed as long as all theories have an equality-matching sampling and only models without pp-algebraicity. For that we use a higher-dimensional version of the matrix defined in the proof, where a relation $R \in \tau_i$ holds on a tuple t if only if any two entries of t either differ in all their coordinates or are equal in all their coordinates and the projection to the i-th dimension of each element of t is in R as defined in the respective sample for T_i.

Note that if $\mathfrak{A}$ has a finite signature and is without pp-algebraicity, then all models of $\mathrm{Th}(\mathfrak{A})$ are without pp-algebraicity. This holds because for each primitive positive formula $\phi(x_1, \ldots, x_k)$ and $n \in \mathbb{N}$, the theory $\mathrm{Th}(\mathfrak{A})$ contains a sentence expressing that for any choice of parameters $x_2, \ldots, x_k$ any satisfying assignment for x_1 is either equal to one of the parameters or there are at least n different satisfying assignments for x_1. If one of the theories, say T_1, does not satisfy the conditions of Theorem 1 because it has models with pp-algebraicity, we can prove the following.

Proposition 6. *Let T_1 be a theory with finite relational signature and let $\mathfrak{A}_2$ be an infinite structure with signature τ_2 whose relations are first-order definable over the empty signature. If T_1 has an equality-matching sampling (L_n) and only infinite models, then the expansion of the samples in (L_n) with relations in τ_2 by their first-order definitions is an equality-matching sampling for $T_1 \cup \mathrm{Th}(\mathfrak{A}_2)$.*

Proof. Fix $n \in \mathbb{N}$ and let τ_1 be the signature of T_1. Call the expanded sampling (L'_n). Let ϕ_i be a conjunction of atomic τ_i formulas. Then $\phi_2(x_1, \ldots, x_n)$ is equivalent to $\bigvee_{i \in [k]} \psi_i(x_1, \ldots, x_n)$, where each ψ_i specifies by a conjunction of equalities and disequalities which variables must be equal and which must differ. However, for every $i \in [k]$ the formula $\phi_1 \wedge \psi_i$ is satisfiable in some element of L_n if and only if it is satisfiable in some model of T_1 because (L_n) is equality-matching. Therefore, $\phi_1 \wedge \phi_2$ is satisfiable in some model of T_1 if and only if it is satisfiable in some structure in L'_n.

There are also theories with a sampling but without an equality-matching sampling: for example, $\mathfrak{A} := (\mathbb{Z}; R_a, R_m)$ where $R_a := \{(x, y, z) \mid x + y = z\}$ and $R_m := \{(x, y, z) \mid x \cdot y = z\}$ has a trivial CSP and therefore a sampling. If there exists an equality-matching sampling for $\mathrm{Th}(\mathfrak{A})$ we can construct a sampling for $T := \mathrm{Th}(\mathfrak{A}) \cup \mathrm{Th}(\mathbb{Z}; \neq)$ by Proposition 6. Then we can define $z = 1$ by the primitive positive formula $\exists x, y \, (x \cdot z = x \wedge y \cdot z = y \wedge x \neq y)$. It is now easy to see that Hilbert's tenth problem, which is undecidable, is many-to-one reducible to $\mathrm{CSP}(T)$, contradicting Proposition 3. The following example shows that we cannot drop the assumption of no pp-algebraicity in Theorem 1.

Example 3. Let succ be the successor relation on $\mathbb{N}$. Let P_0, P_1 be two disjoint, infinite sets (two colors). Then $T_1 := \mathrm{Th}(\mathbb{N}; \mathrm{succ})$ and $T_2 := \mathrm{Th}(P_0 \uplus P_1; P_0, P_1)$ both have an equality-matching sampling which can be computed in polynomial time. However, any sampling $(L_n)_{n \in \mathbb{N}}$ of $T_1 \cup T_2$ has $|L_n| \geq 2^n$ for all $n \in \mathbb{N}$, and therefore no polynomial sampling exists.

To prove this, first notice that we can construct a model $\mathfrak{A}$ for $T := T_1 \cup T_2$ such that $\mathrm{CSP}(\mathfrak{A}) = \mathrm{CSP}(T)$. This can be done by giving each natural number the color P_0 or P_1 in such a way that the resulting sequence over $\{0,1\}$ includes any binary number as consecutive subsequence. Therefore, when examining lower bounds for $|L_n|$, we may assume by Proposition 2 that for each n there is only one element $\mathfrak{B}_n \in S_n(T)$ in L_n. Now observe the following:

1. In any n-sample $\mathfrak{B}_n$, no element x can satisfy $P_0(x) \wedge P_1(x)$ and there is no pp-formula which can force a node to have no color Hence, if some node in $\mathfrak{B}_n$ has no color, we can color this node arbitrarily and the result is again in $S_n(T)$. Therefore, without loss of generality, each node in the sampling has exactly one color

2. When we fix a node c in $\mathfrak{B}_n$ such that $\phi_c := \operatorname{succ}(c, x_2) \wedge \ldots \wedge \operatorname{succ}(x_{n-1}, x_n)$ is satisfiable in $\mathfrak{B}_n$, then there exists exactly one map $s\colon [n] \to \{0,1\}$ such that $\psi_{c,s} := \phi_c \wedge \bigwedge_{i \in [n]} P_{s(i)}(x_i)$ is satisfiable in $\mathfrak{B}_n$. If there were two distinct maps s and s', then $\psi_{x_1,s} \wedge \psi_{x_1,s'}$ would be satisfiable in $\mathfrak{B}_n$, but not in $\mathfrak{A}$.

Now observe that atomic $\tau_1 \cup \tau_2$-formulas with n variables can encode a binary number b of length n via $\operatorname{succ}(x_1, x_2) \wedge \ldots \wedge \operatorname{succ}(x_{n-1}, x_n) \wedge \bigwedge_{i \in [n]} P_{b_i}(x_i)$. By item (2) each element of $\mathfrak{B}_n$ is the start of at most one binary number and therefore, $\mathfrak{B}_n$ must have at least 2^n elements.

We would like to remark that for all n there exists $\mathfrak{B}_n \in S_n(T)$ of size 2^n such that $(\mathfrak{B}_n)$ is an equality-matching sampling of T. It can be constructed via a de-Brujin sequence. However, the smallest n-universal substructure of a model of T has size $2^n + n - 1$, which is larger.

Even though we cannot drop no-pp-algebraicity in general, there are structures with pp-algebraicity where the sets definable by primitive positive formulas are somewhat tame and an equality-matching sampling of the union of their theories exists and is computable in polynomial time. We will demonstrate this with the following example, which will also occur in the next section.

Example 4. Let E_1 be the relation $\{(2a, 2a + 1), (2a + 1, 2a) \mid a \in \mathbb{N}\}$. Let E_2 be a copy of E_1. Then we consider $T := \operatorname{Th}(\mathbb{N}; E_1) \cup \operatorname{Th}(\mathbb{N}; E_2)$. For $n \in \mathbb{N}$ we will now construct $\mathfrak{B}_n \in S_n(T)$ such that $(\mathfrak{B}_n)_{n \in \mathbb{N}}$ is an equality-matching sampling for T computable in polynomial time. Consider formulas γ_k and δ_k describing an *alternating sequence* and an *alternating cycle*, both of length $2k$, respectively. Formally, we define $\gamma_k(x_1, \ldots, x_{2k+1})$ as $\bigwedge_{i \in [k]} (E_1(x_{2i-1}, x_{2i}) \wedge E_2(x_{2i}, x_{2i+1}))$ and $\delta_k(x_1, \ldots, x_{2k})$ as the formula $\gamma_k(x_1, \ldots, x_{2k}, x_1)$. Let $\mathfrak{B}_n$ be the structure containing $\lceil \frac{n}{2k} \rceil$ many copies of $D(\delta_k(x_1, x_2, \ldots, x_{2k}))$, for each $k \in \{1, \ldots, \lceil \frac{n}{2} \rceil\}$. Then, $\mathfrak{B}_n$ has size $O(n^2)$ and $(\mathfrak{B}_n)_{n \in \mathbb{N}}$ is a sampling for T (see [4] for a proof).

4   Exemplary Application to CSPs

We finally show how to use the sampling (L_n) constructed in Theorem 1 in order to prove the polynomial-time tractability of $\operatorname{CSP}(T_1 \cup T_2)$. To do this, we use algorithms for the CSPs of the structures $\mathfrak{B}_n \in L_n$ which run in *uniform polynomial time*, i.e., the runtime is polynomial in the size of the instance and in $|B_n|$. The following generalizes a result for CSPs of structures by Bodirsky, Macpherson, and Thapper [6] to CSPs of theories.

Proposition 7. *Let T be a theory with finite relational signature and let (L_n) be a sampling of T computable in polynomial time. If there is an algorithm that solves $\mathrm{CSP}(\mathfrak{B}_n)$ for every $\mathfrak{B}_n \in L_n$ in uniform polynomial time, then $\mathrm{CSP}(T)$ is polynomial-time tractable.*

To describe classes of finite structures whose CSP can be be solved by a uniform polynomial-time algorithm, the following concepts from universal algebra are important.

Definition 8. *Let $\mathfrak{A}$ be a relational structure with signature τ and let f be an operation of arity k on $\mathfrak{A}$. We call f a polymorphism of $\mathfrak{A}$ if it is a homomorphism from $\mathfrak{A}^k$ to $\mathfrak{A}$, i.e., whenever $t_1, \ldots, t_k \in R^{\mathfrak{A}}$, for some $R \in \tau$, then $f(t_1, \ldots, t_k) \in R^{\mathfrak{A}}$, where f is applied componentwise. An operation $f \colon A^k \to A$ is* totally symmetric *if for all $x_1, \ldots, x_k, y_1, \ldots, y_k \in A$ we have $f(x_1, \ldots, x_k) = f(y_1, \ldots, y_k)$ whenever $\{x_1, \ldots, x_k\} = \{y_1, \ldots, y_k\}$. If $k \geq 3$ and for all $a, b \in A$ we have $f(a, b, b, \ldots, b) = f(b, a, b, b, \ldots, b) = \cdots = f(b, b, \ldots, b, a) = b$, then f is called a* near-unanimity *operation.*

Proposition 8 (Corollary 3.6 in [14]). *There is an algorithm that solves $\mathrm{CSP}(\mathfrak{B})$ in uniform polynomial time for all finite relational structures $\mathfrak{B}$ with a near-unanimity polymorphism.*

Results about the applicability of fast uniform algorithms for CSPs of finite relational structures with a near-unanimity polymorphism can be found in the work of Kozik (2016). Proposition 8 and Proposition 7 can be applied to Example 4 with the following near-unanimity operation f defined on $\mathfrak{B}_n$:

$$f(x, y, z) := \begin{cases} y \text{ if } y = z, \\ x \text{ otherwise.} \end{cases}$$

Note that f is a polymorphism of $\mathfrak{B}_n$, for all n, because if $(t_{1,1}, t_{1,2})$, $(t_{2,1}, t_{2,2})$ and $(t_{3,1}, t_{3,2})$ are in E_k and $t_{i,1} = t_{j,1}$, then $t_{i,2} = t_{j,2}$ and therefore $f(t_1, t_2, t_3) = (t_{i,1}, t_{i,2}) \in E_k$ for all $k \in [2], i, j \in [3], i \neq j$. In particular, $\mathrm{CSP}(T)$ with T from Example 4 can be solved in polynomial time. An example for a totally symmetric polymorphism is the minimum operation over $(\mathbb{Q}; <)$. Also, we can define minimum as an operation of any arity. The following result builds on results of Feder and Vardi [11].

Theorem 2 (Section 3 in [9]). *Let $\mathfrak{B}$ be a finite structure with finite relational signature. Then the arc-consistency procedure solves $\mathrm{CSP}(\mathfrak{B})$ iff $\mathfrak{B}$ has totally symmetric polymorphisms of all arities.*

The Arc-consistency algorithm can be implemented so that its worst-case running time is in $O(n^2 m^2)$ where n is the number of variables in the instance and m is the size of the domain [8]. Theorem 2 and Proposition 7 immediately yield the following.

Corollary 1. *Let (L_n) be a sampling for T which is computable in polynomial time. If all samples in (L_n) have totally symmetric polymorphism of all arities, then $\mathrm{CSP}(T)$ is polynomial-time tractable.*

We can slightly relax the requirement that all the structures in L_n have totally symmetric polymorphisms.

Proposition 9. *Let T be a theory with finite relational signature and let (L_n) be a sampling of T computable in polynomial time. If for all $n \in \mathbb{N}$ and all $\mathfrak{B} \in L_n$ there exists a model $\mathfrak{A}_{\mathfrak{B}}$ of T and a homomorphism $h \colon \mathfrak{B} \to \mathfrak{A}_{\mathfrak{B}}$ such that $h(\mathfrak{B})$ has totally symmetric polymorphisms of all arities, then $\mathrm{CSP}(T)$ is polynomial-time tractable.*

We conclude this section with an application of the developed methods to Example 1. By Lemma 2 and Lemma 3, the theories T_1 and T_2 in Example 1 have polynomial-time computable samplings, and both structures have no pp-algebraicity. Hence, by Theorem 1 there exists a polynomial-time computable sampling (L_n) for $T_1 \cup T_2$. Let τ_i be the signature of $\mathfrak{A}_i$, for $i \in \{1, 2\}$. For every $n \in \mathbb{N}$ and every $\mathfrak{B} \in L_n$ there exists an injective homomorphism h_1 from $\mathfrak{B}^{\tau_1}$ to $\mathfrak{A}_1$ and an injective homomorphism h_2 from $\mathfrak{B}^{\tau_2}$ to $\mathfrak{A}_2$; this follows by inspection of the construction of the sampling in the proof of Theorem 1 and the proofs of Lemma 2 and Lemma 3. As $\mathfrak{A}_1$ and $\mathfrak{A}_2$ are both countably infinite and h_1 and h_2 are injective, there exists a bijection f between A_1 and A_2 such that $f(h_1(a)) = h_2(a)$ for all $a \in B$, inducing a fusion $\mathfrak{A}$ of $\mathfrak{A}_1$ and $\mathfrak{A}_2$. By construction of $\mathfrak{A}$, the map h_1 is a homomorphism from $\mathfrak{B}$ to $\mathfrak{A}$.

Finally notice that we have chosen $\mathfrak{A}_1$ such that the minimum operation is a polymorphism of $\mathfrak{A}_1$. Furthermore, min is also a polymorphism of unary relations and therefore of $\mathfrak{A}$. Hence, Proposition 9 implies that $\mathrm{CSP}(T_1 \cup T_2)$ is polynomial-time tractable. Example 1 is not covered by the conditions of Nelson and Oppen, since $\mathrm{Th}(\mathfrak{A}_1)$ is *not convex*: the formula $R(x, y, z) \wedge x \neq y$ is satisfiable, the formula $R(x, y, z) \wedge y \neq z$ is satisfiable, but the formula $R(x, y, z) \wedge x \neq y \wedge y \neq z$ is not satisfiable in $\mathfrak{A}_1$.

We mention that the polynomial-time tractability of $\mathrm{CSP}(\mathfrak{A}_1)$ in our example was already known in the SMT community [2]. It is straightforward to generalize the example to any finite number m of robots, by replacing the structure $\mathfrak{A}_2$ by the structure $(\mathbb{Q}; P_1, \ldots, P_m)$ that we have already encountered in Lemma 3.

References

1. Baader, F., Schulz, K.U.: Combining constraint solving. In: Goos, G., Hartmanis, J., van Leeuwen, J., Comon, H., Marché, C., Treinen, R. (eds.) CCL 1999. LNCS, vol. 2002, pp. 104–158. Springer, Heidelberg (2001). https://doi.org/10.1007/3-540-45406-3_3

2. Bezem, M., Nieuwenhuis, R., Rodríguez-Carbonell, E.: The max-atom problem and its relevance. In: Cervesato, I., Veith, H., Voronkov, A. (eds.) LPAR 2008. LNCS (LNAI), vol. 5330, pp. 47–61. Springer, Heidelberg (2008). https://doi.org/10.1007/978-3-540-89439-1_4

3. Bodirsky, M., Greiner, J.: The complexity of combinations of qualitative constraint satisfaction problems. Log. Methods Comput. Sci. **16**(1) (2020). https://lmcs.episciences.org/6129

4. Bodirsky, M., Greiner, J.: Tractable combinations of theories via sampling (2020). https://arxiv.org/abs/2012.01199
5. Bodirsky, M., Grohe, M.: Non-dichotomies in constraint satisfaction complexity. In: Aceto, L., Damgård, I., Goldberg, L.A., Halldórsson, M.M., Ingólfsdóttir, A., Walukiewicz, I. (eds.) ICALP 2008. LNCS, vol. 5126, pp. 184–196. Springer, Heidelberg (2008). https://doi.org/10.1007/978-3-540-70583-3_16
6. Bodirsky, M., Macpherson, D., Thapper, J.: Constraint satisfaction tractability from semi-lattice operations on infinite sets. Trans. Comput. Log. (ACM-TOCL) **14**(4), 1–30 (2013)
7. Bodirsky, M., Nešetřil, J.: Constraint satisfaction with countable homogeneous templates. J. Log. Comput. **16**(3), 359–373 (2006)
8. Cooper, M.C.: An optimal k-consistency algorithm. Artif. Intell. **41**(1), 89–95 (1989). https://doi.org/10.1016/0004-3702(89)90080-5
9. Dalmau, V., Pearson, J.: Closure functions and width 1 problems. In: Jaffar, J. (ed.) CP 1999. LNCS, vol. 1713, pp. 159–173. Springer, Heidelberg (1999). https://doi.org/10.1007/978-3-540-48085-3_12
10. De Moura, L., Bjørner, N.: Satisfiability modulo theories: introduction and applications. Commun. ACM **54**(9), 69–77 (2011). https://doi.org/10.1145/1995376.1995394
11. Feder, T., Vardi, M.Y.: The computational structure of monotone monadic SNP and constraint satisfaction: a study through Datalog and group theory. SIAM J. Comput. **28**, 57–104 (1999)
12. Gol'dberg, M.K., Livshits, E.M.: On minimal universal trees. Math. Notes Acad. Sci. USSR **4**, 713–717 (1968). https://doi.org/10.1007/BF01116454
13. Hodges, W.: Model Theory. Cambridge University Press, Cambridge (1993)
14. Jeavons, P., Cohen, D., Cooper, M.: Constraints, consistency and closure. Artif. Intell. **101**(1–2), 251–265 (1998)
15. Lozin, V., Rudolf, G.: Minimal universal bipartite graphs. Ars Comb. **84**, 345–356 (2007)
16. Moon, J.W.: On minimal n-universal graphs. Proc. Glasgow Math. Assoc. **7**(1), 32–33 (1965). https://doi.org/10.1017/S2040618500035139
17. Nelson, G., Oppen, D.C.: Simplification by cooperating decision procedures. ACM Trans. Program. Lang. Syst. **1**(2), 245–257 (1979). https://doi.org/10.1145/357073.357079
18. Oppen, D.C.: Complexity, convexity and combinations of theories. Theor. Comput. Sci. **12**(3), 291–302 (1980). https://doi.org/10.1016/0304-3975(80)90059-6
19. Schulz, K.U.: Why combined decision problems are often intractable. In: Kirchner, H., Ringeissen, C. (eds.) FroCoS 2000. LNCS (LNAI), vol. 1794, pp. 217–244. Springer, Heidelberg (2000). https://doi.org/10.1007/10720084_15
20. Tinelli, C., Ringeissen, C.: Unions of non-disjoint theories and combinations of satisfiability procedures. Theor. Comput. Sci. **290**(1), 291–353 (2003). https://doi.org/10.1016/S0304-3975(01)00332-2

Analyzing Unit Read-Once Refutations in Difference Constraint Systems

K. Subramani$^{(\boxtimes)}$ and Piotr Wojciechowski

LDCSEE, West Virginia University, Morgantown, WV, USA
{k.subramani,pwojciec}@mail.wvu.edu

Abstract. In this paper, we investigate the refutability of Difference Constraint Systems (DCSs) in the Unit Read-once Refutation (UROR) system. Recall that a difference constraint is a linear relationship of the form: $x_i - x_j \leq b_{ij}$ and a DCS is a conjunction of such constraints. DCSs arise in a number of application domains such as program verification and scheduling. It follows that efficient refutation methodologies for these systems are of paramount interest. The UROR system is **incomplete**, in that unsatisfiable difference constraint systems may not have a refutation in this system. However, this refutation system provides a useful tool for proving if a DCS is infeasible because of a restriction on the values the variables can take. Note that without any absolute constraints, the values of the variable in a solution to a DCS can be uniformly increased or decreased without changing the validity of the solution. Thus, the UROR refutations of a DCS depend upon the restrictions placed on the values variables can take. This is in contrast to unrestricted refutations, which need not depend on these restrictions. Investigating **weak** (incomplete) refutation systems leads to a better understanding of the inference rules required for establishing the infeasibility of the given constraint system.

1 Introduction

This paper is concerned with refutations of difference constraint systems. Recall that a difference constraint is a linear relationship of the form: $x_i - x_j \leq b_{ij}$. A conjunction of such constraints is called a Difference Constraint System (DCS) and can be written in matrix form as: $\mathbf{A} \cdot \mathbf{x} \leq \mathbf{b}$. DCSs occur in a number of application domains such as abstract interpretation [4,5] and image segmentation [6]. Thus, efficient refutation procedures are of paramount interest. In this paper, we analyze a restricted refutation system, viz., Unit Read-once Refutation (UROR) for DCSs.

Refutations can be thought of as negative certificates. Certificates (and certifying algorithms) enhance the reliability of software. Our goal in this paper is to investigate the algorithmic complexity of finding negative certificates for DCSs

This research was supported in part by the Air-Force Research Laboratory, Rome through Contract FA8750-17-S-7007 and in part by the Air-Force Office of Scientific Research through Grant FA9550-19-1-0177.

© Springer Nature Switzerland AG 2021
W. Faber et al. (Eds.): JELIA 2021, LNAI 12678, pp. 147–161, 2021.
https://doi.org/10.1007/978-3-030-75775-5_11

within the UROR refutation system. It is worth noting that if a UROR of a DCS exists, then it must be "short". This means that the length of the refutation is polynomial in the size of the input system.

Note that the problem of finding UROR refutations is interesting since it provides domain specific refutations, i.e., these refutations prove that a DCS is infeasible on account of its current set of absolute (one variable) constraints. However, such a refutation does not establish the infeasibility of the underlying relative (two-variable) constraints (see Sect. 2). This is a marked difference from unrestricted linear refutations, which do not necessarily find domain-specific refutations.

It is important to note that UROR is an incomplete refutation system. However, incomplete systems have been studied extensively in propositional proof complexity. For instance, [14] details the computational complexity of read-once refutations in CNF formulas. Likewise, [16] discusses read-once refutations in Horn formulas. Read-once refutation systems have also been studied for linear constraint systems [24].

The principal contributions of this paper are as follows: 1. Establishing that the problem of checking if a DCS has a UROR is **NP-complete**. 2. The design of a fixed parameter tractable (**FPT**) algorithm for checking if a DCS has a UROR. 3. The design of an exact exponential algorithm for checking if a DCS has a UROR. 4. Establishing that the problem of finding the shortest UROR of a DCS is **NPO PB-complete**.

2   Statement of Problems

In this section, we define the problems under consideration.

Definition 1. *A system of constraints* $\mathbf{A} \cdot \mathbf{x} \leq \mathbf{b}$ *is said to be a Difference Constraint System (DCS) if: 1. The entries in* $\mathbf{A}$ *belong to the set* $\{0, 1, -1\}$. *2. Each row of* $\mathbf{A}$ *contains at most one positive entry. 3. Each row of* $\mathbf{A}$ *contains at most one negative entry. 4.* $\mathbf{x}$ *is a real valued vector. 5.* $\mathbf{b}$ *is an integral vector.*

In a constraint $\mathbf{a} \cdot \mathbf{x} \leq b_1$, b_1 is called the defining constant and in the constraint system $\mathbf{A} \cdot \mathbf{x} \leq \mathbf{b}$, $\mathbf{b}$ is referred to as the defining constant vector. Additionally, the terms x_i and $-x_i$ in a difference constraint are referred to as literals.

If a difference constraint has only one non-zero coefficient, then it is called an absolute constraint. Otherwise, it is called a relative constraint.

We are interested in certificates of infeasibility. In linear programs (systems of linear inequalities), refutations use the following rule:

$$\text{ADD}: \frac{\sum_{i=1}^{n} a_i \cdot x_i \leq b_1 \qquad \sum_{i=1}^{n} a_i' \cdot x_i \leq b_2}{\sum_{i=1}^{n} (a_i + a_i') \cdot x_i \leq b_1 + b_2} \qquad (1)$$

We refer to Rule (1) as the **ADD rule**. This rule is analogous to resolution in clausal formulas. It is easy to see that Rule (1) is sound since any assignment that satisfies the hypotheses also satisfies the consequent. Additionally, the rule is **complete**. This means that repeated application of Rule (1) will result in a contradiction of the form: $0 \leq b$, $b < 0$ for every linearly infeasible system. The completeness of the ADD rule was established by Farkas [9], in a lemma that is famously known as Farkas' Lemma for systems of linear inequalities [20].

Farkas' lemma provides a compact proof of infeasibility for linear systems. Additionally, basic feasible solutions provide a compact proof of linear feasibility for linear programs. Together, these two properties establish that the linear programming problem is in the complexity class **NP ∩ coNP**. Farkas' lemma is one of several lemmata that consider pairs of linear systems in which exactly one element of the pair is feasible. These lemmata are collectively referred to as "Theorems of the Alternative" [17].

Definition 2. *A* linear refutation *is a sequence of applications of the ADD rule that results in a contradiction of the form* $0 \leq b$, $b \leq -1$.

In general, applying the ADD rule to an infeasible system $\mathbf{A} \cdot \mathbf{x} \leq \mathbf{b}$, could result in a contradiction of the form $0 \leq b$, $b < 0$. However, in case of DCSs (with integral defining constants), we must have $b \leq -1$.

Our principal focus is on the number of inferences used in a refutation.

Definition 3. *The* **length** *of a refutation is the number of inferences (applications of the ADD rule) in the refutation.*

The length of a refutation R is denoted as $|R|$. Note that in general, the problem of finding a shortest refutation of a DCS can be solved in polynomial time [22,23].

In this paper, we study a restricted version of the ADD rule, known as the unit-ADD rule. In the unit-ADD rule, at least one of the constraints must be an absolute constraint. In DCSs, this rule has the following form:

$$\text{unit-ADD} : \frac{a_i \cdot x_i \leq b_1 \qquad a_j \cdot x_j - a_i \cdot x_i \leq b_2}{a_j \cdot x_j \leq b_1 + b_2}$$

A linear refutation using only the unit-ADD rule is called a unit refutation.

In this paper, we utilize the network construction associated with difference constraints [2]. From a DCS $\mathbf{D}$, this construction creates a directed graph $\mathbf{G} = \langle \mathbf{V}, \mathbf{E}, \mathbf{c} \rangle$ as follows:

1. For each variable x_i in the DCS, create the vertex v_i.
2. Create the vertex v_0.
3. For each constraint l_k in the DCS:
   (a) If l_k is of the form $x_i - x_j \leq b_{ij}$, then create the edge (i, j) of weight $\mathbf{c}(i, j) = b_{ij}$ from v_j to v_i.
   (b) If l_k is of the form $x_i \leq b_i$, then create the edge $(0, i)$ of weight $\mathbf{c}(0, i) = b_i$ from v_0 to v_i.
   (c) If l_k is of the form $-x_i \leq b_i$, then create the edge $(i, 0)$ of weight $\mathbf{c}(i, 0) = b_i$ from v_i to v_0.

Example 1. Figure 1 shows a DCS **D** and its corresponding directed graph **G**.

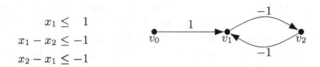

$$x_1 \leq 1$$
$$x_1 - x_2 \leq -1$$
$$x_2 - x_1 \leq -1$$

Fig. 1. Example DCS and its corresponding directed graph.

DCS **D** has the following refutation:

1. ADD $x_1 - x_2 \leq -1$ and $x_2 - x_1 \leq -1$ to get $0 \leq -2$.

However, DCS **D** does not have a unit refutation. Observe that $x_1 \leq 1$ is the only absolute constraint in **D**, thus it must be used in a unit refutation of **D**. It is easy to see that a unit refutation of **D**, if one existed, would have the following form:

1. ADD $x_1 \leq 1$ and $x_2 - x_1 \leq -1$ to get $x_2 \leq 0$.
2. ADD $x_2 \leq 0$ and $x_1 - x_2 \leq -1$ to get $x_1 \leq -1$.

3. $\vdots$

D does not have any unit constraints that cancel either x_1 from the constraint $x_1 \leq -1$ or that cancel x_2 from the constraint $x_2 \leq 0$. Thus, there is no way to complete this unit refutation.

Since unit refutation is a restriction of linear refutation, it is clearly a sound refutation system. However, it is not length preserving (proof omitted due to space requirements).

We now introduce the notion of read-once refutations.

Definition 4. *A **read-once** refutation is a refutation in which each constraint can be used at most once.*

Note that the restriction of being used at most once applies to constraints present in the original system and those derived as a result of previous applications of the ADD rule.

We now formally define the type of refutation discussed in this paper.

Definition 5. *A **Unit Read-once Refutation** (UROR) is a refutation in which each inference is an application of the unit-ADD rule and each constraint can be used at most once.*

Note that a UROR is both a unit refutation and a read-once refutation. However, a DCS can have both a unit refutation and a read-once refutation, but not have a UROR.

Example 2. Figure 2 shows a DCS **D** and its corresponding directed graph **G**.

$$x_1 \leq \quad 1000$$
$$-x_1 \leq -1$$
$$x_1 - x_2 \leq -1$$
$$x_2 - x_1 \leq -1$$

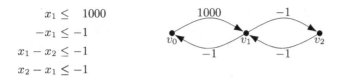

Fig. 2. Example DCS and its corresponding directed graph.

DCS **D** has the following unit refutation:

1. ADD $x_1 \leq 1000$ and $x_2 - x_1 \leq -1$ to get $x_2 \leq 999$.
2. ADD $x_2 \leq 999$ and $x_1 - x_2 \leq -1$ to get $x_1 \leq 998$.

3. $\vdots$
4. ADD $x_2 \leq 1$ and $x_1 - x_2 \leq -1$ to get $x_1 \leq 0$.
5. ADD $x_1 \leq 0$ and $-x_1 \leq -1$ to get $0 \leq -1$.

Additionally, **D** has the following read-once refutation: ADD $x_2 - x_1 \leq -1$ and $x_1 - x_2 \leq -1$ to get $0 \leq -2$.

Note that any unit refutation of **D** must use the constraint $x_1 \leq 1000$. Thus, **D** does not have a UROR.

3 Motivation and Related Work

In this paper, we examine the problem of finding specific forms of refutations for systems of difference constraints. These refutations serve as negative certificates for the DCS feasibility problem. In other words, they are used to prove that a given DCS has no linear or integer solutions.

The focus on unit (read-once) refutations in this paper stems from a fundamental difference between absolute constraints and relative constraints in DCSs. Since absolute constraints only place bounds on a single variable, they can be used to define the domain over which feasibility is considered. Meanwhile, relative constraints define the relationship between variables and can be considered domain agnostic. This difference in the two types of difference constraints carries over to create a difference between unit and non-unit refutations.

A unit refutation relies on the absolute constraints in the underlying DCS. Thus, a unit refutation serves as a domain-specific refutation. This is in contrast to an unrestricted refutation that may be domain agnostic. Thus, a study of unit refutations is important since it reveals the structure of such domain-specific refutations.

Note that unit refutations may be required to use specific constraints within a DCS. As a result, a unit refutation may be exponentially longer than an unrestricted refutation of the same system (proof in full paper). Because of this inflated length, this paper studies unit read-once refutations. These refutations combine the restrictions of unit refutations and read-once refutations to generate domain specific refutations that are guaranteed to be short.

For the feasibility problem in various constraint systems, certificates can be divided into two main categories, positive certificates and negative certificates. For a given constraint system $\mathbf{P} : \mathbf{A} \cdot \mathbf{x} \leq \mathbf{b}$, any satisfying assignment to the system serves as a positive certificate. However, the form negative certificates take depends on the form of the constraint system.

The infeasibility of linear systems is commonly established using Farkas' lemma [9]. As a result of Farkas' lemma, a proof of linear infeasibility can simply be a non-negative vector $\mathbf{y}$, such that $\mathbf{y} \cdot \mathbf{A} = \mathbf{0}$, $\mathbf{y} \cdot \mathbf{b} < \mathbf{0}$. This vector $\mathbf{y}$ is called the Farkas witness of the infeasibility of $\mathbf{P}$. Similarly, the elements of $\mathbf{y}$ are called Farkas variables.

Note that the Farkas vector $\mathbf{y}$ corresponds to a summation of the constraints in $\mathbf{P}$. Such a refutation can be broken up into individual summations, each between a pair of constraints. These summations correspond to applications of the ADD inference rule. This provides an additional form for refutations of linear programs that corresponds to a step by step refutation procedure. In the summation version of the refutation, we can examine different structural properties (tree-like refutations vs. Dag-like refutations) and restrictions (read-once refutations and unit refutations).

In a UROR, the ADD rule plays a role, similar to that of resolution in refutations of clausal systems. Resolution was introduced in [19] as a refutation system used to establish the unsatisfiability of clausal Boolean formulas. Resolution is only one of many refutation systems used for clausal formulas [25]. Resolution is both sound and complete. However, it is not considered to be an efficient refutation system [12].

This paper focuses specifically on systems of difference constraints. In particular, we focus on the problem of finding short refutations of DCSs. The problem of finding the shortest refutation (not necessarily unit) of a DCS is motivated by a number of applications, as discussed in [22], including program verification [3,18,21], real-time scheduling [11,13], and incremental shortest paths in weighted networks [8]. The first polynomial-time algorithm for this problem was proposed in [22] and runs in $O(n^3 \cdot \log K)$ time, where n is the number of vertices in the corresponding network $\mathbf{G}$ [2], and K is the length of the refutation. The current fastest deterministic algorithm runs in $O(m \cdot n \cdot K)$ time [23], where m is the number of edges in $\mathbf{G}$.

In this paper, we focus on a restricted version of linear refutations, viz., unit read-once refutations. In particular, we focus on refutations in which each inference must use an absolute constraint and each constraint can be used at most once. Note that placing these restrictions on a refutation system can cause the refutation system to become **incomplete**. Additionally, we study how this restriction affects refutation length.

There are several reasons to consider restricted refutation systems, viz.

1. Restricted refutations tend to be compact (polynomial in the size of the input). For instance, URORs are at most linear in the size of the input.
2. For specific constraint systems, the existence of these restricted refutations can be checked efficiently. For example, [22] showed every infeasible DCS has

a read-once refutation and that such a refutation can be found in polynomial time. While systems of Unit Two Variable Per Inequality (UTVPI) constraints do not always have read-once refutations, these refutations can still be found in polynomial time [24]. Note that UTVPI constraints are a more general form of difference constraints in which constraints of the form $x_i + x_j \leq b_{ij}$ and $-x_i - x_j \leq b_{ij}$ are permitted.

4 The UROR Refutation System

In this section, we examine the problem of checking if a DCS has a UROR. We also examine the problem of finding the shortest UROR of a DCS.

4.1 The Feasibility Problem

We first show that the problem of checking if a DCS **D** has a UROR is **NP-complete**. This is done by a reduction from the Hamiltonian Cycle problem:

From a directed graph **G** with n vertices and m edges we construct a DCS **D** as follows: 1. For each vertex v_i in **G**, create the variables x_i^+ and x_i^-. Additionally, create the constraint $x_i^+ - x_i^- \leq 0$ for each $i > 1$. 2. For each edge (v_i, v_j) in **G**, create the constraint $x_j^- - x_i^+ \leq -1$. 3. Create the constraints $x_1^+ \leq n - 1$ and $-x_1^- \leq 0$.

Example 3. Figure 3 shows a directed graph **G** and its corresponding DCS **D**.

$$
\begin{aligned}
x_1^+ &\leq 3 & -x_1^- &\leq 0 \\
x_2^+ - x_2^- &\leq 0 & x_3^+ - x_3^- &\leq 0 \\
x_4^+ - x_4^- &\leq 0 & x_1^- - x_2^+ &\leq -1 \\
x_3^- - x_1^+ &\leq -1 & x_2^- - x_3^+ &\leq -1 \\
x_2^- - x_4^+ &\leq -1 & x_4^- - x_3^+ &\leq -1
\end{aligned}
$$

Fig. 3. Example directed graph and its corresponding DCS

We now show that **D** has a UROR if and only if **G** has a Hamiltonian Cycle.

Lemma 1. *Let* **G** *be a directed graph.* **G** *has a Hamiltonian Cycle, if and only if the corresponding DCS* **D** *has a UROR.*

Proof. First, suppose that **G** has a Hamiltonian Cycle C. Let $v_{C(k)}$ be the kth vertex in the cycle. Assume without loss of generality that $v_{C(1)} = v_1$. We construct a UROR R of **D** as follows:

1. Start with the constraint $x_1^+ \leq n - 1$.
2. The edge $(v_1, v_{C(2)})$ is in C. Thus, the constraint $x_{C(2)}^- - x_1^+ \leq -1$ is in **D**. Apply the ADD rule to this constraint and $x_1^+ \leq n - 1$ to get $x_{C(2)}^- \leq n - 2$.

3. The constraint $x_{C(2)}^+ - x_{C(2)}^- \leq 0$ is in **D**. Apply the ADD rule to this constraint and $x_{C(2)}^- \leq n - 2$ to get $x_{C(2)}^+ \leq n - 2$.
4. The edge $(v_{C(2)}, v_{C(3)})$ is in C. Thus, the constraint $x_{C(3)}^- - x_{C(2)}^+ \leq -1$ is in **D**. Apply the ADD rule to this constraint and $x_{C(2)}^+ \leq n - 2$ to get $x_{C(3)}^- \leq n - 3$.
5. Continue this process until the constraint $x_{C(n)}^+ \leq 0$ is derived.
6. The edge $(v_{C(n)}, v_1)$ is in C. Thus, the constraint $x_1^- - x_{C(n)}^+ \leq -1$ is in **D**. Apply the ADD rule to this constraint and $x_{C(n)}^+ \leq 0$ to get $x_1^- \leq -1$.
7. Apply the ADD rule to the constraints $x_1^- \leq -1$ and $-x_1^- \leq 0$ to get the contradiction $0 \leq -1$.

Since C is a Hamiltonian Cycle, no edge or vertex in C is repeated. Thus, R uses each constraint at most once. This means that R is a UROR as desired.

Now suppose that **D** has a UROR R. From R we construct a Hamiltonian Cycle C as follows: For each constraint of the form $x_j^- - x_i^+ \leq -1$ in R add the edge (x_i, x_j) to C. We make the following observations about the structures of R and C:

1. Recall that R must use a constraint of the form $x_i \leq b$. By construction, the only constraint in **D** of this form is $x_1^+ \leq n - 1$. Thus, this constraint must be in R.
2. Since R is a refutation, the constant in the derived constraint must be negative. Thus R must use at least n constraints of the form $x_j^- - x_i^+ \leq -1$. This means that C contains at least n edges.
3. The constraint $x_i^+ - x_i^- \leq 0$ is used at most once by R. By construction, this is the only constraint with the terms x_i^+ and $-x_i^-$. Thus, at most one constraint in R has the term $-x_i^+$ and at most once constraint in R has the term x_i^-. This means that C has at most one edge entering the vertex v_i and at most one edge leaving the vertex v_i.
4. Thus, C must be a Hamiltonian Cycle as desired.   □

Theorem 1. *The problem of checking if a DCS* **D** *has a UROR is* **NP-complete**.

Proof. Since each constraint in a UROR is used at most once, we know that the length of any UROR of **D** is polynomial in the size of **D**. Thus, the problem of checking if **D** has a UROR is in **NP**.

From Lemma 1, we can reduce the problem of checking if a graph **G** has a Hamiltonian Cycle to the problem of checking if the corresponding DCS **D** has a UROR. Since the problem of checking if **G** has a Hamiltonian Cycle is **NP-complete**, the problem of checking if **D** has a UROR is **NP-hard**. Thus, this problem is **NP-complete**.   □

4.2   An FPT Algorithm

We now present an FPT algorithm for finding a UROR R of a DCS **D** parameterized by k, the length of R. Let **G** be the corresponding directed graph.

This algorithm proceeds by first partitioning the constraints of $\mathbf{D}$ into the sets $S_1, \ldots, S_k$. Let $S(i, j)$ be the set containing edge (i, j). Then the algorithm finds the shortest path from v_0 to itself using at most one edge from each partition. We refer to such a walk as a partitioned walk.

Let $H \subseteq \{S_1, \ldots, S_k\}$, and let $L(i, H)$ be the length of the shortest path from v_0 to v_i using exactly one edge from the set S_l for each $S_l \in H$ and no edges from any other set. Note that $L(i, \{S(0, i)\}) = \mathbf{c}(0, i)$ for each vertex v_i adjacent to v_0 (see Sect. 2). We now show that $L(i, H) = \min_{\{v_j : S(i,j) \in H\}} \mathbf{c}(i, j) + L(j, H \setminus \{S(i, j)\})$.

Theorem 2. $L(i, H)$ *is governed by the recurrence relation*
$$L(i, H) = \min_{\{v_j : S(i,j) \in H\}} \mathbf{c}(i, j) + L(j, H \setminus \{S(i, j)\}).$$

Proof. Consider the shortest path p from v_0 to v_i using exactly one edge from the set S_l for each $S_l \in H$ and no edges from any other set. Assume that $L(j, H')$ correctly computes the length of the shortest paths for each $H' \subset H$.

Note that the last edge of p must be an edge from some v_j to v_i. Let this edge belong to the set $S(i, j) \in H$. Thus, the remaining path must be the shortest path from v_0 to v_j using exactly one edge from each set in $H \setminus \{S(i, j)\}$ and no edges from any other set. The length of this path is precisely $L(j, H \setminus \{S(i, j)\})$. Thus, $L(i, H) = \min_{\{v_j : S(i,j) \in H\}} \mathbf{c}(i, j) + L(j, H \setminus \{S(i, j)\})$. $\square$

First, we provide a randomized algorithm for finding a UROR of a DCS $\mathbf{D}$ with m constraints over n variables. This is represented by Algorithm 4.1.

DCS-UROR_RAND (system $\mathbf{D}$ of difference constraints)
1: Create the sets S_1 through S_k.
2: Create the directed graph $\mathbf{G}$ corresponding to $\mathbf{D}$.
3: Create the function $L(i, H)$ and define $L(i, \{(0, i)\}) = \mathbf{c}(0, i)$ for each vertex v_i.
4: **for** (each edge (i, j) in $\mathbf{G}$) **do**
5:     Randomly assign (i, j) to a set S_l. {Let $S(i, j)$ denote this set.}
6: **for** (each vertex v_i and each $H \subseteq \{S_1, \ldots, S_k\}$) **do**
7:     $L(i, H) = \min_{\{v_j : S(i,j) \in H\}} \mathbf{c}(i, j) + L(j, H \setminus \{S(i, j)\})$.
8: **if** ($L(0, H) < 0$ for any $H \subseteq \{S_1, \ldots, S_k\}$) **then**
9:     **return** $\mathbf{D}$ has a UROR.
10: **return** $\mathbf{D}$ has no UROR.

Algorithm 4.1. Randomized UROR algorithm for DCS

Note that once $L(j, H')$ is known for each j and $H' \subset H$, $L(i, H)$ can be found in $O(n)$ time. Thus, Algorithm 4.1 runs in $O(2^k \cdot n^2)$ time.

We now show that $\mathbf{D}$ has a UROR if Algorithm 4.1 returns **true**. We also show that if $\mathbf{D}$ has a UROR that uses k constraints, then Algorithm 4.1 returns **true** with a probability of at least $\frac{1}{e^k}$.

Theorem 3. *If Algorithm 4.1 returns true, then* $\mathbf{D}$ *has a UROR.*

Proof. Assume Algorithm 4.1 returns **true**. Thus, there exist sets S_1 through S_k such that there exists a negative weight partitioned walk through v_0. Since this is a negative weight closed walk in G that uses each edge at most once, it corresponds to a UROR of **D**. $\square$

Theorem 4. *If* **D** *has a UROR that uses at most* k *constraints, then Algorithm 4.1 will return* **true** *with probability at least* $\frac{1}{e^k}$.

Proof. Let R be a UROR of **D** that uses at most k constraints. We want to find the probability that each edge in R is assigned to a different set S_l. Note that there are k^m different ways to assign the edges of **G** to sets and in $k! \cdot k^{m-k}$ of there the edges corresponding to R are assigned to different sets. This has probability $\frac{k!}{k^k} > \frac{1}{e^k}$. $\square$

To obtain an FPT algorithm for finding a UROR, we derandomize this algorithm as described in [7]. This derandomization utilizes (m, k)-perfect hash families that are defined as follows:

Definition 6. *Let S be a set of size m. An (m, k)-perfect hash family is a family U of functions F that partition S into S_1 through S_k such that for any set $R \subseteq S$ of size k, there exists a function that assigns each element of R to a different partition.*

Let R be a UROR of **D** of that uses at most k constraints. Let U be an (m, k)-perfect hash family for **D**. Then, for some $F \in U$, we have that every edge corresponding to R is assigned to different S_i. Note that we can construct an (m, k)-perfect hash family for **D** of size $e^k \cdot k^{O(\log k)} \cdot \log m$ in $O(e^k \cdot k^{O(\log k)} \cdot m \cdot \log m)$ time [7].

Thus, given k, checking if **D** has a UROR using at most k constraints can be done as follows: 1. Construct an (m, k)-perfect hash family set U for **D**. Note that U contains $e^k \cdot k^{O(\log k)} \cdot \log m$ partitions of **D**. This can be done in time $O(e^k \cdot k^{O(\log k)} \cdot m \cdot \log m)$. 2. For each partition, check if **D** has a negative cycle through v_0 using at most one edge from each set S_i. Using the method described previously, this takes $O(2^k \cdot n^2)$ time for each of the $e^k \cdot k^{O(\log k)} \cdot \log m$ partitions. This algorithm runs in time $O((2 \cdot e)^k \cdot k^{O(\log k)} \cdot n^2 \cdot \log m)$. Thus, this is an FPT algorithm for finding a UROR of a DCS.

4.3   An Exact Exponential Algorithm

We now present an exact exponential algorithm DCS-UROR_EXP(**D**) for finding a UROR R of a DCS **D**. Since this procedure involves a polynomial-time check for each subset of constraints in **D**, it runs in time $O^*(2^m)$. We now establish that this algorithm correctly determines if **D** has a UROR.

Theorem 5. *Let* **D** *be a DCS, Algorithm 4.2 correctly determines if* **D** *has a UROR.*

DCS-UROR_EXP (system **D** of difference constraints)
1: **for** (each subset S of **D**) **do**
2:     Construct the graph $\mathbf{G}_S$ corresponding to S.
3:     **if** ($\mathbf{G}_S$ is strongly connected, S contains an absolute constraint, and summing the constraints in S results in $0 \leq b$, $b < 0$.) **then**
4:         **return D** has a UROR.
5: **return D** has no UROR.

Algorithm 4.2. Exact Exponential UROR algorithm for DCS

Proof. If Algorithm 4.2 declares that **D** has a read-once refutation, then there exists a subset S of **D** such that S has the following properties: 1. The directed graph $\mathbf{G}_S$ corresponding to S is strongly connected. 2. S contains an absolute constraint. 3. Summing the constraints in S results in a constraint of the form $0 \leq b$ where $b < 0$.

Since summing the constraints in S results in a contradiction, each variable appears the same number of times with coefficient 1 as it does with coefficient -1. Thus, each vertex in $\mathbf{G}_S$ has the same number of inbound edges as outbound edges. Consequently, since $\mathbf{G}_S$ is strongly connected it contains an Eulerian Tour [10]. Since S contains an absolute constraint, $\mathbf{G}_S$ contains the vertex v_0. If we start with the absolute constraint corresponding to the edge leaving x_0, we can sum the constraints in the order corresponding to the order of the edges in the Eulerian Tour. Each summation in this process involves a unit constraint, thus this summation is a unit refutation of **D**. Since each constraint is used at most once in this summation, this is a UROR of **D**.   □

Note that a naive approach needs to test all possible orders of constraints. This results in a running time of $O^*(m!)$. The $O^*(2^m)$ algorithm presented here represents an improvement over this naive approach.

5   Approximability

We now show that the problem of approximating the length of the shortest UROR of a DCS **D** is **NPO PB-complete**. This is done by a strict reduction from the shortest path with forbidden pairs problem [1].

This problem is defined as follows: Given a graph **G**, l forbidden pairs of vertices r_1 through r_l, source s, and target t find the shortest path from s to t using at most one vertex from each pair. This problem is known to be **NPO PB-complete** [15].

From a directed graph **G** with n vertices and m edges we construct a DCS **D** as follows:

1. For each vertex v_i in **G**, create the variables $x_{i,0}$ thorough $x_{i,l}$. Additionally, create the constraints $x_{i,0} - x_{i,1} \leq 0$ through $x_{i,l-1} - x_{i,l} \leq 0$ for each $i > 1$.
2. For each forbidden pair $r_w = \{v_i, v_j\}$, create the vertex y_w and the constraints $x_{i,w} - y_l \leq 0$, $x_{j,w} - y_l \leq 0$, $y_{l+1} - x_{i,w} \leq 0$, and $y_{l+1} - x_{j,w} \leq 0$

3. For each edge (v_i, v_j) in $\mathbf{G}$, create the constraint $x_{j,l} - x_{i,0} \leq 0$.
4. For each edge (s, v_i) in $\mathbf{G}$, create the constraint $x_{i,l} \leq 0$.
5. For each edge (v_i, t) in $\mathbf{G}$, create the constraint $t - x_{i,0} \leq 0$.
6. Create the constraints $y_1 - t \leq -1$ and $-y_{k+1} \leq 0$.

Observe that the above reduction can be performed in polynomial time.

We now show that $\mathbf{D}$ has a UROR of length $(l+1) \cdot (k+1)$ if and only if $\mathbf{G}$ has a path with forbidden pairs of length k from s to t.

Lemma 2. *Let $\mathbf{G}$ be a directed graph. $\mathbf{G}$ has a path with forbidden pairs of length k from s to t, if and only if the corresponding DCS $\mathbf{D}$ has a UROR of length $(l+1) \cdot (k+1)$.*

Proof. First, suppose that $\mathbf{G}$ has a valid path P (no forbidden pairs) of length k, from s to t. Let $v_{P(r)}$ be the rth vertex in the path. We construct a UROR R of $\mathbf{D}$ as follows:

1. Start with the constraint $x_{P(1),l} \leq 0$.
2. Apply the ADD rule to this constraint an the constraints $x_{P(1),l-1} - x_{P(1),l} \leq 0$ through $x_{P(1),0} - x_{P(1),1} \leq 0$.
3. The edge $(v_{P(1)}, v_{P(2)})$ is in P. Thus, the constraint $x_{P(2),l} - x_{P(1),0} \leq 0$ is in $\mathbf{D}$. Apply the ADD rule to this constraint and $x_{P(1),0} \leq 0$ to get $x_{P(2),l} \leq 0$.
4. The the constraints $x_{P(2),l-1} - x_{P(2),l} \leq 0$ through $x_{P(2),0} - x_{P(2),1} \leq 0$ are in $\mathbf{D}$. Apply the ADD rule to these constraints and $x_{P(2),l} \leq 0$ to get $x_{P(2),0} \leq 0$.
5. The edge $(v_{P(2)}, v_{P(3)})$ is in P. Thus, the constraint $x_{P(3),l} - x_{P(2),0} \leq 0$ is in $\mathbf{D}$. Apply the ADD rule to this constraint and $x_{P(2),0} \leq 0$ to get $x_{P(3),l} \leq 0$.
6. Continue this process until the constraint $t \leq 0$ is derived.

Since P does not use both vertices of any forbidden pair we can derive the constraint $-t \leq 1$ without reusing a constraint. Thus, R uses each constraint at most once. This means that R is a UROR as desired. Note that R has $(k+1) \cdot (l+1)$ uses of the ADD rule.

Now suppose that $\mathbf{D}$ has a UROR R. From R we construct a valid path P as follows: For each constraint of the form $x_{j,l} - x_{i,0} \leq 0$ in R add the edge (x_i, x_j) to P. We make the following observations about the structures of R and P:

1. Recall that R must use a constraint of the form $x_{i,l} \leq b$. By construction, the only constraints in $\mathbf{D}$ of this form correspond to edges leaving s.
2. Since R is a refutation, the constant in the derived constraint must be negative. Thus R must use the constraint of the form $y_1 - t \leq -1$. This means that P contains a path from s to t.
3. The constraint $x_{i,r} - x_{i,r+1} \leq 0$ is used at most once by R. By construction, this is the only constraint with the terms $x_{i,r}$ and $-x_{i,r+1}$. Thus, at most one constraint in R has the term $-x_{i,r}$ and at most once constraint in R has the term $x_{i,r+1}$. This means that P has at most one edge entering the vertex v_i and at most one edge leaving the vertex v_i.

4. R must derive a contradiction from the constraint $y_1 \leq -1$. To cancel each y_j, R must use a constraint of the form $x_{i,r} - y_j \leq 0$ for some x_i in the rth forbidden pair. Thus, the original path cannot use both vertices from the pair.

Note that an edge is added to P for each $(l+1)$ inferences in R. This is followed by an additional $(l+1)$ inferences. Thus, if R has length $(l+1) \cdot (k+1)$, then P has length k.   □

Example 4. Figure 4 shows a directed graph **G** with forbidden pair (v_1, v_2) and its corresponding DCS **D**.

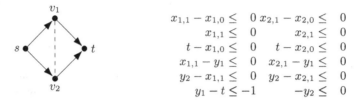

$$
\begin{array}{ll}
x_{1,1} - x_{1,0} \leq 0 & x_{2,1} - x_{2,0} \leq 0 \\
x_{1,1} \leq 0 & x_{2,1} \leq 0 \\
t - x_{1,0} \leq 0 & t - x_{2,0} \leq 0 \\
x_{1,1} - y_1 \leq 0 & x_{2,1} - y_1 \leq 0 \\
y_2 - x_{1,1} \leq 0 & y_2 - x_{2,1} \leq 0 \\
y_1 - t \leq -1 & -y_2 \leq 0
\end{array}
$$

Fig. 4. Example directed graph and its corresponding DCS

Theorem 6. *The problem of finding the shortest UROR of a DCS* **D** *is* **NPO PB-complete**.

Proof. Since the refutation is read-once, the length of the shortest UROR of a DCS with m constraints is at most m. Thus, this problem is in **NPO PB**. From Lemma 2, if we can approximate the shortest UROR of a DCS to within a factor of α, then we can approximate the length of a shortest path with forbidden pairs to within a factor of α. Thus, this reduction is a strict reduction. Recall that the shortest path with forbidden pairs problem is **NPO PB-complete**. Thus, the problem of finding a shortest UROR of a DCS is **NPO PB-complete**.   □

6   Conclusion

In this paper, we studied an incomplete refutation system, viz., UROR, for difference constraint systems. For the UROR system in DCSs, we established **NP-hardness** for the feasibility problem and discussed a fixed-parameter tractable algorithm and an exact exponential algorithm for the same. We also considered the problem of finding the shortest refutation of a DCS in the UROR system and showed that it is **NPO PB-complete**. As discussed before, the study of unit read-once refutations is well-motivated.

References

1. Ausiello, G., Crescenzi, P., Gambosi, G., Kann, V., Marchetti-Spaccamela, A., Protasi, M.: Complexity and Approximation: Combinatorial Optimization and Their Approximability Properties, 1st edn. Springer, Heidelberg (1999). https://doi.org/10.1007/978-3-642-58412-1
2. Cormen, T.H., Leiserson, C.E., Rivest, R.L., Stein, C.: Introduction to Algorithms, 3rd edn. The MIT Press, Cambridge (2009)
3. Cotton, S., Asarin, E., Maler, O., Niebert, P.: Some progress in satisfiability checking for difference logic. In: Lakhnech, Y., Yovine, S. (eds.) FORMATS/FTRTFT -2004. LNCS, vol. 3253, pp. 263–276. Springer, Heidelberg (2004). https://doi.org/10.1007/978-3-540-30206-3_19
4. Cotton, S., Maler, O.: Fast and flexible difference constraint propagation for DPLL(T). In: Biere, A., Gomes, C.P. (eds.) SAT 2006. LNCS, vol. 4121, pp. 170–183. Springer, Heidelberg (2006). https://doi.org/10.1007/11814948_19
5. Cousot, P., Cousot, R.: Abstract interpretation: a unified lattice model for static analysis of programs by construction or approximation of fixpoints. In: POPL, pp. 238–252 (1977)
6. Cox, I.J., Rao, S.B., Zhong, Y.: Ratio regions: a technique for image segmentation. In: Proceedings of the International Conference on Pattern Recognition, pp. 557–564. IEEE, August 1996
7. Cygan, M., et al.: Parameterized Algorithms. Springer, Cham (2015). https://doi.org/10.1007/978-3-319-21275-3
8. Demtrescu, C., Italiano, G.F.: A new approach to dynamic all pairs shortest paths. J. ACM $51(6)$, 968–992 (2004)
9. Farkas, G.: Über die Theorie der Einfachen Ungleichungen. J. für die Reine und Angewandte Mathematik $124(124)$, 1–27 (1902)
10. Fleury, P.-H.: Deux problèmes de géométrie de situation. J. de mathématiques élémentaires, 2nd ser. 2, 257–261 (1883). (in French)
11. Gerber, R., Pugh, W., Saksena, M.: Parametric dispatching of hard real-time tasks. IEEE Trans. Comput. $44(3)$, 471–479 (1995)
12. Haken, A.: The intractability of resolution. Theor. Comput. Sci. $39(2–3)$, 297–308 (1985)
13. Han, C.C., Lin, K.J.: Job scheduling with temporal distance constraints. Technical report UIUCDCS-R-89-1560, University of Illinois at Urbana-Champaign, Department of Computer Science (1989)
14. Iwama, K., Miyano, E.: Intractability of read-once resolution. In: Proceedings of the 10th Annual Conference on Structure in Complexity Theory (SCTC 1995), Los Alamitos, CA, USA, pp. 29–36. IEEE Computer Society Press, June 1995
15. Kann, V.: Polynomially bounded minimization problems that are hard to approximate. Nord. J. Comput. $1(3)$, 317–331 (1994)
16. Kleine Büning, H., Wojciechowski, P., Subramani, K.: Read-once resolutions in horn formulas. In: Chen, Y., Deng, X., Lu, M. (eds.) FAW 2019. LNCS, vol. 11458, pp. 100–110. Springer, Cham (2019). https://doi.org/10.1007/978-3-030-18126-0_9
17. Nemhauser, G.L., Wolsey, L.A.: Integer and Combinatorial Optimization. Wiley, New York (1999)
18. Nieuwenhuis, R., Oliveras, A.: DPLL(T) with exhaustive theory propagation and its application to difference logic. In: Etessami, K., Rajamani, S.K. (eds.) CAV 2005. LNCS, vol. 3576, pp. 321–334. Springer, Heidelberg (2005). https://doi.org/10.1007/11513988_33

19. John Alan Robinson: A machine-oriented logic based on the resolution principle. J. ACM **12**(1), 23–41 (1965)
20. Schrijver, A.: Theory of Linear and Integer Programming. Wiley, New York (1987)
21. Seshia, S.A., Lahiri, S.K., Bryant, R.E.: A hybrid sat-based decision procedure for separation logic with uninterpreted functions. In: DAC, pp. 425–430 (2003)
22. Subramani, K.: Optimal length resolution refutations of difference constraint systems. J. Autom. Reason. (JAR) **43**(2), 121–137 (2009). https://doi.org/10.1007/s10817-009-9139-4
23. Subramani, K., Williamson, M., Gu, X.: Improved algorithms for optimal length resolution refutation in difference constraint systems. Formal Aspects Comput. **25**(2), 319–341 (2013). https://doi.org/10.1007/s00165-011-0186-3
24. Subramani, K., Wojciechowki, P.: A polynomial time algorithm for read-once certification of linear infeasibility in UTVPI constraints. Algorithmica **81**(7), 2765–2794 (2019). https://doi.org/10.1007/s00453-019-00554-z
25. Urquhart, A.: The complexity of propositional proofs. Bull. Symb. Log. **1**(4), 425–467 (1995)

Residuation for Soft Constraints: Lexicographic Orders and Approximation Techniques

Fabio Gadducci[1(✉)] and Francesco Santini[2]

[1] Dipartimento di Informatica, Università di Pisa, Pisa, Italy
fabio.gadducci@unipi.it
[2] Dipartimento di Matematica e Informatica, Università di Perugia, Perugia, Italy
francesco.santini@unipg.it

Abstract. Residuation theory concerns the study of partially ordered algebraic structures, most often monoids, equipped with a weak inverse for the monoidal operator. One of its area of application has been constraint programming, whose key requirement is the presence of an aggregator operator for combining preferences. Given a residuated monoid of preferences, the paper first shows how to build a new residuated monoid of (possibly infinite) tuples, which is based on the lexicographic order. Second, it introduces a variant of an approximation technique (known as Mini-bucket) that exploits the presence of the weak inverse.

1 Introduction

Residuation theory [5] concerns the study of partially ordered algebraic structures, most often just monoids, equipped with an operator that behaves as a weak inverse to the monoidal one, without the structure being necessarily a group. Such structures have since long been investigated in mathematics and computer science. Concerning e.g. logics, residuated monoids form the basis for the semantics of substructural logics [18]. As for e.g. discrete event systems such as weighted automata, the use of tropical semirings put forward the adoption of residuals for the approximated solution of inequalities [1].

One of the recent area of application of residuation theory has been constraint programming. Roughly, a *Soft Constraint Satisfaction Problem* is given by a relation on a set of variables, plus a preference score to each assignment of such variables [3,23]. They key requirement is the presence of an aggregator operator for combining preferences, making such a set a monoid, and a large body of work has been devoted to enrich such a structure, guaranteeing that resolution techniques can be generalised by a parametric formalism for designing metrics and algorithms. An example are *local-consistency* algorithms [2], devised for safely moving costs towards constraints involving a smaller number of variables,

Research partially supported by the MIUR PRIN 2017FTXR7S "IT-MaTTerS" and by GNCS-INdAM ("Gruppo Nazionale per il Calcolo Scientifico").

© Springer Nature Switzerland AG 2021
W. Faber et al. (Eds.): JELIA 2021, LNAI 12678, pp. 162–176, 2021.
https://doi.org/10.1007/978-3-030-75775-5_12

without changing the set of solutions and their preference. In order to "move" quantities, we need to "subtract" costs somewhere and "add" them elsewhere.

The paper focuses on residuated monoids for constraint programming. Their relevance for local-consistency, as mentioned above, has been spotted early on [4,7], and various extensions has been proposed [15], as well as applications to languages based on the Linda paradigm, such as *Soft Concurrent Constraint Programming*, where a process may be *telling* and *asking* constraints to a centralised store [17]. More precisely, we tackle here two aspects. On the one side, we consider lexicographic orders, as used in contexts with multi-objective problems. That is, the preference values are obtained by the combination of separate concerns, and the order of the combination matters. On the other side, we introduce a soft version of *Bucket* and *Mini-bucket* elimination algorithms, well-known exact and approximated techniques for inference, which exploits the presence of a residuated monoid: in order to have an estimation of the approximation on the preference level of a solution, it is necessary to use a removal operator. Finally we present a *Depth-First Branch-and-Bound* algorithm, which exploits upper and lower bounds to prune search. Our proposals generalise the original soft versions of these approximation techniques presented in [21].

Lexicographic orders are potentially useful in applications that involve multiple objectives and attributes, and as such have been extensively investigated in the literature on soft constraints. However, usually the connection has been established by encoding a lexicographic *hard* constraint problem, where the preference structure is a Boolean algebra, into a soft constraint formalism. For example, in [13] the authors show how to encode a lexicographic order and how the resulting structure can support specialised algorithms such as *Branch-and-bound*. *Hierarchical Constraint Logic Programming* [24] frameworks allow to handle both hard constraints and several preference levels of soft constraints, whose violations need to be minimised, and such levels are usually managed following a lexicographic order [22]. However, even if lifting the algebraic structure of a preference set to the associated set of (possibly infinite) tuples with a point-wise order is straightforward, doing the same for the lexicographic order is not, and this result cannot be directly achieved for the formalisms in [3,23]. The solution advanced in [14,22] is to drop some preference values from the domain carrier of the set of tuples. The present work builds on this proposal by dealing with sets of preferences that form residuated monoids, systematising and extending the case of infinite tuples tackled in [11] to tuples of any length.

The paper has the following structure: in Sect. 2 we present the background on partially ordered residuated monoids, which is the structure we adopt to model preferences. In Sect. 3 we consider the collapsing elements of a monoid, which will be used to define an ad-hoc algebraic structure representing (possibly infinite) lexicographically ordered tuples of elements of the chosen monoid, which is given in Sect. 4. The latter section also presents our main construction, introducing residuation for these lexicographically ordered monoids. Section 5 shows how residuation helps to find a measure of goodness between an algorithm and its tractable approximation. Finally, in Sect. 6 we wrap up the paper with concluding remarks and ideas about future works.

The proof for the results presented in the paper are available in [16].

2   Preliminaries

This section recalls some of the basic algebraic structures needed for defining the set of preference values. In particular, we propose elements of *partially ordered monoids* as preferences, which allows to compare and compose preference values.

2.1   Ordered Monoids

The first step is to define an algebraic structure for modelling preferences. We refer to [15] for the missing proofs as well as for an introduction and a comparison with other proposals.

Definition 1 (Orders). *A partial order (PO) is a pair $\langle A, \leq \rangle$ such that A is a set and $\leq \, \subseteq A \times A$ is a reflexive, transitive, and anti-symmetric relation. A join semi-lattice (simply semi-lattice, SL) is a POs such that any finite subset of A has a least upper bound (LUB); a complete lattice (CL) is a PO such that any subset of A has a LUB.*

The LUB of a subset $X \subseteq A$ is denoted $\bigvee X$, and it is unique. Note that we require the existence of $\bigvee \emptyset$, which is the bottom of the order, denoted as $\bot$, and sometimes we will talk about a PO with bottom element (POB). The existence of LUBs for any subset of A (thus including $\emptyset$) guarantees that CLs also have greatest lower bounds (GLBs) for any subset X of A: it will be denoted by $\bigwedge X$. Whenever it exists, $\bigvee A$ corresponds to the top of the order, denoted as $\top$.

Definition 2 (Ordered monoids). *A (commutative) monoid is a triple $\langle A, \otimes, 1 \rangle$ such that $\otimes : A \times A \to A$ is a commutative and associative function and $1 \in A$ is its identity element, i.e., $\forall a \in A.\, a \otimes 1 = a$.*

A partially ordered monoid (POM) is a 4-tuple $\langle A, \leq, \otimes, 1 \rangle$ such that $\langle A, \leq \rangle$ is a PO and $\langle A, \otimes, 1 \rangle$ a monoid. A semi-lattice monoid (SLM) and a complete lattice monoid (CLM) are POMs such that their underlying PO is a SL, a CL respectively.

For ease of notation, we use the infix notation: $a \otimes b$ stands for $\otimes(a, b)$.

Example 1 (Power set). Given a (possibly infinite) set V of variables, we consider the monoid $\langle 2^V, \cup, \emptyset \rangle$ of (possibly empty) subsets of V, with union as the monoidal operator. Since the operator is idempotent (i.e., $\forall a \in A.\, a \otimes a = a$), the natural order ($\forall a, b \in A.\, a \leq b$ iff $a \otimes b = b$) is a partial order, and it coincides with subset inclusion: in fact, $\langle 2^V, \subseteq, \cup, \emptyset \rangle$ is a CLM.

In general, the partial order $\leq$ and the multiplication $\otimes$ can be unrelated. This is not the case for distributive CLMs.

Definition 3 (Distributivity). *A SLM* $\langle A, \leq, \otimes, 1 \rangle$ *is finitely distributive if*

$$\forall X \subseteq_f A. \forall a \in A. \quad a \otimes \bigvee X = \bigvee \{a \otimes x \mid x \in X\}.$$

A CLM is distributive is the equality holds also for any subset.

In the following, we will sometimes write $a \otimes X$ for the set $\{a \otimes x \mid x \in X\}$.

Remark 1. Note that $a \leq b$ is equivalent to $\bigvee \{a, b\} = b$ for all $a, b \in A$. Hence, finite distributivity implies that $\otimes$ is monotone with respect to $\leq$ (i.e., $\forall a, b, c \in A. a \leq b \Rightarrow a \otimes c \leq b \otimes c$) and that $\bot$ is the zero element of the monoid (i.e., $\forall a \in A. a \otimes \bot = \bot$). The power-set CLM in Example 1 is distributive.

Example 2 (Extended integers). The extended integers $\langle \mathbb{Z} \cup \{\pm\infty\}, \leq, +, 0 \rangle$, where $\leq$ is the natural order, such that for $k \in \mathbb{Z}$

$$-\infty \leq k \leq +\infty,$$

$+$ is the natural addition, such that for $k \in \mathbb{Z} \cup \{+\infty\}$

$$\pm\infty + k = \pm\infty, \qquad +\infty + (-\infty) = -\infty,$$

and 0 is the identity element constitutes a distributive CLM, and $+\infty$ and $-\infty$ are respectively the top and the bottom element of the CL.

Remark 2. Finitely distributive SLMs precisely corresponds to *tropical* semirings by defining the (idempotent) sum operator as $a \oplus b = \bigvee \{a, b\}$ for all $a, b \in A$. If, moreover, 1 is the top of the SLM we end up with *absorptive* semirings [19], which are known as *c*-semirings in the soft constraint jargon [3]. Together with monotonicity, imposing 1 to coincide with $\top$ means that preferences are negative (i.e., $a \leq 1$ for all $a \in A$).

Distributive CLMs are known in the literature as *quantales* [20].

Remark 3. Given two distributive CLMs, it is easy to show that their Cartesian product, whose elements are pairs and where the partial order and the monoidal operator are defined point-wise, is a distributive CLM. In particular, in the following we consider the Cartesian product of $\langle \mathbb{Z} \cup \{\pm\infty\}, \leq, +, 0 \rangle$ with itself: its set of elements is $(\mathbb{Z} \cup \{\pm\infty\})^2$, the identity element is $(0, 0)$, and the top and bottom elements are $(+\infty, +\infty)$ and $(-\infty, -\infty)$, respectively.

2.2 Residuated Monoids

We first introduce *residuation*, which allows us to define a "weak" inverse operator $\ominus$ with respect to the monoidal operator $\otimes$. In this way, besides aggregating values together, it is also possible to remove one from another. Residuation theory [19] is concerned with the study of sub-solutions of the equation $b \otimes x = a$, where x is a "divisor" of a with respect to b. The set of sub-solutions of an equation contains also the possible solutions, whenever they exist, and in that case the maximal element is also a solution.

Definition 4 (residuation). *A residuated POM is a 5-tuple $\langle A, \leq, \otimes, \ominus, 1 \rangle$ such that $\langle A, \leq \rangle$ is a PO, $\langle A, \otimes, 1 \rangle$ is a monoid, and $\ominus : A \times A \to A$ is a function such that*

– $\forall a, b, c \in A.\ b \otimes c \leq a \iff c \leq a \ominus b.$

In the following, we will sometimes write $a \ominus X$ and $X \ominus a$ for the set $\{a \ominus x \mid x \in X\}$ and $\{x \ominus a \mid x \in X\}$, respectively.

Remark 4. It is easy to show that residuation is monotone on the first argument and anti-monotone on the second. In fact, in a SML $\bigvee(X \ominus a) \leq \bigvee X \ominus a$, and the same in a CLM with respect to infinite sub-sets. However, the equality does not hold, e.g. in the Cartesian product of the CLM $\langle N \cup \{\infty\}, \geq, +, 0 \rangle$ with itself.

Also, $a \ominus \bigvee X \leq \bigwedge(a \ominus X)$ whenever the latter exists, as it does in CLMs.

Remark 5. As for distributivity, given two residuated POMs, it is easy to show that their Cartesian product is a residuated POM.

Residuation implies distributivity (see e.g. [15, Lemma 2.2]).

Lemma 1. *Let $\langle A, \leq, \otimes, 1 \rangle$ be a residuated POM. Then it is monotone. If additionally it is a SLM (CLM), then it is finitely distributive (distributive).*

Conversely, it is noteworthy that CLMs are always residuated, and the following folklore fact holds.

Lemma 2. *Let $\langle A, \leq, \otimes, 1 \rangle$ be a distributive CLM. It is residuated and $\forall a, b \in A.\ a \ominus b = \bigvee\{c \mid b \otimes c \leq a\}$.*

We close with a simple lemma relating residuation with the top and bottom elements of a POM.

Lemma 3. *Let $\langle A, \leq, \otimes, \ominus, 1 \rangle$ be a residuated POM. If it has the bottom element $\bot$, then it also has the top element $\top$ and $\forall a \in A.\ a \ominus \bot = \top$. Viceversa, if it has the top element $\top$, then $\forall b \in A.\ \top \ominus b = \top$.*

Remark 6. Nothing can be stated for $\bot \ominus a$, since there could be elements that are $\bot$-divisors: see again the Cartesian product of the CLM $\langle \mathbb{N} \cup \{\infty\}, \geq, +, 0 \rangle$ with itself, where $\langle \infty, 3 \rangle \otimes \langle 4, \infty \rangle = \langle \infty, \infty \rangle$.

Similarly, nothing can be stated for $a \ominus \top$: see the Cartesian product of the CLM $\langle \mathbb{N} \cup \{\infty\}, \geq, +, 0 \rangle$ with its dual CLM $\langle \mathbb{N} \cup \{\infty\}, \leq, +, 0 \rangle$.

3   The Ideal of Collapsing Elements

As shown in [14], the first step for obtaining SLMs based on a lexicographic order is to restrict the carrier of the monoid.

Definition 5. *Let $\langle A, \otimes, 1 \rangle$ be a monoid. Its sub-set $I(A)$ of cancellative elements is defined as $\{c \mid \forall a, b \in A.\ a \otimes c = b \otimes c \implies a = b\}$.*

We recall a well-known fact.

Lemma 4. *Let* $\langle A, \otimes, \mathbf{1} \rangle$ *be a monoid. Then* $I(A)$ *is a sub-monoid of* A *and* $C(A) = A \backslash I(A)$ *is a prime ideal of* A.

Explicitly, $C(A) = \{c \mid \exists a, b \in A.\ a \neq b \wedge a \otimes c = b \otimes c\}$. Being an ideal means that $\forall a \in A, c \in C(A).\ a \otimes c \in C(A)$, and being prime further states that $\forall a, b \in A.\ a \otimes b \in C(A) \implies a \in C(A) \vee b \in C(A)$. All the proofs are straightforward, and we denote $C(A)$ as the set of *collapsing* elements of A.

Note that an analogous closure property does not hold for LUBs.

Example 3. Consider the monoid of natural numbers $\langle \mathbb{N}, +, 0 \rangle$ and the (non distributive) CLM with elements $\mathbb{N} \cup \{\bot, \top\}$ obtained by lifting the flat order (i.e., $a \not\leq b$ for any $a, b \in \mathbb{N}$ as well as $a + \bot = \bot = \top + \bot$ and $a + \top = \top$ for any $a \in \mathbb{N}$). Then, $I(\mathbb{N} \cup \{\bot, \top\}) = \mathbb{N}$ is not closed under finite LUBs.

Now, let us consider the distributive CLM with elements $\mathbb{N} \cup \{\infty\}$ obtained by lifting the natural order induced by addition. We have that $I(\mathbb{N} \cup \{\infty\}) = \mathbb{N}$ is a (finitely distributive) SLM, yet it is not closed with respect to infinite LUBs.

We now present a simple fact that is needed later on.

Lemma 5. *Let* A_1, A_2 *be POMs and* $A_1 \times A_2$ *their Cartesian product. Then we have* $C(A_1 \times A_2) = C(A_1) \times A_2 \cup A_1 \times C(A_2)$.

Example 4. Let us consider the tropical SLM $\langle \mathbb{N} \cup \{\infty\}, \geq, +, 0 \rangle$ and the Cartesian product with itself. Clearly, $C(\mathbb{N} \times \mathbb{N})$ is not closed under finite LUBs: it suffices to consider $X = \{\langle \infty, 3 \rangle, \langle 4, \infty \rangle\} \subseteq C(\mathbb{N} \times \mathbb{N})$, since $\bigvee X = \langle 3, 4 \rangle \notin C(\mathbb{N} \times \mathbb{N})$. Neither is $C(\mathbb{N} \times \mathbb{N})$ closed under residuation, as suggested by Lemma 3, since the top element is not necessarily collapsing. Indeed, in $C(\mathbb{N} \times \mathbb{N})$ we have $\langle \infty, 4 \rangle \oplus \langle \infty, 3 \rangle = \langle 0, 1 \rangle$.

Remark 7. Note that in an absorptive CLM A we have that $a \oplus b = \mathbf{1}$ whenever $b \leq a$. Hence $C(A)$ is usually not closed under residuation, since $\mathbf{1}$ is cancellative.

3.1 A Different View on Collapsing Elements

When the first presentation of lexicographic SLMs was provided [14], a different set of collapsing elements was considered.

Definition 6 ([14]). *Let* $\langle A, \leq, \otimes, \mathbf{1} \rangle$ *be a POM. Its sub-set* $C'(A)$ *is defined as* $\{c \mid \exists a, b \in A.\ a < b \wedge a \otimes c = b \otimes c\}$.

Clearly, $C'(A) \subseteq C(A)$. However, we can replicate Lemma 4.

Lemma 6. *Let* $\langle A, \otimes, \mathbf{1} \rangle$ *be a monoid. Then* $C'(A)$ *is an ideal of* A. *If* $\otimes$ *is monotone, then* $I'(A) = A \backslash C'(A)$ *is a sub-monoid of* A *and* $C'(A)$ *a prime ideal of* A.

Explicitly, $I'(A) = \{c \mid \forall a, b \in A.\ a \otimes c = b \otimes c \implies a \not< b\}$. The definitions we encounter in the next section could then be rephrased with minimal adjustments using $I'(A)$ and $C'(A)$ istead of $I(A)$ and $C(A)$, confirming the proposal in [14].[1]

However, what is in fact noteworthy is that the two approaches are coincident whenever distributivity holds, as shown by the lemma below.

Lemma 7. *Let $\langle A, \leq, \otimes, 1 \rangle$ be a finitely distributive SLM. Then $C'(A) = C(A)$.*

Remark 8. Consider the (non distributive) CLM $\langle [0 \ldots n] \cup \{\bot, \top\}, +, 0 \rangle$ obtained by lifting the initial segment $[0 \ldots n]$ of the natural numbers with the flat order (as done for the CLM of all natural numbers in Example 3). Here addition is capped, so that e.g. $n + m = n$ for all m. Hence, $C([0 \ldots n] \cup \{\bot, \top\}) = [1 \ldots n] \cup \{\bot, \top\}$ that is, all elements except 0. Instead, $C'([0 \ldots n] \cup \{\bot, \top\})) = \{\bot, \top\}$.

4 On Lexicographic Orders

We now move to lexicographic orders, taking into account the results in Sect. 3.

Proposition 1. *Let $\langle A, \leq, \otimes, 1 \rangle$ be a POM with bottom element $\bot$. Then we can define a family $\langle Lex_k(A), \leq_k, \otimes^k, 1^k \rangle$ of POMs with bottom element $\bot^k$ such that $\otimes^k$ is defined point-wise, $Lex_1(A) = A$ and $\leq_1\ =\ \leq$, and*

- *$Lex_{k+1}(A) = I(A)Lex_k(A) \cup C(A)\{\bot\}^k$,*
- *$a_1 \ldots a_k \leq_k b_1 \ldots b_k$ if $a_1 < b_1$ or $a_1 = b_1$ and $a_2 \ldots a_k \leq_{k-1} b_2 \ldots b_k$.*

Note that $Lex_k(A)$ is contained in the k-times Cartesian product A^k, and the definitions of $\otimes^k$, 1^k, and $\bot^k$ coincide. Also, the bottom element is needed for padding the tuples, in order to make simpler the definition of the order.

We can provide an alternative definition for such POMs.

Lemma 8. *Let $\langle A, \leq, \otimes, 1 \rangle$ be a POM with bottom element $\bot$. Then $Lex_{k+1}(A) = \bigcup_{i \leq k} I(A)^i A\{\bot\}^{k-i}$ for all k.*

Now, given a tuple a of elements in A^k, for $i \leq k$ we denote with a_i its i-th component and with $a_{|i}$ its prefix $a_1 \ldots a_i$, with the obvious generalisation for a set $X \subseteq A^k$, noting that $a_1 = a_{|1}$.

Theorem 1. *Let $\langle A, \leq, \otimes, 1 \rangle$ be a finitely distributive SLM (distributive CLM). Then so is $\langle Lex_k(A), \leq_k, \otimes^k, 1^k \rangle$ for all k.*

---

[1] And in fact, the lemma holds also for a property that is weaker than monotonicity: it suffices that $\forall a, b, c.\ a \leq b \implies (a \otimes c \leq b \otimes c) \vee (b \otimes c \leq a \otimes c)$.

4.1   On Lexicographic Residuation

The fact that $Lex_k(A)$ is a CLM if so is A tells us that $Lex_k(A)$ is also residuated.

Example 5. Let us consider the usual tropical CLM of natural numbers with inverse order, and the CLM $Lex_2(\mathbb{N})$. Clearly $C(\mathbb{N}) = +\infty$. We then have for example that

$$(3,6)\ominus_2(4,2) = \bigvee\{(x,y) \mid (4+x, 2+y) \leq_2 (3,6)\} = (0,0)$$

Indeed, $(4+x, 2+y) \leq_2 (3,6)$ holds for any possible choice of (x,y), since $4+x < 3$ for all x, hence $(0,0)$ as the result.

Note that for the CLM obtained via the Cartesian product $\mathbb{N} \times \mathbb{N}$, the result would have been $(0,4)$.

Indeed, this can be proved in general for POMs. First, we need some additional definitions and technical lemmas.

Definition 7. *Let* $\langle A, \leq, \otimes, \oplus, \mathbf{1}\rangle$ *be a residuated POM with bottom and* $a, b \in Lex_k(A)$. *Then*

$-\ \gamma(a,b) = min\{i \mid (a_i \ominus b_i) \in C(A)\}$
$-\ \delta(a,b) = min\{i \mid (a_i \ominus b_i) \otimes b_i < a_i\}$

with the convention that the result is $k+1$ *whenever the set is empty.*

Lemma 9. *Let* $\langle A, \leq, \otimes, \oplus, \mathbf{1}\rangle$ *be a residuated POM with bottom and* $a, b \in Lex_k(A)$. *Then either* $\delta(a,b) = k+1$ *or* $\delta(a,b) \leq \gamma(a,b)$.

We can then present the definition of residuation for lexicographic POMs only for the cases identified by the proposition above.

Proposition 2. *Let* $\langle A, \leq, \otimes, \ominus, \mathbf{1}\rangle$ *be a residuated POM with bottom and* $a, b \in Lex_k(A)$. *If* $\delta(a,b) = \gamma(a,b) = k+1$ *then their residuation* $a\ominus_k b$ *in* $Lex_k(A)$ *exists and it is given by*

$$(a_1 \ominus b_1)\dots(a_k \ominus b_k)$$

Note that $a\ominus_k b$ here coincides with the residuation $a\ominus^k b$ on the Cartesian product. Furthermore, we have that $(a\ominus_k b) \otimes^k b = a$.

Proposition 3. *Let* $\langle A, \leq, \otimes, \ominus, \mathbf{1}\rangle$ *be a residuated POM with bottom and* $a, b \in Lex_k(A)$. *If* $\delta(a,b) < \gamma(a,b)$ *then their residuation* $a\ominus_k b$ *in* $Lex_k(A)$ *exists and it is given by*

$$(a_1 \ominus b_1)\dots(a_{\delta(a,b)} \ominus b_{\delta(a,b)})(\bigvee Lex_{k-\delta(a,b)}(A))$$

Additionally, please note that $\bigvee Lex_n(A)$ can be easily characterised: it coincides with $\top^n$ if $\top \in I(A)$, and with $\top\bot^{n-1}$ otherwise.

Proposition 4. *Let $\langle A, \leq, \otimes, \oplus, 1 \rangle$ be a residuated POM with bottom element $\perp$ and $a, b \in Lex_k(A)$. If either $\delta(a,b) = \gamma(a,b) \leq k$ or $\gamma(a,b) < \delta(a,b) = k+1$ then their residuation $a \oplus_k b$ in $Lex_k(A)$ exists and it is given by*

$$(a_1 \oplus b_1) \ldots (a_{\gamma(a,b)} \oplus b_{\gamma(a,b)}) \perp^{k-\gamma(a,b)}$$

From the propositions above it is straightforward to derive Theorem 2, which states that, given a residuated POM, it is possible to define a lexicographic order on its tuples, which is a residuated POM as well.

Theorem 2. *Let $\langle A, \leq, \otimes, \oplus, 1 \rangle$ be a residuated POM with bottom element $\perp$. Then so is $\langle Lex_k(A), \leq_k, \otimes^k, \oplus_k, 1^k \rangle$ for all k, with $\oplus_k$ defined as*

$$a \oplus_k b = \begin{cases} (a_1 \ominus b_1) \ldots (a_k \ominus b_k) & \text{if } k+1 = \gamma(a,b) = \delta(a,b) \\ (a_1 \ominus b_1) \ldots (a_{\gamma(a,b)} \ominus b_{\gamma(a,b)}) \perp^{k-\gamma(a,b)} & \text{if } k+1 \neq \gamma(a,b) \leq \delta(a,b) \\ (a_1 \ominus b_1) \ldots (a_{\delta(a,b)} \ominus b_{\delta(a,b)}) (\bigvee Lex_{k-\delta(a,b)}(A)) & \text{otherwise} \end{cases}$$

4.2 Infinite Tuples

We can now move to POMs whose elements are tuples of infinite length.

Proposition 5. *Let $\langle A, \leq, \otimes, 1 \rangle$ be a POM with bottom element $\perp$. Then we can define a POM $\langle Lex_\omega(A), \leq_\omega, \otimes^\omega, 1^\omega \rangle$ with bottom element $\perp^\omega$ such that $\otimes^\omega$ is defined point-wise and*

– $Lex_\omega(A) = I(A)^\omega \cup I(A)^* A \{\perp\}^\omega$
– $a \leq_\omega b$ *if* $a_{\leq k} \leq_k b_{\leq k}$ *for all k*

A straightforward adaptation of Proposition 1. Thus, we can define a POM of infinite tuples simply by lifting the family of POMs of finite tuples.

Remark 9. Note that the seemingly obvious POM structure cannot be added to $\bigcup_k Lex_k(A) = I(A)^* A \{\perp\}^*$: it would be missing the identity of the monoid.

Proposition 6. *Let $\langle A, \leq, \otimes, 1 \rangle$ be a finitely distributive SLM (distributive CLM). Then so is $\langle Lex_\omega(A), \leq_\omega, \otimes^\omega, 1^\omega \rangle$.*

Also a straightforward adaptation, this time of Theorem 1.

Proposition 7. *Let $\langle A, \leq, \otimes, \oplus, 1 \rangle$ be a residuated POM with bottom. Then so is $\langle Lex_\omega(A), \leq_\omega, \otimes^\omega, \oplus_\omega, 1^\omega \rangle$, with $\oplus_\omega$ defined as*

$$a \oplus_\omega b = \begin{cases} (a_1 \oplus b_1) \ldots (a_k \oplus b_k) \ldots & \text{if } \infty = \gamma(a,b) = \delta(a,b) \\ (a_1 \oplus b_1) \ldots (a_{\gamma(a,b)} \oplus b_{\gamma(a,b)}) \perp^\omega & \text{if } \infty \neq \gamma(a,b) \leq \delta(a,b) \\ (a_1 \oplus b_1) \ldots (a_{\delta(a,b)} \oplus b_{\delta(a,b)}) (\bigvee Lex_\omega(A)) & \text{otherwise} \end{cases}$$

It follows from Theorem 2, via the obvious extension of Lemma 9. Note that $\bigvee Lex_\omega(A)$ is $\top^\omega$ if $\top \in I(A)$, and $\top \perp^\omega$ otherwise.

5   Mini-bucket Elimination for Residuated POMs

This section shows an application of residuation to a general approximation algorithms for soft CSPs, *Mini-Bucket Elimination* (MBE) [9], a relaxation of a well-known complete inference algorithm, *Bucket Elimination* (BE) [10].

BE first partitions the constraints into *buckets*, where the bucket of a variable stores those constraints whose *support*[2] contains that variable and none that is higher in the ordering: variables are previously sorted according to some criteria (e.g., just lexicographically on their names: $v_1, v_2, \ldots$). The next step is to process the buckets from top to bottom. When the bucket of variable v is processed, an *elimination procedure* is performed over the constraints in its bucket, yielding a new constraint defined over all the variables mentioned in the bucket, excluding v. This constraint summarises the "effect" of v on the remainder of the problem. The new constraint ends up in a lower bucket.

BE finds the preference of the optimal solution and not an approximation of it; however, BE is exponential in the induced width, which measures the acyclicity of a problem. MBE takes advantage of a control parameter z: it partitions the buckets into smaller subsets called *mini-buckets*, such that their arity is bounded by z. Therefore, the cost of computing this approximation is now exponential in z, which allows trading off time and space for accuracy. MBE is often used for providing bounds in branch-and-bound algorithms (see Sect. 5.1).

Algorithm 1 extends MBE to work on residuated monoids, hence including also the framework of preferences presented in Sect. 3 and Sect. 4. The algorithm takes as input a problem P defined as $P = \langle V, D, C \rangle_{POM}$, where V is the set of variables $\{v_1, \ldots, v_n\}$, D is a set of domains $\{D_1, \ldots, D_n\}$ (where $v_1 \in D_1, \ldots, v_n \in D_n$), C is a set of constraints where $\bigcup_{c \in C} supp(c) = V$,[3] and finally, the problem is given on a residuated SLM.

We define a *projection* operator $\Downarrow$ for a constraint c and variable v as $(c \Downarrow_v) = \bigvee_{d \in D_v} c[v := d]$. Projection decreases the support: $supp(c \Downarrow_v) \subseteq supp(c) \backslash \{v\}$. In Algorithm 1 we use this operator to eliminate variables from constraints.

At line 4 Algorithm 1 finds bucket $\mathfrak{B}_i$, which contains all the constraints having v_i in their support. Then at line 5 we find a partition of $\mathfrak{B}_i$ into p mini-buckets $\mathfrak{Q}$ limited by z. All the mini-buckets are projected over v_i, thus eliminating it from the support and obtaining a new constraint $g_{i,j}$ as result (line 7). Finally, the bucket $\mathfrak{B}_i$ is discarded from the problem while adding p new constraints g (line 8). The elimination of the last variable produces an empty-support constraints, whose composition provides the desired upper bound (that is, a solution of P cannot have a better preference than this bound).

Bucket elimination is defined in Algorithm 2. The second part (from line 7 to 14) has been modified with respect to the one in e.g. [10] in order to manage partially ordered preferences (as POMs can do). Note that the $\cdot$ operator extends an assignment tuple t with a new element. The set I stores all the domain values

---

[2] The *support* of a constraint is the set of variables on which assignment it depends.
[3] For instance, a binary constraint c with $supp(c) = \{v_1, v_2\}$ is a function $c : (V \longrightarrow D) \longrightarrow A$ that depends only on the assignment of variables $\{v_1, v_2\} \subseteq V$.

Algorithm 1. Mini-Bucket for Residuated POMs.

Input: $P = \langle V, D, C \rangle_{POM}$ and control parameter z
Output: An upper bound of $(\bigotimes_{c \in C}) \Downarrow_V$

1: **function** MBE
2:     $\{v_1, v_2, \ldots, v_n\} := compute\_order(P)$
3:     **for** $i = n$ to 1 **do**
4:         $\mathfrak{B}_i := \{c \in C \mid v_i \in supp(c)\}$
5:         $\{\mathfrak{Q}_1, \mathfrak{Q}_2, \ldots, \mathfrak{Q}_p\} := partition(\mathfrak{B}_i, z)$
6:         **for** $j = 1$ to p **do**
7:             $g_{i,j} := (\bigotimes_{c \in \mathfrak{Q}_j} c) \Downarrow_{v_i}$
8:         $C := (C \cup \{g_{i,1}, \ldots, g_{i,j}\}) - \mathfrak{B}_i$
9:     **return** $(\bigotimes_{c \in C} c)$

Algorithm 2. Bucket for Residuated POMs.

Input: $P = \langle V, D, C \rangle_{POM}$
Output: The set of best solutions of P

1: **function** BE
2:     $\{v_1, v_2, \ldots, v_n\} := compute\_order(P)$
3:     **for** $i = n$ to 1 **do**
4:         $\mathfrak{B}_i := \{c \in C \mid v_i \in supp(c)\}$
5:         $g_i := (\bigotimes_{c \in \mathfrak{B}_j} c) \Downarrow_{v_i}$
6:         $C := (C \cup \{g_i\}) - \mathfrak{B}_i$
7:     $BSols := \{\langle\rangle\}$ ▷ The empty tuple
8:     **for** $i = 1$ to $|V|$ **do**
9:         $T = \emptyset$
10:         **for all** $t \in BSols$ **do**
11:             $I := \{d \mid \nexists d'.(\bigotimes \mathfrak{B}_i)(t \cdot (x_i = d)) < (\bigotimes \mathfrak{B}_i)(t \cdot (x_i = d'))\}$
12:             $T := T \cup \{t \cdot (x_i = d) \mid \exists d \in I\}$
13:         $BSols := T \backslash \{t \in T \mid \exists t' \in T.(\bigotimes \mathfrak{B}_i)(t) < (\bigotimes \mathfrak{B}_i)(t')\}$
14:     **return** $(g_1, BSols)$

---

that produce new undominated tuples, which are saved in T. This is repeated for all the assignments in the set of partial solutions, which is finally updated in $BSols$ with undominated solutions only (line 13); g_1 is the empty-support constraint which represents the (best) preference of such solutions.

By having available residuation, it is now possible to use it in order to have an estimation about how far a partitioning is from buckets: we can use $\oplus$ to compute good bucket partitions, similarly to the method adopted in [21]. Let us consider a partition $\mathfrak{Q} = \{\mathfrak{Q}_1, \mathfrak{Q}_2, \ldots, \mathfrak{Q}_p\}$ of a bucket $\mathfrak{B}_i$, which contains all the constraints with variable v_i in the support. We say that $\mathfrak{Q}$ is a z partition if the support size of its mini-buckets is smaller than z, i.e., if $\forall i.|supp(\mathfrak{Q}_i)| \leq z$. The approximation $\mu^{\mathfrak{Q}}$ of the bucket is computed as

$$\mu^{\mathfrak{Q}} = \bigotimes_{j=1}^{p} \left(\left(\bigotimes \mathfrak{Q}_j\right) \Downarrow_{v_i} \right)$$

It is noteworthy that residuation may help in quantifying the distance between a bucket and its partitioning

$$\left(\left(\bigotimes \mathfrak{B} \right) \Downarrow_{v_i} \right) \oplus \left(\bigotimes_{j=1}^{p} \left(\left(\bigotimes \mathfrak{Q}_j \right) \Downarrow_{v_i} \right) \right)$$

We can compute a refined approximation for a mini-bucket $app_{\mathfrak{Q}_j}$ with respect to the partitioned bucket as

$$\left(\left(\left(\bigotimes \mathfrak{B} \right) \oplus \left(\bigotimes (\mathfrak{B} \backslash \mathfrak{Q}_j) \right) \right) \Downarrow_{v_i} \right) \oplus \left(\left(\bigotimes \mathfrak{Q}_j \right) \Downarrow_{v_i} \right)$$

If we compose this approximation for each mini-bucket we get an approximation between a bucket and its partitioning

$$approx_{\mu\mathfrak{Q}} = \bigotimes_j approx_{\mathfrak{Q}_j}$$

Algorithm 3. Soft Depth-First Branch-and-Bound.

```
1: function SoftDFBB(t, LB)
2:     if (supp(t) = V) then
3:         return ⊗ C(t)
4:     else
5:         let v_i ∈ U                          ▷ U is the set of unassigned variables
6:         for all d ∈ D_{v_i} do
7:             H := UB(t · (v_i = d))
8:             if (∃u ∈ H, ∃l ∈ LB. l ≤_{POM} u) then
9:                 LB := LB ∪ SoftDFBB(t · (v_i = d), LB)
10:                LB := LB\{e ∈ LB | ∃e' ∈ LB.e <_{POM} e'}
11:        return LB
```

5.1   Soft Branch-and-Bound

Algorithms like MBE can be used to obtain a lower bound that underestimates the best solution of a given problem $P = \langle V, D, C \rangle_{POM}$. This bound can be then passed as input to a search algorithm in order to increase its pruning efficiency [12]. In the following of this section, we describe an example of search that can be used to find all the solutions of a (possibly lexicographic) soft CSP. Note that this algorithm is designed to deal with partially ordered solutions. On the contrary, in [23] the solution of *Lex-VCSP* (and in general *Valued CSPs*, i.e., *VCSPs*) is associated with a set of totally ordered preferences.

The family of *Soft Branch-and-Bound* algorithms explores the state space of a soft CSP as a tree. A *Depth-First Branch-and-Bound* (*DFBB*) (see Algorithm 3) performs a depth-first traversal of the search tree. Given a partial assignment t of V, an upper bound $ub(t)$ is an overestimation of the acceptance degree of any possible complete assignment involving t. A lower bound $lb(t)$ is instead a minimum acceptance degree that we are willing to accept during the search.

With each node in the search tree is associated a set of variables $X \subseteq V$ that have been already assigned (and the set of unassigned ones is given by

$U = V \backslash X$), along with the associated (partial) assignment t to those variables ($supp(t) = X$). A leaf node is associated with a complete assignment ($supp(t) = V$). Each time a new internal node is created, a variable $v_i \in U$ to assign next is chosen, as well as an element $d \in D_{v_i}$ of its domain. Note that the procedure in Algorithm 3 prunes the search space at line 8, since it only explores those assignments $v_i = d$ such that there exists an upper bound $u \in UB$ that is better than a lower bound $l \in LB$.

The efficiency of Soft DFBB depends largely on its pruning capacity, which relies on the quality of its bounds: the higher lb and the lower ub (still ensuring they are actual bounds of optimal solutions), the better Soft DFBB performs. Note that, in order to deal with partial orderings of preferences, Algorithm 3 has to manage sets of undominated upper UB and lower LB bounds of (partial) solutions, differently from classical Branch-and-Bound. In Algorithm 3, LB returns a set of lower bounds for a given partial assignment. When all the variables are assigned (line 2), the procedure stops with a solution.

6   Conclusions and Future Works

In this paper we considered a formal framework for soft CSP based on a residuated monoid of partially ordered preferences. This allows for using the classical solving algorithms that need preference removal, as for instance arc consistency where values need to be moved from binary to unary constraints, or for proving a cost estimation to be used during the search for solutions, as for instance branch-and-bound algorithms. The contribution of this paper is twofold. On the one side, we proved the adequacy of the formalism for modelling lexicographic orders. On the other side, we showed how it can enable heuristics for efficiently solving soft CSPs, such as the Bucket and Mini-bucket elimination.

Our focus on soft CSP includes its computational counterparts based on constraints, such as soft CCP [17], and in fact, considering infinite tuples enables to model temporal reasoning, as shown for soft constraint automata [11]. However, the framework is reminiscent, and is in fact an extension, of previous formalisms such as monotonic logic programming [8], whose semantics is given in terms of residuated lattices of truth-values. And it fits in the current interests on the development of sequent systems for substructural logics, as witnessed by current research projects [6]: well-known examples are Lukasiewicz's many-valued logics, relevance logics and linear logics.

All the connections sketched above deserve further investigations. For the time being, we leave to future work some related extensions. Mini-bucket is often used for providing an upper bound in branch-and-bound algorithms: for this reason we will investigate this technique, as well as other solving methods used in the solution of lexicographic problems [13]. We will also study ad-hoc heuristics for selecting the order in Algorithm 1, directly depending on lexicographic orders.

Acknowledgements. We are grateful to the reviewers for their comments. In particular, we are indebted to the referee pointing out the connection of our work to monotonic logic programming, which we plan to further explore.

References

1. Baccelli, F., Cohen, G., Olsder, G., Quadrat, J.P.: Synchronization and Linearity: An Algebra for Discrete Event Systems. Wiley, Hoboken (1992)
2. Bessiere, C.: Constraint propagation. In: Rossi, F., van Beek, P., Walsh, T. (eds.) Handbook of Constraint Programming, pp. 29–83. Elsevier (2006)
3. Bistarelli, S., Montanari, U., Rossi, F.: Semiring-based constraint satisfaction and optimization. J. ACM **44**(2), 201–236 (1997)
4. Bistarelli, S., Gadducci, F.: Enhancing constraints manipulation in semiring-based formalisms. In: Brewka, G., Coradeschi, S., Perini, A., Traverso, P. (eds.) ECAI 2006. FAIA, vol. 141, pp. 63–67. IOS Press (2006)
5. Blyth, T.S., Janowitz, M.F.: Residuation Theory. Elsevier, Amsterdam (2014)
6. Ciabattoni, A., Genco, F.A., Ramanayake, R.: Substructural logics: semantics, proof theory, and applications. Report on the second SYSMICS workshop. ACM SIGLOG News **5**(2), 58–60 (2018)
7. Cooper, M., Schiex, T.: Arc consistency for soft constraints. Artif. Intell. **154**(1–2), 199–227 (2007)
8. Damásio, C.V., Pereira, L.M.: Monotonic and residuated logic programs. In: Benferhat, S., Besnard, P. (eds.) ECSQARU 2001. LNCS (LNAI), vol. 2143, pp. 748–759. Springer, Heidelberg (2001). https://doi.org/10.1007/3-540-44652-4_66
9. Dechter, R.: Mini-buckets: a general scheme for generating approximations in automated reasoning. In: IJCAI 1997, pp. 1297–1302. Morgan Kaufmann (1997)
10. Dechter, R.: Bucket elimination: a unifying framework for reasoning. Artif. Intell. **113**(1–2), 41–85 (1999)
11. Dokter, K., Gadducci, F., Lion, B., Santini, F.: Soft constraint automata with memory. Log. Algebraic Methods Program. **118**, 100615 (2021)
12. Domshlak, C., Prestwich, S.D., Rossi, F., Venable, K.B., Walsh, T.: Hard and soft constraints for reasoning about qualitative conditional preferences. Heuristics **12**(4–5), 263–285 (2006). https://doi.org/10.1007/s10732-006-7071-x
13. Freuder, E.C., Heffernan, R., Wallace, R.J., Wilson, N.: Lexicographically-ordered constraint satisfaction problems. Constraints **15**(1), 1–28 (2010). https://doi.org/10.1007/s10601-009-9069-0
14. Gadducci, F., Hölzl, M., Monreale, G.V., Wirsing, M.: Soft constraints for lexicographic orders. In: Castro, F., Gelbukh, A., González, M. (eds.) MICAI 2013. LNCS (LNAI), vol. 8265, pp. 68–79. Springer, Heidelberg (2013). https://doi.org/10.1007/978-3-642-45114-0_6
15. Gadducci, F., Santini, F.: Residuation for bipolar preferences in soft constraints. Inf. Process. Lett. **118**, 69–74 (2017)
16. Gadducci, F., Santini, F.: Residuation for soft constraints: lexicographic orders and approximation techniques. CoRR abs/2103.06741 (2021)
17. Gadducci, F., Santini, F., Pino, L.F., Valencia, F.D.: Observational and behavioural equivalences for soft concurrent constraint programming. Log. Algebraic Methods Program. **92**, 45–63 (2017)
18. Galatos, N., Jipsen, P., Kowalski, T., Ono, H.: Residuated Lattices: An Algebraic Glimpse at Substructural Logics. Springer, Heidelberg (2007)
19. Golan, J.S.: Semirings and Their Applications. Springer, Heidelberg (2013)
20. Kruml, D., Paseka, J.: Algebraic and categorical aspects of quantales. In: Hazewinkel, M. (ed.) Handbook of Algebra, vol. 5, pp. 323–362. North-Holland (2008)

21. Rollon, E., Larrosa, J., Dechter, R.: Semiring-based mini-bucket partitioning schemes. In: Rossi, F. (ed.) IJCAI 2013, pp. 644–650. IJCAI/AAAI (2013)
22. Schiendorfer, A., Knapp, A., Steghöfer, J.-P., Anders, G., Siefert, F., Reif, W.: Partial valuation structures for qualitative soft constraints. In: De Nicola, R., Hennicker, R. (eds.) Software, Services, and Systems. LNCS, vol. 8950, pp. 115–133. Springer, Cham (2015). https://doi.org/10.1007/978-3-319-15545-6_10
23. Schiex, T., Fargier, H., Verfaillie, G.: Valued constraint satisfaction problems: hard and easy problems. In: IJCAI 1995, pp. 631–639. Morgan Kaufmann (1995)
24. Wilson, M., Borning, A.: Hierarchical constraint logic programming. Log. Program. **16**(3), 277–318 (1993)

Description Logics and Ontological Reasoning

Exploiting Forwardness: Satisfiability and Query-Entailment in Forward Guarded Fragment

Bartosz Bednarczyk[1,2(✉)] (iD)

[1] Computational Logic Group, Technische Universität Dresden, Dresden, Germany
[2] Institute of Computer Science, University of Wrocław, Wrocław, Poland
bartosz.bednarczyk@cs.uni.wroc.pl

Abstract. We study the complexity of two standard reasoning problems for Forward Guarded Logic ($\mathcal{FGF}$), obtained as a restriction of the Guarded Fragment in which variables appear in atoms only in the order of their quantification. We show that $\mathcal{FGF}$ enjoys the higher-arity-forest-model property, which results in ExpTime-completeness of its (finite and unrestricted) knowledge-base satisfiability problem. Moreover, we show that $\mathcal{FGF}$ is well-suited for knowledge representation. By employing a generalisation of Lutz's spoiler technique, we prove that the conjunctive query entailment problem for $\mathcal{FGF}$ remains in ExpTime.

We find that our results are quite unusual as $\mathcal{FGF}$ is, up to our knowledge, the first decidable fragment of First-Order Logic, extending standard description logics like $\mathcal{ALC}$, that offers unboundedly many variables and higher-arity relations while keeping its complexity surprisingly low.

1 Introduction

The *guarded fragment of first-order logic* ($\mathcal{GF}$) is a prominent fragment of first-order logic ($\mathcal{FO}$) that finds application in ontology-based reasoning and in database theory [4,6,24]. In particular, $\mathcal{GF}$ embeds standard modal logics (like K) as well as description logics (DLs) *e.g.* $\mathcal{ALC}$ [8]. The guarded fragment is obtained from $\mathcal{FO}$ by requiring that first-order quantification is appropriately relativised by atoms. It was introduced by Andréka, Németi and van Benthem [1] who proved that its satisfiability problem is decidable. A year later, Grädel [9] proved that $\mathcal{GF}$ has the finite model property and is 2ExpTime-complete. In this work we study the complexity of a certain fragment of $\mathcal{GF}$.

1.1 Our Motivation and Related Work

Our motivation is two-fold. The first comes from applications of $\mathcal{GF}$ to databases and description logics, where query entailment under ontologies plays a vital role. In this scenario a relational database $\mathcal{D}$ and a set of constraints $\mathcal{T}$ (a.k.a. ontology) are given as an input. The input database may not satisfy the given constraints and hence, we look at possible ways of expanding it in a way so that

© Springer Nature Switzerland AG 2021
W. Faber et al. (Eds.): JELIA 2021, LNAI 12678, pp. 179–193, 2021.
https://doi.org/10.1007/978-3-030-75775-5_13

the axioms of $\mathcal{T}$ are finally fulfilled. We are interested in the question whether a query q has a certain answer in the (expanded) database. It boils down to the problem of checking if all models of $(\mathcal{D}, \mathcal{T})$ entail q. Such a question is obviously undecidable in general [3] and the ongoing works concentrate on identifying relevant fragments of $\mathcal{FO}$ for which the problem is decidable [4] and has manageable complexity.

The second motivation is complexity-theoretic. Since the complexity of the Guarded Fragment is relatively high, it is natural to ask whether there exists a fragment of $\mathcal{GF}$ having reasonable complexity while still being expressive enough to capture description logics like $\mathcal{ALC}$. A few such restrictions have already been proposed. Grädel [9] has shown that the complexity of $\mathcal{GF}$ can be lowered to EXPTIME either by bounding the number of variables, or the arity of relational symbols. This however, does not seem to be well-suited for applications in database theory, as databases may have arbitrarily large schemas. We would prefer a solution leading to lower complexity that does not restrict the number of variables or the arity of relations. Moreover, Grädel's restriction does not help to lower the complexity of the query entailment problem: his logic captures the DL $\mathcal{ALCI}$, known to have 2EXPTIME-hard query entailment problem [18]. Another idea was recently suggested by Kieroński [15]. In [15] the author proposed a family of one-dimensional guarded logics that restrict quantification patterns in $\mathcal{GF}$ by leaving each maximal block of quantifiers in it with at most one free variable. Their satisfiability problem is NEXPTIME-complete (so probably lower than 2EXPTIME) but the complexity of the query entailment problem is still 2EXPTIME-hard. The culprit is again the ability to speak about inverses of relations, giving us a way to capture $\mathcal{ALCI}$.

1.2   Our Results

In this work we present a sublogic of $\mathcal{GF}$ that overcomes the problems mentioned in the previous section, which is inspired by Fluted Logic [22,23]. We call our logic the *Forward Guarded Fragment* ($\mathcal{FGF}$) of First-Order Logic. $\mathcal{FGF}$ restricts quantification patterns of $\mathcal{GF}$ in such a way that tuples of variables appearing in atoms are infixes of the sequence of the already quantified-variables (in the order of their quantification). This "forwardness" prohibits the logic from capturing the inverse relations from $\mathcal{ALCI}$ but it still is expressive enough to capture $\mathcal{ALC}$. Moreover, the logic offers a non-trivial use of higher-arity relations, so it can be employed to reason about real-life relational databases.

In the paper we exploit "forwardness" to show that $\mathcal{FGF}$-knowledge-bases enjoy the *higher-arity-forest-model property*, a tailored version of the forest-model property from $\mathcal{GF}$ in which the higher-arity relations link elements from different levels of a tree only in a contiguous ascending order. This property is then employed to establish EXPTIME-completeness for the knowledge-base satisfiability problem, which also relies on the fact that there are only exponentially many different relevant types of tuples of the domain elements. The culmination point of the paper is the EXPTIME-completeness proof of the CQ entailment problem, achieved by a generalisation of Lutz's spoiler technique from [19], carefully tailored towards higher-arity relations.

Our proof techniques are similar to those introduced in [9,19]. However, the devil is in the details and higher-arity relations made the problem significantly more difficult. Missing proofs were delegated to the technical report.

2 Preliminaries

In this paper, we employ the standard terminology from finite model theory [17]. Usually, we refer to structures with fraktur letters, and to their universes with the corresponding Roman letters. When working with structures, we always assume that they have non-empty domains. We employ countable *signatures* of individual constants $\mathbf{N_I}$ and predicates (of various positive arities) Σ. The arity of $R \in \Sigma$ is denoted with $\mathsf{ar}(R)$. We refer to domain elements with $c, d, e, \ldots$ and usually employ $\vec{c}, \vec{d}, \vec{e}, \ldots$ to denote tuples of domain elements. We frequently use variables $x, y, \ldots$ from a countably-infinite set $\mathbf{N_V}$ and individual names $a, b, \ldots$ from $\mathbf{N_I}$. We write $\varphi(\vec{x})$ to indicate that all free variables of φ are in $\vec{x}$. A sentence is a formula without free variables. For a unary function f we write $f(\vec{x})$ to denote the tuple resulting from applying f to each element of $\vec{x}$. Given a structure $\mathfrak{A}$ and a set $B \subseteq A$ we define the *restriction* of $\mathfrak{A}$ to B as the structure $\mathfrak{A}{\restriction}_B$.

Let $\mathcal{L}$ be a fragment of $\mathcal{FO}$ with its standard syntax and semantics. Given φ with free variables in $\vec{x}$ we say that a tuple of domain elements $\vec{d}$ from $\mathfrak{A}$ *satisfies* $\varphi(\vec{x})$ iff $\mathfrak{A} \models \varphi[\vec{x}/\vec{d}]$ holds. An $\mathcal{L}$-theory $\mathcal{T}$ is a finite set of $\mathcal{L}$-formulae over Σ. An $\mathcal{L}$-database is a finite set of facts, *i.e.* expressions of the form $R(\vec{a})$, where $\vec{a}$ is a tuple of individual names. We denote the set of individual names appearing in $\mathcal{D}$ with $\mathsf{ind}(\mathcal{D})$. An $\mathcal{L}$-knowledge-base (a kb for short) is a pair $\mathcal{K} = (\mathcal{D}, \mathcal{T})$ composed of $\mathcal{L}$-database $\mathcal{D}$ and $\mathcal{L}$-theory $\mathcal{T}$. We say that a structure $\mathfrak{A}$ satisfies a theory $\mathcal{T}$ (written: $\mathfrak{A} \models \mathcal{T}$) if it satisfies all of its formulae. Similarly, $\mathfrak{A}$ satisfies a database $\mathcal{D}$ if it satisfies all its facts (with individual names treated as constants). We say that $\mathfrak{A}$ satisfies a kb $\mathcal{K}$ (written: $\mathfrak{A} \models \mathcal{K}$) if it satisfies both its components.

In the *satisfiability* (resp. *knowledge base satisfiability*) problem for a logic $\mathcal{L}$ we ask whether an input formula (resp. knowledge-base) from $\mathcal{L}$ has a *model*.

2.1 Queries

Conjunctive queries (CQs) are conjunctions of positive atoms with variables from $\mathbf{N_V}$. The set of variables appearing in q is denoted with $\mathsf{Var}(q)$ and the number of atoms of q (*i.e.* the size of q) is denoted with $|q|$. The fact that $R(\vec{x})$ appears in q is indicated with $R(\vec{x}) \in q$. Whenever some subset $V \subseteq \mathsf{Var}(q)$ is given, with $q{\restriction}_V$ we denote a sub-query of q where all the atoms containing any variable outside V are removed.

Let $\pi : \mathsf{Var}(q) \rightarrow A$ be a *variable assignment*. We write $\mathfrak{A} \models_\pi R(\vec{x})$ if $\pi(\vec{x}) \in R^{\mathfrak{A}}$. Similarly, we write $\mathfrak{A} \models_\pi q_1 \wedge q_2$ iff $\mathfrak{A} \models_\pi q_1$ and $\mathfrak{A} \models_\pi q_2$, for some CQs

q_1, q_2. We say that π is a *match* for $\mathfrak{A}$ and q if $\mathfrak{A} \models_\pi q$ holds and that $\mathfrak{A}$ *satisfies* q (denoted with: $\mathfrak{A} \models q$) whenever $\mathfrak{A} \models_\pi q$ for some match π. The definitions are lifted to kbs: q is *entailed* by a kb $\mathcal{K}$ (written: $\mathcal{K} \models q$) if all models $\mathfrak{A}$ of $\mathcal{K}$ satisfy q. When $\mathfrak{A} \models \mathcal{K}$ but $\mathfrak{A} \not\models q$, we call $\mathfrak{A}$ a *countermodel* for $\mathcal{K}$ and q. Note that q is entailed by $\mathcal{K}$ iff there are no countermodels for $\mathcal{K}$ and q. In the *CQ entailment problem* for a logic $\mathcal{L}$ we ask if an input $\mathcal{L}$-kb $\mathcal{K}$ entails an input CQ q.

Observe that a conjunctive query q can be seen as a structure $\mathfrak{H}_q$, with the domain $\mathrm{Var}(q)$, having the interpretation of relations fixed as $\mathrm{R}^{\mathfrak{H}_q} = \{\, \vec{x} \mid \mathrm{R}(\vec{x}) \in q \,\}$. We will call it a *query hypergraph* of q. Hence, any match π for $\mathfrak{A}$ and q can be seen as a homomorphism from $\mathfrak{H}_q$ to $\mathfrak{A}$.

3   Forward Guarded Fragment

We introduce the Forward Guarded Fragment (denoted with $\mathcal{FGF}$) of First-Order Logic defined as the intersection of the Guarded Fragment [1] and the Forward Fragment, sharing the spirit of the Fluted Fragment [23]. We define their syntax first. We stress that the considered logics do not allow for constants and equality.

3.1   Logics

Recall that the *guarded fragment* ($\mathcal{GF}$) is obtained from $\mathcal{FO}$ by requiring that first-order quantification is appropriately relativised by atoms. Formally $\mathcal{GF}$ is the smallest set containing all atomic formulae, closed under boolean connectives and whenever $\varphi(\vec{x}, \vec{y})$ is in $\mathcal{GF}$ and $\alpha(\vec{x}, \vec{y})$ is an atom containing all free variables of φ then both $\forall \vec{y} \, (\alpha(\vec{x}, \vec{y}) \rightarrow \varphi(\vec{x}, \vec{y}))$ and $\exists \vec{y} \, (\alpha(\vec{x}, \vec{y}) \wedge \varphi(\vec{x}, \vec{y}))$ are in $\mathcal{GF}$. The atom α is called a *guard*.

Next we define the *forward fragment* ($\mathcal{FF}$) of $\mathcal{FO}$. It is inspired by the Fluted Fragment $\mathcal{FL}$ [23] and the Ordered Fragment of $\mathcal{FO}$ [11]: the main difference is that we allow the variable sequences appearing in formulae to be infixes of the already quantified variables, not only suffixes (as in $\mathcal{FL}$) or prefixes (as in the ordered fragment). Turing our attention to the formal definition of $\mathcal{FF}$, let us fix a sequence $\vec{x_\omega} = x_1, x_2, \ldots$ of variables from $\mathbf{N_V}$. For simplicity, we write $\vec{x}_{i\ldots j}$ to denote the (gap-free!) sequence $x_i, x_{i+1}, \ldots, x_j$. We start by defining the set of $\mathcal{FF}^{[n]}$ formulae over Σ for all natural n:

- an atom $\alpha(\vec{x})$ belongs to $\mathcal{FF}^{[n]}$ if $\vec{x} = \vec{x}_{k\ldots\ell}$ for some infix $[k, \ell]$ of $[1, n]$
- $\mathcal{FF}^{[n]}$ is closed under boolean connectives $\wedge, \vee, \neg, \rightarrow$;
- If $\varphi(\vec{x}_{1\ldots n+1})$ is in $\mathcal{FF}^{[n+1]}$ then both $\exists x_{n+1} \, \varphi(\vec{x}_{1\ldots n+1})$ and $\forall x_{n+1} \, \varphi(\vec{x}_{1\ldots n+1})$ belong to $\mathcal{FF}^{[n]}$.

We define $\mathcal{FF}$ as the set $\mathcal{FF}^{[0]}$, which is composed exclusively of sentences. We stress that $\mathcal{FF}$ was not studied in the literature before but it can be polynomially reduced to the Fluted Fragment $\mathcal{FL}$.

Finally, we define the *forward guarded fragment* ($\mathcal{FGF}$) as $\mathcal{GF} \cap \mathcal{FF}$, thus combining both mentioned restrictions. To gain more intuitions on $\mathcal{FGF}$, we encourage the reader to consult the following correct $\mathcal{FGF}$ formula φ_1^{ok} as well as three incorrect formulae φ_{1-3}^{bad}:

$$\varphi_1^{ok} = \forall x_1 \; A(x_1) \rightarrow \exists x_2 \; \big[S(x_1, x_2) \wedge \neg U(x_1, x_2) \wedge \neg A(x_2) \wedge$$
$$\forall x_3 \forall x_4 \; (T(x_1, x_2, x_3, x_4) \rightarrow P(x_2, x_3, x_4) \wedge A(x_4)) \big]$$

$$\varphi_1^{bad} = \forall x_1 \; R(x_1, x_1), \quad \varphi_2^{bad} = \forall x_1 \forall x_2 \; S(x_1, x_2) \rightarrow R(x_2, x_1),$$
$$\varphi_3^{bad} = \forall x_1 \forall x_2 \forall x_3 \; R(x_1, x_2) \wedge R(x_2, x_3) \rightarrow R(x_1, x_3)$$

Note that all of the aforementioned incorrect formulae are not in $\mathcal{FGF}$ due to the fact that sequences of variables appearing in atoms are not infixes of $x_1, \ldots, x_k$, with k being the number of the last quantified variable. One can also observe that there is another reason for the third formula to be incorrect: the quantifiers in φ_3^{bad} are not guarded, *i.e.* the atom $\alpha(x_1, x_2, x_3)$ after the last quantifier is missing. The atom $S(x_1, x_2)$ in φ_2^{bad} is an example of a correct guard. The formula φ_1^{bad} demonstrates why the equality predicate is disallowed in $\mathcal{FGF}$.

3.2   Simplified Forms and Forward Types

While working with $\mathcal{FGF}$ formulae it is convenient to convert them into an appropriate normal form. The proof goes via a routine renaming.

Lemma 1. *For any $\mathcal{FGF}$-kb $\mathcal{K} = (\mathcal{D}, \mathcal{T})$ we can compute (in polynomial time) an equi-satisfiable kb $\mathcal{K}_{simpl} = (\mathcal{D}_+, \{\varphi_\forall, \varphi_{\forall\exists}\})$ (over an extended signature) with*

$$\varphi_\forall = \bigwedge_{i=0}^{m_\forall} \forall \vec{x}_{1\ldots k_i} \; R_{\forall_i}(\vec{x}_{1\ldots k_i}) \rightarrow \psi_{\forall_i}(\vec{x}_{1\ldots k_i})$$

$$\varphi_{\forall\exists} = \bigwedge_{i=0}^{m_{\forall\exists}} \forall \vec{x}_{1\ldots k_i} \; R_{\forall\exists_i}(\vec{x}_{1\ldots k_i}) \rightarrow \exists \vec{x}_{k_i+1 \ldots k_i + \ell_i} \; S_{\forall\exists_i}(\vec{x}_{1\ldots k_i + \ell_i}) \wedge \psi_{\forall\exists_i}(\vec{x}_{1\ldots k_i + \ell_i}),$$

where (possibly decorated) R, S and ψ denote, respectively, predicates and quantifier-free $\mathcal{FGF}$ formulae. We refer to such a $\mathcal{K}_{simpl}$ as a simplified $\mathcal{K}$.

We next introduce a notion of a *forward type* useful to reason about $\mathcal{FGF}$-definable properties. Fix finite signature Σ and positive n. A (Σ, n)-*forward type* is an $\mathcal{FO}$ formula with n free-variables $\vec{x}_{1\ldots n}$ s.t. for all symbols $R \in \Sigma$ of arity ℓ not bigger than n and for all $1 \leq i \leq n+1-\ell$ a type contains as a conjunct either $R(\vec{x}_{i\ldots i+\ell-1})$ or its negation. We write $\mathsf{tp}_{\mathfrak{A}}^{\Sigma}(\vec{d})$ to denote the *unique* forward type satisfying $\mathfrak{A} \models \mathsf{tp}_{\mathfrak{A}}^{\Sigma}(\vec{d})$. We also say that $\vec{d}$ *realises* the forward type $\mathsf{tp}_{\mathfrak{A}}^{\Sigma}(\vec{x})$. By elementary counting we can see that the number of (Σ, n)-forward types is exponential in $|\Sigma| + n$ while their sizes are only polynomial.

Lemma 2. *Up to isomorphism, there are at most $2^{|\Sigma| \cdot n^2}$ (Σ, n)-forward types. Moreover, each (Σ, n)-forward type has at most $|\Sigma| \cdot n$ conjuncts.*

Finally, by unfolding definitions, one can show that whenever two tuples have equal forward types then they satisfy the same formulae from simplified kbs.

3.3 Higher-Arity-Forest-(Counter)Model Property

Here we introduce the notion of higher-arity forests, which are forest reflecting
the essence of forwardness. We say that a structure $\mathfrak{F}$ is a *higher-arity forest* (HAF) if its domain is a prefix-closed subset of sequences from $\mathbb{N}^+$ and for
all relational symbols R of arity k we have that $\vec{d} \in R^{\mathfrak{F}}$ implies:

- either all the elements from $\vec{d}$ are natural numbers (= one-element sequences)
- or $\vec{d} = (c_1, \ldots, c_\ell, e_1, e_2, \ldots e_{\ell'})$, where each member of $\vec{c}$ is a number and there
  exist numbers $n_1, n_2, \ldots, n_{\ell'}$ such that $e_i = c_\ell \cdot n_1 \cdot \ldots \cdot n_i$ for all $\ell' \geq i \geq 0$
- or $\vec{d} = (d_1, \ldots, d_k)$, with $d_1 \notin \mathbb{N}$, such that for each index i there exist a
  number n_i such that $d_{i+1} = d_i \cdot n_i$.

The elements from $F \cap \mathbb{N}$ are simply the *roots* of $\mathfrak{F}$. A forest with a single root
is called a *tree*. We also use the prefix ordering $\prec_{\text{pref}}$ to speak about children,
parents, siblings in the usual (graph-theoretic) way. Observe that, intuitively,
higher-arity forests are just forests in which relations either arbitrarily traverse
roots or connect other elements but only in a level-by-level ascending order.

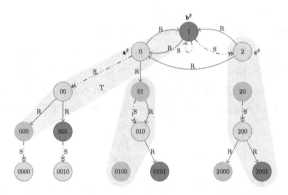

Fig. 1. An example higher-arity forest. The coloured areas in the picture indicates
higher-arity relations, *e.g.* the red area means $T(1, 0, 00, 000)$. (Color figure online)

A model $\mathfrak{A}$ of a kb $\mathcal{K} = (\mathcal{D}, \mathcal{T})$ is a *HAF model* iff $\mathfrak{A}$ is a HAF with the set of
roots being equal to the set of interpretations of individuals from $\text{ind}(\mathcal{D})$ in $\mathfrak{A}$.

We show $\mathcal{FGF}$ enjoys the *HAF-model property*, useful to design an EXPTIME
decision procedure for deciding $\mathcal{FGF}$. In the proof we take any model $\mathfrak{A}$ of $\mathcal{K}$
and construct an infinite sequence of forest of growing sizes. The first of them is
simply $\mathfrak{A}$ restricted to the interpretation of database constants. The others are
obtained as follows: whenever some forest $\mathfrak{F}$ contains a tuple $\vec{d}$ of elements does
not have a witness to satisfy a conjunct of $\varphi_{\forall\exists}$ we expand the domain of $\mathfrak{F}$ with a
fresh copy of its original witnesses taken from $\mathfrak{A}$ and connect it to $\vec{d}$, mimicking
the connections in $\mathfrak{A}$. The limit of this process will be a HAF-model of $\mathcal{K}$.

Lemma 3. *Any satisfiable simplified $\mathcal{FGF}$ kb $\mathcal{K}$ has a HAF model. Moreover, if
there is a countermodel for $\mathcal{K}$ and a CQ q then there is also a HAF countermodel.*

3.4   ExpTime-Completeness of the kb Satisfiability Problem

The notion of forward types and higher-arity forests will now be employed to design an alternating PSPACE procedure for deciding the satisfiability for $\mathcal{FGF}$ knowledge bases. Since APSPACE = EXPTIME [5] we derive an EXPTIME upper bound for $\mathcal{FGF}$. The matching lower bound is inherited from $\mathcal{ALC}$ [2]. The forthcoming algorithm is a variant of Grädel's algorithm for $\mathcal{GF}$ [9].

We sketch the main ideas. As a preliminary step, we first transform the input $\mathcal{K}$ into $\mathcal{K}_{smpl} = (\mathcal{D}_+, \{\varphi_\forall, \varphi_{\forall\exists}\})$. Then the rest of the procedure is responsible for constructing a higher-arity forest-model $\mathfrak{F}$ of $\mathcal{K}_{smpl}$. We start from guessing the "roots" $\mathfrak{R}$ of $\mathfrak{F}$. Note that we cannot simply guess $\mathfrak{R}$: once Σ contains an n-ary predicate, such a predicate might be composed of $|R|^n$ different tuples and thus we cannot fully store it in polynomial space. Fortunately we do not need to do it. It turns out that for the feasibility of our procedure it suffices to keep only the forward types of tuples appearing in $\mathcal{D}_+$ (the number of which is bounded polynomially, see: Lemma 2). Since the guessed structure is of polynomial size, we can perform the standard $\mathcal{FO}$ model-checking algorithm [25] to ensure that $\mathfrak{R}$ satisfies both $\mathcal{D}_+$ and $\varphi_\forall$. It could be, however, that $\varphi_{\forall\exists}$ is not satisfied (yet). We then iterate over all conjuncts λ from $\varphi_{\forall\exists}$, universally choosing a tuple $\vec{d}$ of elements for whose the antecedent of λ is satisfied but the consequent of λ is not. For such a tuple we introduce fresh elements $\vec{e}$ and guess the forward type of $\vec{d} \cdot \vec{e}$. Next, we check that $\vec{d} \cdot \vec{e}$ indeed satisfies λ and whether its type does not violate $\varphi_\forall$ (we reject otherwise). Finally, we recursively repeat the procedure for the substructure containing only $\vec{d} \cdot \vec{e}$. The procedure accepts when the number of steps exceeds the total number of (Σ, n)-forward-types – by pigeonhole principle it follows that one of the (Σ, n)-forward-types necessarily occurs twice, so if the procedure has not rejected the input yet it means that we can safely repeat the process over and over, making exactly the same choices as it did before.

Our pseudo-code and its correctness proof are available in the full paper. From it we conclude the first main theorem of the paper. Since $\mathcal{GF}$ has the finite model property [9] (even in the presence of constants that can simulate DBs) our algorithm for $\mathcal{FGF}$ can also be applied to the finite-model reasoning.

Theorem 4. *Kb (finite) satisfiability problem for $\mathcal{FGF}$ is* EXPTIME-*complete.*

4   Query Answering

This section provides a worst-case complexity-optimal algorithm for deciding query entailment over $\mathcal{FGF}$ knowledge-bases. The main technique employed here is a generalisation of the so-called *spoiler technique* by Lutz [19, Sec. 3], carefully tailored to work over structures having relations of arity greater than 2.

We first give a rather informal explanation of the technique. We recall that to decide $\mathcal{K} \models q$ it suffices to check the existence of a HAF countermodel for $\mathcal{K}$ and q (see: Lemma 3). In the ideal situation, we would know how to prepare a knowledge-base $\mathcal{K}_{\neg q}$ that characterises the class of all HAF countermodels for q. Note that the existence of $\mathcal{K}_{\neg q}$ would immediately imply that any model of

$\mathcal{K} \cup \mathcal{K}_{\neg q}$ is, by definition, also a countermodel for $\mathcal{K}$ and q. The problematic part is, of course, the construction of $\mathcal{K}_{\neg q}$. To decide satisfiability of $\mathcal{K} \cup \mathcal{K}_{\neg q}$ we would like axioms of $\mathcal{K}_{\neg q}$ to be written in $\mathcal{FGF}$, which seems to be challenging since the matches of q may have arbitrary complex shapes. On the positive side, there is a simple way of detecting matches of tree-shaped queries, based on the well-known *rolling-up technique* [13, Sec. 4]: we basically describe tree-shaped matches as unary predicates by defining their trees in a bottom-up manner and then we enforce their emptiness in all models of $\mathcal{K}_{\neg q}$. Here we exploit the fact that countermodels can be made HAFs and combine the rolling-up technique with so-called *splittings*, that detects query matches of arbitrary shape over forests. In order to block such matches, we parallelise the construction of $\mathcal{K}_{\neg q}$. Rather than construing one huge kb we divide it into smaller chunks $\mathcal{K}_s$ called *spoilers* with an intuitive meaning that the consistency of any of $\mathcal{K} \cup \mathcal{K}_s$ spoils the entailment $\mathcal{K} \models q$. Once we show that each spoiler is of polynomial size and there are only exponentially many of them, we can reduce the entailment question to exponentially many satisfiability checks for kbs of polynomial size (hence in ExpTime by Theorem 4), deducing the ExpTime-completeness of CQ entailment problem for $\mathcal{FGF}$.

4.1   Rolling-Up: Detecting Matches of Tree-Shaped Queries

We consider a modification of the *rolling-up technique* that transforms tree-shaped queries into $\mathcal{FGF}$. In our scenario, the name "tree-shaped" indicates that the underlying hypergraph $\mathfrak{H}_q$ of a query q is a (connected) higher-arity tree. Henceforth we always assume that whenever $R(\vec{x}_{1...k}) \in q$ then also $R_i(\vec{x}_{1...i}) \in q$ for fresh relation names R_i. We call such CQs *closed* and by the *closure* of q, denoted with $\mathrm{cl}(q)$, we mean the query obtained from q by extending q in a minimal way to make it closed. Note that the entailment problem of CQs and closed CQs over $\mathcal{FGF}$ kbs coincides, since we can always extend the input kb with fresh relations R_i and the rules $\forall \vec{x}_{1...\mathrm{ar}(R)} \ R(\vec{x}_{1...\mathrm{ar}(R)}) \leftrightarrow \bigwedge_{i=1}^{\mathrm{ar}(R)} R_i(\vec{x}_{1...i})$ for all non-unary predicates R appearing in q. Abusing slightly the notation, we call the kbs extended in the above way their q-*closures*.

In what follows we are going to construct, for every variable $v \in \mathrm{Var}(q)$, a unary predicate $\mathrm{Subt}_q^v(x)$ with the indented meaning that $d \in (\mathrm{Subt}_q^v)^{\mathfrak{A}}$ holds whenever the subtree of $\mathfrak{H}_q$ rooted at the variable v can be mapped below d in $\mathfrak{A}$. In order to adjust the rolling-up technique to non-binary relations that may appear in trees, we employ additional non-binary predicates $\mathrm{Subt}_q^{\vec{v},u}(\vec{x}, y)$ that do the same job as $\mathrm{Subt}_q^u(y)$ but in contrast they memorise the path $\vec{v}$ leading to u, so the higher-arity relations can be retrieved from the construction.

An inductive definition is given next. The main idea behind it is to traverse the input tree in a bottom-up manner, describing its shape in $\mathcal{FGF}$, and gradually "rolling-up" the input tree into smaller chunks until its root is reached.

Definition 5. *For a given closed tree-shaped CQ q and any sequence of variables $\vec{v}u$ from $\mathrm{Var}(q)$ (that follows the level-by-level order in $\mathfrak{H}_q$) we define an*

$(|\vec{v}|+1)$-ary predicate $\mathrm{Subt}_q^{\vec{v},u}(\vec{x}_{1\ldots|\vec{v}|+1})$ as follows. The empty conjunction is treated as $\top$.

1. We initially set $\mathrm{Subt}_q^{\vec{v},u}(\vec{x}_{1\ldots|\vec{v}|+1})$ to be equal:

$$\bigwedge_{R(\vec{v}_{k\ldots|\vec{v}|}u)\in q} R(\vec{x}_{k\ldots|\vec{v}|+1}) \wedge \bigwedge_{A(u)\in q} A(x_{|\vec{v}|+1})$$

2. Additionally, when u is not a leaf of $\mathfrak{H}_q$, we supplement the above formula with some extra conjuncts for each children variable $w \in \mathrm{Var}(q)$ of u in $\mathfrak{H}_q$. Take a longest suffix $\vec{v}_{suff}$ of $\vec{v}$ for which $R(\vec{v}_{suff}, u, w) \in q$ (if there is no such suffix then keep $\vec{v}_{suff}$ empty) and append the formula:

$$\exists x_{|\vec{v}|+2}\,\mathrm{Subt}_q^{\vec{v}_{suff},u,w}(\vec{x}_{|\vec{v}|-|\vec{v}_{suff}|+1\ldots|\vec{v}|+2})$$

We use $\mathrm{Match}_q(x)$ as a shorthand for $\mathrm{Subt}_q^{x_r}(x)$ with x_r being the root of $\mathfrak{H}_q$. We stress that due to the closedness of q and the fact that we keep the variables appropriately ordered, the definition of $\mathrm{Match}_q(x)$ is in $\mathcal{FGF}$.

From the presented construction we can easily see that the size (i.e. the number of atoms) of Match_q is polynomial in $|q|$. The next lemma, claiming correctness of the presented definition, can be shown by induction.

Lemma 6. *For any higher-arity forest $\mathfrak{A}$ and a closed tree-shaped conjunctive query q we have $(\mathrm{Match}_q)^{\mathfrak{A}} \neq \emptyset$ iff there exists a homomorphism $\mathfrak{h} : \mathfrak{H}_q \to \mathfrak{A}$.*

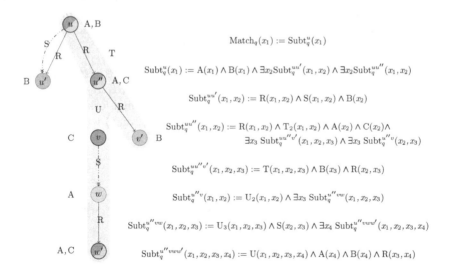

Fig. 2. An example CQ q together with the resulting rolling-up predicates. In the picture we omitted additional relations appearing in q due to its closedness. Moreover, in the definitions of predicates Subt_q we omitted S_1, R_1, T_1, U_1.

The presented rolling-up technique shows us how to detect matches of tree-shaped queries. Its direct consequence is the forthcoming theorem telling us that such query matches can be effectively blocked and giving us a robust reduction from query entailment problem for tree-shaped queries to kb satisfiability problem.

Theorem 7. *Let* $\mathcal{K} = (\mathcal{D}, \mathcal{T})$ *be a closed satisfiable kb and let* q *be a closed tree-shaped CQ. Then* $\mathcal{K} \not\models q$ *iff the kb* $\mathcal{K} \cup \{\forall x_1 \neg \mathrm{Match}_q(x_1)\}$ *is satisfiable.*

Unfortunately, the above theorem does not transfer beyond tree-shaped CQs since our match-detecting mechanism is too weak. To detect matches of arbitrary CQs, we introduce the notions of forks and splittings.

4.2   Fork Rewritings: Describing Different Collapsings of a Query

Observe that a connected conjunctive query can induce several different query matches, depending on how its variables "glue" together. We formalise this concept with the forthcoming notion of fork rewritings [19, p. 4]. Moreover, as it will turn out soon, the only relevant trees for detecting query matches are exactly those trees being subtrees of the maximal fork rewritings.

Definition 8. *Let* q, q' *be conjunctive queries. We say that* q' *is obtained from* q *by fork elimination, and denote this fact with* $q \leadsto_{\mathsf{fe}} q'$, *if* q' *can be obtained from* q *by selecting two atoms* $\mathrm{R}(\vec{z}, \vec{y_1}, x)$, $\mathrm{S}(\vec{y_2}, x)$ *of* q *(where* $\vec{z}$ *might be empty,* R *and* S *are not necessarily different and* $|\vec{y_1}| = |\vec{y_2}|$ *holds) and componentwise identifying the tuples* $\vec{y_1}, \vec{y_2}$. *We also say that* q' *is a fork rewriting of* q *if* q' *is obtained from* q *by applying fork elimination on* q *possibly multiple times. When the fork elimination process is applied exhaustively on* q *we say that the resulting query, denoted with* $\mathsf{maxfr}(q)$, *is a maximal fork rewriting of* q.

Example 9. Consider a CQ $q = \mathrm{R}(x, y) \wedge \mathrm{S}(v, y) \wedge \mathrm{R}(x, z) \wedge \mathrm{R}(v, z) \wedge \mathrm{T}(y, x, z) \wedge \mathrm{T}(y, v, z)$ with atoms α_{1-6}. Note that q has three forks: (α_1, α_2), (α_3, α_4) and (α_5, α_6). By eliminating any of them we obtain the maximal fork rewriting of q, namely $\mathsf{maxfr}(q) = \mathrm{R}(xv, y) \wedge \mathrm{R}(xv, z) \wedge \mathrm{S}(xv, y) \wedge \mathrm{T}(y, xv, z)$ with fresh xv.

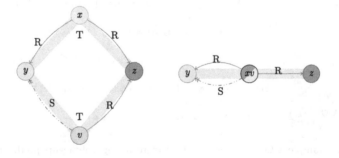

By employing a special naming schemes for variables and by induction over the number of fork eliminations we can show the following lemma:

Lemma 10. *Every CQ q has the unique (up to renaming)* maxfr(q).

A rather immediate application of Definition 8 is that entailment of a fork rewriting of a query implies entailment of the input query itself. The proof goes via an induction over the number of fork eliminations.

Lemma 11. *Let q, q' be conjunctive queries, such that q' is obtained from q by fork elimination, and let $\mathfrak{A}$ be a structure. Then $\mathfrak{A} \models q'$ implies $\mathfrak{A} \models q$.*

4.3 Splittings: Describing Query Matches in an Abstract Way

The next notion, namely *splittings* [19, p. 4], are partitions of query variables that provide an abstract way to reason on how (a fork rewriting of) a conjunctive query matches a forest structure, without referring to either to a concrete forest or to a concrete match. Intuitively, when a query q matches a forest, its match induces a partition of variables $x \in \text{Var}(q)$, according to the following scenarios:

- either x is mapped to one of the roots of the intended forest,
- or x, together with some other variables, constitute to a subtree dangling from one of the forests' roots,
- or otherwise x is mapped somewhere far inside the forest, not being directly connected to the forests' roots.

Splittings capture the above intuitions. Their definition is provided below.

Definition 12. *A splitting Π_q w.r.t. $\mathcal{K} = (\mathcal{T}, \mathcal{D})$ of q is a tuple*

$$\Pi_q = (\text{Roots}, \text{name}, \text{SubTree}_1, \text{SubTree}_2, \ldots, \text{SubTree}_n, \text{root-of}, \text{Trees}),$$

where the sets Roots, SubTree$_1, \ldots,$ SubTree$_n$, Trees *induce a partition of* Var(q), name : Roots $\rightarrow$ ind($\mathcal{D}$) *is a function naming the roots and* root-of : $\{1, 2, \ldots, n\} \rightarrow$ Roots *assigns to each* SubTree$_i$ *an element from* Roots. *Moreover, Π_q satisfies:*

(a) *the query $q{\restriction}_{\text{Trees}}$ is a variable-disjoint union of tree-shaped queries,*
(b) *the queries $q{\restriction}_{\text{SubTree}_i}$ are tree-shaped for all indices $i \in \{1, 2, \ldots, n\}$,*
(c) *for any atom $R(\vec{x}) \in q$ the variables from $\vec{x}$ either belong to the same set or $\vec{x} = (\vec{y}, u, v, \vec{z})$ [with possibly empty $\vec{y}, \vec{z}$], where:*
    - *all variables from $\vec{y}, u$ belong to* Roots,
    - *there is an index $i \in \{1, 2, \ldots, n\}$ witnessing* root-of$(i) = u$,
    - *$v \in$ SubTree$_i$ is the root of $q{\restriction}_{\text{SubTree}_i}$ and variables from $\vec{z}$ are in* SubTree$_i$.
(d) *For any index $i \in \{1, 2, \ldots, n\}$ there is an atom $R(\vec{y}, \text{root-of}(i), x_i) \in q$ [where $\vec{y}$ is possibly empty] with x_i being the root of $q{\restriction}_{\text{SubTree}_i}$.*

It helps to think that a splitting consists of named roots, corresponding to the database part of the model, together with some of their subtrees and of some auxiliary trees lying somewhere far from the roots.

Example 13. Consider a HAF $\mathfrak{A}$ with roots $a, \dot{b}, c$ and a (non-tree-shaped) CQ:

$$q = (A(x_0) \wedge R(x_0, x_1) \wedge R(x_1, x_0) \wedge B(x_1)) \wedge (S(x_0, x_{00}) \wedge R(x_{00}, x_{000})) \wedge$$
$$(R(x_0, x_{01}) \wedge S(x_{01}, x_{010}) \wedge R(x_{010}, x_{0100})) \wedge (A(x_{200}) \wedge R(x_{200}, x_{2001}) \wedge B(x_{2001})) .$$

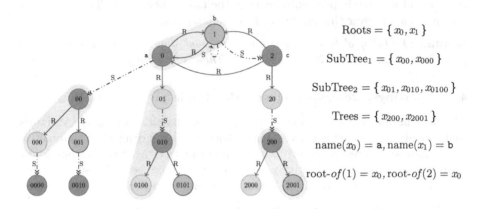

$$\text{Roots} = \{\, x_0, x_1 \,\}$$

$$\text{SubTree}_1 = \{\, x_{00}, x_{000} \,\}$$

$$\text{SubTree}_2 = \{\, x_{01}, x_{010}, x_{0100} \,\}$$

$$\text{Trees} = \{\, x_{200}, x_{2001} \,\}$$

$$\text{name}(x_0) = a, \text{name}(x_1) = b$$

$$\text{root-}of(1) = x_0, \text{root-}of(2) = x_0$$

Fig. 3. Splitting Π_q of q, compatible with $\mathfrak{A}$. Coloured areas partition variables.

We conclude the section by showing that splittings indeed correspond to query matches over forests. In order to do it, we first introduce an auxiliary definition of *compatibility* of a splitting with a HAF. Intuitively, the first item detects distant trees with the rolling-up technique, the second one describes the connections between roots and the last one detects subtrees dangling from some root.

Definition 14. *Let $\mathcal{K}$ be a closed $\mathcal{FGF}$ knowledge-base, q be a closed CQ and $\mathfrak{A}$ a HAF model of $\mathcal{K}$. A splitting Π_q w.r.t $\mathcal{K}$ of q is compatible with $\mathfrak{A}$ if it satisfies all the conditions below:*

(A) for all connected components $\hat{q}$ of Trees there is a $d \in A$ s.t. $d \in (\text{Match}_{\hat{q}})^{\mathfrak{A}}$,

(B) for all $R(\vec{x}) \in q$ with all $x_i \in \text{Roots}$ we have $(\text{name}(x_1)^{\mathfrak{A}}, \dots, \text{name} (x_{|\vec{x}|})^{\mathfrak{A}}) \in R^{\mathfrak{A}}$,

(C) Take all indices $i \in \{1, 2, \dots, n\}$ and let v_i be the root variable of $q\!\restriction_{\text{SubTree}_i}$. Take any $\vec{u}$ composed only of Roots with the last element $\text{root-}of(i)$, s.t. $R(\vec{u}, v_i) \in q$. Then the tuple $(\text{name}(u_1)^{\mathfrak{A}}, \dots, \text{name}(u_{|\vec{u}|})^{\mathfrak{A}})$ satisfies

$$\exists x_{|\vec{u}|+1}\, \text{Subt}^{\vec{u}, v_i}_{q\restriction_{\{\vec{u}, v_i\} \cup \text{SubTree}_i}} (\vec{x}_{1\dots|\vec{u}|+1})$$

We stress that the difficulties in Item (C) comes from a possible presence of higher-arity relations that link other roots before reaching $\text{root-}of(i)$.

The lemma below gathers the notions presented so far.

Lemma 15. *Let $\mathcal{K}$ be a closed $\mathcal{FGF}$-kb, q a closed CQ and a HAF model $\mathfrak{A}$ of $\mathcal{K}$. Then $\mathfrak{A} \models q$ iff there is a fork rewriting q' of q and a splitting $\Pi_{q'}$ w.r.t. $\mathcal{K}$ of q' compatible with $\mathfrak{A}$.*

4.4   Spoilers: Blocking Query Matches

Spoilers are knowledge bases dedicated to blocking compatibility of a given splitting. We define them similarly to Definition 14, in a way that there will be a
tight correspondence between the cases below and those from Definition 14.

Definition 16. *Let q be a closed CQ, $\mathcal{K}$ be a closed $\mathcal{FGF}$-kb and let $\Pi_q =$
(Roots, name, SubTree$_1$, . . . , SubTree$_n$, root-of, Trees) be a splitting w.r.t $\mathcal{K}$ of
q. A spoiler $\mathcal{K}_{\neg \Pi_q} = (\mathcal{D}_{\neg \Pi_q}, \mathcal{T}_{\neg \Pi_q})$ for Π_q is an $\mathcal{FGF}$-kb satisfying one of:*

(A) $\forall x \; \neg \mathrm{Match}_{\hat{q}}(x) \in \mathcal{T}_{\neg \Pi_q}$ for some tree-shaped query $\hat{q}$ from Trees,
*(B) $\neg \mathrm{R}(\mathrm{name}(x_1), \dots, \mathrm{name}(x_k)) \in \mathcal{D}_{\neg \Pi_q}$ for some atom $\mathrm{R}(\vec{x}) \in q$ with all x_i
    in Roots,*
*(C) there is an index $i \in \{1, 2, \dots, n\}$, a tuple of variables $\vec{u}$ composed only of
    Roots with the last element root-of(i), s.t. $\mathrm{R}(\vec{u}, v_i) \in q$, where v_i is the root
    variable of $q\lceil_{\mathrm{SubTree}_i}$, but*

$$\left(\neg \exists x_{|\vec{u}|+1} \; \mathrm{Subt}_{q\lceil_{\vec{u}\cup\{v_i\}\cup\mathrm{SubTree}_i}}^{\vec{u}, v_i} (\vec{x}_{1\dots|\vec{u}|+1}) \right) \left(\mathrm{name}(u_1), \dots, \mathrm{name}(u_{|\vec{u}|}) \right) \in \mathcal{D}_{\neg \Pi_q}.$$

The definition of spoilers is now lifted to the case for the whole closed CQs.

Definition 17. *A super-spoiler for a closed CQ q and a closed $\mathcal{FGF}$ kb $\mathcal{K}$ is
a minimal (in the sense the of number of axioms) $\mathcal{FGF}$ kb $\mathcal{K}_{\neg q}$ s.t. for all fork
rewritings q' of q and all splittings $\Pi_{q'}$ w.r.t $\mathcal{K}$ of q', $\mathcal{K}_{\neg q}$ is a spoiler for $\Pi_{q'}$.*

The following crucial property of super-spoilers is shown next.

Lemma 18. *Let $\mathcal{K}$ be a closed $\mathcal{FGF}$ kb and let q be a closed CQ. Then $\mathcal{K} \not\models q$
iff there is a super-spoiler $\mathcal{K}_{\neg q}$ for q and $\mathcal{K}$ such that $\mathcal{K} \cup \mathcal{K}_{\neg q}$ is satisfiable.*

We now bound the total number and the sizes of super-spoilers. It is easy
to see that there are only exponentially many super-spoilers, since the facts
that appear in super-spoilers are also present in the input knowledge base. The
challenging part is to show that super-spoilers are of polynomial size in $|\mathcal{K}| + |q|$.
In order to do it, we observe that all trees that appear in spoilers are actually
subtrees of the maximal fork rewriting of q. Trivially, there are only polynomially
many subtrees of $\mathrm{maxfr}(q)$, so we are done. Finally, we will see that candidates
for super-spoilers can be enumerated in exponential time.

Lemma 19. *Let $\mathcal{K}$ be closed $\mathcal{FGF}$ kb and q be a closed CQ. The following
properties hold true: (a) super-spoilers have sizes polynomial in $|\mathcal{K}|+|q|$; (b) there
are only exponentially many (in $|\mathcal{K}|+|q|$) candidates for super-spoilers; (c) super-
spoilers can be enumerated in time exponential in $|\mathcal{K}| + |q|$.*

From the presented lemma we can deduce an algorithm for solving CQ entailment over $\mathcal{FGF}$ kbs. As a preliminary step we "close" both input CQ q and input
kb $\mathcal{K}$. Second, we exhaustively enumerate all possible candidates $\mathcal{K}_{\neg q}$ for being
a super-spoiler for $\mathcal{K}$ and q. Note that the enumeration process can be done in
exponential time due to Lemma 19. After ensuring that $\mathcal{K}_{\neg q}$ is indeed a super-
spoiler, we test whether $\mathcal{K} \cup \mathcal{K}_{\neg q}$ is satisfiable. The satisfiability test can be

performed in ExpTime due to the polynomial size of $\mathcal{K}_{\neg q}$ and Theorem 4. If some $\mathcal{K} \cup \mathcal{K}_{\neg q}$ is satisfiable, by Lemma 18, we conclude $\mathcal{K} \not\models q$. Otherwise we have that $\mathcal{K} \models q$. The overall process can be implemented in ExpTime, thus we conclude the second main theorem of the paper.

Theorem 20. *CQ entailment problem for $\mathcal{FGF}$ is* ExpTime-*complete.*

Note that the lower bounds are inherited from kb satisfiability problem. For readers interested in CQ entailment over finite models we can also infer ExpTime-completness of the finitary version of the problem. A (non-trivial) argument is that $\mathcal{GF}$ is *finite controllable* [7] (a CQ is entailed over all models iff it is entailed over finite models), which obviously applies also to $\mathcal{FGF}$. Hence, we obtain:

Corollary 21. *CQ finite entailment problem for $\mathcal{FGF}$ is* ExpTime-*complete.*

In the real-life applications, we usually measure the *data complexity* of both satisfiability and entailment problems, *i.e.* the case when the size of the input theory and query is treated as a constant and only $|\mathcal{D}|$ matters. The upper bound follows from $\mathcal{GF}$ [7] and the lower bound holds already for $\mathcal{ALC}$.

Corollary 22. *(Finite) satisfiability and CQ (finite) entailment problems for $\mathcal{FGF}$ are, respectively,* NP-*complete and* coNP-*complete in data-complexity.*

5   Conclusions and Future Work

In the paper we introduced a novel logic $\mathcal{FGF}$ that combines ideas of guarded quantification and forwardness. By exploiting the HAF-model property of the logic we have shown that both kb satisfiability problems and CQ entailment problems are ExpTime-complete, also in the finite.

Our results are quite encouraging and there is a lot of space for future research. We conclude by discussing some interesting open problems.

- Understanding model theory of $\mathcal{FGF}$. One can develop an appropriate notion of bisimulation for $\mathcal{FGF}$ and show an analogous of Van Benthem & Rosen characterisation theorem in the spirit of [10,20]. In the light of [12] it would be interesting to investigate Craig Interpolation and Beth Definability for $\mathcal{FGF}$.
- Understanding extensions of $\mathcal{FGF}$ with counting, constants or transitivity. We conjuncture that the extensions of $\mathcal{FGF}$ with counting quantifiers à la [21] or constants are decidable and can be shown with techniques from Sect. 3.4. Another idea is to $\mathcal{FGF}$ with transitive guards, denoted with $\mathcal{FGF}$+TG, that captures the DL $\mathcal{SH}$. Its two-variable fragment is known to be ExpSpace-complete (without database though) [14]. We believe that the combination of our techniques and those from [14,16] can be applied to infer an ExpSpace upper bound for kb sat problem for the full logic. Finally, CQ entailment for $\mathcal{GF}$+TG is undecidable [7], but we hope that it is not the case for $\mathcal{FGF}$+TG.

Acknowledgements. The author apologises for all mistakes and grammar issues that appear in the paper. He thanks A. Karykowska and P. Witkowski for proofreading, E. Kieroński for his help with the introduction, W. Faber for deadline extension and anonymous JELIA's reviewers for many useful comments.
    This work was supported by the ERC Consolidator Grant No. 771779 (DeciGUT).

References

1. Andréka, H., Németi, I., van Benthem, J.: Modal languages and bounded fragments of predicate logic. J. Philos. Logic (1998)
2. Baader, F., Horrocks, I., Lutz, C., Sattler, U.: An Introduction to Description Logic. Cambridge University Press, Cambridge (2017)
3. Beeri, C., Vardi, M.Y.: The Implication Problem for Data Dependencies. In: ICALP (1981)
4. Calí, A., Gottlob, G., Kifer, M.: Taming the infinite chase: query answering under expressive relational constraints. J. Artif. Intell. Res. (2013)
5. Chandra, A.K., Kozen, D., Stockmeyer, L.J.: Alternation. J. ACM (1981)
6. Figueira, D., Figueira, S., Baque, E.P.: Finite Controllability for Ontology-Mediated Query Answering of CRPQ. KR (2020)
7. Gottlob, G., Pieris, A., Tendera, L.: Querying the Guarded Fragment with Transitivity. In: ICALP (2013)
8. Grädel, E.: Description Logics and Guarded Fragments of First Order Logic. DL (1998)
9. Grädel, E.: On the restraining power of guards. J. Symb. Log. (1999)
10. Grädel, E., Otto, M.: The Freedoms of (Guarded) Bisimulation (2013)
11. Herzig, A.: A new decidable fragment of first order logic. In: Third Logical Biennial, Summer School and Conference in Honour of S. C. Kleene (1990)
12. Hoogland, E., Marx, M., Otto, M.: Beth Definability for the Guarded Fragment. LPAR (1999)
13. Horrocks, I., Tessaris, S.: Answering Conjunctive Queries over DL ABoxes: A Preliminary Report. DL (2000)
14. Kieronski, E.: On the complexity of the two-variable guarded fragment with transitive guards. Inf. Comput. (2006)
15. Kieronski, E.: One-Dimensional Guarded Fragments. MFCS (2019)
16. Kieronski, E., Malinowski, A.: The triguarded fragment with transitivity. LPAR (2020)
17. Libkin, L.: Elements of finite model theory. In: Libkin, L. (ed.) Texts in Theoretical Computer Science. Springer, Heidelberg (2004). https://doi.org/10.1007/978-3-662-07003-1
18. Lutz, C.: Inverse Roles Make Conjunctive Queries Hard. DL (2007)
19. Lutz, C.: Two Upper Bounds for Conjunctive Query Answering in SHIQ. DL (2008)
20. Otto, M.: Elementary Proof of the van Benthem-Rosen Characterisation Theorem. Technical Report (2004)
21. Pratt-Hartmann, I.: Complexity of the guarded two-variable fragment with counting quantifiers. J. Log. Comput. (2007)
22. Pratt-Hartmann, I., Szwast, W., Tendera, L.: The fluted fragment revisited. J. Symb. Log. (2019)
23. Quine, W.: The Ways of Paradox and Other Essays, Revised edn. Harvard University Press, Cambridge (1976)
24. Rosati, R.: On the decidability and finite controllability of query processing in databases with incomplete information. PODS (2006)
25. Stockmeyer, L.: The Complexity of Decision Problems in Automata Theory and Logic (1974)

An Algebraic View on p-Admissible Concrete Domains for Lightweight Description Logics

Franz Baader$^{(\boxtimes)}$ and Jakub Rydval

Institute of Theoretical Computer Science, TU Dresden, Dresden, Germany
{franz.baader,jakub.rydval}@tu-dresden.de

Abstract. Concrete domains have been introduced in Description Logics (DLs) to enable reference to concrete objects (such as numbers) and predefined predicates on these objects (such as numerical comparisons) when defining concepts. To retain decidability when integrating a concrete domain into a decidable DL, the domain must satisfy quite strong restrictions. In previous work, we have analyzed the most prominent such condition, called ω-admissibility, from an algebraic point of view. This provided us with useful algebraic tools for proving ω-admissibility, which allowed us to find new examples for concrete domains whose integration leaves the prototypical expressive DL $\mathcal{ALC}$ decidable.

When integrating concrete domains into lightweight DLs of the $\mathcal{EL}$ family, achieving decidability is not enough. One wants reasoning in the resulting DL to be tractable. This can be achieved by using so-called p-admissible concrete domains and restricting the interaction between the DL and the concrete domain. In the present paper, we investigate p-admissibility from an algebraic point of view. Again, this yields strong algebraic tools for demonstrating p-admissibility. In particular, we obtain an expressive numerical p-admissible concrete domain based on the rational numbers. Although ω-admissibility and p-admissibility are orthogonal conditions that are almost exclusive, our algebraic characterizations of these two properties allow us to locate an infinite class of p-admissible concrete domains whose integration into $\mathcal{ALC}$ yields decidable DLs.

Keywords: Description logic · Concrete domains · p-admissibility · Convexity · ω-admissibility · Finite boundedness · Tractability · Decidability · Constraint satisfaction

1 Introduction

Description Logics (DLs) [3,5] are a well-investigated family of logic-based knowledge representation languages, which are frequently used to formalize ontologies for application domains such as the Semantic Web [25] or biology

Supported by DFG GRK 1763 (QuantLA) and TRR 248 (cpec, grant 389792660).

W. Faber et al. (Eds.): JELIA 2021, LNAI 12678, pp. 194–209, 2021.
https://doi.org/10.1007/978-3-030-75775-5_14

and medicine [24]. A DL-based ontology consists of inclusion statements (so-called GCIs) between concepts defined using the DL at hand. For example, the GCI *Human* ⊑ ∃*parent.Human*, which says that every human being has a human parent, uses concepts expressible in $\mathcal{EL}$. This GCI clearly implies the inclusion *Human* ⊑ ∃*parent.*∃*parent.Human*, i.e., *Human* is subsumed by ∃*parent.*∃*parent.Human* w.r.t. any ontology containing the above GCI. Keeping the subsumption problem decidable, and preferably of a low complexity, is an important design goal for DLs. While subsumption in the lightweight DL $\mathcal{EL}$ is tractable (i.e., decidable in polynomial time), it is ExpTime-complete in $\mathcal{ALC}$, which is obtain from $\mathcal{EL}$ by adding negation [5].

If information about the age of human beings is relevant in the application at hand, then one would like to associate humans with their ages and formulate constraints on these numbers. This becomes possible by integrating concrete domains into DLs [4]. Using the concrete domain $(\mathbb{Q}, >)$, we can express that children cannot be older than their parents with the GCI $>$(*age, parent age*) ⊑ ⊥, where ⊥ is the bottom concept (always interpreted as the empty set) and *age* is a concrete feature that maps from the abstract domain populating concepts into the concrete domain $(\mathbb{Q}, >)$. While integrating $(\mathbb{Q}, >)$ leaves $\mathcal{ALC}$ decidable [30], this is no longer the case if we integrate $(\mathbb{Q}, +_1)$, where $+_1$ is a binary predicate that is interpreted as incrementation [5,7]. In [31], ω-admissibility was introduced as a condition on concrete domains that ensures decidability. It was shown in that paper that Allen's interval logic [1] as well as the region connection calculus RCC8 [33] can be represented as ω-admissible concrete domains. Since ω-admissibility is a collection of rather complex technical conditions, it is not easy to show that a given concrete domain satisfies this property. In [7], we relate ω-admissibility to well-known notions from model theory, which allows us to prove ω-admissibility of certain concrete domains (among them Allen and RCC8) using known results from model theory. A different algebraic condition (called *EHD*) that ensures decidability was introduced in [18], and used in [29] to show decidability and complexity results for a concrete domains based on the integers.

When integrating a concrete domain into a lightweight DL like $\mathcal{EL}$, one wants to preserve tractability rather than just decidability. To achieve this, the notion of p-admissible concrete domains was introduced in [2] and paths of length > 1 were disallowed in concrete domain constraints. Regarding the latter restriction, note that, in the above example, we have used the path *parent age*, which has length 2. The restriction to paths of length 1 means (in our example) that we can no longer compare the ages of different humans, but we can still define concepts like teenager, using the GCI

$$Teenager \sqsubseteq Human \sqcap \geq_{10}(age) \sqcap \leq_{19}(age),$$

where $\geq_{10}$ and $\leq_{19}$ are unary predicates respectively interpreted as the rational numbers greater equal 10 and smaller equal 19. In a p-admissible concrete domain, satisfiability of conjunctions of atomic formulae and validity of implications between such conjunctions must be tractable. In addition, the concrete domain must be *convex*, which roughly speaking means that a conjunction cannot imply a true disjunction. For example, the concrete domain $(\mathbb{Q}, >, =, <)$ is ω-admissible [7], but it is not convex since $x < y \wedge x < z$ implies $y < z \vee y = z \vee y > z$, but none of the disjuncts. In [2], two p-admissible concrete domains were exhibited, where one of them is based on $\mathbb{Q}$ with unary predicates $=_p, >_p$ and binary predicates $+_p, =$. To the best of our knowledge, since then no other p-admissible concrete domains have been described in the literature.

One of the main contributions of the present paper is to devise algebraic characterizations of convexity in different settings. We start by noting that the definition of convexity given in [2] is ambiguous, and that what was really meant is what we call *guarded* convexity. However, in the presence of the equality predicate (which is available in the two p-admissible concrete domains introduced in [2]), the two notions of convexity coincide. Then we devise a general characterization of convexity based on the notion of *square embeddings*, which are embeddings of the product $\mathfrak{B}^2$ of a relational structure $\mathfrak{B}$ into $\mathfrak{B}$. We investigate the implications of this characterization further for so-called ω-categorical structures, finitely bounded structures, and numerical concrete domains. For ω-*categorical structures*, the square embedding criterion for convexity can be simplified, and we use this result to obtain new p-admissible concrete domains: countably infinite vector spaces over finite fields. *Finitely bounded structures* can be defined by specifying finitely many forbidden patterns, and are of great interest in the constraint satisfaction (CSP) community [15]. We show that, for such structures, convexity is a necessary *and sufficient* condition for p-admissibility. This result provides use with many examples of p-admissible concrete domains, but their usefulness in practice still needs to be investigated. Regarding *numerical concrete domains*, we exhibit a new and quite expressive p-admissible concrete domain based on the rational numbers, whose predicates are defined by linear equations over $\mathbb{Q}$.

Next, the paper investigates the connection between p-admissibility and ω-admissibility. We show that only trivial concrete domains can satisfy both properties. However, by combining the results on finitely bounded structures of the present paper with results in [7], we can show that convex finitely bounded homogeneous structures, which are p-admissible, can be integrated into $\mathcal{ALC}$ (even without the length 1 restriction on role paths) without losing decidability. Whereas these structures are not ω-admissible, they can be expressed in an ω-admissible concrete domain [7]. Finally, we show that, in general, the restriction to paths of length 1 is needed when integrating a p-admissible concrete domain into $\mathcal{EL}$, not only to stay tractable, but even to retain decidability.

2 Preliminaries

In this section, we introduce the algebraic and logical notions that will be used in the rest of the paper. The set $\{1, \ldots, n\}$ is denoted by $[n]$. We use the bar notation for tuples; for a tuple $\bar{t}$ indexed by a set I, the value of $\bar{t}$ at the position $i \in I$ is denoted by $\bar{t}[i]$. For a function $f \colon A^k \to B$ and n-tuples $\bar{t}_1, \ldots, \bar{t}_k \in A^n$, we use $f(\bar{t}_1, \ldots, \bar{t}_k)$ as a shortcut for the tuple $\big(f(\bar{t}_1[1], \ldots \bar{t}_k[1]), \ldots, f(\bar{t}_1[n], \ldots, \bar{t}_k[n])\big)$.

From a mathematical point of view, concrete domains are relational structures. A *relational signature* τ is a set of *relation symbols*, each with an associated natural number called *arity*. For a relational signature τ, a *relational τ-structure* $\mathfrak{A}$ (or simply τ-structure or structure) consists of a set A (the *domain*) together with the relations $R^{\mathfrak{A}} \subseteq A^k$ for each relation symbol $R \in \tau$ of arity k. Such a structure $\mathfrak{A}$ is *finite* if its domain A is finite. We often describe structures by listing their domain and relations, i.e., we write $(A, R_1^{\mathfrak{A}}, R_2^{\mathfrak{A}}, \dots)$.

An *expansion* of a τ-structure $\mathfrak{A}$ is a σ-structure $\mathfrak{B}$ with $A = B$ such that $\tau \subseteq \sigma$ and $R^{\mathfrak{B}} = R^{\mathfrak{A}}$ for each relation symbol $R \in \tau$. Conversely, we call $\mathfrak{A}$ a *reduct* of $\mathfrak{B}$. The *product* of a family $(\mathfrak{A}_i)_{i \in I}$ of τ-structures is the τ-structure $\prod_{i \in I} \mathfrak{A}_i$ over $\prod_{i \in I} A_i$ such that, for each $R \in \tau$ of arity k, we have $(\bar{a}_1, \dots, \bar{a}_k) \in R^{\prod_{i \in I} \mathfrak{A}_i}$ iff $(\bar{a}_1[i], \dots, \bar{a}_k[i]) \in R^{\mathfrak{A}_i}$ for every $i \in I$. We denote the binary product of a structure $\mathfrak{A}$ with itself as $\mathfrak{A}^2$.

A *homomorphism* $h \colon \mathfrak{A} \to \mathfrak{B}$ for τ-structures $\mathfrak{A}$ and $\mathfrak{B}$ is a mapping $h \colon A \to B$ that *preserves* each relation of $\mathfrak{A}$, i.e., if $\bar{t} \in R^{\mathfrak{A}}$ for some k-ary relation symbol $R \in \tau$, then $h(\bar{t}) \in R^{\mathfrak{B}}$. A homomorphism $h \colon \mathfrak{A} \to \mathfrak{B}$ is *strong* if it additionally satisfies the inverse condition: for every k-ary relation symbol $R \in \tau$ and $\bar{t} \in A^k$ we have $h(\bar{t}) \in R^{\mathfrak{B}}$ only if $\bar{t} \in R^{\mathfrak{A}}$. An *embedding* is an injective strong homomorphism. We write $\mathfrak{A} \hookrightarrow \mathfrak{B}$ if $\mathfrak{A}$ embeds into $\mathfrak{B}$. The class of all finite τ-structures that embed into $\mathfrak{B}$ is denoted by $\mathrm{Age}(\mathfrak{B})$. A *substructure* of $\mathfrak{B}$ is a structure $\mathfrak{A}$ over the domain $A \subseteq B$ such that the inclusion map $i \colon A \to B$ is an embedding. Conversely, we call $\mathfrak{B}$ an extension of $\mathfrak{A}$. An *isomorphism* is a surjective embedding. Two structures $\mathfrak{A}$ and $\mathfrak{B}$ are *isomorphic* (written $\mathfrak{A} \cong \mathfrak{B}$) if there exists an isomorphism from $\mathfrak{A}$ to $\mathfrak{B}$. An *automorphism* of $\mathfrak{A}$ is an isomorphism from $\mathfrak{A}$ to $\mathfrak{A}$.

Given a relational signature τ, we can build first-order formulae using the relation symbols of τ in the usual way. Relational τ-structures then coincide with first-order interpretations. In the context of p-admissibility, we are interested in quite simple formulae. A τ-atom is of the form $R(x_1, \dots, x_n)$, where $R \in \tau$ is an n-ary relation symbol and $x_1, \dots, x_n$ are variables. For a fixed τ-structure $\mathfrak{A}$, the *constraint satisfaction problem (CSP)* for $\mathfrak{A}$ [11] asks whether a given finite conjunction of atoms is satisfiable in $\mathfrak{A}$. An *implication* is of the form $\forall \bar{x}. (\phi \Rightarrow \psi)$ where ϕ is a conjunction of atoms, ψ is a disjunction of atoms, and the tuple $\bar{x}$ consists of the variables occurring in ϕ or ψ. Such an implication is a *Horn-implication* if ψ is the empty disjunction (corresponding to falsity $\bot$) or a single atom. The CSP for $\mathfrak{A}$ can be reduced in polynomial time to the validity problem for Horn-implications since ϕ is satisfiable in $\mathfrak{A}$ iff $\forall \bar{x}. (\phi \Rightarrow \bot)$ is not valid in $\mathfrak{A}$. Conversely, validity of Horn implications in a structure $\mathfrak{A}$ can be reduced in polynomial time to the CSP in the expansion $\mathfrak{A}^\neg$ of $\mathfrak{A}$ by the complements of all relations. In fact, the Horn implication $\forall \bar{x}. (\phi \Rightarrow \psi)$ is valid in $\mathfrak{A}$ iff $\phi \wedge \neg\psi$ is not satisfiable in $\mathfrak{A}^\neg$. In the signature of $\mathfrak{A}^\neg$, $\neg\psi$ can then be expressed by an atom.

3   Integrating p-Admissible Concrete Domains into $\mathcal{EL}$

Given countably infinite sets $\mathsf{N_C}$ and $\mathsf{N_R}$ of concept and role names, $\mathcal{EL}$ concepts are built using the concept constructors top concept ($\top$), conjunction ($C \sqcap D$), and existential restriction ($\exists r.C$). The semantics of the constructors is defined in the usual way (see, e.g., [3,5]). It assigns to every $\mathcal{EL}$ concept C a set $C^{\mathcal{I}} \subseteq \Delta^{\mathcal{I}}$, where $\Delta^{\mathcal{I}}$ is the interpretation domain of the given interpretation $\mathcal{I}$.

As mentioned before, a concrete domain is a τ-structure $\mathfrak{D}$ with a relational signature τ. To integrate such a structure into $\mathcal{EL}$, we complement concept and role names with a set of *feature names* $\mathsf{N_F}$, which provide the connection between the abstract domain $\Delta^{\mathcal{I}}$ and the concrete domain D. A *path* is of the form $r\,f$ or f where $r \in \mathsf{N_R}$ and $f \in \mathsf{N_F}$. In our example in the introduction, *age* is both a feature name and a path of length 1, and *parent age* is a path of length 2. The DL $\mathcal{EL}(\mathfrak{D})$ extends $\mathcal{EL}$ with the new concept constructor

$$R(p_1, \ldots, p_k) \quad \text{(concrete domain restriction)},$$

where $p_1, \ldots, p_k$ are paths, and $R \in \tau$ is a k-ary relation symbol. We use $\mathcal{EL}[\mathfrak{D}]$ to denote the sublanguage of $\mathcal{EL}(\mathfrak{D})$ where paths in concrete domain restrictions are required to have length 1. Note that $\mathcal{EL}(\mathfrak{D})$ is the restriction to $\mathcal{EL}$ of the way concrete domains were integrated into $\mathcal{ALC}$ in [31], whereas our definition of $\mathcal{EL}[\mathfrak{D}]$ describes how concrete domains were integrated into $\mathcal{EL}$ in [2].

To define the semantics of concrete domain restrictions, we assume that an interpretation $\mathcal{I}$ assigns functional binary relations $f^{\mathcal{I}} \subseteq \Delta^{\mathcal{I}} \times D$ to feature names $f \in \mathsf{N_F}$, where *functional* means that $(a, d) \in f^{\mathcal{I}}$ and $(a, d') \in f^{\mathcal{I}}$ imply $d = d'$. We extend the interpretation function to paths of the form $p = r\,f$ by setting $(r\,f)^{\mathcal{I}} = \{(a, d) \in \Delta^{\mathcal{I}} \times D \mid \text{there is } b \in \Delta^{\mathcal{I}} \text{ such that } (a, b) \in r^{\mathcal{I}} \text{ and } (b, d) \in f^{\mathcal{I}}\}$. The semantics of concrete domain restrictions is now defined as follows:

$$R(p_1, \ldots, p_k)^{\mathcal{I}} = \{a \in \Delta^{\mathcal{I}} \mid \text{there are } d_1, \ldots, d_k \in D \text{ such that} \\ (a, d_i) \in p_i^{\mathcal{I}} \text{ for all } i \in [k] \text{ and } (d_1, \ldots, d_k) \in R^{\mathfrak{D}}\}.$$

As usual, an $\mathcal{EL}(\mathfrak{D})$ TBox is defined to be a finite set of GCIs $C \sqsubseteq D$, where C, D are $\mathcal{EL}(\mathfrak{D})$ concepts. The interpretation $\mathcal{I}$ is a *model* of such a TBox if $C^{\mathcal{I}} \subseteq D^{\mathcal{I}}$ holds for all GCIs $C \sqsubseteq D$ occurring in it. Given $\mathcal{EL}(\mathfrak{D})$ concept descriptions C, D and an $\mathcal{EL}(\mathfrak{D})$ TBox $\mathcal{T}$, we say that C is *subsumed by* D w.r.t. $\mathcal{T}$ (written $C \sqsubseteq_{\mathcal{T}} D$) if $C^{\mathcal{I}} \subseteq D^{\mathcal{I}}$ holds for all models of $\mathcal{T}$. For the subsumption problem in $\mathcal{EL}[\mathfrak{D}]$, to which we restrict our attention for the moment, only $\mathcal{EL}[\mathfrak{D}]$ concepts may occur in $\mathcal{T}$, and C, D must also be $\mathcal{EL}[\mathfrak{D}]$ concepts.

Subsumption in $\mathcal{EL}$ is known to be decidable in polynomial time [16]. For $\mathcal{EL}[\mathfrak{D}]$, this is the case if the concrete domain is p-admissible [2]. According to [2], a concrete domain $\mathfrak{D}$ is *p-admissible* if it satisfies the following conditions: (i) satisfiability of conjunctions of atoms and validity of Horn implications in $\mathfrak{D}$ are tractable; and (ii) $\mathfrak{D}$ is convex. Unfortunately, the definition of convexity in [2] (below formulated using our notation) is ambiguous:

($*$) If a conjunction of atoms of the form $R(x_1, \ldots, x_k)$ implies a disjunction of such atoms, then it also implies one of its disjuncts.

The problem is that this definition does not say anything about which variables may occur in the left- and right-hand sides of such implications. To illustrate this, let us consider the structure $\mathfrak{N} = (\mathbb{N}, E, O)$ in which the unary predicates E and O are respectively interpreted as the even and odd natural numbers. If the right-hand side of an implication considered in the definition of convexity may contain variables not occurring on the left-hand side, then $\mathfrak{N}$ is not convex: $\forall x, y. (E(x) \Rightarrow E(y) \vee O(y))$ holds in $\mathfrak{N}$, but neither $\forall x, y. (E(x) \Rightarrow E(y))$ nor $\forall x, y. (E(x) \Rightarrow O(y))$ does. However, for *guarded implications*, where all variables occurring on the right-hand side must also occur on the left-hand side, the structure $\mathfrak{N}$ satisfies the convexity condition $(*)$. We say that a structure is *convex* if $(*)$ is satisfied without any restrictions on the occurrence of variables, and *guarded convex* if $(*)$ is satisfied for guarded implications. Clearly, any convex structure is guarded convex, but the converse implication does not hold, as exemplified by $\mathfrak{N}$.

We claim that, what was actually meant in [2], was guarded convexity rather than convexity. In fact, it is argued in that paper that non-convexity of $\mathfrak{D}$ allows one to express disjunctions in $\mathcal{EL}[\mathfrak{D}]$, which makes subsumption in $\mathcal{EL}[\mathfrak{D}]$ ExpTime-hard. However, this argument works only if the counterexample to convexity is given by a guarded implication. Let us illustrate this again on our example $\mathfrak{N}$. Whereas $\forall x, y. (E(x) \Rightarrow E(y) \vee O(y))$ holds in $\mathfrak{N}$, the subsumption $E(f) \sqsubseteq_\emptyset E(g) \sqcup O(g)$ does not hold in the extension of $\mathcal{EL}[\mathfrak{D}]$ with disjunction since the feature g need not have a value. For this reason, we use guarded convexity rather than convexity in our definition of p-admissibility. For the same reason, we also restrict the tractability requirement in this definition to validity of guarded Horn implications.

Definition 1. *A relational structure* $\mathfrak{D}$ *is p-admissible if it is guarded convex and validity of guarded Horn implications in* $\mathfrak{D}$ *is tractable*

Using this notion, the main results of [2] concerning concrete domains can now be summarized as follows.

Theorem 1 (Baader, Brandt, and Lutz [2]). *Let* $\mathfrak{D}$ *be a relational structure. Then subsumption in* $\mathcal{EL}[\mathfrak{D}]$ *is*

1. *decidable in polynomial time if* $\mathfrak{D}$ *is p-admissible;*
2. *ExpTime-hard if* $\mathfrak{D}$ *is not guarded convex.*

The two p-admissible concrete domains introduced in [2] have equality as one of their relations. For such structures, convexity and guarded convexity obviously coincide since one can use $x = x$ as a trivially true guard. For example, the extension $\mathfrak{N}_=$ of $\mathfrak{N}$ with equality is no longer guarded convex since the implication $\forall x. (x = x \Rightarrow E(x) \vee O(x))$ holds in $\mathfrak{N}_=$, but neither $\forall x. (x = x \Rightarrow E(x))$ nor $\forall x. (x = x \Rightarrow O(x))$.

In the next section, we will show algebraic characterizations of (guarded) convexity. Regarding the tractability condition in the definition of p-admissibility, we have seen that it is closely related to the constraint satisfaction problem for $\mathfrak{D}$ and $\mathfrak{D}^{\urcorner}$. Characterizing tractability of the CSP in a given structure is a very hard problem. Whereas the Feder-Vardi conjecture [20] has recently been confirmed after 25 years of intensive research in the field by giving an algebraic criterion that can distinguish between *finite* structures with tractable and with NP-complete CSPs [17,34], finding comprehensive criteria that ensure tractability for the case of infinite structures is a wide open problem, though first results for special cases have been found (see, e.g., [13,14]).

4   Algebraic Characterizations of Convexity

Before we can formulate our characterization of (guarded) convexity, we need to introduce a semantic notion of guardedness. We say that the relational τ-structure $\mathfrak{A}$ is *guarded* if for every $a \in A$ there is a relation $R \in \tau$ such that a appears in a tuple in $R^{\mathfrak{A}}$.

Theorem 2. *For a relational τ structure $\mathfrak{B}$, the following are equivalent:*

1. $\mathfrak{B}$ *is* guarded *convex.*
2. *For every finite $\sigma \subseteq \tau$ and every $\mathfrak{A} \in \mathrm{Age}\,(\mathfrak{B}^2)$ whose σ-reduct is guarded, there exists a strong homomorphism from the σ-reduct of $\mathfrak{A}$ to the σ-reduct of $\mathfrak{B}$.*

We concentrate here on proving "2 ⇒ 1" since this is the direction that will be used later on. Alternatively, we could obtain "2 ⇒ 1" by adapting the proof of McKinsey's lemma [22]. A proof of the other direction can be found in [6].

Proof of "2 ⇒ 1" of Theorem 2. Suppose to the contrary that the implication $\forall x_1, \ldots, x_n. (\phi \Rightarrow \psi)$ is valid in $\mathfrak{B}$, where ϕ is a conjunction of atoms such that each variable x_i is present in some atom of ϕ, and ψ is a disjunction of atoms $\psi_1, \ldots, \psi_k$, but we also have $\mathfrak{B} \not\models \forall x_1, \ldots, x_n. (\phi \Rightarrow \psi_i)$ for every $i \in [k]$. Without loss of generality, we assume that $\phi, \psi_1, \ldots, \psi_k$ all have the same free variables $x_1, \ldots, x_n$, some of which might not influence their truth value. For every $i \in [k]$, there exists a tuple $\bar{t}_i \in B^n$ such that

$$\mathfrak{B} \models \phi(\bar{t}_i) \wedge \neg\psi_i(\bar{t}_i). \tag{$*$}$$

We show by induction on i that, for every $i \in [k]$, there exists a tuple $\bar{s}_i \in B^n$ that satisfies the *induction hypothesis*

$$\mathfrak{B} \models \phi(\bar{s}_i) \wedge \neg \bigvee_{\ell \in [i]} \psi_\ell(\bar{s}_i). \tag{$\dagger$}$$

In the *base case* $(i = 1)$, it follows from $(*)$ that $\bar{s}_1 := \bar{t}_1$ satisfies $(\dagger)$.

In the *induction step* $(i \to i+1)$, let $\bar{s}_i \in B^n$ be any tuple that satisfies $(\dagger)$. Let $\sigma \subseteq \tau$ be the finite set of relation symbols occurring in the implication $\forall x_1, \ldots, x_n. (\phi \Rightarrow \psi)$, and let $\mathfrak{A}_i$ be the substructure of $\mathfrak{B}^2$ on the set $\{(\bar{s}_i[1], \bar{t}_{i+1}[1]), \ldots, (\bar{s}_i[n], \bar{t}_{i+1}[n])\}$. Since $\mathfrak{B} \models \phi(\bar{s}_i)$ by $(\dagger)$, $\mathfrak{B} \models \phi(\bar{t}_{i+1})$ by $(*)$, and ϕ contains an atom for each variable x_i, we conclude that the σ-reduct of $\mathfrak{A}_i$ is guarded. By 2., there exists a strong homomorphism f_i from the σ-reduct of $\mathfrak{A}_i$ to the σ-reduct of $\mathfrak{B}$. Since ϕ is a conjunction of atoms and f_i is a homomorphism, we have that $\mathfrak{B} \models \phi\big(f_i(\bar{s}_i, \bar{t}_{i+1})\big)$. Suppose that $\mathfrak{B} \models \psi_{i+1}\big(f_i(\bar{s}_i, \bar{t}_{i+1})\big)$. Since f_i is a strong homomorphism, we get $\mathfrak{B} \models \psi_{i+1}(\bar{t}_{i+1})$, a contradiction to (∗). Now suppose that $\mathfrak{B} \models \psi_j\big(f_i(\bar{s}_i, \bar{t}_{i+1})\big)$ for some $j \leq i$. Since f_i is a strong homomorphism, we get $\mathfrak{B} \models \psi_j(\bar{s}_i)$, a contradiction to (†). We conclude that $\bar{s}_{i+1} := f_i(\bar{s}_i, \bar{t}_{i+1})$ satisfies (†).

Since $\mathfrak{B} \models \forall x_1, \ldots, x_n . (\phi \Rightarrow \psi)$, the existence of a tuple $\bar{s}_i \in B^n$ that satisfies (†) for $i = k$ leads to a contradiction. □

As an easy consequence of Theorem 2, we also obtain a characterization of (unguarded) convexity. This is due to the fact that the structure $\mathfrak{B}$ is convex iff its expansion with the full unary predicate (interpreted as B) is guarded convex. In addition, in the presence of this predicate, any structure is guarded.

Corollary 1. *For a relational τ-structure $\mathfrak{B}$, the following are equivalent:*

1. *$\mathfrak{B}$ is convex.*
2. *For every finite $\sigma \subseteq \tau$ and every $\mathfrak{A} \in \mathrm{Age}(\mathfrak{B}^2)$, there exists a strong homomorphism from the σ-reduct of $\mathfrak{A}$ to the σ-reduct of $\mathfrak{B}$.*

As an example, the structure $\mathfrak{N} = (\mathbb{N}, E, O)$ introduced in the previous section is guarded convex, but not convex. According to the corollary, the latter should imply that there is a finite substructure $\mathfrak{A}$ of $\mathfrak{N}^2$ that has no strong homomorphism to $\mathfrak{N}$. In fact, if we take as $\mathfrak{A}$ the substructure of $\mathfrak{N}^2$ induced by the tuple $(1, 2)$, then this tuple belongs neither to E nor to O in the product. However, a strong homomorphism to $\mathfrak{N}$ would need to map this tuple either to an odd or an even number. But then the tuple would need to belong to either E or O since the homomorphism is strong. This example does not work for the case of guarded convexity, because the considered substructure is not guarded. In fact, a guarded substructure of $\mathfrak{N}^2$ can only contain tuples where both components are even or both components are odd. In the former case, the tuple can be mapped to an even number, and in the latter to an odd number.

In the presence of the equality predicate, strong homomorphisms are embeddings and guarded convexity is the same as convexity.

Corollary 2. *For a structure $\mathfrak{B}$ with a relational signature τ with equality, the following are equivalent:*

1. *$\mathfrak{B}$ is convex.*
2. *For every finite $\sigma \subseteq \tau$ and every $\mathfrak{A} \in \mathrm{Age}(\mathfrak{B}^2)$, the σ-reduct of $\mathfrak{A}$ embeds into the σ-reduct of $\mathfrak{B}$.*

5   Examples of Convex and p-Admissible Structures

We consider three different kinds of structures (ω-categorical, finitely bounded, numerical) and show under which conditions such structures are convex. This provides us with new examples for p-admissible concrete domains.

5.1   Convex ω-Categorical Structures

A structure is called ω-*categorical* if its first-order theory has a unique countable model up to isomorphism. A well-known example of such a structure is $(\mathbb{Q}, <)$, whose first-order theory is the theory of linear orders without first and last element. Such structures have drawn considerable attention in the CSP community since their CSPs can, to some extent, be investigated using the algebraic tools originally developed for finite structures. Countably infinite ω-categorical structures can be characterized using automorphisms and orbits. For every structure $\mathfrak{A}$, the set of all automorphisms of $\mathfrak{A}$, denoted by $\mathrm{Aut}(\mathfrak{A})$, forms a permutation group with composition as group operation [23]. The *orbit* of a tuple $\bar{t} \in A^k$ under $\mathrm{Aut}(\mathfrak{A})$ is the set $\{(g(\bar{t}[1]), ..., g(\bar{t}[k])) \mid g \in \mathrm{Aut}(\mathfrak{A})\}$. The following result is due to Engeler, Ryll-Nardzewski, and Svenonius (see Theorem 6.3.1 in [23]).

Theorem 3. *For a countably infinite structure $\mathfrak{D}$ with a countable signature, the following are equivalent:*

1. $\mathfrak{D}$ *is ω-categorical.*
2. *Every relation preserved by $\mathrm{Aut}(\mathfrak{D})$ has a first-order definition in $\mathfrak{D}$.*
3. *For every $k \geq 1$, there are only finitely many orbits of k-tuples under $\mathrm{Aut}(\mathfrak{D})$.*

For countably infinite ω-categorical structures the characterization of convexity of Corollary 2 can be improved to the following simpler statement.

Theorem 4. *For a countably infinite ω-categorical relational structure $\mathfrak{B}$ with a countable signature τ with equality, the following are equivalent:*

1. $\mathfrak{B}$ *is convex.*
2. $\mathfrak{B}^2$ *embeds into $\mathfrak{B}$.*

The proof of this theorem combines the proof of Corollary 2 with the following two facts, which are implied by ω-categoricity of $\mathfrak{B}$. First, there exists a strong homomorphism from $\mathfrak{B}^2$ to $\mathfrak{B}$ iff there exists a strong homomorphism from $\mathfrak{A}$ to $\mathfrak{B}$ for every $\mathfrak{A} \in \mathrm{Age}(\mathfrak{B}^2)$ (see, e.g., Lemma 3.1.5 in [11]). Second, to deal with the fact that τ may be infinite (which is problematic for the proof of "1 $\Rightarrow$ 2"), we can use Theorem 3, which ensures that, for every $k \geq 1$, there are only finitely many inequivalent k-ary formulae over $\mathfrak{B}$ consisting of a single τ-atom.

In the CSP literature, one can find two examples of countably infinite ω-categorical structure that satisfy the square embedding condition of the above theorem: atomless Boolean algebras and countably infinite vector spaces over finite fields. Since the CSP for atomless Boolean algebras is NP-complete [9], this example does not provide us with a p-admissible concrete domain. Things are more rosy for the vector space example. As shown in [12], the relational representation $\mathfrak{V}_q = (V_q, R^+, R^{s_0}, ..., R^{s_{q-1}})$ of the countably infinite vector space over a finite field $\mathrm{GF}(q)$ is ω-categorical, satisfies $\mathfrak{V}_q^2 \cong \mathfrak{V}_q$, and its CSP is decidable in polynomial time, even if the complements of all predicates are added. Here R^+ is a ternary predicate corresponding to addition of vectors, and the R^{s_i} are binary predicates corresponding to scalar multiplication of a vector with the element s_i of $\mathrm{GF}(q)$. We can show that these properties are preserved if we add finitely many unary predicates R^{e_i} that correspond to unit vectors $e_1, \ldots, e_k$ [6].

Corollary 3. *The structure $\mathfrak{V}_q$ expanded with predicates $R^{e_1}, \ldots, R^{e_k}$ for unit vectors $e_1, \ldots, e_k$ is p-admissible.*

For the case $q = 2$, the vectors in V_q are one-sided infinite tuples of zeros and ones containing only finitely many ones, which can be viewed as representing finite subsets of $\mathbb{N}$. For example, $(0, 1, 1, 0, 1, 0, 0, \ldots)$ represents the set $\{1, 2, 4\}$. Thus, if we use $\mathfrak{V}_2$ as concrete domain, the features assign finite sets of natural numbers to individuals. For example, assume that the feature *daughters-ages* assigns the set of ages of female children to a person, and *sons-ages* the set of ages of male children. Then $R^+(\textit{daughters-ages, sons-ages, zero})$ describes persons that, for every age, have either both a son and a daughter of this age, or no child at all of this age. The feature *zero* is supposed to point to the zero vector, which can, e.g., be enforced using the GCI $\top \sqsubseteq R^+(\textit{zero, zero, zero})$.

5.2 Convex Structures with Forbidden Patterns

For a class $\mathcal{F}$ of τ-structures, $\mathrm{Forb}_e(\mathcal{F})$ stands for the class of all finite τ-structures that do not embed any member of $\mathcal{F}$. A structure $\mathfrak{B}$ is *finitely bounded* if its signature is finite and $\mathrm{Age}(\mathfrak{B}) = \mathrm{Forb}_e(\mathcal{F})$ for some finite set $\mathcal{F}$ of *bounds*. Alternatively, one can say that $\mathfrak{B}$ is finitely bounded if its signature is finite and there is a universal first-order sentence Φ with equality such that $\mathrm{Age}(\mathfrak{B})$ consists precisely of the finite models of Φ [8]. A well-known example of a finitely bounded structure is $(\mathbb{Q}, >, =)$, for which the self loop, the 2-cycle, the 3-cycle, and two isolated vertices can be used as bounds (see Fig. 1 in [7]). As universal sentence defining $\mathrm{Age}(\mathbb{Q}, >, =)$ we can take the conjunction of the usual axioms defining linear orders. For finitely bounded structures, p-admissibility turns out to be equivalent to convexity.

Theorem 5. *Let $\mathfrak{B}$ be a finitely bounded τ-structure with equality. Then the following statements are equivalent:*

1. *$\mathfrak{B}$ is convex,*
2. *$\mathrm{Age}(\mathfrak{B})$ is defined by a conjunction of Horn implications,*
3. *$\mathfrak{B}$ is p-admissible.*

The structure $(\mathbb{Q}, >, =)$ is not convex. In fact, since it is also ω-categorical, convexity would imply that its square $(\mathbb{Q}, >, =) \times (\mathbb{Q}, >, =)$ embeds into $(\mathbb{Q}, >, =)$, by Theorem 4. This cannot be the case since the product contains incomparable elements, whereas $(\mathbb{Q}, >, =)$ does not. In the universal sentence defining $\mathrm{Age}(\mathbb{Q}, >, =)$, the totality axiom $\forall x, y. (x < y \vee x = y \vee x > y)$ is the culprit since it is not Horn. If we remove this axiom, we obtain the theory of strict partial orders.

Example 1. It is well-known that there exists a unique countable homogeneous[1] strict partial order $\mathfrak{O}$ [32], whose age is defined by the universal sentence $\forall x, y, z. \, (x < y \wedge y < z \Rightarrow x < z) \wedge \forall x. \, (x < x \Rightarrow \bot)$, which is a Horn implication. Thus, $\mathfrak{O}$ extended with equality is finitely bounded and convex. Using $\mathfrak{O}$ as a concrete domain means that the feature values satisfy the theory of strict partial orders, but not more. One can, for instance, use this concrete domain to model preferences of people; e.g., the concept *Italian* $\sqcap >(pizzapref, pastapref)$ describes Italians that like pizza more than pasta. Using $\mathfrak{O}$ here means that preferences may be incomparable. As we have seen above, adding totality would break convexity and thus p-admissibility.

Beside finitely bounded structures, the literature also considers structures whose age can be described by a finite set of forbidden homomorphic images [19, 26]. For a class $\mathcal{F}$ of τ-structures, $\mathrm{Forb}_h(\mathcal{F})$ stands for the class of all finite τ-structures that do not contain a homomorphic image of any member of $\mathcal{F}$. A structure is *connected* if its so-called Gaifman graph is connected.

Theorem 6 (Cherlin, Shelah, and Shi [19]). *Let $\mathcal{F}$ be a finite family of connected relational structures with a finite signature τ. Then there exists an ω-categorical τ-structure $\mathrm{CSS}(\mathcal{F})$ that is a reduct of a finitely bounded homogeneous structure and such that $\mathrm{Age}\,(\mathrm{CSS}(\mathcal{F})) = \mathrm{Forb}_h(\mathcal{F})$.*

We can show [6] that the structures of the form $\mathrm{CSS}(\mathcal{F})$ provided by this theorem are always p-admissible.

Proposition 1. *Let $\mathcal{F}$ be a finite family of connected relational structures with a finite signature τ. Then the expansion of $\mathrm{CSS}(\mathcal{F})$ by the equality predicate is p-admissible.*

This proposition actually provides us with infinitely many examples of countable p-admissible concrete domains, which all yield a different extension of $\mathcal{EL}$: the so-called Henson digraphs [21] (see [6] for details). The usefulness of these concrete domains for defining interesting concepts is, however, unclear.

5.3   Convex Numerical Structures

We exhibit two new p-admissible concrete domain that are respectively based on the real and the rational numbers, and whose predicates are defined by linear equations. Let $\mathfrak{D}_{\mathbb{R},\mathrm{lin}}$ be the relational structure over $\mathbb{R}$ that has, for every linear equation system $A\bar{x} = \bar{b}$ over $\mathbb{Q}$, a relation consisting of all its solutions in $\mathbb{R}$. We define $\mathfrak{D}_{\mathbb{Q},\mathrm{lin}}$ as the substructure of $\mathfrak{D}_{\mathbb{R},\mathrm{lin}}$ on $\mathbb{Q}$. For example, using the matrix $A = (2\ 1\ -1)$ and the vector $\bar{b} = (0)$ one obtains the ternary relation $\{(p, q, r) \in \mathbb{Q}^3 \mid 2p + q = r\}$ in $\mathfrak{D}_{\mathbb{Q},\mathrm{lin}}$.

Theorem 7. *The relational structures $\mathfrak{D}_{\mathbb{R},\mathrm{lin}}$ and $\mathfrak{D}_{\mathbb{Q},\mathrm{lin}}$ are p-admissible.*

---

[1] A structure is *homogeneous* if every isomorphism between its finite substructures extends to an automorphism of the whole structure.

To prove this theorem for $\mathbb{R}$, we start with the well-known fact that $(\mathbb{R}, +, 0)^2$ and $(\mathbb{R}, +, 0)$ are isomorphic [28], and show that it can be extended to $\mathfrak{D}_{\mathbb{R},\text{lin}}$. This yields convexity of $\mathfrak{D}_{\mathbb{R},\text{lin}}$. For $\mathbb{Q}$, we cannot employ the same argument since $(\mathbb{Q}, +, 0)^2$ is not isomorphic to $(\mathbb{Q}, +, 0)$. Instead, we use the well-known fact that the structures $(\mathbb{Q}, +, 0)$ and $(\mathbb{R}, +, 0)$ satisfy the same first-order-sentences [28] to show that convexity of $\mathfrak{D}_{\mathbb{R},\text{lin}}$ implies convexity of $\mathfrak{D}_{\mathbb{Q},\text{lin}}$. Tractability can be shown for both structures using a variant of the Gaussian elimination procedure. A detailed proof can be found in [6].

It is tempting to claim that $\mathfrak{D}_{\mathbb{Q},\text{lin}}$ is considerably more expressive than the p-admissible concrete domain $\mathfrak{D}_{\mathbb{Q},\text{dist}}$ with domain $\mathbb{Q}$, unary predicates $=_p, >_p$, and binary predicates $+_p, =$ exhibited in [2]. However, formally speaking, this is not true since the relations $>_p$ cannot be expressed in $\mathfrak{D}_{\mathbb{Q},\text{lin}}$. In fact, adding such a relation to $\mathfrak{D}_{\mathbb{Q},\text{lin}}$ would destroy convexity. Conversely, adding the ternary addition predicate, which is available in $\mathfrak{D}_{\mathbb{Q},\text{lin}}$, to $\mathfrak{D}_{\mathbb{Q},\text{dist}}$ also destroys convexity. Using these observations, we can actually show that the expressive powers of $\mathfrak{D}_{\mathbb{Q},\text{dist}}$ and $\mathfrak{D}_{\mathbb{Q},\text{lin}}$ are incomparable [6]. We expect, however, that $\mathfrak{D}_{\mathbb{Q},\text{lin}}$ will turn out to be more useful in practice than $\mathfrak{D}_{\mathbb{Q},\text{dist}}$.

6 ω-Admissibility versus p-Admissibility

The notion of ω-admissibility was introduced in [31] as a condition on concrete domains $\mathfrak{D}$ that ensures that the subsumption problem in $\mathcal{ALC}(\mathfrak{D})$ w.r.t. TBoxes remains decidable. This is a rather complicated condition, but for our purposes it is sufficient to know that, according to [31], an ω-admissible concrete domain $\mathfrak{D}$ has finitely many binary relations, which are jointly exhaustive (i.e., their union yields $D \times D$) and pairwise disjoint (i.e., for two different relation symbols R_i, R_j we have $R_i^{\mathfrak{D}} \cap R_j^{\mathfrak{D}} = \emptyset$). In the presence of equality, these two conditions do not go well together with convexity.

Proposition 2. *Let $\mathfrak{D}$ be a structure with a finite binary relational signature that includes equality. If $\mathfrak{D}$ is convex, jointly exhaustive, and pairwise disjoint, then its domain D satisfies $|D| \leq 1$.*

This proposition shows that there are no non-trivial concrete domains with equality that are at the same time p-admissible and ω-admissible. Without equality, there are some, but they are still not very interesting [6]. Nevertheless, by combining the results of Sect. 5.2 with Corollary 2 in [7], we obtain non-trivial p-admissible concrete domains with equality for which subsumption in $\mathcal{ALC}(\mathfrak{D})$ is decidable.

Corollary 4. *Let $\mathfrak{D}$ be a finitely bounded convex structure with equality that is a reduct of a finitely bounded homogeneous structure. Then subsumption w.r.t. TBoxes is tractable in $\mathcal{EL}[\mathfrak{D}]$ and decidable in $\mathcal{ALC}(\mathfrak{D})$.*

The Henson digraphs already mentioned in Sect. 5.2 provide us with infinitely many examples of structures that satisfy the conditions of this corollary.

In general, however, p-admissibility of $\mathfrak{D}$ does *not* guarantee decidability of subsumption in $\mathcal{ALC}(\mathfrak{D})$. For example, subsumption w.r.t. TBoxes is undecidable in $\mathcal{ALC}(\mathfrak{D}_{\mathbb{Q},\text{dist}})$ and $\mathcal{ALC}(\mathfrak{D}_{\mathbb{Q},\text{lin}})$ since this is already true for their common reduct $(\mathbb{Q}, +_1)$ [7].

Even for $\mathcal{EL}$, integrating a p-admissible concrete domain may cause undecidability if we allow for role paths of length 2. To show this, we consider the relational structure $\mathfrak{D}_{\mathbb{Q}^2,\text{aff}}$ over $\mathbb{Q}^2$, which has, for every affine transformation $\mathbb{Q}^2 \to \mathbb{Q}^2 : \bar{x} \mapsto A\bar{x} + \bar{b}$, the binary relation $R_{A,\bar{b}} := \{(\bar{x}, \bar{y}) \in (\mathbb{Q}^2)^2 \mid \bar{y} = A\bar{x} + \bar{b}\}$.

Theorem 8. *The relational structure $\mathfrak{D}_{\mathbb{Q}^2,\text{aff}}$ is p-admissible, which implies that subsumption w.r.t. TBoxes is tractable in $\mathcal{EL}[\mathfrak{D}_{\mathbb{Q}^2,\text{aff}}]$. However, subsumption w.r.t. TBoxes is undecidable in $\mathcal{EL}(\mathfrak{D}_{\mathbb{Q}^2,\text{aff}})$.*

In [6], we show p-admissibility of $\mathfrak{D}_{\mathbb{Q}^2,\text{aff}}$ using the fact that $\mathfrak{D}_{\mathbb{Q},\text{lin}}$ is p-admissible. Tractability of subsumption in $\mathcal{EL}[\mathfrak{D}_{\mathbb{Q}^2,\text{aff}}]$ is then an immediate consequence of Theorem 1. Undecidability of subsumption w.r.t. TBoxes in $\mathcal{EL}(\mathfrak{D}_{\mathbb{Q}^2,\text{aff}})$ can be shown by a reduction from *2-Dimensional Affine Reachability*, which is undecidable by Corollary 4 in [10]. For this problem, one is given vectors $\bar{v}, \bar{w} \in \mathbb{Q}^2$ and a finite set S of affine transformations from $\mathbb{Q}^2$ to $\mathbb{Q}^2$. The question is then whether $\bar{w}$ can be obtained from $\bar{v}$ by repeated application of transformations from S. It is not hard to show that 2-Dimensional Affine Reachability can effectively be reduced to subsumption w.r.t. TBoxes in $\mathcal{EL}(\mathfrak{D}_{\mathbb{Q}^2,\text{aff}})$.

7 Conclusion

The notion of p-admissible concrete domains was introduced in [2], where it was shown that integrating such concrete domains into the lightweight DL $\mathcal{EL}$ (and even the more expressive DL $\mathcal{EL}^{++}$) leaves the subsumption problem tractable. The paper [2] contains two examples of p-admissible concrete domains, and since then no new examples have been exhibited in the literature. This appears to be mainly due to the fact that it is not easy to show the convexity condition required by p-admissibility "by hand". The main contribution of the present paper is that it provides us with a useful algebraic tool for showing convexity: the square embedding condition. We have shown that this tool can indeed be used to exhibit new p-admissible concrete domains, such as countably infinite vector spaces over finite field, the countable homogeneous partial order, and numerical concrete domains over $\mathbb{R}$ and $\mathbb{Q}$ whose relations are defined by linear equations. The usefulness of these numerical concrete domains for defining concepts should be evident. For the other two we have indicated their potential usefulness by small examples.

We have also shown that, for finitely bounded structures, convexity is equivalent to p-admissibility, and that this corresponds to the finite substructures being definable by a conjunction of Horn implications. Interestingly, this provides us with infinitely many examples of countable p-admissible concrete domains, which all yield a different extension of $\mathcal{EL}$: the Henson digraphs. From a theoretical point of view, this is quite a feat, given that before only two p-admissible concrete domains were known.

Finitely bounded structures also provide us with examples of structures $\mathfrak{D}$ that can be used both in the context of $\mathcal{EL}$ and $\mathcal{ALC}$, in the sense that subsumption is tractable in $\mathcal{EL}[\mathfrak{D}]$ and decidable in $\mathcal{ALC}(\mathfrak{D})$. Finally, we have shown that, when embedding p-admissible concrete domains into $\mathcal{EL}$, the restriction to paths of length 1 in concrete domain restrictions (indicated by the square brackets) is needed since there is a p-admissible concrete domains $\mathfrak{D}$ such that subsumption in $\mathcal{EL}(\mathfrak{D})$ is undecidable.

References

1. Allen, J.F.: Maintaining knowledge about temporal intervals. Commun. ACM **26**(11), 832–843 (1983)
2. Baader, F., Brandt, S., Lutz, C.: Pushing the $\mathcal{EL}$ envelope. In: Kaelbling, L.P., Saffiotti, A. (eds.) Proceedings of the 19th International Joint Conference on Artificial Intelligence (IJCAI 2005), Los Altos, Edinburgh (UK), pp. 364–369. Morgan Kaufmann (2005)
3. Baader, F., Calvanese, D., McGuinness, D., Nardi, D., Patel-Schneider, P.F. (eds.): The Description Logic Handbook: Theory, Implementation, and Applications. Cambridge University Press, Cambridge (2003)
4. Baader, F., Hanschke, P.: A schema for integrating concrete domains into concept languages. In: Proceedings of the 12th International Joint Conference on Artificial Intelligence (IJCAI 1991), pp. 452–457 (1991)
5. Baader, F., Horrocks, I., Lutz, C., Sattler, U.: An Introduction to Description Logic. Cambridge University Press, Cambridge (2017)
6. Baader, F., Rydval, J.: An algebraic view on p-admissible concrete domains for lightweight description logics (extended version). LTCS-Report 20-10, Chair of Automata Theory, Institute of Theoretical Computer Science, Technische Universität Dresden, Dresden, Germany (2020). https://tu-dresden.de/inf/lat/reports# BaRy-LTCS-20-10
7. Baader, F., Rydval, J.: Description logics with concrete domains and general concept inclusions revisited. In: Peltier, N., Sofronie-Stokkermans, V. (eds.) IJCAR 2020. LNCS (LNAI), vol. 12166, pp. 413–431. Springer, Cham (2020). https://doi. org/10.1007/978-3-030-51074-9_24
8. Baader, F., Rydval, J.: Using model-theory to find ω-admissible concrete domains. LTCS-Report 20-01, Chair of Automata Theory, Institute of Theoretical Computer Science, Technische Universität Dresden, Dresden, Germany (2020). https://tu-dresden.de/inf/lat/reports#BaRy-LTCS-20-01
9. Barto, L., Kompatscher, M., Olšák, M., Van Pham, T., Pinsker, M.: Equations in oligomorphic clones and the Constraint Satisfaction Problem for ω-categorical structures. J. Math. Logic **19**(2), 1950010 (2019)
10. Bell, P., Potapov, I.: On undecidability bounds for matrix decision problems. Theoret. Comput. Sci. **391**(1–2), 3–13 (2008)
11. Bodirsky, M.: Complexity classification in infinite-domain constraint satisfaction. Mémoire d'Habilitation à Diriger des Recherches, Université Diderot - Paris 7 (2012). https://arxiv.org/abs/1201.0856
12. Bodirsky, M., Chen, H., Kára, J., von Oertzen, T.: Maximal infinite-valued constraint languages. Theoret. Comput. Sci. **410**(18), 1684–1693 (2009)

13. Bodirsky, M., Kára, J.: The complexity of temporal constraint satisfaction problems. J. ACM (JACM) **57**(2), 1–41 (2010)
14. Bodirsky, M., Madelaine, F., Mottet, A.: A universal-algebraic proof of the complexity dichotomy for monotone monadic SNP. In: Proceedings of the 33rd Annual ACM/IEEE Symposium on Logic in Computer Science (LICS 2018), pp. 105–114 (2018)
15. Bodirsky, M., Pinsker, M., Pongrácz, A.: Projective clone homomorphisms. J. Symbolic Logic, 1–13 (2019). https://doi.org/10.1017/jsl.2019.23
16. Brandt, S.: Polynomial time reasoning in a description logic with existential restrictions, GCI axioms, and–what else? In: de Mántaras, R.L., Saitta, L. (eds.) Proceedings of the 16th European Conference on Artificial Intelligence (ECAI 2004), pp. 298–302 (2004)
17. Bulatov, A.A.: A dichotomy theorem for nonuniform CSPs. In: Proceedings of the 58th Annual Symposium on Foundations of Computer Science (FOCS 2017), pp. 319–330. IEEE (2017)
18. Carapelle, C., Turhan, A.: Description logics reasoning w.r.t. general TBoxes is decidable for concrete domains with the EHD-property. In: Kaminka, G.A., et al. (eds.) Proceedings of the 22nd European Conference on Artificial Intelligence (ECAI 2016). Frontiers in Artificial Intelligence and Applications, vol. 285, pp. 1440–1448. IOS Press (2016)
19. Cherlin, G., Shelah, S., Shi, N.: Universal graphs with forbidden subgraphs and algebraic closure. Adv. Appl. Math. **22**(4), 454–491 (1999)
20. Feder, T., Vardi, M.Y.: Homomorphism closed vs. existential positive. In: Proceedings of the 18th Annual IEEE Symposium of Logic in Computer Science (LICS 2003), pp. 311–320. IEEE (2003)
21. Henson, C.W.: A family of countable homogeneous graphs. Pac. J. Math. **38**(1), 69–83 (1971)
22. Hodges, W.: Model Theory. Cambridge University Press, Cambridge (1993)
23. Hodges, W.: A Shorter Model Theory. Cambridge University Press, Cambridge (1997)
24. Hoehndorf, R., Schofield, P.N., Gkoutos, G.V.: The role of ontologies in biological and biomedical research: a functional perspective. Brief. Bioinform. **16**(6), 1069–1080 (2015)
25. Horrocks, I., Patel-Schneider, P.F., van Harmelen, F.: From SHIQ and RDF to OWL: the making of a web ontology language. J. Web Semant. **1**(1), 7–26 (2003)
26. Hubička, J., Nešetřil, J.: Homomorphism and embedding universal structures for restricted classes. J. Mult.-Valued Log. Soft Comput. **27**, 229–253 (2016). https://arxiv.org/abs/0909.4939
27. Jaax, S., Kiefer, S.: On affine reachability problems. In: Esparza, J., Král', D. (eds.) Proceedings of the 45th International Symposium on Mathematical Foundations of Computer Science (MFCS 2020). Leibniz International Proceedings in Informatics (LIPIcs), vol. 170, pp. 48:1–48:14. Schloss Dagstuhl-Leibniz-Zentrum für Informatik, Dagstuhl, Germany (2020)
28. Kegel, O.H., Wehrfritz, B.A.: Locally Finite Groups. Elsevier, Amsterdam (2000)
29. Labai, N., Ortiz, M., Simkus, M.: An ExpTime upper bound for $\mathcal{ALC}$ with integers. In: Calvanese, D., Erdem, E., Thielscher, M. (eds.) Proceedings of the 17th International Conference on Principles of Knowledge Representation and Reasoning (KR 2020), pp. 614–623 (2020)
30. Lutz, C.: Combining interval-based temporal reasoning with general TBoxes. Artif. Intell. **152**(2), 235–274 (2004)

31. Lutz, C., Milicic, M.: A tableau algorithm for description logics with concrete domains and general Tboxes. J. Autom. Reason. **38**(1–3), 227–259 (2007)
32. Pach, P.P., Pinsker, M., Pluhár, G., Pongrácz, A., Szabó, C.: Reducts of the random partial order. Adv. Math. **267**, 94–120 (2014)
33. Randell, D.A., Cui, Z., Cohn, A.G.: A spatial logic based on regions and connection. In: Proceedings of the 3rd International Conference on the Principles of Knowledge Representation and Reasoning (KR 1992), Los Altos. pp. 165–176. Morgan Kaufmann (1992)
34. Zhuk, D.: A proof of CSP dichotomy conjecture. In: Proceedings of the 58th Annual Symposium on Foundations of Computer Science (FOCS 2017), pp. 331–342. IEEE (2017)

ReAD: AD-Based Modular Ontology Classification

Haoruo Zhao$^{(\boxtimes)}$, Bijan Parsia⬀, and Uli Sattler

University of Manchester, Oxford Rd M13 9PL, UK
{haoruo.zhao,bijan.parsia,uli.sattler}@manchester.ac.uk

Abstract. For OWL ontologies, classification is the central reasoning task, and several highly-optimised reasoners have been designed for different fragments of OWL. Some of these exploit different notions of modularity, including the atomic decomposition (AD), to further optimise their performance, but this is a complex task due to ontology modules overlapping, thereby possibly causing duplication of subsumption tests.

In this paper, we use the AD to avoid both this duplication as well as other subsumption tests that can be avoided by inspecting the AD. We have designed and implemented a new AD-informed and MORe-inspired algorithm that uses Hermit and ELK as delegate reasoners, but avoids any duplicate subsumption tests between these two reasoners and further minimises these tests. We have thoroughly evaluated the effects of these two kinds of avoidance on the overall classification time on a corpus of complex ontologies.

Keywords: OWL · Description logic · Classification · Reasoning

1 Introduction

Reasoning in decidable, expressive ontology languages, such as the Web Ontology Language OWL 2 DL [4,12,26], has a high worst case complexity (entailment testing is N2EXPTIME-complete) [12,27]. Given this fact and the large sizes OWL ontologies can reach (with several examples having hundreds of thousands of terms and correspondingly large numbers of axioms), there has been interest in exploiting recent work in logically sound modularity analysis [7,11,13,36] of ontologies to support a robust divide and conquer strategy to ontology reasoning, in particular classification. Suitable modules, as approximations of uniform interpolants [1,11,17,29,30,38,42,43], allow classification of each module independently and combining the results to achieve sound and complete classification of the original ontology. These strong properties support a black box approach to modular reasoning where each delegate reasoner treats each module as if it were a stand alone ontology. The only information shared between delegates is the results for each module.

While implementing a coalition modular reasoner is, in principle, easy—no modification of the delegate reasoners needed—the performance gains have not

© Springer Nature Switzerland AG 2021
W. Faber et al. (Eds.): JELIA 2021, LNAI 12678, pp. 210–224, 2021.
https://doi.org/10.1007/978-3-030-75775-5_15

been as dramatic as one might expect [33]. One issue is that locality-based modules often do not partition an ontology which means that considerable amounts of redundant work might be performed. One mitigation is to look for larger, mostly distinct modules which approximately partition the ontology. Unfortunately, extensive experimentation in [31] suggest that partition-like sets of locality-based modules are not common and, when they do exist, only yield a few large modules. This induces the opposite problem, to wit, that modular reasoner is forced to do work that they could have avoided with more granular exploitation of the modular structure of the ontology.

In this paper, we explore the effect of redundant and wholly unnecessary work on modular reasoner performance. We build the theoretical foundation of the distribution of subsumption tests in locality-based modules using the atomic decomposition. We extend the MORe algorithm, a prominent approach to modular ontology classification, and modify it and one of the component reasoners so as to fully avoid unnecessary subsumption tests using our theoretical results. We test 3 variants of the modified MORe (called ReAD): the original, duplication avoiding, and combined avoiding algorithms against the 2017 BioPortal corpus [32] used in the last ORE competition [34].

2   Background and Related Work

We assume the reader to be familiar with *Description Logics* (DLs), a family of knowledge representation languages underlying OWL 2 [12] that are basically decidable fragments of First Order Logic [6], and only fix the notation used. In this paper, we use $\mathcal{O}$ for an ontology and Σ for a *signature*, i.e., a set of concept and role names. For an axiom, a module, or an ontology X, we use $\widetilde{X}$ to denote its signature. We consider $\mathcal{SROIQ}$ [12] ontologies that are TBoxes, i.e., without concept or role assertions, or their OWL DL counterparts.

Ontology Classification. In this paper, we use $\mathbf{N_C}$ to represent *atomic concept names* (e.g. Person, Animal). To *classify* an ontology $\mathcal{O}$, we first check whether $\mathcal{O}$ is consistent. If it is, we check for all $A, B \in \widetilde{\mathcal{O}} \cap \mathbf{N_C}$, $A \neq B$, whether $\mathcal{O} \models^? A \sqsubseteq B, \mathcal{O} \models^? A \sqsubseteq \bot$ and $\mathcal{O} \models^? \top \sqsubseteq B$; these checks are called *subsumption tests (STs)* and have a high worst-case complexity (2NExpTime-complete for OWL 2 [27]). Naively, this results in a quadratic number of entailment tests. To avoid these, DL reasoners employ a form of *traversal algorithm* to reduce the number of STs [5,18]. In practice, these are highly effective, almost always reducing the number of STs to at most $n * \log n$ [33]. To classify (lightweight) $\mathcal{EL}^{++}$ ontologies, one-pass algorithms have been developed and implemented that avoid traversal and classify an ontology in polynomial time in one go [2,3,28]. In this paper, we concentrate on ST avoidance.

Modularity and Atomic Decomposition. In the following, we focus on $\bot$-*locality based modules* [10] (called *modules* for short). These are subsets of an ontology that have certain properties which are important for their use in classification optimization. Let $\mathcal{M} = \mathcal{M}(\Sigma, \mathcal{O})$ be such a $\bot$-locality based module of $\mathcal{O}$ for the signature Σ. Then $\mathcal{M}$

1. preserves all entailments of $\mathcal{O}$ over Σ,
2. preserves all entailments of $\mathcal{O}$ over $\widetilde{\mathcal{M}}$,
3. is unique, i.e., there is no other $\bot$-locality based module of $\mathcal{O}$ for Σ,
4. is subsumer-preserving, i.e., for $A \in \widetilde{\mathcal{M}}$ and $B \in \widetilde{\mathcal{O}}$ concept names, $\mathcal{O} \models A \sqsubseteq B$ implies $\mathcal{M} \models A \sqsubseteq B$, and
5. is monotonic, i.e., if $\Sigma_1 \subseteq \Sigma_2$, then $\mathcal{M}(\Sigma_1, \mathcal{O}) \subseteq \mathcal{M}(\Sigma_2, \mathcal{O})$.

The *atomic decomposition (AD)* [16] partitions an ontology into logically inseparable sets of axioms, so-called *atoms* $\mathfrak{a}$, and relates these atoms via a *dependency relation* $\succeq$.

Definition 1 *[16]. Given two axioms $\alpha, \beta \in \mathcal{O}$, we say $\alpha \sim_{\mathcal{O}} \beta$ if, for all modules $\mathcal{M}$ of $\mathcal{O}$, we have $\alpha \in \mathcal{M}$ iff $\beta \in \mathcal{M}$. The atoms of an ontology $\mathcal{O}$ are the equivalence classes $\sim_{\mathcal{O}}$. Given two atoms $\mathfrak{a}, \mathfrak{b}$, we say that $\mathfrak{a}$ is dependent on $\mathfrak{b}$, written $\mathfrak{a} \succeq \mathfrak{b}$ if, for any module $\mathcal{M}$, $\mathfrak{a} \subseteq \mathcal{M}$ implies that $\mathfrak{b} \subseteq \mathcal{M}$. The AD of $\mathcal{O}$, $\mathfrak{A}(\mathcal{O})$, consists of the set of $\mathcal{O}$'s atoms and the partial order $\succeq$.*

For an atom $\mathfrak{a} \in \mathfrak{A}(\mathcal{O})$, its *principal ideal* $\downarrow \mathfrak{a} = \{\alpha \in \mathfrak{b} \mid \mathfrak{b} \in \mathfrak{A}(\mathcal{O}), \mathfrak{a} \succeq \mathfrak{b}\}$ is the union of all atoms it depends on and has been shown to be a module [16]. The following lemma is an immediate consequence of the fact that the signature of $\top \sqsubseteq \bot$ is empty and that modules are monotonic [11].

Lemma 1. *If $\mathcal{O}$ is inconsistent, then there is an atom $\mathfrak{a}$ in $\mathfrak{A}(\mathcal{O})$ with $\downarrow \mathfrak{a} = \mathfrak{a} \models \top \sqsubseteq \bot$ and $\mathfrak{b} \succeq \mathfrak{a}$ for all $\mathfrak{b}$ in $\mathfrak{A}(\mathcal{O})$.*

Modular Reasoning. Modules and the AD have been explored for improving the performance of reasoning in general [8,23,24,33,35,39], and it is helpful to distinguish between two potential benefits for classification. First, modules can be used to make STs easier by reducing the number of axioms considered for each ST (*easification*) and by enabling us to use specialised reasoners for inexpressive modules, so-called *delegate reasoners*. In [33], it is shown that easification is unlikely to lead to a significant performance gain. Secondly, given properties like the above mentioned preservation of subsumptions, we can *avoid* STs by exploiting the modular structure, e.g., the AD [40].

Several reasoners use modules and AD for incremental reasoning [9] or classification optimisation; e.g., MORe [35] uses modules and Chainsaw [39] uses the AD to identify suitable modules. These techniques, however, fail to provide dramatic performance improvement [21], possibly due to the overhead involved and, more importantly, due to duplication of STs caused by modules overlapping. In this paper, we are focusing on solving this problem.

Duplication of STs. MORe splits the ontology into two modules of different expressivity, and then uses a fast, *delegate* reasoner on the inexpressive module, thereby further easifying tests in the inexpressive module. In its empirical evaluation, MORe uses ELK [28] to classify the module in $\mathcal{EL}^{++}$ [2,3] and HermiT [19] for the remaining OWL 2 module. In case these two modules overlap, HermiT duplicates STs already checked by ELK.

Example 1. Consider the ontology $\mathcal{O} = \{\alpha_1 : A \sqsubseteq \exists r.B, \alpha_2 : C \sqcap D \sqsubseteq A, \alpha_3 : E \sqsubseteq F \sqcup A\}$. Now module $\mathcal{M}_1 = \{\alpha_1, \alpha_2\}$ is classified by ELK and module $\mathcal{M}_2 = \{\alpha_1, \alpha_3\}$ is classified by HermiT. The subsumption relation between A and B is potentially checked by two reasoners.

In this paper, we design a MORe-like framework that exploits delegate reasoners for inexpressive modules but avoids ST duplication by using the AD. Moreover, in our framework, the inexpressive subset classified by the delegate reasoner does not need to be a module and can thus be larger.

3   Theoretical Foundations

In this section, we explain the foundations of using the AD for avoiding STs during classification. Using the AD, we identify a (hopefully small) set of subsumption tests $\mathsf{Subs}(\mathcal{O})$ that are sufficient for classification. Provided that the AD has a "good" structure, i.e., no large atoms, this results in a low number of STs for a reasoner to carry out, plus the opportunity to use delegate reasoners on inexpressive modules as well as to classify modules in parallel.

First, we fix some notation. Let A be a concept name, $\mathfrak{a}$ an atom, and $\mathcal{O}$ an ontology. We define the following sets:

$$\begin{aligned}
\mathsf{Ats}(A) &:= \{\mathfrak{a} \in \mathfrak{A}(\mathcal{O}) \mid A \in \tilde{\mathfrak{a}}\} && \text{the \textit{atoms of } } A \\
\mathsf{MinAts}(A) &:= \{\mathfrak{a} \in \mathsf{Ats}(A) \mid \nexists\mathfrak{b} \in \mathsf{Ats}(A) \text{ with } \mathfrak{a} \succ \mathfrak{b}\} && \text{the \textit{lowest atoms of } } A \\
\mathsf{CanS}(\mathfrak{a}) &:= \{A \mid \mathfrak{a} \in \mathsf{MinAts}(A) \text{ and } \#\mathsf{MinAts}(A) = 1\} && \text{an atom's \textit{candidate set}} \\
\mathsf{BTop}(\mathcal{O}) &:= \{A \mid A \in \tilde{\mathcal{O}} \cap \mathbf{N_C} \text{ and } \#\mathsf{MinAts}(A) > 1\} && \text{\textit{concept names below } } \top
\end{aligned}$$

As we will discuss below, the *candidate set* $\mathsf{CanS}(\mathfrak{a})$ of an atom $\mathfrak{a}$ are those concept names for which STs need to be run for $\mathfrak{a}$, and concepts in $\mathsf{BTop}(\mathcal{O})$ have only trivial subsumers. In Fig. 1, we illustrate these new definitions using our example ontology.

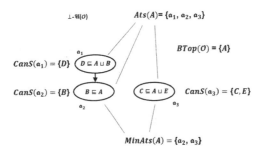

Fig. 1. The AD of $\mathcal{O}$ from Example 1 and applications of the new definitions.

Lemma 2. *1.* $\tilde{\mathcal{O}} \cap \mathbf{N_C} = \bigcup_{\mathfrak{a} \in \mathfrak{A}(\mathcal{O})} \mathsf{CanS}(\mathfrak{a}) \cup \mathsf{BTop}(\mathcal{O})$,
2. for each $\mathfrak{a} \in \mathfrak{A}(\mathcal{O})$, $\mathsf{CanS}(\mathfrak{a}) \cap \mathsf{BTop}(\mathcal{O}) = \emptyset$, *and*
3. for each $\mathfrak{a}, \mathfrak{b} \in \mathfrak{A}(\mathcal{O})$ *with* $\mathfrak{a} \neq \mathfrak{b}$, $\mathsf{CanS}(\mathfrak{a}) \cap \mathsf{CanS}(\mathfrak{b}) = \emptyset$.

Proof. (1). Since $\mathfrak{A}(\mathcal{O})$ partitions $\mathcal{O}$, we have that $\tilde{\mathcal{O}} \cap \mathbf{N_C} = \bigcup_{\mathfrak{a} \in \mathfrak{A}(\mathcal{O})} \tilde{\mathfrak{a}} \cap \mathbf{N_C}$, and
thus for each concept name $A \in \tilde{\mathcal{O}} \cap \mathbf{N_C}$, $\#\mathsf{MinAts}(A) > 0$. If $\#\mathsf{MinAts}(A) = 1$,
we thus have some $\mathfrak{a} \in \mathfrak{A}(\mathcal{O})$ with $\mathfrak{a} \in \mathsf{MinAts}(A)$ and hence $A \in \mathsf{CanS}(\mathfrak{a})$.
Otherwise, $\#\mathsf{MinAts}(A) > 1$ and $A \in \mathsf{BTop}(\mathcal{O})$. The "$\supseteq$" direction holds by
definition of $\mathsf{CanS}(\mathfrak{a})$ and $\mathsf{BTop}(\mathcal{O})$.

(2). This follows immediately from the facts that $A \in \mathsf{BTop}(\mathcal{O})$ implies that
$\#\mathsf{MinAts}(A) > 1$ and $A \in \mathsf{CanS}(\mathfrak{a})$ implies that $\#\mathsf{MinAts}(A) = 1$.

(3). Let $A \in \mathsf{CanS}(\mathfrak{a})$. By definition, $\mathfrak{a} \in \mathsf{MinAts}(A)$. Assume there was some
$\mathfrak{b} \neq \mathfrak{a}$ with $A \in \mathsf{CanS}(\mathfrak{b})$; this would mean $\mathfrak{b} \in \mathsf{MinAts}(A)$, contradicting
$\#\mathsf{MinAts}(A) = 1$.

$\square$

Theorem 1. *Given a concept name $A \in \mathsf{BTop}(\mathcal{O})$, we have*

1. $\mathcal{M}(\{A\}, \mathcal{O}) = \emptyset$,
2. $\mathcal{O} \not\models A \sqsubseteq \bot$, *and*
3. *there is no concept name $B \neq A$, $B \in \tilde{\mathcal{O}}$ with $\mathcal{O} \models A \sqsubseteq B$.*

Proof. (1). Let $A \in \mathsf{BTop}(\mathcal{O})$. Hence $\#\mathsf{MinAts}(A) > 1$, and thus there are two
distinct atoms $\mathfrak{a}, \mathfrak{b} \in \mathsf{MinAts}(A)$. By definition of $\mathsf{MinAts}(A)$, $\mathfrak{a} \not\succ \mathfrak{b}$ and $\mathfrak{b} \not\succ \mathfrak{a}$.
Now assume $\mathcal{M}(\{A\}, \mathcal{O}) \neq \emptyset$; due to monotonicity and $\{A\}$ being a singleton
signature, there is some $\mathfrak{c}$ with $\mathcal{M}(\{A\}, \mathcal{O}) = \downarrow\mathfrak{c}$. Since $\bot$-locality based modules are monotonic, $\mathcal{M}(\{A\}, \mathcal{O}) \subseteq \downarrow\mathfrak{a}$ and $\mathcal{M}(\{A\}, \mathcal{O}) \subseteq \downarrow\mathfrak{b}$ which, together
with $\mathfrak{a}, \mathfrak{b} \in \mathsf{MinAts}(A)$ and $A \in \tilde{\mathfrak{c}}$, contradicts the minimality condition in the
definition of $\mathsf{MinAts}(A)$.

(2). This is a direct consequence of (1) $\mathcal{M}(\{A\}, \mathcal{O}) = \emptyset$: $\bot$-locality based modules capture deductive (and model) conservativity, hence $\mathcal{M}(\{A\}, \mathcal{O}) = \emptyset$
implies that $\mathcal{O}$ cannot entail $A \sqsubseteq \bot$.

(3). This is also a direct consequence of (1) and the fact that $\bot$-locality based
modules are closed under subsumers [11].

$\square$

Based on Theorem 1, for a concept name $A \in \mathsf{BTop}(\mathcal{O})$, we can avoid checking
$\mathcal{O} \models^? A \sqsubseteq \bot$ and subsumptions of the form $\mathcal{O} \models^? A \sqsubseteq B$. Next, we use the
AD to identify a (hopefully small) set of STs $\mathsf{Subs}(\mathcal{O})$ that are sufficient for
classification.

Definition 2. *The set of STs $\mathsf{Subs}(\mathfrak{a})$ of an atom $\mathfrak{a}$ is defined as follows:*

$$\mathsf{Subs}(\mathfrak{a}) := \{(A, B) \mid A \in \mathsf{CanS}(\mathfrak{a}), B \in \widetilde{\downarrow\mathfrak{a}}, \text{ and } A \neq B\} \cup$$
$$\{(A, \bot) \mid A \in \mathsf{CanS}(\mathfrak{a})\} \cup$$
$$\{(\top, B) \mid B \in \mathsf{CanS}(\mathfrak{a})\}.$$

*Given a module $\mathcal{M} = \mathfrak{a}_1 \cup \mathfrak{a}_2 \ldots \cup \mathfrak{a}_n$, the set of STs $\mathsf{Subs}(\mathcal{M})$ of $\mathcal{M}$ is defined as
follows:*

$$\mathsf{Subs}(\mathcal{M}) := \mathsf{Subs}(\mathfrak{a}_1) \cup \ldots \cup \mathsf{Subs}(\mathfrak{a}_n).$$

Finally, $\mathsf{Subs}(\mathcal{O}) := \bigcup_{\mathfrak{a} \in \mathfrak{A}(\mathcal{O})} \mathsf{Subs}(\mathfrak{a}) \cup \{(\top, A) \mid A \in \mathsf{BTop}(\mathcal{O})\} \cup \{(\top, \bot)\}$.

As a consequence of the following theorem, a reasoner that tests only STs in $\mathsf{Subs}(\mathcal{O})$ during classification will (a) test all required, non-trivial[1] STs and (b) never duplicate a test.[2]

Theorem 2. *For $A, B \in \widetilde{\mathcal{O}} \cap N_C \cup \{\top, \bot\}$ with $\bot \neq A \neq B \neq \top$. If $\mathcal{O} \models A \sqsubseteq B$ then $(A, B) \in \mathsf{Subs}(\mathcal{O})$, and (A, B) is either in exactly one $\mathsf{Subs}(\mathfrak{a})$ or of the form $(\top, A)$ or $(\top, \bot)$.*

Proof. Let A, B be as described in Theorem 2 and let $\mathcal{O} \models A \sqsubseteq B$. If $A \neq \top$, then $A \notin \mathsf{BTop}(\mathcal{O})$ by Theorem 1.3. By Lemma 2.1, there is an atom $\mathfrak{a}$ with $A \in \mathsf{CanS}(\mathfrak{a})$, and by Lemma 2.3, this atom $\mathfrak{a}$ is unique. By definition of candidate sets, $\mathsf{CanS}(\mathfrak{a}) \subseteq \widetilde{\mathfrak{a}} \subseteq \downarrow\! \mathfrak{a}$, and thus $A \in \downarrow\! \mathfrak{a}$ and, by definition of AD, $\downarrow\! \mathfrak{a}$ is a module. If $B \neq \bot$, by definition of modules, we have $B \in \downarrow\! \mathfrak{a}$. By definition of $\mathsf{Subs}(\cdot)$, $(A, B) \in \mathsf{Subs}(\mathfrak{a})$. If $B = \bot$, we find $(A, \bot) \in \mathsf{Subs}(\mathfrak{a})$ by Definition 2.

If $A = \top$ and $B = \bot$, by definition of $\mathsf{Subs}(\mathcal{O})$, we have $(\top, \bot) \in \mathsf{Subs}(\mathcal{O})$. If $A = \top$ and $B \neq \bot$, by Lemma 2.1, $B \in \bigcup_{\mathfrak{a} \in \mathfrak{A}(\mathcal{O})} \mathsf{CanS}(\mathfrak{a}) \cup \mathsf{BTop}(\mathcal{O})$. If $B \in \mathsf{BTop}(\mathcal{O})$, by definition of $\mathsf{Subs}(\mathcal{O})$, we have $(\top, B) \in \mathsf{Subs}(\mathcal{O})$. If $B \in \bigcup_{\mathfrak{a} \in \mathfrak{A}(\mathcal{O})} \mathsf{CanS}(\mathfrak{a})$, Lemma 2.3, there is exactly one atom with $B \in \mathsf{CanS}(\mathfrak{a})$, and thus by definition of $\mathsf{Subs}(\mathcal{O})$, $(\top, B) \in \mathsf{Subs}(\mathfrak{a})$.   □

In [15], it is shown that the decomposition of many ontologies results in an AD with many small atoms with a rather shallow and wide dependency relation. As a consequence, we should be able to exploit the AD and the insights captured in Theorem 2 to avoid almost all subsumption tests in a novel, AD-informed alternative to well-known enhanced traversal algorithms [5,18].

4   AD-Based Classification with Delegate Reasoners

In this section, we first explain how the results from Sect. 3 can be exploited to make use of *delegate* reasoners that are optimized for tractable (or less complex) fragments, and then describe an AD-based classification algorithm.

Assume we have, for $1 \leq i \leq n$ modules $\mathcal{M}_i \subseteq \mathcal{O}$ that are in a specific description logic $\mathcal{L}$ for which we have a specialised, optimised reasoner.[3] Based on our observations in Sect. 3, we can partition our subsumption tests as follows:

$$\mathsf{Subs}(\mathcal{O}) = \bigcup_{\substack{\mathfrak{a} \in \mathfrak{A}(\mathcal{O}), \\ \mathfrak{a} \not\subseteq \mathcal{M}_1 \cup \ldots \cup \mathcal{M}_n}} \mathsf{Subs}(\mathfrak{a}) \cup \bigcup_{\substack{\mathfrak{a} \in \mathfrak{A}(\mathcal{O}), \\ \mathfrak{a} \subseteq \mathcal{M}_1 \cup \ldots \cup \mathcal{M}_n}} \mathsf{Subs}(\mathfrak{a}) \cup \{(\top, A) \mid A \in \mathsf{BTop}(\mathcal{O})\} \cup \{(\top, \bot)\}. \quad (1)$$

Of course, the "global" subsumption test $(\top, \bot)$ should be carried out first.

Next, we will discuss briefly how the choice of "lightweight" modules $\mathcal{M}_i$ affect the overall ST load. Consider the ontology whose AD is shown in Fig. 2

---

[1] Of course we avoid testing tautologies.

[2] It may, though, include a test (A, C) in addition to (A, B) and (B, C).

[3] It is straightforward to extend this to more than one DL and more than one specialised, optimised reasoner.

with 7 atoms, and with atoms $\mathfrak{a}_1$, $\mathfrak{a}_2$, $\mathfrak{a}_5$, $\mathfrak{a}_6$, $\mathfrak{a}_7$ being in (the lightweight DL) $\mathcal{L}$. This means there are four modules $\mathcal{M}_1$, $\mathcal{M}_2$, $\mathcal{M}_6$, $\mathcal{M}_7$ in $\mathcal{L}$.

Now we can use a delegate reasoner for $\mathcal{L}$ to classify the set of axioms $\mathcal{M}_1 \cup \mathcal{M}_2 \cup \mathcal{M}_6$. The leaves us with the subsumption tests $\mathsf{Subs}(\mathfrak{a}_3)$, $\mathsf{Subs}(\mathfrak{a}_4)$, $\mathsf{Subs}(\mathfrak{a}_5)$. For these we have the choice to carry them out w.r.t. the whole of $\mathcal{O}$ or we can test $\mathsf{Subs}(\mathfrak{a}_i)$ w.r.t. $\mathcal{M}_i$.

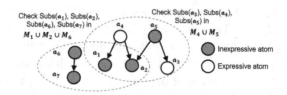

Fig. 2. Modules with different expressivity and their $\mathsf{Subs}(\mathfrak{a})$

Please recall that, in general, a union of modules is not necessarily a module, and thus in our example $\mathcal{M}_1 \cup \mathcal{M}_2 \cup \mathcal{M}_6 \cup \mathcal{M}_7$ is not guaranteed to be a module. Nevertheless, Theorem 2 guarantees that our split of $\mathcal{O}$ and usage of delegate reasoners is correct for classification.

4.1   An AD-Based Classification Algorithm

In this section, we introduce a specific classification algorithm based on the observations above and its implementation in our DL meta reasoner ReAD, as sketched in Algorithm 1. For ReAD, we have chosen to set $\mathcal{L} = \mathcal{EL}^{++}$ and use ELK as delegate $\mathcal{EL}^{++}$ reasoner. We use HermiT as the OWL DL reasoner for the remaining STs.

Firstly, we compute the AD and get the union of $\mathcal{EL}^{++}$ modules $\mathcal{T}_{\mathsf{EL}}$. Then we use ELK to classify $\mathcal{T}_{\mathsf{EL}}$ and store the resulting subsumption relations in the hierarchy $\mathcal{H}$, provided that $\mathcal{T}_{\mathsf{EL}}$ is consistent (otherwise, we stop and return the inconsistency). For the union of modules outside $\mathcal{EL}^{++}$, called $\mathcal{T}_{\mathsf{RAs}}$, we have modified HermiT to ensure that it tests exactly the STs in last three terms of Eq. 1.

HermiT works in three phases [18]: 1) it checks consistency of the input ontology, 2) it tests all concept names for satisfiability, 3) it traverses a graph whose nodes correspond to satisfiable concepts while recording, as labelled edges, the results of STs (both positive and negative results, as well as disjointness relations). The graph traversal algorithm is highly optimised and exploits transitivity of the subsumption relation as well as its interaction with the disjointness relation (the latter becomes available as "free" knowledge from STs).

The modification for HermiT is described in lines 14 to 26 in Algorithm 1. In lines 14–19, we test consistency of $\mathcal{O}$ only if $\mathcal{O}$ has no ELAtoms as per Lemma 1. In case $\mathcal{O}$ is consistent, we run HermiT's second and third phase on (hopefully small) $\mathcal{T}_{\mathsf{RAs}}$, and test only the STs as per Eq. 1. For the second phase, this is done

Algorithm 1. AD-aware Classification

Require: an ontology $\mathcal{O}$
1: Initialize a hierarchy $\mathcal{H} := \{(\bot, \top)\}$
2: Compute the $\bot\text{-}\mathfrak{A}(\mathcal{O})$
3: ELAtoms $:= \{\mathfrak{a} \in \bot\text{-}\mathfrak{A}(\mathcal{O}) \mid \downarrow\mathfrak{a}$ is in $\mathcal{EL}^{++}\}$ {Find all $\mathcal{EL}^{++}$ modules}
4: $\mathcal{T}_{\mathsf{EL}} := \bigcup_{\mathfrak{a} \in \mathsf{ELAtoms}} \mathfrak{a}$ {Compute union of $\mathcal{EL}^{++}$ modules}
5: Classify($\mathcal{T}_{\mathsf{EL}}$)   {use ELK for this}
6: **if** $\mathcal{T}_{\mathsf{EL}}$ is consistent **then**
7:      add resulting hierarchy to $\mathcal{H}$
8: **else**
9:      **return** "$\mathcal{O}$ is inconsistent"
10: **end if**
11: RemainingAtoms $:= \bot\text{-}\mathfrak{A}(\mathcal{O}) \setminus \mathsf{ELAtoms}$
12: AllCanS $:= \{A \mid$ there is some $\mathfrak{a} \in$ RemainingAtoms with $A \in \mathsf{CanS}(\mathfrak{a})\}$
13: $\mathcal{T}_{\mathsf{RAs}} := \{\alpha \in \downarrow\mathfrak{a} \mid \mathfrak{a} \in$ RemainingAtoms$\}$
14: **if** ELAtoms $= \emptyset$ **then**
15:     Check whether $\mathcal{O} \models \top \sqsubseteq \bot$ {use HermiT for this}
16:     **if** $\mathcal{O}$ is inconsistent **then**
17:         **return** "$\mathcal{O}$ is inconsistent"
18:     **end if**
19: **end if**
20: **for** each concept name $A \in$ AllCanS **do**
21:     **if** $\mathcal{T}_{\mathsf{RAs}} \models (A, \bot)$ {use HermiT for this} **then**
22:         add $(A, \bot)$ to $\mathcal{H}$
23:     **else**
24:         Initialize HermiT with neg. subsumptions $(A, B) \notin$ Subs($\mathfrak{a}$) for $\mathfrak{a} \in$ RemainingAtoms
25:     **end if**
26: **end for**
27: Classify $\mathcal{T}_{\mathsf{RAs}}$ and add resulting hierarchy to $\mathcal{H}$ {use HermiT for this}
28: **return** $\mathcal{H}$

in line 20–22. For the third phase, we initialise HermiT's traversal graph with negative subsumptions for all non-subsumption captured in (the complement of) Subs($\mathfrak{a}$). In this way, we preserve HermiT's sophisticated traversal algorithm but

– exploit both ELK as a delegate reasoner for the set of all $\mathcal{EL}^{++}$ modules,
– ensure that HermiT avoids STs for
  • all non-subsumptions we can infer from the AD, and
  • all STs concerning concept names of the $\mathcal{EL}^{++}$ part,
  i.e., we use HermiT only for STs in Subs($\mathfrak{a}$) for non-$\mathcal{EL}^{++}$ atoms $\mathfrak{a}$, and
– possibly easify STs by focusing HermiT on $\mathcal{T}_{\mathsf{RAs}}$.

As a consequence, we combine the AD-informed avoidance described in [41] with HermiT's traversal algorithm and with a MORe-inspired usage of a delegate reasoner—but avoid any overlap in testing STs between both reasonsers.

5 Implementation and Evaluation

In this section, we report on the empirical evaluation of our algorithm. In particular, we answer the following research questions:

1. Compared to the size of the whole ontology, what is the size of the union of $\mathcal{EL}^{++}$ modules? This will help us to understand the potential benefits of using ELK.
2. How many maximal modules are in the union of $\mathcal{EL}^{++}$ modules? This will help us to understand the potential benefit of our approach compared to MORe's usage of a single maximal $\mathcal{EL}^{++}$ module.
3. What is ReAD's performance in terms of classification time and the number of STs carried out, and how do these compare to those of Hermit?

5.1 Experimental Setting

Corpus In our experiment, we used the snapshot of the NCBO BioPortal ontology repository[4] from [31], which contains 438 ontologies. Firstly, we removed ABox axioms for these 438 ontologies since we want to know how the classification algorithm behaves on the TBox axioms. Then we removed those ontologies that are empty after removing ABox axioms (18) or are not in OWL 2 DL (69). We also removed those ontologies for which we cannot compute an AD (6) or which HermiT cannot handle (37);[5] this leaves us with 308 ontologies.

We further discarded the 164 ontologies that are either purely $\mathcal{EL}^{++}$ (122 ontologies) or have no $\mathcal{EL}^{++}$ modules (42 ontologies). This leaves us with a corpus of 144 ontologies, which we split into two parts: 63 ontologies with *non-deterministic tableaux graphs* and 81 ontologies with *deterministic tableaux graphs*; for the latter, HermiT does not enter phase 3 (see Sect. 4.1) as the concept name satisfiability tests produce, as a side-effect, all subsumers of each concept name. This corpus is described in Table 1 in terms of the number of (TBox) axioms and the length of its ontologies.[6]

Table 1. A summary of 144 ontologies. The 50th (median), 90th, 95th, 99th, 100th (maximum) percentiles are shown for the size (i.e. number of axioms) and the length (i.e., sum of length of axioms) of ontologies.

	Mean	StdDev	P50	P90	P95	P99	P100
Size	9,296	31,071	474	13,356	32,917	145,425	233,439
Length	23,618	81,506	1,125	30,705	85,058	461,319	538,100

---

[4] https://bioportal.bioontology.org.
[5] HermiT threw OutOfMemory exceptions or timed-out after 10 h for 11 ontologies; it failed to handle 26 ontologies due to unsupported syntax or syntax errors.
[6] The length used here is standard and defined in [14] Page 24.

Implementation. The implementation of ReAD is based on the OWL API [25] Version 3.4.3, especially on the implementation of the AD[7] that is part of the OWL API, namely the one available via Maven Central (maven.org) with an artifactId of owlapi-tools. We use the reasoner HermiT version 1.3.8[8] both as is and modified in ReAD, and we use the reasoner ELK version 0.4.2 as a delegate reasoner. We also use code from MORe[9] for testing whether axioms are in $\mathcal{EL}^{++}$. All experiments have been performed on Intel(R) Core(TM) i7-6700HQ CPU 2.60 GHz RAM 8 GB, allocating Java heap memory of between 1 GB and 8 GB. Time is measured in CPU time.

5.2 $\mathcal{EL}^{++}$-Part and Modules

To answer Research Question 1, we computed the union of $\mathcal{EL}^{++}$ modules for these ontologies (see line 3 of Algorithm 1); in the following, we call this union *the $\mathcal{EL}^{++}$-part* of an ontology. Figure 3 is a scatter plot with both axes on a logarithmic scale where each ontology is represented as a blue dot: the x-axis indicates their size (number of axioms) and the y-axis that of their $\mathcal{EL}^{++}$-part. We find that the size of the $\mathcal{EL}^{++}$-part varies widely across the ontologies in our corpus, independently of the size of the ontologies but with many ontologies having $\mathcal{EL}^{++}$-parts of substantial to large size.

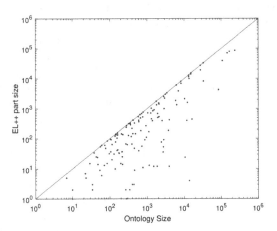

Fig. 3. The size of the 144 ontologies and their $\mathcal{EL}^{++}$-part in our corpus.

To answer our Research Question 2, we consider how the number of (subset-) maximal $\mathcal{EL}^{++}$ modules in the $\mathcal{EL}^{++}$-parts varies across the ontologies in our

---

[7] AD implementation is only supported in OWL API version 5. We transformed this one to OWL API version 3 so that it can be used with HermiT.

[8] The code of this version can be found in http://www.hermit-reasoner.com.

[9] https://github.com/anaphylactic/MORe.

corpus. In our corpus, only one ontology has only one such maximal $\mathcal{EL}^{++}$ module, the mean number of such modules is 1,938, more than half of our ontologies have at least 110 such modules, and 10% have over 2,500. As mentioned before, a union of modules is not necessarily a module. Among our corpus, however, we find that only 13% of ontologies (19/144) are such that the union of their (numerous) $\mathcal{EL}^{++}$ modules is *not* a module.

5.3   Classification Time and Number of STs Carried Out

Next, we compare ReAD's performance with that of (unmodified) HermiT on our corpus of 144 ontologies, and we do this separately for the 63 non-deterministic and the 81 deterministic ontologies since, as mentioned above, HermiT avoids all STs on the latter. For ReAD, the computation time excludes the time used for computing the AD. We classified each ontology five times: the runtime was so stable that we decided to measure single runs.

Following [20, 22], we split our corpus into three bins: into those ontologies $\mathcal{O}$ that HermiT can classify in (1) less than 1 s; (2) more than 1 s and less than 10 s; (3) more than 10 s. For 121/144 ontologies, (fastest) classification requires less than 1 s, 13/144 ontologies require 1 s–10 s, and 10/144 ontologies require more than 10 s. As described in [41] and rather unsurprisingly, ReAD classification time improves over that of HermiT with the relative size of the $\mathcal{EL}^{++}$ part.

In the following analysis, we use EL-ModPer as the size of the $\mathcal{EL}^{++}$ part relative to the size of the ontology (as percentage). Similarly, we use DupliPer as the size of the intersection of the $\mathcal{EL}^{++}$ part and the ontology considered by HermiT, i.e., $\mathcal{T}$, relative to the size of the ontology (as percentage). We use $\mathsf{CTH}(\mathcal{O})$ to represent the time HermiT takes to classify $\mathcal{O}$ and $\mathsf{CTR}(\mathcal{O})$ for ReAD's classification time on $\mathcal{O}$. To compare classification times better, we consider the (relative) *improvement*, i.e., the percentage of $(\mathsf{CTH}(\mathcal{O}) - \mathsf{CTR}(\mathcal{O}))/\mathsf{CTH}(\mathcal{O})$.

Deterministic ontologies are classified by HermiT without a single ST, hence any performance improvement we see in ReAD comes from the usage of ELK and from avoiding duplication of satisfiability tests in lines 21 of Algorithm 1. To understand the contribution of these factors, we have implemented a variant ReAD$_{\mathsf{wiDupli}}$ of ReAD by removing lines 14–26 in Algorithm 1, i.e., that only exploits ELK. In Fig. 4, we see that the major relative improvement is due to the usage of ELK for the 7 (non-trivial, deterministic) ontologies in bins (2) and (3), and that avoiding duplication adds a smaller but still considerable improvement.

For *non-deterministic ontologies*, the performance improvement can stem from three factors: the usage of ELK, the avoidance of duplicate STs between HermiT and ELK, and the avoidance of STs via the AD in line 24 in Algorithm 1. Again, to understand the contribution of these factors, we have implemented a variant

- ReAD$_{\mathsf{wiDupli\&noAvoid}}$ that avoids no duplication of STs between HermiT and ELK and does not use the AD to avoid STs; this variant is again obtained by removing lines 14–26 in Algorithm 1.

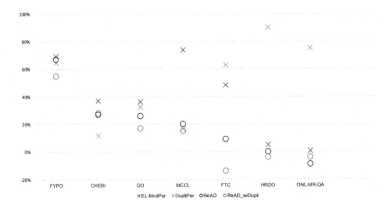

Fig. 4. The classification time improvements of the 7 deterministic ontologies in bins (2) and (3) with their EL-ModPer and DupliPer.

- ReAD$_{noAvoid}$ that does avoid duplication of STs between HermiT and ELK but does not use the AD to avoid STs; this variant is again obtained by modifying line 24 in Algorithm 1.

In Fig. 5, we see that, on the 16 (non-trivial, non-deterministic) ontologies, all three factors play a notable role.

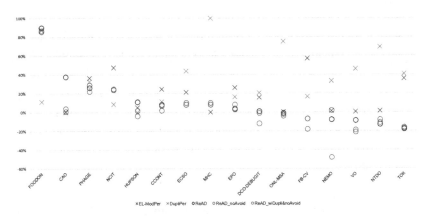

Fig. 5. The classification time improvement of 16 non-deterministic ontologies with their $\mathcal{EL}^{++}$ ModPer and DupliPer in bins (2) and (3).

Our corpus is too small to consider correlations between EL-ModPer, DupliPer, and the improvements we get from ReAD or its "restricted" variants, so we will discuss some interesting examples. In general, we see that ReAD can improve classification time substantially despite the $\mathcal{EL}^{++}$ part being small, but only for non-deterministic ontologies. Consider the deterministic ontology GO: it has a large

$\mathcal{EL}^{++}$ part (36% EL-ModPer) that overlaps modestly with $\mathcal{T}$ (33% DupliPer); ReAD gets a good improvement of 26% (835 s to 619 s), but ReAD$_{wiDupli}$ improvement is close with 17% (835 s to 695 s). Contrast this with the deterministic ontology FTC: it has an even larger $\mathcal{EL}^{++}$ part (48% EL-ModPer) that overlaps largely with $\mathcal{T}$ (63% DupliPer); hence it is no surprise that its ReAD$_{wiDupli}$ "improvement" is −14% 1446 s to1646 s) whereas its ReAD improvement is 9% 1446 s to1322 s). The non-deterministic ontology CAO also has a tiny $\mathcal{EL}^{++}$ part (0.67% EL-ModPer) but we get a strong ReAD improvement 38% 1071 s to 667 s) due to avoiding STs in HermiT classification.

Finally, we compare the number of STs carried out by HermiT with those carried out by HermiT during ReAD classification, see Table 2: overall, ReAD halves the number of STs.

Table 2. A summary of the number of STs carried out for the 63 non-deterministic ontologies in our corpus. The 50th (median), 90th,..., 100th (maximum) percentiles are shown for the STs number in HermiT and HermiT-in-ReAD.

	Mean	StdDev	P50	P90	P95	P99	P100
#STs in HermiT	387	834	64	849	2,359	4,094	4,130
#STs in HermiT-in-ReAD	178	528	11	481	660	2,730	3,465

6 Conclusion

In this paper, we have described the theoretical foundations of an AD-based classification algorithm, as well as its implementation as a modification of HermiT with ELK as a delegate reasoner. We have evaluated our approach and took care to investigate the effect of three factors (usage of ELK, avoiding re-testing STs in HermiT that were already tested in ELK, avoiding STs in HermiT using information from the AD), and learned that all three factors are clearly beneficial.

In the future, we also want to explore how our algorithm interacts with the Enhanced Traversal algorithm as described in [5], and we can further refine our algorithm to understand whether/which kinds of *easification* are beneficial; these refinements are easily realised by adapting lines 21 and/or 26 in Algorithm 1 to consider suitable modules.

Finally, we are currently exploring whether ReAD can deal with really hard ontologies such as non-$\mathcal{EL}^{++}$ versions of SNOMED CT.

References

1. Armas Romero, A., Kaminski, M., Cuenca Grau, B., Horrocks, I.: Module extraction in expressive ontology languages via Datalog reasoning. J. Artif. Intell. Res. **55**, 499–564 (2016)
2. Baader, F., Brandt, S., Lutz, C.: Pushing the $\mathcal{EL}$ envelope. In: Proceedings of IJCAI 2005 (2005)

3. Baader, F., Brandt, S., Lutz, C.: Pushing the $\mathcal{EL}$ envelope further. In: Proceedings of OWLED 2008 (2008)
4. Baader, F., Calvanese, D., McGuinness, D., Nardi, D., Patel-Schneider, P.F. (eds.): The Description Logic Handbook: Theory, Implementation, and Applications, 2nd edn. Cambridge University Press, Cambridge (2007)
5. Baader, F., Hollunder, B., Nebel, B., Profitlich, H.J., Franconi, E.: An empirical analysis of optimization techniques for terminological representation systems. Appl. Intell. **4**(2), 109–132 (1994). https://doi.org/10.1007/BF00872105
6. Baader, F., Horrocks, I., Lutz, C., Sattler, U. (eds.): An Introduction to Description Logic. Cambridge University Press, Cambridge (2017)
7. Bao, J., Voutsadakis, G., Slutzki, G., Honavar, V.: Package-based Description Logics. In: Stuckenschmidt, H., et al. (ed.) [37], pp. 349–371 (2009)
8. Chen, J., Alghamdi, G., Schmidt, R.A., Walther, D., Gao, Y.: Ontology extraction for large ontologies via modularity and forgetting. In: Proceedings of K-CAP 2019, pp. 45–52. ACM (2019)
9. Cuenca Grau, B., Halaschek-Wiener, C., Kazakov, Y., Suntisrivaraporn, B.: Incremental classification of description logics ontologies. J. Autom. Reasoning **44**(4), 337–369 (2010). https://doi.org/10.1007/s10817-009-9159-0
10. Cuenca Grau, B., Horrocks, I., Kazakov, Y., Sattler, U.: Just the right amount: extracting modules from ontologies. In: WWW 2007, pp. 717–726. ACM (2007)
11. Cuenca Grau, B., Horrocks, I., Kazakov, Y., Sattler, U.: Modular reuse of ontologies: theory and practice. J. Artif. Intell. Res. **31**(1), 273–318 (2008)
12. Cuenca Grau, B., Horrocks, I., Motik, B., Parsia, B., Patel-Schneider, P.F., Sattler, U.: OWL 2: the next step for OWL. J. Web Semant. **6**(4), 309–322 (2008)
13. Cuenca Grau, B., Parsia, B., Sirin, E.: Ontology integration using $\mathcal{E}$-connections. In: Stuckenschmidt, H., et al. (eds.) [37], pp. 293–320 (2009)
14. Del Vescovo, C.: The modular structure of an ontology: atomic decomposition and its applications. Ph.D. thesis, University of Manchester (2013). http://www.cs.man.ac.uk/~delvescc/thesis.pdf
15. Del Vescovo, C., Horridge, M., Parsia, B., Sattler, U., Schneider, T., Zhao, H.: Modular structures and atomic decomposition in ontologies. J. Artif. Intell. Res. **69**, 963–1021 (2020)
16. Del Vescovo, C., Parsia, B., Sattler, U., Schneider, T.: The modular structure of an ontology: atomic decomposition. In: IJCAI, pp. 2232–2237 (2011)
17. Ghilardi, S., Lutz, C., Wolter, F.: Did I damage my ontology? A case for conservative extensions in description logics. In: KR, pp. 187–197. AAAI Press (2006)
18. Glimm, B., Horrocks, I., Motik, B., Shearer, R., Stoilos, G.: A novel approach to ontology classification. J. Web Semant. **14**, 84–101 (2012)
19. Glimm, B., Horrocks, I., Motik, B., Stoilos, G., Wang, Z.: HermiT: an OWL 2 reasoner. J. Autom. Reasoning **53**(3), 245–269 (2014). https://doi.org/10.1007/s10817-014-9305-1
20. Goncalves, J.R.: Impact analysis in description logic ontologies. Ph.D. thesis, The University of Manchester (2014)
21. Gonçalves, R.S., et al.: OWL reasoner evaluation (ORE) workshop 2013 results. In: ORE, pp. 1–18 (2013)
22. Gonçalves, R.S., Parsia, B., Sattler, U.: Performance heterogeneity and approximate reasoning in description logic ontologies. In: Cudré-Mauroux, P., et al. (eds.) ISWC 2012. LNCS, vol. 7649, pp. 82–98. Springer, Heidelberg (2012). https://doi.org/10.1007/978-3-642-35176-1_6
23. Guimaraes, R., Sattler, U., Wassermann, R.: Ontology stratification methods: acomparative study. In: MedRACER+ WOMoCoE@ KR, pp. 51–62 (2018)

24. Horridge, M., Bail, S., Parsia, B., Sattler, U.: Toward cognitive support for OWL justifications. Knowl.-Based Syst. **53**, 66–79 (2013)
25. Horridge, M., Bechhofer, S.: The OWL API: a java API for OWL ontologies. Semant. web **2**(1), 11–21 (2011)
26. Horrocks, I., Patel-Schneider, P.F., van Harmelen, F.: From SHIQ and RDF to OWL: the making of a web ontology language. J. Web Semant. **1**(1), 7–26 (2003)
27. Kazakov, Y.: $\mathcal{RIQ}$ and $\mathcal{SROIQ}$ are harder than $\mathcal{SHOIQ}$. In: Proceedings of KR 2008, pp. 274–284. AAAI Press (2008)
28. Kazakov, Y., Krötzsch, M., Simančík, F.: The incredible ELK. J. Autom. Reasoning **53**(1), 1–61 (2014). https://doi.org/10.1007/s10817-013-9296-3
29. Konev, B., Lutz, C., Ponomaryov, D., Wolter, F.: Decomposing description logic ontologies. In: KR 2010, pp. 236–246. AAAI Press (2010)
30. Koopmann, P., Schmidt, R.A.: Count and forget: uniform interpolation of $\mathcal{SHQ}$-ontologies. In: Demri, S., Kapur, D., Weidenbach, C. (eds.) IJCAR 2014. LNCS (LNAI), vol. 8562, pp. 434–448. Springer, Cham (2014). https://doi.org/10.1007/978-3-319-08587-6_34
31. Matentzoglu, N., Parsia, B.: BioPortal Snapshot 30 March 2017 (data set) (2017). http://doi.org/10.5281/zenodo.439510
32. Matentzoglu, N., Bail, S., Parsia, B.: A snapshot of the OWL web. In: Alani, H., et al. (eds.) ISWC 2013. LNCS, vol. 8218, pp. 331–346. Springer, Heidelberg (2013). https://doi.org/10.1007/978-3-642-41335-3_21
33. Matentzoglu, N., Parsia, B., Sattler, U.: Owl reasoning: subsumption test hardness and modularity. J. Autom. Reasoning **60**(4), 385–419 (2018). https://doi.org/10.1007/s10817-017-9414-8
34. Parsia, B., Matentzoglu, N., Gonçalves, R.S., Glimm, B., Steigmiller, A.: The OWL reasoner evaluation (ORE) 2015 competition report. J. Autom. Reasoning **59**(4), 455–482 (2017). https://doi.org/10.1007/s10817-017-9406-8
35. Armas Romero, A., Cuenca Grau, B., Horrocks, I.: MORe: modular combination of OWL reasoners for ontology classification. In: Cudré-Mauroux, P., et al. (eds.) ISWC 2012. LNCS, vol. 7649, pp. 1–16. Springer, Heidelberg (2012). https://doi.org/10.1007/978-3-642-35176-1_1
36. Serafini, L., Tamilin, A.: Composing modular ontologies with distributed description logics. In: Stuckenschmidt, H., et al. (eds.) [37], pp. 321–347 (2009)
37. Stuckenschmidt, H., Parent, C., Spaccapietra, S. (eds.): Modular Ontologies: Concepts, Theories and Techniques for Knowledge Modularization. LNCS, vol. 5445. Springer, Heidelberg (2009). https://doi.org/10.1007/978-3-642-01907-4
38. Suntisrivaraporn, B.: Module extraction and incremental classification: a pragmatic approach for $\mathcal{EL}^+$ ontologies. In: Bechhofer, S., Hauswirth, M., Hoffmann, J., Koubarakis, M. (eds.) ESWC 2008. LNCS, vol. 5021, pp. 230–244. Springer, Heidelberg (2008). https://doi.org/10.1007/978-3-540-68234-9_19
39. Tsarkov, D., Palmisano, I.: Chainsaw: a metareasoner for large ontologies. In: Proceedings of ORE 2012 (2012)
40. Zhao, H., Parsia, B., Sattler, U.: Avoiding subsumption tests during classification using the atomic decomposition. In: DL 2019, vol. 573 (2019)
41. Zhao, H., Parsia, B., Sattler, U.: ReAD: delegate OWL reasoners for ontology classification with atomic decomposition. In: Proceedings of WOMoCoE 2020 (2020)
42. Zhao, Y., Schmidt, R.A.: Role forgetting for $\mathcal{ALCOQH}(\nabla)$-ontologies using an Ackermann-based approach. In: IJCAI 2017, pp. 1354–1361 (2017). ijcai.org
43. Zhao, Y., Schmidt, R.A.: On concept forgetting in description logics with qualified number restrictions. In: IJCAI 2018, pp. 1984–1990 (2018). ijcai.org

Weighted Defeasible Knowledge Bases and a Multipreference Semantics for a Deep Neural Network Model

Laura Giordano$^{(\boxtimes)}$ and Daniele Theseider Dupré

DISIT - Università del Piemonte Orientale, Alessandria, Italy
{laura.giordano,dtd}@uniupo.it

Abstract. In this paper we investigate the relationships between a multipreferential semantics for defeasible reasoning in knowledge representation and a deep neural network model. Weighted knowledge bases for description logics are considered under a "concept-wise" multipreference semantics. The semantics is further extended to fuzzy interpretations and exploited to provide a preferential interpretation of Multilayer Perceptrons, under some condition.

1 Introduction

Preferential approaches have been used to provide axiomatic foundations of non-mono-tonic and common sense reasoning [5,18,37,38,42,45,46]. They have been extended to description logics (DLs), to deal with inheritance with exceptions in ontologies, by allowing for non-strict forms of inclusions, called *typicality or defeasible inclusions*, with different preferential semantics [10,26,27], and closure constructions [11–13,23,28,47].

In this paper, we exploit a concept-wise multipreference semantics as a semantics for weighted knowledge bases, i.e. knowledge bases in which defeasible or typicality inclusions of the form $\mathbf{T}(C) \sqsubseteq D$ (meaning "the typical C's are D's" or "normally C's are D's") are given a positive or negative weight. This multipreference semantics, which takes into account preferences with respect to different concepts, has been first introduced as a semantics for ranked DL knowledge bases [20]. For weighted knowledge bases, we develop a different semantic closure construction, although in the spirit of other semantic constructions in the literature. We further extend the multipreference semantics to the fuzzy case.

The concept-wise multipreference semantics has been shown to have some desired properties from the knowledge representation point of view [20,21], and a related semantics with multiple preferences has also been proposed in the first-order logic setting by Delgrande and Rantsaudis [19]. In previous work [24], the concept-wise multipreference semantics has been used to provide a preferential interpretation of Self-Organising Maps [35], psychologically and biologically plausible neural network models. In this paper, we aim at investigating its relationships with another neural network model, Multilayer Perceptrons.

© Springer Nature Switzerland AG 2021
W. Faber et al. (Eds.): JELIA 2021, LNAI 12678, pp. 225–242, 2021.
https://doi.org/10.1007/978-3-030-75775-5_16

We consider a multilayer neural network after the training phase, when the synaptic weights have been learned, to show that the neural network can be given a preferential DL semantics with multiple preferences, as well as a semantics based on fuzzy DL interpretations and another one combining fuzzy interpretations with multiple preferences. The three semantics allow the input-output behavior of the network to be captured by interpretations built over a set of input stimuli through a simple construction, which exploits the activity level of neurons for the stimuli. Logical properties can be verified over such models by model checking.

To prove that the fuzzy multipreference interpretations, built from the network for a given set of input stimuli, are models of the neural network in a logical sense, we map the multilayer network to a conditional knowledge base, i.e., a set of weighted defeasible inclusions. A logical interpretation of a neural network can be useful from the point of view of explainability, in view of a trustworthy, reliable and explainable AI [1,2,29], and can potentially be exploited as the basis for an integrated use of symbolic reasoning and neural models.

2   The Description Logics $\mathcal{ALC}$ and $\mathcal{EL}$

In this section we recall the syntax and semantics of the description logic $\mathcal{ALC}$ [4] and of its lightweight fragment $\mathcal{EL}$ [3] at the basis of OWL2 EL Profile.

Let N_C be a set of concept names, N_R a set of role names and N_I a set of individual names. The set of $\mathcal{ALC}$ *concepts* (or, simply, concepts) can be defined inductively as follows: (1) $A \in N_C$, $\top$ and $\bot$ are concepts; (2) if C and D are concepts, and $r \in N_R$, then $C \sqcap D$, $C \sqcup D$, $\neg C$, $\forall r.C$, $\exists r.C$ are concepts.

A knowledge base (KB) K is a pair $(\mathcal{T}, \mathcal{A})$, where $\mathcal{T}$ is a TBox and $\mathcal{A}$ is an ABox. The TBox $\mathcal{T}$ is a set of concept inclusions (or subsumptions) $C \sqsubseteq D$, where C, D are concepts. The ABox $\mathcal{A}$ is a set of assertions of the form $C(a)$ and $r(a, b)$ where C is a concept, a an individual name in N_I and r a role name in N_R.

An $\mathcal{ALC}$ *interpretation* is defined as a pair $I = \langle \Delta, \cdot^I \rangle$ where: Δ is a domain— a set whose elements are denoted by $x, y, z, \ldots$ —and $\cdot^I$ is an extension function that maps each concept name $C \in N_C$ to a set $C^I \subseteq \Delta$, each role name $r \in N_R$ to a binary relation $r^I \subseteq \Delta \times \Delta$, and each individual name $a \in N_I$ to an element $a^I \in \Delta$. It is extended to complex concepts as follows:

$$\top^I = \Delta, \qquad \bot^I = \emptyset, \qquad (\neg C)^I = \Delta \backslash C^I,$$
$$(\exists r.C)^I = \{x \in \Delta \mid \exists y.(x,y) \in r^I \text{ and } y \in C^I\}, \qquad (C \sqcap D)^I = C^I \cap D^I,$$
$$(\forall r.C)^I = \{x \in \Delta \mid \forall y.(x,y) \in r^I \Rightarrow y \in C^I\}, \qquad (C \sqcup D)^I = C^I \cup D^I.$$

The notion of satisfiability of a KB in an interpretation and the notion of entailment are defined as follows:

Definition 1 (Satisfiability and entailment). *Given an $\mathcal{LC}$ interpretation* $I = \langle \Delta, \cdot^I \rangle$:

- *I satisfies an inclusion $C \sqsubseteq D$ if $C^I \subseteq D^I$;*
- *I satisfies an assertion $C(a)$ (resp., $r(a, b)$) if $a^I \in C^I$ (resp., $(a^I, b^I) \in r^I$).*

Given a KB $K = (\mathcal{T}, \mathcal{A})$, an interpretation I satisfies $\mathcal{T}$ (resp. $\mathcal{A}$) if I satisfies all inclusions in $\mathcal{T}$ (resp. all assertions in $\mathcal{A}$); I is a model *of K if I satisfies $\mathcal{T}$ and $\mathcal{A}$.*

A subsumption $F = C \sqsubseteq D$ (resp., an assertion $C(a)$, $r(a,b)$), is entailed by K, written $K \models F$, if for all models $I = \langle \Delta, \cdot^I \rangle$ of K, I satisfies F.

Given a knowledge base K, the *subsumption* problem is the problem of deciding whether an inclusion $C \sqsubseteq D$ is entailed by K.

In the logic $\mathcal{EL}$ [3], concepts are restricted to $C := A \mid \top \mid C \sqcap C \mid \exists r.C$, i.e., union, complement and universal restriction are not $\mathcal{EL}$ constructs. In the following, we will also consider the boolean fragment of $\mathcal{ALC}$ only including constructs $\sqcap$, $\sqcup$, $\neg$.

3 Fuzzy Description Logics

Fuzzy description logics have been widely studied in the literature for representing vagueness in DLs [7,8,41,50,51], based on the idea that concepts and roles can be interpreted as fuzzy sets and fuzzy binary relations.

As in Mathematical Fuzzy Logic [14] a formula has a degree of truth in an interpretation, rather than being either true or false, in a fuzzy DL axioms are associated with a degree of truth (usually in the interval $[0,1]$). In the following we shortly recall the semantics of a fuzzy extension of $\mathcal{ALC}$ referring to the survey by Lukasiewicz and Straccia [41]. We limit our consideration to a few features of a fuzzy DL and, in particular, we omit considering datatypes.

A *fuzzy interpretation* for $\mathcal{ALC}$ is a pair $I = \langle \Delta, \cdot^I \rangle$ where: Δ is a non-empty domain and $\cdot^I$ is *fuzzy interpretation function* that assigns to each concept name $A \in N_C$ a function $A^I : \Delta \to [0,1]$, to each role name $r \in N_R$ a function $r^I : \Delta \times \Delta \to [0,1]$, and to each individual name $a \in N_I$ an element $a^I \in \Delta$. A domain element $x \in \Delta$ belongs to the extension of A to some degree in $[0,1]$, i.e., A^I is a fuzzy set. The interpretation function $\cdot^I$ is extended to complex concepts as follows:

$$\begin{array}{ll} \top^I(x) = 1, \qquad \perp^I(x) = 0, & (\neg C)^I(x) = \ominus C^I(x), \\ (\exists r.C)^I(x) = sup_{y \in \Delta}\ r^I(x,y) \otimes C^I(y), & (C \sqcup D)^I(x) = C^I(x) \oplus D^I(x) \\ (\forall r.C)^I(x) = inf_{y \in \Delta}\ r^I(x,y) \rhd C^I(y), & (C \sqcap D)^I(x) = C^I(x) \otimes D^I(x) \end{array}$$

where $x \in \Delta$ and $\otimes$, $\oplus$, $\rhd$ and $\ominus$ are arbitrary but fixed t-norm, s-norm, implication function, and negation function, chosen among the combination functions of various fuzzy logics (we refer to [41] for details).

The interpretation function $\cdot^I$ is also extended to non-fuzzy axioms (i.e., to strict inclusions and assertions of an $\mathcal{ALC}$ knowledge base) as follows:

$$(C \sqsubseteq D)^I = inf_{x \in \Delta} C^I(x) \rhd D^I(x), \qquad (C(a))^I = C^I(a^I), \qquad (R(a,b))^I = R^I(a^I, b^I).$$

A *fuzzy $\mathcal{ALC}$ knowledge base* K is a pair $(\mathcal{T}, \mathcal{A})$ where $\mathcal{T}$ is a fuzzy TBox and $\mathcal{A}$ a fuzzy ABox. A fuzzy TBox is a set of *fuzzy concept inclusions* of the form $C \sqsubseteq D \; \theta \; n$, where $C \sqsubseteq D$ is an $\mathcal{ALC}$ concept inclusion axiom, $\theta \in \{\geq, \leq, >, <\}$ and $n \in [0,1]$. A fuzzy ABox $\mathcal{A}$ is a set of *fuzzy assertions* of the form $C(a)\theta n$ or $r(a,b)\theta n$, where C is an $\mathcal{ALC}$ concept, $r \in N_R$, $a, b \in N_I$, $\theta \in \{\geq, \leq, >, <\}$ and $n \in [0,1]$. Following Bobillo and Straccia [7], we assume that fuzzy interpretations are *witnessed*, i.e., the sup and inf are attained at some point of the involved domain. The notions of satisfiability of a KB in a fuzzy interpretation and of entailment are defined in the natural way.

Definition 2 (Satisfiability and entailment for fuzzy KBs). *A fuzzy interpretation I satisfies a fuzzy $\mathcal{ALC}$ axiom E (denoted $I \models E$), as follows, for $\theta \in \{\geq, \leq, >, <\}$:*

- *I satisfies a fuzzy $\mathcal{ALC}$ inclusion axiom $C \sqsubseteq D \; \theta \; n$ if $(C \sqsubseteq D)^I \theta \; n$;*
- *I satisfies a fuzzy $\mathcal{ALC}$ assertion $C(a) \; \theta \; n$ if $C^I(a^I)\theta \; n$;*
- *I satisfies a fuzzy $\mathcal{ALC}$ assertion $r(a,b) \; \theta \; n$ if $r^I(a^I, b^I)\theta \; n$.*

Given a fuzzy KB $K = (\mathcal{T}, \mathcal{A})$, a fuzzy interpretation I satisfies $\mathcal{T}$ (resp. $\mathcal{A}$) if I satisfies all fuzzy inclusions in $\mathcal{T}$ (resp. all fuzzy assertions in $\mathcal{A}$). A fuzzy interpretation I is a model *of K if I satisfies $\mathcal{T}$ and $\mathcal{A}$. A fuzzy axiom E is entailed by a fuzzy knowledge base K, written $K \models E$, if for all models $I = \langle \Delta, \cdot^I \rangle$ of K, I satisfies E.*

4   A Concept-Wise Multipreference Semantics for Weighted KBs

In this section we develop an extension of $\mathcal{EL}$ with defeasible inclusions having positive and negative weights, based on a concept-wise multipreference semantics first introduced for ranked $\mathcal{EL}_\bot^+$ knowledge bases [20], where defeasible inclusions have positive integer ranks. In addition to standard $\mathcal{EL}$ inclusions $C \sqsubseteq D$ (called *strict* inclusions in the following), the TBox $\mathcal{T}$ will also contain typicality inclusions of the form $\mathbf{T}(C) \sqsubseteq D$, where C and D are $\mathcal{EL}$ concepts. A typicality inclusion $\mathbf{T}(C) \sqsubseteq D$ means that "typical C's are D's" or "normally C's are D's" and corresponds to a conditional implication $C \mathrel{|\!\sim} D$ in Kraus, Lehmann and Magidor's (KLM) preferential approach [37,38]. Such inclusions are defeasible, i.e., admit exceptions, while strict inclusions must be satisfied by all domain elements. We assume that with each typicality inclusion is associated a weight w, a real number. A positive weight supports the plausibility of a defeasible inclusion; a negative weight supports its implausibility.

4.1   Weighted $\mathcal{EL}$ Knowledge Bases

Let $\mathcal{C} = \{C_1, \ldots, C_k\}$ be a set of distinguished $\mathcal{EL}$ concepts, the concepts for which defeasible inclusions are defined. A weighted TBox $\mathcal{T}_{C_i}$ is defined for each distinguished concept $C_i \in \mathcal{C}$ as a set of defeasible inclusions of the form $\mathbf{T}(C_i) \sqsubseteq D$ with a weight.

A *weighted $\mathcal{EL}$ knowledge base K over $\mathcal{C}$* is a tuple $\langle \mathcal{T}_{strict}, \mathcal{T}_{C_1}, \ldots, \mathcal{T}_{C_k}, \mathcal{A} \rangle$, where $\mathcal{T}_{strict}$ is a set of strict concept inclusions, $\mathcal{A}$ is an ABox and, for each

$C_j \in \mathcal{C}$, $\mathcal{T}_{C_j}$ is a weighted TBox of defeasible inclusions, $\{(d_h^i, w_h^i)\}$, where each d_h^i is a typicality inclusion of the form $\mathbf{T}(C_i) \sqsubseteq D_{i,h}$, having weight w_h^i, a real number.

Consider, for instance, the ranked knowledge base $K = \langle \mathcal{T}_{strict}, \mathcal{T}_{Employee}, \mathcal{T}_{Student}, \mathcal{A} \rangle$, over the set of distinguished concepts $\mathcal{C} = \{Employee, Student\}$, with empty ABox, and with $\mathcal{T}_{strict}$ containing the set of strict inclusions:

$Employee \sqsubseteq Adult \quad Adult \sqsubseteq \exists has\_SSN.\top \quad PhdStudent \sqsubseteq Student$

The weighted TBox $\mathcal{T}_{Employee}$ contains the following weighted defeasible inclusions:

(d_1) $\mathbf{T}(Employee) \sqsubseteq Young$,   - 50
(d_2) $\mathbf{T}(Employee) \sqsubseteq \exists has\_boss.Employee$,   100
(d_3) $\mathbf{T}(Employee) \sqsubseteq \exists has\_classes.\top$,   -70;

the weighted TBox $\mathcal{T}_{Student}$ contains the defeasible inclusions:

(d_4) $\mathbf{T}(Student) \sqsubseteq Young$,   90
(d_5) $\mathbf{T}(Student) \sqsubseteq \exists has\_classes.\top$,   80
(d_6) $\mathbf{T}(Student) \sqsubseteq \exists hasScholarship.\top$,   -30

The meaning is that, while an employee normally has a boss, he is not likely to be young or have classes. Furthermore, between the two defeasible inclusions (d_1) and (d_3), the second one is considered less plausible than the first one. Given two employees Tom and Bob such that Tom is not young, has no boss and has classes, while Bob is not young, has no classes and has a boss who is an employee, in the following, considering the weights above, we will regard Bob as being more typical than Tom as an employee.

4.2   The Concept-Wise Preferences from Weighted Knowledge Bases

The concept-wise multipreference semantics has been recently introduced as a semantics for ranked $\mathcal{EL}_\bot^+$ knowledge bases [20], which are inspired by Brewka's framework of basic preference descriptions [9]. For each concept $C_i \in \mathcal{C}$, a preference relation $<_{C_i}$ describes the preference among domain elements with respect to concept C_i. Each $<_{C_i}$ has the properties of preference relations in KLM-style ranked interpretations [38], that is, $<_{C_i}$ is a modular and well-founded strict partial order. In particular, $<_{C_i}$ is *well-founded* if, for all $S \subseteq \Delta$, if $S \neq \emptyset$, then $min_{<_{C_i}}(S) \neq \emptyset$; $<_{C_i}$ is *modular* if, for all $x, y, z \in \Delta$, $x <_{C_j} y$ implies $(x <_{C_j} z$ or $z <_{C_j} y)$.

In the following we will recall the concept-wise semantics for $\mathcal{ALC}$, which extends to its fragments considered in the following. An $\mathcal{ALC}$ interpretation, is extended with a collection of preference relations, one for each concept in $\mathcal{C}$.

Definition 3 (Multipreference interpretation). *A multipreference interpretation is a tuple* $\mathcal{M} = \langle \Delta, <_{C_1}, \ldots, <_{C_k}, \cdot^I \rangle$, *where:*

(a) Δ *is a domain, and* $\cdot^I$ *an interpretation function, as in* $\mathcal{ALC}$ *interpretations;*

(b) *the* $<_{C_i}$ *are irreflexive, transitive, well-founded and modular relations over* Δ.

The preference relation $<_{C_i}$ determines the relative typicality of domain individuals with respect to concept C_i. For instance, Tom may be more typical than Bob as a student ($tom <_{Student} bob$), but more exceptional as an employee ($bob <_{Employee} tom$). The minimal C_i-elements with respect to $<_{C_i}$ are regarded as the most typical C_i-elements.

While preferences do not need to agree, arbitrary conditional formulas cannot be evaluated with respect to a single preference relation. For instance, evaluating the inclusion "Are typical employed students young?" would require both the preferences $<_{Student}$ and $<_{Employee}$ to be considered. The approach proposed in [20] is that of *combining* the preference relations $<_{C_i}$ into a single *global preference* relation $<$, and than exploit the global preference for interpreting the typicality operator **T**, which may be applied to arbitrary concepts. A natural way to define the notion of global preference $<$ is by Pareto combination of the relations $<_{C_1}, \ldots, <_{C_k}$, as follows:

$$x < y \text{ iff } \quad (i) \; x <_{C_i} y, \text{ for some } C_i \in \mathcal{C}, \text{ and}$$
$$(ii) \; \text{for all } C_j \in \mathcal{C}, \; x \leq_{C_j} y.$$

A slightly more sophisticated notion of preference combination, which exploits a modified Pareto condition taking into account the specificity relation among concepts (such as, for instance, the fact that concept *PhdStudent* is more specific than concept *Student*), has been considered for ranked knowledge bases [20].

The addition of the global preference relation, leads to the definition of a notion of *concept-wise multipreference interpretation*, where concept **T**(C) is interpreted as the set of all $<$-minimal C elements.

Definition 4. *A concept-wise multipreference interpretation (or cw^m-interpretation) is a multipreference interpretation $\mathcal{M} = \langle \Delta, <_{C_1}, \ldots, <_{C_k}, <, \cdot^I \rangle$, according to Definition 3, such that the global preference relation $<$ is defined as above and $(\mathbf{T}(C))^I = min_<(C^I)$, where $Min_<(S) = \{u : u \in S \text{ and } \nexists z \in S \text{ s.t.} z < u\}$.*

In the following, we define a notion of cw^m-model of a weighted $\mathcal{EL}$ knowledge base K as a cw^m-interpretation in which the preference relations $<_{C_i}$ are constructed from the typicality inclusions in the $\mathcal{T}_{C_i}$'s.

4.3   A Semantics Closure Construction for Weighted Knowledge Bases

Given a weighted knowledge base $K = \langle \mathcal{T}_{strict}, \mathcal{T}_{C_1}, \ldots, \mathcal{T}_{C_k}, \mathcal{A} \rangle$, where $\mathcal{T}_{C_i} = \{(d_h^i, w_h^i)\}$ for $i = 1, \ldots, k$, and an $\mathcal{EL}$ interpretation $I = \langle \Delta, \cdot^I \rangle$ satisfying all the strict inclusions in $\mathcal{T}_{strict}$ and assertions in $\mathcal{A}$, we define a preference relation $<_{C_j}$ on Δ for each distinguished concepts $C_i \in \mathcal{C}$ through a *semantic closure construction*, a construction similar in spirit to the one considered by Lehmann for the lexicographic closure [39], but based on a different seriousness ordering. In order to define $<_{C_i}$ we consider the sum of the weights of the defeasible inclusions for C_i satisfied by each domain element $x \in \Delta$; higher preference wrt $<_{C_i}$ is given to the domain elements whose associated sum (wrt C_i) is higher.

First, let us define when a domain element $x \in \Delta$ satisfies/violates a typicality inclusion for C_i wrt an $\mathcal{EL}$ interpretation I. As $\mathcal{EL}$ has the *finite model property* [3], we will restrict to $\mathcal{EL}$ interpretations with a *finite* domain. We say that $x \in \Delta$ *satisfies* $\mathbf{T}(C_i) \sqsubseteq D$ in I, if $x \notin C_i^I$ or $x \in D^I$ (otherwise x *violates* $\mathbf{T}(C_i) \sqsubseteq D$ in I). Note that, in an interpretation I, any domain element which is not an instance of C_i trivially satisfies all defeasible inclusions $\mathbf{T}(C_i) \sqsubseteq D$. Such domain elements will be given the lowest preference with respect to $<_{C_i}$.

Given an $\mathcal{EL}$ interpretation $I = \langle \Delta, \cdot^I \rangle$ and a domain element $x \in \Delta$, we define the *weight of x wrt C_i in I*, $W_i(x)$, considering the inclusions $(\mathbf{T}(C_i) \sqsubseteq D_{i,h}, w_h^i) \in \mathcal{T}_{C_i}$:

$$W_i(x) = \begin{cases} \sum_{h:x \in D_{i,h}^I} w_h^i & \text{if } x \in C_i^I \\ -\infty & \text{otherwise} \end{cases} \tag{1}$$

where $-\infty$ is added at the bottom of all real values.

Informally, given an interpretation I, for $x \in C_i^I$, the weight $W_i(x)$ of x wrt C_i is the sum of the weights of all the defeasible inclusions for C_i satisfied by x in I. The more plausible are the satisfied inclusions, the higher is the weight of x. For instance, in the example (Sect. 4.1), assuming that elements $tom, bob \in Employee^I$, and that the typicality inclusion (d_3) is satisfied by tom, while $(d_1), (d_2)$ are satisfied by bob, for $C_i = Employee$, we would get $W_i(tom) = -70$ and $W_i(bob) = 100 - 70 = 30$.

Based on this notion of weight of a domain element with respect to a concept, one can construct a preference relation $<_{C_i}$ from a given $\mathcal{EL}$ interpretation I. A domain element x is preferred to element y wrt C_i if the weight of the defaults in $\mathcal{T}_{C_i}$ satisfied by x is higher than weight of defaults in $\mathcal{T}_{C_i}$ satisfied by y.

Definition 5 (Preference relation $<_{C_i}$ constructed from $\mathcal{T}_{C_i}$). *Given a ranked knowledge base K where, for all j, $\mathcal{T}_{C_j} = \{(d_h^i, r_h^i)\}$, and an $\mathcal{EL}$ interpretation $I = \langle \Delta, \cdot^I \rangle$, a preference relation $\leq_{C_i}$ can be defined as follows: For $x, y \in \Delta$,*

$$x \leq_{C_i} y \quad \textit{iff} \quad W_i(x) \geq W_i(y) \tag{2}$$

$\leq_{C_j}$ is a total preorder relation on Δ. A strict preference relation (a strict modular partial order) $<_{C_j}$ and an equivalence relation $\sim_{C_j}$ can be defined on Δ by letting: $x <_{C_j} y$ iff $(x \leq_{C_j} y$ and not $y \leq_{C_j} x)$, and $x \sim_{C_j} y$ iff $(x \leq_{C_j} y$ and $y \leq_{C_j} x)$. Note that the domain elements which are instances of C_i are all preferred (wrt $<_{C_i}$) to the domain elements which are not instances of C_i. Furthermore, for all domain elements $x, y \notin C_j^I$, $x \sim_{C_j} y$ holds. The higher is the weight of an element wrt C_i the more preferred is the element. In the example, $W_i(bob) = 30 > W_i(tom) = -70$ (for $C_i = Employee$) and, hence, $bob <_{Employee} tom$, i.e., Bob is more typical than Tom as an employee.

Following the same approach as for ranked $\mathcal{EL}$ knowledge bases [20], we define a notion of cw^m-*model* for a weighted knowledge base K, where each preference relation $<_{C_j}$ in the model is constructed from the weighted TBox $\mathcal{T}_{C_j}$ according to Definition 5 above, and the global preference is defined by combining the $<_i$'s.

Definition 6 (cw^m-model of K). *Let* $K = \langle \mathcal{T}_{strict}, \mathcal{T}_{C_1}, \ldots, \mathcal{T}_{C_k}, \mathcal{A} \rangle$ *be a weighted $\mathcal{EL}$ knowledge base over $\mathcal{C}$, and $I = \langle \Delta, \cdot^I \rangle$ an $\mathcal{EL}$ interpretation for K. A concept-wise multipreference model (cw^m-model) of K is a cw^m-interpretation $\mathcal{M} = \langle \Delta, <_{C_1}, \ldots, <_{C_k}, <, \cdot^I \rangle$ such that: $\mathcal{M}$ satisfies all strict inclusions in $\mathcal{T}_{strict}$ and assertions in $\mathcal{A}$, and for all $j = 1, \ldots, k$, $<_{C_j}$ is defined from $\mathcal{T}_{C_j}$ and I, according to Definition 5.*

As preference relations $<_{C_j}$, defined according to Definition 5, are irreflexive, transitive, modular, and well-founded relations over Δ (for well-foundedness, remember that we are considering finite models), the notion of cw^m-model $\mathcal{M}$ introduced above is well-defined. By definition of cw^m-model, $\mathcal{M}$ must satisfy all strict inclusions and assertions in K, but it is not required to satisfy all typicality inclusions $\mathbf{T}(C_j) \sqsubseteq D$ in K, unlike other preferential typicality logics [26]. This happens in a similar way in the multipreferential semantics for $\mathcal{EL}^+_\bot$ ranked knowledge bases, and we refer to [20] for an example showing that the cw^m-semantics is more liberal (in this respect) than standard KLM preferential semantics.

Observe that the notion of weight $W_i(x)$ of x wrt C_i, defined above as the sum of the weights of the satisfied defaults, is just a possible choice for the definition of the preference relations $<_i$ with respect to a concept C_i. A different notion of preference $<_{C_i}$ has been defined from a ranked TBox $\mathcal{T}_{C_j}$ [20], by exploiting the (positive) integer ranks of the defeasible inclusions in $\mathcal{T}_{C_j}$ and the (lexicographic) # strategy in the framework of basic preference descriptions [9]. The sum of weights/ranks has been first used in Penalty Logic [48], where weigths are positive real numbers, and in Kern-Isberner's c-interpretations [33,34], which also consider the sum of the weights $\kappa_i^- \in \mathbb{N}$, representing penalty points for *falsified* conditionals. Here, we sum the (positive or negative) weights of the satisfied defaults, and we do it in a concept-wise manner.

A notion of *concept-wise entailment* (or cw^m-entailment) can be defined in a natural way to establish when a defeasible concept inclusion follows from a weighted knowledge base K. We can restrict our consideration to (finite) *canonical* models, i.e., models which are large enough to contain all the relevant domain elements[1].

Definition 7 (cw^m-entailment). *An inclusion $\mathbf{T}(C) \sqsubseteq D$ is cw^m-entailed from a weighted knowledge base K if $\mathbf{T}(C) \sqsubseteq D$ is satisfied in all canonical cw^m-models $\mathcal{M}$ of K.*

As for ranked $\mathcal{EL}$ knowledge bases [20], it can be proved that this notion of cw^m-entailment for weigthed KBs satisfies the KLM postulates of a preferential consequence relation [20]. This is an easy consequence of the fact that the global preference relation $<$, which is used to evaluate typicality, is a strict partial order. As $<$ is not necessarily modular, cw^m-entailment does not necessarily satisfy rational monotonicity [38].

---

[1] This is a standard assumption in the semantic characterizations of rational closure for DLs, and in other semantic constructions. See [20] for the definition of canonical models for $\mathcal{EL}$.

The problem of deciding cw^m-entailment is Π_2^p-complete for ranked $\mathcal{EL}_\bot^+$ knowledge bases [20]; cw^m-entailment can be proven as well to be in Π_2^p for weighted knowledge bases, based on a similar reformulation of cw^m-entailment as a problem of computing preferred answer sets. The proof of the result is similar to the proof of Proposition 7 in the online Appendix of [20], apart from minor differences due to the different notion of preference $<_{C_i}$ used here with respect to the one for ranked knowledge bases.

5 Weighted Tboxes and Multipreference Fuzzy Interpretations

In this section, we move to consider fuzzy interpretations, and investigate the possibility of extending the previous multipreference semantic construction to the fuzzy case.

Definition 8 (Fuzzy multipreference interpretation). *A fuzzy multipreference interpretation (or fm-interpretation) is a tuple* $\mathcal{M} = \langle \Delta, <_{C_1}, \ldots, <_{C_k}, \cdot^I \rangle$, *where:*

(a) $(\Delta, \cdot^I)$ *is a fuzzy interpretation;*

(b) the $<_{C_i}$ *are irreflexive, transitive, well-founded and modular relations over* Δ.

Let K be a weighted knowledge base $\langle \mathcal{T}_{strict}, \mathcal{T}_{C_1}, \ldots, \mathcal{T}_{C_k}, \mathcal{A} \rangle$, where each axiom in $\mathcal{T}_{strict}$ has the form $\langle \alpha \geq 1 \rangle$, and $\mathcal{T}_{C_i} = \{(d_h^i, w_h^i)\}$ is a set of typicality inclusions $d_h^i = \mathbf{T}(C_i) \sqsubseteq D_{i,h}$ with weight w_h^i.

Given a fuzzy interpretation $I = \langle \Delta, \cdot^I \rangle$, satisfying all the strict inclusions in $\mathcal{T}_{strict}$ and all assertions in $\mathcal{A}$, we aim at constructing a concept-wise multipreference interpretation from I, by defining a preference relation $<_{C_j}$ on Δ for each $C_i \in \mathcal{C}$, based on a closure construction similar to the one developed in Sect. 4.3. The definition of $W_i(x)$ in (1) can be reformulated as follows:

$$W_i(x) = \begin{cases} \sum_h w_h^i \, D_{i,h}^I(x) & \text{if } C_i^I(x) > 0 \\ -\infty & \text{otherwise} \end{cases} \tag{3}$$

by regarding the interpretation $D_{i,h}^I$ of concept $D_{i,h}$ as a two valued function from Δ to $\{0,1\}$ (rather than a subset of Δ). And similarly for $C_i^I(x)$. Definition (3) can be taken as the definition of the weight function $W_i(x)$ when I is a fuzzy interpretation. Simply, in the fuzzy case, for each default $d_h^i = \mathbf{T}(C_i) \sqsubseteq D_{i,h}$, $D_{i,h}^I(x)$ is a value in $[0,1]$. In the sum, the value $D_{i,h}^I(x)$ of the membership of x in $D_{i,h}$ is weighted by w_h^i.

From this notion of weight of a domain element x wrt a concept $C_i \in \mathcal{C}$, the *preference relation* $\leq_{C_i}$ *associated with* $\mathcal{T}_{C_j}$ *in a fuzzy interpretation* I can be defined as in Sect. 4.3:

$$x \leq_{C_i} y \quad \text{iff} \quad W_i(x) \geq W_i(y) \tag{4}$$

A notion of fuzzy multipreference model of a weighted KB can then be defined.

Definition 9 (fuzzy multipreference model of K). *Let $K = \langle \mathcal{T}_{strict},$ $\mathcal{T}_{C_1}, \ldots, \mathcal{T}_{C_k}, \mathcal{A} \rangle$ be a weighted $\mathcal{EL}$ knowledge base over $\mathcal{C}$. A fuzzy multiprefer- ence model (or fm-model) of K is an fm-interpretation $\mathcal{M} = \langle \Delta, <_{C_1}, \ldots, <_{C_k} ,\cdot^I \rangle$ such that: the fuzzy interpretation $I = (\Delta, \cdot^I)$ satisfies all strict inclusions in $\mathcal{T}_{strict}$ and assertions in $\mathcal{A}$ and, for all $j = 1, \ldots, k$, $<_{C_j}$ is defined from $\mathcal{T}_{C_j}$ and I, according to condition (4).*

Note that, as we restrict to witnessed fuzzy interpretations I, for $S \neq \emptyset$, $inf_{x \in S} C_i^I$ is attained at some point in Δ. Hence, $min_{<_{C_i}}(S) \neq \emptyset$, i.e., $<_{C_i}$ is well-founded.

The preference relation $<_{C_i}$ establishes how typical a domain element x is wrt C_i. We can then require that the degree of membership in C_i (given by the fuzzy interpretation I) and the relative typicality wrt C_i (given by the preference relations $<_{C_i}$) are related, and agree with each other.

Definition 10 (Coherent fm-models). *The preference relation $<_{C_i}$ agrees with the fuzzy interpretation $I = \langle \Delta, \cdot^I \rangle$ if, for all $x, y \in \Delta$: $x <_{C_i} y$ iff $C_i^I(x) > C_i^I(y)$.*
An fm-model $\mathcal{M} = \langle \Delta, <_{C_1}, \ldots, <_{C_k}, \cdot^I \rangle$ of K is a coherent fm-model (or cf^m- model) of K if, for all $C_i \in \mathcal{C}$, preference relation $<_{C_i}$ agrees with the fuzzy interpretation I.

In a cf^m-model, the preference relation $<_{C_i}$ over Δ constructed from $\mathcal{T}_{C_i}$ coin- cides with the preference relation induced by C_i^I. As the interpretation function $\cdot^I$ extends to any concept C, for cf^m-models we do not need to introduce a global preference relation $<$, defined by combining the $<_{C_i}$. To define the interpretation of typicality concepts $\mathbf{T}(C)$ in a cf^m-model, we follow a different route and we let, for all concepts C,

$$(\mathbf{T}(C))^I = min_{<_C}(C^I),$$

where $<_C$ is the preference relation over Δ induced by C^I, i.e., for all $x, y \in \Delta$: $x <_C y$ iff $C^I(x) > C^I(y)$. Note that satisfiability in a cf^m-model is now extended to fuzzy inclusion axioms involving typicality concepts, such as $\langle \mathbf{T}(C) \sqsubseteq D \geq \alpha \rangle$.

A notion of *cf^m-entailment* from a weighted knowledge base K can be defined in the obvious way: a fuzzy axiom E is cf^m-entailed by a fuzzy knowledge base K if, for all cf^m-models $\mathcal{M}$ of K, $\mathcal{M}$ satisfies E.

6   Preferential and Fuzzy Interpretations of Multilayer Perceptrons

In this section, we first shortly introduce multilayer perceptrons. Then we develop a preferential interpretation of a neural network after training, as well as a fuzzy-preferential semantics.

Let us first recall from [30] the model of a *neuron* as an information-processing unit in an (artificial) neural network. The basic elements are the following:

– a set of *synapses* or *connecting links*, each one characterized by a *weight*. We let x_j be the signal at the input of synapse j connected to neuron k, and w_{kj} the related synaptic weight;

- the adder for summing the input signals to the neuron, weighted by the respective synapses weights: $\sum_{j=1}^{n} w_{kj} x_j$;
- an *activation function* for limiting the amplitude of the output of the neuron (typically, to the interval $[0, 1]$ or $[-1, +1]$).

The sigmoid, threshold and hyperbolic-tangent functions are examples of activation functions. A neuron k can be described by the following pair of equations: $u_k = \sum_{j=1}^{n} w_{kj} x_j$, and $y_k = \varphi(u_k + b_k)$, where $x_1, \ldots, x_n$ are the input signals and $w_{k1}, \ldots, w_{kn}$ are the weights of neuron k; b_k is the bias, φ the activation function, and y_k is the output signal of neuron k. By adding a new synapse with input $x_0 = +1$ and synaptic weight $w_{k0} = b_k$, one can write: $u_k = \sum_{j=0}^{n} w_{kj} x_j$, and $y_k = \varphi(u_k)$, where u_k is called the *induced local field* of the neuron. The neuron can be represented as a directed graph, where the input signals $x_1, \ldots, x_n$ and the output signal y_k of neuron k are nodes of the graph. An edge from x_j to y_k, labelled w_{kj}, means that x_j is an input signal of neuron k with synaptic weight w_{kj}.

A neural network can then be seen as "a directed graph consisting of nodes with interconnecting synaptic and activation links" [30]: nodes in the graph are the neurons (the processing units) and the weight w_{ij} on the edge from node j to node i represents "the strength of the connection [..] by which unit j transmits information to unit i" [44]. Source nodes (i.e., nodes without incoming edges) produce the input signals to the graph. Neural network models are classified by their synaptic connection topology. In a *feedforward* network the architectural graph is acyclic, while in a *recurrent* network it contains cycles. In a feedforward network neurons are organized in layers. In a *single-layer* network there is an input-layer of source nodes and an output-layer of computation nodes. In a *multilayer feedforward* network there is one or more hidden layer, whose computation nodes are called *hidden neurons* (or hidden units). The source nodes in the input-layer supply the activation pattern (*input vector*) providing the input signals for the first layer computation units. In turn, the output signals of first layer computation units provide the input signals for the second layer computation units, and so on, up to the final output layer of the network, which provides the overall response of the network to the activation pattern. In a recurrent network at least one feedback exists, so that "the output of a node in the system influences in part the input applied to that particular element" [30]. In the following, we do not put restrictions on the topology the network.

"A major task for a neural network is to learn a model of the world" [30]. In supervised learning, a set of input/output pairs, input signals and corresponding desired response, referred as training data, or training sample, is used to train the network to learn. In particular, the network learns by changing the synaptic weights, through the exposition to the training samples. After the training phase, in the generalization phase, the network is tested with data not seen before. "Thus the neural network not only provides the implicit model of the environment in which it is embedded, but also performs the information-processing function of interest" [30]. In the next section, we try to make this model explicit as a multipreference model.

6.1 A Multipreference Interpretation of Multilayer Perceptrons

Assume that the network $\mathcal{N}$ has been trained and the synaptic weights w_{kj} have been learned. We associate a concept name $C_i \in N_C$ to any unit i in $\mathcal{N}$ (including input units and hidden units) and construct a multi-preference interpretation over a (finite) *domain* Δ of input stimuli, the input vectors considered so far, for training and generalization. In case the network is not feedforward, we assume that, for each input vector v in Δ, the network reaches a stationary state [30], in which $y_k(v)$ is the activity level of unit k.

Let $\mathcal{C} = \{C_1, \ldots, C_n\}$ be a subset of N_C, the set of concepts C_i for a distinguished subset of units i, the units we are focusing on (for instance, $\mathcal{C}$ might be associated to the set of output units, or to all units). We can associate to $\mathcal{N}$ and Δ a (two-valued) concept-wise multipreference interpretation over the boolean fragment of $\mathcal{ALC}$ (with no roles and no individual names), based on Definition 4, as follows:

Definition 11. *The cw^m interpretation $\mathcal{M}_{\mathcal{N}}^{\Delta} = \langle \Delta, <_{C_1}, \ldots, <_{C_n}, <, \cdot^I \rangle$ over Δ for network $\mathcal{N}$ wrt $\mathcal{C}$ is a cw^m-interpretation where:*
- *the interpretation function $\cdot^I$ is defined for named concepts $C_k \in N_C$ as: $x \in C_k^I$ if $y_k(x) \neq 0$, and $x \notin C_k^I$ if $y_k(x) = 0$.*
- *for $C_k \in \mathcal{C}$, relation $<_{C_k}$ is defined for $x, x' \in \Delta$ as: $x <_{C_k} x'$ iff $y_k(x) > y_k(x')^2$.*

The relation $<_{C_k}$ is a strict partial order, and $\leq_{C_k}$ and $\sim_{C_k}$ are defined as usual. In particular, $x \sim_{C_k} x'$ for $x, x' \notin C_k^I$. Clearly, the boundary between the domain elements which are in C_k^I and those which are not could be defined differently, e.g., by letting $x \in C_k^I$ if $y_k(x) > 0.5$, and $x \notin C_k^I$ if $y_k(x) \leq 0.5$. This would require only a minor change in the definition of the $<_{C_k}$.

This model provides a multipreference interpretation of the network $\mathcal{N}$, based on the input stimuli considered in Δ. For instance, when the neural network is used for categorization and a single output neuron is associated to each category, each concept C_h associated to an output unit h corresponds to a learned category. If $C_h \in \mathcal{C}$, the preference relation $<_{C_h}$ determines the relative typicality of input stimuli wrt category C_h. This allows to verify typicality properties concerning categories, such as $\mathbf{T}(C_h) \sqsubseteq D$ (where D is a boolean concept built from the named concepts in N_C), by *model checking* on the model $\mathcal{M}_{\mathcal{N}}^{\Delta}$. According to the semantics of typicality concepts, this would require to identify typical C_h-elements and checking whether they are instances of concept D. General typicality inclusion of the form $\mathbf{T}(C) \sqsubseteq D$, with C and D boolean concepts, can as well be verified on the model $\mathcal{M}_{\mathcal{N}}^{\Delta}$. However, the identification of $<$-minimal C-elements requires computing, for all pairs of elements $x, y \in \Delta$, the relation $<$ and the relations $<_{C_i}$ for $C_i \in \mathcal{C}$. This may be challenging as Δ can be large.

Evaluating properties involving hidden units might be of interest, although their meaning is usually unknown. In the well known Hinton's family example

---

[2] $y_k(x)$ is the output signal of unit k for input vectors x. Differently from Sect. 6, here (and below) the dependency of the output y_k of neuron k on the input vector x is made explicit.

[31], one may want to verify whether, normally, given an old Person 1 and relationship Husband, Person 2 would also be old, i.e., $\mathbf{T}(Old_1 \sqcap Husband) \sqsubseteq Old_2$ is satisfied. Here, concept Old_1 (resp., Old_2) is associated to a (known, in this case) hidden unit for Person 1 (and Person 2), while Husband is associated to an input unit.

6.2 A Fuzzy Interpretation of Multilayer Perceptrons

The definition of a fuzzy model of a neural network $\mathcal{N}$, under the same assumptions as in Sect. 6.1, is straightforward. Let N_C be the set containing a concept name C_i for each unit i in $\mathcal{N}$, including hidden units. Let us restrict to the boolean fragment of $\mathcal{ALC}$ with no individual names. We define a *fuzzy interpretation* $I_\mathcal{N} = \langle \Delta, \cdot^I \rangle$ for $\mathcal{N}$ as follows: (*i*) Δ is a (finite) set of input stimuli; (*ii*) the interpretation function $\cdot^I$ is defined for named concepts $C_k \in N_C$ as: $C_k^I(x) = y_k(x)$, $\forall x \in \Delta$; where $y_k(x)$ is the output signal of neuron k, for input vector x.

The verification that a fuzzy axiom $\langle C \sqsubseteq D \geq \alpha \rangle$ is satisfied in the model $I_\mathcal{N}$, can be done based on satisfiability in fuzzy DLs, according to the choice of the t-norm and implication function. It requires $C_k^I(x)$ to be recorded for all $k = 1, \ldots, n$ and $x \in \Delta$. Of course, one could restrict N_C to the concepts associated to input and output units in $\mathcal{N}$, so to capture the input/output behavior of the network.

In the next section, starting from this fuzzy interpretation of a neural network $\mathcal{N}$, we define a fuzzy multipreference interpretation $\mathcal{M}_\mathcal{N}^{f,\Delta}$, and prove that it is a coherent fm-model of the conditional knowledge base $K_\mathcal{N}$ associated to $\mathcal{N}$, under some condition.

6.3 Multilayer Perceptrons as Conditional Knowledge Bases

Let N_C be as in Sect. 6.2, and let $\mathcal{C} = \{C_1, \ldots, C_n\}$ be a subset of N_C. Given the *fuzzy interpretation* $I_\mathcal{N} = \langle \Delta, \cdot^I \rangle$ as defined in Sect. 6.2, a fuzzy multipreference interpretation $\mathcal{M}_\mathcal{N}^{f,\Delta} = \langle \Delta, <_{C_1}, \ldots, <_{C_n}, \cdot^I \rangle$ over $\mathcal{C}$ can be defined by letting $<_{C_k}$ to be the preference relation induced by the interpretation $I_\mathcal{N}$, as follows: for $x, x' \in \Delta$,

$$x <_{C_k} x' \text{ iff } y_k(x) > y_k(x'). \tag{5}$$

Interpretation $\mathcal{M}_\mathcal{N}^{f,\Delta}$ makes the preference relations induced by $I_\mathcal{N}$ explicit. We aim at proving that $\mathcal{M}_\mathcal{N}^{f,\Delta}$ is indeed a coherent fm-model of the neural network $\mathcal{N}$. A weighted conditional knowledge base $K^\mathcal{N}$ is associated to the neural network $\mathcal{N}$ as follows.

For each unit k, we consider all the units $j_1, \ldots, j_m$ whose output signals are the input signals of unit k, with synaptic weights $w_{k,j_1}, \ldots, w_{k,j_m}$. Let C_k be the concept name associated to unit k and $C_{j_1}, \ldots, C_{j_m}$ the concept names associated to units $j_1, \ldots, j_m$, respectively. We define for each unit k the following set $\mathcal{T}_{C_k}$ of typicality inclusions, with their associated weights: $\mathbf{T}(C_k) \sqsubseteq C_{j_1}$ with w_{k,j_1}, ..., $\mathbf{T}(C_k) \sqsubseteq C_{j_m}$ with w_{k,j_m}. Given $\mathcal{C}$, the knowledge base extracted from network $\mathcal{N}$ is defined as the tuple: $K^{\mathcal{N}} = \langle \mathcal{T}_{strict}, \mathcal{T}_{C_1}, \ldots, \mathcal{T}_{C_n}, \mathcal{A} \rangle$, where $\mathcal{T}_{strict} = \mathcal{A} = \emptyset$ and $K^{\mathcal{N}}$ contains the set $\mathcal{T}_{C_k}$ of weighted typicality inclusions associated to neuron k (defined as above), for each $C_k \in \mathcal{C}$. $K^{\mathcal{N}}$ is a weighted knowledge base over the set of distinguished concepts $\mathcal{C} = \{C_1, \ldots, C_n\}$. For multilayer feedforward networks, $K^{\mathcal{N}}$ corresponds to an acyclic conditional knowledge base, and defines a (defeasible) subsumption hierarchy among concepts. Given a network $\mathcal{N}$, it can be proved that (see [22] for the proof):

Proposition 1. $\mathcal{M}_{\mathcal{N}}^{f,\Delta}$ *is a cf^m-model of the knowledge base $K^{\mathcal{N}}$, provided the activation functions φ of all units are monotonically increasing and have value in $(0,1]$.*

Under the given conditions, that hold, for instance, for the sigmoid activation function, for any choice of $\mathcal{C} \subseteq N_C$ and for any choice of the domain Δ of input stimuli (all leading to a stationary state of $\mathcal{N}$), the fm-interpretation $\mathcal{M}_{\mathcal{N}}^{f,\Delta}$ is a coherent fuzzy multipreference model of the defeasible knowledge base $K^{\mathcal{N}}$. The knowledge base $K^{\mathcal{N}}$ does not provide a logical characterization of the neural network $\mathcal{N}$, as the requirement of coherence does not determine the activation functions of neurons. For this reason, the knowledge base $K^{\mathcal{N}}$ captures the behavior of all the networks $\mathcal{N}'$, obtained from $\mathcal{N}$ by replacing the activation function of the units in $\mathcal{N}$ with other monotonically increasing activation functions with values in $(0,1]$ (but retaining the synaptic weights as in $\mathcal{N}$). That is, an interpretation $\mathcal{M}_{\mathcal{N}'}^{f,\Delta}$, constructed from a network $\mathcal{N}'$ and any Δ as above, is as well a cf^m-model of $K^{\mathcal{N}}$. This means that the logical formulas cf^m-entailed from $K^{\mathcal{N}}$ hold in all the models $\mathcal{M}_{\mathcal{N}'}^{f,\Delta}$ built from $\mathcal{N}'$. They are properties of $\mathcal{N}'$, as well as of network $\mathcal{N}$. cf^m-entailment from $K^{\mathcal{N}}$ is sound for $\mathcal{N}$ and for each $\mathcal{N}'$ as above.

7   Conclusions

In this paper, we have investigated the relationships between defeasible knowledge bases, under a fuzzy multipreference semantics, and multilayer neural networks. Given a network after training, we have seen that one can construct a (fuzzy) multipreference interpretation starting from a domain containing a set of input stimuli, and using the activity level of neurons for the stimuli. We have proven that such interpretations are models of the conditional knowledge base associated to the network, corresponding to a set of weighted defeasible inclusions in a simple DL.

The correspondence between neural network models and fuzzy systems has been first investigated by Bart Kosko in his seminal work [36]. In his view, "at each instant the n-vector of neuronal outputs defines a fuzzy unit or a fit vector. Each fit value indicates the degree to which the neuron or element belongs to the n-dimentional fuzzy set." Our fuzzy interpretation of a multilayer perceptron regards, instead, each concept (representing a single neuron) as a fuzzy set. This is the usual way of viewing concepts in fuzzy DLs [6,40,51], and we have used fuzzy concepts within a multipreference semantics based on a semantic closure construction, in the line of Lehmann's semantics for lexicographic closure [39] and of Kern-Isberner's c-interpretations [33,34].

Much work has been devoted, in recent years, to the combination of neural networks and symbolic reasoning, leading to the definition of new computational models [15,16,32,49], and to extensions of logic programming languages with neural predicates [43,53]. Among the earliest systems combining logical reasoning and neural learning are the KBANN [52] and the CLIP [17] systems and Penalty Logic [48], a non-monotonic reasoning formalism used to establish a correspondence with symmetric connectionist networks . None on these approaches provides a semantics of neural networks in terms of concept-wise multipreference interpretations with typicality. This conditional interpretation may be of interest from the standpoint of explainable AI [1,2,29].

Several issues may deserve investigation as future work. An open problem is whether the notion of cf^m-entailment is decidable (even for the small fragment of $\mathcal{EL}$ without roles), under which choice of fuzzy logic combination functions, and whether decidable approximations can be defined. Another issue is whether the multipreference semantics can provide a semantic interpretation of other neural network models, besides self-organising maps [35], whose multipreference semantics is investigated in [24,25].

Acknowledgement. This research is partially supported by INDAM-GNCS Project 2020.

References

1. Adadi, A., Berrada, M.: Peeking inside the black-box: a survey on explainable artificial intelligence (XAI). IEEE Access **6**, 52138–52160 (2018)
2. Barredo Arrieta, A., et al.: Explainable artificial intelligence (XAI): concepts, taxonomies, opportunities and challenges toward responsible AI. Inf. Fusion **58**, 82–115 (2020)
3. Baader, F., Brandt, S., Lutz, C.: Pushing the $\mathcal{EL}$ envelope. In: Kaelbling, L.P., Saffiotti, A. (eds.), Proceedings of the 19th International Joint Conference on Artificial Intelligence (IJCAI 2005), Edinburgh, Scotland, UK, August 2005, pp. 364–369. Professional Book Center (2005)
4. Baader, F., Calvanese, D., McGuinness, D.L., Nardi, D., Patel-Schneider, P.F.: The Description Logic Handbook - Theory, Implementation, and Applications, 2nd edn. Cambridge University Press, Cambridge (2007)
5. Benferhat, S., Dubois, D., Prade, H.: Possibilistic logic: from nonmonotonicity to logic programming. In: Clarke, M., Kruse, R., Moral, S. (eds.) ECSQARU 1993. LNCS, vol. 747, pp. 17–24. Springer, Heidelberg (1993). https://doi.org/10.1007/BFb0028177
6. Bobillo, F., Straccia, U.: The fuzzy ontology reasoner fuzzyDL. Knowl. Based Syst. **95**, 12–34 (2016)
7. Bobillo, F., Straccia, U.: Reasoning within fuzzy OWL 2 EL revisited. Fuzzy Sets Syst. **351**, 1–40 (2018)
8. Borgwardt, S., Distel, F., Peñaloza, R.: The limits of decidability in fuzzy description logics with general concept inclusions. Artif. Intell. **218**, 23–55 (2015)

9. Brewka, G.: A rank based description language for qualitative preferences. In: Proceedings of the 16th European Conference on Artificial Intelligence, ECAI 2004, Valencia, Spain, 22–27 August 2004, pp. 303–307 (2004)
10. Britz, K., Heidema, J., Meyer, T.: Semantic preferential subsumption. In: Brewka, G., Lang, J. (eds.) Principles of Knowledge Representation and Reasoning: Proceedings of the 11th International Conference (KR 2008), Sidney, Australia, September 2008, pp. 476–484. AAAI Press (2008)
11. Casini, G., Meyer, T., Varzinczak, I.J., Moodley, K.: Nonmonotonic reasoning in description logics: rational closure for the ABox. In: 26th International Workshop on Description Logics (DL 2013), CEUR Workshop Proceedings, vol. 1014, pp. 600–615 (2013)
12. Casini, G., Straccia, U.: Rational closure for defeasible description logics. In: Janhunen, T., Niemelä, I. (eds.) Proceedings 12th European Conference on Logics in Artificial Intelligence (JELIA 2010). LNCS, Helsinki, Finland, September 2010, vol. 6341, pp. 77–90. Springer, Heidelberg (2010). https://doi.org/10.1007/978-3-642-15675-5_9
13. Casini, G., Straccia, U., Meyer, T.: A polynomial time subsumption algorithm for nominal safe elo⊥ under rational closure. Inf. Sci. **501**, 588–620 (2019)
14. Cintula, P., Hájek, P., Noguera, C. (eds.): Handbook of Mathematical Fuzzy Logic, vol. 37–38. College Publications, Norcross (2011)
15. d'Avila Garcez, A.S., Gori, M., Lamb, L.C., Serafini, L., Spranger, M., Tran., S.N.: Neural-symbolic computing: an effective methodology for principled integration of machine learning and reasoning. FLAP **6**(4), 611–632 (2019)
16. d'Avila Garcez, A.S., Lamb, L.C., Gabbay, D.M.: Neural-symbolic cognitive reasoning. In: Cognitive Technologies. Springer, Heidelberg (2009). https://doi.org/10.1007/978-3-540-73246-4
17. d'Avila Garcez, A.S., Zaverucha, G.: The connectionist inductive learning and logic programming system. Appl. Intell. **11**(1), 59–77 (1999). https://doi.org/10.1023/A:1008328630915
18. Delgrande, J.: A first-order conditional logic for prototypical properties. Artif. Intell. **33**(1), 105–130 (1987)
19. Delgrande, J., Rantsoudis, C.: A preference-based approach for representing defaults in first-order logic. In: Proceedings of the 18th International Workshop on Non-Monotonic Reasoning, NMR 2020, 12th–14th September 2020 (2020)
20. Giordano, L., Theseider Dupré, D.: An ASP approach for reasoning in a concept-aware multipreferential lightweight DL. Theory Pract. Log. Program. **20**(5), 751–766 (2020). Online Appendix in CoRR, abs/2006.04387
21. Giordano, L., Theseider Dupré, D.: A framework for a modular multi-concept lexicographic closure semantics. In: Proceedings of the 18th International Workshop on Non-Monotonic Reasoning, NMR 2020, 12th–14th September 2020 (2020)
22. Giordano, L., Theseider Dupré, D.: Weighted defeasible knowledge bases and a multipreference semantics for a deep neural network model. CoRR, abs/2012.13421 (2020)
23. Giordano, L., Gliozzi, V.: A reconstruction of multipreference closure. Artif. Intell. **290**, 103398 (2021)
24. Giordano, L., Gliozzi, V., Theseider Dupré, D.:On a plausible concept-wise multipreference semantics and its relations with self-organising maps. In: Calimeri, F., Perri, S., Zumpano, E. (eds.) Proceedings of the 35th Italian Conference on Computational Logic - CILC 2020, Rende, Italy, 13–15 October 2020, CEUR Workshop Proceedings, vol. 2710, pp. 127–140 (2020). CEUR-WS.org

25. Giordano, L., Gliozzi, V., Theseider Dupré, D.: A conditional, a fuzzy and a probabilistic interpretation of self-organising maps (2021)
26. Giordano, L., Gliozzi, V., Olivetti, N., Pozzato, G.L.: Preferential description logics. In: Dershowitz, N., Voronkov, A. (eds.) LPAR 2007. LNCS (LNAI), vol. 4790, pp. 257–272. Springer, Heidelberg (2007). https://doi.org/10.1007/978-3-540-75560-9_20
27. Giordano, L., Gliozzi, V., Olivetti, N., Pozzato, G.L.: ALC+T: a preferential extension of Description Logics. Fundamenta Informaticae **96**, 1–32 (2009)
28. Giordano, L., Gliozzi, V., Olivetti, N., Pozzato, G.L.: Semantic characterization of rational closure: from propositional logic to description logics. Artif. Intell. **226**, 1–33 (2015)
29. Guidotti, R., Monreale, A., Ruggieri, S., Turini, F., Giannotti, F., Pedreschi, D.: A survey of methods for explaining black box models. ACM Comput. Surv. **51**(5), 93:1–93:42 (2019)
30. Haykin, S.: Neural Networks - A Comprehensive Foundation. Pearson, London (1999)
31. Hinton, G.: Learning distributed representation of concepts. In: Proceedings 8th Annual Conference of the Cognitive Science Society. Erlbaum, Hillsdale (1986)
32. Hohenecker, P., Lukasiewicz, T.: Ontology reasoning with deep neural networks. J. Artif. Intell. Res. **68**, 503–540 (2020)
33. Kern-Isberner, G. (ed.): Conditionals in Nonmonotonic Reasoning and Belief Revision. LNCS (LNAI), vol. 2087. Springer, Heidelberg (2001). https://doi.org/10.1007/3-540-44600-1
34. Kern-Isberner, G., Eichhorn, C.: Structural inference from conditional knowledge bases. Stud. Logica **102**(4), 751–769 (2014). https://doi.org/10.1007/s11225-013-9503-6
35. Kohonen, T., Schroeder, M.R., Huang, T.S. (eds.) Self-Organizing Maps, 3rd edn. Springer Series in Information Sciences. Springer, Heidelberg (2001). https://doi.org/10.1007/978-3-642-56927-2
36. Kosko, B.: Neural Networks and Fuzzy Systems: A Dynamical Systems Approach to Machine Intelligence. Prentice Hall, Upper Saddle River (1992)
37. Kraus, S., Lehmann, D., Magidor, M.: Nonmonotonic reasoning, preferential models and cumulative logics. Artif. Intell. **44**(1–2), 167–207 (1990)
38. Lehmann, D., Magidor, M.: What does a conditional knowledge base entail? Artif. Intell. **55**(1), 1–60 (1992)
39. Lehmann, D.J.: Another perspective on default reasoning. Ann. Math. Artif. Intell. **15**(1), 61–82 (1995). https://doi.org/10.1007/BF01535841
40. Lukasiewicz, T., Straccia, U.: Managing uncertainty and vagueness in description logics for the semantic web. J. Web Semant. **6**(4), 291–308 (2008)
41. Lukasiewicz, T., Straccia, U.: Description logic programs under probabilistic uncertainty and fuzzy vagueness. Int. J. Approx. Reason. **50**(6), 837–853 (2009)
42. Makinson, D.: General theory of cumulative inference. In: Reinfrank, M., de Kleer, J., Ginsberg, M.L., Sandewall, E. (eds.) NMR 1988. LNCS, vol. 346, pp. 1–18. Springer, Heidelberg (1989). https://doi.org/10.1007/3-540-50701-9_16
43. Manhaeve, R., Dumancic, S., Kimmig, A., Demeester, T., De Raedt, L.: DeepProbLog: neural probabilistic logic programming. In: Advances in Neural Information Processing Systems 31: Annual Conference on Neural Information Processing Systems, NeurIPS 2018, 3–8 December 2018, Montréal, Canada, pp. 3753–3763 (2018)
44. McLeod, P., Plunkett, K., Rolls, E.T. (eds.): Introduction to Connectionist Modelling of Cognitive Processes. Oxford university Press, Oxford (1998)

45. Pearl, J.: Probabilistic Reasoning in Intelligent Systems Networks of Plausible Inference. Morgan Kaufmann, Burlington (1988)
46. Pearl, J.: System Z: a natural ordering of defaults with tractable applications to nonmonotonic reasoning. In: Proceedings of the 3rd Conference on Theoretical Aspects of Reasoning about Knowledge (TARK 1990), Pacific Grove, CA, USA, March 1990, pp. 121–135. Morgan Kaufmann, Burlington (1990)
47. Pensel, M., Turhan, A.: Reasoning in the defeasible description logic $EL_\perp$ - computing standard inferences under rational and relevant semantics. Int. J. Approx. Reasoning **103**, 28–70 (2018)
48. Pinkas, G.: Reasoning, nonmonotonicity and learning in connectionist networks that capture propositional knowledge. Artif. Intell. **77**(2), 203–247 (1995)
49. Serafini, L., d'Avila Garcez, A.S.: Learning and reasoning with logic tensor networks. In: Adorni, G., Cagnoni, S., Gori, M., Maratea, M. (eds.) AI*IA 2016. LNCS (LNAI), vol. 10037, pp. 334–348. Springer, Cham (2016). https://doi.org/10.1007/978-3-319-49130-1_25
50. Stoilos, G., Stamou, G.B., Tzouvaras, V., Pan, J.Z., Horrocks, I.: Fuzzy OWL: uncertainty and the semantic web. In: Proceedings of the OWLED 2005 Workshop on OWL: Experiences and Directions, Galway, Ireland, 11–12 November 2005, CEUR Workshop Proceedings, vol. 188. (2005). CEUR-WS.org
51. Straccia, U.: Towards a fuzzy description logic for the semantic web (preliminary report). In: Gómez-Pérez, A., Euzenat, J. (eds.) ESWC 2005. LNCS, vol. 3532, pp. 167–181. Springer, Heidelberg (2005). https://doi.org/10.1007/11431053_12
52. Towell, G.G., Shavlik, J.W.: Knowledge-based artificial neural networks. Artif. Intell. **70**(1–2), 119–165 (1994)
53. Yang, Z., Ishay, A., Lee, J.: NeurASP: embracing neural networks into answer set programming. In: Bessiere, C. (ed.) Proceedings of the Twenty-Ninth International Joint Conference on Artificial Intelligence, IJCAI 2020, pp. 1755–1762 (2020). ijcai.org

Non-classical Logics

A Computationally Grounded Logic of Graded Belief

Emiliano Lorini[1] and François Schwarzentruber[2(✉)]

[1] IRIT-CNRS, Toulouse University, Toulouse, France
[2] Univ Rennes, IRISA, CNRS, Rennes, France
schwarzentruber@ens-rennes.fr

Abstract. We present a logic of graded beliefs with a formal semantics grounded on the notion of belief base. It has modal operators which represent what an agent would believe if she removed k pieces of information from her belief base. We provide a sound and complete axiomatics for our logic as well as an optimal model checking algorithm. To illustrate its expressive power, we apply it to modeling social influence and epistemic explanation.

1 Introduction

Epistemic logic (in the broad sense) captures epistemic attitudes including knowledge and belief. It has been extensively studied by philosophers [27], computer scientists [18,39] and economists [33] and applied to a variety of fields of AI including security protocols [9,22], blockchain protocol [22,38] and epistemic planning [6]. Its language extends that of propositional logic by a modal operator for expressing an agent's knowledge or belief. Multi-agent extensions of epistemic logic have been studied in which modal operators are parameterized by agent names identifying the knower (or the believer) in the system.

Several extensions and variants of epistemic logic dealing with the notion of graded belief have been proposed. This includes logics of probabilistic beliefs [17,31,50] as well as logics of graded belief based on a qualitative or semiqualitative notion of plausibility [1,3,32,49]. As pointed out by [40,51], while in quantitative approaches belief states are represented by classical probabilistic measures or by alternative numerical accounts, such as lexicographic probabilities or conditional probabilities, in a semi-qualitative setting, such as rank-based systems [44] and possibility theory [16], belief states are represented by qualitative measures assigning orders of magnitude. Finally, qualitative approaches employ a plausibility ordering (also called epistemic entrenchment ordering) on possible worlds. Other approaches use graded modalities whereby the degree of a belief is a function of the number of worlds in which the believed formula is true [8,47,48], or of the number of evidences which support it [2]. All these approaches to graded belief use Kripke semantics in which agents' epistemic states are modeled via accessibility relations over possible worlds.

© Springer Nature Switzerland AG 2021
W. Faber et al. (Eds.): JELIA 2021, LNAI 12678, pp. 245–261, 2021.
https://doi.org/10.1007/978-3-030-75775-5_17

Kripke semantics have severe limitations in modeling knowledge. First, the number of possible worlds is huge in real applications: for instance, in a classical card game with four players having each 8 cards among a set of 32 cards, the number of possibilities is $\binom{32}{8} \times \binom{24}{8} \times \binom{16}{8} = 9.95 \times 10^{16}$ possible worlds. For this reason, although the model checking problem of epistemic logic based on Kripke semantics is in polynomial time, in many applications, the model cannot be explicitly constructed. Thus, it is hard to implement graded beliefs through Kripke semantics.

Kripke models and their corresponding accessibility relations can be compactly represented by means of BDDs [46], by Boolean formulas and programs [10–13] or by the notion of visibility [25]. In these approaches, the size of the models scales up, although the corresponding symbolic model checking is PSPACE-complete. However, they capture restricted notions of belief and knowledge and the formal languages they use to succinctly represent the Kripke model are of different nature than the standard epistemic language. This makes it difficult to define the notion of graded belief.

In this paper, we present a novel account of graded belief exploiting the notion of belief base. The belief base approach to knowledge representation is well-established since at least 30 years in a single-agent setting [5,23,30,42]. In this approach, an agent has non-deductively closed explicit beliefs in her belief base and we call implicit belief a statement that can be inferred from her explicit beliefs.

As we aim at a multi-agent setting, we rely on the idea of using belief bases as a semantics for multi-agent epistemic logic which was put forth in [34] and developed in a series of papers with the aim of capturing multi-agent belief dynamics [36,37] and higher-order epistemic reasoning [35], and of elucidating the connection between distributed belief and belief merging [26]. We enrich the logic presented in [34] with a notion of graded belief. It is expressed by modal operators of the form $\square_i^k$, where i is an agent and k is a positive integer capturing the agent's strength of belief. At the semantic level, such operators are interpreted via graded epistemic accessibility relations of type $\mathcal{R}_i^k$, one per $k \in \mathbb{N}$. Such a relation specifies the set of states that agent i considers possible after having removed at most k pieces of information from her belief base. This means that the higher the value of k of a given state for agent i, the higher the degree of plausibility of that state for agent i.[1] Indeed, states with a high degree of plausibility are states which satisfy a large number of information in the agent's belief base. In the extreme case, maximally plausible states for the agent are states to which value 0 is assigned, since they satisfy all information in the agent's belief base. This is a crucial aspect of our approach which distinguishes it from the standard extensional Kripke-style semantics for epistemic logic. While in the standard semantics an agent's plausibility ordering or the corresponding plausibility measure over states is given as a primitive (see, e.g., [1,3,32]), in our approach they are computed from and grounded on the agents' belief base. The latter provides an advantages for formal verification since the model checking

---

[1] This is in line with the theory of qualitative uncertainty by [44].

problem is formulated in our logic in a more compact way than in existing logics of graded belief. Also, from the conceptual point view, our logic offers a minimalistic approach to graded belief in which the only primitive concept is belief base, while the concept of graded implicit belief is derived from it.

Our approach provides a succinct semantics of epistemic states exploiting belief bases as well as a conservative extension of standard epistemic logic by the notions of explicit belief and graded belief.

The paper is organized as follows. In Sect. 2, we introduce the language of our multi-agent epistemic logic of explicit belief and graded implicit belief. Section 3 presents its formal semantics exploiting belief bases. Section 4 presents the first application of our logical framework to modeling the concept of social influence. Section 5 is the core part of the paper and provides an axiomatics proven to be sound and complete relative to the belief base semantics. In Sect. 6, we extend the base logic by conditional belief operators and generalize the completeness result to it. Section 7 presents a model checking algorithm for the base logic and its extension. Section 8 presents the second application of our logic: we illustrate its expressive power to account for a variety of notions of epistemic explanation. Finally, in Sect. 9, we conclude.

2   Graded Doxastic Language

Assume a countably infinite set of atomic propositions Atm and a finite set of agents $Agt = \{1, \ldots, n\}$. We define the language for representing agents' explicit beliefs and agents' graded implicit beliefs in two steps. First, we define the language $\mathcal{L}_0(Atm, Agt)$ for representing agents' explicit beliefs by the grammar:

$$\alpha ::= p \mid \neg\alpha \mid \alpha_1 \wedge \alpha_2 \mid \triangle_i \alpha,$$

where p ranges over Atm and i ranges over Agt. The formula $\triangle_i \alpha$ is read "agent i explicitly believes that α". Second, the language $\mathcal{L}(Atm, Agt)$ extends the language $\mathcal{L}_0(Atm, Agt)$ by graded implicit belief operators. It is is defined by:

$$\varphi ::= \alpha \mid \neg\varphi \mid \varphi_1 \wedge \varphi_2 \mid \Box_i^k \varphi,$$

where α ranges over $\mathcal{L}_0(Atm, Agt)$, i ranges over Agt and k ranges over $\mathbb{N}$. For notational convenience we write $\mathcal{L}_0$ instead of $\mathcal{L}_0(Atm, Agt)$ and $\mathcal{L}$ instead of $\mathcal{L}(Atm, Agt)$, when the context is unambiguous. The other Boolean constructions $\top, \bot, \rightarrow$ and $\leftrightarrow$ are defined in the standard way. For every formula $\varphi \in \mathcal{L}$, we write $Atm(\varphi)$ to denote the set of atomic propositions of type p occurring in φ. Moreover, for every set of formulas $X \subseteq \mathcal{L}$, we define $Atm(X) = \bigcup_{\varphi \in X} Atm(\varphi)$.

The formula $\Box_i^k \varphi$ is read "agent i would implicitly believe φ, for every removal of at most k pieces of information from her belief base". The value k can also be conceived as the extent to which agent i believes that φ. Indeed, the higher the number of information in the belief base that can be removed without affecting the belief, the stronger the belief. Thus, $\Box_i^k \varphi$ can also be read "agent i believes that φ with degree (or strength) at least k". The abbreviation $\Diamond_i^k \varphi \overset{\text{def}}{=} \neg\Box_i^k \neg\varphi$

defines the concept of belief compatibility. The formula $\Diamond_i^k \varphi$ has to be read "φ would be compatible with agent i's explicit beliefs, for some removal of at most k pieces of information from her belief base".

Example 1. Let us discuss the informal meaning of some formulas by means of an example of a single robot i exploring an area. Formula $\triangle_i fire$ says that she explicitly believes there is fire. We could also have $\triangle_i(fire \rightarrow danger)$. Thus, we would have $\Box_i^0 danger$. If now we also have $\triangle_i radiation$ and $\triangle_i(radiation \rightarrow danger)$, we would have $\Box_i^1 danger$. In words, the agent would believe that there is a danger at strength 1, because she would still infer *danger* even if at most one explicit belief is removed.

We denote by $\mathcal{L}^-$ the fragment of language $\mathcal{L}$ obtained by the rule: [4] $\varphi ::= \alpha \mid \neg\varphi \mid \varphi_1 \wedge \varphi_2 \mid \Box_i^0 \varphi$. The abbreviations $\Box_i \varphi \overset{\text{def}}{=} \Box_i^0 \varphi$ and $\Diamond_i \varphi \overset{\text{def}}{=} \Diamond_i^0 \varphi$ define the concepts of ungraded implicit belief and belief compatibility. Moreover, the abbreviation $\Box_i^{=k} \varphi \overset{\text{def}}{=} \Box_i^k \varphi \wedge \neg\Box_i^{k+1} \varphi$ has to be read "agent i believes that φ with degree (or strength) equal to k".

3   Belief Base Semantics

Following [34, 36], we now present a formal semantics for the language $\mathcal{L}$ exploiting belief bases. Unlike the standard Kripke semantics for epistemic logic in which the notions of epistemic alternative and plausibility of a world (or state) are given as primitive, in this semantics they are defined from the primitive concept of belief base.

Definition 1 (State). *A state is a tuple $B = (B_1, \ldots, B_n, S)$ where for every $i \in Agt$, $B_i \subseteq \mathcal{L}_0$ is agent i's finite belief base, and $S \subseteq Atm$ is the actual environment. The set of all states is denoted by $\mathbf{S}$.*

The sublanguage $\mathcal{L}_0(Atm, Agt)$ is interpreted with respect to states, as follows.

Definition 2 (Satisfaction relation). *Let $B = (B_1, \ldots, B_n, S) \in \mathbf{S}$ be a state. Then:*

$$B \models p \Longleftrightarrow p \in S,$$
$$B \models \neg\alpha \Longleftrightarrow B \not\models \alpha,$$
$$B \models \alpha_1 \wedge \alpha_2, \Longleftrightarrow B \models \alpha_1 \text{ and } B \models \alpha_2,$$
$$B \models \triangle_i \alpha \Longleftrightarrow \alpha \in B_i.$$

Observe in particular the set-theoretic interpretation of the explicit belief operator: agent i explicitly believes that α if and only if α is included in her belief base.

It is also worth considering belief correct states, according to which every fact explicitly believed by an agent is true.

Definition 3 (Belief correct state). *A state* $B = (B_1, \ldots, B_n, S)$ *is* belief correct *if and only if, for every agent* $i \in Agt$ *and for every* $\alpha \in B_i$, *we have then* $B \models \alpha$. *The set of all belief correct states is denoted by* $\mathbf{S}_{BC}$.

A multi-agent belief model (MAB) is defined to be a state supplemented with a set of states, called *context*. The latter includes all states compatible with the common ground [45], i.e., the body of information that the agents commonly believe to be the case.

Definition 4 (Multi-agent belief model). *A multi-agent belief model (MAB) is a pair* (B, Cxt), *where* $B \in \mathbf{S}$ *and* $Cxt \subseteq \mathbf{S}$. *The class of MABs is denoted by* $\mathbf{M}$.

Note that in Definition 4 we do not require $B \in Cxt$. The following definition introduces the notion of graded doxastic alternative.

Definition 5 (Graded doxastic alternatives). *Let* $i \in Agt$ *and let* $k \in \mathbb{N}$. *Then,* $\mathcal{R}_i^k$ *is the binary relation on the set* $\mathbf{S}$ *such that, for all* $B = (B_1, \ldots, B_n, S), B' = (B'_1, \ldots, B'_n, S') \in \mathbf{S}$:

$$B\mathcal{R}_i^k B' \text{ if and only if } |\{\alpha \in B_i : B' \models \alpha\}| \geq (|B_i| - k),$$

$B\mathcal{R}_i^k B'$ means that B' is a k-level doxastic alternative for agent i at B, that is to say, B' is a state that at B agent i considers possible after having removed at most k pieces of information from her belief base. Graded doxastic accessibility relations induce a plausibility ordering over states, as in [32,44].[2] For notational convenience, we write $\mathcal{R}_i$ instead of $\mathcal{R}_i^0$. Clearly, $B\mathcal{R}_i B'$ if and only if $B' \models \alpha$, for every $\alpha \in B_i$.

The following definition extends Definition 2 to the full language $\mathcal{L}$. Its formulas are interpreted with respect to MABs. (We omit Boolean cases, as they are defined in the usual way.)

Definition 6 (Satisfaction relation (cont.)). *Let* $(B, Cxt) \in \mathbf{M}$. *Then:*

$$(B, Cxt) \models \alpha \Longleftrightarrow B \models \alpha,$$
$$(B, Cxt) \models \Box_i^k \varphi \Longleftrightarrow \forall B' \in Cxt : \text{if } B\mathcal{R}_i^k B' \text{ then } (B', Cxt) \models \varphi.$$

We consider the subclass of MABs that guarantee correctness of the agents' beliefs.

Definition 7 (Belief correct MAB). *The MAB* (B, Cxt) *is* belief correct *(BC) if and only if* $B \in Cxt$ *and, for every* $i \in Agt$ *and for every* $B' \in Cxt$, $B'\mathcal{R}_i B'$. *The class of MABs satisfying BC is denoted by* $\mathbf{M}_{BC}$.

---

[2] Note that a belief base B_i may contain non-independent formulas p and $p \wedge p$ which count twice when computing relations $\mathcal{R}_i^k$. We could consider non-redundant belief bases in which redundant formulas such as $p \wedge p$ are not allowed. We leave the analysis of the notion of redundancy for future work.

Saying that (B, Cxt) satisfies BC is the same thing as saying that $B \in Cxt$ and, for every $i \in Agt$, the relation $\mathcal{R}_i \cap (Cxt \times Cxt)$ is reflexive. The condition $B \in Cxt$ in Definition 7 is necessary to make the agents' implicit beliefs correct, i.e., to make the formula $\square_i \varphi \rightarrow \varphi$ valid.

As the following proposition highlights, belief correctness for MABs is completely characterized by the fact that the actual world is included in the agents' common ground and that the agents' explicit beliefs are correct in the sense of Definition 3.

Proposition 1. *A MAB (B, Cxt) satisfies BC if and only if $B \in Cxt$ and $Cxt \subseteq \mathbf{S}_{BC}$.*

Let $\varphi \in \mathcal{L}$. We say that φ is valid relative to the class $\mathbf{M}$ (resp. $\mathbf{M}_{BC}$), denoted by $\models_{\mathbf{M}} \varphi$ (resp. $\models_{\mathbf{M}_{BC}} \varphi$), if and only if, for every $(B, Cxt) \in \mathbf{M}$ (resp. $(B, Cxt) \in \mathbf{M}_{BC}$) we have $(B, Cxt) \models \varphi$. We say that φ is satisfiable for the class $\mathbf{M}$ (resp. $\mathbf{M}_{BC}$) if and only if $\neg\varphi$ is not valid for the class $\mathbf{M}$ (resp. $\mathbf{M}_{BC}$).

As the following theorem indicates, graded belief operators add expressivity to the non-graded language $\mathcal{L}^-$.

Theorem 1. *The language $\mathcal{L}$ is strictly more expressive than the language $\mathcal{L}^-$.*

Proof (sketch). By contradiction, suppose there is a formula φ from the single-agent version of $\mathcal{L}^-$ that is equivalent to $\square_1^1 p$. Let us consider a formula $\psi = p \wedge \cdots \wedge p$ such that $\triangle_1 \psi$ does not appear in φ. We have:

- $((\{p, \psi\}, \emptyset), \mathbf{S}) \models \square_1^1 p$;
- $((\{p, \psi\}, \emptyset), \mathbf{S}) \models \varphi$;

- $((\{p\}, \emptyset), \mathbf{S}) \not\models \square_1^1 p$;
- $((\{p\}, \emptyset), \mathbf{S}) \not\models \varphi$

By $((\{p, \psi\}, \emptyset), \mathbf{S}) \models \varphi$, we also have $((\{p\}, \emptyset), \mathbf{S}) \models \varphi$ because φ does not talk about ψ being in the base of 1. □

4   Social Influence

In this section, we apply the language $\mathcal{L}$ and its belief base semantics to the analysis of the concept of social influence. In social sciences [41], social influence is conceived as the causal connection between an agent's belief (or opinion) and other agents' beliefs: an agent (the influencee) believes that α because and as long as she believes that other credible agents (the influencers) believe that α. It has been shown to play a crucial role in information dynamics in multi-agent systems (see, e.g., [14,21,43]).

The belief in the information source's credibility is an essential component of the influence process. Indeed, for a rational agent i to be influenced by another agent j's opinion, i must believe that j's opinion is correct and well-founded, that is to say, j must not have wrong beliefs about the subject at matter.

In line with [15], we assume that an agent i's belief that another agent j's is credible about α is identified with i's belief that 'if agent j believes that α, then α is true'. This captures a form of i's trust in j, namely, i's trust in j's credibility about α. We note the latter by $Trust(i, j, \alpha)$ and define it as follows:

$$Trust(i, j, \alpha) \stackrel{\text{def}}{=} \triangle_i(\triangle_j \alpha \to \alpha).$$

Let $2^{Agt*} = 2^{Agt} \setminus \{\emptyset\}$ and its elements be denoted by $G, G', \ldots$ As the following proposition indicates if an agent i has trusts in the credibility of each information source in group G and explictly believes that each of them explictly believes that α, then she should conclude that α is true with strength at least $|G| - 1$. This means that an agent cumulates information received from different credible information sources to determine her degree of belief: the higher the number of credible sources in support of α, the stronger the influence, the higher the degree of the belief that α. We recall that $\square_i$ is defined by $\square_i^0$. This is the reason why the resulting degree of belief is $|G| - 1$ instead of $|G|$. For example, if G is a singleton, the resulting degree is 0 which means that agent i believes that α.

Proposition 2. *Let $i \in Agt$ and $G \in 2^{Agt*}$. Then,*

$$\models_{\mathbf{M}} \bigwedge_{j \in G} \left(Trust(i, j, \alpha) \wedge \triangle_i \triangle_j \alpha \right) \to \square_i^{|G|-1} \alpha. \tag{1}$$

The following example concretely illustrates the social influence process with the help of the belief base semantics.

Example 2. Suppose agent cb is a chatbot connected to the Internet who has to provide information to a human user about the quality of a certain movie. The chatbot has access to four recommender systems about movies: Netflix (nf), Rotten Tomatoes (rt), IMDb (im) and Amazon (am). Each recommender system provides an evaluation whether the movie is good or not which is used by the chabot to form an opinion about the movie. Consider an arbitrary MAB (B, Cxt) such that agent cb's belief base in B is:

$$B_{\text{cb}} = \bigcup_{j \in \{\text{nf,rt,im,am}\}} \{\triangle_j good \to good, \triangle_j \neg good \to \neg good\} \cup$$
$$\{\triangle_{\text{nf}} good, \triangle_{\text{rt}} good, \triangle_{\text{am}} good, \triangle_{\text{im}} \neg good\}.$$

We have the following:

$$(B, Cxt) \models \bigwedge_{j \in \{\text{nf,rt,im,am}\}} \left(Trust(\text{cb}, j, good) \wedge Trust(\text{cb}, j, \neg good) \right) \wedge$$
$$\triangle_{\text{cb}} \triangle_{\text{nf}} good \wedge \triangle_{\text{cb}} \triangle_{\text{rt}} good \wedge \triangle_{\text{cb}} \triangle_{\text{am}} good \wedge$$
$$\triangle_{\text{cb}} \triangle_{\text{im}} \neg good \wedge \square_{\text{cb}}^{=2} good \wedge \square_{\text{cb}}^{=0} \neg good.$$

This means that in the situation described by the MAB (B, Cxt), (i) cb trusts the credibility of each of the four recommender systems both about the fact that the movie is good and about the fact that the movie is not good, and (ii) cb believes that Netflix, Rotten Tomatoes and Amazon evaluates it as a good movie, while IMDb evaluates it as a not good movie. Furthermore, thanks to (i) and (ii), we have that (iii) cb believes that the movie is good with strength equal to 2 and believes that the movie is not good with strength equal to 0. This means that cb's degree of belief that the movie is good, is strictly higher than the degree of belief that the movie is not good, since there are more credible sources in support of the former than credible sources in support of the latter.

It is worth noting that in Proposition 2, information sources are supposed to be independent. Indeed, formula $Trust(i, j, \alpha)$ relies on the assumption that i believes that j is credible about α, *regardless of what the other agents believe.* This explains why j's opinion contributes to increase i's strength of belief. The situation is different when agent i merely trusts the credibility of a group of information sources including agent j as a whole. In this case, i will not be influenced by j's beliefs unless the other sources have the same belief. This covers the case in which information sources in the group are dependent so that their opinions jointly contribute to increase i's strength of belief, but not individually. To see this formally, let us generalize the previous definition to trust in a group's credibility, as follows:

$$Trust(i, G, \alpha) \stackrel{\text{def}}{=} \triangle_i \big(\big(\bigwedge_{j \in G} \triangle_j \alpha \big) \to \alpha \big) \text{ with } G \in 2^{Agt*}.$$

As the following proposition indicates, trusting a group's credibility about α and believing that each source in the group believes that α is sufficient for forming the belief that α. Nonetheless, it is not sufficient for forming a belief with a stricly higher degree, since the group counts as a single unit of influence.

Proposition 3. *Let $i \in Agt$, $G \in 2^{Agt*}$. Then,*

$$\models_\mathbf{M} \big(Trust(i, G, \alpha) \wedge \bigwedge_{j \in G} \triangle_i \triangle_j \alpha \big) \to \Box_i \alpha, \tag{2}$$

$$\not\models_\mathbf{M} \big(Trust(i, G, p) \wedge \bigwedge_{j \in G} \triangle_i \triangle_j p \big) \to \Box_i^1 p. \tag{3}$$

5 Axiomatics and Decidability

This section is devoted to define two logical systems of explicit belief and graded implicit belief. They are called LGDA and LGDA$_{\mathbf{T}_{\Box_i}}$, where LGDA stands for "Logic of Graded Doxastic Attitudes".

Let us start with the definition of the two logics.

Definition 8 (LGDA). *We define* LGDA *to be the extension of classical propositional logic by the following axioms and rule of inference:*

$$(\Box_i^k \varphi \wedge \Box_i^k(\varphi \rightarrow \psi)) \rightarrow \Box_i^k \psi \tag{$\mathbf{K}_{\Box_i^k}$}$$

$$\Box_i^k \varphi \rightarrow \Box_i^{k'} \varphi \ \text{if} \ k' \leq k \tag{$\mathbf{Mon}_{\Box_i^k}$}$$

$$\Big(\bigwedge_{\alpha \in X} \triangle_i \alpha\Big) \rightarrow \Box_i^k \bigvee_{\substack{X' \subseteq X: \\ |X'| \geq |X| - k}} \bigwedge_{\beta \in X'} \beta \ \text{if} \ |X| > k \tag{$\mathbf{Int}_{\triangle_i, \Box_i}$}$$

$$\frac{\varphi}{\Box_i^k \varphi} \tag{$\mathbf{Nec}_{\Box_i^k}$}$$

We define LGDA$_{\mathbf{T}_{\Box_i}}$ *to be the extension of the logic* LGDA *by the following axiom:*

$$\Box_i \varphi \rightarrow \varphi \tag{$\mathbf{T}_{\Box_i}$}$$

Axiom $\mathrm{K}_{\Box_i^k}$ and the rule of inference $\mathrm{Nec}_{\Box_i^k}$ are the basic principles of the normal modal operator $\Box_i^k$ for graded implicit belief. Axiom $\mathbf{Mon}_{\Box_i^k}$ is a monotonicity principle for graded implicit belief: implicitly believing that φ with degree at least k implies implicitly believing that φ with degree at least k' if $k' \leq k$. Finally, Axiom $\mathbf{Int}_{\triangle_i, \Box_i}$ is the interaction principle between explicit and graded implicit belief: if an agent explicitly believes every fact in X, then she should implicitly believe with degree at least k that there exists a subset X' of X such that $|X'| \geq |X| - k$ and every fact in X' is true. The reason why we do not consider the case $|X| \leq k$ is that if $|X| \leq k$ then $\Box_i^k(\bigvee_{X' \subseteq X: |X'| \geq |X| - k} \bigwedge_{\beta \in X'} \beta)$ is equivalent to $\Box_i^k \top$ which in turn is equivalent to $\top$. It is also worth noting that if $|X| = 1$ then Axiom $\mathbf{Int}_{\triangle_i, \Box_i}$ acquires the simpler form $\triangle_i \alpha \rightarrow \Box_i \alpha$.

As the following theorem highlights, the two logics are sound and complete relative to the belief base semantics defined in the previous section.

Theorem 2. *The logic* LGDA *is sound and complete for the class of MABs, whereas the logic* LGDA$_{\mathbf{T}_{\Box_i}}$ *is sound and complete for the class of belief correct MABs.*

Proof (sketch). The theorem relies on the fact that the belief base semantics for the language $\mathcal{L}$ given in Sect. 2 is equivalent to a "weaker" semantics exploiting enriched Kripke structures of the form $M = (W, \mathcal{D}, \mathcal{N}, \mathcal{V})$ where W is a non-empty set of worlds, $\mathcal{D} : Agt \times W \longrightarrow 2^{\mathcal{L}_0}$ with $\mathcal{D}(i, w)$ finite for every $i \in Agt$ and $w \in W$, $\mathcal{N} : Agt \times W \times \mathbb{N} \longrightarrow 2^W$ and $\mathcal{V} : Atm \longrightarrow 2^W$ such that for all $i \in Agt$, for all $w \in W$ and for all $k, k' \in \mathbb{N}$:

$$\mathcal{N}(i, w, k) \subseteq \big\{ v \in W : |Sat_M(i, w, v)| \geq (|\mathcal{D}(i, w)| - k) \big\},$$
$$\mathcal{N}(i, w, k') \subseteq \mathcal{N}(i, w, k) \ \text{if} \ k' \leq k,$$

and with respect to which $\mathcal{L}$-formulas are interpreted as follows (boolean cases are omitted for simplicity): (i) $(M, w) \models p$ iff $w \in \mathcal{V}(p)$, (ii) $(M, w) \models \triangle_i \alpha$

iff $\alpha \in \mathcal{D}(i,w)$, (iii) $(M,w) \models \square_i^k \varphi$ iff $\forall v \in \mathcal{N}(i,w,k) : (M,v) \models \varphi$, with $Sat_M(i,w,v) = \{\alpha \in \mathcal{D}(i,w) : (M,v) \models \alpha\}$. $\square$

The following decidability result is a consequence of the finite model property for logics LGDA and LGDA$_{\mathbf{T}_{\square_i}}$.

Theorem 3. *The satisfiability problem of* LGDA *(resp.* LGDA$_{\mathbf{T}_{\square_i}}$*) relative to the class of MABs (resp. belief correct MABs) is decidable.*

6   Conditional Belief Operators

In this section, we extend the language $\mathcal{L}$ by conditional belief operators of type $\square_i^{+X}$ and $\square_i^{-X}$. They capture, respectively, what agent i would implicitly believe if she added all information in X to her belief base, and what she would believe if she removed all information in X from her belief base. The new language is denoted by $\mathcal{L}_{cond}$. The semantic interpretation of these new operators is given in the following definition.

Definition 9. *Let* $(B, Cxt) \in \mathbf{M}$ *with* $B = (B_1, \dots, B_n, S)$. *Then,*

$$(B, Cxt) \models \square_i^{+X} \varphi \ \textit{iff} \ (B^{i+X}, Cxt) \models \square_i \varphi,$$
$$(B, Cxt) \models \square_i^{-X} \varphi \ \textit{iff} \ (B^{i-X}, Cxt) \models \square_i \varphi,$$

where $B^{i+X} = (B_1^{i+X}, \dots, B_n^{i+X}, S^{i+X})$ *and* $B^{i-X} = (B_1^{i-X}, \dots, B_n^{i-X}, S^{i-X})$ *with:*

$$B_i^{i+X} = B_i \cup X, \qquad\qquad\qquad B_i^{i-X} = B_i \setminus X,$$
$$B_j^{i+X} = B_j^{i-X} = B_j \ \textit{if} \ i \neq j, \qquad\qquad S^{i+X} = S^{i-X} = S.$$

Interestingly, the following axioms show that the new operators $\square_i^{+X}$ and $\square_i^{-X}$ do not add expressivity to the language.

$$\square_i^{+X} \varphi \leftrightarrow \square_i \big((\bigwedge_{\alpha \in X} \alpha) \to \varphi\big) \tag{+X}$$

$$\square_i^{-X} \varphi \leftrightarrow \bigwedge_{X' \subseteq X} \Big(\big((\bigwedge_{\alpha \in X'} \triangle_i \alpha) \wedge (\bigwedge_{\alpha \in X \setminus X'} \neg \triangle_i \alpha)\big) \to$$
$$\bigwedge_{X'' \subseteq X'} \square_i^{|X''|} \big((\bigwedge_{\alpha \in X''} \neg \alpha) \to \varphi\big)\Big) \tag{-X}$$

In axiom +X, we simply evaluate φ-states, possible for agent i, that satisfy the guard $\bigwedge_{\alpha \in X} \alpha$. Axiom -X mimics the removing of X. To do that, we first identify the subset X' of formulas in X that actually appear in the base of agent i. Formulas in X' are the formulas that are indeed removed while formulas in $X \setminus X'$ are not present in the base of agent i. Then we should impose that φ

holds in all possible worlds when formulas in X' are not enforced anymore. In particular, the clause for $X'' = X'$ says that if we remove $|X'|$ formulas, and if these $|X'|$ removed formulas are those in X' and are false (the guard $\bigwedge_{\alpha \in X'} \neg\alpha$) then φ holds. The definition of axiom -X is more subtle. As some formulas in $\alpha \in X'$ cannot be made false (because they are tautologies), we consider all guards $\bigwedge_{\alpha \in X''} \neg\alpha$ for all subsets X'' of X'.

Theorem 4. *Axioms +X and -X are valid.*

We call LGCDA (Logic of Graded and Conditional Doxastic Attitudes) the extension of logic LGDA by the previous Axioms -X and -X, and LGCDA$_{\mathbf{T}_{\square_i}}$ the corresponding extension of the logic LGDA$_{\mathbf{T}_{\square_i}}$. It is routine exercise to check that these axioms are valid relative to the class of MABs. Thus, by Corollary 2, we have the following completeness result for the logics LGCDA and LGCDA$_{\mathbf{T}_{\square_i}}$.

Theorem 5. *The logic LGCDA is sound and complete for the class of MABs, whereas the logic LGCDA$_{\mathbf{T}_{\square_i}}$ is sound and complete for the class of belief correct MABs.*

The following theorem is a direct consequence of Theorem 3.

Theorem 6. *The satisfiability problem of LGCDA (resp. LGCDA$_{\mathbf{T}_{\square_i}}$) relative to the class of MABs (resp. belief correct MABs) is decidable.*

7   Model Checking

Consider these compact formulations of the model checking problems for the language $\mathcal{L}_{cond}$.

Model checking

Given: $\varphi \in \mathcal{L}_{cond}$, $\alpha \in \mathcal{L}_0$ and a finite $B \in \mathbf{S}$.
Question: Do we have $(B, \mathbf{S}(\alpha)) \models \varphi$?
with $\mathbf{S}(\alpha) = \{B \in \mathbf{S} : B \models \alpha\}$.

Belief correct model checking

Given: $\varphi \in \mathcal{L}_{cond}$, $\alpha \in \mathcal{L}_0$ and a finite $B \in \mathbf{S}_{BC}$ with $B \models \alpha$.
Question: Do we have $(B, \mathbf{S}_{BC}(\alpha)) \models \varphi$?
with $\mathbf{S}_{BC}(\alpha) = \{B \in \mathbf{S}_{BC} : B \models \alpha\}$.

---

where the state $B = (B_1, \dots, B_n, S)$ is said to be finite if S and every B_i are finite. Note that, thanks to Proposition 1 and the fact that $B \models \alpha$, the MAB $(B, \mathbf{S}_{BC}(\alpha))$ in the belief correct variant of model checking belongs to the model class $\mathbf{M}_{BC}$, as expected.

In [35], it is proved that the previous two problems are PSPACE-hard, already for the fragment of $\mathcal{L}$ with only implicit belief operators of type $\square_i$.

We are going to focus on the complexity upper bound. To this aim, we follow the approach given in [26]. The algorithm given in Fig. 1 checks that a formula φ is true in a given finite state B. Checking $B' \models \alpha$ (see Definition 5) can be done in polynomial time because α does not contain any implicit belief operator; thus it is reducible to the propositional problem by stating any explicit belief as a fresh proposition. Once $|\{\alpha \in B_i : B' \models \alpha\}|$ is computed, the comparison $|\{\alpha \in B_i : B' \models \alpha\}| \geq (|B_i| - k)$, can be done in polynomial time. Furthermore checking that B' is in $\mathbf{S}(\alpha)$ (or $\mathbf{S}_{BC}(\alpha)$) can be done in polynomial time. So checking $B\mathcal{R}_i^k B'$ can be done in polynomial time and space. We are now ready to establish the PSPACE upper bound for the two model checking problems.

Theorem 7. *Both the model checking problem and the belief correct model checking problem are in PSPACE.*

Proof (sketch). The number of nested calls in $mc(B, \varphi)$ is bounded by the size of φ. The local memory used by the recursive call is polynomial in the size of the initial B and the size of φ. Loops "**for** all B'..." are performed by enumerating the B' containing correct subformulas of formulas in the initial B and in the initial formula φ. Despite there is an exponential number of such B', storing the current B' only requires a polynomial amount of space.

The algorithm for the belief correct model checking is similar: we just check each time that the states B' under consideration are correct (Definition 3).   □

```
procedure mc(B, φ)
    match φ do
        case p: return B ⊨ p
        case ¬ψ: return not mc(B, ψ)
        case ψ₁ ∧ ψ₂: return mc(B, ψ₁) and mc(B, ψ₂)
        case △ᵢα: return α ∈ Bᵢ
        case □ᵢᵏψ:
            for all B' such that BRᵢᵏB' do
                if not mc(B', ψ) return false
        case □ᵢ⁺ˣψ:
            for all B' such that B⁺ˣRᵢ⁰B' do
                if not mc(B', ψ) return false
        case □ᵢ⁻ˣψ:
            for all B' such that B⁻ˣRᵢ⁰B' do
                if not mc(B', ψ) return false
    return true          // when all tests in for loops failed
```

Fig. 1. Generic algorithm for model checking.

8 Epistemic Explanation

In this section, we leverage the language $\mathcal{L}_{cond}$ to model a variety of notions of epistemic explanation. The standard notion of explanation [24, 29] is relative to some background theory which together with the *explanans* is used to explain the *explanandum*. As emphasized by [7], epistemic explanation is relative to an agent's epistemic state: the agent explains a given fact or observation in the light of her background knowledge. Existing formal models of epistemic explanation including [7,19,20] focus on the single agent case. We generalize the analysis of epistemic explanation to the multi-agent case in which (i) different agents may have diverging explanations of the same fact, and (ii) an agent may include other agents' beliefs in the explanation of a given fact.

Following [7], we distinguish *factual* explanation from *hypothetical* explanation. In factual explanation both the explanans and the explanandum are believed by the explaining agent, while they are not in hypothetical explanation. Specifically, a factual explanation is a body of information in the agent's belief base which supports an actual belief of the agent. A hypothetical explanation is relative to a fact that is not actually believed by the agent but that the agent would have believed, if she had believed that the explanans is true. Let us first define factual explanation:

$$FactExpl_i(X, \varphi) \stackrel{\text{def}}{=} \left(\bigwedge_{\alpha \in X} \triangle_i \alpha \right) \wedge \square_i \varphi \wedge \neg \square_i^{-X} \varphi.$$

Formula $FactExpl_i(X, \varphi)$ has to be read "according to agent i, X is a factual explanation of φ", where X is the explanans and φ is the explanandum. This means that (i) i explicitly believes all facts in X, (ii) i implicitly believes φ, and (iii) if i removed all information in X from her belief base, she would not believe φ anymore. In other words, a factual explanation is a subset of the agent's belief base which is necessary for the agent to derive φ. Note that this notion of factual explanation can be used by the agent to detect and explain inconsistency of her belief base. In particular, $FactExpl_i(X, \bot)$ means that, according to agent i, inconsistency of her belief base depends on the body of information X.

Most formal theories of explanation [4,28] agree on a minimality requirement. In order to account for minimality of factual explanation, we need to assume that, for every strict subset X' of X, removing all information in X' from the belief base does not affect i's belief that φ. That is, we define:

$$MinFactExpl_i(X, \varphi) \stackrel{\text{def}}{=} FactExpl_i(X, \varphi) \wedge \bigwedge_{\alpha \in X} \square_i^{-(X \setminus \{\alpha\})} \varphi,$$

where $MinFactExpl_i(X, \varphi)$ has to be read "according to agent i, X is a minimal factual explanation of φ". Like $FactExpl_i(X, \varphi)$ the size of $MinFactExpl_i(X, \varphi)$ is polynomial in the size of X. Note that since $\square_i^{-X} \varphi$ implies $\square_i^{-X'} \varphi$ for $X' \subset X$, the second conjunct in the definition of $MinFactExpl_i(X, \varphi)$ is equivalent to $\bigwedge_{X' \subset X} \square_i^{-X'} \varphi$.

The following example illustrates the notion of minimal factual explanation.

Example 3. Let us go back to the example of Sect. 4. By the model checking algorithm of Fig. 1, we can verify that:

$$(B, Cxt) \models MinFactExpl_{cb}(\{\triangle_{nf} good, \triangle_{rt} good, \triangle_{am} good\}, good).$$

This means that the fact that every agent in $\{nf, rt, am\}$ explicitly believes the movie is good is for agent cb a minimal factual explanation that the movie is good. Thus, the body of information $\{\triangle_{nf} good, \triangle_{rt} good, \triangle_{am} good\}$ is necessary for cb to conclude $good$.

We end this section with a definition of hypothetical explanation:

$$HypExpl_i(X, \varphi) \overset{\text{def}}{=} \big(\bigwedge_{\alpha \in X} \neg\triangle_i\alpha \big) \wedge \Box_i^{+X}\varphi \wedge \neg\Box_i^{+X}\bot.$$

$HypExpl_i(X, \varphi)$ has to be read "according to agent i, X is a hypothetical explanation of φ", in the sense that: (i) no piece of information in X is included in i's belief base, (ii) i does not believe that φ, (iii) the body of information X would be sufficient for agent i to consistently conclude φ. Similarly to factual explanation, minimality is captured by assuming that there is no strict subset X' of X that is sufficient for agent i to conclude φ:

$$MinHypExpl_i(X, \varphi) \overset{\text{def}}{=} HypExpl_i(X, \varphi) \wedge \bigwedge_{\alpha \in X} \neg\Box_i^{+(X\setminus\{\alpha\})}\varphi.$$

$MinHypExpl_i(X, \varphi)$ has to be read "according to agent i, X is a minimal hypothetical explanation of φ". Note that since $\Box_i^{+X'}\varphi$ implies $\Box_i^{+X}\varphi$ for $X' \subset X$, the second conjunct in the definition of $MinHypExpl_i(X, \varphi)$ is equivalent to $\bigwedge_{X'\subset X} \neg\Box_i^{+X'}\varphi$.

9   Conclusion

We defined a graded doxastic language $\mathcal{L}$ to reason about an agent's implicit beliefs, when a given *number* of explicit beliefs are removed from her belief base.

Our approach could be relevant in many applications: the agents receive beliefs (including higher-order beliefs, e.g., agent 1 knows that agent 2 knows that p) from different sources, or different reasoners. Moreover, the model checking procedure presented in the paper helps to understand what an agents still believes if some beliefs are removed from her belief base. Also, non-AI experts do not need to learn several languages: in our approach, we emphasize that the query language (e.g., does drone 1 believes that drone 2 believes the area is safe?), the inner state description (formulas in bases), and the language for explanation are the *same*.

Concerning the contributions, we showed that the language $\mathcal{L}$ is strictly more expressive that the ungraded doxastic language $\mathcal{L}^-$. We also introduced the language $\mathcal{L}_{cond}$ to reason about an agent's implicit beliefs when a given *set* of explicit beliefs are added/removed to/from her belief base. The languages $\mathcal{L}$ and $\mathcal{L}_{cond}$ are equally expressive and we provided a sound and complete axiomatization for both of them.

Directions of future work are manifold. On the theoretical side, we plan to study complexity of the satisfiability checking problem for $\mathcal{L}$ and $\mathcal{L}_{cond}$. On the practical side, we plan to implement the model checking algorithm for $\mathcal{L}$ and $\mathcal{L}_{cond}$. We also plan to propose a tool for automatic verification and generation of epistemic explanations in multi-agent scenarios involving autonomous agents endowed with epistemic states.

Acknowledgements. Support from the ANR-3IA Artificial and Natural Intelligence Toulouse Institute and from the ANR project CoPains (grant number ANR-18-CE33-0012) is gratefully acknowledged.

References

1. Aucher, G.: A combined system for update logic and belief revision. In: Barley, M.W., Kasabov, N. (eds.) PRIMA 2004. LNCS (LNAI), vol. 3371, pp. 1–17. Springer, Heidelberg (2005). https://doi.org/10.1007/978-3-540-32128-6_1
2. Balbiani, P., Fernández-Duque, D., Herzig, A., Lorini, E.: Stratified evidence logics. In: Proceedings of the Twenty-Eighth International Joint Conference on Artificial Intelligence (IJCAI 2019), pp. 1523–1529 (2019)
3. Baltag, A., Smets, S.: A qualitative theory of dynamic interactive belief revision. In: Bonanno, G., van der Hoek, W., Wooldridge, M. (eds.) Logic and the Foundations of Game and Decision Theory, volume 3 of Texts in Logic and Games, pp. 13–60. Amsterdam University Press (2008)
4. Benferhat, S., Dubois, D., Prade, H.: Some syntactic approaches to the handling of inconsistent knowledge bases: a comparative study part 1: the flat case. Stud. Logica. **58**, 17–45 (1997)
5. Benferhat, S., Dubois, D., Prade, H., Williams, M.-A.: A practical approach to revising prioritized knowledge bases. Stud. Logica. **70**(1), 105–130 (2002)
6. Bolander, T., Andersen, M.B.: Epistemic planning for single- and multi-agent systems. J. Appl. Non-Classical Logics **21**(1), 656–680 (2011)
7. Boutilier, C., Beche, V.: Abduction as belief revision. Artif. Intell. **77**(1), 43–94 (1995)
8. Budzynska, K., Kacprzak, M.: A logic for reasoning about persuasion. Fund. Inform. **85**, 51–65 (2008)
9. Burrows, M., Abadi, M., Needham, R.: A logic of authentication. ACM Trans. Comput. Syst. **8**(1), 18–36 (1990)
10. Charrier, T., Pinchinat, S., Schwarzentruber, F.: Symbolic model checking of public announcement protocols. J. Logic Comput. **29**(8), 1211–1249 (2019)
11. Charrier, T., Schwarzentruber, F.: Arbitrary public announcement logic with mental programs. In: Proceedings of the 2015 International Conference on Autonomous Agents and Multiagent Systems (AAMAS 2015), pp. 1471–1479. ACM (2015)
12. Charrier, T., Schwarzentruber, F.: A succinct language for dynamic epistemic logic. In: Proceedings of the 16th Conference on Autonomous Agents and MultiAgent Systems (AAMAS 2017), pp. 123–131. ACM (2017)
13. Charrier, T., Schwarzentruber, F.: Complexity of dynamic epistemic logic with common knowledge. In: Proceedings of the 12th conference on Advances in Modal Logic 12, pp. 103–122. College Publications (2018)
14. Christoff, Z.: A logic for social influence through communication. In: Proceedings of the Eleventh European Workshop on Multi-Agent Systems (EUMAS 2013), volume 1113 of CEUR Workshop Proceedings, pp. 31–39. CEUR-WS.org (2013)

15. Demolombe, R.: Reasoning about trust: a formal logical framework. In: Jensen, C., Poslad, S., Dimitrakos, T. (eds.) iTrust 2004. LNCS, vol. 2995, pp. 291–303. Springer, Heidelberg (2004). https://doi.org/10.1007/978-3-540-24747-0_22

16. Dubois, D., Prade, H.: Possibility Theory: An Approach to Computerized Processing of Uncertainty. Plenum Press (1988)

17. Fagin, R., Halpern, J.: Reasoning about knowledge and probability. J. Assoc. Comput. Mach. **41**(2), 340–367 (1994)

18. Fagin, R., Halpern, J., Moses, Y., Vardi, M.: Reasoning about Knowledge. MIT Press, Cambridge (1995)

19. Falappa, M.A., Kern-Isberner, G., Simari, G.R.: Explanations, belief revision and defeasible reasoning. Artif. Intell. **141**, 1–28 (2002)

20. Gärdenfors, P.: A pragmatic approach to explanations. Philos. Sci. **47**(3), 404–423 (1980)

21. Grandi, U., Lorini, E., Perrussel, L.: Propositional opinion diffusion. In: Proceedings of the 2015 International Conference on Autonomous Agents and Multiagent Systems (AAMAS 2015), pp. 989–997. ACM (2015)

22. Halpern, J.Y., Pass, R.: A knowledge-based analysis of the blockchain protocol. In: Proceedings of the Sixteenth Conference on Theoretical Aspects of Rationality and Knowledge (TARK 2017), pp. 324–335. EPTCS (2017)

23. Hansson, S.O.: Theory contraction and base contraction unified. J. Symbolic Logic **58**(2), 602–625 (1993)

24. Hempel, C., Oppenheim, P.: Studies in the logic of explanation. Philos. Sci. **15**, 135–175 (1948)

25. Herzig, A., Lorini, E., Maffre, F.: A poor man's epistemic logic based on propositional assignment and higher-order observation. In: van der Hoek, W., Holliday, W.H., Wang, W. (eds.) LORI 2015. LNCS, vol. 9394, pp. 156–168. Springer, Heidelberg (2015). https://doi.org/10.1007/978-3-662-48561-3_13

26. Herzig, A., Lorini, E., Perrotin, E., Romero, F., Schwarzentruber, F.: A logic of explicit and implicit distributed belief. In: Proceedings of the 24th European Conference on Artificial Intelligence (ECAI 2020), vol. 325, pp. 753–760. IOS Press (2020)

27. Hintikka, J.: Knowledge and Belief. Cornell University Press, New York (1962)

28. De Kleer, J.: An assumption-based TMS. Artif. Intell. **28**, 127–162 (1986)

29. Kment, B.: Counterfactuals and explanation. Mind **115**(458), 261–310 (2006)

30. Konolige, K.: What awareness isn't: a sentential view of implicit and explicit belief. In: Proceedings of the 1st Conference on Theoretical Aspects of Reasoning about Knowledge, Monterey, CA, USA, March 1986, pp. 241–250. Morgan Kaufmann (1986)

31. Kooi, B.P.: Probabilistic dynamic epistemic logic. J. Logic Lang. Inf. **12**, 381–408 (2003)

32. Laverny, N., Lang., J.: From knowledge-based programs to graded belief-based programs part I: on-line reasoning. In: Proceedings of the 16th European Conference on Artificial Intelligence, (ECAI'2004), pp. 368–372. IOS Press (2004)

33. Lismont, L., Mongin, P.: On the logic of common belief and common knowledge. Theory Decis. **37**, 75–106 (1994)

34. Lorini, E.: In praise of belief bases: Doing epistemic logic without possible worlds. In: Proceedings of the Thirty-Second AAAI Conference on Artificial Intelligence (AAAI-18), pp. 1915–1922. AAAI Press (2018)

35. Lorini, E.: Exploiting belief bases for building rich epistemic structures. In: Moss, L.S. (ed.) Proceedings of the Seventeenth Conference on Theoretical Aspects of Rationality and Knowledge (TARK 2019), volume 297 of EPTCS, pp. 332–353 (2019)
36. Lorini, E.: Rethinking epistemic logic with belief bases. Artif. Intell. **282**, 103233 (2020)
37. Lorini, E., Romero, F.: Decision procedures for epistemic logic exploiting belief bases. In: Proceedings of the 18th International Conference on Autonomous Agents and MultiAgent Systems (AAMAS 2019), pp. 944–952. IFAAMAS (2019)
38. Marinkovic, B., Glavan, P., Ognjanovic, Z., Studer, T.: A temporal epistemic logic with a non-rigid set of agents for analyzing the blockchain protocol. J. Logic Comput. **29**(5), 803–830 (2019)
39. Meyer, J.J., van der Hoek, W.: Epistemic Logic for AI and Computer Science. Cambridge University Press, Cambridge (1995)
40. Pearl, J.: From conditional oughts to qualitative decision theory. In: Heckerman, D., Mamdani, E.H., (eds.) Proceedings of UAI 1993, pp. 12–22. Morgan Kaufmann (1993)
41. Rashotte, L.: Social influence. In: Ritzer, G., Ryan, J.M. (eds.) Concise Blackwell Encyclopedia of Sociology. Blackwell (2009)
42. Rott, H.: Just because: Taking belief bases seriously. In: Logic Colloquium, vol. 98, pp. 387–408 (1998)
43. Schwind, N., Inoue, K., Bourgne, G., Konieczny, S., Marquis, P.: Belief revision games. In: Proceedings of the Twenty-Ninth AAAI Conference on Artificial Intelligence, pp. 1590–1596. AAAI Press (2015)
44. Spohn, W.: Ordinal conditional functions: a dynamic theory of epistemic states. In: Harper, W.L., Skyrms, B. (eds.) Causation in decision, belief change and statistics, pp. 105–134. Kluwer (1988)
45. Stalnaker, R.: Common ground. Linguist. Philos. **25**(5–6), 701–721 (2002)
46. van Benthem, J., van Eijck, J., Gattinger, M., Su, K.: Symbolic model checking for dynamic epistemic logic - S5 and beyond. J. Logic Comput. **28**(2), 367–402 (2018)
47. van der Hoek, W.: Modalities for Reasoning about Knowledge and Quantities. PhD thesis, Free University of Amsterdam (1992)
48. van der Hoek, W., Meyer, J.-J.C.: Graded modalities in epistemic logic. Logique Anal. **133–134**, 251–270 (1991)
49. van Ditmarsch, H.: Prolegomena to dynamic logic for belief revision. Synthese **147**(2), 229–275 (2005)
50. van Eijck, J., Schwarzentruber, F.: Epistemic probability logic simplified. In: Advances in Modal Logic 10, pp. 158–177. College Publications (2014)
51. Weydert, E.: General belief measures. In: de Mántaras, R.L., Poole, D., (eds.) Proceedings of UAI 1994, pp. 575–582. Morgan Kaufmann (1994)

Tractability Frontiers in Probabilistic Team Semantics and Existential Second-Order Logic over the Reals

Miika Hannula[1] and Jonni Virtema[2(✉)]

[1] University of Helsinki, Helsinki, Finland
miika.hannula@helsinki.fi
[2] Leibniz Universität Hannover, Hannover, Germany
virtema@thi.uni-hannover.de

Abstract. Probabilistic team semantics is a framework for logical analysis of probabilistic dependencies. Our focus is on the complexity and expressivity of probabilistic inclusion logic and its extensions. We identify a natural fragment of existential second-order logic with additive real arithmetic that captures exactly the expressivity of probabilistic inclusion logic. We furthermore relate these formalisms to linear programming, and doing so obtain PTIME data complexity for the logics. Moreover, on finite structures, we show that the full existential second-order logic with additive real arithmetic can only express NP properties.

1 Introduction

Metafinite model theory, introduced by Grädel and Gurevich [12], generalizes the approach of *finite model theory* by shifting to two-sorted structures that extend finite structures with another (often infinite) domain with some arithmetic (such as the reals with multiplication and addition), and weight functions bridging the two sorts. Finite structures enriched with real arithmetic are called $\mathbb{R}$-*structures*. *Blum-Shub-Smale machines* [3] (BSS machine for short) are essentially random access machines with registers that can store arbitrary real numbers and which can compute rational functions over reals in a single time step, and are thus perfectly suited to compute properties of $\mathbb{R}$-structures. *Descriptive complexity theory* for BSS machines and logics on metafinite structures was initiated by Grädel and Meer who showed that $\text{NP}_{\mathbb{R}}$ (i.e., non-deterministic polynomial time on BSS machines) is captured by a variant of existential second-order logic ($\text{ESO}_{\mathbb{R}}$) over $\mathbb{R}$-structures [14]. Since the work by Grädel and Meer, others (see, e.g., [6,17,19,29]) have shed more light upon *the descriptive complexity over the reals* mirroring the development of classical descriptive complexity.

In addition to metafinite structures, the connection between logical definability encompassing numerical structures and computational complexity has

The first author is supported by the Academy of Finland grant 308712. The second author is supported by the DFG grant VI 1045/1-1.

© Springer Nature Switzerland AG 2021
W. Faber et al. (Eds.): JELIA 2021, LNAI 12678, pp. 262–278, 2021.
https://doi.org/10.1007/978-3-030-75775-5_18

received attention in *constraint databases* [1,13,28]. A constraint database models, e.g., geometric data by combining a numerical *context structure*, such as the real arithmetic, with a finite set of quantifier-free formulae defining infinite database relations [23].

Renewed interest to logics on frameworks analogous to metafinite structures, and related descriptive complexity theory, is motivated by the need to model inferences utilizing numerical data values in the fields of machine learning and artificial intelligence. See e.g. [15,33] for declarative frameworks for machine learning utilizing logic, [5,31] for very recent works on logical query languages with arithmetic, and [22] for applications of descriptive complexity in machine learning.

Team semantics is the semantical framework of modern logics of dependence and independence. Introduced by Hodges [20] and adapted to dependence logic by Väänänen [32], team semantics defines truth in reference to collections of assignments, called *teams*. Team semantics is particularly suitable for a formal analysis of properties, such as the functional dependence between variables, which only arise in the presence of multiple assignments. In the past decade numerous research articles have, via re-adaptations of team semantics, shed more light into the interplay between logic and dependence. A common feature, and limitation, in all these endeavors has been their preoccupation with notions of dependence that are *qualitative* in nature. That is, notions of dependence and independence that make use of quantities, such as conditional independence in statistics, have usually fallen outside the scope of these studies.

The shift to quantitative dependencies in team semantics setting is relatively recent. While the ideas of probabilistic teams trace back to the works of Galliani [9] and Hyttinen et al. [21], a systematic study on the topic can be traced to [7,8]. In *probabilistic team semantics* the basic semantic units are probability distributions (i.e., *probabilistic teams*). This shift from set based semantics to distribution based semantics enables probabilistic notions of dependence to be embedded to the framework. In [8] probabilistic team semantics was studied in relation to the dependence concept that is most central in statistics: conditional independence. Mirroring [10,14,27] the expressiveness of probabilistic independence logic (FO($\perp\!\!\!\perp_c$)), obtained by extending first-order logic with conditional independence, was in [8,17] characterised in terms of arithmetic variants of existential second-order logic. In [17] the data complexity of FO($\perp\!\!\!\perp_c$) was also identified in the context of BSS machines and the existential theory of the reals. In [16] the focus was shifted to the expressivity hierarchies between probabilistic logics defined in terms of different quantitative dependencies.

Of all the dependence concepts thus far investigated in team semantics, that of *inclusion* has arguably turned out to be the most intriguing and fruitful. One reason is that *inclusion logic*, which arises from this concept, can only define properties of teams that are decidable in polynomial time [11]. In contrast, other natural team-based logics, such as dependence and independence logic, capture non-deterministic polynomial time [10,27,32], and many variants, such as team logic, have an even higher complexity [26]. Thus it should come as no surprise if quantitative variants of many team-based logics turn out be intractable; in principle, adding arithmetical operations and/or counting cannot be a mitigating factor when it comes to complexity.

In this paper we focus on the complexity and expressivity of *probabilistic inclusion logic*, which is the extension of first-order logic with so-called *marginal identity atoms* defined on probabilistic teams. The marginal identity atom $x \approx y$ states that the probability of x being a is the same as the probability of y being a, for all values a.

Our Contribution. We use strong results from linear programming to obtain the following complexity results restricted to finite structures. We identify a natural fragment of additive $\mathrm{ESO}_{\mathbb{R}}$ (that is, *almost conjunctive* $(\ddot{\exists}^* \forall^*)_{\mathbb{R}}[\leq, +, \mathrm{SUM}, 0, 1]$) which captures P on ordered structures (see page 4 for a definition). In contrast, we show that the full additive $\mathrm{ESO}_{\mathbb{R}}$ captures NP. Moreover, we establish that the so-called *loose fragments*, almost conjunctive $\mathrm{L}\text{-}(\ddot{\exists}^* \forall^*)_{d[0,1]}[=, \mathrm{SUM}, 0, 1]$ and $\mathrm{L}\text{-}\mathrm{ESO}_{d[0,1]}[=, \mathrm{SUM}, 0, 1]$, of the aforementioned logics have the same expressivity as probabilistic inclusion logic and its extension with dependence atoms, respectively. The characterizations of P and NP hold also for these fragments. Finally, we show that inclusion logic can be conservatively embedded into its probabilistic variant, when restricted to probabilistic teams that are uniformly distributed. From this we obtain an alternative proof through linear systems (that is entirely different from the original proof of Galliani and Hella [11]) for the fact that inclusion logic can express only polynomial time properties.

2   Existential Second-Order Logics on $\mathbb{R}$-Structures

In addition to finite relational structures, we consider their numerical extensions by adding real numbers ($\mathbb{R}$) as a second domain sort and functions that map tuples over the finite domain to $\mathbb{R}$. Throughout the paper structures are assumed to have at least two elements. In the sequel, τ and σ will always denote a finite relational and a finite functional vocabulary, respectively. The arities of function variables f and relation variables R are denoted by $\mathrm{ar}(f)$ and $\mathrm{ar}(R)$, resp. If f is a function with domain $\mathrm{Dom}(f)$ and A a set, we define $f \restriction A$ to be the function with domain $\mathrm{Dom}(f) \cap A$ that agrees with f for each element in its domain. Given a finite set S, a function $f \colon S \to [0, 1]$ that maps elements of S to elements of the closed interval $[0, 1]$ of real numbers such that $\sum_{s \in S} f(s) = 1$ is called a *(probability) distribution*, and the *support* of f is defined as $\mathrm{Supp}(f) := \{s \in S \mid f(s) > 0\}$. Also, f is called *uniform* if $f(s) = f(s')$ for all $s, s' \in \mathrm{Supp}(f)$.

Definition 1 ($\mathbb{R}$-structures). *A tuple* $\mathfrak{A} = (A, \mathbb{R}, (R^{\mathfrak{A}})_{R \in \tau}, (g^{\mathfrak{A}})_{g \in \sigma})$, *where the reduct of* $\mathfrak{A}$ *to* τ *is a finite relational structure, and each* $g^{\mathfrak{A}}$ *is a function from* $A^{\mathrm{ar}(g)}$ *to* $\mathbb{R}$, *is called an $\mathbb{R}$-structure of vocabulary* $\tau \cup \sigma$. *Additionally,* $\mathfrak{A}$ *is also called (i) an S-structure, for* $S \subseteq \mathbb{R}$, *if each* $g^{\mathfrak{A}}$ *is a function from* $A^{\mathrm{ar}(g)}$ *to* S, *and (ii) a d[0, 1]-structure if each* $g^{\mathfrak{A}}$ *is a distribution. We call* $\mathfrak{A}$ *a finite structure, if* $\sigma = \emptyset$.

Our focus is on a variant of functional existential second-order logic with numerical terms ($\text{ESO}_{\mathbb{R}}$) that is designed to describe properties of $\mathbb{R}$ structures. As first-order terms we have only first-order variables. For a set σ of function symbols, the set of numerical σ-terms i is generated by the following grammar: $i ::= c \mid f(\boldsymbol{x}) \mid i + i \mid i \times i \mid \text{SUM}_y\, i$, where the interpretations of $+, \times, \text{SUM}$ are the standard addition, multiplication, and summation of real numbers, respectively, and $c \in \mathbb{R}$ is a real constant denoting itself.

Definition 2 (Syntax of $\text{ESO}_{\mathbb{R}}$). *Let $O \subseteq \{+, \times, \text{SUM}\}$, $E \subseteq \{=, <, \leq\}$, and $C \subseteq \mathbb{R}$. The set of $\tau \cup \sigma$-formulae of $\text{ESO}_{\mathbb{R}}[O, E, C]$ is defined via the grammar:*

$$\phi ::= \; x = y \mid \neg x = y \mid i\, e\, j \mid \neg i\, e\, j \mid R(\boldsymbol{x}) \mid \neg R(\boldsymbol{x}) \mid \phi \wedge \phi \mid \phi \vee \phi \mid \exists x \phi \mid \forall x \phi \mid \exists f \psi,$$

where i and j are numerical σ-terms constructed using operations from O and constants from C; $e \in E$; $R \in \tau$ is a relation symbol; f is a function variable; x, y, and $\boldsymbol{x}$ are (tuples of) first-order variables; and ψ is a $\tau \cup (\sigma \cup \{f\})$-formula of $\text{ESO}_{\mathbb{R}}[O, E, C]$.

The semantics of $\text{ESO}_{\mathbb{R}}[O, E, C]$ is defined via $\mathbb{R}$-structures and assignments analogous to first-order logic, however the interpretations of function variables f range over functions $A^{\text{ar}(f)} \to \mathbb{R}$. Furthermore, given $S \subseteq \mathbb{R}$, we define $\text{ESO}_S[O, E, C]$ as the variant of $\text{ESO}_{\mathbb{R}}[O, E, C]$ in which quantification of functions range over $h \colon A^{\text{ar}(f)} \to S$.

Loose Fragment. For $S \subseteq \mathbb{R}$, define $\text{L-ESO}_S[O, E, C]$ as the *loose fragment* of $\text{ESO}_S[O, E, C]$ in which negated numerical atoms $\neg i\, e\, j$ are disallowed.

Almost Conjunctive. A formula $\phi \in \text{ESO}_S[O, E, C]$ is *almost conjunctive*, if for every subformula $(\psi_1 \vee \psi_2)$ of ϕ, no numerical term occurs in ψ_i, for some $i \in \{1, 2\}$.

Prefix Classes. For a regular expression L over the alphabet $\{\ddot{\exists}, \exists, \forall\}$, we denote by $L_S[O, E, C]$ the formulae of $\text{ESO}_S[O, E, C]$ in prefix form whose quantifier prefix is in the language defined by L, where $\ddot{\exists}$ denotes existential function quantification, and $\exists$ and $\forall$ first-order quantification.

Expressivity Comparisons. Let $\mathcal{L}$ and $\mathcal{L}'$ be some logics defined above, and let $X \subseteq \mathbb{R}$. For $\phi \in \mathcal{L}$, define $\text{Struc}_X(\phi)$ ($\text{Struc}_{\text{fin}}(\phi)$, resp.) to be the class of pairs $(\mathfrak{A}, s)$ where $\mathfrak{A}$ is an X-structure (finite structure, resp.) and s an assignment such that $\mathfrak{A} \models_s \phi$. Additionally, $\text{Struc}_{d[0,1]}(\phi)$ is the class of $(\mathfrak{A}, s) \in \text{Struc}_{[0,1]}(\phi)$ such that each $f^{\mathfrak{A}}$ is a distribution. If X is a set of reals or from $\{\,\text{``}d[0,1]\text{''}, \text{``fin''}\,\}$, we write $\mathcal{L} \leq_X \mathcal{L}'$ if for all formulae $\phi \in \mathcal{L}$ there is a formula $\psi \in \mathcal{L}'$ such that $\text{Struc}_X(\phi) = \text{Struc}_X(\psi)$. For formulae without free first-order variables, we omit s from the pairs $(\mathfrak{A}, s)$ above. As usual, the shorthand $\equiv_X$ stands for $\leq_X$ in both directions. For $X = \mathbb{R}$, we write simply $\leq$ and $\equiv$.

3   Data Complexity of Additive $\text{ESO}_{\mathbb{R}}$

On finite structures $\text{ESO}_{\mathbb{R}}[\leq, +, \times, 0, 1]$ is known to capture the complexity class $\exists \mathbb{R}$ [4,14,30], which lies somewhere between NP and PSPACE. Here we focus on the additive fragment of the logic. It turns out that the data complexity of the additive fragment is NP and thus no harder than that of ESO. Furthermore, we obtain a tractable fragment of the logic, which captures P on finite ordered structures.

3.1   A Tractable Fragment

Next   we   show   P   data   complexity   for   almost   conjunctive $(\exists^*\exists^*\forall^*)_\mathbb{R}[\leq, +, \mathrm{SUM}, 0, 1]$.

Proposition 3. *Let ϕ be an almost conjunctive $\mathrm{ESO}_\mathbb{R}[\leq, +, \mathrm{SUM}, 0, 1]$-formula in which no existential first-order quantifier is in a scope of a universal first-order quantifier. There is a polynomial-time reduction from $\mathbb{R}$-structures $\mathfrak{A}$ and assignments s to families of systems of linear inequations $\mathcal{S}$ such that $\mathfrak{A} \models_s \phi$ if and only if there is a system $S \in \mathcal{S}$ that has a solution. If ϕ has no free function variables, the systems of linear inequations in $\mathcal{S}$ have integer coefficients.*

Proof. Fix ϕ. We assume, w.l.o.g., that variables quantified in ϕ are quantified exactly once, the sets of free and bound variables of ϕ are disjoint, and that the domain of s is the set of free variables of ϕ. Moreover, we assume that ϕ is of the form $\exists \boldsymbol{y} \exists \boldsymbol{f} \forall \boldsymbol{x} \theta$, where $\boldsymbol{f}$ is a tuple of function variables and θ is quantifier-free. We use X and Y to denote the sets of variables in $\boldsymbol{x}$ and $\boldsymbol{y}$, respectively, and $\boldsymbol{g}$ to denote the free function variables of ϕ.

We describe a polynomial-time process of constructing a family of systems of linear inequations $\mathcal{S}_{\mathfrak{A},s}$ from a given $\tau \cup \sigma$-structure $\mathfrak{A}$ and an assignment s. We introduce

- a fresh variable $z_{\boldsymbol{a},f}$, for each k-ary function symbol f in $\boldsymbol{f}$ and k-tuple $\boldsymbol{a} \in A^k$.

In the sequel, the variables $z_{\boldsymbol{a},f}$ will range over real numbers.

Let $\mathfrak{A}$ be a $\tau \cup \sigma$-structure and s an assignment for the free variables in ϕ. In the sequel, each interpretation for the variables in $\boldsymbol{y}$ yields a system of linear equations. Given an interpretation $v \colon Y \to A$, we will denote by S_v the related system of linear equations to be defined below. We then set $\mathcal{S}_{\mathfrak{A},s} := \{S_v \mid v \colon Y \to A\}$. The system of linear equations S_v is defined as $S_v := \bigcup_{u \colon X \to A} S_v^u$, where S_v^u is defined as follows. Let s_v^u denote the extension of s that agrees with u and v. We let θ_v^u denote the formula obtained from θ by the following simultaneous substitution: If $(\psi_1 \vee \psi_2)$ is a subformula of θ such that no function variable occurs in ψ_i, then $(\psi_1 \vee \psi_2)$ is substituted with $\top$, if

$$\mathfrak{A} \models_{s_v^u} \psi_i, \tag{1}$$

and with ψ_{3-i} otherwise. The set S_v^u is now generated from θ_v^u together with u and v. Note that θ_v^u is a conjunction of first-order or numerical atoms θ_i, $i \in I$, for some index set I. For each conjunct θ_i in which some $f \in \boldsymbol{f}$ occurs, add $(\theta_i)_{s_v^u}$ to S_v^u, where $(\psi)_{s_v^u}$ is defined recursively as follows:

$$(\neg\psi)_{s_v^u} := \neg(\psi)_{s_v^u}, \qquad (i.e.j)_{s_v^u} := (i)_{s_v^u} \, e \, (j)_{s_v^u}, \text{ for each } e \in \{=,<,\leq,+\},$$

$$(f(\boldsymbol{z}))_{s_v^u} := z_{s_v^u(\boldsymbol{z}),f}, \qquad (\mathrm{SUM}_z i)_{s_v^u} := \sum_{a \in A^{|z|}} (i)_{s_v^u(a/z)},$$

$$(g(\boldsymbol{z}))_{s_v^u} := g^{\mathfrak{A}}(s_v^u(\boldsymbol{z})), \quad (x)_{s_v^u} := s_v^u(x), \text{ for every variable } x.$$

Let θ^* be the conjunction of those conjuncts of θ_v^u in which no $f \in \boldsymbol{f}$ occurs. If $\mathfrak{A} \not\models_{s_v^u} \theta^*$, remove S_v from $\mathcal{S}_{\mathfrak{A},s}$.

Since ϕ is fixed, it is clear that $\mathcal{S}_{\mathfrak{A},s}$ can be constructed in polynomial time with respect to $|\mathfrak{A}|$. Moreover, it is straightforward to show that there exists a solution for some $S \in \mathcal{S}_{\mathfrak{A},s}$ exactly when $\mathfrak{A} \models_s \phi$.

Assume first that there exists an $S \in \mathcal{S}_{\mathfrak{A},s}$ that has a solution. Let $w \colon Z \to \mathbb{R}$, where $Z := \{z_{a,f} \mid f \in \boldsymbol{f} \text{ and } a \in A^{\mathrm{ar}(f)}\}$, be the function given by a solution for S. By construction, $S = S_v$, for some $v \colon Y \to A$. Let $\mathfrak{A}'$ be the expansion of $\mathfrak{A}$ that interprets each $f \in \boldsymbol{f}$ as the function $a \mapsto w(z_{a,f})$. By construction, $\mathfrak{A}' \models_{s_v^u} \theta_v^u$ for every $u \colon X \to A$. Now, from (1) and the related substitutions, we obtain that $\mathfrak{A}' \models_{s_v^u} \theta$ for every $u \colon X \to A$, and hence $\mathfrak{A}' \models_{s_v} \forall x_1 \dots \forall x_n \theta$. From this $\mathfrak{A} \models_s \phi$ follows.

For the converse, assume that $\mathfrak{A} \models_s \phi$. Hence there exists an extension s_v of s and an expansion $\mathfrak{A}'$ of $\mathfrak{A}$ such that $\mathfrak{A}' \models_{s_v} \forall x_1 \dots \forall x_n \theta$. Now, by construction, it follows that $S_v \in \mathcal{S}_{\mathfrak{A},s}$ and $\mathfrak{A}' \models_{s_v^u} \theta_v^u$, for every $u \colon X \to A$. Moreover, it follows that the function defined by $z_{a,f} \mapsto f^{\mathfrak{A}'}(a)$, for $f \in \boldsymbol{f}$ and $a \in A^{\mathrm{ar}(f)}$, is a solution for S_v. □

The above proposition could be strengthened by relaxing the almost conjunctive requirement in any way such that (1) can be still decided (i.e., it suffices that the satisfaction of ψ_is do not depend on the interpretations of the functions in $\boldsymbol{f}$).

Theorem 4. *The data complexity of almost conjunctive* $\mathrm{ESO}_{\mathbb{R}}[\leq,+,\mathrm{SUM},0,1]$*-formulae without free function variables and where no existential first-order quantifiers are in a scope of a universal first-order quantifier is in* P.

Proof. Fix an almost conjunctive $\mathrm{ESO}_{\mathbb{R}}[\leq,+,\mathrm{SUM},0,1]$-formula ϕ of relational vocabulary τ of the required form. Given a $\tau \cup \emptyset$ structure $\mathfrak{A}$ and an assignment s for the free variables of ϕ, let $\mathcal{S}$ be the related polynomial size family of polynomial size systems of linear inequations with integer coefficients given by Proposition 3. Deciding whether a system of linear inequalities with integer coefficients has solutions can be done in polynomial time [24]. Thus checking whether there exists a system of linear inequalities $S \in \mathcal{S}$ that has a solution can be done in P as well, from which the claim follows. □

We later show that probabilistic inclusion logic captures P on finite ordered structures (Corollary 22) and can be translated to almost conjunctive $\mathrm{L}\text{-}(\ddot{\exists}^*\forall^*)_{[0,1]}[\leq,\mathrm{SUM},0,1]$ (Lemma 16). Hence already almost conjunctive $\mathrm{L}\text{-}(\ddot{\exists}^*\forall^*)_{\mathbb{R}}[\leq,\mathrm{SUM},0,1]$ captures P.

Corollary 5. *Almost conjunctive* $\mathrm{L}\text{-}(\ddot{\exists}^*\forall^*)_{\mathbb{R}}[\leq,\mathrm{SUM},0,1]$ *captures* P *on finite ordered structures.*

3.2 Full Additive ESO$_\mathbb{R}$

The goal of this subsection is to prove the following theorem:

Theorem 6. ESO$_\mathbb{R}[\leq, +, \text{SUM}, 0, 1]$ *captures* NP *on finite structures.*

First observe that SUM is definable in ESO$_\mathbb{R}[\leq, +, 0, 1]$: Already ESO$_\mathbb{R}[=]$ subsumes ESO, and thus we may assume a built-in successor function S and its associated minimal and maximal elements min and max on k-tuples over the finite part of the $\mathbb{R}$-structure. Then, for a k-ary tuple of variables $\boldsymbol{x}$, SUM$_{\boldsymbol{x}} i$ agrees with $f(\max)$, for any function variable f satisfying $f(\min) = i(\boldsymbol{x} \mapsto \min)$ and $f(S(\boldsymbol{x})) = f(\boldsymbol{x}) + i(S(\boldsymbol{x}))$.

As ESO$_\mathbb{R}[\leq, +, 0, 1]$ subsumes ESO, by Fagin's theorem, it can express all NP properties. Thus we only need to prove that any ESO$_\mathbb{R}[\leq, +, 0, 1]$-definable property of finite structures is recognizable in NP. The proof relies on (descriptive) complexity theory over the reals. The fundamental result in this area is that existential second-order logic over the reals (ESO$_\mathbb{R}[\leq, +, \times, (r)_{r \in \mathbb{R}}]$) corresponds to non-deterministic polynomial time over the reals (NP$_\mathbb{R}$) for BSS machines [14, Theorem 4.2]. To continue from this, some additional terminology is needed. We refer the reader to [2] for more information about BSS machines. Let $C_\mathbb{R}$ be a complexity class over the reals.

- C_{add} is $C_\mathbb{R}$ restricted to *additive* BSS machines (i.e., without multiplication).
- $C_\mathbb{R}^0$ is $C_\mathbb{R}$ restricted to BSS machines with machine constants 0 and 1 only.
- BP($C_\mathbb{R}$) is $C_\mathbb{R}$ restricted to languages of strings that contain only 0 and 1.

A straightforward adaptation of [14, Theorem 4.2] yields the following theorem.

Theorem 7 [14]. ESO$_\mathbb{R}[\leq, +, 0, 1]$ *captures* NP$^0_{\text{add}}$ *on $\mathbb{R}$-structures.*

If we can establish that BP(NP$^0_{\text{add}}$), the so-called *Boolean part* of NP$^0_{\text{add}}$, collapses to NP, we have completed the proof of Theorem 6. Observe that another variant of this theorem readily holds; ESO$_\mathbb{R}[=, +, (r)_{r \in \mathbb{R}}]$-definable properties of $\mathbb{R}$-structures are recognizable in NP$_{\text{add}}$ branching on equality, which in turn, over Boolean inputs, collapses to NP [25, Theorem 3]. Here, restricting branching to equality is crucial. With no restrictions in place (the BSS machine by default branches on inequality and can use arbitrary reals as machine constants) NP$_{\text{add}}$ equals NP/poly over Boolean inputs [25, Theorem 11]. What we show next is that disallowing machine constants other than 0 and 1, but allowing branching on inequality, is a mixture that leads to a collapse to NP. The proof adapts arguments from [25] and can be found in the full version [18].

Theorem 8. BP(NP$^0_{\text{add}}$) = NP.

Proof. Clearly NP $\leq$ BP(NP$^0_{\text{add}}$); a Boolean guess for an input x can be constructed by comparing to zero each component of a real guess y, and a polynomial-time Turing computation can be simulated by a polynomial-time BSS computation.

For the converse, let $L \subseteq \{0,1\}^*$ be a Boolean language that belongs to $\mathsf{BP}(\mathsf{NP}^0_{\mathrm{add}})$; we need to show that L belongs also to NP. Let M be a BSS machine such that its running time is bounded by some polynomial p, and for all Boolean inputs $x \in \{0,1\}^*$, $x \in L$ if and only if there is $y \in \mathbb{R}^{p(|x|)}$ such that M accepts (x, y).

The non-deterministic computation of M on x can be described by guessing the whole non-deterministic polynomial time computation including the outcomes of the comparisons in the BSS computation. During the computation the value of each register is a linear function of the values of the registers in the previous time step, and ultimately from the constants 0 and 1, the input x, and the real guess y of polynomial length. Thus it is possible to construct in polynomial time a system $\mathcal{S}$ of linear inequations on y that has a solution if and only if M accepts x. For a complete proof see the ArXiv version [18]. □

4   Probabilistic Team Semantics and Additive $\mathsf{ESO}_{\mathbb{R}}$

4.1   Probabilistic Team Semantics

Let D be a finite set of first-order variables and A a finite set. A *team* X is a set of assignments from D to A. A *probabilistic team* is a distribution $\mathbb{X} \colon X \to [0,1]$, where X is a finite team. Also the empty function is considered a probabilistic team. We call D the variable domain of both X and $\mathbb{X}$, written $\mathrm{Dom}(\mathbb{X})$ and $\mathrm{Dom}(X)$. A is called the *value domain* of X and $\mathbb{X}$.

Let $\mathbb{X} \colon X \to [0,1]$ be a probabilistic team, x a variable, $V \subseteq \mathrm{Dom}(\mathbb{X})$ a set of variables, and A a set. The *projection* of $\mathbb{X}$ on V is defined as $\mathrm{Pr}_V(\mathbb{X}) \colon X \upharpoonright V \to [0,1]$ such that $s \mapsto \sum_{t \upharpoonright V = s} \mathbb{X}(t)$, where $X \upharpoonright V := \{t \upharpoonright V \mid t \in X\}$. Define $\mathrm{S}_{x,A}(\mathbb{X})$ as the set of all probabilistic teams $\mathbb{Y}$ with variable domain $\mathrm{Dom}(\mathbb{X}) \cup \{x\}$ such that $\mathrm{Pr}_{\mathrm{Dom}(\mathbb{X}) \setminus \{x\}}(\mathbb{Y}) = \mathrm{Pr}_{\mathrm{Dom}(\mathbb{X}) \setminus \{x\}}(\mathbb{X})$ and A is a value domain of $\mathbb{Y} \upharpoonright \{x\}$. We denote by $\mathbb{X}[A/x]$ the unique $\mathbb{Y} \in \mathrm{S}_{x,A}(\mathbb{X})$ such that

$$\mathbb{Y}(s) = \frac{\mathrm{Pr}_{\mathrm{Dom}(\mathbb{X}) \setminus \{x\}}(\mathbb{X})(s \upharpoonright \mathrm{Dom}(\mathbb{X}) \setminus \{x\})}{|A|}.$$

If x is a fresh variable, then this equation becomes $\mathbb{Y}(s(a/x)) = \frac{\mathbb{X}(s)}{|A|}$. We also define $X[A/x] := \{s(a/x) \mid s \in X, a \in A\}$, and write $\mathbb{X}[a/x]$ and $X[a/x]$ instead of $\mathbb{X}[\{a\}/x]$ and $X[\{a\}/x]$, for singletons $\{a\}$.

Let us also define some function arithmetic. Let α be a real number, and f and g be functions from a shared domain into real numbers. The scalar multiplication αf is a function defined by $(\alpha f)(x) := \alpha f(x)$. The addition $f + g$ is defined as $(f + g)(x) = f(x) + g(x)$, and the multiplication fg is defined as $(fg)(x) := f(x)g(x)$. In particular, if f and g are probabilistic teams and $\alpha + \beta = 1$, then $\alpha f + \beta g$ is a probabilistic team.

We define first probabilistic team semantics for first-order formulae. As is customary in the team semantics context, we restrict attention to formulae in negation normal form.

Definition 9 (Probabilistic team semantics). *Let $\mathfrak{A}$ be a τ-structure over a finite domain A, and $\mathbb{X}\colon X \to [0,1]$ a probabilistic team. The satisfaction relation $\models_{\mathbb{X}}$ for first-order logic is defined as follows:*

$$
\begin{aligned}
\mathfrak{A} \models_{\mathbb{X}} l \quad &\Leftrightarrow \forall s \in \mathrm{Supp}(\mathbb{X}) : \mathfrak{A} \models_s l, \text{ where } l \text{ is a literal}\\
\mathfrak{A} \models_{\mathbb{X}} (\psi \wedge \theta) &\Leftrightarrow \mathfrak{A} \models_{\mathbb{X}} \psi \text{ and } \mathfrak{A} \models_{\mathbb{X}} \theta\\
\mathfrak{A} \models_{\mathbb{X}} (\psi \vee \theta) &\Leftrightarrow \mathfrak{A} \models_{\mathbb{Y}} \psi \text{ and } \mathfrak{A} \models_{\mathbb{Z}} \theta \text{ for some } \mathbb{Y}, \mathbb{Z},\\
&\qquad \alpha \in [0,1] \text{ such that } \alpha\mathbb{Y} + (1-\alpha)\mathbb{Z} = \mathbb{X}\\
\mathfrak{A} \models_{\mathbb{X}} \forall x \psi \quad &\Leftrightarrow \mathfrak{A} \models_{\mathbb{X}[A/x]} \psi\\
\mathfrak{A} \models_{\mathbb{X}} \exists x \psi \quad &\Leftrightarrow \mathfrak{A} \models_{\mathbb{Y}} \psi \text{ for some } \mathbb{Y} \in S_{x,A}(\mathbb{X})
\end{aligned}
$$

The satisfaction relation $\models_s$ denotes the Tarski semantics of first-order logic. If ϕ is a *sentence* (i.e., without free variables), then $\mathfrak{A}$ *satisfies* ϕ, written $\mathfrak{A} \models \phi$, if $\mathfrak{A} \models_{\mathbb{X}_\emptyset} \phi$, where $\mathbb{X}_\emptyset$ is the distribution that maps the empty assignment to 1.

We make use of a generalization of probabilistic team semantics where the requirement of being a distribution is dropped. A *weighted team* is any non-negative weight function $\mathbb{X}\colon X \to \mathbb{R}_{\geq 0}$. Given a first-order formula α, we write $\mathbb{X}_\alpha$ for the restriction of the weighted team $\mathbb{X}$ to the assignments of X satisfying α (with respect to the underlying structure). Moreover, the *total weight* of a weighted team $\mathbb{X}$ is $|\mathbb{X}| := \sum_{s \in X} \mathbb{X}(s)$.

Definition 10 (Weighted semantics). *Let $\mathfrak{A}$ be a τ-structure over a finite domain A, and $\mathbb{X}\colon X \to \mathbb{R}_{\geq 0}$ a weighted team. The satisfaction relation $\models_{\mathbb{X}}^{w}$ for first-order logic is defined exactly as in Definition 9, except that for $\vee$ we define instead:*

$$
\mathfrak{A} \models_{\mathbb{X}}^{w} (\psi \vee \theta) \quad\Leftrightarrow\quad \mathfrak{A} \models_{\mathbb{Y}} \psi \text{ and } \mathfrak{A} \models_{\mathbb{Z}} \theta \text{ for some } \mathbb{Y}, \mathbb{Z} \text{ s.t. } \mathbb{Y} + \mathbb{Z} = \mathbb{X}.
$$

We consider logics with the following atomic dependencies:

Definition 11 (Dependencies). *Let $\mathfrak{A}$ be a finite structure with universe A, $\mathbb{X}$ a weighted team, and X a team.*

- **Marginal identity and inclusion atoms.** *If $\boldsymbol{x}, \boldsymbol{y}$ are variable sequences of length k, then $\boldsymbol{x} \approx \boldsymbol{y}$ is a marginal identity atom and $\boldsymbol{x} \subseteq \boldsymbol{y}$ is an inclusion atom with satisfactions defined as:*

$$
\mathfrak{A} \models_{\mathbb{X}}^{w} \boldsymbol{x} \approx \boldsymbol{y} \Leftrightarrow |\mathbb{X}_{\boldsymbol{x}=\boldsymbol{a}}| = |\mathbb{X}_{\boldsymbol{y}=\boldsymbol{a}}| \text{ for each } \boldsymbol{a} \in A^k,
$$
$$
\mathfrak{A} \models_X \boldsymbol{x} \subseteq \boldsymbol{y} \Leftrightarrow \text{ for all } s \in X \text{ there is } s' \in X \text{ such that } s(\boldsymbol{x}) = s'(\boldsymbol{y}).
$$

- **Dependence atom.** *For a sequence of variables $\boldsymbol{x}$ and a variable y, $=(\boldsymbol{x}, y)$ is a dependence atom with satisfaction defined as:*

$$
\mathfrak{A} \models_X =(\boldsymbol{x}, y) \Leftrightarrow \text{ for all } s, s' \in X : \text{ if } s(\boldsymbol{x}) = s'(\boldsymbol{x}), \text{ then } s(y) = s'(y).
$$

For probabilistic teams $\mathbb{X}$, the satisfaction relation is written without the superscript w.

Observe that any dependency α over team semantics can also be interpreted in probabilistic team semantics: $\mathfrak{A} \models_{\mathbb{X}} \alpha$ iff $\mathfrak{A} \models_{\mathrm{Supp}(\mathbb{X})} \alpha$. For a list $\mathcal{C}$ of dependencies, we write $\mathrm{FO}(\mathcal{C})$ for the extension of first-order logic with the dependencies in $\mathcal{C}$. The logics $\mathrm{FO}(\approx)$ and $\mathrm{FO}(\subseteq)$, in particular, are called *probabilistic inclusion logic* and *inclusion logic*, respectively. We write $\mathrm{Fr}(\phi)$ for the set free variables of $\phi \in \mathrm{FO}(\mathcal{C})$, defined as usual. We conclude this section with a list of useful equivalences. We omit the proofs, which are straightforward structural inductions ((ii) was also proven in [16] and (v) follows from (i) and the flatness property of team semantics).

Proposition 12. *Let* $\phi \in \mathrm{FO}(\mathcal{C})$, $\psi \in \mathrm{FO}(\approx, \mathcal{C})$, *and* $\theta \in \mathrm{FO}$, *where* $\mathcal{C}$ *is a list of dependencies over team semantics. Let* $\mathfrak{A}$ *be a structure,* $\mathbb{X}$ *a weighted team, and* r *any positive real. The following equivalences hold:*

(i) $\mathfrak{A} \models_{\mathbb{X}}^{w} \phi \Leftrightarrow \mathfrak{A} \models_{\mathrm{Supp}(\mathbb{X})} \phi$.

(ii) $\mathfrak{A} \models_{\mathbb{X}}^{w} \psi \Leftrightarrow \mathfrak{A} \models_{\frac{1}{|\mathbb{X}|}\mathbb{X}}^{w} \psi$.

(iii) $\mathfrak{A} \models_{\mathbb{X}}^{w} \psi \Leftrightarrow \mathfrak{A} \models_{r\mathbb{X}}^{w} \psi$.

(iv) $\mathfrak{A} \models_{\mathbb{X}}^{w} \psi \Leftrightarrow \mathfrak{A} \models_{\mathbb{X}\restriction V}^{w} \psi$, *where* $\mathrm{Fr}(\psi) \subseteq V$.

(v) $\mathfrak{A} \models_{\mathbb{X}}^{w} \theta \Leftrightarrow \mathfrak{A} \models_{s} \theta$, *for all* $s \in \mathrm{Supp}(X)$.

4.2 Expressivity of Probabilistic Inclusion Logic

We turn to the expressivity of probabilistic inclusion logic and its extension with dependence atoms. In particular, we relate these logics to existential second-order logic over the reals. We show that probabilistic inclusion logic extended with dependence atoms captures a fragment in which arithmetic is restricted to summing. Furthermore, we show that leaving out dependence atoms is tantamount to restricting to sentences in almost conjunctive form with $\exists^* \forall^*$ quantifier prefix.

Expressivity Comparisons. Fix a list of atoms $\mathcal{C}$ over probabilistic team semantics. For a probabilistic team $\mathbb{X}$ with variable domain $\{x_1, \ldots, x_n\}$ and value domain A, the function $f_{\mathbb{X}} : A^n \to [0,1]$ is defined as the probability distribution such that $f_{\mathbb{X}}(s(\boldsymbol{x})) = \mathbb{X}(s)$ for all $s \in X$. For a formula $\phi \in \mathrm{FO}(\mathcal{C})$ of vocabulary τ and with free variables $\{x_1, \ldots, x_n\}$, the class $\mathrm{Struc}_{d[0,1]}(\phi)$ is defined as the class of $d[0,1]$-structures $\mathfrak{A}$ over $\tau \cup \{f\}$ such that $(\mathfrak{A} \restriction \tau) \models_{\mathbb{X}} \phi$, where $f_{\mathbb{X}} = f^{\mathfrak{A}}$ and $\mathfrak{A} \restriction \tau$ is the finite τ-structure underlying $\mathfrak{A}$. Let $\mathcal{L}$ and $\mathcal{L}'$ be two logics of which one is defined over (probabilistic) team semantics. We write $\mathcal{L} \leq \mathcal{L}'$ if for every formula $\phi \in \mathcal{L}$ there is $\phi' \in \mathcal{L}'$ such that $\mathrm{Struc}_{d[0,1]}(\phi) = \mathrm{Struc}_{d[0,1]}(\phi')$; again, $\equiv$ is a shorthand for $\leq$ both ways.

Theorem 13. *The following equivalences hold:*

(i) $\mathrm{FO}(\approx, =(\cdots)) \equiv \mathrm{L\text{-}ESO}_{[0,1]}[=, +, 0, 1]$.

(ii) $\mathrm{FO}(\approx) \equiv$ *almost conjunctive* $\mathrm{L\text{-}}(\exists^* \forall^*)_{[0,1]}[=, \mathrm{SUM}, 0, 1]$.

We divide the proof of Theorem 13 into two parts. In Sect. 4.3 we consider the direction from probabilistic team semantics to existential second-order logic over the reals, and in Sect. 4.4 we shift attention to the converse direction. In order to simplify the presentation in the forthcoming subsections, we start by showing how to replace existential function quantification by distribution quantification. The following lemma in its original form includes multiplication (see [17, Lemma 6.4]) but works also without it. Its proof does not preserve the almost conjunctive form, and thereby we need to deal with that case separately in Proposition 15 (for a proof see the full version [18] in ArXiv). This proposition also uses the fact that real constants 0 and 1 are definable in almost conjunctive L-$(\ddot{\exists}^*\forall^*)_{d[0,1]}[=, \text{SUM}]$ by the following construction that eliminates 0 and 1 in θ:

$$\exists n \exists f \exists h \forall x \forall y \forall z \big(f(x) = h(x,x) \wedge \big(y = z \vee \theta(h(y,z)/0, n/1)\big)\big)$$

Lemma 14 [17]. L-$\text{ESO}_{[0,1]}[=, +, 0, 1] \equiv_{d[0,1]}$ L-$\text{ESO}_{d[0,1]}[=, \text{SUM}]$.

Proposition 15. L-$\text{ESO}_{[0,1]}[=, \text{SUM}, 0, 1]$ $\equiv_{[0,1]}$ L-$\text{ESO}_{d[0,1]}[=, \text{SUM}]$. *The same holds when both logics are restricted to almost conjunctive formulae of the prefix class $\ddot{\exists}^*\forall^*$.*

4.3 From Probabilistic Team Semantics to Existential Second-Order Logic

Let c and d be two distinct constants. Let $\phi(\boldsymbol{x}) \in \text{FO}(\approx, =(\cdots))$ be a formula whose free variables are from the sequence $\boldsymbol{x} = (x_1, \ldots, x_n)$. We now construct recursively an L-$\text{ESO}_{[0,1]}[=, \text{SUM}, 0, 1]$-formula $\phi^*(f)$ that contains one free n-ary function variable f. In this formula, a probabilistic team $\mathbb{X}$ is represented as a function $f_{\mathbb{X}}$ such that $\mathbb{X}(s) = f_{\mathbb{X}}(s(x_1), \ldots, s(x_n))$.

(1) If $\phi(\boldsymbol{x})$ is a first-order literal, then $\phi^*(f) := \forall \boldsymbol{x}\big(f(\boldsymbol{x}) = 0 \vee \phi(\boldsymbol{x})\big)$.
(2) If $\phi(\boldsymbol{x})$ is a dependence atom of the form $=(\boldsymbol{x_0}, \boldsymbol{x_1})$, then
$\phi^*(f) := \forall \boldsymbol{x}\boldsymbol{x}'\big(f(\boldsymbol{x}) = 0 \vee f(\boldsymbol{x}') = 0 \vee \boldsymbol{x}_0 \neq \boldsymbol{x}'_0 \vee x_1 = x'_1\big)$.
(3) If $\phi(\boldsymbol{x})$ is $\boldsymbol{x_0} \approx \boldsymbol{x_1}$, where $\boldsymbol{x} = \boldsymbol{x_0}\boldsymbol{x_1}\boldsymbol{x_2}$, then
$\phi^*(f) := \forall \boldsymbol{y}\, \text{SUM}_{\boldsymbol{x_1},\boldsymbol{x_2}} f(\boldsymbol{y}, \boldsymbol{x_1}, \boldsymbol{x_2}) = \text{SUM}_{\boldsymbol{x_0},\boldsymbol{x_2}} f(\boldsymbol{x_0}, \boldsymbol{y}, \boldsymbol{x_2})$.
(4) If $\phi(\boldsymbol{x})$ is of the form $\psi_0(\boldsymbol{x}) \wedge \psi_1(\boldsymbol{x})$, then $\phi^*(f) := \psi_0^*(f) \wedge \psi_1^*(f)$.
(5) If $\phi(\boldsymbol{x})$ is of the form $\psi_0(\boldsymbol{x}) \vee \psi_1(\boldsymbol{x})$, then define $\phi^*(f)$ as
$\exists g \forall \boldsymbol{x}(\text{SUM}_y g(\boldsymbol{x}, y) = f(\boldsymbol{x}) \wedge \forall y(y = c \vee y = d \vee g(\boldsymbol{x}, y) = 0) \wedge \psi_0^*(g^c) \wedge \psi_1^*(g^d))$,
where g^i is of the same arity as f and defined as $g^i(\boldsymbol{x}) = g(\boldsymbol{x}, i)$.
(6) If $\phi(\boldsymbol{x})$ is $\exists y \psi(\boldsymbol{x}, y)$, then $\phi^*(f) := \exists g\big((\forall \boldsymbol{x}\, \text{SUM}_y g(\boldsymbol{x}, y) = f(\boldsymbol{x})) \wedge \psi^*(g)\big)$.
(7) If $\phi(\boldsymbol{x})$ is of the form $\forall y \psi(\boldsymbol{x}, y)$, then
$\phi^*(f) := \exists g\big(\forall \boldsymbol{x}(\forall y \forall z g(\boldsymbol{x}, y) = g(\boldsymbol{x}, z) \wedge \text{SUM}_y g(\boldsymbol{x}, y) = f(\boldsymbol{x})) \wedge \psi^*(g)\big)$.

This translation leads to the following lemma, the proof of which can be found in the full version [18]. The claim (ii) follows when the translation for dependence atoms $=(\boldsymbol{x_0}, x_1)$ and $\boldsymbol{x} = \boldsymbol{x_0}\boldsymbol{x_1}\boldsymbol{x_2}$ is modified to $\forall \boldsymbol{x_0} \exists x_1 \text{SUM}_{\boldsymbol{x_2}} f(\boldsymbol{x}) = \text{SUM}_{\boldsymbol{x_1}\boldsymbol{x_2}} f(\boldsymbol{x})$. Finally (iii) follows when the case for dependence atoms is omitted.

Lemma 16. *The following hold:*

(i) $\mathrm{FO}(\approx, =(\cdots)) \leq \mathrm{L}\text{-}(\ddot{\exists}^*\forall^*)_{[0,1]}[=, \mathrm{SUM}, 0, 1]$.

(ii) $\mathrm{FO}(\approx, =(\cdots)) \leq$ *almost conjunctive* $\mathrm{L}\text{-}(\ddot{\exists}^*\forall^*\exists^*)_{[0,1]}[=, \mathrm{SUM}, 0, 1]$.

(iii) $\mathrm{FO}(\approx) \leq$ *almost conjunctive* $\mathrm{L}\text{-}(\ddot{\exists}^*\forall^*)_{[0,1]}[=, \mathrm{SUM}, 0, 1]$.

This completes the "$\leq$" direction of Theorem 13. For (i), this follows from (i) of Lemma 16, Proposition 15, and Lemma 14. For (ii), only (iii) of Lemma 16 is needed.

Recall from Proposition 3 that almost conjunctive $(\ddot{\exists}^*\exists^*\forall^*)_{\mathbb{R}}[\leq, +, \mathrm{SUM}, 0, 1]$ is in PTIME in terms of data complexity. Since dependence logic captures NP [32], the previous lemma indicates that we have found, in some regard, a maximal tractable fragment of additive existential second-order logic. That is, dropping either the requirement of being almost conjunctive, or that of having the prefix form $\ddot{\exists}^*\exists^*\forall^*$, leads to a fragment that captures NP; that NP is also an upper bound for these fragments follows by Theorem 6.

Corollary 17. $\mathrm{FO}(\approx, =(\cdots))$ *captures* NP *on finite structures.*

4.4 From Existential Second-Order Logic to Probabilistic Team Semantics

Due to Lemma 14 and Proposition 15, our aim is to translate $\mathrm{L}\text{-}\mathrm{ESO}_{d[0,1]}[=, \mathrm{SUM}]$ and almost conjunctive $\mathrm{L}\text{-}\mathrm{ESO}_{d[0,1]}[=, \mathrm{SUM}]$ to $\mathrm{FO}(\approx, =(\cdots))$ and $\mathrm{FO}(\approx)$, resp. The following lemma states that we may restrict attention to formulae in Skolem normal form.[1]

Lemma 18 [8]. *For every formula* $\phi \in \mathrm{L}\text{-}\mathrm{ESO}_{d[0,1]}[=, \mathrm{SUM}]$ *there is a formula* $\phi^* \in \mathrm{L}\text{-}(\ddot{\exists}^*\forall^*)_{d[0,1]}[=, \mathrm{SUM}]$ *such that* $\mathrm{Struc}_{d[0,1]}(\phi) = \mathrm{Struc}_{d[0,1]}(\phi^*)$, *and any second sort identity atom in* ϕ^* *is of the form* $f_i(\boldsymbol{w}) = \mathrm{SUM}_{\boldsymbol{v}} f_j(\boldsymbol{u}, \boldsymbol{v})$ *for distinct* f_i *and* f_j *of which at least one is quantified. Furthermore,* ϕ^* *is almost conjunctive if* ϕ *is almost conjunctive and in* $\mathrm{L}\text{-}(\ddot{\exists}^*\forall^*)_{d[0,1]}[=, \mathrm{SUM}]$.

The translation presented next is similar to one found in [8], with the exception that probabilistic independence atoms cannot be used here. Without loss of generality each structure is enriched with two distinct constants c and d; such constants are definable in $\mathrm{FO}(\approx, =(\cdots))$ by $\exists cd(=(c) \wedge =(d) \wedge c \neq d)$, and for almost conjunctive formulae they are not needed. Let $\phi(f) = \exists \boldsymbol{f} \forall \boldsymbol{x}\, \theta(f, \boldsymbol{x}) \in \mathrm{L}\text{-}(\ddot{\exists}^*\forall^*)_{d[0,1]}[=, \mathrm{SUM}]$ be of the form described in the previous lemma, with one free variable f. We define

$$\Phi := \exists \boldsymbol{y}_1 \ldots \exists \boldsymbol{y}_n \forall \boldsymbol{x} \Theta(\boldsymbol{x}, \boldsymbol{y}_1, \ldots, \boldsymbol{y}_n),$$

---

[1] The corresponding Lemma 3 in [8] includes multiplication but the proof works also without it. We would like to thank Richard Wilke for noting that the construction used in [8] to prove Lemma 18 had an element that yields circularity. It is, fortunately, straightforward to mend the proof such that the issue is avoided. See the full version [18] for the fixed proof.

where $\boldsymbol{y}_i$ are sequences of variables of length $\mathrm{ar}(f_i)$, and Θ is built inductively from θ:

(1) If θ is a literal of the first sort, let $\Theta := \theta$.
(2) If θ is of the form $f_i(\boldsymbol{x}_i) = \mathrm{SUM}_{\boldsymbol{x}_{j0}} f_j(\boldsymbol{x}_{j0}\boldsymbol{x}_{j1})$, let $\Theta := \exists\alpha\beta\psi$ for ψ given as

$$(\alpha = x \leftrightarrow \boldsymbol{x}_i = \boldsymbol{y}_i) \wedge (\beta = x \leftrightarrow \boldsymbol{x}_{j1} = \boldsymbol{y}_{j1}) \wedge \boldsymbol{x}\alpha \approx \boldsymbol{x}\beta, \qquad (2)$$

where x is any variable from $\boldsymbol{x}$, and the first-order variable sequence $\boldsymbol{y}_j$ that corresponds to function variable f_j is thought of as a concatenation of two sequences $\boldsymbol{y}_{j0}$ and $\boldsymbol{y}_{j1}$ whose respective lenghts are $|\boldsymbol{x}_{j0}|$ and $|\boldsymbol{x}_{j1}|$.
(3) If θ is $\theta_0 \wedge \theta_1$, let $\Theta := \Theta_0 \wedge \Theta_1$
(4) If θ is $\theta_0 \vee \theta_1$, let $\Theta := \exists z\Big(=(\boldsymbol{x}, \boldsymbol{z}) \wedge \big((\Theta_0 \wedge z = c) \vee (\Theta_1 \wedge z = d)\big)\Big)$.

Alternatively, if θ_0 contains no numerical terms, let $\Theta := \theta_0 \vee (\theta_0^- \wedge \Theta_1)$, where θ_0^- is obtained from $\neg\theta_0$ by pushing $\neg$ in front of atomic formulae.

The full proof of the next lemma can be found in the full version [18].

Lemma 19. *Let* $\phi(f) \in \mathrm{L\text{-}}(\overset{\ddots}{\exists}{}^*\forall^*)_{d[0,1]}[=, \mathrm{SUM}]$ *be of the form described in Lemma 18, with one free variable* f. *Then there is a formula* $\Phi(\boldsymbol{x}) \in \mathrm{FO}(\approx , = (\cdots))$ *such that for all structures* $\mathfrak{A}$ *and probabilistic teams* $\mathbb{X} := f^{\mathfrak{A}}$, $\mathfrak{A} \models_{\mathbb{X}} \Phi \iff (\mathfrak{A}, f) \models \phi$. *Furthermore, if* $\phi(f)$ *is almost conjunctive, then* $\Phi(\boldsymbol{x}) \in \mathrm{FO}(\approx)$.

The "$\geq$" direction of item (i) in Theorem 13 follows by Lemmata 14, 18, and 19; that of item (ii) follows similarly, except that Proposition 15 is used instead of Lemma 14. This concludes the proof of Theorem 13.

5   Interpreting Inclusion Logic in Probabilistic Team Semantics

Next we turn to the relationship between inclusion and probabilistic inclusion logics. The logics are comparable for, as shown in Propositions 12, team semantics embeds into probabilistic team semantics conservatively. The seminal result by Galliani and Hella shows that inclusion logic captures PTIME over ordered structures [11]. We show that restricting to finite structures, or uniformly distributed probabilistic teams, inclusion logic is in turn subsumed by probabilistic inclusion logic. There are two immediate consequences for this. First, the result by Galliani and Hella readily extends to probabilistic inclusion logic. Second, their result obtains an alternative, entirely different proof through linear systems.

We utilize another result of Galliani stating that inclusion logic is equiexpressive with *equiextension logic* [10], defined as the extension of first-order logic with *equiextension* atoms $\boldsymbol{x}_1 \bowtie \boldsymbol{x}_2 := \boldsymbol{x}_1 \subseteq \boldsymbol{x}_2 \wedge \boldsymbol{x}_2 \subseteq \boldsymbol{x}_1$. In the sequel, we relate equiextension atoms to probabilistic inclusion atoms.

For a natural number $k \in \mathbb{N}$ and an equiextension atom $\boldsymbol{x}_1 \bowtie \boldsymbol{x}_2$, where $\boldsymbol{x}_1$ and $\boldsymbol{x}_2$ are variable tuples of length m, define $\psi^k(\boldsymbol{x}_1, \boldsymbol{x}_2)$ as

$$\forall \boldsymbol{u} \exists v_1 v_2 \forall \boldsymbol{z}' \exists \boldsymbol{z} ((\boldsymbol{x}_1 = \boldsymbol{u} \leftrightarrow v_1 = y) \wedge (\boldsymbol{x}_2 = \boldsymbol{u} \leftrightarrow v_2 = y) \wedge \tag{3}$$
$$(\boldsymbol{z}' = \boldsymbol{y} \to \boldsymbol{z} = \boldsymbol{y}) \wedge (\neg \boldsymbol{z} = \boldsymbol{y} \vee \boldsymbol{u} v_1 \approx \boldsymbol{u} v_2)),$$

where $\boldsymbol{z}$ and $\boldsymbol{z}'$ are variable tuples of length k, and $\boldsymbol{y}$ is obtained by concatenating k times some variable y in $\boldsymbol{u}$. Intuitively (3) expresses that a probabilistic team $\mathbb{X}$, extended with universally quantified $\boldsymbol{u}$, decomposes to $\mathbb{Y} + \mathbb{Z}$, where $\mathbb{Y}(s) = f_s \mathbb{X}(s)$ for some variable coefficient $f_s \in [\frac{1}{n^k}, 1]$, and $|\mathbb{Y}_{\boldsymbol{x}_1 = \boldsymbol{u}}| = |\mathbb{Y}_{\boldsymbol{x}_2 = \boldsymbol{u}}|$, for any $\boldsymbol{u}$. Thus (3) readily implies that $\boldsymbol{x}_1 \bowtie \boldsymbol{x}_2$. On the other hand, $\boldsymbol{x}_1 \bowtie \boldsymbol{x}_2$ implies (3) if each assignment weight $\mathbb{X}(s)$ equals $g_s |\mathbb{X}|$ for some $g_s \in [\frac{1}{n^k}, 1]$. In this case, one finds the decomposition $\mathbb{Y} + \mathbb{Z}$ by balancing the weight differences between values of $\boldsymbol{x}_1$ and $\boldsymbol{x}_2$. A more formal proof for the following lemma can be found in the full version [18].

Lemma 20. *Let k be a positive integer, $\mathfrak{A}$ a finite structure with universe A of size n, and $\mathbb{X} : X \to \mathbb{R}_{\geq 0}$ a weighted team.*

(i) If $\mathfrak{A} \models^w_\mathbb{X} \boldsymbol{x}_1 \bowtie \boldsymbol{x}_2$ and $\forall s \in X : \mathbb{X}(s) = 0$ or $\mathbb{X}(s) \geq \frac{|\mathbb{X}|}{n^k}$, then $\mathfrak{A} \models^w_\mathbb{X} \phi^k(\boldsymbol{x}, \boldsymbol{y})$.
(ii) If $\mathfrak{A} \models^w_\mathbb{X} \phi^k(\boldsymbol{x}, \boldsymbol{y})$, then $\mathfrak{A} \models^w_\mathbb{X} \boldsymbol{x}_1 \bowtie \boldsymbol{x}_2$.

We next establish that inclusion logic is subsumed by probabilistic inclusion logic at the level of sentences.

Theorem 21. $\mathrm{FO}(\subseteq) \leq \mathrm{FO}(\approx)$ *with respect to sentences.*

Proof. As $\mathrm{FO}(\subseteq) \equiv \mathrm{FO}(\bowtie)$ [10], it suffices to show $\mathrm{FO}(\bowtie) \leq \mathrm{FO}(\approx)$ over sentences. Let $\phi \in \mathrm{FO}(\bowtie)$ be a sentence, and let k be the number of disjunctions and quantifiers in ϕ. Let ϕ^* be obtained from ϕ by replacing all equiextension atoms of the form $\boldsymbol{x}_1 \bowtie \boldsymbol{x}_2$ with $\psi^k(\boldsymbol{x}_1, \boldsymbol{x}_2)$. We can make three simplifying assumption without loss of generality. First, we may restrict attention to weighted semantics by item (ii) of Proposition 12. Thus, we assume that $\mathfrak{A} \models^w_\mathbb{X} \phi$ for some weighted team $\mathbb{X}$ and a finite structure $\mathfrak{A}$ with universe of size n. Second, we may assume that the support of $\mathbb{X}$ consists of the empty assignment by item (iv) of Proposition 12. Third, since $\mathrm{FO}(\bowtie)$ is insensitive to assignment weights, we may assume that the satisfaction of ϕ by $\mathbb{X}$ is witnessed by uniform semantic operations. That is, existential and universal quantification split an assignment to at most n equally weighted extensions, and disjunction can only split an assignment to two equally weighted parts. It follows from these assumptions that in any weighted team $\mathbb{Y}$, obtained from $\mathbb{X}$ for some subformula of ϕ, all the assignment weights are greater than or equal to $\frac{|\mathbb{Y}|}{n^k}$. We then obtain by the previous lemma and a simple inductive argument that $\mathfrak{A} \models^w_\mathbb{X} \phi^*$. The converse direction follows similarly by the previous lemma. $\square$

Consequently, probabilistic inclusion logic captures P, for this holds already for inclusion logic [11]. Another consequence is an alternative proof, through probabilistic inclusion logic (Theorem 21) and linear programs (Theorems 13 and 4), for the PTIME upper bound of the data complexity of inclusion logic. For this, note also that quantification of functions, whose range is the unit interval, is clearly expressible in $\mathrm{ESO}_\mathbb{R}[\leq, \mathrm{SUM}, 0, 1]$.

Corollary 22. *Sentences of* $\mathrm{FO}(\approx)$ *capture* P *on finite ordered structures.*

Theorem 21 also extends to formulae over uniform teams. Recall that a function f is uniform if $f(s) = f(s')$ for all $s, s' \in \mathrm{Supp}(f)$.

Theorem 23. $\mathrm{FO}(\subseteq) \leq \mathrm{FO}(\approx)$ *over uniform probabilistic teams.*

Proof. Recall that $\mathrm{FO}(\subseteq) \equiv \mathrm{FO}(\bowtie)$. Let ϕ be an $\mathrm{FO}(\bowtie)$ formula, $\mathfrak{A}$ a finite structure, and $\mathbb{X}$ a uniform probabilistic team. Let $*$ denote the translation of Theorem 21. Now

$$
\begin{aligned}
\mathfrak{A} \models_\mathbb{X} \phi \quad &\Leftrightarrow \quad (\mathfrak{A}, R := X) \models \forall x_1 \ldots x_n \big(\neg R(x_1 \ldots x_n) \vee \big(R(x_1 \ldots x_n) \wedge \phi\big)\big) \\
&\Leftrightarrow \quad (\mathfrak{A}, R := X) \models \forall x_1 \ldots x_n \big(\neg R(x_1 \ldots x_n) \vee \big(R(x_1 \ldots x_n) \wedge \phi\big)\big)^* \\
&\Leftrightarrow \quad (\mathfrak{A}, R := X) \models \forall x_1 \ldots x_n \big(\neg R(x_1 \ldots x_n) \vee \big(R(x_1 \ldots x_n) \wedge \phi^*\big)\big) \\
&\Leftrightarrow \quad \mathfrak{A} \models_\mathbb{X} \phi^*,
\end{aligned}
$$

where X is the support of $\mathbb{X}$ and $\mathrm{Dom}(\mathbb{X}) = \{x_1, \ldots, x_n\}$. $\square$

6 Conclusion

Our investigations gave rise to the following expressiveness and complexity picture:

$$
\mathrm{P} \equiv_{\text{fin-ord}} \mathrm{FO}(\approx) \equiv \text{almost conjunctive } \mathrm{L\text{-}}(\ddot{\exists}^* \forall^*)_{[0,1]}[=, \mathrm{SUM}, 0, 1]
$$
$$
< \mathrm{L\text{-}ESO}_{[0,1]}[=, +, 0, 1] \equiv \mathrm{FO}(\approx, =(\cdots)) \equiv_{\text{fin}} \mathrm{NP},
$$

where the strict inclusion was shown in [16]. Its worth to note that almost conjunctive $(\ddot{\exists}^* \ddot{\exists}^* \forall^*)_\mathbb{R}[\leq, +, \mathrm{SUM}, 0, 1]$ is in some regard a maximal tractable fragment of additive existential second-order logic as dropping either the requirement of being almost conjunctive, or that of having the prefix form $\ddot{\exists}^* \ddot{\exists}^* \forall^*$, leads to a fragment that captures NP. We also showed that the full additive existential second-order logic (with inequality and constants 0 and 1) collapses to NP, a result which as far as we know has not been stated previously.

References

1. Benedikt, M., Grohe, M., Libkin, L., Segoufin, L.: Reachability and connectivity queries in constraint databases. J. Comput. Syst. Sci. **66**(1), 169–206 (2003)
2. Blum, L., Cucker, F., Shub, M., Smale, S.: Complexity and Real Computation. Springer-Verlag, Berlin, Heidelberg (1997)
3. Blum, L., Shub, M., Smale, S.: On a theory of computation and complexity over the real numbers: *np*-completeness, recursive functions and universal machines. Bull. Amer. Math. Soc. (N.S.) **21**(1), 1–46 (1989)

4. Bürgisser, P., Cucker, F.: Counting complexity classes for numeric computations II: algebraic and semialgebraic sets. J. Complexity **22**(2), 147–191 (2006)
5. Console, M., Hofer, M., Libkin, L.: Queries with arithmetic on incomplete databases. In: Suciu, D., Tao, Y., Wei, Z. (eds.) Proceedings of the 39th ACM SIGMOD-SIGACT-SIGAI Symposium on Principles of Database Systems, PODS 2020, Portland, OR, USA, 14–19 June 2020, pp. 179–189. ACM (2020)
6. Cucker, F., Meer, K.: Logics which capture complexity classes over the reals. J. Symb. Log. **64**(1), 363–390 (1999)
7. Durand, A., Hannula, M., Kontinen, J., Meier, A., Virtema, J.: Approximation and dependence via multiteam semantics. Ann. Math. Artif. Intell. **83**(3–4), 297–320 (2018)
8. Durand, A., Hannula, M., Kontinen, J., Meier, A., Virtema, J.: Probabilistic team semantics. In: Foundations of Information and Knowledge Systems - 10th International Symposium, FoIKS 2018, Budapest, Hungary, 14–18 May 2018, Proceedings, pp. 186–206 (2018)
9. Galliani, P.: Game Values and Equilibria for Undetermined Sentences of Dependence Logic. MSc Thesis. ILLC Publications, MoL-2008-08 (2008)
10. Galliani, P.: Inclusion and exclusion dependencies in team semantics: on some logics of imperfect information. Ann. Pure Appl. Logic **163**(1), 68–84 (2012)
11. Galliani, P., Hella, L.: Inclusion logic and fixed point logic. In: Ronchi, S., Rocca, D., (eds.) Computer Science Logic 2013 (CSL 2013), volume 23 of Leibniz International Proceedings in Informatics (LIPIcs), Dagstuhl, Germany, pp. 281–295 (2013)
12. Grädel, E., Gurevich, Y.: Metafinite model theory. Inf. Comput. **140**(1), 26–81 (1998)
13. Grädel, E., Kreutzer, S.: Descriptive complexity theory for constraint databases. In: Computer Science Logic, 13th International Workshop, CSL 1999, 8th Annual Conference of the EACSL, Madrid, Spain, 20–25 September 1999, Proceedings, pp. 67–81 (1999)
14. Grädel, E., Meer, K.: Descriptive complexity theory over the real numbers. In: Proceedings of the Twenty-Seventh Annual ACM Symposium on Theory of Computing, 29 May-1 June 1995, Las Vegas, Nevada, USA, pp. 315–324 (1995)
15. Grohe, M., Ritzert, M.: Learning first-order definable concepts over structures of small degree. In: 32nd Annual ACM/IEEE Symposium on Logic in Computer Science, LICS 2017, Reykjavik, Iceland, 20–23 June 2017, pp. 1–12. IEEE Computer Society (2017)
16. Hannula, M., Hirvonen, Å., Kontinen, J., Kulikov, V., Virtema, J.: Facets of distribution identities in probabilistic team semantics. In: Logics in Artificial Intelligence - 16th European Conference, JELIA 2019, Rende, Italy, 7–1 May 2019, Proceedings, pp. 304–320 (2019)
17. Hannula, M., Kontinen, J., Van den Bussche, J., Virtema, J.: Descriptive complexity of real computation and probabilistic independence logic. In: Hermanns, H., Zhang, L., Kobayashi, N., Miller, D., (eds.) LICS 2020: 35th Annual ACM/IEEE Symposium on Logic in Computer Science, Saarbrücken, Germany, 8–1 July 2020, pp. 550–563. ACM (2020)
18. Hannula, M., Virtema, J.: Tractability frontiers in probabilistic team semantics and existential second-order logic over the reals. CoRR, abs/2012.12830 (2020)
19. Uffe Flarup Hansen and Klaus Meer: Two logical hierarchies of optimization problems over the real numbers. Math. Log. Q. **52**(1), 37–50 (2006)
20. Hodges, W.: Compositional semantics for a language of imperfect information. J. Interest Group Pure Appl. Logics **5**(4), 539–563 (1997)

21. Hyttinen, T., Paolini, G., Väänänen, J.: A logic for arguing about probabilities in measure teams. Arch. Math. Logic **56**(5–6), 475–489 (2017)
22. Jordan, C., Kaiser, L.: Machine learning with guarantees using descriptive complexity and SMT solvers. CoRR, abs/1609.02664 (2016)
23. Kanellakis, P.C., Kuper, G.M., Revesz, P.Z.: Constraint query languages. J. Comput. Syst. Sci. **51**(1), 26–52 (1995)
24. Khachiyan, L.G.: A polynomial algorithm in linear programming. Dokl. Akad. Nauk SSSR **244**, 1093–1096 (1979)
25. Koiran, P.: Computing over the reals with addition and order. Theor. Comput. Sci. **133**(1), 35–47 (1994)
26. Kontinen, J., Nurmi, V.: Team logic and second-order logic. In: Ono, H., Kanazawa, M., de Queiroz, R. (eds.) Logic. Language, Information and Computation, volume 5514 of Lecture Notes in Computer Science, pp. 230–241. Springer, Berlin / Heidelberg (2009)
27. Kontinen, J., Väänänen, J.: On definability in dependence logic. J. Logic, Lang. Inf. **3**(18), 317–332 (2009)
28. Kreutzer, S.: Fixed-point query languages for linear constraint databases. In: Proceedings of the Nineteenth ACM SIGMOD-SIGACT-SIGART Symposium on Principles of Database Systems, 15–17 May 2000, Dallas, Texas, USA, pp. 116–125 (2000)
29. Meer, K.: Counting problems over the reals. Theor. Comput. Sci. **242**(1–2), 41–58 (2000)
30. Schaefer, M., Stefankovic, D.: Fixed points, nash equilibria, and the existential theory of the reals. Theory Comput. Syst. **60**(2), 172–193 (2017)
31. Torunczyk, S.: Aggregate queries on sparse databases. In: Suciu, D., Tao, Y., Wei, Z., (eds.) Proceedings of the 39th ACM SIGMOD-SIGACT-SIGAI Symposium on Principles of Database Systems, PODS 2020, Portland, OR, USA, 14–19 June 2020, pp. 427–443. ACM (2020)
32. Väänänen, J.: Dependence Logic. Cambridge University Press, Cambridge (2007)
33. van Bergerem, S., Schweikardt, N.: Learning concepts described by weight aggregation logic. In: Baier, C., Goubault-Larrecq, J. (eds.) 29th EACSL Annual Conference on Computer Science Logic, CSL 2021, January 25-28, 2021, Ljubljana, Slovenia (Virtual Conference), LIPIcs, vol. 183, pp. 10:1–10:18. Schloss Dagstuhl - Leibniz-Zentrum für Informatik (2021). https://doi.org/10.4230/LIPIcs.CSL.2021.10. https://dblp.org/rec/conf/csl/BergeremS21.bib

An Epistemic Probabilistic Logic
with Conditional Probabilities

Šejla Dautović[1(✉)], Dragan Doder[2], and Zoran Ognjanović[1]

[1] Mathematical Institute of Serbian Academy of Sciences and Arts, Belgrade, Serbia
{shdautovic,zorano}@mi.sanu.ac.rs
[2] Utrecht University, Utrecht, The Netherlands
d.doder@uu.nl

Abstract. We present a proof-theoretical and model-theoretical approach to reasoning about knowledge and conditional probability. We extend both the language of epistemic logic and the language of linear weight formulas, allowing statements like "Agent Ag knows that the probability of A given B is at least a half". We axiomatize this logic, provide corresponding semantics and prove that the axiomatization is sound and strongly complete. We also show that the logic is decidable.

Keywords: Probabilistic logic · Epistemic logic · Completeness

1 Introduction

Epistemic logics are formal models designed in order to reason about the knowledge of agents and their knowledge of each other's knowledge. During the last couple of decades, they have found applications in various fields such as game theory, the analysis of multi-agent systems in computer science and artificial intelligence, and for analyzing the behavior and interaction of agents in a distributed system [7,8,24]. In parallel, uncertain reasoning has emerged as one of the main fields in artificial intelligence, with many different tools developed for representing and reasoning with uncertain knowledge. A particular line of research concerns the formalization in terms of logic, and the questions of providing an axiomatization and decision procedure for *probabilistic logic* attracted the attention of researchers and triggered investigation about formal systems for probabilistic reasoning [1,6,9–11,19,20].

Fagin and Halpern [5] emphasised the need for combining those two fields for many application areas, and in particular in distributed systems applications, when one wants to analyze randomized or probabilistic programs. They developed a joint framework for reasoning about knowledge and probability, proposed a complete axiomatization and investigated decidability of the framework. Based on the seminal paper by Fagin, Halpern and Meggido [6], they extended the propositional epistemic language with formulas which express linear combinations of probabilities, called *linear weight formulas*, i.e., the formulas of the

© Springer Nature Switzerland AG 2021
W. Faber et al. (Eds.): JELIA 2021, LNAI 12678, pp. 279–293, 2021.
https://doi.org/10.1007/978-3-030-75775-5_19

form $a_1 w(\alpha_1) + \ldots + a_k w(\alpha_k) \geq r$, where a_j's and r are rational numbers. They proposed a finitary axiomatization and proved weak completeness, using a small model theorem.

In this paper, we extend the logic from [5] by also allowing formulas that can represent conditional probability. Thus, our language contains both knowledge operators K_i (one for each agent i) and conditional probability formulas of the form $a_1 w_i(\alpha_1, \beta_1) + \ldots + a_k w_i(\alpha_k, \beta_k) \geq r$. The expressions of the form $w_i(\alpha, \beta)$ represent conditional probabilities that agent i places on events according to Kolmogorov definition: $P(A|B) = \frac{P(A \cap B)}{P(B)}$ if $P(B) > 0$, while $P(A|B)$ is undefined when $P(B) = 0$. The corresponding semantics consists of enriched Kripke models, with a probability measure assigned to every agent in each world.

Our main results are a sound and complete axiomatization for the logic and decidability result. We prove strong completeness (every consistent set of formulas is satisfiable) using an adaptation of Henkin's construction, modifying some of our earlier methods [2–4,16,18,19,21]. Our axiom system contains infinitary rules of inference, whose premises and conclusions are in the form of k-nested implications (Definition 6). This form of infinitary rules is a technical solution already used in probabilistic, epistemic and temporal logics for obtaining various *strong necessitation* results [13,15,17,22,23]. An obvious alternative to an infinitary axiomatization would be to develop a finitary system which would be weakly complete (strong completeness of a finitary system is impossible due to the noncompactness phenomena for probability logics, see [11]). We do not know a finitary axiomatization for this rich language. Moreover, even for logics which need to express conditional probabilities only (i.e., without knowledge operators), the task of developing a finitary system turned out to be very hard to accomplish. Fagin, Halpern and Meggido [6] faced problems when they tried to represent conditional probabilities by adding multiplication to the syntax of linear weight formulas, and they needed to introduce a first-order extension of the language in order to obtain completeness. The only finitary axiomatization we are aware of is the fuzzy approach of Marchioni and Godo [14], who consider the probability of a conditional event of the form "α given β" as the truth-value of the fuzzy proposition $P(\alpha|\beta)$ which is read as "$P(\alpha|\beta)$ is probable."

In the last part of this paper, we prove that satisfiability problem for our logic is decidable. From the technical point of view, we combine the method of filtration [12] and a reduction to a system of inequalities.

2 Syntax and Semantics

Let $\mathcal{P} = \{p, q, r, \ldots\}$ be a set of propositional letters and let $\mathbf{A}$ be a finite set of agents. Let $\mathcal{Q}$ denote the set of all rational numbers and let $[0,1]_Q = [0,1] \cap \mathcal{Q}$.

Definition 1 (Formula). *The set For of all formulas of the logic is the smallest set such that:*

- *$\mathcal{P} \subset For$;*
- *If $\alpha \in For$ then $K_i \alpha \in For$.*

- For any $i \in \mathbf{A}$ and $k \geq 1$, if $\alpha_1, \alpha_1', \ldots, \alpha_k, \alpha_k' \in For$ and $a_1, \ldots, a_k, r \in \mathcal{Q}$, then $a_1 w_i(\alpha_1, \alpha_1') + \cdots + a_k w_i(\alpha_k, \alpha_k') \geq r \in For$,
- If α and β are formulas then $\neg\alpha, \alpha \wedge \beta \in For$.

The meaning of formula $K_i\alpha$ is "agent i knows α", while the expression $w_i(\alpha, \beta)$ denotes conditional probability of α given β, according to the agent i.

An expression of the form $a_1 w_i(\alpha_1, \alpha_1') + \cdots + a_k w_i(\alpha_k, \alpha_k')$ is called *term*. Following [5], we do not allow appearance of multiple agents inside of a term. We denote terms with f_i, g_i and h_i.

The propositional connectives, $\vee, \rightarrow$ and $\leftrightarrow$, are introduced as abbreviations, in the usual way. We define $\top$ to be an abbreviation for the formula $p \vee \neg p$ where p is a propositional letter, while $\bot$ is $\neg\top$. We also use abbreviations to define other types of inequalities; for example: $w_i(\alpha, \beta) \geq w_i(\alpha', \beta')$ as an abbreviation for $w_i(\alpha, \beta) - w_i(\alpha', \beta') \geq 0$, $w_i(\alpha, \beta) \leq w_i(\alpha', \beta')$ for $w_i(\alpha', \beta') \geq w_i(\alpha, \beta)$, $w_i(\alpha, \beta) = w_i(\alpha', \beta')$ for $(w_i(\alpha, \beta) \geq w_i(\alpha', \beta')) \wedge (w_i(\alpha, \beta) \leq w_i(\alpha', \beta'))$, and $w_i(\alpha, \beta) > w_i(\alpha', \beta')$ for $(w_i(\alpha, \beta) \geq w_i(\alpha', \beta')) \wedge \neg(w_i(\alpha, \beta) = w_i(\alpha', \beta'))$.

Now we introduce the semantics of our logic CKL.

Definition 2 (CKL-structure). *A* CKL-*structure is a tuple* $(W, \mathcal{K}, Prob, v)$ *where:*

1. W *is a non-empty set of objects called* worlds.
2. $v : W \times \mathcal{P} \rightarrow \{true, false\}$ *assigns to each world* $u \in W$ *a two-valued evaluation* $v(u, \cdot)$ *of propositional letters,*
3. $\mathcal{K} = \{\mathcal{K}_i \mid i \in \mathbf{A}\}$ *is a set of binary equivalence relations on* W. *We denote* $\mathcal{K}_i(u) = \{u' \mid (u', u) \in \mathcal{K}_i\}$, *and write* $u\mathcal{K}_i u'$ *if* $u' \in \mathcal{K}_i(u)$,
4. $Prob$ *assigns to every* $i \in \mathbf{A}$ *and* $u \in W$ *a probability space* $Prob(i, u) = (W_i(u), H_i(u), \mu_i(u))$, *where*
   - $W_i(u)$ *is a non-empty subset of* W,
   - $H_i(u)$ *is an algebra of subsets of* $W_i(u)$, *i.e. a set such that*
     (a) $W_i(u) \in H_i(u)$,
     (b) if $A \in H_i(u)$, *then* $W_i(u) \setminus A \in H_i(u)$, *and*
     (c) if $A, B \in H_i(u)$, *then* $A \cup B \in H_i(u)$.
   - $\mu_i(u) : H_i(u) \longrightarrow [0, 1]$ *is a finitely additive measure, i.e.,*
     (a) $\mu_i(u)(W_i(u)) = 1$,
     (b) $\mu_i(u)(A \cup B) = \mu_i(u)(A) + \mu_i(u)(B)$, *whenever* $A \cap B = \emptyset$.

The elements of $H_i(u)$ *are called* measurable sets.

Definition 3 (Satisfiability). *Let* M *be a CKL-structure and let* u *be some world from* M. *The satisfiability relation* $\models$ *is defined recursively as follows:*

1. *If* $\alpha \in \mathcal{P}$ *then* $M, u \models \alpha$ *iff* $v(u, \alpha) = true$,
2. $M, u \models K_i\alpha$ *iff* $M, u' \models \alpha$ *for all* $u' \in \mathcal{K}_i(u)$,
3. $M, u \models \sum_{k=1}^{n} a_k w_i(\alpha_k, \beta_k) \geq r$ *if* $\mu_i(u)(\{u' \in W_i(u) \mid M, u' \models \beta_k\}) > 0$ *for every* $k \in \{1, \ldots, n\}$ *and* $\sum_{k=1}^{n} a_k \mu_i(u)(\{u' \in W_i(u) \mid M, u' \models \alpha_k\} | \{u' \in W_i(u) \mid M, u' \models \beta_k\}) \geq r$,
4. $M, u \models \neg\alpha$ *iff* $M, u \not\models \alpha$,
5. $M, u \models \alpha \wedge \beta$ *iff* $M, u \models \alpha$ *and* $M, u \models \beta$.

We denote by $[\alpha]_{i,M,u}$ the set of all worlds from $W_i(u)$ in which α holds, i.e.,

$$[\alpha]_{i,M,u} = \{u' \in W_i(u) \mid M, u' \models \alpha\}.$$

We write $[\alpha]$ instead of $[\alpha]_{i,M,u}$ when i, M and u are clear from the context. Note that the satisfiability relation defined in Definition 3 is a partial relation, i.e., it is not in general defined for all formulas. The reason is that a formula $\sum_{k=1}^{n} a_k w_i(\alpha_k, \beta_k) \geq r$ can be evaluated in u only if all the sets $[\alpha_k]_{i,M,u}$ and $[\beta_k]_{i,M,u}$ are measurable. In order to keep the relation $\models$ *total* (i.e., well-defined for all the formulas), in this paper we consider only the models in which all those sets are indeed measurable.

Definition 4 (CKL-measurable structure). *A CKL-structure M is CKL-measurable iff $[\alpha]_{i,u} \in H(u)$ for every world u from M, every $\alpha \in For$ and every $i \in \mathbf{A}$. We denote the set of all measurable structures with* $\mathrm{CKL}_{\mathrm{Meas}}$.

Note that, according to Definition 3, the formula $w_i(\alpha, \beta) \geq r \vee w_i(\alpha, \beta) \leq r$ is not necessary satisfied in a model; the reason is that unconditional probability is simply undefined if probability of the condition is zero.

Definition 5 (Model, entailment). *For an $M = (W, Prob, K, v) \in \mathrm{CKL}_{\mathrm{Meas}}$, $u \in W$ and a set of formulas T, we say that M, u is a model of T, and write $M, u \models T$, iff $M, u \models \alpha$ for every $\alpha \in T$. The set T is satisfiable, if there is $M \in \mathrm{CKL}_{\mathrm{Meas}}$ and a world u from M such that $M, u \models T$. Formula α is valid if $\neg\alpha$ is not satisfiable. We say that T entails α and write $T \models \alpha$, if for every $M = (W, Prob, K, v) \in \mathrm{CKL}_{\mathrm{Meas}}$ and every $u \in W$ if $M, u \models T$ then $M, u \models \alpha$.*

3   Axiomatization

In this section we present an axiomatization of our logic, which we denote $Ax(\mathrm{CKL})$. First we need to introduce a useful notion which we use for the proof of Theorem 2.

Definition 6 (k-nested implication). *Let $\alpha \in For$ be a formula and let $k \in \mathbb{N}$. Let $\theta = (\theta_0, \ldots, \theta_k)$ be a sequence of k formulas, and $X = (X_1, \ldots, X_k)$ a sequence of knowledge operators from $\{K_i \mid i \in \mathbf{A}\}$. The k-nested implication formula $\Phi_{k,\theta,X}(\alpha)$ is defined recursively as follows:*

$$\Phi_{0,\theta,X}(\alpha) = \theta_0 \rightarrow \alpha$$

$$\Phi_{k,\theta,X}(\alpha) = \theta_k \rightarrow X_k \Phi_{k-1,\theta_{j=0}^{k-1},X_{j=0}^{k-1}}(\alpha)$$

For example, if $X = (K_a, K_b, K_c)$, $a, b, c \in \mathbf{A}$, then $\Phi_{3,\theta,X}(\alpha) = \theta_3 \rightarrow K_c(\theta_2 \rightarrow K_b(\theta_1 \rightarrow K_a(\theta_0 \rightarrow \top)))$.

$Ax(\text{CKL})$ contains the following axiom schemas and inference rules. It is straightforward to check that $Ax(\text{CKL})$ is sound with respect to CKL_{Meas}.

Axiom and rule for propositional reasoning

(A1) All instances of classical propositional tautologies.
(R1) From $\{\alpha, \alpha \to \beta\}$ infer β

Axioms and rules for reasoning about knowledge

(A2) $(K_i\alpha \wedge K_i(\alpha \to \beta)) \to K_i\beta$, for every $i \in G$
(A3) $K_i\alpha \to \alpha$,
(A4) $K_i\alpha \to K_iK_i\alpha$,
(A5) $\neg K_i\alpha \to K_i\neg K_i\alpha$,
(R2) From α infer $K_i\alpha$.

Axioms for reasoning about linear inequalities

(A6) $((a_1w_i(\alpha_1,\alpha_1') + \cdots + a_kw_i(\alpha_k,\alpha_k') \leq r) \wedge (w_i(\alpha_{k+1}',\top) > 0)) \leftrightarrow (a_1w_i(\alpha_1,\alpha_1') + \cdots + a_kw_i(\alpha_k,\alpha_k') + 0w_i(\alpha_{k+1},\alpha_{k+1}') \leq r)$
(A7) $(a_1w_i(\alpha_1,\alpha_1') + \cdots + a_kw_i(\alpha_k,\alpha_k') \leq r) \to (a_{j_1}w_i(\alpha_{j_1},\alpha_{j_1}') + \cdots + a_{j_k}w_i(\alpha_{j_k},\alpha_{j_k}') \leq r)$ where $j_1,\ldots j_k$ is a permutation of $1,\ldots k$.
(A8) $(a_1w_i(\alpha_1,\alpha_1') + \cdots + a_kw_i(\alpha_k,\alpha_k') \leq r) \wedge (a_1'w_i(\alpha_1,\alpha_1') + \cdots + a_k'w_i(\alpha_k,\alpha_k') \leq r') \to ((a_1+a_1')w_i(\alpha_1,\alpha_1') + \cdots + (a_k+a_k')w_i(\alpha_k,\alpha_k') \leq r+r')$
(A9) $(a_1w_i(\alpha_1,\alpha_1') + \cdots + a_kw_i(\alpha_k,\alpha_k') \leq r) \leftrightarrow (da_1w_i(\alpha_1,\alpha_1') + \cdots + da_kw_i(\alpha_k,\alpha_k') \leq dr)$ where $d > 0$.
(A10) $\bigwedge_{i=0}^{n} w_i(\alpha_i',\top) > 0 \to ((a_1w_i(\alpha_1,\alpha_1') + \cdots + a_kw_i(\alpha_k,\alpha_k') \leq r) \vee (a_1w_i(\alpha_1,\alpha_1') + \cdots + a_kw_i(\alpha_k,\alpha_k') \geq r)$
(A11) $(f_i \geq r) \to (f_i > r')$ for $r > r'$

Axioms and rule for reasoning about probabilities

(A12) $w_i(\alpha,\top) \geq 0$
(A13) $w_i(\alpha \wedge \beta,\top) + w_i(\alpha \wedge \neg\beta,\top) = w_i(\alpha,\top)$
(A14) $w_i(\alpha,\top) = w_i(\beta,\top)$ if $\alpha \leftrightarrow \beta$ is an instance of propositional tautology
(A15) $\sum_{j=1}^{n} a_jw_i(\alpha_j,\beta_j) \geq r \to w_i(\beta_j,\top) > 0$ for every $j \in \{1,\ldots,n\}$
(A16) $(w_i(\beta,\top) \geq s \wedge w_i(\alpha,\beta) \geq r) \to w_i(\alpha \wedge \beta,\top) \geq sr$
(R3) From α infer $w_i(\alpha,\top) \geq 1$
(R4) From the set of premises $\{\Phi_{k,\theta,X}(f_i \geq r - \frac{1}{k}) \mid k \in \mathbb{N}\}$ infer $\Phi_{k,\theta,X}(f_i \geq r)$
(R5) From the set of premises $\{\Phi_{k,\theta,X}(w_i(\beta,\top) > 0)\} \cup \{\Phi_{k,\theta,X}((w_i(\beta,\top) \geq s \to w_i(\alpha \wedge \beta,\top) \geq rs) \mid s \in [0,1]_Q\}$ infer $\Phi_{k,\theta,X}(w_i(\alpha,\beta) \geq r)$

The given axioms and rules are divided into four groups, according to the type of reasoning. The axioms A6–A14 are adapted from axiom system from [5] to our approach to conditional probabilities. The axioms A15 and A16, together with the rule R5 properly capture the third condition of Definition 3. The rules R4 and R5 are infinitary inference rules. R4 is a variant of so called Archimedean rule, whose role is to prevent nonstandard values. Intuitively, it says that is the value of a term is infinitely close to r, then it must be equal to r.

Let us now define some basic notions of proof theory.

Definition 7 (Theorem, proof). *A formula α is a* theorem, *denoted by $\vdash \alpha$, if there is a sequence of formulas $\alpha_0, \alpha_1, \ldots, \alpha_{\lambda+1}$ (λ is finite or countable ordinal), such that $\alpha_{\lambda+1} = \alpha$ and every α_i, $i \le \lambda + 1$, is an axiom, or it is derived from the preceding formulas by an inference rule.*

A formula α is deducible *from a set $T \subseteq For$ ($T \vdash_{Ax(\mathrm{CKL})} \alpha$) if there is a sequence of formulas $\alpha_0, \alpha_1, \ldots, \alpha_{\lambda+1}$ (λ is finite or countable ordinal), such that $\alpha_{\lambda+1} = \alpha$ and every α_i is an axiom or a formula from T, or it is derived from the preceding formulas by an inference rule, with the exception that e R2 and R3 can be applied to the theorems only. The sequence $\alpha_0, \alpha_1, \ldots, \alpha$ is a* proof *of α from T. We write $\vdash$ instead of $\vdash_{Ax_{\mathrm{CKL}}}$ when it is clear from context.*

Note that the length of a proof is any countable successor ordinal.

Definition 8 (Consistency). *A set of formulas T is* inconsistent *if $T \vdash \perp$, otherwise it is* consistent. *T is a* maximal consistent set *(mcs) of formulas if it is consistent and every proper superset of T is inconsistent.*

4 Completeness

In this section we show that the axiomatization $Ax(\mathrm{CKL})$ is strongly complete for the logic CKL, i.e., we prove that every consistent set of formulas has a model. First we prove several auxiliary statements.

Theorem 1 (Deduction theorem). *Let T be a set of formula and α and β a formulas. Then*

$$T \cup \{\alpha\} \vdash \beta \text{ iff } T \vdash \alpha \rightarrow \beta.$$

Deduction theorem can be proven using transfinite induction on the length of the inference. For the cases when we apply infinitary inference rules, we refer the reader to [23], when a similar proof is presented, using the form of k-nested implications in the infinitary rules.

Theorem 2 (Strong necessitation). *If T is a set of formulas and $T \vdash \alpha$, then $K_i T \vdash K_i \alpha$, for all $i \in \mathbf{A}$, where $K_i T = \{K_i \alpha \mid \alpha \in T\}$.*

Proof. Let $T \vdash \alpha$. We will prove the theorem by using the transfinite induction on the length of the proof of $T \vdash \alpha$. Here we will only consider the application of the rule R5. Let α be the formula $\Phi_{k,\theta,X}(w_i(\gamma, \beta) \ge r)$ which was obtained by the rule R5. Then we have

$T \vdash \Phi_{k,\theta,X}(w_i(\beta, \top) > 0)$
$T \vdash \Phi_{k,\theta,X}(w_i(\beta, \top) \ge s \rightarrow w_i(\gamma \wedge \beta, \top) \ge rs)$ for all $s \in [0,1]_Q$
$K_i T \vdash K_i \Phi_{k,\theta,X}(w_i(\beta, \top) > 0)$ by IH
$K_i T \vdash K_i \Phi_{k,\theta,X}(w_i(\beta, \top) \ge s \rightarrow w_i(\gamma \wedge \beta, \top) \ge rs)$ for all $s \in [0,1]_Q$, by IH
$K_i T \vdash \top \rightarrow K_i \Phi_{k,\theta,X}(w_i(\beta, \top) > 0)$
$K_i T \vdash \top \rightarrow K_i \Phi_{k,\theta,X}(w_i(\beta, \top) \ge s \rightarrow w_i(\gamma \wedge \beta, \top) \ge rs)$ for all $s \in [0,1]_Q$
$K_i T \vdash \Phi_{k+1,\overline{\theta},\overline{X}}(w_i(\beta, \top) > 0)$, $\overline{\theta} = (\theta, \top)$, $\overline{X} = (X, K_i)$

$K_iT \vdash \Phi_{k+1,\overline{\theta},\overline{X}}(w_i(\beta, \top) \geq s \to w_i(\gamma \wedge \beta, \top) \geq rs)$ for all $s \in [0,1]_Q$,
$K_iT \vdash \Phi_{k+1,\overline{\theta},\overline{X}}(w_i(\gamma, \beta) \geq r)$, by R5
$K_iT \vdash \top \to K_i\Phi_{k,\theta,X}(w_i(\gamma, \beta) \geq r)$
$K_iT \vdash K_i\alpha.$ $\qquad\qquad\qquad\qquad\qquad\qquad\qquad\qquad\qquad\qquad\qquad$ $\square$

Next we prove some crucial statements which we need for the proof of the completeness theorem.

Theorem 3 (Lindenbaum's Theorem). *Every consistent set of formulas can be extended to a maximal consistent set.*

Proof. Let T be an arbitrary consistent set of formulas. Assume that $\{\gamma_i \mid i = 0, 1, 2, \dots\}$ is an enumeration of all formulas from *For*. We construct the set T^* recursively, in the following way:

1. $T_0 = T$.
2. If the formula γ_i is consistent with T_i, then $T_{i+1} = T_i \cup \{\gamma_i\}$.
3. If the formula γ_i is not consistent with T_i, then:
   (a) If $\gamma_i = \Phi_{k,\theta,X}(f_i \geq r)$ and $f_i = w_i(\alpha, \beta)$, then we define $T_{i+1} = T_i \cup \{\neg\gamma_i, \neg\Phi_{k,\theta,X}(f_i \geq r - \frac{1}{m}), \gamma"_i\}$ where
   $\gamma"_i = \neg\Phi_{k,\theta,X}(w_i(\beta, \top) > 0)$, if $T_i \cup \{\neg\Phi_{k,\theta,X}(w_i(\beta, \top) > 0\} \not\vdash \bot$
   $\gamma"_i = \neg\Phi_{k,\theta,X}(w_i(\beta, \top) \geq s \to w_i(\alpha \wedge \beta, \top) \geq sr)$, otherwise,
   for some $m \in \mathbb{N}$ and $s \in [0,1]_Q$ such that T_{i+1} is consistent.
   (b) If $\gamma_i = \Phi_{k,\theta,X}(f_i \geq r)$ and $f_i \neq w_i(\alpha, \beta)$ then we define $T_{i+1} = T_i \cup \{\neg\gamma_i, \neg\Phi_{k,\theta,X}(f_i \geq r - \frac{1}{m})\}$ for some $m \in \mathbb{N}$, such that T_{i+1} is consistent.
   (c) Otherwise, $T_{i+1} = T_i \cup \{\neg\gamma_i\}$.
4. $T^* = \bigcup_{n=0}^{\infty} T_n$.

First we will show that the set T^* is correctly defined, i.e., there exist $m \in \mathbb{N}$ from (3a) and (3b) and rational number s from the step (3a) of the construction. Let us prove correctness in step (3a) exists.

Let us assume that $T'_i = T_i \cup \{\Phi_{k,\theta,X}(w_i(\alpha, \beta) \geq r)\}$ is inconsistent. From Theorem 1 we obtain $T_i \vdash \neg\Phi_{k,\theta,X}(w_i(\alpha, \beta) \geq r)$. Suppose that the set $T_i \cup \{\neg\Phi_{k,\theta,X}(w_i(\alpha, \beta) \geq r - \frac{1}{m})\}$ inconsistent for every $m \in \mathbb{N}$. By Theorem 1, we have $T_i \vdash \Phi_{k,\theta,X}(w_i(\alpha, \beta) \geq r - \frac{1}{m})$ for every $m \in \mathbb{N}$. Then by the rule R3 we have $T_i \vdash \Phi_{k,\theta,X}(w_i(\alpha, \beta) \geq r)$. Contradiction. Now suppose that the set $T'_i \cup \{\neg\Phi_{k,\theta,X}(w_i(\beta, \top) > 0)\}$ is inconsistent, and that the set $T'_i \cup \{\neg\Phi_{k,\theta,X}(w_i(\beta, \top) \geq s \to w_i(\alpha \wedge \beta, \top) \geq sr)\}$ is inconsistent for every s. By Theorem 1, we obtain that $T'_i \vdash \Phi_{k,\theta,X}(w_i(\beta, \top) > 0)$ and $T'_i \vdash \Phi_{k,\theta,X}(w_i(\beta, \top) \geq s \to w_i(\alpha \wedge \beta, \top) \geq sr)$, for every s. By the rule R4 we have $T'_i \vdash \Phi_{k,\theta,X}(w_i(\alpha, \beta) \geq r)$. Contradiction.

Next we prove that T^* is a maximal consistent set. Note that every T_i is consistent by the construction. This still doesn't imply consistency of $T^* = \bigcup_{n=0}^{\infty} T_n$, since we have infinitary rules. First we show that for every $\gamma' \in For$ either $\gamma' \in T^*$ or $\neg\gamma' \in T^*$ holds. Let i and j be the nonnegative integers such that $\gamma_i = \gamma'$ and $\gamma_j = \neg\gamma'$. Then, either γ' or $\neg\gamma'$ is consistent with $T_{max\{i,j\}}$. If $T_{max\{i,j\}}$ is not consistent with γ' and $\neg\gamma'$ then by Theorem 1, $T_{max\{i,j\}}$ will be inconsistent. Then either $\gamma' \in T_{i+1}$ or $\neg\gamma' \in T_{j+1}$, so either $\gamma' \in T^*$ or $\neg\gamma' \in T^*$.

In order to prove the consistency of T^*, we will show that T^* is deductively closed. If the formula γ is an instance of some axiom, then $\gamma \in T^*$ by the construction of T^*. Here we show that T^* is closed under the rule R5; the other cases are similar. Suppose $T^* \vdash \Phi_{k,\theta,X}(w_i(\alpha,\beta) \geq r)$ was obtained by R5, where $\Phi_{k,\theta,X}(w_i(\beta,\top) > 0) \in T^*$ and $\Phi_{k,\theta,X}(w_i(\beta,\top) \geq s \rightarrow w_i(\alpha \wedge \beta,\top) \geq sr) \in T^*$ for all $s \in [0,1]_Q$. Assume that $\Phi_{k,\theta,X}(w_i(\alpha,\beta) \geq r) \notin T^*$. Let j be the positive integer such that $\gamma_j = \Phi_{k,\theta,X}(w_i(\alpha,\beta) \geq r)$. Then, $T_j \cup \{\gamma_j\}$ is inconsistent, since otherwise $\Phi_{k,\theta,X}(w_i(\alpha,\beta) \geq r) \in T_{j+1} \subset T^*$. By the step (3a) $\neg\Phi_{k,\theta,X}(w_i(\beta,\top) > 0) \in T_{j+1}$ or there is $s' \in [0,1]_Q$ such that $\neg\Phi_{k,\theta,X}(w_i(\beta,\top) \geq s' \rightarrow w_i(\alpha \wedge \beta,\top) \geq s'r) \in T_{j+1}$. Suppose $\neg\Phi_{k,\theta,X}(w_i(\beta,\top) > 0) \in T_{j+1}$ and from $\Phi_{k,\theta,X}(w_i(\beta,\top) > 0) \in T^*$ there is nonegative integer k such that $\Phi_{k,\theta,X}(w_i(\beta,\top) > 0) \in T_k$. Then $T_{\max\{k,j+1\}} \vdash \bot$, a contradiction.

Now suppose that $\neg\Phi_{k,\theta,X}(w_i(\beta,\top) \geq s' \rightarrow w_i(\alpha \wedge \beta,\top) \geq s'r) \in T_{j+1}$, where $s' \in [0,1]_Q$. We have that $\Phi_{k,\theta,X}(w_i(\beta,\top) \geq s \rightarrow w_i(\alpha \wedge \beta,\top) \geq sr) \in T^*$ for all $s \in [0,1]_Q$, so we have $\Phi_{k,\theta,X}(w_i(\beta,\top) \geq s' \rightarrow w_i(\alpha \wedge \beta,\top) \geq s'r) \in T^*$. Then, there is nonegative integer k' such that $\Phi_{k,\theta,X}(w_i(w_i(\beta,\top) \geq s' \rightarrow w_i(\alpha \wedge \beta,\top) \geq s'r) \in T'_k$. Then $T_{\max\{k',j+1\}} \vdash \bot$, a contradiction. Consequently, the set T^* is deductively closed.

From the fact that T^* is deductively closed we can prove that T^* is consistent. Indeed, if T^* is inconsistent, there is $\gamma' \in For$ such that $T^* \vdash \gamma' \wedge \neg\gamma'$. But then there is a nonnegative integer i such that $\gamma' \wedge \neg\gamma' \in T_i$, a contradiction. $\qquad\square$

Next we introduce some notation, that we use in definition of the canonical model. For a given $T \subseteq For$ and $i \in \mathbf{A}$, we define the set T/K_i as follows:

$$T/K_i = \{\alpha \mid K_i\alpha \in T\}.$$

Definition 9 (Canonical model). *The canonical model* $M_C = (W, \mathcal{K}, Prob, v)$ *is defined as follows:*

- $W = \{u \mid u$ *is maximal consistent set*$\}$,
- *for every world* u *and every propositional letter* $p \in \mathcal{P}$, $v(u,p) = true$ *iff* $p \in u$,
- $\mathcal{K} = \{\mathcal{K}_i \mid i \in \mathbf{A}\}$ *where* $\mathcal{K}_i = \{(u',u) \mid u'/K_i \subset u\}$
- $Prob(i,u) = (W_i(u), H_i(u), \mu_i(u))$ *such that:*
  - $W_i(u) = W$,
  - $H_i(u) = \{\{u' \in W \mid \alpha \in u'\} \mid \alpha \in For\}$,
  - $\mu_i(u) : H_i(u) \rightarrow [0,1]$ *such that* $\mu_i(u)(\{u' \in W \mid \alpha \in u'\}) = \sup\{r \in [0,1]_Q \mid w_i(\alpha,\top) \geq r \in u\}$.

We use the following notation to refer to the elements of $H_i(u)$ from the canonical model:

$$[\alpha] = \{u' \in W \mid \alpha \in u'\}.$$

Lemma 1. *Let* u *be a world of* M_C. *If* $f_i = a_1 w_i(\alpha_1, \alpha'_1) + \cdots + a_k w_i(\alpha_k, \alpha'_k)$ *then* $a_1\mu_i(u)([\alpha_1]|[\alpha'_1]) + \cdots + a_k\mu_i(u)([\alpha_k]|[\alpha'_k]) = \sup\{s \mid u \vdash f_i \geq s\}$.

Proof. First we will show that $\mu_i(u)([\![\alpha]\!]|[\![\beta]\!]) = \sup\{r \in [0,1]_Q \mid w_i(\alpha,\beta) \geq r \in u\}$. Note that if $\mu_i(u)([\![\beta]\!]) = 0$ then both $\mu_i(u)([\![\alpha]\!]|[\![\beta]\!])$ and $\sup\{r \in [0,1]_Q \mid w_i(\alpha,\beta) \geq r \in u\}$ are undefined.

Suppose that $w_i(\alpha,\beta) \geq r \in u$ and let $\{s_n \mid n \in \mathbb{N}\}$ be strictly increasing sequence of numbers from $[0,1]_Q$, such that $\lim_{n \to \infty} s_n = \mu_i(u)([\![\beta]\!])$. Let n be any number from $\mathbb{N}$. Then $u \vdash w_i(\beta,\top) \geq s_n$. Using the assumption $w_i(\alpha,\beta) \geq r \in u$, the axioms A15 and A16 and propositional reasoning, we obtain $u \vdash w_i(\beta,\top) > 0$ and $u \vdash w_i(\alpha \wedge \beta,\top) \geq rs_n$. Finally, by Definition 9 we have $\mu_i(u)([\![\beta]\!]) > 0$ and $\mu_i(u)([\![\alpha \wedge \beta]\!]) \geq \lim_{n \to \infty} rs_n = r\mu_i(u)([\![\beta]\!])$, i.e., $\mu_i(u)([\![\beta]\!]) > 0$ and $\mu_i(u)([\![\alpha]\!]|[\![\beta]\!]) \geq r$. We can conclude that $\mu_i(u)([\![\alpha]\!]|[\![\beta]\!]) \geq \sup\{r \in [0,1]_Q \mid w_i(\alpha,\beta) \geq r \in u\}$.

Let now $\mu_i(u)([\![\alpha]\!]|[\![\beta]\!]) \geq t$ and $\mu_i(u)([\![\beta]\!]) > 0$. We want to show that $u \vdash w_i(\beta,\top) > 0$ and $u \vdash w_i(\beta,\top) \geq s \to w_i(\alpha \wedge \beta,\top) \geq ts$ for all $s \in [0,1]_Q$.

If $u \nvdash w_i(\beta,\top) > 0$ then $u \vdash w_i(\beta,\top) = 0$, i.e., $\mu_i(u)([\![\beta]\!]) = 0$, contradiction. If $s > \mu_i(u)([\![\beta]\!])$, than $u \vdash \neg(w_i(\beta,\top) \geq s)$, so $u \vdash w_i(\beta,\top) \geq s \to w_i(\alpha \wedge \beta,\top) \geq ts$. Let now $s \leq \mu_i(u)([\![\beta]\!])$, then $st \leq \mu_i(u)([\![\alpha \wedge \beta]\!])$, so $u \vdash w_i(\alpha \wedge \beta,\top) \geq ts$. Now, we have that for every $s \in [0,1]_Q$, $u \vdash w_i(\beta,\top) \geq s \to w_i(\alpha \wedge \beta,\top) \geq ts$, by the rule R5 we get $u \vdash w_i(\alpha,\beta) \geq t$. So $\mu_i(u)([\![\alpha]\!]|[\![\beta]\!]) \leq \sup\{r \in [0,1]_Q \mid w_i(\alpha,\beta) \geq r \in u\}$.

Let $f_i = a_1 w_i(\alpha_1,\alpha_1') + \cdots + a_k w_i(\alpha_k,\alpha_k')$. By the properties of supremum and A8, $a_1\mu_i(u)([\![\alpha_1]\!]|[\![\alpha_1']\!]) + \cdots + a_k\mu_i(u)([\![\alpha_k]\!]|[\![\alpha_k']\!]) = a_1 \sup\{s_1 \mid u \vdash w_i(\alpha_1,\alpha_1') \geq s_1\} + \cdots + a_k \sup\{s_k \mid u \vdash w_i(\alpha_k,\alpha_k') \geq s_k\} = \sup\{s \mid u \vdash f_i \geq s\}$. □

Lemma 2. *The canonical model M_C is a CKL-structure.*

Proof. The proof that every $H_i(u)$ from M_C is an algebra of sets is trivial. The fact that every $\mu_i(u)$ is a finitely additive probability measure follows from the axioms for reasoning about probabilities and Lemma 1. □

On the other hand, in order to show that $M_C \in \mathrm{CKL}_{\mathrm{Meas}}$, we need to prove that $[\alpha]_{i,M_C,u} = [\![\alpha]\!]$, for every i and u. This follows form the following lemma.

Lemma 3 (Truth lemma). *Let M_C be the canonical model and $\gamma \in For$. Then for every world u from M_C*

$$\gamma \in u \text{ iff } M_C, u \models \gamma.$$

Proof. We use induction on the complexity of the formula γ. If γ is a propositional letter, the statement follows from the construction of M_C. The cases when γ is a conjunction or a negation are straightforward.

Suppose $\gamma = K_i\beta$. Let $K_i\beta \in u$. Since $\beta \in u/K_i$, then $\beta \in u'$ for every u' such that $(u,u') \in \mathcal{K}_i$ (by the definition of $\mathcal{K}_i$). Therefore, $M_C, u' \models \beta$ by induction hypothesis (β is subformula of $K_i\beta$), and then $M_C, u \models K_i\beta$.

Let now $M_C, u \models K_i\beta$. Assume the opposite, that $K_i\beta \notin u$. Then, $u/K_i \cup \{\neg\beta\}$ must be consistent. If it would not be consistent, then $u/K_i \vdash \beta$ by the Deduction theorem and $u \supset K_i(u/K_i) \vdash K_i\beta$ by Theorem 2, i.e., $K_i\beta \in u$, which is a contradiction. Therefore, $u/K_i \cup \{\neg\beta\}$ can be extended to a maximal consistent U, so $u\mathcal{K}_i U$. Since $\neg\beta \in U$, then $M_C, U \models \neg\beta$ by induction hypothesis, so we get the contradiction $M_C, u \not\models K_i\beta$.

Let $f_i = a_1 w_i(\alpha_1, \alpha_1') + \cdots + a_k w_i(\alpha_k, \alpha_k')$. We suppose that $f_i \geq r \in u$, then $r \leq \sup\{s \mid u \vdash f_i \geq s\}$ and $w_i(\alpha_j', \top) > 0 \in u$ for every $j \in \{1, \ldots, k\}$. Then by Lemma 1, $M_C, u \models f_i \geq r$.

For the other direction, assume that $M_C, u \models f_i \geq r$. Suppose that $f_i \geq r \notin u$. Then we have $w_i(\alpha_j', \top) = 0 \in u$ for some $j \in \{1, \ldots, k\}$ or $f_i < r \in u$. If $w_i(\alpha_j', \top) = 0$ for some j then $M_C, u \not\models f_i \geq r$, a contradiction. Let $f_i < r \in u$, then, reasoning as above we conclude $M_C, u \models f_i < r$, a contradiction.   □

Consequently, we have shown that for every $\alpha \in For$, every $i \in \mathbb{A}$ and every world u from M_C the equality $[\alpha]_{i,M_C,u} = [\![\alpha]\!]$ holds, so M_C is a CKL-measurable structure.

Theorem 4 (Strong completeness of CKL). *A set of formulas T is consistent iff T is* CKL_{Meas}*-satisfiable.*

Proof. The direction form right to left is straightforward. For the other direction, suppose that T is a consistent set of formulas. By Theorem 3, there is a maximal consistent superset T^* of T. Since $M_C \in \text{CKL}_{\text{Meas}}$, we only need to show that M_C is a model of T^*. By Lemma 3, if T is consistent set we know that T^* is a world in M_C, so we obtain $M_C, T^* \models T$.   □

5   Decidability of CKL

In this section, we prove that the logic CKL is decidable. Recall the satisfiability problem: given a CKL-formula α, we want to determine if there exists a world u in a CKL_{Meas}-model M such that $M, u \models \alpha$. First, we show that a CKL-formula is satisfiable iff it is satisfiable in a measurable structure with a finite number of worlds.

For a formula α we denote $Subf(\alpha)$ the set of all subformulas of α.

Theorem 5. *If a CKL-formula α is satisfiable in a model $M \in \text{CKL}_{\text{Meas}}$, then it is satisfied in a model $M^* \in \text{CKL}_{\text{Meas}}$ with at most $2^{|Subf(\alpha)|}$ number of worlds.*

Proof. Let s be a world from M such that $M, s \models \alpha$. Let $Subf(\alpha)$ be the set of all subformulas of α and $k = |Subf(\alpha)|$. By $\sim$ we denote the equivalence relation over $W \times W$, where $s \sim s'$ iff for every $\beta \in Subf(\alpha)$, $M, s \models \beta$ iff $M, s' \models \beta$. The quotient set $W_{/\sim}$ is finite and $|W_{/\sim}| \leq 2^{|Subf(\alpha)|}$. Now, for every class C_i we choose an element and denote it s_i^*. We consider the model $M^* = (W^*, \mathcal{K}^*, Prob^*, v^*)$, where:

- $W^* = \{s_i^* \mid C_i \in W_{/\sim}\}$,
- $\mathcal{K}^* = \{\mathcal{K}_a^* \mid a \in \mathbf{A}\}$ is a set of binary relations on W^* where $(s_i^*, s_j^*) \in \mathcal{K}_a^*$ iff for every $K_a\phi \in Subf(\alpha)$, $M, s_i^* \models K_a\phi$ iff $M, s_j^* \models K_a\phi$
- For every agent a and $s_i^* \in W^*$, $Prob^*(a, s_i^*) = (W_a^*(s_i^*), H_a^*(s_i^*), \mu_a^*(s_i^*))$ is defined as follows:

- $W_a^*(s_i^*) = \{s_j^* \in W^* \mid (\exists u \in C_j)u \in W_a(s_i)\}$,
- $H_a^*(s_i^*)$ is the power set of $W_a^*(s_i^*)$,
- $\mu_a^*(s_i^*)(\{s_j^*\}) = \mu_a(s_i^*)(C_j(s_i^*))$, where $C_j(s_i^*) = C_j \cap W_a^*(s_i^*)$ and for any $D \in H_a^*(s_i^*)$, $\mu_a^*(s_i^*)(D) = \sum_{s_j^* \in D} \mu_a^*(s_i^*)(\{s_j^*\})$,

- $v^*(s_i, p) = v(s_i, p)$.

It can be shown that $M^* \in \mathrm{CKL}_{\mathrm{Meas}}$.

Finally, using induction on the complexity of the formulas, one can show that for any $\beta \in Subf(\alpha)$, $M, s \models \beta$ iff $M^*, s_i^* \models \beta$ where s_i^* represents C_s in M^*. $\square$

Note that there are infinitely many finite models from $\mathrm{CKL}_{\mathrm{Meas}}$ with at most $2^{|Subf(\alpha)|}$ worlds, because there are infinitely many possibilities for real-valued probabilities. Thus, the previous theorem does not directly imply decidability, and the further complementary steps are needed. In order to show decidability we will translate the problem of satisfiability of a formula to the problem of satisfiability of finite sets of equations and inequalities.

Theorem 6. *Satisfiability problem for* CKL *is decidable.*

Proof. Let α be a CKL-formula. We want to check whether there is a $\mathrm{CKL}_{\mathrm{Meas}}$-structure M and a world s form M such that $M, s \models \alpha$. Using the previous theorem, we will consider only the structures with l worlds, where $l \leq 2^{|Subf(\alpha)|}$.

The idea is to see is there any structure with at least l worlds whom we can join a valuation, a set of binary equivalence relations and finitely additive probabilities such that the formula α is satisfied in some world of the structure. For this we will use potential structures which we call pre-structures. In pre-structures we do not specify probability measures (in order to avoid infinitely many cases), but we want to specify enough information about measures from which we can determine satisfiability of all subformulas of α.

Let $Subf(\alpha)$ be the set of subformulas of α, let $\mathcal{P}^\alpha = \mathcal{P} \cap Subf(\alpha)$ and let $SubP(\alpha)$ be the set of all subformulas of α of the form $\sum_{k=1}^n a_k w_i(\alpha_k, \beta_k) \geq r$. For every $l \leq 2^{|Subf(\alpha)|}$ we consider pre-structures $\overline{M} = (\overline{W}, \overline{\mathcal{K}}, \overline{S}, \overline{v})$ such that:

- $\overline{W}$ is a set of worlds such that $|\overline{W}| = l$
- $\overline{v} : \overline{W} \times \mathcal{P}^\alpha \to \{true, false\}$.
- $\overline{\mathcal{K}} = \{\overline{\mathcal{K}}_a \mid a \in \mathbf{A}\}$ on $\overline{W}$.
- $\overline{S} : \overline{W} \times SubP(\alpha) \to \{true, false\}$.

Note that for every number l we have finitely many possibilities for the choice of pre-structures, i.e., we have finite number of choices of valuation, binary equivalence relations and function $\overline{S}$. This pre-structure is not a CKL-structure, but we can check if a subformula of α holds in a world of a pre-structure $\overline{M}$ using the relation $\Vdash$, defined as follows:

1. If $\gamma \in \mathcal{P}^\alpha$ then $\overline{M}, s \Vdash \gamma$ iff $\overline{v}(s, \gamma) = true$,
2. $\overline{M}, s \Vdash \overline{K}_a \gamma$ iff $\overline{M}, s' \Vdash \gamma$ for all $s' \in \overline{\mathcal{K}}_a(s)$,
3. $\overline{M}, s \Vdash \sum_{k=1}^n a_k w_a(\gamma_k, \beta_k) \geq r$ iff $\overline{S}(s, \sum_{k=1}^n a_k w_a(\gamma_k, \beta_k) \geq r) = true$
4. $\overline{M}, s \Vdash \neg\gamma$ iff $\overline{M}, s \nVdash \gamma$,
5. $\overline{M}, s \Vdash \gamma \wedge \beta$ iff $\overline{M}, s \Vdash \gamma$ and $\overline{M}, s \Vdash \gamma$.

We will consider only those $\overline{M} = (\overline{W}, \overline{\mathcal{K}}, \overline{S}, \overline{v})$ such that $\overline{M}, s \Vdash \alpha$ for some world $s \in \overline{W}$. For each such $\overline{M}$ we want to check whether $\overline{M}$ can be extended to a structure, i.e., whether there is a measurable structure $M = (\overline{W}, \overline{\mathcal{K}}, Prob, v)$ such that $\overline{v}$ is a restriction of v and for every agent a and every $s \in \overline{W}$ and $\sum_{k=1}^{n} a_k w_a(\gamma_k, \beta_k) \geq r \in SubP(\alpha)$ we have $M, s \models \sum_{k=1}^{n} a_k w_a(\gamma_k, \beta_k) \geq r$ iff $\overline{S}(s, \sum_{k=1}^{n} a_k w_a(\gamma_k, \beta_k) \geq r) = true$. It is straightforward to check that for such M we have $M, s \models \beta$ iff $\overline{M}, s \Vdash \beta$ holds for every $\beta \in Subf(\alpha)$. Since the way v extends $\overline{v}$ is irrelevant, it suffices to check whether $\overline{S}$ can be replaced with $Prob$ in some $\overline{M} = (\overline{W}, \overline{\mathcal{K}}, \overline{S}, \overline{v})$ such that $\overline{M}, s \Vdash \alpha$ for some world $s \in \overline{W}$. For that purpose, for each such $\overline{M}$ we consider specific equations and inequalities, that we describe below. We chose the variables of the form y_{a,s_i,s_j} which represent the values $\mu_a(s_i)(\{s_j\})$. Now we state the equations and inequalities:

(1) $y_{a,s_i,s_j} \geq 0$, for every world s_j

(2) $\displaystyle\sum_{s_j \in \overline{M}} y_{a,s_i,s_j} = 1$

(3) $\displaystyle\sum_{w_j : M^l, w_j \Vdash \beta_k} y_{a,s_i,s_j} > 0$ for every $k \in \{1, \ldots, n\}$, and

$$\sum_{k=1}^{n} \left(a_k \sum_{s_j : \overline{M}, s_j \Vdash \beta_k \wedge \gamma_k} y_{a,s_i,s_j} \prod_{t \neq k, t=1}^{n} \sum_{s_j : \overline{M}, s_j \Vdash \beta_t} y_{a,s_i,s_j} \right) \geq$$

$$r \prod_{k=1}^{n} \sum_{s_j : \overline{M}, s_j \Vdash \beta_k} y_{a,s_i,s_j}, \text{ for every formula } \sum_{k=1}^{n} a_k w_a(\gamma_k, \beta_k) \geq r$$

such that $\overline{S}(s_i, \sum_{k=1}^{n} a_k w_a(\gamma_k, \beta_k) \geq r) = true$

(4) $\displaystyle\bigvee_{k=1}^{n} \left(\sum_{s_j : \overline{M}, s_j \Vdash \beta_k} y_{a,s_i,s_j} = 0 \right)$ or

$$\sum_{k=1}^{n} \left(a_k \sum_{s_j : \overline{M}, s_j \Vdash \beta_k \wedge \gamma_k} y_{a,s_i,s_j} \prod_{t \neq k, t=1}^{n} \sum_{s_j : \overline{M}, s_j \Vdash \beta_t} y_{a,s_i,s_j} \right) <$$

$$r \prod_{k=1}^{n} \sum_{s_j : \overline{M}, s_j \Vdash \beta_k} y_{a,s_i,s_j}, \text{ for every formula } \sum_{k=1}^{n} a_k w_a(\gamma_k, \beta_k) \geq r$$

such that $\overline{S}(s_i, \sum_{k=1}^{n} a_k w_a(\gamma_k, \beta_k) \geq r) = false$

The inequality (1) above assures that all the probability measures are non-negative, and the equality (2) states that the probability of the set of all possible worlds has to be equal to 1. The equality (3) states that the probabilities of the sets of all evidences in a formula are greater than 0 and the linear combination of probabilities is greater than r, from the corresponding formula. It is easy to see that (3) corresponds to the third condition of the satisfiability relation from Definition 3, after we clean the denominators. Similarly, (4), corresponds to the combination of the fourth and the third condition from Definition 3.

The equations and inequalities (1)–(4) form not one, but a number of finite systems of equations and inequalities. Note that adding (4) to any system Sys of equations and inequalities results with a disjunction of at least two different extensions of Sys. For the purpose of this proof, the fact that we always have finitely many systems is sufficient, and it is enough if one of the systems is solvable. Those systems are represented in the language of real closed fields, and it is well known that the theory of real closed fields is decidable. Since we have finitely many possibilities for the choice of l, and for every l finitely many possibilities for the choice of pre-structure, our logic is decidable as well.   □

6 Conclusion

We have investigated a propositional logic of knowledge and conditional probability that allows explicit reasoning about probabilities. We have been able to obtain strongly complete axiomatization and decision procedure for our logic. Following [5], we proposed the most general case, where no semantic relationship is posed between the modalities for knowledge and probability. Fagin and Halpern [5] also consider some modification of the semantics, by posing relations between the sample spaces $W_i(u)$ and possible worlds $\mathcal{K}_i(u)$, which model some typical situations in the multi-agent systems. For example, they consider a natural assumption $W_i(u) \subseteq \mathcal{K}_i(u)$, which forbids an agent to place positive probabilities to the events she knows to be false. The paper [5] provides characterization of all those semantic assumptions in terms of corresponding axioms. (for example, $W_i(u) \subseteq \mathcal{K}_i(u)$ corresponds to $K_i\alpha \to w_i(\alpha) = 1$). Adding those axioms to our system would also make it complete for the considered semantics.

Acknowledgments. This work has been partially funded by the Science Fund of the Republic of Serbia through the project Advanced artificial intelligence techniques for analysis and design of system components based on trustworthy BlockChain technology - AI4TrustBC (the first and the third author).

References

1. Alechina, N.: Logic with probabilistic operators. In: Proceedings of the ACCO-LADE 1994, pp. 121–138 (1995)
2. Doder, D., Marinković, B., Maksimović, P., Perović, A.: A logic with conditional probability operators. Publications de L'Institut Mathematique Ns **87**(101), 85–96 (2010)
3. Doder, D., Ognjanović, Z.: Probabilistic logics with independence and confirmation. Studia Logica **105**(5), 943–969 (2017)

4. Doder, D., Ognjanovic, Z.: A probabilistic logic for reasoning about uncertain temporal information. In: Meila, M., Heskes, T. (eds.) Proceedings of the Thirty-First Conference on Uncertainty in Artificial Intelligence, UAI 2015, Amsterdam, The Netherlands, pp. 248–257. AUAI Press (2015)
5. Fagin, R., Halpern, J.Y.: Reasoning about knowledge and probability. J. ACM 41(2), 340–367 (1994)
6. Fagin, R., Halpern, J.Y., Megiddo, N.: A logic for reasoning about probabilities. Inf. Comput. 87, 78–128 (1990)
7. Fagin, R., Geanakoplos, J., Halpern, J.Y., Vardi, M.Y.: The hierarchical approach to modeling knowledge and common knowledge. Int. J. Game Theory 28(3), 331–365 (1999)
8. Fagin, R., Halpern, J.Y., Moses, Y., Vardi, M.Y.: Reasoning About Knowledge. MIT Press, Cambridge, MA (2003)
9. Frisch, A., Haddawy, P.: Anytime deduction for probabilistic logic. Artif. Intell. 69, 93–122 (1994)
10. Halpern, J.Y., Pucella, R.: A logic for reasoning about evidence. J. Artif. Intell. Res. 26, 1–34 (2006)
11. van der Hoek, W.: Some considerations on the logic pfd. J. Appl. Non-Classical Logics 7(3) (1997)
12. Hughes, G.E., Cresswell, M.J.: A Companion to Modal Logic. Methuen London, New York (1984)
13. de Lavalette, G.R.R., Kooi, B., Verbrugge, R.: A strongly complete proof system for propositional dynamic logic. In: AiML2002–Advances in Modal Logic (Conference Proceedings), pp. 377–393 (2002)
14. Marchioni, E., Godo, L.: A logic for reasoning about coherent conditional probability: a modal fuzzy logic approach. In: Alferes, J.J., Leite, J. (eds.) JELIA 2004. LNCS (LNAI), vol. 3229, pp. 213–225. Springer, Heidelberg (2004). https://doi.org/10.1007/978-3-540-30227-8_20
15. Marinkovic, B., Glavan, P., Ognjanovic, Z., Studer, T.: A temporal epistemic logic with a non-rigid set of agents for analyzing the blockchain protocol. J. Logic Comput. (2019)
16. Marinkovic, B., Ognjanovic, Z., Doder, D., Perovic, A.: A propositional linear time logic with time flow isomorphic to ω^2. J. Appl. Log. 12(2), 208–229 (2014)
17. Milošević, M., Ognjanović, Z.: A first-order conditional probability logic. Logic J. IGPL 20(1), 235–253 (2012)
18. Ognjanovic, Z., Markovic, Z., Raskovic, M., Doder, D., Perovic, A.: A propositional probabilistic logic with discrete linear time for reasoning about evidence. Ann. Math. Artif. Intell. 65(2–3), 217–243 (2012)
19. Ognjanović, Z., Rašković, M., Marković, Z.: Probability Logics: Probability-based Formalization of Uncertain Reasoning. Springer, New York (2016). https://doi.org/10.1007/978-3-319-47012-2
20. Rašković, M., Ognjanović, Z., Marković, Z.: A logic with conditional probabilities. In: Alferes, J.J., Leite, J. (eds.) JELIA 2004. LNCS (LNAI), vol. 3229, pp. 226–238. Springer, Heidelberg (2004). https://doi.org/10.1007/978-3-540-30227-8_21
21. Savic, N., Doder, D., Ognjanovic, Z.: Logics with lower and upper probability operators. Int. J. Approx. Reason. 88, 148–168 (2017)
22. Tomović, S., Ognjanović, Z., Doder, D.: Probabilistic common knowledge among infinite number of agents. In: Destercke, S., Denoeux, T. (eds.) ECSQARU 2015. LNCS (LNAI), vol. 9161, pp. 496–505. Springer, Cham (2015). https://doi.org/10.1007/978-3-319-20807-7_45

23. Tomovic, S., Ognjanovic, Z., Doder, D.: A first-order logic for reasoning about knowledge and probability. ACM Trans. Comput. Log. **21**(2), 16:1–16:30 (2020)
24. Wolter, F.: First order common knowledge logics. Studia Logica **65**(2), 249–271 (2000)

Logic Programming and Answer Set Programming

On Syntactic Forgetting Under Uniform Equivalence

Ricardo Gonçalves[1] ⓘ, Tomi Janhunen[2] ⓘ, Matthias Knorr[1(✉)] ⓘ, and João Leite[1] ⓘ

[1] Universidade Nova de Lisboa, Caparica, Portugal
{rjrg,mkn,jleite}@fct.unl.pt
[2] Tampere University, Tampere, Finland
tomi.janhunen@tuni.fi

Abstract. Forgetting in Answer Set Programming (ASP) aims at reducing the language of a logic program without affecting the consequences over the remaining language. It has recently gained interest in the context of modular ASP where it allows simplifying a program of a module, making it more declarative, by omitting auxiliary atoms or hiding certain atoms/parts of the program not to be disclosed. Unlike for arbitrary programs, it has been shown that forgetting for modular ASP can always be applied, for input, output and hidden atoms, and preserve all dependencies over the remaining language (in line with uniform equivalence). However, the definition of the result is based solely on a semantic characterization in terms of HT-models. Thus, computing an actual result is a complicated process and the result commonly bears no resemblance to the original program, i.e., we are lacking a corresponding syntactic operator. In this paper, we show that there is no forgetting operator that preserves uniform equivalence (modulo the forgotten atoms) between the given program and its forgetting result by only manipulating the rules of the original program that contain the atoms to be forgotten. We then present a forgetting operator that preserves uniform equivalence and is syntactic whenever this is suitable. We also introduce a special class of programs, where syntactic forgetting is always possible, and as a complementary result, establish it as the largest known class where forgetting while preserving all dependencies is always possible.

Keywords: Answer Set Programming · Forgetting · Uniform equivalence

1 Introduction

Forgetting, also known as variable elimination, aims at reducing the language of a knowledge base while preserving all direct and indirect relationships over the remaining language. First studied in the context of classical logic [5,14,27,32, 33,39], it gained considerable interest in a wide variety of formalisms (cf. the recent survey [12]) and found applications in, e.g., cognitive robotics [30,31,35],

ⓒ Springer Nature Switzerland AG 2021
W. Faber et al. (Eds.): JELIA 2021, LNAI 12678, pp. 297–312, 2021.
https://doi.org/10.1007/978-3-030-75775-5_20

conflict resolution [13, 27, 28, 41], and ontology abstraction and comparison [24–26, 38]. In more general terms, its usefulness stems from the fact that auxiliary variables can be eliminated, resulting in a more declarative representation of (certain parts of) a knowledge base, as well as that certain pieces of information can be omitted/hidden for reasons of privacy or legal requirements.

In Answer Set Programming (ASP), forgetting has also been extensively studied, where its non-monotonic nature has created unique challenges resulting in a wide variety of different appproaches [4, 10, 13, 15, 18, 23, 36, 37, 40, 41]. Among the many proposals of operators and desirable properties (cf. the survey on forgetting in ASP [16]), arguably, forgetting in ASP is best captured by *strong persistence* [23], a property which requires that the answer sets of a program and its forgetting result be in correspondence, even in the presence of additional rules over the remaining language. However, it is not always possible to forget and satisfy strong persistence [17, 19].

Recently, forgetting has also gained interest in the context of modular ASP [2, 9, 20, 22, 34]. In general, modular programming is fundamental to facilitate the creation and reuse of large programs, and modular ASP allows the creation of answer set programs equipped with well-defined input-output interfaces whose semantics is compositional on the individual modules. For modules with input-output interfaces, strong persistence can be relaxed to *uniform persistence* that only varies additional sets of facts (the inputs), and it has been shown that forgetting for modular ASP can always be applied and preserves all dependencies over the remaining language [15].

Uniform persistence is closely related to uniform equivalence, which in turn is closely connected to one of the central ideas of ASP: a problem is specified as an abstract program, and varying instances, represented by sets of facts, are combined with it to obtain concrete solutions. Thus, arguably, uniform persistence seems the better alternative when considering forgetting in ASP in general, but its usage is hindered by the lack of practically usable forgetting operators: the definition of a result in [15] is based solely on an advanced semantic characterization in terms of HT-models, so computing an actual result is a complicated process and the result, though semantically correct w.r.t. uniform persistence, commonly bears no resemblance to the original program. What is missing is a syntactic operator that computes results of forgetting, ideally only by manipulating the rules of the original program that contain the atoms to be forgotten.

Concrete syntactic forgetting operators have been considered infrequently in the literature. Zhang and Foo [41] define two such operators in the form of strong and weak forgetting, but neither of them does even preserve the answer sets of the original program (modulo the forgotten atoms) [13]. Eiter and Wang [13] present a syntactic operator for their semantic forgetting, but it only preserves the answer sets themselves and does not satisfy uniform nor strong persistence. Knorr and Alferes [23] provide an operator that aims at aligning with strong persistence which is not possible in general. Thus, it is only defined for a non-standard class of programs, and cannot be iterated in general, as the operator is not closed for this non-standard class, nor does it satisfy uniform persistence.

Berthold et al. [4] introduce an operator that satisfies strong persistence whenever possible, but it does not satisfy uniform persistence, nor is it closed for the non-standard class defined in [23]. Finally, based on the idea of forks [1], a forgetting operator is provided [3] that introduces so-called anonymous cycles when forgetting in the sense of strong persistence is not possible. However, rather than reducing the language this operator does introduce new auxiliary atoms to remove existing ones, though only in a restricted way. Thus, no syntactic forgetting operator exists in the literature that satisfies uniform persistence.

In this paper, we research whether there exists such a syntactic forgetting operator that satisfies uniform persistence. Somewhat surprisingly, we answer this question negatively in the general case. This raises several questions:

- When is it possible/suitable to forget syntactically while preserving uniform persistence?
- Are there meaningful classes of programs where syntactic forgetting is always possible while preserving uniform persistence?
- Can such an operator be iterated, i.e., is it closed for the class of programs for which it is defined?
- Are there correspondences to existing operators in restricted settings (to clarify relations to related work)?

Our contributions can be summarized as follows:
- We show that there is no forgetting operator that preserves uniform equivalence (modulo the forgotten atoms) between the given program and its forgetting result, by only manipulating the rules of the original program that contain the atoms to be forgotten (as formalized in the property $(\mathbf{SI_u})$).
- We argue that forgetting an atom for which there are rules of the form $p \leftarrow not\,not\,p$ is indeed not suitable in a syntactic manner, even for cases where such result could still be constructed based alone on the rules of the original program that contain the atoms to be forgotten.
- We present a forgetting operator that preserves uniform equivalence while forgetting, and is syntactic whenever this is suitable. We show that this operator can indeed be iterated in the general case.
- In addition, we present a special case of our operator for stratified programs, without disjunction and loops over (double) negation, and show that syntactic forgetting is always possible while preserving uniform equivalence.
- We also show that, for stratified programs, this operator corresponds to an existing forgetting operator that aims at preserving all dependencies whenever possible, and we establish this class of programs as the largest known class where forgetting while preserving all dependencies is always possible.

The remainder of our paper is structured as follows. We recall relevant notions and notations in Sect. 2. In Sect. 3, we first introduce our operator for stratified programs, before we establish our main impossibility result in the general case and present our general operator in Sect. 4. We conclude in Sect. 5.

2 Preliminaries

Let us first recall relevant notions on logic programs under answer set semantics and forgetting in Answer Set Programming (ASP).

An *(extended) rule* r is an expression of the form

$$a_1 \vee \cdots \vee a_k \leftarrow b_1, \ldots, b_l, not\, c_1, \ldots, not\, c_m, not\, not\, d_1, \ldots, not\, not\, d_n, \quad (1)$$

where $a_1, \ldots, a_k, b_1, \ldots, b_l, c_1, \ldots, c_m$, and $d_1, \ldots, d_n$ are atoms of a given propositional alphabet $\mathcal{A}$.[1] We also write such rules as

$$H(r) \leftarrow B^+(r), not\, B^-(r), not\, not\, B^{--}(r), \quad (2)$$

where $H(r) = \{a_1, \ldots, a_k\}$, $B^+(r) = \{b_1, \ldots, b_l\}$, $B^-(r) = \{c_1, \ldots, c_m\}$, and $B^{--}(r) = \{d_1, \ldots, d_n\}$, and we will use both forms interchangeably.[2] Given a rule r, $H(r)$ is called the *head* of r, and $B(r) = B^+(r) \cup not\, B^-(r) \cup not\, not\, B^{--}(r)$ the *body* of r, where, for a set L of literals (elements of the form a, $not\, a$, or $not\, not\, a$, for $a \in \mathcal{A}$), $not\, L = \{not\, \ell \mid \ell \in L\}$, where $not\, not\, not\, \ell$ systematically simplifies as $not\, \ell$. An *(extended) logic program* is a finite set of rules. By $\mathcal{A}(P)$ we denote the set of atoms appearing in P and by $\mathcal{C}_e$ the class of extended programs. We call r *disjunctive* if $B^{--}(r) = \emptyset$; *normal* if, additionally, $H(r)$ has at most one element; *Horn* if on top of that $B^-(r) = \emptyset$; and *fact* if also $B^+(r) = \emptyset$. The classes of *disjunctive*, *normal* and *Horn programs*, $\mathcal{C}_d$, $\mathcal{C}_n$, and $\mathcal{C}_H$, are defined as usual. Given a program P and an *interpretation* I, i.e., a set $I \subseteq \mathcal{A}$, the *reduct* P^I is defined as:

$$P^I = \{H(r) \leftarrow B^+(r) \mid r \text{ of the form (2) in } P, B^-(r) \cap I = \emptyset, B^{--}(r) \subseteq I\}.$$

An *HT-interpretation* is a pair $\langle X, Y \rangle$ s.t. $X \subseteq Y \subseteq \mathcal{A}$. Given a program P, an HT-interpretation $\langle X, Y \rangle$ is an *HT-model of P* if $Y \models P$ and $X \models P^Y$, where $\models$ stands for the standard satisfaction relation of classical logic. The set of *all HT-models of P* is denoted by $\mathcal{HT}(P)$, and we admit that the set of HT-models of a program P can be restricted to $\mathcal{A}(P)$ even if $\mathcal{A}(P) \subset \mathcal{A}$. Given a program P, a set of atoms $Y \subseteq \mathcal{A}(P)$ is an *answer set* of P if $\langle Y, Y \rangle \in \mathcal{HT}(P)$ and there is no $X \subset Y$ s.t. $\langle X, Y \rangle \in \mathcal{HT}(P)$. The set of all answer sets of P is denoted by $\mathcal{AS}(P)$. Given a set $V \subseteq \mathcal{A}$, the *V-exclusion* of a set of answer sets (a set of HT-interpretations) $\mathcal{M}$, denoted $\mathcal{M}_{\|V}$, is $\{X \backslash V \mid X \in \mathcal{M}\}$ ($\{\langle X \backslash V, Y \backslash V \rangle \mid \langle X, Y \rangle \in \mathcal{M}\}$). Two programs P_1 and P_2 are *equivalent*, denoted by $P_1 \equiv_n P_2$, if $\mathcal{AS}(P_1) = \mathcal{AS}(P_2)$, *strongly equivalent*, denoted by $P_1 \equiv P_2$, if $\mathcal{AS}(P_1 \cup R) = \mathcal{AS}(P_2 \cup R)$ for any $R \in \mathcal{C}_e$ (alternatively, if $\mathcal{HT}(P_1) = \mathcal{HT}(P_2)$ by [29]), and *uniformly equivalent*, denoted by $P_1 \equiv_u P_2$, if $\mathcal{AS}(P_1 \cup R) = \mathcal{AS}(P_2 \cup R)$, for any set of facts R.

Strongly or uniformly equivalent programs can be syntactically different, e.g., due to the occurrence of non-minimal or tautological rules, i.e., rules that if removed would not affect its HT-models in any way. To facilitate the presentation

---

[1] Note that double negation is standard in the context of forgetting in ASP.
[2] Thus, there cannot be any duplicates in any of the rule components.

in this paper, and in line with related work, we restrict our considerations to programs in normal form following the definition introduced in [4]. Formally, a rule r in P is *minimal* if there is no rule $r' \in P$ such that $H(r') \subseteq H(r) \wedge B(r') \subset B(r)$ or $H(r') \subset H(r) \wedge B(r') \subseteq B(r)$. We also recall that a rule r is *tautological* if $H(r) \cap B^+(r) \neq \emptyset$, or $B^+(r) \cap B^-(r) \neq \emptyset$, or $B^-(r) \cap B^{--}(r) \neq \emptyset$.

Definition 1. *A program P is in* normal form *if the following conditions hold:*

1. *for every $a \in \mathcal{A}(P)$ and $r \in P$, at most one of a, $(not\ a)$ or $(not\ not\ a)$ is in $B(r)$;*
2. *if $a \in H(r)$, then neither a, nor $(not\ a)$ are in $B(r)$;*
3. *all rules in P are minimal.*

It is shown in [4], that, for a given program P, a strongly equivalent normal form $NF(P)$ can be obtained in polynomial time.

A *forgetting operator* over a class $\mathcal{C}$ of programs[3] over $\mathcal{A}$ is a partial function $f : \mathcal{C} \times 2^{\mathcal{A}} \to \mathcal{C}$ s.t. the *result of forgetting about V from P*, $f(P, V)$, is a program over $\mathcal{A}(P) \backslash V$, for each $P \in \mathcal{C}$ and $V \subseteq \mathcal{A}$. We denote the domain of f by $\mathcal{C}(f)$. The operator f is called *closed* for $\mathcal{C}' \subseteq \mathcal{C}(f)$ if $f(P, V) \in \mathcal{C}'$, for every $P \in \mathcal{C}'$ and $V \subseteq \mathcal{A}$. A *class* F *of forgetting operators (over $\mathcal{C}$)* is a set of forgetting operators f s.t. $\mathcal{C}(f) \subseteq \mathcal{C}$.

Among the many properties introduced for different classes of forgetting operators in ASP [16], *strong persistence* **(SP)** [23] is arguably the one that should intuitively hold, since it imposes the preservation of all original direct and indirect dependencies between atoms not to be forgotten. I.e., closely related to strong equivalence, the answer sets of $f(P, V)$ correspond to those of P, no matter what programs R over $\mathcal{A} \backslash V$ we add to both. However, as shown in [17,19], there is no forgetting operator that satisfies **(SP)** and that is defined for all pairs $\langle P, V \rangle$, called *forgetting instances*, where P is a program and V is a set of atoms to be forgotten from P. Thus, a relaxation of property **(SP)** was introduced in [15], called *uniform persistence* **(UP)**, that only considers R consisting of facts. We recall both properties, where F is a class of forgetting operators.

(SP) F satisfies *Strong Persistence* if, for each $f \in \mathsf{F}$, $P \in \mathcal{C}(f)$ and $V \subseteq \mathcal{A}$, we have $\mathcal{AS}(f(P, V) \cup R) = \mathcal{AS}(P \cup R)_{\parallel V}$, for all programs $R \in \mathcal{C}(f)$ with $\mathcal{A}(R) \subseteq \mathcal{A} \backslash V$.

(UP) F satisfies *Uniform Persistence* if, for each $f \in \mathsf{F}$, $P \in \mathcal{C}(f)$ and $V \subseteq \mathcal{A}$, we have $\mathcal{AS}(f(P, V) \cup R) = \mathcal{AS}(P \cup R)_{\parallel V}$, for all sets of facts R with $\mathcal{A}(R) \subseteq \mathcal{A} \backslash V$.

A class of forgetting operators $\mathsf{F_{UP}}$ is defined in [15] based on semantic definition over HT-models, that is shown to satisfy this property **(UP)**, and it is shown that an operator exists for that class relying on the countermodels of the semantic characterization in terms of HT-models [7] – a construction previously used for computing concrete results of forgetting for classes of forgetting operators based on HT-models [19,36,37].

---

[3] In this paper, we only consider the very general class of programs introduced before, but, often, subclasses of it appear in the literature of ASP and forgetting in ASP.

In light of the general impossibility result for **(SP)** for arbitrary context programs R, and the fact that **(UP)** is satisfiable for sets of facts R, one may wonder whether it is possible to find a property that uses programs R in a class in between these two extremes such that it is possible to forget and preserve all dependencies. As it turns out, this is not possible.

Proposition 1. (UP) *is the strongest relaxation of* **(SP)** *w.r.t. the class of programs R such that there is a forgetting operator over $\mathcal{C} \supseteq \mathcal{C}_n$ that satisfies it.*

This novel result stresses the importance of **(UP)** and of finding syntactic operators that satisfy this property.

3   Uniform Forgetting from Stratified Programs

In this section, we introduce a syntactic operator for forgetting from a restricted class of programs that aligns with the ideas of uniform persistence by only manipulating the rules of the original program that contain the atoms to be forgotten. We focus first on this restricted class of programs with the intuition to ease the reading and to facilitate comparisons to the few existing syntactic forgetting operators in the literature. As usual, this operator will be defined for forgetting a single atom first. Several atoms can then be forgotten iteratively, after showing that the operator can indeed be iterated.

We start by formalizing our restricted forms of programs, called stratified programs that do not allow cycles over (double) negation nor disjunctions. For that purpose, we introduce notation to refer to all rules in P that include some specific atom in one of its components. Namely, P_p^H refers to the rules r in P with $p \in H(r)$, P_p^+ refers to the rules r in P with $p \in B^+(r)$, P_p^- refers to the rules r in P with $p \in B^-(r)$, and P_p^{--} refers to the rules r in P with $p \in B^{--}(r)$.

Definition 2. *Let P be a logic program. We call P stratified if:*

1. *all of its rules of the form (1) are s.t. $k \leq 1$;*
2. *P can be partitioned into disjoint P_i s.t., for each $p \in \mathcal{A}$,*
   (a) all rules $r \in P_p^H$ occur in one P_i;
   (b) if $p \in B^+(r)$ with $r \in P_i$, then $P_p^H \subseteq P_j$ with $j \leq i$;
   (c) if $p \in (B^-(r) \cup B^{--}(r))$ with $r \in P_i$, then $P_p^H \subseteq P_j$ with $j < i$.

This not only avoids cycles over negation between atoms, it also prohibits in the case of normal forms that any atom occurs in more than one part of a rule.

We now proceed towards introducing the new stratified uniform forgetting operator f_{su}. For that purpose, we require some further notation and we introduce it along with motivating examples that provide intuitions on how to obtain desired results. To ease the notation, we usually consider forgetting p from P.

Example 1. Consider P containing the following rules:

$$p \leftarrow s \qquad p \leftarrow not\, q, r \qquad t \leftarrow p \qquad v \leftarrow not\, p$$

If we add $s \leftarrow$ to P, then p becomes derivable, thus also t. So, when forgetting about p, we want to preserve that adding s makes t derivable, which can be achieved by introducing a rule $t \leftarrow s$, i.e. by replacing the body atom p with the body whose rule head is p, in a way quite similar to wGPPE [6]. For the same reason, a rule $t \leftarrow not\, q, r$ should appear in the result of forgetting, passing along that, if q is false and r is true, then t is true. This kind of replacement of p in some body does not directly transfer to the replacement of $not\, p$ in another body. In fact, v will be derivable if none of the bodies of rules with head p is true. For example, we want a rule $v \leftarrow not\, s, not\, not\, q$ in the result of forgetting to capture one such case. It can be verified in that case that $not\, p$ is true if one of the two conjuncts, $not\, s$ and $not\, not\, q$, is true, and false otherwise, and that adding further rules to capture the remaining combinations allows one to preserve the dependency between v and the cases in which $not\, p$ is true.   □

To be able to capture these dependencies in the case of negated atoms, [4] extends the ideas of the as-dual from [23] inspired by [13]. The as-dual is a set of conjunctions of literals, each of which can be used to replace some negated atom, but preserves its truth value. Here, and in the following, we identify by $B^{\backslash p}(r) = B(r)\backslash\{p, not\, p, not\, not\, p\}$ the set of body literals of r after removing every occurrence of p.

Definition 3. *Let P be a logic program, $p \in \mathcal{A}(P)$, and $P_p^H = \{r_1, \dots, r_n\}$. We define the* as-dual *of P for p as follows:*

$$\mathcal{D}_{as}^p(P) = \{not\,\{l_1, \dots, l_n\} \mid l_i \in B^{\backslash p}(r_i), 1 \leq i \leq n\}.$$

Note that for a stratified program in normal form, $B(r_i)$ cannot contain any form of p, but we prefer to keep this definition general, so that it be applicable in the general case.

Example 2. Recall program P from Example 1. Among these rules, only two contain p in the head, and we obtain $\mathcal{D}_{as}^p(P) = \{\{not\, s, not\, r\}, \{not\, s, not\, not\, q\}\}$. We can verify that whenever all elements in one of these sets are true, p cannot be true in any answer set of P.   □

Based on that, we can formalize our first operator.

Definition 4. *Let P be a stratified program over $\mathcal{A}$, $N = NF(P)$ the normal form of P, and $p \in \mathcal{A}$. The result of forgetting about p from P, $\mathsf{f}_{su}(P, p)$, is $NF(S)$ where S is obtained from N as follows:*

1. *replace $r \in N_p^+$ with rules $H(r) \leftarrow B^{\backslash p}(r) \cup B(r_1)$ for each $r_1 \in N_p^H$;*
2. *replace $r \in N_p^{--}$ with rules $H(r) \leftarrow B^{\backslash p}(r) \cup not\, not\, B(r_1)$ for each $r_1 \in N_p^H$;*
3. *replace $r \in N_p^-$ with rules $H(r) \leftarrow B^{\backslash p}(r) \cup D$ s.t. $D \in \mathcal{D}_{as}^p(N_p^H)$;*
4. *omit N_p^H.*

Example 3. Consider P, a slight variation of the program in Example 1.

$$p \leftarrow s \qquad p \leftarrow not\, q, r \qquad t \leftarrow p \qquad v \leftarrow not\, p \qquad w \leftarrow not\, not\, p$$

We have $\mathcal{D}_{as}^{p}(P) = \{\{not\, s, not\, r\}, \{not\, s, not\, not\, q\}\}$ from Example 2 and the following result of forgetting:

$$
\begin{array}{lll}
t \leftarrow s & w \leftarrow not\, not\, s & v \leftarrow not\, s, not\, not\, q \\
t \leftarrow not\, q, r & w \leftarrow not\, q, not\, not\, r & v \leftarrow not\, s, not\, r
\end{array}
$$

We can verify that no matter which set of facts over the remaining $\mathcal{A}$ is added to the forgetting result, the induced answer sets coincide with those of the original program modulo the forgotten atoms. □

Note that the normal form of a stratified program is also a stratified program.

Lemma 1. *Given a stratified program P, $NF(P)$ is a stratified program.*

This allows us to show that forgetting an atom p from P using f_{su}, results in a stratified program not mentioning the atom to be forgotten.

Proposition 2. *Let P be a stratified program over signature $\mathcal{A}$ and $p \in \mathcal{A}$. Then $f_{su}(P, p)$ is a stratified program over $\mathcal{A} \setminus \{p\}$.*

This result is important as it allows us to iterate the operator, which can be used to iteratively forget a set of atoms. For that purpose, we define how such iteration can be achieved for any operator defined for forgetting a single atom.

Definition 5. *Let P be a logic program over Σ, $V = \{v_1, v_2, \ldots, v_n\} \subseteq \mathcal{A}$ an ordered sequence of atoms, and f an operator defined for forgetting a single atom. Then, we define $f(P, V)$ inductively as follows:*

- $f(P, \{v_1\}) = f(P, v_1)$;
- $f(P, \{v_1, v_2, \ldots, v_n\}) = f(f(P, \{v_1\}), \{v_2, \ldots, v_n\})$.

We need to fix an order on the set of atoms to be forgotten (lexicographic for example) to ensure that the result of forgetting is indeed a unique program. This raises the question as to whether the order in which we forget the elements of such a set matters. To answer this question for f_{su}, we first relate to existing work in the literature. In fact, due to the restriction to stratified programs, for many of the syntactic operators presented in the literature, we can show that our operator does coincide with them, though on different levels.

Theorem 1. *Let P be a stratified program and $p \in \mathcal{A}$. We have:*

1. $f_{su}(P, p) = f_{SP}(P, p)$ *for* f_{SP} *defined in [4];*
2. $f_{su}(P, p) \equiv f_{Sas}(P, p)$ *for* f_{Sas} *defined in [23];*
3. $f_{su}(P, p) \equiv_n \mathsf{forget}_3(P, p)$ *for* forget_3 *defined in [13] if P does not contain double negation.*

Thus, for stratified programs, the syntactic operator that aims at satisfying **(SP)** whenever possible, f_{SP}, coincides with our operator; the one that aims at satisfying **(SP)** in a rather restricted non-standard setting, f_{Sas}, provides strongly equivalent forgetting results, and the one defined for preserving answer sets, forget_3, only provides equivalent results, and is only defined for disjunctive programs originally, though it is shown in [13] that for N-acyclic programs, i.e., programs that satisfy conditions (a) and (c) for $r \in P_p^{--}$ of Definition 1, double negation can simply be omitted.[4] In the latter two cases, the reason why the correspondence is not stronger lies mainly in the preprocessing applied: the normal form in [23] does not eliminate non-minimal rules, and the transformations applied in [13] to simplify the program based on its answer sets before forgetting do not preserve strong equivalence (e.g. Positive Reduction). There are further syntactic forgetting operators [41], but these do not even preserve equivalence [13], thus no correspondence result exists.

Among the results of Theorem 1, the first one is of particular interest, as it relates to an operator that aims at preserving **(SP)** whenever possible. In the case of stratified programs, we can improve on that premise and show that it is always possible to forget while preserving **(SP)**.

Theorem 2. *The operator f_{su} satisfies* **(SP)***.*

Since **(SP)** is stronger than **(UP)**, the following corollary is straightforward.

Corollary 1. *The operator f_{su} satisfies* **(UP)***.*

As shown in [17,19] no class of forgetting operators can satisfy **(SP)** on any class of programs including normal programs. Thus, Theorem 2 is an interesting result in its own right as it presents the first operator for which it has been shown that it can be iterated and satisfies **(SP)** on a class of programs beyond Horn programs, unlike previous work in [4,13,23].

The relevance of this class of programs is further witnessed by the following complementary result, that shows that three classes of forgetting operators [18, 19] do coincide on stratified programs.

Proposition 3. *For stratified programs, the classes* $\mathsf{F_{SP}}$, $\mathsf{F_R}$ *and* $\mathsf{F_M}$ *do coincide.*

This is interesting, as these classes have been shown to satisfy different minimal relaxations of **(SP)** and were assumed to be different in a more general setting, as such coincidence was only known for Horn programs.

Finally, Theorem 2 also helps determine that the order of iteration does not affect the final result w.r.t. strong equivalence.

---

[4] The semantics in [13] then only considers the minimal models of the resulting program, but for the sake of the comparison of the operators as such, this is irrelevant.

Proposition 4. *Let P be a stratified program over $\mathcal{A}$ and $V_1, V_2 \subseteq \mathcal{A}$. Then,*

$$\mathsf{f}_{su}(\mathsf{f}_{su}(P, V_1), V_2) \equiv \mathsf{f}_{su}(\mathsf{f}_{su}(P, V_2), V_1).$$

Hence, for f_{su}, indeed any order for atoms can be chosen in the sense of Definition 5.

4   Uniform Forgetting in General

In this section, we present the general impossibility result of a syntactic operator that satisfies (**UP**), and then define an operator that does satisfy (**UP**) and is syntactic whenever suitable. To lift our ideas presented for stratified programs, according to Definition 2, we need to consider in addition how to deal with disjunction and with cycles involving negation. In the following, we first discuss the actual challenges resulting from admitting these and we start with disjunction.

Example 4. Consider forgetting about p from program P just consisting of a single rule $p \vee q \leftarrow$. We have $\mathcal{AS}(P) = \{\{p\}, \{q\}\}$, and thus, according to (**UP**) the answer sets of the forgetting result must be $\{\}$ and $\{q\}$. A program over q with these answer sets is the program containing a single rule $q \leftarrow not\ not\ q$. Though it is not immediately clear how to obtain this program in a syntactic manner, it helps to consider the following program P' consisting of two rules, $p \leftarrow not\ q$ and $q \leftarrow not\ p$. Both programs have the same answer sets, and though it is well-known that they are not strongly equivalent, they are uniformly equivalent. Moreover, the result of forgetting p is exactly the same, and in the case of P', Definition 4 could be applied to obtain precisely that result.   □

Building on the notion of semi-shifting [13], we formalize the ideas presented in the previous example to remove rules containing disjunctions including a particular atom, replacing them with rules without disjunction.

Definition 6. *Let P be a logic program and p an atom in $\mathcal{A}(P)$. The result of semi-shifting P w.r.t. p, $SH(P, p)$, is defined as replacing any rule $r \in P$ s.t. $H(r) = p \vee a_1 \vee \cdots \vee a_k$ and $k \geq 1$, by the two rules $p \leftarrow not\ a_1, \ldots, not\ a_k, B(r)$ and $a_1 \vee \cdots \vee a_k \leftarrow not\ p, B(r)$.*

Inspecting Definition 4, we note that if the normal form of P, $N = NF(P)$, is such that $N_p^H \cap N_p^{--} = \emptyset$, then we can apply f_{su} to $SH(P, p)$ for forgetting p. To make this precise, and to make this operator applicable to non-stratified programs, we define a new operator as follows.

Definition 7. *Let P be a program over $\mathcal{A}$, $N = NF(P)$ the normal form of P and $p \in \mathcal{A}$ s.t. $N_p^H \cap N_p^{--} = \emptyset$. We extend f_{su} to this class of programs by:*

$$\mathsf{f}_{du}(P, p) = \mathsf{f}_{su}(SH(P, p), p).$$

We can prove that f_{du} defined over this broader class of programs still satisfies (**UP**) when forgetting a single atom.

Proposition 5. *Let P be a program over $\mathcal{A}$, $N = NF(P)$ its normal form, and $p \in \mathcal{A}$ s.t. $N_p^H \cap N_p^{--} = \emptyset$. Then, for all sets of facts R with $\mathcal{A}(R) \subseteq \mathcal{A}\backslash\{p\}$:*

$$\mathcal{AS}(\mathsf{f}_{du}(P, p) \cup R) = \mathcal{AS}(P \cup R)_{\|\{p\}}.$$

This result shows that we can forget an atom p from a program P in normal form by syntactically manipulating its rules, even if P is not stratified, as long as $P_p^H \cap P_p^{--} = \emptyset$. In that regard, note that restricting to normal or disjunctive programs does not help as f_{du} may introduce double negation.

This brings us to the question of what happens if we want to forget p from a program that contains such rules. The difficulty resides in the fact that a rule $p \leftarrow not\, not\, p$ admits two models, $\{p\}$ and $\{\}$, and so forgetting about p has to correctly propagate this choice to all occurrences of p in rule bodies.

Example 5. Consider forgetting about p from program P containing the rules

$$p \leftarrow not\, not\, p, B(r_1) \qquad r \leftarrow p, B(r_2) \qquad s \leftarrow p, B(r_3) \qquad q \leftarrow not\, p, B(r_4)$$

where the $B(r_i)$ represent the remaining rule bodies. If all these $B(r_i)$ are empty, then, by **(UP)**, the answer sets of P, i.e., $\{p, r, s\}$ and $\{q\}$, should be preserved (modulo p). Moreover, adding, e.g., $\{r \leftarrow\}$ should still admit two answer sets, while adding, e.g., $\{r \leftarrow; s \leftarrow; q \leftarrow\}$ should admit precisely one answer set, which means that no simple syntactic transformation as used so far can achieve this. Instead, we have to look at which rule heads depend on p (r and s) and which on $not\, p$ (q). This information can first be used to create rules to represent the models of the resulting program of forgetting, by combining these opposing rule heads in all possible ways, i.e., either the elements supported by p are true, or those supported by $not\, p$, but not both.

$$r \leftarrow not\, q \qquad s \leftarrow not\, q \qquad q \leftarrow not\, r \qquad q \leftarrow not\, s \qquad (3)$$

However, this does not suffice, since we still need to guarantee that the answer sets are preserved in the presence of an additional set R of facts not containing p. This can be remedied by adding the following rules:

$$r \leftarrow not\, not\, r, not\, not\, s, q \qquad s \leftarrow not\, not\, s, not\, not\, r, q \qquad q \leftarrow not\, not\, q, r, s \qquad (4)$$

Now, whenever q is derivable (independently), r and s may both either be simultaneously true or false. This can be generalized to rules with non-empty $B(r_i)$ by adding $\bigcup_i B(r_i)$ for the involved i to each rule mentioned in (3) and (4), i.e., such model generators only apply if the remaining bodies are true. E.g., we obtain $r \leftarrow not\, not\, r, not\, not\, s, q, B(r_1), B(r_2)$ in the case of $r \leftarrow not\, not\, r, not\, not\, s, q$. However, if, e.g., $B(r_3)$ is false, then so is s, and therefore r and s will no longer be simultaneously true, namely, we need to add a rule $r \leftarrow not\, not\, r, q, B(r_1), B(r_2), not\, B(r_3)$, and similarly for the other cases. I.e., in general we have to create rules matching the different possible combinations of true and false rule bodies over the rules containing p in the body. $\qquad \square$

This example indicates that we cannot forget p from P in a syntactic manner if $P_p^H \cap P_p^{--}$ is not empty: rather than replacing (possibly negated) occurrences of p in the body with (parts of) the bodies of the rules with head p, a set of rules is created that rebuilds the semantic relations based on that choice between p and $not\, p$. This hardly resembles the original program in general and the possibly resulting combinatorial representation is not desirable. One could argue that, presumably, at least this problem is restricted to the rules mentioning the atom to be forgotten. I.e., implicitly we have used so far the following property that characterizes the fact that, when forgetting, we can focus just on the rules that contain the atom to be forgotten.

(SI$_u$). A class F of forgetting operators satisfies *Strong Invariance with respect to uniform equivalence* if, for each $f \in F$, $P \in \mathcal{C}(f)$ and $V \subseteq \mathcal{A}$, we have $f(P,V) \cup R \equiv_u f(P \cup R, V)$, for all programs $R \in \mathcal{C}(f)$ with $\mathcal{A}(R) \subseteq \mathcal{A}\backslash V$.

This property is a relaxation of the property strong invariance **(SI)** (see, e.g., [16]), referring to uniform equivalence rather than strong equivalence.

Unfortunately, it turns out that **(UP)** and **(SI$_u$)** are in general incompatible.

Theorem 3. *There is no forgetting operator over $\mathcal{C}_e$ that satisfies both* **(UP)** *and* **(SI$_u$)**.

This shows that the problems observed in Example 5 are in fact a consequence of a more general incompatibility between the two properties: it is in general not possible to have a completely syntactic operator that satisfies **(UP)**.

In light of this result, the rather convoluted hinted construction of a possible result in Example 5, and the fact that forgetting p can be obtained nicely if $P_p^H \cap P_p^{--}$ is empty, we argue that it is not suitable to forget syntactically if $P_p^H \cap P_p^{--}$ is not empty, even in corner cases where such result exists, despite Theorem 3. We thus propose an operator that combines our syntactic approach whenever this is suitable, and use a semantic operator only for the remaining cases.

For this purpose, let f_{UP} be the semantic operator sketched in [15] (based on the countermodel construction [7]), which satisfies **(UP)**.

Definition 8. *Let P be a program over $\mathcal{A}$, $N = NF(P)$ the normal form of P, and $p \in \mathcal{A}$. The result of forgetting about p from P, $f_u(P,p)$, is $NF(S)$ where:*

$$S = \begin{cases} f_{du}(P,p) & \text{if } N_p^H \cap N_p^{--} = \emptyset \\ f_{UP}(P,p) & \text{otherwise} \end{cases}$$

Example 6. As an example for f_{UP}, consider P from Example 5 with all $B(r_i)$ empty. The HT-models of the forgetting result coincide with the HT-models obtained for f_{UP} [15]. The countermodel construction provides 15 rules, including one of those in (4) and the other two with one double negation omitted. Also, variants of the rules in (3) appear together with constraints to obtain the desired HT-models. This result can be further simplified following work on minimal programs [8], and that, in all, the resulting program is rather similar to ours supporting our stance that in such a case the forgetting result is not truly syntactic.   □

The resulting operator is defined for every program P and any atom p to be forgotten, and forgetting p from P according to f_u provides program without p.

Proposition 6. *Let P be a program over signature $\mathcal{A}$ and $p \in \mathcal{A}$. Then $f_u(P, p)$ is a program over $\mathcal{A} \setminus \{p\}$.*

This result naturally allows the extension of f_u to sets of atoms using Definition 5. We are able to prove that f_u indeed satisfies **(UP)**.

Theorem 4. *The operator f_u satisfies* **(UP)**.

We have thus defined the first general operator that can be iterated and that satisfies **(UP)** and that, whenever this is possible and suitable, produces a result of forgetting that corresponds to a syntactic manipulation of the rules of the original program that contain the atoms to be forgotten.
    In addition, we can show that the order of iteration does not affect the final result w.r.t. uniform equivalence.

Proposition 7. *Let P be a program over $\mathcal{A}$ and $V_1, V_2 \subseteq \mathcal{A}$. Then,*

$$f_u(f_u(P, V_1), V_2) \equiv_u f_u(f_u(P, V_2), V_1).$$

Thus, we can forget a set of atoms in any order, which may allow us to prioritize atoms where syntactic forgetting is possible and suitable, resulting in a uniformly equivalent program, but possibly syntactically closer to the original program.
    Finally, it is not surprising that computing such forgetting results is worst-case exponential in the size of the input program, due to the as-dual in the case of f_{du} and the computation of the countermodels in the case of f_{UP} (for f_{du} alone exponential in the size of rules mentioning the atom to be forgotten).

5   Conclusions

In this paper, we have investigated syntactic forgetting under uniform equivalence in modular ASP. We have studied this problem first for stratified programs and shown that even strong equivalence is preserved while forgetting, establishing interesting results to existing operators of forgetting and novel results as to when these coincide. We then considered the general case and showed that it is not always possible to syntactically forget using only the rules that mention the atom(s) to be forgotten while preserving uniform persistence. This can be traced back to rules of the form $p \leftarrow not\, not\, p$ which are known to break the antichain property of answer sets. We argue that syntactic forgetting in such cases is not suitable, as it would result in a semantic reconstruction of possible ways of assigning truth to the involved atoms. We thus establish an operator that is syntactic whenever this is possible and suitable, and we show that this operator can be iterated and preserves strong persistence.

To add to the discussion of related work in the introduction, we note that [4], which is closest in spirit to our work, provides an operator that is syntactic, as the class for which it is defined satisfies strong invariance, i.e., it is amenable to restrict forgetting only to the rules that mention the atom(s) to be forgotten. Still, it has been observed that the construction is particularly complicated whenever there are rules of the form $p \leftarrow not\, not\, p$, often with rules in the forgetting result that are not easily associated to the rules in the original program.

Possible future work includes investigating the precise relationship of **(UP)** to the notion of relativized uniform equivalence [11], to gain further insights into semantic operators, study in more detail minimization of logic programs [8] for simplifying the results of semantic operators, and investigate other impossibility results in the context of ASP for similarities, such as embedding ASP into propositional logic [21], where knowing individual rules does not suffice and a more holistic view is required.

Acknowledgments. We thank the anonymous reviewers for their helpful comments. Authors R. Gonçalves, M. Knorr, and J. Leite were partially supported by FCT project FORGET (PTDC/CCI-INF/32219/2017) and by FCT project NOVA LINCS (UIDB/04516/2020). T. Janhunen was partially supported by the Academy of Finland projects ETAIROS (251170) and AI-ROT (335718).

References

1. Aguado, F., Cabalar, P., Fandinno, J., Pearce, D., Pérez, G., Vidal, C.: Forgetting auxiliary atoms in forks. Artif. Intell. **275**, 575–601 (2019)
2. Baral, C., Dzifcak, J., Takahashi, H.: Macros, macro calls and use of ensembles in modular answer set programming. In: Etalle, S., Truszczyński, M. (eds.) ICLP 2006. LNCS, vol. 4079, pp. 376–390. Springer, Heidelberg (2006). https://doi.org/10.1007/11799573_28
3. Berthold, M., Gonçalves, R., Knorr, M., Leite, J.: Forgetting in answer set programming with anonymous cycles. In: Moura Oliveira, P., Novais, P., Reis, L.P. (eds.) EPIA 2019. LNCS (LNAI), vol. 11805, pp. 552–565. Springer, Cham (2019). https://doi.org/10.1007/978-3-030-30244-3_46
4. Berthold, M., Gonçalves, R., Knorr, M., Leite, J.: A syntactic operator for forgetting that satisfies strong persistence. Theory Pract. Log. Program. **19**(5–6), 1038–1055 (2019)
5. Bledsoe, W.W., Hines, L.M.: Variable elimination and chaining in a resolution-based prover for inequalities. In: Bibel, W., Kowalski, R. (eds.) CADE 1980. LNCS, vol. 87, pp. 70–87. Springer, Heidelberg (1980). https://doi.org/10.1007/3-540-10009-1_7
6. Brass, S., Dix, J.: Semantics of (disjunctive) logic programs based on partial evaluation. J. Log. Program. **40**(1), 1–46 (1999)
7. Cabalar, P., Ferraris, P.: Propositional theories are strongly equivalent to logic programs. TPLP **7**(6), 745–759 (2007)

8. Cabalar, P., Pearce, D., Valverde, A.: Minimal logic programs. In: Dahl, V., Niemelä, I. (eds.) ICLP 2007. LNCS, vol. 4670, pp. 104–118. Springer, Heidelberg (2007). https://doi.org/10.1007/978-3-540-74610-2_8

9. Dao-Tran, M., Eiter, T., Fink, M., Krennwallner, T.: Modular nonmonotonic logic programming revisited. In: Hill, P.M., Warren, D.S. (eds.) ICLP 2009. LNCS, vol. 5649, pp. 145–159. Springer, Heidelberg (2009). https://doi.org/10.1007/978-3-642-02846-5_16

10. Delgrande, J.P., Wang, K.: A syntax-independent approach to forgetting in disjunctive logic programs. In: Bonet, B., Koenig, S. (eds.) Proceedings of AAAI, pp. 1482–1488. AAAI Press (2015)

11. Eiter, T., Fink, M., Woltran, S.: Semantical characterizations and complexity of equivalences in answer set programming. ACM Trans. Comput. Log. **8**(3) (2007)

12. Eiter, T., Kern-Isberner, G.: A brief survey on forgetting from a knowledge representation and reasoning perspective. Künstliche Intell. **33**(1), 9–33 (2019)

13. Eiter, T., Wang, K.: Semantic forgetting in answer set programming. Artif. Intell. **172**(14), 1644–1672 (2008)

14. Gabbay, D.M., Schmidt, R.A., Szalas, A.: Second Order Quantifier Elimination: Foundations, Computational Aspects and Applications. College Publications (2008)

15. Gonçalves, R., Janhunen, T., Knorr, M., Leite, J., Woltran, S.: Forgetting in modular answer set programming. In: AAAI, pp. 2843–2850. AAAI Press (2019)

16. Goncalves, R., Knorr, M., Leite, J.: The ultimate guide to forgetting in answer set programming. In: Baral, C., Delgrande, J., Wolter, F. (eds.) Proceedings of KR, pp. 135–144. AAAI Press (2016)

17. Gonçalves, R., Knorr, M., Leite, J.: You can't always forget what you want: on the limits of forgetting in answer set programming. In: Fox, M.S., Kaminka, G.A. (eds.) Proceedings of ECAI, pp. 957–965. IOS Press (2016)

18. Gonçalves, R., Knorr, M., Leite, J., Woltran, S.: When you must forget: beyond strong persistence when forgetting in answer set programming. TPLP **17**(5–6), 837–854 (2017)

19. Gonçalves, R., Knorr, M., Leite, J., Woltran, S.: On the limits of forgetting in answer set programming. Artif. Intell. **286**, 103307 (2020)

20. Harrison, A., Lierler, Y.: First-order modular logic programs and their conservative extensions. TPLP **16**(5–6), 755–770 (2016)

21. Janhunen, T.: Some (in)translatability results for normal logic programs and propositional theories. J. Appl. Non Class. Logics **16**(1–2), 35–86 (2006)

22. Janhunen, T., Oikarinen, E., Tompits, H., Woltran, S.: Modularity aspects of disjunctive stable models. J. Artif. Intell. Res. (JAIR) **35**, 813–857 (2009)

23. Knorr, M., Alferes, J.J.: Preserving strong equivalence while forgetting. In: Fermé, E., Leite, J. (eds.) JELIA 2014. LNCS (LNAI), vol. 8761, pp. 412–425. Springer, Cham (2014). https://doi.org/10.1007/978-3-319-11558-0_29

24. Konev, B., Ludwig, M., Walther, D., Wolter, F.: The logical difference for the lightweight description logic EL. J. Artif. Intell. Res. (JAIR) **44**, 633–708 (2012)

25. Konev, B., Lutz, C., Walther, D., Wolter, F.: Model-theoretic inseparability and modularity of description logic ontologies. Artif. Intell. **203**, 66–103 (2013)

26. Kontchakov, R., Wolter, F., Zakharyaschev, M.: Logic-based ontology comparison and module extraction, with an application to DL-Lite. Artif. Intell. **174**(15), 1093–1141 (2010)

27. Lang, J., Liberatore, P., Marquis, P.: Propositional independence: formula-variable independence and forgetting. J. Artif. Intell. Res. (JAIR) **18**, 391–443 (2003)

28. Lang, J., Marquis, P.: Reasoning under inconsistency: a forgetting-based approach. Artif. Intell. **174**(12–13), 799–823 (2010)
29. Lifschitz, V., Pearce, D., Valverde, A.: Strongly equivalent logic programs. ACM Trans. Comput. Log. **2**(4), 526–541 (2001)
30. Lin, F., Reiter, R.: How to progress a database. Artif. Intell. **92**(1–2), 131–167 (1997)
31. Liu, Y., Wen, X.: On the progression of knowledge in the situation calculus. In: Walsh, T. (ed.) Proceedings of IJCAI, pp. 976–982. IJCAI/AAAI (2011)
32. Middeldorp, A., Okui, S., Ida, T.: Lazy narrowing: strong completeness and eager variable elimination. Theoret. Comput. Sci. **167**(1&2), 95–130 (1996)
33. Moinard, Y.: Forgetting literals with varying propositional symbols. J. Log. Comput. **17**(5), 955–982 (2007)
34. Oikarinen, E., Janhunen, T.: Achieving compositionality of the stable model semantics for Smodels programs. TPLP **8**(5–6), 717–761 (2008)
35. Rajaratnam, D., Levesque, H.J., Pagnucco, M., Thielscher, M.: Forgetting in action. In: Baral, C., Giacomo, G.D., Eiter, T. (eds.) Proceedings of KR. AAAI Press (2014)
36. Wang, Y., Wang, K., Zhang, M.: Forgetting for answer set programs revisited. In: Rossi, F. (ed.) Proceedings of IJCAI, pp. 1162–1168. IJCAI/AAAI (2013)
37. Wang, Y., Zhang, Y., Zhou, Y., Zhang, M.: Knowledge forgetting in answer set programming. J. Artif. Intell. Res. (JAIR) **50**, 31–70 (2014)
38. Wang, Z., Wang, K., Topor, R.W., Pan, J.Z.: Forgetting for knowledge bases in DL-Lite. Ann. Math. Artif. Intell. **58**(1–2), 117–151 (2010)
39. Weber, A.: Updating propositional formulas. In: Expert Database Conference, pp. 487–500 (1986)
40. Wong, K.S.: Forgetting in logic programs. Ph.D. thesis, The University of New South Wales (2009)
41. Zhang, Y., Foo, N.Y.: Solving logic program conflict through strong and weak forgettings. Artif. Intell. **170**(8–9), 739–778 (2006)

Solving a Multi-resource Partial-Ordering Flexible Variant of the Job-Shop Scheduling Problem with Hybrid ASP

Giulia Francescutto[1](✉) ⓘ, Konstantin Schekotihin[2] ⓘ,
and Mohammed M. S. El-Kholany[2] ⓘ

[1] Infineon Technologies Austria AG, Siemensstrasse 2, 9500 Villach, Austria
`giulia.francescutto@infineon.com`
[2] University of Klagenfurt, Universitaetsstrasse 65-67, Klagenfurt, Austria
{`konstantin.schekotihin,mohammed.el-kholany`}`@aau.at`

Abstract. Many complex activities in production cycles, such as quality control or fault analysis, require highly experienced specialists to perform various operations on (semi)finished products using different tools. In practical scenarios, the next operation selection is complicated since each expert has only a local view on the entire set of operations to be performed. As a result, decisions made by the specialists are suboptimal and might cause high costs. In this paper, we consider a *Multi-resource Partial-ordering Flexible Job-shop Scheduling* (MPF-JSS) problem where partially-ordered sequences of operations must be scheduled on multiple required resources, such as tools and specialists. The resources are flexible and can perform one or more operations depending on their properties. We model the problem using Answer Set Programming (ASP), which can efficiently handle time assignments using Difference Logic. Moreover, we suggest two multi-shot solving strategies aiming to identify the time bounds allowing for a solution to the schedule optimization problem. Experiments conducted on a set of instances extracted from a medium-sized semiconductor fault analysis lab indicate that our approach can find schedules for 87 out of 91 considered real-world instances.

Keywords: Scheduling · ASP · Difference logic · Multi-shot solving

1 Introduction

Digitalization of manufacturing brings many advantages to the modern industry. Nevertheless, the work of highly experienced specialists cannot be substituted by machines in many fields like quality control, fault analysis, or research and development. In such scenarios, the experts use their knowledge of the application domain and apply sophisticated tools to perform various operations on

This work was partially funded by KWF project 28472, cms electronics GmbH, FunderMax GmbH, Hirsch Armbänder GmbH, incubed IT GmbH, Infineon Technologies Austria AG, Isovolta AG, Kostwein Holding GmbH, and Privatstiftung Kärntner Sparkasse.

ⓒ Springer Nature Switzerland AG 2021
W. Faber et al. (Eds.): JELIA 2021, LNAI 12678, pp. 313–328, 2021.
https://doi.org/10.1007/978-3-030-75775-5_21

queued jobs. In the absence of automated support, the specialists select jobs and perform operations that appear to be best according to their awareness of the situation. That is, they are making locally best decisions according to numerous heuristics such as deadlines of the jobs, availability of tools and colleagues experienced in specific operations, or given preferences of jobs. However, missed deadlines as well as idle time of machines and experts can be quite costly.

In manufacturing settings, the reduction of operational costs is often achieved by applying automated schedulers. *Job-Shop Scheduling* (JSS) [22] is one of the most well-known problems in which, given a set of machines and a set of jobs represented as a sequence of operations, the goal is to assign operations to machines such that: *(i)* each operation can be processed by one machine at a time; *(ii)* all jobs are processed independently of other jobs; and *(iii)* the execution of operations cannot be interrupted (no preemption). Practical scheduling applications resulted in various extensions of JSS, such as *flexible* JSS [8] in which an operation can be performed by various resources, e.g., machines or engineers; *multi-resource* JSS with *non-linear routing* [10], where an operation may need multiple resources for its execution, e.g., an engineer and a machine, and may have different preceding and succeeding operations. Another well-known extension is the Resource-Constrained Project Scheduling Problem (RCPSP) [20], where each operation might consume some amount of available resources. Similarly, as for JSS, there are various RCPSP extensions, such as a *multi-skill* variant [7], where human resources might require skills to perform operations, or *multi-mode* operations [28], which can be performed in different ways, e.g., using different tools and procedures.

In this paper, we consider a Multi-resource Partial-ordering Flexible JSS (MPF-JSS) problem, which can informally be described as: Given a set of jobs, represented as *partially-ordered* sets of operations, and *two sets of resources* that can *perform multiple operations*, i.e., tools and engineers trained to operate them, find a schedule of operations for all resources that is optimal wrt. predefined criteria such as tardiness. The latter is defined as the difference between the completion time of a job and its deadline, or 0 otherwise. The partial order of operations indicates that the sequence of some operations of a job is not essential. For instance, engineers can do various non-invasive inspection operations using different tools in an arbitrary order. Selection of a specific order can, however, improve the schedule since the availability of resources, like tools or engineers, might be limited.

To solve the problem, we propose an encoding using Answer Set Programming (ASP) [24] with Difference Logic [21]. The introduction of difference constraints allows one to express timing requirements compactly and thus to avoid grounding issues that might occur if the number of possible time points required to find a schedule is too large. Nevertheless, as our evaluation shows, conventional reasoning and optimization methods of ASP solvers cannot find solutions to real-world instances in a predefined time. Therefore, we suggest two search strategies based on multi-shot solving techniques [18], allowing for the identification of tighter upper time bounds on the schedule. The evaluation of our approach was conducted on instances extracted from the historical data representing ten operational days of an Infineon Fault Analysis lab. Each complete instance representing a whole day was then split into smaller instances enabling a detailed assessment of the solving performance. The results show that the basic ASP encoding was unable to solve any of the complete instances, while the suggested multi-shot approaches could find optimal schedules for eight or nine days, respectively. In total, these approaches solved 87 out of 91 instances considered in our full evaluation.

2   Preliminaries

Answer Set Programming. A normal ASP program Π is a finite set of rules of the form

$$h \leftarrow b_1, \ldots, b_m, \sim b_{m+1}, \ldots, \sim b_n \qquad (1)$$

where h and $b_1, \ldots b_n$, for $n \geq 0$, are atoms and $\sim$ is *negation as failure*. An *atom* is either $\bot$, representing the constant *false*, or an expression of the form $p(t_1, \ldots, t_l)$, where p is a predicate symbol and $t_1, \ldots, t_l$ are *terms*. Each term is either a *variable* or a *constant*. A *literal* l is either an atom (positive) or its negation (negative). Given a rule r of the form (1), $H(r) = h$ denotes the *head* atom and the *body* $B(r) = B^+(r) \cup B^-(r)$ comprises the positive $B^+(r) = \{b_1, \ldots, b_m\}$ and negative $B^-(r) = \{b_{m+1}, \ldots, b_n\}$ atoms. A rule r is a *fact* if $B(r) = \emptyset$ and a *constraint* if $H(r) = \bot$.

The semantics of an ASP program Π is given in terms of its ground instantiation Π_G, obtained from Π by substituting the variables in each rule $r \in \Pi$ with constants appearing in Π. An *interpretation* I is a set of (*true*) ground atoms occurring in Π_G that does not contain $\bot$. A rule $r \in \Pi_G$ is *satisfied* by I if $B^+(r) \subseteq I$ and $B^-(r) \cap I = \emptyset$ imply $H(r) \in I$, and I is a *model* of Π if it satisfies each $r \in \Pi_G$. As originally defined in [19], a model I of Π is *stable* (an *answer set*) if it is a $\subseteq$-minimal model of the reduct $\{H(r) \leftarrow B^+(r) \mid r \in \Pi_G, B^-(r) \cap I = \emptyset\}$.

Multi-shot Solving. ASP allows for a flexible reasoning process suitable for controlled solving of continuously changing logic programs, i.e., multi-shot solving [18]. Thus, *clingo* enhances the ASP declarative language [9] with control capacities. This is accomplished by introducing a new `#program` directive in the ASP program that allows to structure it into subprograms, making the solving process fully modular. Flexibility is provided by an imperative programming interface (API) that allows a continuous assembly of the program and gives control over the grounding and solving functions. Each subprogram has a name and an optional list of parameters. It gathers all the rules up to the next `#program` directive. Subprogram *base* is a dedicated subprogram where all the rules not preceded by any `#program` directive are collected. `#external` directives are used within subprograms to set external atoms to some truth value via the *clingo* API.

ASP Modulo Difference Logic. *clingo*[DL] extends the input language of *clingo* by theory atoms representing difference constraints [16,17,21]. Difference constraints are represented by specific constraint atoms of the form &diff$\{x-y\} \leq k$ where x and y are ASP terms, which are internally interpreted as integer variables' names, and k is a constant. *clingo*[DL] therefore provides the following extension of the rule (1):

$$\text{\&diff}\{x - y\} \leq k \leftarrow b_1, \ldots, b_m, \sim b_{m+1}, \ldots, \sim b_n.$$

Such rules express that, whenever the body holds, the linear inequality represented by the head has to be satisfied as well.

3 Problem Formalization

In this paper, we consider a novel variant of the JSS problem, which occurs in scenarios when multiple resources have to be combined in order to process incoming jobs. In particular, MPF-JSS extends the standard problem in three ways: *(i) Multi-resource* – there is more than one resource type needed to execute an operation; *(ii) Partially-ordered* – some operations of a job can be executed in an arbitrary order; and *(iii) Flexible* – an operation can be executed by various resources.

3.1 MPF-JSS Definition

Let $O = \{(o_1, p_1), \ldots, (o_m, p_m)\}$ be a set of *operations*, where o_i denotes the operation identifier and $p_i \in \mathbb{N}$ its duration, and C be a set of available *classes of resources*, which represent groups of equivalent instances of a resource. Then, $R = \{(i, c, O_r) \mid i \in \mathbb{N}, c \in C, O_r \subseteq O\}$ is a set of available *resources*, where each resource $r = (i, c, O_r)$ is a triple defining an *instance* i of the resource, its class, and a set of operations O_r it can execute. In addition, the set $D = \{(o, C_d) \mid o \in O, C_d \subseteq C\}$ provides *demands* of operations in O for instances of resource classes C_d. Finally, a set of *jobs* is defined as $J = \{(O_j, P_j, d) \mid O_j \subseteq O, P_j \subseteq O_j \times O_j, d \in \mathbb{N}\}$, where $O_j \subseteq O$ is a set of operations that must be executed for the job, P_j defines their (partial) order, and d indicates the deadline.

Given an MPF-JSS instance (J, D, R), a *schedule* S is a set of assignments $\{(R_s, o_j, t) \mid R_s \subseteq R, o_j \in O, t \in \mathbb{N}\}$. Each triple (R_s, o_j, t) indicates that an operation o_j of a given job and a required set of resources R_s is assigned to a time point t. In addition, the following constraints must hold:

- the set R_s must comprise all resources demanded by an operation o_j;
- the schedule is non-preemptive, i.e., operations cannot be interrupted once started;
- any two operations of a job cannot be executed simultaneously;
- each resource instance is assigned to only one operation at a time; and
- operations of a job j must be scheduled wrt. to the given partial order, i.e., for any pair $(o_i, o_k) \in P_j$ the corresponding schedule assignments (R_i, o_i, t_i) and (R_k, o_k, t_k) must satisfy the inequality $t_i \leq t_k$.

A schedule is *optimal* if it has the minimal *total tardiness* $T = \sum_{j \in J} \max(0, C_j - d_j)$, where C_j and d_j denote the completion time and the deadline of a job j, respectively.

Example. Let us exemplify the MPF-JSS problem definition on a small instance. Suppose we have five operations $(o_1, 1), \ldots, (o_5, 1)$ and two classes of resources – a worker and a machine – denoted by w and m, respectively. The set of resources is defined as

$$R = \{(1, w, \{o_1, o_2\}), (2, w, \{o_4, o_5\}), (3, w, \{o_2, o_3, o_4\})\} \cup$$
$$\{(1, m, \{o_3\}), (2, m, \{o_4\}), (3, m, \{o_4\}), (4, m, \{o_5\})\}$$

For instance, in this set $(1, w, \{o_1, o_2\})$ indicates that the first worker is trained to execute operations o_1 and o_2, and $(1, m, \{o_3\})$ denotes that the first machine can be used to process o_3. Moreover, the definition of the operation demand D states that the operations o_1 and o_2 are processed only by workers, whereas the operations o_3, o_4 and o_5 require both a worker and a machine:

$$D = \{(o_1, \{w\}), (o_2, \{w\}), (o_3, \{w, m\}), (o_4, \{w, m\}), (o_5, \{w, m\})\}$$

Assume that the shop got three new jobs with a deadline 3 each. The first job has to undergo three operations, where o_1 must be completed before both o_2 and o_4. Operations of the second job can be done in an arbitrary order. Finally, the third job comprises four operations such that o_3 must be done before o_2 and o_1 before o_2 and o_5.

$$J = \{(\{o_1, o_2, o_4\}, \{(o_1, o_2), (o_1, o_4)\}, 3),$$
$$(\{o_3, o_4\}, \emptyset, 3),$$
$$(\{o_1, o_2, o_3, o_5\}, \{(o_3, o_2), (o_1, o_2), (o_1, o_5)\}, 3)\}$$

One of the possible solutions of the given instance is shown in Figs. 1 and 2. The found schedule assigns operations to the provided resources and time points in a way that minimizes the tardiness optimization criterion. As a result, two jobs are finished in time, i.e., completion times of the first and second jobs are $C_1 = 3$ and $C_2 = 2$. The third job has tardiness $C_3 - d_3 = 1$ since it is impossible to complete the four operations with a duration of 1 each in time without executing operations of a job in parallel.

3.2   Modeling MPF-JSS with Hybrid ASP

Answer Set Programming (ASP) has been widely used in the literature to solve scheduling problems. For instance, [25] applies ASP to develop a system for computing suitable allocations of personnel on the international seaport of Gioia Tauro, and [2] addresses a similar problem of workforce scheduling. ASP has also been used for approaching scheduling problems in healthcare, like assigning patients to operating rooms [12] and scheduling chemotherapy treatments [11].

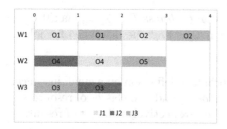

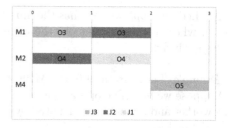

Fig. 1. Workers allocations   **Fig. 2.** Machines allocations

Listing 1. Problem instance

```
1   op(o1,1).  op(o2,1).  op(o3,1).  op(o4,1).  op(o5,1).
2   needs(o1,w).  needs(o2,w).  needs(o3,m).  needs(o3,w).
3   needs(o4,m).  needs(o4,w).  needs(o5,m).  needs(o5,w).

5   res(w1,w,o1).  res(w1,w,o2).  res(w2,w,o4).  res(w2,w,o5).
6   res(w3,w,o2).  res(w3,w,o3).  res(w3,w,o4).
7   res(m1,m,o3).  res(m2,m,o4).  res(m3,m,o4).  res(m4,m,o5).

9   job(j1,3).  job(j2,3).  job(j3,3).
10  recipe(j1,o1).  recipe(j1,o2).  recipe(j1,o4).
11  recipe(j2,o3).  recipe(j2,o4).
12  recipe(j3,o1).  recipe(j3,o2).  recipe(j3,o3).  recipe(j3,o5).
13  prec(j1,o1,o2).  prec(j1,o1,o4).
14  prec(j3,o3,o2).  prec(j3,o1,o2).  prec(j3,o1,o5).
```

In addition, ASP was applied to solve the course timetabling problem [6,23]. These approaches, however, indicated one of the major problems of ASP in scheduling applications – grounding issues occurring while dealing with a large number of possible time points. Therefore, in the literature, a number of extensions have been proposed to integrate ASP with Constraint Programming (CP) constraints, such as the hybrid solvers *clingcon* [5], *ascass* [29], and *ezcsp* [3,4]. The *ezcsp* system has been used to solve the problem of allocating jobs to devices in the context of industrial printing [4], and *clingcon* was successfully applied to production scheduling in [15]. In this paper, we use ASP modulo Difference Logic, which is also applied in [1] to schedule railroad traffic, for modeling the MPF-JSS problem.

Problem Instances. In order to encode the MPF-JSS problem in ASP, we first define a number of predicates representing the input instances. The set of operations is encoded using the predicate op/2 where the first term is indicating the operation identifier, and the second the expected processing times. The demands of operations for resources are described with the needs/2 predicate, see lines 1-3 in Listing 1 encoding the example presented in the previous section.

The set of resources is represented with atoms over the res/3 predicate. An atom res(r,c,o) provides an identifier r of a resource instance, a class c of the

Listing 2. Encoding of the resource allocation

```
1  {alloc(R,J,O,M) : res(M,R,O)}=1 :- recipe(J,O), needs(O,R).

3  allocated(R,M) :- alloc(R,J,O,M).
4  :- alloc(R,J,O,N), res(M,R,O), M < N, not allocated(R,M).
```

required resource, and an operation o it can execute. Thus, the set of required resources can be encoded as shown in lines 5–7.

Finally, the jobs are encoded using three predicates job/2, recipe/2, and prec/3. Atoms over the first predicate provide identifiers of the jobs and their deadlines. Recipes are used to define the set of operations that must be executed for a job, and the partial order of the operations is specified by the atoms over the prec/3 predicate. Respective facts encoding the jobs of our example are given in lines 9–14.

MPF-JSS Encoding. The problem encoding is split into three parts:

1. *base*: encodes all the definitions and constraints for the scheduling requirements (Listings 2, 3, and 4);
2. *incremental*: implements an incremental search strategy as well as weak constraints for the tardiness optimization (Listing 5); and
3. *exponential*: uses multi-shot solving to find the upper bound on the tardiness for a given instance using exponential search (Listing 6).

The first section of the *base* subprogram, presented in Listing 2, addresses the allocation of resources, expressed by atoms alloc(R,J,O,M), required to execute an operation of a job. Each operation O of a job J requiring a resource of type R should be executed by exactly one instance M of this resource. Since the instances of a resource are equivalent, we introduce a symmetry-breaking constraint in lines 3–4. This constraint avoids unnecessary allocation variants by requiring the solver to select resources starting from the ones with the lexicographically smallest identifier.

Listing 3 shows the second part of the *base* subprogram. The rule in lines 6–7 specifies that the order in which two operations of a job are executed can be arbitrary when these operations are not subject to the job's precedence relation. Similarly, an arbitrary order is possible if two operations of different jobs require the same resource (lines 8–9). For the operations that need an ordering, expressed by atoms over the ord/4 predicate, we generate an execution sequence – denoted by the seq/4 predicate – using the rules in lines 10 and 11. The sequence of operations whose precedence is given in the input instance is forced by the rule in line 12.

Finally, in Listing 4 we introduce the difference constraints encoding the starting times of operations. We represent the starting time of an operation O of job J by an integer variable (J,O). The first constraint in line 13 requires the starting time of each operation to be greater or equal to 0. The second constraint enforces the starting times to be compatible with the order provided by atoms

Listing 3. Encoding of operation sequences

```
6   ord(J,01,J,02)        :- recipe(J,01), recipe(J,02), 01 < 02,
7                            not prec(J,01,02), not prec(J,02,01).
8   ord(J1,01,J2,02)      :- alloc(R,J1,01,M), alloc(R,J2,02,M),
9                            J1 < J2.
10  {seq(J1,01,J2,02)}:- ord(J1,01,J2,02).
11  seq(J2,02,J1,01)      :- ord(J1,01,J2,02), not seq(J1,01,J2,02).
12  seq(J,01,J,02)        :- prec(J,01,02).
```

Listing 4. Difference constraints on operations' starting times

```
13  &diff{0 - (J,0)}<=0  :- recipe(J,0).
14  &diff{(J1,01) - (J2,02)}<=-P1 :- seq(J1,01,J2,02), op(01,P1).
```

over the seq/4 predicate. That is, an operation (J2,02) coming after (J1,01) must not start before (J1,01) is finished.

Multi-shot Solving. Finding solutions of minimal tardiness for MPF-JSS instances can be hard since, without the knowledge of any reasonable bounds on the scheduling time interval, a solver may have to enumerate a large number of possible solutions. Finding such bounds can be complicated and simple heuristics, like determining a maximal sum of operation durations for a particular resource, often provide very imprecise approximations. Therefore, we exploit the power of multi-shot solving to find an upper bound on the tardiness and thus provide a good starting point for the optimization methods of an ASP solver.

In the following, we present two approaches to search for feasible solutions to a given problem instance incrementally. Such techniques were already introduced and used for similar purposes in SAT solving. For instance, Eén and Sörensson [13] apply an incremental SAT solver to model and solve the temporal induction problem for finite state machines, where a given property is incrementally proven over reachable states of the machine. In further work [14], the authors also use an incremental SAT solver to solve pseudo-boolean constraints, where an optimum is found by incrementally solving constraints with different bounds. Similarly, Rintanen et al. [26] suggest geometric and exponential search schemes automatically identifying a suitable planning horizon. To this end, multiple SAT solvers are run concurrently, providing each solver with a computation time budget determined by the applied scheme. For instance, the exponential scheme grants solvers exponentially less time to find a plan as the horizon increases.

The idea of the first approach is to incrementally increase the upper bound on the tardiness of each job in order to identify an interval for which a schedule exists. That is, the algorithm starts by considering the 0 tardiness bound, and if this yields unsatisfiability (UNSAT), it starts to increment the tardiness bounds by a constant. As a result, the algorithm implements a tumbling window search strategy. The corresponding subprogram step(m,n), shown in Listing 5, takes the parameters m and n to indicate the lower and upper bounds of the interval

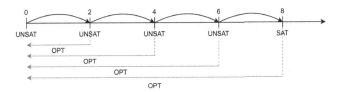

Fig. 3. Incremental approach

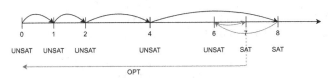

Fig. 4. Exponential approach

considered in the current iteration. The parameter values are set via a Python control script, which shifts them by the considered window size in each iteration. The control is implemented using the #external directive, providing a mechanism to activate or deactivate constraints by assigning a corresponding tardiness(n) atom to *true* or *false*, respectively. Figure 3 illustrates a sample execution of the incremental search algorithm, where a tumbling window of size 2 is moved in each iteration until the target interval for which a schedule exists is found.

Once the admissible upper bound n (and a corresponding lower bound m) is identified, ASP optimization methods search for an optimal solution within this interval, where the truth of an end(J,N) atom for N in-between 1 and n expresses that the tardiness of job J is less than N. Such atoms can be guessed to be *true* via the choice rule in line 21. The constraint in line 22 propagates smaller tardiness up to the upper bound n, and line 23 forces the tardiness of each job to be less than n. Finally, we minimize the number of pairs J,N for which end(J,N) is *false*, i.e., the tardiness of job J is at least N, by means of the weak constraint in line 24. Such an optimization strategy is required since *clingo*[DL] does not directly allow for minimizing a sum of integer variables occurring in its difference constraints. Therefore, in lines 26–27, we force each operation of a job to finish within the corresponding tardiness bound. In an obtained answer set, the end(J,N) atom with the smallest value for N signals the tardiness N-1 for job J.

In the second approach, shown in Listing 6, the additional subprogram iterate(n) is used first to find an upper tardiness bound n for each job such that some schedule exists. This is accomplished by a binary search that exponentially increments n until the first schedule is found, and then converges to the smallest n for which the scheduling problem is still satisfiable (SAT).

Figure 4 illustrates the process converging to the upper bound 7, relative to which the tardiness optimization is performed in the second step. In fact, with the iteration(n) atom from the #external directive in line 30 set to *true*, the constraint in lines 32–33 forces the tardiness of each job to be less than n, and

Listing 5. Step subprogram for incremental approach

```
16   #program step(m,n).
17   #external tardiness(n).

19   current(m..n,n).

21   {end(J,N)} :- job(J,_), current(N,n).
22   :- end(J,N-1), not end(J,N), current(N,n).
23   :- job(J,_), not end(J,n), tardiness(n).
24   :~ job(J,_), not end(J,N), current(N,n). [1,J,N]

26   &diff{(J,0) - 0}<=K :- job(J,D), end(J,N), current(N,n),
27                         recipe(J,O), op(O,P), K=D+N-P.
```

Listing 6. Iterate subprogram for exponential approach

```
29   #program iterate(n).
30   #external iteration(n).

32   &diff{(J,0) - 0}<=K :- job(J,D), iteration(n),
33                         recipe(J,O), op(O,P), K=D+n-P.
```

it remains to add the step(1,n-1) subprogram as above for optimization, yet letting the external atom tardiness(n-1) be *false* to avoid unsatisfiability due to the constraint in line 23.

Discussion. The two presented approaches aim at finding tardiness bounds per job, which can then be used as a starting point for the tardiness optimization. However, the bounds found by both approaches might have a different impact on the total tardiness of the optimal solution. This difference is essential for the quality of the obtained solutions, and both bounds merely approximate the maximal tardiness of some jobs needed for the optimal schedule. Theoretically, there can be situations in which the minimal total tardiness can only be reached when one of the jobs has comparably high tardiness, whereas others can be completed with low or zero tardiness. The upper bounds identified by our search algorithms might result in suboptimal schedules in which jobs, nevertheless, do not have extreme differences in their tardiness. In particular, the exponential approach is geared to find solutions that avoid large tardiness differences between jobs. Such schedules might be advantageous in scenarios where customers can tolerate short waiting times without serious drawbacks. The incremental strategy may admit schedules with smaller total tardiness, given a sufficiently large window size to come to a greater bound than identified by the exponential search. However, the incremental approach can be computationally more expensive since it might result in a larger number of candidate solutions to be considered by the underlying ASP optimization method.

4   Experimental Evaluation

We conduct our experiments on a set of real-world instances of the MPF-JSS problem retrieved from the daily operations history of a semiconductor Fault Analysis (FA) Lab.

Application Domain: FA Lab. In the context of semiconductor industries, the goal of the FA process is to identify the failure that results in an observed incorrect behavior of a semiconductor device [27]. In order to determine the nature and the cause of the failure, a sequence of investigation activities must be performed. Thus, different FA methods are applied to correctly identify different aspects of the failure. Obtained results are then put together to infer the failure mechanism and to understand its causes.

Some FA techniques alter the device permanently, e.g., the chemical alteration of the surface, while others do not affect the device in any way. Consequently, some analyses need to be executed before any alteration of a sample semiconductor device, while others can only be executed after some specific alteration. For example, an initial external visual inspection can only be done on a non-altered device, whereas the internal inspection of the sample is possible only after its decapsulation. This results in some precedence requirements for the sequences of executed investigation methods.[1]

In general, a sequence of FA techniques, required to identify the root cause of a fault, is unknown. Often the next method is selected upon results obtained during the previous steps of the FA process. However, in the specific context we consider in this paper, the FA process is executed to assess the quality of produced devices that have been put under some stress test. Therefore, in this case the set of methods to be executed is known in advance.

Each FA technique is executed by a trained employee possibly using a dedicated machine. For most of the operations, there is more than one employee trained to conduct them using one of the available machines. FA diagnostics of all incoming devices, called jobs, must be finished within a certain predefined deadline. The latter might not be met due to unavoidable reasons, like personnel shortages, unavailability of tools, or large numbers of incoming jobs. However, in practice, most of the missed deadlines are due to ad-hoc scheduling that leads to "forgotten" jobs, bottlenecks by rare and expensive equipment, or personnel allocation. One of the possible solutions is, therefore, to represent the FA problem as MPF-JSS and use modern ASP solvers to find the optimal allocation of jobs' analyses to machines and employees.

Instance Generation. The experimental evaluation is performed on real-world instances provided by our partner Infineon Technologies Austria. The provided data comprises a list of jobs processed in a selected period of time including: *(i)* the list of operations/techniques executed on each job, *(ii)* the processing time of the operations, *(iii)* the job deadlines, *(iv)* job identifiers, *(v)* the list

---

[1] www.eesemi.com.

of machines available, and *(vi)* information about the employees who executed these operations.

Out of this data, we extracted instances for ten random days representing a snapshot of the situation in the lab. However, the information regarding precedence requirements between failure analysis techniques was missing in the provided data. At the moment of data collection, it was impossible to communicate to the experts and to retrieve the missing dependencies between the techniques. Therefore, we decided to take the order of operations given in the data and convert it into an ordering relation, thus providing a strict order in our test instances.[2] The processing time of each operation was set to its average processing time measured in minutes during the selected period. Given the job deadlines in a date format, we computed the difference in minutes between the deadline date and the beginning of the day shift chosen for the computation. For simplicity, we assumed that each day has only one shift, which is eight hours long.

The resulting instances have the following approximate number of fixed components defined by the properties of the studied lab: *(i)* 50 operations, *(ii)* 75 machines, and *(iii)* 45 workers. For each of the days chosen the number of open jobs ranges between 30 and 50. We split each day-instance into sub-instances, with the aim of having instances of increasing size in multiples of 5, which resulted into a total of 91 instances.

Evaluation Results. For each obtained instance, we ran the three ASP programs introduced in Sect. 3.2: *(i) single-shot* – the base program with a tardiness bound precomputed using a heuristic, *(ii) inc* – the incremental variant, and *(iii) exp* – the exponential search approach. We compared the multi-shot approaches to a single-shot version where the bound is computed in advance and given as constant input to the program. In particular, we compute the sum of durations of all operations in an instance, which defines the tardiness bound large enough to allow for finding an optimal solution. Then, we introduce this bound as constant in the ASP single-shot program, and solve the optimization problem using the same idea as for the optimization steps of the multi-shot approaches.

The experiments were conducted on a workstation with Ubuntu 18.05, Intel 3930 K and 64 GB RAM. In our experiments, we use *clingo*[DL] 1.1.0 and *clingo* 5.4.0 with multi-shot solving controlled by the main routine in Python 3.8.5. For each instance, we let the solver run up to a timeout of 2 hours. For the incremental approach, we chose to use a constant tumbling window of 20 min.

Figure 5 shows a comparison of the solving performance of the two multi-shot approaches and the single-shot version. The single-shot program manages to solve only a small subset of the test instances. Thus, it always reached the timeout for instances with more than 20 jobs and only managed to find a schedule for instances with 15 jobs for two days – Day 2 and Day 9. Interestingly, the total tardiness of all schedules found by the single-shot and by multi-shot approaches was equal. The two multi-shot approaches significantly outperformed

---

[2] See the paper website for the encodings and instances.

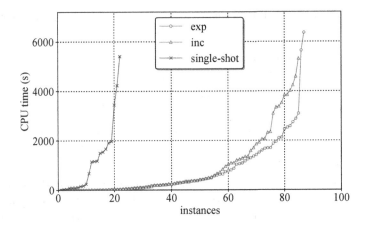

Fig. 5. Cactus plot of solving times

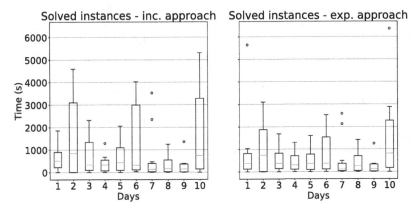

Fig. 6. Box plot of solving times for the instances from ten days and the two multi-shot approaches. The incremental approach reached the timeout for five instances in Day 1 and one instance in Day 10, and the exponential approach reached the timeout for four instances in Day 1.

the single-shot version. The exponential version solved 87 instances and reached the timeout only for four instances, all of which belong to Day 1. The incremental version managed to solve 85 instances and reached the timeout for six instances: five instances in Day 1, and the largest instance in Day 10 comprising all recorded jobs for this day. The exponential approach performs slightly better since it was always finding a tighter upper bound for tardiness, thus, leaving fewer choices for the optimization strategy of the ASP solver. Nevertheless, the differences between the approaches discussed in Sect. 3.2 were also confirmed in the evaluation. That is, in our experiments, the incremental variant was able to obtain better solutions for three instances with an average total tardiness improvement of 80 min.

Table 1. Search and optimization times in seconds for multi-shot approaches on largest instances

	Day1	Day2	Day3	Day4	Day5	Day6	Day7	Day8	Day9	Day10
inc_search	362	285	174	131	140	150	165	251	281	173
inc_opt	TO	4311	2145	1156	1920	3869	3360	987	1074	TO
exp_search	151	77	49	39	75	47	52	41	15	208
exp_opt	TO	3020	1640	1256	1442	2476	2528	1384	1233	6154

The box plot in Fig. 6 summarizes the solving times measured over instances from each day. We observe that the exponential approach generally needs less time. The outliers in the plot of the exponential search correspond to instances that the incremental version did not manage to solve within the timeout. Nevertheless, if we consider only the solved instances, then the solving times required by both multi-shot approaches are quite close with a slight advantage of the exponential search. The reason is that *clingo*[DL] could rather quickly decide whether an instance is satisfiable for a given tardiness bound or not. For the largest instances, the exponential and incremental strategies required 75 and 211, respectively, seconds on average for finding a bound, while substantially more time was spent on the optimization performed wrt. this bound.

Table 1 shows the times needed by the two multi-shot approaches for their search and optimization steps on the largest instance per day. In general, the exponential approach is faster to find a tardiness bound than the incremental strategy. In Day 1, both approaches reached the timeout of 7200 seconds in the optimization step, and in Day 10 only the exponential approach managed to find an optimal solution within the timeout.

5   Conclusions

In this paper, we introduce a Multi-resource Partial-ordering Flexible Job-Shop Scheduling (MPF-JSS) problem and provide an encoding using hybrid ASP modulo Difference Logic. We present two multi-shot solving strategies to find reasonable approximations of tardiness bounds. These approaches were tested on a set of real-world instances provided by Infineon Technologies Austria, where they showed to enable the optimization of daily schedules for a Fault Analysis lab, while single-shot solving could not accomplish the optimization within the same time limit. In the future, we plan to test the proposed encodings on different problem types to reinforce the assessment. In addition, we are going to extend the suggested approach in two ways. First, we intend to develop novel optimization techniques for Difference Logic allowing for the minimization of sums of integer variables, which must in the current approach be simulated by means of underlying ASP optimization methods. Second, we aim to devise multi-shot solving strategies that can take advantage of historical data, which is often available in industrial application scenarios. In particular, we are going to study combinations of ASP with (supervised) machine learning models trained to guide the search procedure of a solver by giving preference to operations to schedule in successive solving steps.

References

1. Abels, D., Jordi, J., Ostrowski, M., Schaub, T., Toletti, A., Wanko, P.: Train scheduling with hybrid ASP. In: LPNMR, pp. 3–17 (2019)
2. Abseher, M., Gebser, M., Musliu, N., Schaub, T., Woltran, S.: Shift design with answer set programming. FI **147**(1), 1–25 (2016)
3. Balduccini, M.: Representing constraint satisfaction problems in answer set programming. In: ASPOCP, pp. 16–30 (2009)
4. Balduccini, M.: Industrial-size scheduling with ASP+CP. In: Delgrande, J.P., Faber, W. (eds.) LPNMR 2011. LNCS (LNAI), vol. 6645, pp. 284–296. Springer, Heidelberg (2011). https://doi.org/10.1007/978-3-642-20895-9_33
5. Banbara, M., Kaufmann, B., Ostrowski, M., Schaub, T.: Clingcon: the next generation. TPLP **17**(4), 408–461 (2017)
6. Banbara, M., Soh, T., Tamura, N., Inoue, K., Schaub, T.: Answer set programming as a modeling language for course timetabling. TPLP **13**(4–5), 783–798 (2013)
7. Bellenguez-Morineau, O.: Methods to solve multi-skill project scheduling problem. 4OR **6**(1), 85–88 (2008). https://doi.org/10.1007/s10288-007-0038-4
8. Brucker, P., Schlie, R.: Job-shop scheduling with multi-purpose machines. Computing **45**(4), 369–375 (1990). https://doi.org/10.1007/BF02238804
9. Calimeri, F., et al.: ASP-Core-2 input language format. TPLP **20**(2), 294–309 (2020)
10. Dauzère-Pérès, S., Roux, W., Lasserre, J.: Multi-resource shop scheduling with resource flexibility. EJOR **107**(2), 289–305 (1998)
11. Dodaro, C., Galatà, G., Maratea, M., Mochi, M., Porro, I.: Chemotherapy treatment scheduling via answer set programming. In: CILC, pp. 342–356 (2020)
12. Dodaro, C., Galatà, G., Khan, M.K., Maratea, M., Porro, I.: An ASP-based solution for operating room scheduling with beds management. In: Fodor, P., Montali, M., Calvanese, D., Roman, D. (eds.) RuleML+RR 2019. LNCS, vol. 11784, pp. 67–81. Springer, Cham (2019). https://doi.org/10.1007/978-3-030-31095-0_5
13. Eén, N., Sörensson, N.: Temporal induction by incremental SAT solving. ENTCS **89**(4), 543–560 (2003)
14. Eén, N., Sörensson, N.: Translating pseudo-boolean constraints into SAT. JSAT **2**, 1–26 (2006)
15. Friedrich, G., et al.: Representing production scheduling with constraint answer set programming. In: OR, pp. 159–165 (2014)
16. Gebser, M., et al.: Potassco user guide (2019). http://potassco.org
17. Gebser, M., Kaminski, R., Kaufmann, B., Ostrowski, M., Schaub, T., Wanko, P.: Theory solving made easy with clingo 5. In: ICLP (Technical Communications), pp. 2:1–2:15 (2016)
18. Gebser, M., Kaminski, R., Kaufmann, B., Schaub, T.: Multi-shot ASP solving with clingo. TPLP **19**(1), 27–82 (2019)
19. Gelfond, M., Lifschitz, V.: The stable model semantics for logic programming. In: ICLP/SLP, pp. 1070–1080 (1988)
20. Hartmann, S., Briskorn, D.: A survey of variants and extensions of the resource-constrained project scheduling problem. EJOR **207**(1), 1–14 (2010)

21. Janhunen, T., Kaminski, R., Ostrowski, M., Schellhorn, S., Wanko, P., Schaub, T.: Clingo goes linear constraints over reals and integers. TPLP **17**(5–6), 872–888 (2017)
22. Johnson, S.: Optimal two-and three-stage production schedules with setup times included. NRLQ **1**(1), 61–68 (1954)
23. Kahraman, M.K., Erdem, E.: Personalized course schedule planning using answer set programming. In: Alferes, J.J., Johansson, M. (eds.) PADL 2019. LNCS, vol. 11372, pp. 37–45. Springer, Cham (2019). https://doi.org/10.1007/978-3-030-05998-9_3
24. Lifschitz, V.: Answer Set Programming. Springer, Heidelberg (2019). https://doi.org/10.1007/978-3-030-24658-7
25. Ricca, F., et al.: Team-building with answer set programming in the Gioia-Tauro seaport. TPLP **12**(3), 361–381 (2012)
26. Rintanen, J., Heljanko, K., Niemelä, I.: Planning as satisfiability: parallel plans and algorithms for plan search. AIJ **170**(12–13), 1031–1080 (2006)
27. Ross, R. (ed.): Microelectronics Failure Analysis: Desk Reference. ASM International, Russell (2011)
28. Sprecher, A., Hartmann, S., Drexl, A.: An exact algorithm for project scheduling with multiple modes. OR Spectrum **19**(3), 195–203 (1997). https://doi.org/10.1007/BF01545587
29. Teppan, E., Friedrich, G.: Heuristic constraint answer set programming for manufacturing problems. In: Advances in Hybridization of Intelligent Methods, pp. 119–147 (2018)

Tractable Reasoning Using Logic Programs with Intensional Concepts

Jesse Heyninck[1]([✉])(iD), Ricardo Gonçalves[2](iD), Matthias Knorr[2](iD), and João Leite[2](iD)

[1] Technische Universität Dortmund, Dortmund, Germany
jesse.heyninck@tu-dortmund.de

[2] NOVA LINCS, Departamento de Informática, Faculdade de Ciências e Tecnologia, Universidade Nova de Lisboa, Caparica, Portugal
{rjrg,mkn,jleite}@fct.unl.pt

Abstract. Recent developments triggered by initiatives such as the Semantic Web, Linked Open Data, the Web of Things, and geographic information systems resulted in the wide and increasing availability of machine-processable data and knowledge in the form of data streams and knowledge bases. Applications building on such knowledge require reasoning with modal and intensional concepts, such as time, space, and obligations, that are defeasible. E.g., in the presence of data streams, conclusions may have to be revised due to newly arriving information. The current literature features a variety of domain-specific formalisms that allow for defeasible reasoning using specific intensional concepts. However, many of these formalisms are computationally intractable and limited to one of the mentioned application domains. In this paper, we define a general method for obtaining defeasible inferences over intensional concepts, and we study conditions under which these inferences are computable in polynomial time.

1 Introduction

In this paper, we develop a solution that allows us to tractably reason with intensional concepts, such as time, space and obligations, providing defeasible/non-monotonic inferences in the presence of large quantities of data.

Initiatives such as the Semantic Web, Linked Open Data, and the Web of Things, as well as modern Geographic Information Systems, resulted in the wide and increasing availability of machine-processable data and knowledge in the form of data streams and knowledge bases. To truly take advantage of this kind of knowledge, it is paramount to be able to reason in the presence of *intensional* or *modal* concepts, which has resulted in an increased interest in formalisms, often based on rules with defeasible inferences, that allow for reasoning with time [5,10,12,14,26,41], space [13,28,39,42], and possibility or obligations [11, 25,27,36]. Examples of such concepts may be found in applications with data referring for example to time (e.g., operators such as "next", "at time", "during

© Springer Nature Switzerland AG 2021
W. Faber et al. (Eds.): JELIA 2021, LNAI 12678, pp. 329–345, 2021.
https://doi.org/10.1007/978-3-030-75775-5_22

interval T") or space (e.g., "at place P", "within a given radius", "connected to"), but also legal reasoning (e.g., "is obliged to", "is permitted").

Example 1. In a COVID-19-inspired setting, we consider an app for contact-tracing. It tracks where people move and stores their networks of persons, i.e., their colleagues and family whom they meet regularly. Once a person tests positive, the app informs anyone at risk (e.g. someone who was in the proximity of an infected person for a longer amount of time or because someone in their network is at risk) that they have to stay in quarantine for 10 days. If a negative test result can be given, this quarantine is not obligatory anymore. It is important that the app can explain to persons being orderd in quarantine the reason for their being at risk (e.g. since they were in contact with an infected person for a longer amount of time) while preserving anonymity to abide with laws of data protection (e.g. someone being ordered into quarantine should *not* be able to see who is the reason for this).

In this context, efficient reasoning with non-monotonic rules over intensional concepts is indeed mandatory, since a) rules allow us to encode monitoring and intervention guidelines and policies in a user-friendly and declarative manner; b) conclusions may have to be revised in the presence of newly arriving information; c) different intensional concepts need to be incorporated in the reasoning process; d) timely decisions are required, even in the presence of large amounts of data, as in streams; e) intensional concepts can preserve anonymity, e.g. in user-friendly explanations without having to change the rules. However, relevant existing work usually deals with only one kind of intensional concepts (as detailed before), and, in general, the computational complexity of the proposed formalisms is too high, usually due to both the adopted underlying formalism and the unrestricted reasoning with expressive intensional concepts.

In this paper, we introduce a formalism that allows us to seamlessly represent and reason with defeasible knowledge over different intensional concepts. We build on so-called intensional logic programs [34], extended with non-monotonic default negation, and equip them with a novel three-valued semantics with favorable properties. In particular, we define a well-founded model in the line of the well-founded semantics for logic programs [22]. Provided the adopted intensional operators satisfy certain properties, which turn out to be aligned with practical applications such as the one outlined in Example 1, the well-founded model is unique, minimal among the three-valued models, in the sense of only providing derivable consequences, and, crucially, its computation is tractable. Our approach allows us to add to relevant related work in the sense of providing a well-founded semantics to formalisms that did not have one so far, which we illustrate on a relevant fragment of LARS programs [10].

We introduce intensional logic programs in Sect. 2, define our three-valued semantics in Sect. 3, show how to compute the well-founded model in Sect. 4, discuss the complexity and related work in Sects. 5 and 6, respectively, before we conclude.

2 Intensional Logic Programs

In this section, building on previous work by Orgun and Wadge [34], we introduce intensional logic programs, a very expressive framework that allows us to reason with intensional concepts, such as time, space, and obligations, in the presence of large quantities of data, including streams of data. Intensional logic programs are based on rules, as used in normal logic programs, enriched with atoms that introduce the desired intensional concepts. The usage of default negation in the rules is a distinctive feature compared to the original work [34] and particularly well-suited to model non-monotonic and defeasible reasoning [23] and allows us to capture many other forms of non-monotonic reasoning, see, e.g., [16,19]. To assign meaning to intensional programs, we rely on the framework of neighborhood semantics [35], a generalization of the Kripke semantics, that easily allows us to capture a wide variety of intensional operators.

We start by defining the basic elements of our language. We consider a function-free first-order signature $\Sigma = \langle P, C \rangle$, a set X of variables, and a set of *operation symbols* $\mathcal{O}$, such that the sets P (of predicates), C (of constants), X and $\mathcal{O}$ are mutually disjoint. The set of atoms over Σ and X is defined in the usual way. We say that an atom is ground if it does not contain variables, and we denote by $\mathcal{A}_\Sigma$ the set of all ground atoms over Σ. In what follows, and without loss of generality, we leave the signature Σ implicit and consider only the set of ground atoms over Σ, denoted by $\mathcal{A}$.

The set $\mathcal{O}$ contains the symbols representing the various intensional operators ∇. Based on these, we introduce the set of intensional atoms $\mathcal{I}_{\mathcal{O}}^{\mathcal{A}}$.

Definition 1. *Given a set of atoms $\mathcal{A}$ and a set of operation symbols $\mathcal{O}$, the set $\mathcal{I}_{\mathcal{O}}^{\mathcal{A}}$ of* intensional atoms *over $\mathcal{A}$ and $\mathcal{O}$ is defined as $\mathcal{I}_{\mathcal{O}}^{\mathcal{A}} = \{\nabla p \mid p \in \mathcal{A} \text{ and } \nabla \in \mathcal{O}\}$[1], and the set of* program atoms *$\mathcal{L}_{\mathcal{O}}^{\mathcal{A}}$ is defined as $\mathcal{L}_{\mathcal{O}}^{\mathcal{A}} = \mathcal{A} \cup \mathcal{I}_{\mathcal{O}}^{\mathcal{A}}$.*

We can define intensional logic programs as sets of rules with default negation, denoted by $\sim$, over program atoms.

Definition 2. *Given a set of atoms $\mathcal{A}$ and a set of operation symbols $\mathcal{O}$, an* intensional logic program *$\mathcal{P}$ over $\mathcal{A}$ and $\mathcal{O}$ is a finite set of rules r of the form:*

$$A \leftarrow A_1, \ldots, A_n, \sim B_1, \ldots, \sim B_m \tag{1}$$

where $A, A_1, \ldots, A_n, B_1, \ldots, B_m \in \mathcal{L}_{\mathcal{O}}^{\mathcal{A}}$. We distinguish between the head *of r, A, and its* body, *$A_1, \ldots, A_n, \sim B_1, \ldots, \sim B_m$.*

We also call $\mathcal{P}$ simply a *program* when this does not cause confusion and *positive* if it does not contain default negation. Intensional logic programs are highly expressive as intensional operators can appear arbitrarily anywhere in the rules, in particular in rule heads and in scope of default negation.

---

[1] For simplicity, we restrict ourselves to non-nested (or equivalently in view of Definition 2, composed) intensional atoms. This does not result in any loss of generality, since nested operators can straightforwardly be modelled as non-nested operators, see Remark 1.

Example 2. Let a set of agents $A = \{a, b, r\}$ (for Anita, Bonnie and Ruth) be given, a set of locations $L = \{\alpha, \beta, \gamma, \ldots\}$ and a set of time points $T = \{1, 2, \ldots, \}$. We also assume that every agent has a network $N_i \subseteq A$ which represents the people the agent has regular close contact with (e.g. family, colleagues or partner). In our example, $N_a = \{b\}$, $N_b = \{a\}$ and $N_r = \emptyset$. We furthermore assume a function $\nu : L \to \wp(L)$ which assigns to each place ℓ the places in its vicinity $\nu(\ell)$. In our example, for simplicity's sake, we just assume that $\nu(\alpha) = \{\beta\}$. We define the following operators for our use-case as $\mathcal{O}_1 = \{[i]_\ell, [i], [i]^t, [t, t'], \triangleright_t^i, \hat{\ell}^i, \langle A \rangle_\ell, \langle N_i \rangle \mid i \in A, \ell \in L, t \in T\}$ with the following informal interpretations: $[i]_\ell \phi$ says that ϕ is true for agent i at location ℓ; $[i]\phi$ says that ϕ is true for agent i; $[i]^t \phi$ says that ϕ is true for agent i at time t; $[t, t']\phi$ means that ϕ is the case in the interval between t and t'; $\triangleright_t^i \phi$ means ϕ is the case at or after time t for agent i; $\hat{\ell}^i \phi$ says that ϕ is true for an agent i in the vicinity of ℓ; $\langle A \rangle_\ell^t \phi$ says that ϕ is true for some agent $i \in A$ at location ℓ; and $\langle N_i \rangle \phi$ says that ϕ is true for some agent in i's network.

We use the atoms `risk`, `reside`, `inf`, `neg.test`, `quar`, and `spread`, which represent that someone is at risk of infection, is residing, is infected, has a negative test result, is imposed quarantine, and is a potential spreader, respectively. We can now, for example, succinctly write the following program (for any $i \in A$, $\ell \in L$ and $t \in T$):

$$[i]_\ell \text{spread} \leftarrow [i]\text{inf}, [i]_\ell \text{reside}$$

$$[i]^t \text{risk} \leftarrow [t, t+x]\hat{\ell}^i \text{reside}, [t, t+x]\langle A \rangle_\ell \text{spread}$$

$$[i]\text{risk} \leftarrow \langle N_i \rangle \text{risk}$$

$$[t, t+10][i]\text{quar} \leftarrow [i]^t \text{risk}, \sim \triangleright_t^i \text{neg.test}$$

These rules express that someone who is infected and resides at ℓ is a potential spreader at place ℓ; if agent i is in the vicinity of a potential spreader for at least x time units, i is at risk: if someone in agent i's network is at risk, so is i; if i is at risk at time t and does not have a negative test result after time t, i is imposed quarantine for the time between t and $t+10$.

In order to give semantics to intensional operators, we follow the ideas employed by Orgun and Wadge [34] and consider the neighborhood semantics, a strict generalization of Kripke-style semantics that allows capturing intensional operators [35] such as temporal, spatial, or deontic operators, even those that do not satisfy the normality property imposed by Kripke frames [18]. We start by recalling neighborhood frames.

Definition 3. *Given a set of operation symbols $\mathcal{O}$, a* neighborhood frame *(over $\mathcal{O}$) is a pair $\mathfrak{F} = \langle W, N \rangle$ where W is a non-empty set (of worlds) and $N = \{\theta_\nabla \mid \nabla \in \mathcal{O}\}$ is a set of* neighborhood functions *$\theta_\nabla : W \to \wp(\wp(W))$.*[2]

---

[2] Note that we often leave $\mathcal{O}$ implicit as N allows to uniquely determine all elements from $\mathcal{O}$. Also, to ease the presentation, we only consider unary intensional operators. Others can then often be represented using rules (see also [34]).

Thus, in comparison to Kripke frames, instead of a relation over W, neighborhood frames have functions for each operator that map worlds to a set of sets of worlds. These sets intuitively represent the atoms necessary (according to the corresponding intensional operator) at that world.

Example 3. The operators from Example 2 are given semantics using a neighborhood frame. We define worlds $w \in W$ as triples (i, ℓ, t) where $i \in A$, $\ell \in L$ and $t \in T$. These represent the space-time locations for an agent i.

The neighborhoods of $\mathcal{O}_1$ are defined, for $t, t', t^\star \in T$, $\ell, \ell' \in L$ and $i, i' \in A$:

- $\theta_{[i]_\ell}((i', \ell', t)) = \{W' \subseteq W \mid (i, \ell, t) \in W'\}$.
- $\theta_{[i]^t}((i', \ell, t')) = \{W' \subseteq W \mid (i, \ell, t) \in W'\}$.
- $\theta_{[i]}((i', \ell, t)) = \{W' \subseteq W \mid (i, \ell, t) \in W'\}$.
- $\theta_{[t,t']}((i, \ell, t^\dagger)) = \{W' \subseteq W \mid \{(i, \ell, t^\star) \mid t^\star \in [t, t']\} \subseteq W'\}$.
- $\theta_{\vartriangleleft_t^i}((i, \ell, t')) = \{W' \subseteq W \mid \{(i, \ell, t^\star) \mid \ell \in L\} \subseteq W' \text{ for some } t^\star \leq t\}$.
- $\theta_{\hat{\rho}^i}((i', \ell', t)) = \{W' \subseteq W \mid (i, \ell^\star, t) \in W' \text{ for some } \ell^\star \in \nu(\ell)\}$.
- $\theta_{\langle A\rangle_\ell}((i', \ell', t')) = \{W' \subseteq W \mid (i^\star, \ell, t) \in W' \text{ for some } i^\star \in A\}$.
- $\theta_{\langle N_i\rangle_\ell^t}((i', \ell', t')) = \{W' \subseteq W \mid (i^\star, \ell, t) \in W' \text{ for some } i^\star \in N_i\}$.

Intuitively, e.g., $\theta_{[i]_\ell}((i', \ell', t))$ consists of all the sets of worlds that include the world (i, ℓ, t) that shares a time component with the world (i', ℓ', t), but has ℓ and i as spatial and agent components; $\theta_{[t,t']^i}$ consists of all the sets of worlds that include all worlds $(i, \ell, t^\star)$ with some time component $t^\star$ between or equal to t and t' (for every place $\ell \in L$); and a set of worlds is contained in $\theta_{\langle A\rangle_\ell^t}$ if it contains at least one world with time component t and space component ℓ and some agent component i.

As the example above shows, neighborhood functions θ can be both invariant under the input w or variate depending on w (e.g., $\theta_{\langle A\rangle^{t,\ell}}$ and $\theta_{[t,t']^i}$ are invariant, while $\theta_{[i]_\ell}$ and $\theta_{[i]^t}$ variate depending on w). This is why the above definitions of neighborhood functions that depend on w need to explicit the components of the world w, i.e., (i, ℓ, t).

3 Three-Valued Semantics

In this section, we define a three-valued semantics for intensional logic programs as an extension of the well-founded semantics for logic programs [22] that incorporates reasoning over intensional concepts. The benefit of this approach over the more commonly used two-valued models is that, although there are usually several such three-valued models, we can determine a unique minimal one – intuitively the one which contains all the minimally necessary consequences of a program – which can be efficiently computed. Recall that even for programs without intensional concepts, a unique two-valued minimal model does not usually exist [24].

We consider three truth values, "true", "false", and "undefined", where the latter corresponds to neither true nor false. Given a neighborhood frame, we start by defining interpretations that contain a valuation function which indicates in which worlds (of the frame) an atom from $\mathcal{A}$ is true ($W^\top$), and in which ones it is true or undefined (W^u), i.e., not false[3].

Definition 4. *Given a set of atoms $\mathcal{A}$ and a frame $\mathfrak{F} = \langle W, N \rangle$, an interpretation I over $\mathcal{A}$ and $\mathfrak{F}$ is a tuple $\langle W, N, V \rangle$ with a valuation function $V : \mathcal{A} \to \wp(W) \times \wp(W)$ s.t., for every $p \in \mathcal{A}$, $V(p) = (W^\top, W^u)$ with $W^\top \subseteq W^u$. If, for every $p \in \mathcal{A}$, $W^\top = W^u$, then we call I total.*

The subset inclusion on the worlds ensures that no $p \in \mathcal{A}$ can be true and false in some world simultaneously. This intuition of the meaning is made precise with the denotation of program atoms for which we use the three truth values. We denote the truth values true, undefined and false with $\top$, u, and $\perp$, respectively, and we assume that the language $\mathcal{L}_{\hat{\mathcal{O}}}^{\mathcal{A}}$ contains a special atom u (associated to u).

Definition 5. *Given a set of atoms $\mathcal{A}$, a frame $\mathfrak{F}$, and an interpretation $I = \langle W, N, V \rangle$, we define the denotation of $A \in \mathcal{L}_{\hat{\mathcal{O}}}^{\mathcal{A}}$ in I:*

- $\|p\|_I^\dagger = W^\dagger$ *if $A = p \in \mathcal{A}$, with $V(p) = (W^\top, W^u)$ and $\dagger \in \{\top, u\}$;*
- $\|u\|^u = W$ *and* $\|u\|^\top = \emptyset$*, if $A = $ u;*
- $\|\nabla p\|_I^\dagger = \{w \in W \mid \|p\|_I^\dagger \in \theta_\nabla(w)\}$ *if $A = \nabla p \in \mathcal{I}_{\hat{\mathcal{O}}}^{\mathcal{A}}$ and $\dagger \in \{\top, u\}$;*
- $\|A\|_I^\perp = W \setminus \|A\|_I^u$ *for $A \in \mathcal{L}_{\hat{\mathcal{O}}}^{\mathcal{A}}$.*

For a formula $A \in \mathcal{L}_{\hat{\mathcal{O}}}^{\mathcal{A}}$ and an interpretation I, $\|A\|_I^\top$ is the set of worlds in which A is true, $\|A\|_I^u$ is the set of worlds in which A is not false, i.e., undefined or true, and $\|A\|_I^\perp$ is the set of worlds in which A is false. For atoms $p \in \mathcal{A}$, the denotation is straightforwardly derived from the interpretation I, i.e., from the valuation function V, and for the special atom u it is defined as expected (undefined in all worlds). For an intensional atom ∇p, w is in the denotation $\|\nabla p\|_I^\dagger$ of ∇p if the denotation of p (according to I) is a neighborhood of ∇ for w, i.e. $\|p\|_I^\dagger \in \theta_\nabla(w)$.

We often leave the subscript I from $\|A\|_I^\dagger$ as well as the reference to $\mathcal{A}$ and $\mathfrak{F}$ for interpretations and programs implicit.

Example 4. Consider $I_1 = \langle W_1, \mathcal{O}_1, V \rangle$ with the set of worlds W_1 and the neighborhoods as in Example 3 where:

$V(\texttt{reside}) = (\{(a, \alpha, 1)\}, \{(a, \alpha, 1)\})$

Then the following are examples of denotations of intensional atoms:

$\|[a]^\alpha \texttt{reside}\|_{I_1}^\top = \{(i, \ell, 1) \mid i \in A, \ell \in L\}$

$\|\hat{\beta}^a \texttt{reside}\|_{I_1}^\top = \{(i, \ell, 1), (i, \ell, 2) \mid i \in A, \ell \in L\}$

We explain the first denotation $\|[a]^\alpha \texttt{reside}\|_{I_1}^\top$ as follows: since reside is true for agent a at α and time 1, $[a]^\alpha \texttt{reside}$ is true at every world with time stamp 1. More formally, this can be seen since the set of worlds in which reside is true is a neighborhood $\theta_{[a]^\alpha}$.

---

[3] We follow the usual notation in modal logic and interpretations explicitly include the corresponding frame.

Based on the denotation, we can now define our model notion, which is inspired by partial stable models [38], which come with two favorable properties, minimality and support. The former captures the idea of minimal assumption, the latter provides traceable inferences from rules. We adapt this notion here by defining a reduct that, given an interpretation, transforms programs into positive ones, for which a satisfaction relation and a minimal model notion are defined.

Remark 1. Operators can be straightforwardly combined within our framework. Indeed, given two operators ∇_1 and ∇_2, the nesting of them, $\nabla_1\nabla_2$, can be seen as an operator $\nabla_1 \oplus \nabla_2$, where the neighborhood $\theta_{\nabla_2 \oplus \nabla_1}(w)$ is defined as follows. First we define $\theta_\nabla^{-1} : W \to W$ as $\theta_\nabla^{-1}(W') = \{w' \in W \mid W' \in \theta_\nabla(w')\}$. Intuitively, this is the set of worlds w' for which W' is a ∇-neighborhood of w', i.e. $w' \in \theta_\nabla^{-1}(W')$ iff $W' \in \theta_\nabla(w')$. We then define the neighborhood of the composition of ∇_1 and ∇_2 as:

$$\theta_{\nabla_2 \oplus \nabla_1}(w) = \{W' \subseteq W \mid \theta_{\nabla_1}^{-1}(W') \in \theta_{\nabla_2}(w)\}$$

It is not hard to see that for any $\phi \in \mathcal{A}$, $w \in \|\nabla_2 \oplus \nabla_1 \phi\|^\dagger$ iff $\|\nabla_1 \phi\|^\dagger \in \theta_{\nabla_2}(w)$ (for any $\dagger \in \top, u\}$). In other words, $\nabla_2 \oplus \nabla_1 \phi$ is true at w iff the worlds at which $\nabla_1 \phi$ is true is a neighborhood of ∇_2, as expected from a sound definition of nested operators.

Example 5. As an example of the neighborhood of a nesting of operators, consider $[t, t+x]\hat{\ell}^i$ as it occurs in the second rule of Example 2. Since $\theta_{\hat{\ell}^i}^{-1}(W') = \{(i', \ell', t) \mid t \in T$ for which $(i, l^\star, t) \in W'$ for some $l^\star \in \nu(l), \ell' \in L, i' \in A\}$, one can observe:

$$\theta_{[t,t+x]\hat{\ell}^i}(w) = \{W' \subseteq W_1 \mid \forall t^\star \in [t, t+x] \; \exists l^\star \in \nu(l) \text{ s.t. } (i, l^\star, t^\star) \in W'\}$$

In other words, a formula $[t, t+x]\hat{\ell}^i \phi$ is true at (at world w) iff ϕ is true for agent i at some place $l^\star$ in the vicinity of l for every time point $t^\star$ within the inteval $[t, t+x]$.

We first adapt two orders for interpretations, the truth ordering, $\sqsubseteq$, and the knowledge ordering, $\sqsubseteq_k$. The former prefers higher truth values in the order $\bot < u < \top$, the latter more knowledge (i.e., less undefined knowledge). Formally, for interpretations I and I', and every $p \in \mathcal{A}$: $I \sqsubseteq I'$ iff $\|p\|_I^\dagger \subseteq \|p\|_{I'}^\dagger$ for every $\dagger \in \{\top, u\}$; $I \sqsubseteq_k I'$ iff $\|p\|_I^\top \subseteq \|p\|_{I'}^\top$ and $\|p\|_I^\bot \subseteq \|p\|_{I'}^\bot$. We write $I \prec I'$ if $I \preceq I'$ and $I' \not\preceq I$ for $\preceq \in \{\sqsubseteq, \sqsubseteq_k\}$.

We now generalize the notion of reduct to programs with intensional atoms.

Definition 6. *Let $\mathcal{A}$ be set of atoms, and $\mathfrak{F} = \langle W, N \rangle$ a frame. $\mathcal{P}/I_w$, the reduct of a program $\mathcal{P}$ at $w \in W$ w.r.t. an interpretation I, contains for each $r \in \mathcal{P}$ of the form (1):*

- $A \leftarrow A_1, \ldots, A_n$ *if* $w \notin \bigcup_{i \le m} \|B_i\|^u$
- $A \leftarrow A_1, \ldots, A_n, u$ *if* $w \in \bigcup_{i \le m} \|B_i\|^u \setminus \bigcup_{i \le m} \|B_i\|^\top$

Intuitively, for each rule r of $\mathcal{P}$, the reduct $\mathcal{P}/I_w$ contains either (a) a rule of the first form, if all negated program atoms in the body of r are false at w (or the body does not have negated atoms), or (b) a rule of the second form, if none of the negated program atoms in the body of r are true at w, but some of these are undefined at w, or (c) none, otherwise. This also explains why the reduct is defined at w: truth and undefinedness vary for different worlds. The special atom u is applied to ensure that rules for the second case cannot impose the truth of the head in the notion of satisfaction for positive programs.

As reducts are positive programs, we can define a notion of satisfaction as follows.

Definition 7. *Let $\mathcal{A}$ be a set of atoms, and $\mathfrak{F} = \langle W, N \rangle$ a frame. An interpretation I satisfies a positive program $\mathcal{P}$ at $w \in W$ iff for each $r \in \mathcal{P}$ of the form (1), we have that $w \in \bigcap_{i \leq n} \|A_i\|^\dagger$ implies $w \in \|A\|^\dagger$ (for any $\dagger \in \{\top, u\}$)[4].*

Stable models can now be defined by imposing minimality w.r.t. the truth ordering on the corresponding reduct.

Definition 8. *Let $\mathcal{A}$ be set of atoms, and $\mathfrak{F} = \langle W, N \rangle$ a frame. An interpretation I is a stable model of a program $\mathcal{P}$ if:*

- *for every $w \in W$, I satisfies $\mathcal{P}/I_w$ at w, and*
- *there is no interpretation I' s.t. $I' \sqsubset I$ and, for each $w \in W$, I' satisfies $\mathcal{P}/I_w$ at w.*

Example 6. We consider the following program on the basis of $\mathcal{P}$ from Example 2, zooming in on the part restricted to considerations pertaining to the network of an agent (rules 3 and 4 of that example) and adding the information that Anita was at risk at place α on time 1. This results in the following program $\mathcal{P}'$:

$$[i]\mathbf{risk} \leftarrow \langle N_i \rangle \mathbf{risk} \quad [t, t+10]^i \mathbf{quar} \leftarrow [i]^t \mathbf{risk}, \sim \rhd_t^i \mathbf{neg.test} \quad [a]_a^1 \mathbf{risk} \leftarrow$$

Consider $\mathfrak{F} = \langle W_1, \mathcal{O}_1 \rangle$ as in Example 3 and the total interpretation I_1 defined by:

$$\|\mathbf{risk}\|_{I_1}^\top = \{(a, \alpha, 1), (b, \alpha, 1)\} \quad \|\mathbf{quar}\|_{I_1}^\top = \{(i, \alpha, t), \mid t \leq 10, i \in \{a, b\}\}$$
$$\|\mathbf{neg.test}\|_{I_1}^\top = \emptyset$$

We see that, for any $w \in W_1$, $\mathcal{P}'/(I_1)_w$ consists of the following rules:

$$[i]\mathbf{risk} \leftarrow \langle N_i \rangle \mathbf{risk} \quad [t, t+10]^i \mathbf{quar} \leftarrow [i]^t \mathbf{risk} \quad [a]_\ell^t \mathbf{risk} \leftarrow$$

It can be checked that I_1 satisfies minimality and is therefore a stable model of $\mathcal{P}$.

---

[4] Since the intersection of an empty sequence of subsets of a set is the entire set, then, for n=0, i.e., when the body of the rule is empty, the satisfaction condition is just $w \in \|A\|^\dagger$ for any $\dagger \in \{\top, u\}$.

Consider now the following total interpretation I_2 defined by:

$$\|\mathtt{risk}\|_{I_2}^\top = \{(a, \alpha, 1)\} \qquad \|\mathtt{quar}\|_{I_2}^\top = \emptyset \qquad \|\mathtt{neg.test}\|_{I_2}^\top = \emptyset$$

We see that for any $w \in W_1$, $\mathcal{P}'/(I_2)_w = \mathcal{P}'/(I_1)_w$. Notice that I_1 is not a stable model of $\mathcal{P}$, since for $(a, \alpha, 1) \in \|\langle N_b \rangle \mathtt{risk}\|_{I_1}^\top$ yet $(a, \alpha, 1) \notin \|[b]\mathtt{risk}\|_{I_1}^\top$, since $(b, \alpha, 1) \notin \|\mathtt{risk}\|_{I_1}^\top$.

We can show that our model notion is faithful w.r.t. partial stable models of normal logic programs [38], i.e., if we consider a program without intensional atoms, then its semantics corresponds to that of partial stable models.

Proposition 1. *Let $\mathcal{A}$ be set of atoms, $\mathfrak{F}$ a frame, and $\mathcal{P}$ a program with no intensional atoms. Then, there is a one-to-one correspondence between the stable models of $\mathcal{P}$ and the partial stable models of the normal logic program $\mathcal{P}$.*

While partial stable models are indeed truth-minimal, this turns out not to be the case for intensional programs due to non-monotonic intensional operators.

Example 7. Consider the operator $|j, k|_a$ representing that an atom is true during all time points in $[j, k]$ for agent a, and not in any interval properly containing $[j, k]$. This operator has the following neighborhood (given W_1 from Example 3): $\theta_{|j,k|_a}((i, \ell, t)) = \{W' \subseteq W_1 \mid \{(a, \ell, j), (a, \ell, j+1), \ldots, (a, \ell, k)\} \subseteq W'$ and $(a, \ell, j-1), (a, \ell, k+1) \notin W'\}$. Consider the following program $\mathcal{P}$:

$$[a]_1\mathtt{resides} \leftarrow \qquad [a]_2\mathtt{resides} \leftarrow \qquad [a]_3\mathtt{resides} \leftarrow \sim |1, 2|_a\mathtt{resides}$$

For simplicity we restrict ourselves to $W_1^\alpha = \{(i, \alpha, t) \mid i \in A, t \in T\}$. Then this program has two stable models, and one of them is not minimal. Namely, these interpretations are stable: I_1 with $\|\mathtt{resides}\|_{I_1}^\top = \|\mathtt{resides}\|_{I_1}^u = \{(a, \alpha, 1), (a, \alpha, 2)\}$ and I_2 with $\|\mathtt{resides}\|_{I_2}^\top = \|\mathtt{resides}\|_{I_2}^u = \{(a, \alpha, 1), (a, \alpha, 2), (a, \alpha, 3)\}$. To see that I_2 is stable, observe first that since $\{(a, \alpha, 1), (a, \alpha, 2), (a, \alpha, 3)\} \notin \theta_{|1,2|_a}(w)$ for any $w \in W_1$, $\||1, 2|_a\mathtt{resides}\|_{I_2}^\top = \emptyset$, which means that $\mathcal{P}/I_2 = \{[a]_1\mathtt{resides} \leftarrow; [a]_2\mathtt{resides} \leftarrow; [a]_3\mathtt{resides} \leftarrow\}$. Clearly, I_2 is the $\sqsubseteq$-minimal interpretation that satisfies $\mathcal{P}/I_2$. However, $I_1 \sqsubset I_2$ and thus, I_2 is not a truth-minimal stable model.

To counter that, we consider monotonic operators. Formally, given a set of atoms $\mathcal{A}$ and a frame $\mathfrak{F}$, an intensional operator ∇ is said to be *monotonic* in $\mathfrak{F}$ if, for any two interpretations I and I' such that $I \sqsubseteq I'$, we have that $\|\nabla p\|_I^\dagger \subseteq \|\nabla p\|_{I'}^\dagger$ for every $p \in \mathcal{A}$ and $\dagger \in \{\top, u\}$.

If all intensional operators in a frame are monotonic, then truth-minimality of stable models is guaranteed.

Proposition 2. *Let $\mathcal{A}$ be set of atoms, and $\mathfrak{F}$ a frame in which all intensional operators are monotonic. If I is a stable model of $\mathcal{P}$, then there is no stable model I' of $\mathcal{P}$ such that $I' \sqsubset I$.*

Regarding support, recall that the stable models semantics of normal logic programs satisfies the support property, in the sense that for every atom of a stable model there is a rule that justifies it. In other words, if we remove an atom p from a stable model some rule becomes false in the resulting model. Such rule can be seen as a justification for p being true at the stable model. In the case of intensional logic programs we say that an interpretation $I = \langle W, N, V \rangle$ is *supported* for a program $\mathcal{P}$ if, for every $p \in \mathcal{A}$ and $w \in W$, if $w \in \|p\|^\top$, then there is a rule $r \in \mathcal{P}/I_w$ that is not satisfied by I' at w, where $I' = \langle W, N, V' \rangle$ is such that $V'(q) = V(q)$ for $q \neq p$, and $V'(p) = \langle W^\top \setminus \{w\}, W^u \rangle$ where $V(p) = \langle W^\top, W^u \rangle$.

This notion of supportedness is desirable for intensional logic programs since we also want a justification why each atom is true at each world in a stable model. The following results show that this is indeed the case.

Proposition 3. *Let $\mathcal{A}$ be set of atoms, and $\mathfrak{F}$ a frame. Then, every stable model of a program $\mathcal{P}$ is supported.*

Yet, existence and uniqueness of stable models of a program are not guaranteed, not even for positive programs under the restriction of all operators being monotonic.

Example 8. Let $\mathcal{O} = \{\oplus\}$, $\mathcal{A} = \{p\}$ and $\mathfrak{F} = \langle \{1,2\}, \{\theta_\oplus\} \rangle$ where $\theta_\oplus(1) = \theta_\oplus(2) = \{\{1\}, \{2\}\}$. Let $\mathcal{P} = \{\oplus p \leftarrow\}$. This program has two stable models: I_1 with $V_1(p) = (\{1\}, \{1\})$ and I_2 with $V_2(p) = (\{2\}, \{2\})$.

The existence of two stable models of the above positive program is caused by the non-determinism introduced by the intensional operator in the head of the rule. Formally, an operator θ of a frame $\mathfrak{F} = \langle W, N \rangle$ is *deterministic* if $\bigcap \theta(w) \in \theta(w)$ for every $w \in W$. A program $\mathcal{P}$ is *deterministic in the head* if, for every rule $r \in \mathcal{P}$ of the form (1), if $A = \nabla p$, then θ_∇ is deterministic.

We can show that every positive program that is deterministic in the head and only considers monotonic operators has a single minimal model.

Proposition 4. *Given a set of atoms $\mathcal{A}$ and a frame $\mathfrak{F}$, if $\mathcal{P}$ is a positive program that is deterministic in the head and every $\nabla \in \mathcal{O}$ is monotonic in $\mathfrak{F}$, then it has a unique stable model.*

Due to this result, in what follows, we focus on monotonic operators and programs that are deterministic in the head, as this is important for several of the results we obtain subsequently.

Remark 2. This does not mean that non-montonic intensional operators cannot be used in our framework. In fact, we can take advantage of the default negation operator $\sim$ to *define* non-monotonic formulas on the basis of monotonic operators and default negation. E.g., consider again the operator $|j, k|$ from Example 7. We can use the following rule to define $|j, k|p$ for some atom $p \in \mathcal{A}$: $|j, k|_a^\alpha p \leftarrow [j, k]^\ell[i]p, \sim [a]_{j-1}^\alpha p, \sim [a]_{k+1}^\alpha p$.

Among the stable models of a program, we can distinguish the *well-founded models* as those that are minimal in terms of the knowledge order.

Definition 9. *Given a set of atoms $\mathcal{A}$ and a frame $\mathfrak{F}$, an interpretation $I = \langle W, N, V \rangle$ is a well-founded model of a program $\mathcal{P}$ if it is a stable model of $\mathcal{P}$, and, for every stable model I' of $\mathcal{P}$, it holds that $I \sqsubseteq_k I'$.*

Example 9 (Example 6 continued). Since I_2 is in fact the unique stable model, it is therefore the well-founded model.

Given our assumptions about monotonicity and determinism in the head, we can show that the well-founded model of an intensional program exists and is unique.

Theorem 1. *Given a set of atoms $\mathcal{A}$, and a frame $\mathfrak{F}$, every program $\mathcal{P}$ has a unique well-founded model.*

This is an important result as a unique model can be computed rather than guessed and checked.

4   Alternating Fixpoint

In this section, we show how the well-founded model can be efficiently computed. Essentially, we extend the idea of the alternating fixpoint developed for logic programs [21], that builds on computing, in an alternating manner, underestimates of what is necessarily true, and overestimates of what is not false, with the mechanisms to handle intensional inferences.[5]

First, since different pieces of knowledge are inferable in different worlds, we need a way to distinguish between these. Therefore, we introduce labels referring to worlds and apply them to formulas of a given language as well as programs, resulting in formulas $w : A$ and program rules $w : r$ constituting a labelled language $\mathcal{L}_W$ and a labelled program $\mathcal{P}_W$, respectively.

Secondly, three operators are defined to ensure that information is extracted correctly from rules and intensional atoms:

- the immediate consequence operator $T_{\mathcal{P}_W} : \wp(\mathcal{L}_W) \to \wp(\mathcal{L}_W)$ which allows to derive labelled programs atoms occuring in the head of rules in the labelled program $\mathcal{P}_W$ if the atoms in the body of the rule are in the set we apply the operator to.
- the *intensional extraction operator* $IE_{\mathcal{P}_W}(\Delta)$ which allows, for a labelled intensional atom $w : \nabla A$, to derive the labelled atoms $w' : A$ for $w' \in \bigcap \theta_\nabla(w')$ that are required to guarantee the truth of $w : \nabla A$.
- the *intensional consequence operator* $IC_\nabla(\Delta)$ which maps labelled atoms to intensional atoms that are implied by the former, i.e. it maps $w_1 : A, \ldots, w_n : A$ to $w : \nabla A$ if $\{w_1, \ldots, w_n\} \in \theta_\nabla(w)$.

---

[5] Due to space restrictions, we are not able to provide full details and examples of this procedure.

These three operators allow us to define a closure operator for a a labelled positive program $\mathcal{P}_W$ as the least fixpoint of:

$$ \bigcup_{\nabla \in \mathcal{O}} IC_\nabla \left(\bigcup_{\nabla \in \mathcal{O}^p} IE_\nabla(T_{\mathcal{P}_W}) \right). $$

Based on this closure operator, the alternating fixpoint procedure can now be defined in the usual way as: Given a frame $\mathfrak{F} = \langle W, N \rangle$ and a program $\mathcal{P}$, we define:

$$ \begin{array}{lll} P^0 = \emptyset & P^{i+1} = Cn(\mathcal{P}_W/N^i) & P^\omega = \bigcup_i P^i \\ N^0 = \mathcal{L}_W & N^{i+1} = Cn(\mathcal{P}_W/P^i) & N^\omega = \bigcap_i N^i \end{array} $$

Given a frame $\mathfrak{F}$, for which any $\nabla \in \mathcal{O}$ is monotonic in $\mathfrak{F}$, the alternating fixpoint construction defined above offers a characterization of the well-founded model for programs that are deterministic in the head. In more detail, given a pair $\langle \Delta, \Theta \rangle$ of sets of $\mathcal{L}_W$-formulas, we define a partial interpretation $I(\langle \Delta, \Theta \rangle) = (W, N, V)$ on the basis of Δ as follows: for every $A \in \mathcal{A}$, $V(A) = (\{w \in W \mid w : A \in \Delta\}, \{w \in W \mid w : A \in \Theta\})$. We can then show this correspondence.

Theorem 2. *Given a frame $\mathfrak{F} = \langle W, N \rangle$, and a program $\mathcal{P}$ s.t. every $\nabla \in \mathcal{O}$ is monotonic in $\mathfrak{F}$ and $\mathcal{P}$ is deterministic in the head, then $I(\langle P^\omega, N^\omega \rangle)$ is the well-founded model of $\mathcal{P}$.*

Note that this procedure can be explored for providing explanations for inferences. It is possible to determine the least i such that a labelled program atom is true in P^i. This then allows us to determine justifications building on the construction of the involved operators. We leave exploring this line of research as future work.

5   Computational Complexity

In this section, we study the computational complexity of several of the problems considered. We recall that the problem of satisfiability under neighborhood semantics has been studied for a variety of epistemic structures [40]. Here, we consider the problem of determining models for the two notions we established, stable models and the well-founded model, focussing on the propositional case,[6] and we assume familiarity with standard complexity concepts, including oracles and the polynomial hierarchy.

We first provide a result in the spirit of model-checking for programs $\mathcal{P}$. As we do not impose any semantic properties on the neighborhood frames, determining

---

[6] Corresponding results for the data complexity of this problem for programs with variables can then be achieved in the usual way [20].

a model for a frame that can be arbitrarily chosen is not meaningful. Thus, we assume a fixed frame $\mathfrak{F}$, fixing the worlds and the semantics of the intensional operators.[7]

Proposition 5. *Given a program $\mathcal{P}$ and an interpretation I, deciding whether I is a stable model of $\mathcal{P}$ is in* coNP, *and in* P *if all operators occurring in $\mathcal{P}$ are monotonic.*

This result is due to the minimization of stable models, i.e., we need to check for satisfaction and verify that there is no other interpretation which is smaller (see Definition 8). This also impacts on the complexity of finding a stable model given a fixed frame.

Theorem 3. *Given a program $\mathcal{P}$, deciding whether there is a stable model of $\mathcal{P}$ is in Σ_2^P, and in* NP *if all operators occurring in $\mathcal{P}$ are monotonic.*

Thus, if all operators are monotonic the complexity results do coincide with that of normal logic programs (without intensional atoms) [20], which indicates that monotonic operators do not add an additional burden in terms of computational complexity.

Now, if we in addition consider programs that are deterministic in the head, then we know that there exists the unique well-founded model (see Theorem 1). As we have shown, this model can be computed efficiently (see Theorem 2), and we obtain the following result in terms of computational complexity.

Theorem 4. *Given a program $\mathcal{P}$ that is deterministic in the head and all operators occurring in $\mathcal{P}$ are monotonic, computing the well-founded model of $\mathcal{P}$ is* P-complete.

Note that this result is indeed crucial in contexts were reasoning with a variety of intensional concepts needs to be highly efficient.

6   Related Work

In this section, we discuss related work establishing relations to relevant formalisms in the literature.

Intensional logic programs were first defined by Orgun and Wadge [34] focussing on the existence of models in function of the properties of the intensional operators. Only positive programs are considered, and thus our approach covers the previous work. Since [34] covers classical approaches for intensional reasoning, such as TempLog [1] and MoLog [17], our work applies to these as well.

It also relates to more recent work with intensional operators, and we first discuss two prominent approaches in the area of stream reasoning.

---

[7] This also aligns well with related work, e.g., for reasoning with time, such as stream reasoning where a finite timeline is often assumed, and avoids the exponential explosion on the number of worlds for satisfiability for some epistemic structures [40].

LARS [10] assumes a set of atoms $\mathcal{A}$ and a stream $S = (T, v)$, where T is a closed interval of the natural numbers and v is an evaluation function that defines which atoms are true at each time point of T. Several temporal operators are defined, including expressive window operators, and answer streams, a generalization of FLP-semantics, are employed for reasoning. A number of related approaches are covered including CQL [6], C-SPARQL [8], and CQELS [37]. Among the implementations exists LASER [9], which focuses on a considerable fragment, called plain LARS. We can represent a plain LARS program and have shown (in the appendix) that there is a one-to-one correspondence between answer streams of the program and the total stable models of the corresponding intensional logic program. In addition, we can apply our well-founded semantics, since the operators applied in plain LARS are monotonic and deterministic. Hence, our work also provides a well-founded semantics for plain LARS, i.e., we allow the usage of unrestricted default negation while preserving polynomial reasoning.

ETALIS [5] aims at *complex event processing*. It assumes as input atomic events with a time stamp and uses *complex events*, based on Allen's interval algebra [4], that are associated with a time *interval*, and is therefore considerably different from LARS (which considers time points). It contains no negation in the traditional sense, but allows for a negated pattern among the events. Many of the complex event patterns from ETALIS can be captured as neighborhood functions in our framework. However, ETALIS also makes use of some event patterns that would result in a non-monotonic operator, such as the negated pattern $\mathtt{not}(p)[q, r]$ which expresses that p is not the case in the interval between the end time of q and the starting time of r. We conjecture that such a negation can be modelled with help of the non-monotonic default negation $\sim$ and monotonic operators (see also Remark 2).

Other formalisms that extend logic programming with intensional operators include *Deontic Logic Programs* [25], *Answer Set Programming Modulo Theories extended to the Qualitative Spatial Domain* [42] and *Metric Temporal Answer Set Programming* [15]. In future work, we plan to study instantiations of our general framework that represent (fragments) of these languages.

7   Conclusions

We have presented intensional logic programs that allow defeasible reasoning with intensional concepts and streams of data, and introduced a novel three-valued semantics based on the neighborhood semantics [35] and partial stable models [38]. We have studied the characteristics of our semantics for monotonic intensional operators and programs that only admit deterministic operators in the heads of the rules, and shown that a unique minimal model, the well-founded model, exists and can be computed in polynomial time. Still, several relevant approaches in the literature can be covered, and for one of them our work also provides a well-founded semantics for the first time.

In terms of future work, several generalizations are possible, for example, allowing for first-order formulas in the programs and non-deterministic intensional operators. We can possibly resort to techniques from well-founded semantics for disjunctive logic programs [32] to resolve the non-determinism that occurs when studying the latter. Finally, the integration with taxonomic knowledge in the form of description logic ontologies [7] may also be worth pursuing as applications sometimes require both (see e.g. [2,3,29]). Hybrid MKNF knowledge bases [33] are a more prominent approach among the existing approaches for combining non-monotonic rules and such ontologies, and the well-founded semantics for these [31] together with its efficient implementation [30] may prove fruitful for such an endeavour.

Acknowledgements. The authors are indebted to the anonymous reviewers of this paper for helpful feedback. The authors were partially supported by FCT project RIVER (PTDC/CCI-COM/30952/2017) and by FCT project NOVA LINCS (UIDB/04516/2020). J. Heyninck was also supported by the German National Science Foundation under the DFG-project CAR (Conditional Argumentative Reasoning) KE-1413/11-1.

References

1. Abadi, M., Manna, Z.: Temporal logic programming. J. Symb. Comput. **8**(3), 277–295 (1989)
2. Alberti, M., Gomes, A.S., Gonçalves, R., Leite, J., Slota, M.: Normative systems represented as hybrid knowledge bases. In: Leite, J., Torroni, P., Ågotnes, T., Boella, G., van der Torre, L. (eds.) CLIMA 2011. LNCS (LNAI), vol. 6814, pp. 330–346. Springer, Heidelberg (2011). https://doi.org/10.1007/978-3-642-22359-4_23
3. Alberti, M., Knorr, M., Gomes, A.S., Leite, J., Gonçalves, R., Slota, M.: Normative systems require hybrid knowledge bases. In: AAMAS. IFAAMAS, pp. 1425–1426 (2012)
4. Allen, J.F.: Maintaining knowledge about temporal intervals. In: Readings in Qualitative Reasoning About Physical Systems, pp. 361–372. Elsevier, Amsterdam (1990)
5. Anicic, D., Rudolph, S., Fodor, P., Stojanovic, N.: Stream reasoning and complex event processing in ETALIS. Semant. Web **3**(4), 397–407 (2012)
6. Arasu, A., Babu, S., Widom, J.: The CQL continuous query language: semantic foundations and query execution. VLDB J. **15**(2), 121–142 (2006)
7. Baader, F., Calvanese, D., McGuinness, D.L., Nardi, D., Patel-Schneider, P.F. (eds.): The Description Logic Handbook: Theory, Implementation, and Applications, 2nd edn. Cambridge University Press, Cambridge (2007)
8. Barbieri, D.F., Braga, D., Ceri, S., Valle, E.D., Grossniklaus, M.: C-SPARQL: a continuous query language for RDF data streams. Int. J. Semant. Comput. **4**(1), 3–25 (2010)
9. Bazoobandi, H.R., Beck, H., Urbani, J.: Expressive stream reasoning with laser. In: d'Amato, C., et al. (eds.) ISWC 2017. LNCS, vol. 10587, pp. 87–103. Springer, Cham (2017). https://doi.org/10.1007/978-3-319-68288-4_6

10. Beck, H., Dao-Tran, M., Eiter, T.: LARS: a logic-based framework for analytic reasoning over streams. Artif. Intell. **261**, 16–70 (2018)
11. Beirlaen, M., Heyninck, J., Straßer, C.: Structured argumentation with prioritized conditional obligations and permissions. J. Logic Comput. **29**(2), 187–214 (2019)
12. Brandt, S., Kalayci, E.G., Ryzhikov, V., Xiao, G., Zakharyaschev, M.: Querying log data with metric temporal logic. J. Artif. Intell. Res. **62**, 829–877 (2018)
13. Brenton, C., Faber, W., Batsakis, S.: Answer set programming for qualitative spatio-temporal reasoning: Methods and experiments. In: Technical Communications of ICLP. OASICS, vol. 52, pp. 4:1–4:15. Schloss Dagstuhl - Leibniz-Zentrum fuer Informatik (2016)
14. Brewka, G., Ellmauthaler, S., Gonçalves, R., Knorr, M., Leite, J., Pührer, J.: Reactive multi-context systems: Heterogeneous reasoning in dynamic environments. Artif. Intell. **256**, 68–104 (2018)
15. Cabalar, P., Dieguez, M., Schaub, T., Schuhmann, A.: Towards metric temporal answer set programming. Theory Pract. Logic Program. **20**(5), 783–798 (2020)
16. Caminada, M., Sá, S., Alcântara, J., Dvořák, W.: On the equivalence between logic programming semantics and argumentation semantics. Int. J. Approx. Reasoning **58**, 87–111 (2015)
17. del Cerro, L.F.: MOLOG: a system that extends PROLOG with modal logic. New Gener. Comput. **4**(1), 35–50 (1986). https://doi.org/10.1007/BF03037381
18. Chellas, B.F.: Modal Logic: An Introduction. Cambridge University Press, Cambridge (1980)
19. Chen, Y., Wan, H., Zhang, Y., Zhou, Y.: dl2asp: implementing default logic via answer set programming. In: Janhunen, T., Niemelä, I. (eds.) JELIA 2010. LNCS (LNAI), vol. 6341, pp. 104–116. Springer, Heidelberg (2010). https://doi.org/10.1007/978-3-642-15675-5_11
20. Dantsin, E., Eiter, T., Gottlob, G., Voronkov, A.: Complexity and expressive power of logic programming. ACM Comput. Surv. **33**(3), 374–425 (2001)
21. Gelder, A.V.: The alternating fixpoint of logic programs with negation. In: Proceedings of SIGACT-SIGMOD-SIGART, pp. 1–10. ACM Press (1989)
22. Gelder, A.V., Ross, K.A., Schlipf, J.S.: The well-founded semantics for general logic programs. J. ACM **38**(3), 620–650 (1991)
23. Gelfond, M.: Answer sets. In: Handbook of Knowledge Representation, Foundations of Artificial Intelligence, vol. 3, pp. 285–316. Elsevier, Amsterdam (2008)
24. Gelfond, M., Lifschitz, V.: Classical negation in logic programs and disjunctive databases. New Gener. Comput. **9**(3–4), 365–385 (1991). https://doi.org/10.1007/BF03037169
25. Gonçalves, R., Alferes, J.J.: Specifying and reasoning about normative systems in deontic logic programming. In: Proceedings of AAMAS. IFAAMAS, pp. 1423–1424 (2012)
26. Gonçalves, R., Knorr, M., Leite, J.: Evolving multi-context systems. In: ECAI. Frontiers in Artificial Intelligence and Applications, vol. 263, pp. 375–380. IOS Press, Amsterdam (2014)
27. Governatori, G., Rotolo, A., Riveret, R.: A deontic argumentation framework based on deontic defeasible logic. In: Miller, T., Oren, N., Sakurai, Y., Noda, I., Savarimuthu, B.T.R., Cao Son, T. (eds.) PRIMA 2018. LNCS (LNAI), vol. 11224, pp. 484–492. Springer, Cham (2018). https://doi.org/10.1007/978-3-030-03098-8_33
28. Izmirlioglu, Y., Erdem, E.: Qualitative reasoning about cardinal directions using answer set programming. In: Proceedings of AAAI, pp. 1880–1887. AAAI Press (2018)

29. Kasalica, V., Gerochristos, I., Alferes, J.J., Gomes, A.S., Knorr, M., Leite, J.: Telco network inventory validation with NoHR. In: Balduccini, M., Lierler, Y., Woltran, S. (eds.) Logic Programming and Nonmonotonic Reasoning. LPNMR 2019. Lecture Notes in Computer Science, vol. 11481, pp. 18–31. Springer, Cham (2019). https:// doi.org/10.1007/978-3-030-20528-7_2
30. Kasalica, V., Knorr, M., Leite, J., Lopes, C.: NoHR: An Overview. Künstl Intell, Heidelberg (2020)
31. Knorr, M., Alferes, J.J., Hitzler, P.: Local closed world reasoning with description logics under the well-founded semantics. Artif. Intell. **175**(9–10), 1528–1554 (2011)
32. Knorr, M., Hitzler, P.: A comparison of disjunctive well-founded semantics. In: FAInt. CEUR Workshop Proceedings, vol. 277 (2007). CEUR-WS.org
33. Motik, B., Rosati, R.: Reconciling description logics and rules. J. ACM **57**(5), 30:1–30:62 (2010)
34. Orgun, M.A., Wadge, W.W.: Towards a unified theory of intensional logic programming. J. Logic Program. **13**(4), 413–440 (1992)
35. Pacuit, E.: Neighborhood Semantics for Modal Logic. Springer, Heidelberg (2017). https://doi.org/10.1007/978-3-319-67149-9
36. Panagiotidi, S., Nieves, J.C., Vázquez-Salceda, J.: A framework to model norm dynamics in answer set programming. In: MALLOW (2009)
37. Le-Phuoc, D., Dao-Tran, M., Xavier Parreira, J., Hauswirth, M.: A native and adaptive approach for unified processing of linked streams and linked data. In: Aroyo, L., et al. (eds.) ISWC 2011. LNCS, vol. 7031, pp. 370–388. Springer, Heidelberg (2011). https://doi.org/10.1007/978-3-642-25073-6_24
38. Przymusinski, T.C.: Stable semantics for disjunctive programs. New Gener. Comput. **9**(3/4), 401–424 (1991). https://doi.org/10.1007/BF03037171
39. Suchan, J., Bhatt, M., Walega, P.A., Schultz, C.P.L.: Visual explanation by high-level abduction: on answer-set programming driven reasoning about moving objects. In: Proceedings of AAAI, pp. 1965–1972. AAAI Press (2018)
40. Vardi, M.Y.: On the complexity of epistemic reasoning. In: Proceedings of LICS. pp. 243–252. IEEE Computer Society (1989)
41. Walega, P.A., Kaminski, M., Grau, B.C.: Reasoning over streaming data in metric temporal datalog. In: Proceedings of AAAI, pp. 3092–3099. AAAI Press (2019)
42. Walega, P.A., Schultz, C.P.L., Bhatt, M.: Non-monotonic spatial reasoning with answer set programming modulo theories. TPLP **17**(2), 205–225 (2017)

Estimating Grounding Sizes of Logic Programs Under Answer Set Semantics

Nicholas Hippen[✉] and Yuliya Lierler

University of Nebraska at Omaha, Omaha, NE 68182, USA
{nhippen,ylierler}@unomaha.edu

Abstract. Answer set programming (ASP) is a declarative logic programming paradigm geared towards solving difficult combinatorial search problems. While different logic programs can encode the same problem, their performance may vary significantly. It is not always easy to identify which version of the program performs the best. We present a system PREDICTOR (and its algorithmic backend) for estimating the grounding size of programs, a metric that can influence a program's performance. We evaluate an impact of PREDICTOR when used as a guide for rewritings produced by the ASP rewriting tool PROJECTOR. The results demonstrate potential to this approach.

Keywords: Answer set programming · Language optimization

1 Introduction

Answer set programming (ASP) [3] is a declarative (constraint) programming paradigm geared towards solving difficult combinatorial search problems. ASP programs model problem specifications/constraints as a set of logic rules. These logic rules define a problem instance to be solved. An ASP system is then used to compute solutions (answer sets) to the program. ASP has been successfully used in scientific and industrial applications.

Intuitive ASP encodings are not always the most optimal/performant making this programming paradigm less attractive to novice users as their first attempts to problem solving may not scale. ASP programs often require careful design and expert knowledge in order to achieve performant results [13]. Figure 1 depicts a typical ASP system architecture. The first step performed by systems called grounders transforms a non-ground logic program (with variables) into a ground/propositional program (without variables). Expert ASP programmers often modify their ASP solution targeting the reduction of grounding size of a resulting program. Size of a ground program has been shown to be a predictive factor of a program's performance, enabling it to be used as an "optimization metric" [13]. Intelligent grounding techniques [10] utilized by grounders such as GRINGO [14] or IDLV [5] also keep such a reduction in mind. Intelligent grounding procedures analyze a given program to produce a smaller propositional program

W. Faber et al. (Eds.): JELIA 2021, LNAI 12678, pp. 346–361, 2021.
https://doi.org/10.1007/978-3-030-75775-5_23

Fig. 1. Typical ASP system architecture

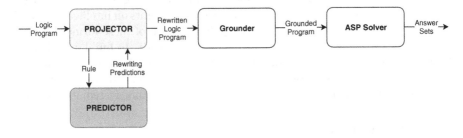

Fig. 2. An ASP system with PROJECTOR and PREDICTOR

without altering the solutions. In addition, researchers looked into automatic program rewriting procedures. Systems such as SIMPLIFY [8,9], LPOPT [1,2], PROJECTOR [15] rewrite non-ground programs targeting the reduction of the grounding size. These systems are meant to be prepossessing tools agnostic to the later choice of ASP solving technology.

Tools such as SIMPLIFY, LPOPT, and PROJECTOR, despite illustrating promising results, often hinder their objective. Sometimes, the original set of rules is better than the rewritten set, when their size of grounding is taken as a metric. Research has been performed to mitigate the negative impact of these rewritings. Mastria et al. [18] demonstrated a novel approach to guiding automatic rewriting techniques performed in IDLV using machine learning with a set of features built from structural properties and domain information. Calimeri et al. [7] illustrated truly successful application of a program rewriting technique stemming from LPOPT by incorporating its procedure inside the intelligent grounding algorithm of grounder IDLV. It was achieved by making a decision on whether to apply an LPOPT rewriting based on the current state of grounding. IDLV accurately estimated the impact of rewriting on grounding and based on this information decided whether to perform a rewriting. This synergy of intelligent grounding and a rewriting technique demonstrates the best performant results. Yet, it makes the transfer of rewriting techniques laborious assuming the need of tight integration of any rewriting within a grounder of choice. Here we propose an algorithm for estimating the size of grounding a program based on (i) mimicking an intelligent grounding procedure documented in [10] and (ii) techniques used in query optimization in relational databases (see, for instance, Chapter 13 in [19]). We then implement this algorithm in a system called PREDICTOR. This tool is meant to be used as a decision support mechanism for ASP program rewriting systems so that they perform a possible rewriting based on estimates produced by PREDICTOR. This work culminates in the integration of tools PREDICTOR and

PROJECTOR depicted in Fig. 2. We illustrate the true success of this synergy by extensive experimental analysis. It is important to note that PREDICTOR is a stand alone tool and can be used as part of any ASP inspired technology where its functionality is of interest.

We start by introducing the subject matter terminology. The key contribution of the work lays in the development of formulas for estimating the grounding size of a logic program based on its structural analysis and insights on intelligent grounding procedures. First, we present the simplified version of these formulas for the case of tight programs. We trust that this helps the reader to build intuitions for the work. Second, the formulas for arbitrary programs are given. We then describe the implementation details of system PREDICTOR. We conclude by experimental evaluation that includes incorporation of PREDICTOR within system PROJECTOR.

2   Preliminaries

An *atom* is an expression $p(t_1, ..., t_k)$, where p is a predicate symbol of arity $k \geq 0$ and $t_1, ..., t_k$ are *terms* – either object constants or variables. As customary in logic programming, variables are marked by an identifier starting with a capital letter. We assume object constants to be numbers. This is an inessential restriction as we can map strings to numbers using, for instance, the lexicographic order. For an atom $p(t_1, ..., t_k)$ and position i ($1 \leq i \leq k$), we define an *argument* denoted by $p[i]$. By $p(t_1, ..., t_k)^0$ and $p(t_1, ..., t_k)^i$ we refer to predicate symbol p and the term t_i, respectively. A *rule* is an expression of the form

$$a_0 \leftarrow a_1, ..., a_m, not\ a_{m+1}, ..., not\ a_n. \tag{1}$$

where $n \geq m \geq 0$, a_0 is either an atom or symbol $\bot$, and $a_1, ..., a_n$ are atoms. We refer to a_0 as the *head* of the rule and an expression to the right hand side of an arrow symbol in (1) as the *body*. An atom a and its negation *not* a is a *literal*. To literals $a_1, ..., a_m$ in the body of rule (1) we refer as *positive*, whereas to literals *not* $a_{m+1}, ..., not\ a_n$ we refer as *negative*. For a rule r, by $\mathbb{H}(r)$ we denote the head atom of r. By $\mathbb{B}^+(r)$ we denote the set of positive literals in the body of r. We obtain the set of variables present in an atom a and a rule r by $vars(a)$ and $vars(r)$, respectively. For a variable X occurring in rule r, by $args(r, X)$ we denote set

$$\{p[i] \mid a \in \mathbb{B}^+(r), a^0 = p, \text{ and } a^i = X\}.$$

A rule r is *safe* if each variable in r appears in $\mathbb{B}^+(r)$. Let r be a safe rule

$$p(A) \leftarrow q(A, B), r(1, A), not\ s(B). \tag{2}$$

Then $vars(r) = \{A, B\}$, $args(r, A) = \{q[1], r[2]\}$, and $args(r, B) = \{q[2]\}$. A *(logic) program* is a finite set of safe rules. We call programs containing variables *non-ground*.

For a program Π, $oc(p[i])$ denotes the set of all object constants occurring within $\{\mathbb{H}(r)^i \mid r \in \Pi \text{ and } \mathbb{H}(r)^0 = p\}$; whereas $oc(\Pi)$ denotes the set of all object constants occurring in the head atoms of the rules in Π. For instance, consider a program, named Π_1:

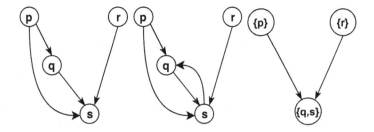

Fig. 3. Left: Graph G_{Π_2}; Center: Graph G_{Π_3}; Right: Graph $G_{\Pi_3}^{sc}$

$$p(1).\ p(2).\ r(3). \tag{3}$$
$$q(X,1) \leftarrow p(X). \tag{4}$$

Then, $oc(p[1]) = \{1,2\}$, $oc(q[1]) = \emptyset$, $oc(q[2]) = \{1\}$ and $oc(\Pi_1) = \{1,2,3\}$. The *grounding* of a program Π, denoted $gr(\Pi)$, is a ground program obtained by instantiating variables in Π with all object constants of the program. For example, $gr(\Pi_1)$ consists of rules in (3) and rules

$$q(1,1) \leftarrow p(1).\quad q(2,1) \leftarrow p(2). \tag{5}$$
$$q(3,1) \leftarrow p(3). \tag{6}$$

Given a program Π, ASP grounders utilizing intelligent grounding are often able to produce a program smaller than its grounding $gr(\Pi)$, but that has the same answer sets as $gr(\Pi)$. For instance, a program obtained from $gr(\Pi_1)$ by dropping rule (6) may be a result of intelligent grounding. The *ground extensions* of a predicate within a grounded program Π are the set of terms associated with the predicate in the program. For instance, in $gr(\Pi_1)$, the ground extensions of predicate q is the set $\{\langle 1,1\rangle, \langle 2,1\rangle, \langle 3,1\rangle\}$ of tuples. For an argument $p[i]$ and a ground program Π, we call the number of distinct object constants occurring in the ground extensions of p in Π at position i the *argument size* of $p[i]$. For instance, for program $gr(\Pi_1)$ argument sizes of $p[1]$, $q[1]$, and $q[2]$ are 3, 3, and 1, respectively.

The *dependency graph* of a program Π is a directed graph $G_\Pi = \langle N, E \rangle$ such that N is the set of predicates appearing in Π and E contains the edge (p,q) if there is a rule r in Π in which p occurs in $\mathbb{B}^+(r)$ and q occurs in the head of r. A program Π is *tight* if G_Π is acyclic, otherwise the program is *non-tight* [11]. For instance, consider program Π_2 constructed from Π_1 by extending it with rules:

$$r(2).\ r(4). \tag{7}$$
$$s(X,Y,Z) \leftarrow r(X), p(X), p(Y), q(Y,Z). \tag{8}$$

Program Π_3 is the program Π_2 extended with the rule:

$$q(Y,X) \leftarrow s(X,Y,Z). \tag{9}$$

Figure 3 shows the dependency graphs G_{Π_2} (left) and G_{Π_3} (center). Program Π_2 is tight, while program Π_3 is not.

3 System PREDICTOR

The key contribution of this work is the development of system PREDICTOR (its algorithmic and software base), whose goal is to provide estimates for the size of an "intelligently" grounded program. PREDICTOR is based on the intelligent grounding procedures implemented by grounder DLV[10]. The key difference is that, instead of building the ground instances of each rule in the program, PREDICTOR constructs statistics about the predicates, their arguments, and rules of the program. This section provides formulas we developed in order to produce the estimates backing up the computed statistics. We conclude with details on the implementation.

Argument Size Estimation. Tight program case: The estimation formulas are based on predicting argument sizes. To understand these it is essential to talk about an order in which we produce estimates for predicate symbols/arguments. Given a program Π, we obtain such an ordering by performing a topological sorting on its dependency graph. We associate each node in this ordering with its position and call it a *level rank* of a predicate. For example, p, q, r, s is one possible ordering for program Π_2. This ordering associates level ranks $1, 2, 3, 4$ with predicates p, q, r, s, respectively.

We now introduce some intermediate formulas for constraining our estimates. These intermediate formulas are inspired by query optimization techniques within relational databases, e.g. see Chapter 13 in [19]. These formulas keep track of information that helps us to guess what the actual values may occur in the grounded program without storing these values themselves. Let $p[i]$ be an argument. We track the range of values that may occur at this argument. To provide intuitions for a process we introduce, consider an intelligent grounding of Π_2 consisting of rules (3), (5), (7), and rules

$$s(2,1,1) \leftarrow r(2), p(2), p(1), q(1,1). \tag{10}$$
$$s(2,1,1) \leftarrow r(2), p(2), p(2), q(2,1). \tag{11}$$

This intelligent grounding produces rules (10), (11) in place of rule (8). Variable X from rule (8) is only ever replaced with object constant 2. Intuitively, this is due to the intersection $oc(p[1]) \cap oc(r[1]) = \{2\}$. We model such a restriction by considering what minimum and maximum values are possible for each argument in an intelligently grounded program (compliant with described principle; all modern intelligent grounders respect such a restriction). We then use these values to define an "upper restriction" of the argument size for each argument.

For a tight program Π, let $p[i]$ be an argument in Π; R be set $\{r \mid r \in \Pi, \mathbb{H}(r)^0 = p$, and $\mathbb{H}(r)^i$ is a variable$\}$. By $\downarrow_{est}^{t\text{-}t} (p[i])$ we denote an estimate of a minimum value that may appear in argument $p[i]$ in Π:

$$\downarrow_{est}^{t\text{-}t} (p[i]) = min\big(oc(p[i])$$
$$\cup \{max\Big(\{\downarrow_{est}^{t\text{-}t} (p'[i']) \mid p'[i'] \in args(r, \mathbb{H}(r)^i)\}\Big) \mid r \in R\}\big)$$

The function $\downarrow_{est}^{t\text{-}t}$ is total because the rank of the predicate occurring on the left hand side of the definition above is strictly greater than the ranks of all of the predicate symbols p' on the right hand side, where rank is understood as a level rank defined before (multiple level rankings are possible; any can be considered here). By $\uparrow_{est}^{t\text{-}t}(p[i])$ we denote an estimate of a maximum value that may appear in argument $p[i]$ in tight program Π. It is computed using formula for $\downarrow_{est}^{t\text{-}t}(p[i])$ with min, max, and $\downarrow_{est}^{t\text{-}t}$ replaced by max, min, and $\uparrow_{est}^{t\text{-}t}$, respectively.

Now that we have estimates for minimum and maximum values, we estimate the size of the range of values. We understand the *range* of an argument to be the number of values we anticipate to see in the argument within an intelligently grounded program if the values were all integers between the minimum and maximum estimates. It is possible that our minimum estimate for a given argument is greater than its maximum estimate. Intuitively, this indicates that no ground rule will contain this argument in its head. The number of values between the minimum and maximum estimates may also be greater than the number of object constants in a considered program. In this case, we restrict the range to the number of object constants occurring in the program. We compute the range, $range_{est}^{t\text{-}t}(p[i])$, as follows:

$$min(\{max(\{0, \uparrow_{est}^{t\text{-}t}(p[i]) - \downarrow_{est}^{t\text{-}t}(p[i]) + 1\}), |oc(\Pi)|\})$$

Recall, program Π_2. The operations required to compute the minimum estimate for argument $s[1]$ in Π_2 follow:

$$\downarrow_{est}^{t\text{-}t}(r[1]) = min(oc(r[1])) = 2$$
$$\downarrow_{est}^{t\text{-}t}(p[1]) = min(oc(p[1])) = 1$$
$$\downarrow_{est}^{t\text{-}t}(s[1]) = min(oc(s[1])$$
$$\cup \{max(\{\downarrow_{est}^{t\text{-}t}(r[1]), \downarrow_{est}^{t\text{-}t}(p[1])\})\}) = min(\emptyset \cup \{2\}) = 2$$

We compute $\uparrow_{est}^{t\text{-}t}(s[1])$ to be 2. Then, $range_{est}^{t\text{-}t}(s[1])$ is

$$min(\{max(\{0, \uparrow_{est}^{t\text{-}t}(s[1]) - \downarrow_{est}^{t\text{-}t}(s[1]) + 1\}), |oc(\Pi_2)|\})$$
$$= min(\{max(\{0, 2 - 2 + 1\}), 4\}) = 1$$

We presented formulas for estimating the range of values in program's arguments. We now show how these estimates are used to assess the *size* of an argument understood as the number of distinct values occurring in this argument upon an intelligent grounding. We now outline intuitions behind a recursive process that we capture in formulas. Let $p[i]$ be an argument. If $p[i]$ is such that predicate p has no incoming edges in the program's dependency graph, then we estimate the size of $p[i]$ as $|oc(p[i])|$. Otherwise, consider rule r such that $\mathbb{H}(r)^0 = p$ and $\mathbb{H}(r)^i$ is a variable. Our goal is to estimate the *number of values* variable $\mathbb{H}(r)^i$ may be replaced with during intelligent grounding. To do so, we consider the argument size estimates for arguments in the positive body of the rule that contain variable $\mathbb{H}(r)^i$. Based on a typical intelligent grounding procedures, variable $\mathbb{H}(r)^i$ may not take more values than the minimum of those argument size estimations. This gives us a possible estimate of the argument size relative to a single rule r. The argument size estimate of $p[i]$ with respect to the entire program may be then computed as the sum of such estimates for all rules such as r (recall that rule r satisfies the requirements $\mathbb{H}(r)^0 = p$ and $\mathbb{H}(r)^i$ is a variable). Yet, the sum over all rules may heavily overestimate the argument size. To milder the effect of overestimation we incorporate range estimates discussed before into the described computations.

For a tight program Π, let $p[i]$ be an argument in Π; R be the set

$$\{r \mid r \in \Pi, \ \mathbb{H}(r)^0 = p, \text{ and } \mathbb{H}(r)^i \text{ is a variable}\}.$$

By $S_{est}^{t\text{-}t}(p[i])$ we denote an estimate of the argument size $p[i]$ in tight program Π. This estimate is computed as follows:

$$S_{est}^{t\text{-}t}(p[i]) = min\Big(\big\{range_{est}^{t\text{-}t}(p[i]), \ |oc(p[i])|$$
$$+ \sum_{r \in R} min(\{S_{est}^{t\text{-}t}(p'[i']) \mid p'[i'] \in args(r, \mathbb{H}(r)^i)\})\big\}\Big)$$

We can argue that the function $S_{est}^{t\text{-}t}$ is total in the same way as we argued that the function $\downarrow_{est}^{t\text{-}t}$ is total.

The following illustrates the computation of the argument size estimates for argument $s[2]$ in program Π_2, given that $range_{est}^{t\text{-}t}(s[2]) = 2$ and $oc(s[2]) = \emptyset$:

$$S_{est}^{t\text{-}t}(p[1]) = |oc(p[1])| = 2$$
$$S_{est}^{t\text{-}t}(q[1]) = min(range_{est}^{t\text{-}t}(q[1]), \{|oc(q[1])|$$
$$+ min(\{S_{est}^{t\text{-}t}(p[1])\})\}) = min(\{2, 0 + min(\{2\})\}) = 2$$
$$S_{est}^{t\text{-}t}(s[2]) = min\big(range_{est}^{t\text{-}t}(s[2]),$$
$$\{|oc(s[2])| + min(\{S_{est}^{t\text{-}t}(p[1]), S_{est}^{t\text{-}t}(q[1])\})\}\big) = 2$$

Arbitrary (nontight) program case: To process arbitrary programs (tight and non-tight), we must manage to resolve the circular dependencies such as present in sample program Π_3 defined in the section on preliminaries. We borrow and simplify a concept of the component graph from [10]. The *component graph* of a program Π is an acyclic directed graph $G_\Pi^{sc} = \langle N, E \rangle$ such that N is the set of strongly connected components in the dependency graph G_Π of Π and E contains the edge (P, Q) if there is an edge (p, q) in G_Π where $p \in P$ and $q \in Q$. For tight programs, we identify its component graph with the dependency graph itself by associating a singleton set annotating a node with its member. Figure 3 (right) shows the component graph for program Π_3. For a program Π, we obtain an ordering on its predicates by performing a topological sorting on its component graph. We associate each node in this ordering with its position and call it a *strong level rank* of each predicate that belongs to a node. For example, $\{p\}, \{r\}, \{q, s\}$ is one possible topological sorting of $G_{\Pi_3}^{sc}$. This ordering associates the following strong level ranks $1, 2, 3, 3$ with predicates p, r, q, s, respectively.

Let C be a node/component in graph G_Π^{sc}. By $\mathcal{P}_C$ we denote the set

$$\{r \mid p \in C, r \in \Pi, \text{ and } \mathbb{H}(r)^0 = p\}.$$

We call this set a *module*. A rule r in module $\mathcal{P}_C$ is a *recursive rule* if there exists an atom a in the positive body of r so that $a^0 = p$ and predicate p occurs in C. Otherwise, rule r is an *exit rule*. For tight programs, all rules are exit rules. It is also possible to have modules with only recursive rules. For instance, the modules in program Π_3 contain

$$\mathcal{P}_{\{p\}} = \{p(1). \quad p(2).\}; \quad \mathcal{P}_{\{r\}} = \{r(2). \quad r(3). \quad r(4).\};$$

and $\mathcal{P}_{\{q,s\}}$ composed of rules (4), (8), and (9). The rules (8) and (9) are recursive.

In the sequel we consider components whose module contains an exit rule. For a component C and its module $\mathcal{P}_C$, we construct a partition $M_1, ..., M_n$ $(n \geq 1)$ in the following way: Every exit rule of $\mathcal{P}_C$ is a member of M_1. A recursive rule r in $\mathcal{P}_C$ is a member of M_k $(k > 1)$ if

- for every predicate $p \in C$ occurring in $\mathbb{B}^+(r)$, there is a rule r' in $M_1 \cup ... \cup M_{k-1}$, where $\mathbb{H}(r')^0 = p$ and
- there is a predicate q occurring in $\mathbb{B}^+(r)$ such that there is a rule r'' in M_{k-1}, where $\mathbb{H}(r'')^0 = q$.

We refer to the unique partition created in this manner as the *component partition* of C; integer n is called its *cardinality*. We call elements of a component partition *groups* (the component partition is undefined for components whose module does not contain an exit rule). The component partition of node $\{q, s\}$ in $G_{\Pi_3}^{sc}$ follows:

$$M_1 = \{q(X, 1) \leftarrow p(X).\}$$
$$M_2 = \{s(X, Y, Z) \leftarrow r(X), p(X), p(Y), q(Y, Z).\}$$
$$M_3 = \{q(Y, X) \leftarrow s(X, Y, Z).\}.$$

For a component partition $M_1, \ldots, M_k, \ldots, M_n$, by $M_k^{p[i]}$ we denote the set

$$\{r \mid r \in M_k, \mathbb{H}(r)^0 = p, \text{ and } \mathbb{H}(r)^i \text{ is a variable}\};$$

and by $M_{1\ldots k}^{p[i]}$ we denote the union $\bigcup_{j=1}^k M_j^{p[i]}$. For instance, for program Π_3 and its argument $q[1]$:

$$M_{1\ldots3}^{q[1]} = \{q(X, 1) \leftarrow p(X). \quad q(Y, X) \leftarrow s(X, Y, Z).\}$$

We now generalize range and argument size estimation formulas for tight programs to the case of arbitrary programs. These formulas are more complex than their "tight versions", yet they perform similar operations at their core. Intuitively, formulas for tight programs relied on argument ordering provided by the program's dependency graph. Now, in addition to an order provided by the component dependency graph, we rely on the orders given to us by the components partitions of the program.

In the remainder of this section, let Π be a program; $p[i]$ be an argument in Π; C be the node in the component graph of Π so that $p \in C$; n be the cardinality of the component partition of C; and j be an integer such that $1 \leq j \leq n$.

If the module of C does not contain an exit rule, then the estimate of the range of an argument $p[i]$, denoted $range_{est}(p[i])$, is assumed 0 and the estimate of the size of an argument $p[i]$, denoted $S_{est}(p[i])$, is assumed 0.

We now consider the case when the module of C contains an exit rule.

By $\downarrow_{est}(p[i])$ we denote an estimate of a minimum value that may appear in argument $p[i]$ in program Π:

$$\downarrow_{est}(p[i]) = \downarrow_{est}^{gr}(p[i], n)$$

$$\downarrow_{est}^{gr}(p[i], j) = min(oc(p[i]) \cup \{\downarrow_{est}^{rule}(p[i], j, r) \mid r \in M_{1...j}^{p[i]}\})$$

$$\downarrow_{est}^{rule}(p[i], j, r) = max(\{\ \downarrow_{est}^{split}(p[i], p'[i'], j) \mid p'[i'] \in args(r, \mathbb{H}(r)^i)\})$$

$$\downarrow_{est}^{split}(p[i], p'[i'], j) = \begin{cases} \downarrow_{est}^{gr}(p'[i'], j - 1), & \text{if } p' \text{ in the same component as } p \\ \downarrow_{est}(p'[i']), & \text{otherwise} \end{cases}$$

We note the strong similarity between the combined definitions of $\downarrow_{est}^{gr}(p[i], j)$ and $\downarrow_{est}^{rule}(p[i], j, r)$ compared to the corresponding "tight" formula $\downarrow_{est}^{t-t}(p[i])$. Formula for $\downarrow_{est}^{split}(p[i], p'[i'], j)$ serves two purposes. If the predicate p' is in the same component as predicate p, we decrement the counter j (intuitively bringing us to preceding groups in component partition). Otherwise, we simply use the minimum estimate for $p'[i']$ that is due to the computation relevant to another component.

We now show that defined functions $\downarrow_{est}$, $\downarrow_{est}^{gr}$, $\downarrow_{est}^{rule}$ and $\downarrow_{est}^{split}$ are total. Consider any strong level ranking of program's predicates. Then, by $rank(p)$ we refer to the corresponding strong level rank of a predicate p. The following table provides ranks associated with expressions used to define functions in question:

Expression	Rank
$\downarrow_{est}(p[i])$	$\omega \cdot (rank(p) + 1)$
$\downarrow_{est}^{gr}(p[i], j)$	$\omega \cdot rank(p) + j$
$\downarrow_{est}^{rule}(p[i], j, r)$	$\omega \cdot rank(p) + j$
$\downarrow_{est}^{split}(p[i], p'[i'], j)$	$\omega \cdot rank(p) + j$

where ω is the smallest infinite ordinal number. It is easy to see that in definitions of functions $\downarrow_{est}$, $\downarrow_{est}^{gr}$, and $\downarrow_{est}^{rule}$ the ranks associated with their expressions do not increase. In definition of $\downarrow_{est}^{split}$ in terms of $\downarrow_{est}$, the rank decreases. Thus, the defined functions are total.

By $\uparrow_{est}(p[i])$ we denote an estimate of a maximum value that may appear in argument $p[i]$ in program Π. It is computed using formula for $\downarrow_{est}(p[i])$ with min, max, $\downarrow_{est}$, $\downarrow_{est}^{gr}$, $\downarrow_{est}^{rule}$, and $\downarrow_{est}^{split}$ replaced with max, min, $\uparrow_{est}$, $\uparrow_{est}^{gr}$, $\uparrow_{est}^{rule}$, and $\uparrow_{est}^{split}$, respectively. The range of an argument $p[i]$, denoted $range_{est}(p[i])$, is computed by the formula of $range_{est}^{t-t}(p[i])$, where we replace $\downarrow_{est}^{t-t}$ and $\uparrow_{est}^{t-t}$ with $\downarrow_{est}$ and $\uparrow_{est}$, respectively.

We define the formula for finding the argument size estimates, $S_{est}(p[i])$, as follows:

$$S_{est}(p[i]) = S_{est}^{gr}(p[i], n)$$

$$S_{est}^{gr}(p[i], j) = min\big(\{range_{est}(p[i]), |oc(p[i])| + \sum_{r \in M_{1...j}^{p[i]}} S_{est}^{rule}(p[i], j, r)\}\big)$$

$$S_{est}^{rule}(p[i], j, r) = min\big(\{S_{est}^{split}(p[i], p'[i'], j) \mid p'[i'] \in args(r, \mathbb{H}(r)^i)\}\big)$$

$$S_{est}^{split}(p[i], p'[i'], j) = \begin{cases} S_{est}^{gr}(p'[i'], j - 1), & \text{if } p' \text{ is in the same component as } p \\ S_{est}(p'[i']), & \text{otherwise} \end{cases}$$

We can argue that the function S_{est} is total in the same way as we argued that the function $\downarrow_{est}$ is total.

Program Size Estimation. Keys. We borrow the concept of a key from relational databases. For some predicate p, we refer to any set of arguments of p that can uniquely identify all ground extensions of p as a *superkey* of p. We call a minimal superkey a *candidate key*. For instance, let the following be the ground extensions of some predicate q:

$$\{\langle 1, 1, a \rangle, \langle 1, 2, b \rangle, \langle 1, 3, b \rangle, \langle 2, 1, c \rangle, \langle 2, 2, c \rangle, \langle 2, 3, a \rangle\}$$

It is easy to see that both $\{q[1], q[2]\}$ and $\{q[1], q[2], q[3]\}$ are superkeys of q, while $\{q[1]\}$ is not a superkey. Only superkey $\{q[1], q[2]\}$ is a candidate key. A *primary key* of a predicate p is a single chosen candidate key. A predicate may have at most one primary key. (For the purposes of this work, the primary key is manually determined.) It is possible that some predicates do not have primary keys specified. To handle such predicates, we define $key(p)$ to mean the following:

$$key(p) = \begin{cases} \text{the primary key of } p, & \text{if } p \text{ has a primary key} \\ \{p[1], ..., p[n]\}, & \text{otherwise} \end{cases}$$

where n is the arity of p. We call an argument $p[i]$ a *key argument* if it is in $key(p)$. For a rule r, by $kvars(r)$ we denote the set of its variables that occur in its key arguments.

Rule size estimation. We now have all the ingredients to provide an estimate for grounding size of each rule in a program. We understand a *grounding size* of a rule as the number of rules produced as a result of intelligently grounding this rule. For a rule r in a program Π, the estimated grounding size, denoted $S_{est}(r)$, is computed as follows:

$$S_{est}(r) = \prod_{X \in kvars(r)} min\big(\{S_{est}(p[i]) \mid p[i] \in args(r, X)\}\big)$$

Implementation Details. System PREDICTOR[1] is developed using the Python 3 programming language. PREDICTOR utilizes PYCLINGO version 5, a Python API sub-system of answer set solving toolkit CLINGO [12]. The PYCLINGO API enables users to easily access and enhance ASP processing steps within Python code, including access to some data in the processing chain. In particular, PREDICTOR uses PYCLINGO to parse a logic program into an abstract syntax tree (AST) representation. After obtaining the AST, PREDICTOR has an immediate access to internal rule structure of the program and computes estimates for the program using the presented formulas. System PREDICTOR is designed for integration with other systems processing ASP programs. It is distributed as a package that can be imported into other systems developed in Python 3, or it can be accessed through a command line interface. In order to ensure that system PREDICTOR is applicable to real world problems, it supports ASP-Core-2 logic programs. For instance, the estimation formulas presented here generalize well to programs with choice rules and disjunction. Rules with aggregates are also supported. Yet, for such rules more sophisticated approaches are required to be more precise at estimations.

4   Experimental Analysis

To evaluate the usefulness of PREDICTOR, two sets of experiments are performed. First, an intrinsic evaluation over accuracy of the predicted grounding size compared to the actual grounding size is examined. Second, an extrinsic evaluation of system PRD-PROJECTOR– a tool resulting from system PROJECTOR enhanced by PREDICTOR– is conducted. In particular, we investigate the utility of system PREDICTOR by integrating it as a decision support mechanism into the ASP rewriting tool PROJECTOR. This integration is illustrated in Fig. 2. Each time system PROJECTOR accounts a rule to which its rewriting is applicable, it performs the rewriting. System PRD-PROJECTOR performs the rewriting of PROJECTOR only if PREDICTOR predicts the reduction in grounding size upon the rewriting. We measure the quality of PREDICTOR by analyzing the impact it has on rewritings by PROJECTOR. We note that the extrinsic evaluation is of a special value illustrating the usefulness and the potential of system PREDICTOR. It assesses PREDICTOR's impact when it is used in practice for its intended purpose as a decision making assistant. The intrinsic evaluation has its value in identifying potential future work directions and pitfalls in estimations. Overall, we will observe intrinsically that our estimates differ frequently in order of magnitude from the reality. Yet, extrinsic evaluation clearly states that PREDICTOR performs as an excellent decision making assistant for the purpose of improving rewriting tools when their performance depends on a decision when rewriting should take place versus not.

---

[1] https://www.unomaha.edu/college-of-information-science-and-technology/natural-language-processing-and-knowledge-representation-lab/software/predictor.php.

Benchmarks were gathered from two different sources. First, programs from the Fifth Answer Set Programming Competition [6] were used. Of the 26 programs in the competition, 13 were selected (these that system PROJECTOR has preformed rewritings on). For each program, the 20 instances (originally selected for the competition) were used. One interesting thing to note about these encodings is that they are generally already well optimized. As such, performing projections often leads to an increase in grounding size. Second, benchmarks were gathered from an application called ASPCCG implementing a natural language parser [17]. This domain has been extensively studied in [4] and was used to evaluate system PROJECTOR in [15]. In that evaluation, the authors considered 3 encodings from ASPCCG: ENC1, ENC7, ENC19. We utilize the same encodings and instances as in the evaluation of PROJECTOR. All tests were conducted on Ubuntu 18.04.3 with an Intel® Xeon® CPU E5-1620 v3 @ 3.50 GHz and 32 GB of RAM. Furthermore, Python version 3.7.3 and PYCLINGO version 5.4.0 are used to run PREDICTOR. Grounding and solving was done by CLINGO version 5.4.0. For all benchmarks execution was limited to 5 min.

Intrinsic Evaluation. Let S be the true grounding size of an instance in a program computed by GRINGO. Let S' be the grounding size predicted by PREDICTOR of the same instance. We define a notion of an *error factor* on a program instance as S'/S. The *average error factor* of a program/benchmark is the average of all error factors across the instances of a program. Table 1 shows the average error factor for all programs. We note that in our tests, keys were manually identified only for root predicate arguments. The average error factor shown was rounded to make comparisons easier. An asterisk ($*$) next to a benchmark name indicates that not all 20 instances of this benchmark were grounded within the allotted time limit. For instance, 19 instances of the *Incremental Scheduling* benchmark were successfully grounded, while the remaining instances timed out. For the $*$ benchmarks we only report the average error factor assuming the instances grounded successfully.

We partition the results into three groups using the average error factor. The partition is indicated by the horizontal lines on Table 1. First, there are five programs where the estimates computed by PREDICTOR are, on average, less than one order of magnitude over. Second, there are eight programs that are, on average, greater than one order of magnitude over. Finally, three programs are predicted to have lower grounding sizes than in reality. It is obvious that the accuracy of system PREDICTOR could still use improvements. In many cases the accuracy is drastically erroneous. These results are not necessarily surprising. We identify five main reasons for observed data on PREDICTOR: (1) Insufficient data modeling is one weak point of PREDICTOR. Since we do not keep track what actual constants could be present in the ground extensions of a predicate, it is often the case that we overestimate argument size due to our inability to identify repetitive values. (2) Since we only identified keys for root predicate arguments, many keys were likely missed. (3) System PREDICTOR has limited support for such common language extensions as aggregates. (4) System PREDICTOR is vulnerable to what is known as *error propagation* [16]. (5) While one might typically

Table 1. Average error factor for benchmark programs

Program	Avg. error factor
Hanoi Tower	1.5
Nomystery	1.5
Perm. Pattern Match.∗	3.8
Solitaire	4.3
Stable Marriage	3.7
Bottle Filling	4.9×10^9
Inc. Scheduling∗	1.1×10^5
Labyrinth∗	1.3×10^1
Minimal Diagnosis	8.2×10^3
Valves Location	$\mathbf{1.3 \times 10^1}$
ASPCCGENC1	$\mathbf{2.9 \times 10^1}$
ASPCCGENC7	$\mathbf{1.3 \times 10^1}$
ASPCCGENC19	2.2×10^1
Knight Tour with Holes	1.9×10^{-4}
Ricochet Robots	$\mathbf{2.0 \times 10^{-1}}$
Weighted Sequence	$\mathbf{6.0 \times 10^{-3}}$

expect PREDICTOR to overestimate due to its limited capabilities in detecting repeated data, the underestimation on *Knight Tour with Holes*, *Ricochet Robots*, and *Weighted Sequence* programs is not surprising due to the fact that these programs are non-tight.

Extrinsic Evaluation. Here, we examine the *relative* accuracy of system PREDICTOR alongside PROJECTOR. In other words, we measure the quality of PREDICTOR by analyzing the impact it has on PROJECTOR performance.

Let S be the grounding size of an instance of a program, where grounding is produced by GRINGO. Let S' be the grounding size of the same instance in a modified (rewritten) version of the program. In this context, the modified version will either be the logic program outputted after using PROJECTOR or the logic program outputted after using PRD-PROJECTOR. The *grounding size factor* of a program's instance is defined as S'/S. As such, a grounding size factor greater than 1 indicates that the modification increased the grounding size, whereas a value less than 1 indicates that the modification improved/decreased the grounding size. The *average grounding size factor* of a benchmark is the average of all grounding size factors across the instances of a benchmark. Table 2 (left) displays the average grounding size factor for PROJECTOR and PRD-PROJECTOR on all benchmark programs. An asterisk (∗) following a program name indicates that not all 20 instances were grounded. In these cases, the average grounding size factor was only computed from instances where all 3 versions of the program (original, PROJECTOR, PRD-PROJECTOR) completed grounding. A dagger

Table 2. Left: Average grounding size factors; Right: Average execution time factors

Program	PROJ	PRD-PROJ	Program	Svd.	PROJ	PRD-PROJ
Hanoi Tower	1.41	1.00	Hanoi Tower	20	1.67	1.00
Inc. Scheduling*	1.14	1.12	Inc. Scheduling	13	1.06	1.10
Minimal Diagnosis	1.06	1.00	Minimal Diagnosis	20	1.04	1.00
Solitaire	1.41	1.00	Solitaire	19	1.32	0.99
Stable Marriage	0.13	0.12	Stable Marriage	19	0.18	0.17
ASPCCG ENC1	0.63	0.49	ASPCCG ENC1	54	0.57	0.52
ASPCCG ENC7	1.40	1.24	ASPCCG ENC7	57	1.37	1.28
ASPCCG ENC19	1.58	1.04	ASPCCG ENC19	59	1.93	1.16
Bottle Filling	1.36	1.36	Bottle Filling	20	1.44	1.43
Labyrinth*	1.11	1.11	Labyrinth	16	5.26	5.27
Perm. Pattern Match.* †	0.13	0.13	Perm. Pattern Match.	16	0.14	0.14
Valves Location†	1.00	1.00	Valves Location	3	1.03	0.93
Weighted Sequence†	1.00	1.00	Weighted Sequence	16	3.05	1.59
Knight Tour with Holes	0.80	0.90	Knight Tour with Holes	1	0.50	2.45
Nomystery	0.62	1.00	Nomystery	7	1.23	1.00
Ricochet Robots	0.91	1.00	Ricochet Robots	20	0.85	1.00

(†) following a program name indicates that there was a slight improvement for PRD-PROJECTOR, however this information was lost for the precision shown.

We partition the results into three sets, indicated by the horizontal lines on Table 2 (left). We note that there are eight programs in which PRD-PROJECTOR reduces the grounding size noticeably when compared to PROJECTOR, five programs in which PRD-PROJECTOR does not impact the grounding size noticeably, and three programs in which PRD-PROJECTOR increases the grounding size noticeably.

While we target improving the grounding size of a program, it is useful to also compare the execution time of the programs, as that is ultimately what we want to reduce. Let S be the execution time of an answer set solver CLINGO on an instance of a benchmark. Let S' be the execution time of CLINGO on the same instance in a modified version of the benchmark. The *execution time factor* of a program's instance is defined as S'/S. The *average execution time factor* of a benchmark is the average of all *execution time factors* across the instances of a benchmark. Table 2 (right) shows the *average execution time factor* of programs rewritten with PROJECTOR and PRD-PROJECTOR. Overall, the results illustrate the validity of PREDICTOR approach.

5 Conclusions

We introduced a method for predicting grounding size of answer set programs. To the best of our knowledge this is *the only* approach for the stated purpose. We implement the described method in stand-alone system PREDICTOR that runs agnostic to any answer set grounder/solver pair. We expect this tool to become a foundation to decision support systems for rewriting/preprocessing tools in

ASP. Indeed, using PREDICTOR as a decision support guide to rewriting system PROJECTOR improves the PROJECTOR's outcome overall. This proves the validity of the proposed approach, especially as further methods for improving estimation accuracy are explored in the future. As such system PREDICTOR is a unique tool unparalleled in earlier research ready for use within preprocessing frameworks in ASP such as SIMPLIFY or LPOPT in a similar manner as we illustrate its use here within the system PRD-PROJECTOR.

Acknowledgments. We would like to thank Mirek Truszczynski, Daniel Houston, Liu Liu, Michael Dingess, Roland Kaminski, Abhishek Parakh, Victor Winter, Parvathi Chundi, and Jorge Fandinno for valuable discussions on the subject of this paper. The work was partially supported by NSF grant 1707371.

References

1. Bichler, M.: Optimizing non-ground answer set programs via rule decomposition. Bachelor Thesis, TU Wien (2015)
2. Bichler, M., Morak, M., Woltran, S.: lpopt: a rule optimization tool for answer set programming. Fund. Inform. **177**(3–4), 275–296 (2020)
3. Brewka, G., Eiter, T., Truszczynski, M.: Answer set programming at a glance. Commun. ACM **54**(12), 92–103 (2011)
4. Buddenhagen, M., Lierler, Y.: Performance tuning in answer set programming. In: Calimeri, F., Ianni, G., Truszczynski, M. (eds.) LPNMR 2015. LNCS (LNAI), vol. 9345, pp. 186–198. Springer, Cham (2015). https://doi.org/10.1007/978-3-319-23264-5_17
5. Calimeri, F., Fusca, D., Perri, S., Zangari, J.: I-DLV: the new intelligent grounder of DLV. Intelligenza Artificiale **11**(1), 5–20 (2017)
6. Calimeri, F., Gebser, M., Maratea, M., Ricca, F.: Design and results of the fifth answer set programming competition. Artif. Intell. **231**, 151–181 (2016)
7. Calimeri, F., Perri, S., Zangari, J.: Optimizing answer set computation via heuristic-based decomposition. Theory Pract. Log. Program. **19**(4), 603–628 (2019)
8. Eiter, T., Fink, M., Tompits, H., Traxler, P., Woltran, S.: Replacements in non-ground answer-set programming. In: Proceedings of International Conference on Principles of Knowledge Representation and Reasoning (KR) (2006)
9. Eiter, T., Traxler, P., Woltran, S.: An implementation for recognizing rule replacements in non-ground answer-set programs. In: Fisher, M., van der Hoek, W., Konev, B., Lisitsa, A. (eds.) JELIA 2006. LNCS (LNAI), vol. 4160, pp. 477–480. Springer, Heidelberg (2006). https://doi.org/10.1007/11853886_41
10. Faber, W., Leone, N., Perri, S.: The intelligent grounder of DLV. In: Erdem, E., Lee, J., Lierler, Y., Pearce, D. (eds.) Correct Reasoning. LNCS, vol. 7265, pp. 247–264. Springer, Heidelberg (2012). https://doi.org/10.1007/978-3-642-30743-0_17
11. Fages, F.: Consistency of Clark's completion and existence of stable models. J. Methods Log. Comput. Sci. **1**, 51–60 (1994)
12. Gebser, M., et al.: Potassco User Guide, 2nd edn. Institute for Informatics, University of Potsdam (2015)
13. Gebser, M., Kaminski, R., Kaufmann, B., Schaub, T.: Challenges in answer set solving. In: Balduccini, M., Son, T.C. (eds.) Logic Programming, Knowledge Representation, and Nonmonotonic Reasoning. LNCS (LNAI), vol. 6565, pp. 74–90. Springer, Heidelberg (2011). https://doi.org/10.1007/978-3-642-20832-4_6

14. Gebser, M., Kaminski, R., König, A., Schaub, T.: Advances in *gringo* series 3. In: Delgrande, J.P., Faber, W. (eds.) LPNMR 2011. LNCS (LNAI), vol. 6645, pp. 345–351. Springer, Heidelberg (2011). https://doi.org/10.1007/978-3-642-20895-9_39
15. Hippen, N., Lierler, Y.: Automatic program rewriting in non-ground answer set programs. In: Alferes, J.J., Johansson, M. (eds.) PADL 2019. LNCS, vol. 11372, pp. 19–36. Springer, Cham (2019). https://doi.org/10.1007/978-3-030-05998-9_2
16. Ioannidis, Y.E., Christodoulakis, S.: On the propagation of errors in the size of join results. Technical report, University of Wisconsin-Madison, Department of Computer Sciences (1991)
17. Lierler, Y., Schueller, P.: Parsing combinatory categorial grammar with answer set programming: preliminary report (2011). http://www.cs.utexas.edu/users/ai-lab/pub-view.php?PubID=127116
18. Mastria, E., Zangari, J., Perri, S., Calimeri, F.: A machine learning guided rewriting approach for asp logic programs. In: 36th International Conference on Logic Programming (ICLP) (2020)
19. Silberschatz, A., Korth, H.F., Sudarshan, S., et al.: Database System Concepts, vol. 4. McGraw-Hill, New York (1997)

Testing in ASP: Revisited Language and Programming Environment

Giovanni Amendola[1], Tobias Berei[2], and Francesco Ricca[1]($\boxtimes$)

[1] University of Calabria, Rende, Italy
{amendola,ricca}@mat.unical.it
[2] University of Applied Sciences Upper Austria, Campus Hagenberg,
Hagenberg, Austria
tobias.berei@students.fh-hagenberg.at

Abstract. Unit testing frameworks are nowadays considered a best practice, foregone in almost all modern software development processes, to achieve rapid development of correct specifications. The first unit testing specification language for Answer Set Programming (ASP) was proposed in 2011 as a feature of the ASPIDE development environment. Later, a more portable unit testing language was included in the LANA annotation language. In this paper we propose a revisited unit testing specification language that allows one to inline tests within ASP program and an ASP-based test execution mechanism. Moreover, we present a programming environment supporting test driven development (TDD) of ASP programs with our language.

Keywords: Answer Set Programming · Unit testing · Test-driven development

1 Introduction

Answer Set Programming (ASP) [8] is a well-known Logic-based formalism developed in the area of knowledge representation and reasoning. ASP combines a purely declarative language based on the stable models semantics [24] with efficient implementations [32]. ASP is known to be suited for rapid prototyping of complex reasoning tasks, and has been effectively used to solve a number of both academic and real-world applications of AI [15]. ASP allows to encode complex computational problems often in an easier and more compact way than mainstream (imperative) programming languages. For instance, the classical NP-complete problem of 3-Colorability is encoded in ASP using only two rules. Nonetheless, it is also easy to write incorrect ASP programs, which seem correct (often due to a misdirecting intuitive reading of rules) but do not work as expected.

To speed-up the development of correct and robust programs, many modern software development processes support some *Test-Driven Development* (TDD) best practices [21] such as *unit testing* [6]. In TDD the following sequence of

W. Faber et al. (Eds.): JELIA 2021, LNAI 12678, pp. 362–376, 2021.
https://doi.org/10.1007/978-3-030-75775-5_24

actions is repeated while developing a new program [6]: (i) add a test that defines a function or improvements of a function, which should be very succinct, so that the developer focuses on the requirements before writing the code; (ii) run all tests and see if the new test fails. This rules out the possibility that the newly introduced test specifies an improvement; (iii) write the code (may be not perfect); (iv) run all tests, to become confident that the new code meets the test requirements, and does not introduce bugs; (v) refactor code to improve it while accommodating the new features.

Tests drive the development because the program is considered improved only if it passes new tests, while the repeated execution of tests allows to find problems early in the development cycle and to isolate the incorrect behavior more easily. This intuition has been subject to further empirical studies which proved that programmers who wrote more tests tended to be more productive [16] and evidenced the superiority of the TDD practice over the traditional test-last approach or testing for correctness approach [34]. Two important best practices of TDD are the following: (i) concentrate on testing possibly small modules/functions/blocks of code; and (ii) adopt frameworks and tools to make the process of testing the program automatic. In the resulting software testing method, complex programs are split in *units*, which are tested in isolation providing (usually) small inputs and checking whether the expected outputs are computed. Tests for program units (i.e., *unit tests*) are directly derived from software requirements and often created before (or while) implementing the corresponding feature. The software is improved to pass the new tests, only.

TDD development practices are nowadays a standard technique used by expert programmers and development teams all over the world, no matter the programming language used. TDD development practices have been already applied also to many AI formalisms, as it is witnessed by the proposals in the literature, such as testing for Description Logics [7], and Constraint Programming [31]. In particular, TDD development practices have been applied to ASP program development. Indeed the first unit testing language for ASP has been introduced in 2011 [18], and was implemented in ASPIDE [19]. Nonetheless, this solution presents some limitations from the perspectives of both the language for specifying unit tests and its implementation. Concerning the language, one drawback is the need for specifying unit tests in separate files with respect to the program to test, which is not very comfortable given that ASP programs might contain (comparatively) few lines of code. Having the possibility to write tests *together* with the source code, without interfering with the actual evaluation of the program itself, would provide clear advantages for the developer. Subsequently [39], a more versatile approach of specifying unit test together with ASP programs was included in the LANA annotation language. However, the prototypical implementation of LANA, called ASPUnit, has never been included in a graphical development environment for ASP. A testing framework integrated in a development environment is comfortable for the developer, who can control the results in the same graphical environment she is using.

In this paper we propose a new unit testing language for ASP, which comprises the key features of both the above-mentioned proposals. The new language is annotation-based as LANA, so to allow the development of test cases inline with ASP code, and keep the assertion-based style for expressing test case conditions from the language of ASPIDE. The resulting annotation style is more similar to the JUnit framework for Java (from which both ASPIDE and LANA proposals were inspired), and should look more familiar to developers that are accustomed to XUnit style languages [6]. Importantly, we present a novel web-based development environment for ASP supporting test driven development of ASP programs that features an integrated implementation of unit testing.

Table 1. Base constructs of the annotation language.

Annotation	Description
`@rule(name="rName",block="bName")`	The name *rName* is assigned to the following rule. Assigning a rule to a block is optional
`@block(name="bName",rules={rList})`	Defines a block with name *bName*. Optionally a block may specify the list of rules that it covers

`@test(`
`  name = "testName",`
`  scope = { referenceList },`
`  programFiles = { programFileList },`
`  input = "aspCode",`
`  inputFiles = { inputFileList },`
`  assert = { assertionList }`
`)`
	Defines a test case with name *testName* and scope *referenceList* which is a list of strings referencing the rules and/or blocks under test. The target file is the current file, if *programFiles* is not defined. An input for the test can be specified in *aspCode* or several files (property *inputFiles*) can be set optionally. Furthermore *assertionList* is a list of assertions (defined in Table 2) that have to be fulfilled for this test case

2   Preliminaries on Answer Set Programming

Let $\mathcal{P}$ be a set of predicates, C of constants, and V of variables. A *term* is a constant or a variable. An atom a of arity k is of the form $p(t_1, ..., t_k)$, where $p \in \mathcal{P}$ and $t_1, ..., t_n$ are terms. A *disjunctive rule* r is of the form

$$a_1 \vee \ldots \vee a_l \leftarrow b_1, \ldots, b_m, \; not \; c_1, \ldots, \; not \; c_n, \qquad (1)$$

where all a_i, b_j, and c_k are atoms; $l, m, n \geq 0$ and $l + m + n > 0$; *not* represents *negation-as-failure*. The set $H(r) = \{a_1, ..., a_l\}$ is the *head* of r; $B^+(r) = \{b_1, ..., b_m\}$ and $B^-(r) = \{c_1, \ldots, c_n\}$ are the *positive body* and the *negative body* of r, respectively; and $B(r) = B^+(r) \cup B^-(r)$ is the *body* of r. A rule r is *safe* if each of its variables occurs in some positive body atom. A rule r is a *fact*, if $B(r) = \emptyset$ (we then omit $\leftarrow$ from the notation); a *constraint* if $H(r) = \emptyset$; *normal* if $|H(r)| \leq 1$; and *positive* if $B^-(r) = \emptyset$. A *(disjunctive logic) program* P is a finite set of disjunctive rules. P is called *normal* [resp. *positive*]

Table 2. Assertions for @test(...) annotation.

Assertion	Description
@noAnswerSet	The test must have no answer set.
@trueInAll(atoms="*atoms*")	The atoms specified in *atoms* must be true in all answer sets
@trueInAtLeast(number=*n*,atoms="*atoms*")	The atoms specified in *atoms* must be true in at least *n* answer sets
@trueInAtMost(number=*n*,atoms="*atoms*")	The atoms specified in *atoms* must be true in at most *n* answer sets
@trueInExactly(number=*n*,atoms="*atoms*")	The atoms specified in *atoms* must be true in exactly *n* answer sets
@constraintForAll(constraint="*c*")	The constraint specified in *c* must be fulfilled in all answer sets
@constraintInAtLeast(number=*n*,constraint="*c*")	The constraint specified in *c* must be fulfilled in at least *n* answer sets
@constraintInAtMost(number=*n*,constraint="*c*")	The constraint specified in *c* must be fulfilled in at most *n* answer sets
@constraintInExactly(number=*n*,constraint="*c*")	The constraint specified in *c* must be fulfilled in exactly *n* answer sets
@bestModelCost(cost=*cv*,level=*lv*)	The best model has to meet the cost of *cv* at level *lv* (for weak constraints)

if each $r \in P$ is normal [resp. positive]. Moreover, a program P is *head-cycle free* if there is a level mapping $\|.\|_h$ of P such that for every rule r of P: (i) For any l in $B^+(r)$, and for any l' in $H(r)$, $\|l\|_h \leq \|l'\|_h$; and (ii) For any pair l, l' of atoms in $H(r)$, $\|l\|_h \neq \|l'\|_h$. We denote by $At(P) = \bigcup_{r \in P} At(r)$ the set of all atoms in P. We restrict attention to programs built on safe rules only.

The *Herbrand universe* of P, denoted by U_P, is the set of all constants appearing in P. If there are no constants in P, we take $U_P = \{a\}$, where a is an arbitrary constant. The *Herbrand base* of P, denoted by B_P, is the set of all ground atoms that can be obtained from the predicate symbols appearing in P and the constants in U_P. Given a rule r of P, a *ground instance* of r is a rule obtained from r by replacing every variable X in r by $\sigma(X)$, where σ is a substitution mapping the variables occurring in r to constants in U_P. The *ground instantiation* of P, denoted by $ground(P)$, is the set of all the ground instances of the rules occurring in P.

Any set $I \subseteq B_P$ is an *interpretation*; it is a *model* of a program P (denoted $I \models P$) if for each rule $r \in ground(P)$, we have $I \cap H(r) \neq \emptyset$ whenever $B^+(r) \subseteq I$ and $B^-(r) \cap I = \emptyset$ (in such case, I is a model of r, denoted $I \models r$). A model M of P is *minimal* if no model $M' \subset M$ of P exists. We denote by $MM(P)$ the set of all minimal models of P. We write P^I for the well-known *Gelfond-Lifschitz reduct* [24] of P w.r.t. I, that is, the set of rules $H(r) \leftarrow B^+(r)$, obtained from rules $r \in ground(P)$ such that $B^-(r) \cap I = \emptyset$. We denote by $AS(P)$ the set of all *answer sets (or stable models)* of P, that is, the set of all interpretations I

such that $I \in MM(P^I)$. We say that a program P is *coherent*, if $AS(P) \neq \emptyset$, otherwise, P is *incoherent*.

Finally, we recall a useful extension of the answer set semantics by the notion of *weak constraint* [9]. A weak constraint ω is of the form:

$$:\sim b_1, \ldots, b_m, \ not\, c_1, \ldots, \ not\, c_n. \ [c@l], \qquad (2)$$

where c and l are nonnegative integers, representing a *cost* and a *level*, respectively. Let $\Pi = P \cup W$, where P is a set of rules and W is a set of weak constraints. We call M an answer set of Π if it is an answer set of P. We denote by $W(l)$ the set of all weak constraints at level l. For every answer set M of Π and any l, the *penalty* of M at level l, denoted by $Penalty_\Pi(M, l)$, is defined as $\sum_{w \in W(l), \ M \models B(\omega)} c$. For any two answer sets M and M' of Π, we say M is *dominated* by M' if there is l s.t. (*i*) $Penalty_\Pi(M', l) < Penalty_\Pi(M, l)$ and (*ii*) for all integers $k > l$, $Penalty_\Pi(M', k) = Penalty_\Pi(M, k)$. An answer set of Π is *optimal* if it is not dominated by another one of Π. We also mention aggregates, an extension of ASP that we do not recall here for keeping simple the description. We refer the reader to [11] for more details.

Example 1. Consider the following set of facts $F = \{node(1); node(2); node(3); edge(1, 2); edge(1, 3); edge(2, 3)\}$, and the ASP program P:

$$col(X, red) \vee col(X, blue) \vee col(X, green) \leftarrow node(X);$$
$$\leftarrow edge(X, Y), \ col(X, C), \ col(Y, C)$$

The set of facts F models a cycle of length 3, while the two rules of the program P model the 3-colorability problem. It can be checked, that $F \cup \{col(1, red), col(2, blue), col(3, green)\}$ is an answer set of $P \cup F$.

3 Unit Testing of Answer Set Programs

We now describe a new annotation-based test specification language that follows the Java annotation style of JUnit, and can be fully embedded in programs compliant with the ASP-Core-2 input language format of ASP competitions [23], which is nowadays a common syntactic fragment supported by the main ASP implementations. An annotation starts with '@' and is enclosed between %** and **% to distinguish multi-line comments, thus avoiding interference with program execution and to not require a separate test definition file (although in principle one could also collect testcases in separate files). The test specification language consists of base annotations and assertion condition annotations (or simply assertion annotations). The base annotations, described in Table 1, allow one to compose test cases, group subprograms in blocks, label rules and sub programs, and refer to the content of files containing programs. These annotations can be written anywhere in the ASP program, except @rule(...), which has to be followed by an ASP rule in order to be assigned correctly. With regards to the @test(...) annotation the property *scope* includes a list of strings as a parameter that reference both rules and blocks under test (by their name). Furthermore the property *assert* holds a list of assertion annotations that are described in Table 2. Basically, the programmer is free to identify the (sub)programs to test, specify the input of a program in a test case, and assert a number of conditions on the expected output, i.e., the basic operations supported by a XUnit testing language [6]. Note that, we have considered in our proposal all the assertions that are both present in the main unit testing languages proposed in the literature and that are more frequent in our experience.

An usage example of the test annotations language can be found in Fig. 1, which contains an instance of the graph coloring problem (3-colorability). This instance produces six answer sets according to the color assignments of the colors to the specified nodes. In order to test whether the rules behave as expected, we have to be able to reference the rules under test. As we do not want to test facts, we assign the names *r1* and *r2* to the rules in Lines 7 and 9. Additionally we assign these rules to a block, which has been defined in Line 4. Afterwards we are able to reference the rules under test inside the *@test(...)* annotation starting in Line 11. First we specify the name of the test case and the rules under test, which is the block *rulesToTest* in this case. While referencing the block is more convenient, we could also reference the rules directly by writing `scope = {"r1", "r2" }`. Input rules can be defined with the property *input*, which are joined with the rules under test during test execution. They are equivalent to the facts of the program in this case, but can be different for more complex test specifications. With the property *assert* we can now define assertions that have to be fulfilled in order to execute the test with positive result. For this simple instance of the graph coloring problem, we can test whether the atom `col(1, red)` is true in exactly two answer sets while the atoms `col(1, red)` in combination with `col(2, blue)` should be true in exactly one answer set (Lines 15 and 16). Note that, the *@test(...)* annotation is very flexible, and allows inputs to be selected freely by picking any sub-program, which plays the role of a *unit* to be tested (and run) in isolation. The *scope* attribute can be filled with any list of references (cfr. Table 1), including single rules, lists of rules (mentioned by name), and rules conveniently collected in a block (as in the example). Thus, it is possible to fine tune tests selecting any subprogram the programmer wants to test. The programmer can also flexibly control the input, inserting specific facts, subprograms, or reading the additional inputs from a file. In spite of being a simple ASP program, Fig. 1 shows how our lightweight annotation language can be used to define test cases without the need for a separate test definition file. The annotations do not interfere with program executability as being part of comments according to ASP-Core-2.

To further highlight the helpfulness of the TDD process for an ASP user, consider the example reported in Fig. 2. The program is a (wrong) ASP encoding for the Hamiltonian Cycle (HC) problem, a classical problem in graph theory. Given a finite directed graph $G = (N, A)$, and a node $a \in N$, the HC problem asks whether a cycle in G exists starting from a and passing through each node in G. In our encoding, the first rule represents a guess for the set of arcs

```
 1 │ %** Test graph **%
 2 │ node(1). node(2). node(3). edge(1,2).
 3 │ edge(1,3). edge(2,3).
 4 │ %** @block(name="ToTest") **%
 5 │ %** @rule(name="r1", block="ToTest") **%
 6 │ col(X,red) | col(X,blue) | col(X,green) :- node(X).
 7 │ %** @rule(name="r2", block="ToTest") **%
 8 │ :- edge(X, Y), col(X,C), col(Y,C).
 9 │ %**@test(name = "checkRules",
10 │        scope = { "ToTest" },
11 │        input = "node(1). node(2). node(3). edge(1,2). edge(1,3).
                 edge(2,3).",
12 │        assert = {
13 │        @trueInExactly(number = 2, atoms = "col(1, red)."),
14 │        @trueInExactly(number = 1, atoms = "col(1, red). col(2, blue)") }
15 │     )
16 │ **%
```

Fig. 1. Testing graph colouring.

of the graph. The second and the third rule model the reachability in a graph. Indeed, the starting node X is reached (rule r2, line 5), and if X is reached and (X, Y) is in the cycle, then Y is also reached (rule r3). Finally, the last three rules are constraints to be satisfied so that the arcs chosen in the cycle form an hamiltonian cycle. Indeed, the first two rules state that there is no more than one outgoing arc (rule r4) and there is no more than one ingoing arc (rule r5); and the last rule state that there is no node X which is not reached (rule r6). Now, if we have found an hamiltonian cycle, we expect to see in each answer set an outgoing arc for each node appearing in the cycle. We can express this condition through a constraint, stating that it is not possible that we have a node X, and there is no arc from X to some other node in the cycle. This condition is modeled by the assertion @constraintForAll in line 19, by meaning that each solution (answer set) must satisfy that condition. If we consider the input $A = \{node(1), node(2), node(3), node(4), arc(1,2), arc(1,4), arc(2,4), arc(3,1), arc(4,3), start(1)\}$ reported in lines 17–18, we expect that an hamiltonian cycle exists. Note that, any programmer would run such kind of "live" test, and maybe more than one, as in any programming language. However, the testing process fails. Indeed, our program on the given input admits the answer set: $A \cup \{inCycle(1,2), inCycle(2,4), inCycle(4,3), outCycle(1,4), outCycle(3,1)\}$, which does not satisfy the assertion. Note that, if you are the author of a piece of code, you are less likely to see a mistake without "trying" the program (you are "expecting" your statements to be correct), and common practice is to run a small instance to see if the result are as we expect. Thus, without an automated testing procedure one should check manually all the answer sets or resort to a script. Automatic testing makes this phase of the development easier and declarative. Note that, since unit tests remain in the source code, once the program is updated, they are not lost (as it happens to manually-handled result-checking

```
1  %** @block(name="hamCycle") **%
2  %** @rule(name="r1", block="hamCycle") **%
3  inCycle(X,Y) | outCycle(X,Y) :- arc(X,Y).
4  %** @rule(name="r2", block="hamCycle") **%
5  reached(X) :- start(X).
6  %** @rule(name="r3", block="hamCycle") **%
7  reached(Y) :- reached(X), inCycle(X,Y).
8  %** @rule(name="r4", block="hamCycle") **%
9  :- inCycle(X,Y), inCycle(X,Z), Y<>Z.
10 %** @rule(name="r5", block="hamCycle") **%
11 :- inCycle(X,Y), inCycle(Z,Y), X<>Z.
12 %** @rule(name="r6", block="hamCycle") **%
13 :- node(X), not reached(X).
14 %** @test(name = "checkProperty",
15          scope = { "hamCycle" },
16          input = "node(1). node(2). node(3). node(4). arc(1,2). arc(1,4).
                     arc(2,4). arc(3,1). arc(4,3). start(1)."
17          assert = { @constraintForAll(":-node(X),
                        #count{Y:inCycle(X,Y)}=0.") }
18      )
19 **%
```

Fig. 2. Testing hamilonian path.

sessions). Tests can be run again gaining all the advantages of *regression* testing [6]. If a test fails, bugs can be identified with a *debugger* [10].

4   The ASP-WIDE Environment

The ASP-WIDE environment implements this paper's unit-testing mechanism and the annotation language. While command line tools are efficient to use, the focus was to build an environment containing a code editor with syntax checking, syntax highlighting and execution/testing capabilities. This development tool offers a convenient environment for writing, executing and testing answer set programs. Since web-based environments, not only for logic programming, but also for conventional languages, are widely used, ASP-WIDE is based mostly on web technologies.

Implementation. As many modern web-based applications, ASP-WIDE consists of a front-end, which is built using the Angular framework, and a back-end implemented in Java utilizing the Spring framework. The communication between front-end and back-end is realized with HTTP-Requests transmitting JSON data. The overall architecture is depicted in Fig. 3. ASP-WIDE is meant to support any ASP solver supporting the ASP-Core-2 input language, such as Clingo and DLV2. The Execution module does not directly interact with an ASP system. Instead it uses the library DLVWrapper [37]. We extended the DLV Wrapper library to handle any ASP systems supporting the output format of the last ASP Competition [23], such as e.g., Clingo [22].

Table 3. Implementation of the assertions. P denotes the scope (i.e., the sub program to test), T_P the program built to implement the assertion, C a constraint, A a set of atoms, k, c, l are integers.

Assertions	Tester program	Test output
@noAnswerSet	P	Return *fail* if T_P admits answer sets, *pass* otherwise
@trueInAll(A)	$P \cup \bigcup_{a \in A}\{\leftarrow a\}$	Return *fail* if T_P admits answer sets, *pass* otherwise
@trueInAtLeast(A,k)	$P \cup \bigcup_{a \in A}\{\leftarrow nota\}$	Return *pass* as soon as the solver on T_P outputs k answer sets, *fail* otherwise
@trueInAtMost(A,k)	$P \cup \bigcup_{a \in A}\{\leftarrow nota\}$	Return *pass* if the solver terminates on T_P outputting at most k answer sets, *fail* otherwise
@trueInExactly(A,k)	$P \cup \bigcup_{a \in A}\{\leftarrow nota\}$	Return *pass* if the solver on T_P outputs k answer sets, *fail* otherwise
@constraintForAll(C)	$P \cup \{f \leftarrow C;\ \leftarrow notf\}$	Return *pass* if T_P admits no answer set, *fail* otherwise
@constraintInAtLeast(C,k)	$P \cup \{C\}$	Return *pass* as soon as the solver on T_P outputs k answer sets, *fail* otherwise
@constraintInAtMost(C,k)	$P \cup \{C\}$	Return *pass* if the solver terminates on T_P outputting at most k answer sets, *fail* otherwise
@constraintInExactly(C,k)	$P \cup \{C\}$	Return *pass* if the solver on T_P outputs k answer sets, *fail* otherwise
@bestModelCost(c,l)	P	Return *pass* if the optimal answer set of T_P has a cost of c at level l, *fail* otherwise

User Interface. The user interface of ASP-WIDE (see Fig. 4) was inspired by ASPIDE and features four main areas of interaction with the user: (i) The toolbar on the top of the environment; (ii) The workspace or file explorer on the left side; (iii) The code editor in the middle/right area (with open tabs on the top); and (iv) The output area on the bottom, which shows answer sets and test results. The toolbar features usual menus for handling files, run programs and adjust settings. Programs can be organized in projects, and the code editor features syntax-highlights and code-completion, i.e., it suggests how to complete predicate names and variables, to assist program and test-case development. Errors and warnings are also immediately displayed, and the modifications are automatically saved, as it is customary in modern web-based interfaces. The output is shown at the bottom.

Performance. The performance of our implementation depends on the underlying solver selected by the user. Our tools inherits for free all improvements to current solving technology, which is already very efficient also when managing problems of industrial size [12,15]. Nonetheless, a rule of thumb for devising good unit tests –that is independent of the language used for implementing the application– is to devise *small meaningful* testcases that are able to quickly isolate and understand the issue. Indeed, for the small-scope hypothesis,

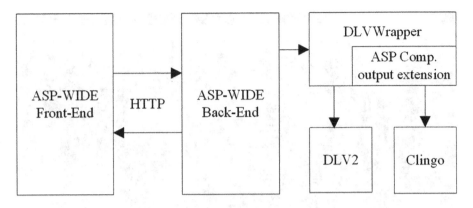

Fig. 3. Architecture of ASP-WIDE.

to detect a bug is sufficient to "analyze programs after grounding them over a small domain" [36]. Thus, despite the high *worst case* complexity of ASP programs, performance is never an issue in practice, provided that the test cases are properly devised. Our experience in developing applications confirms this is the case.

Availability. The ASP-WIDE environment can be installed as a standalone application in any computer with a modern (java-script enabled) web browser and Java 8 installed. ASP-WIDE can be downloaded (the url will be disclosed after acceptance) and the sources are distributed under GPL licence.

5 Related Work

The first paper approaching the problem of systematic testing of ASP programs is [28], where a general framework for structure-based testing of answer set programs, encompassing the definition of test coverage notions for ASP programs, has been proposed. In [28] the complexity issues related to coverage problems and the inherent complexity of relevant decision problems were also studied. An experimental comparison of basic strategies for random testing and structure-based testing of ASP programs has been presented [29]. The results of [29] indicate that random testing is quite effective in catching errors provided that sufficiently many admissible test inputs are considered. It has been empirically demonstrated [36] that the small-scope hypothesis of traditional testing holds also in the case of ASP programs. That is, many errors can be found by testing a program w.r.t. test inputs considering a small number of objects (i.e., from a small scope). More recently, a new tool for random based testing of ASP programs, called Harvey, has been described [27]. In Harvey random testing for ASP has been implemented using ASP itself (i.e., both test-input generation and determining test verdicts is done employing ASP). Harvey achieves uniformity of the test-input selection by using XOR streamlining [25] a technique used also

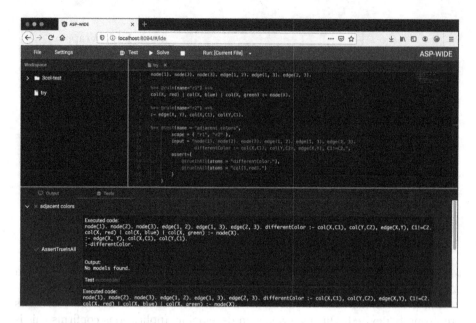

Fig. 4. The ASP-WIDE interface.

in the area of SAT solving [26]. The methods mentioned up to now focus on the problem of generating automatically test suites for ASP programs that are sufficient to identify defects, *after correct programs have been written*. These tools are thus particularly useful in cases in which one wants to improve an encoding, and use a natural (but less efficient) encoding, to check whether a more complicated (but efficient) one is being developed. On the other hand, as outlined in the introduction, the goal of unit testing in software development is to drive the implementation towards working software also when *no previous solution exists*. Indeed, in TDD, test cases are derived from the requirements even before writing the source code [6,21]. Nonetheless, automatic test generation can be combined with unit testing, e.g., in case one is evolving a solution to meet some non functional requirement such as efficient computation.

Focusing on unit testing, the first implementation of an ASP-specific solution was presented and included in the comprehensive development tool ASPIDE [18]. This implementation utilizes rule naming inside of ASP comments in combination with a test definition language for specifying test cases. While rule naming can be accomplished in an annotation-like manner, which does not interfere with program executability, the specification of test cases required a separate test file and a dedicated syntax [18]. Since adding meta-information to programs in form of annotations is known from conventional programming languages as C# and Java, a purely annotation-based test case specification for answer set programs is desirable. With [39] a language for annotating answer set programs (called LANA) is presented. Although LANA is not solely devoted to testing, it does address test case definition inside of ASP comments. Despite fully relying on annotations, its implementation (called ASPUnit) requires each unit test to be defined in a separate file, and was never been integrated in a development environment (to the best of our knowledge). Consequently the desire for a lightweight test definition mechanism that is purely annotation-based and does not necessarily require additional files or external tools that are not included in an environment dedicated to assisted programming remained unfulfilled.

The annotation language presented in this paper, albeit inspired by existing proposals, presents a new syntax that differs from both ASPIDE and LANA proposals, and recalls the well-known annotation style of Java. Since one of our design goals was to keep it simple while considering all the most important features, our language does not support (by design) some of the ASPIDE-specific options (such as automatic extraction of program modules, and run configuration management), and some of the LANA-specific options (such as pre/post conditions, and signatures). We discarded those that are: not strictly-related to program testing (e.g., signatures); can be simulated (e.g. pre/post conditions); are implementation specific (run configuration management); have a not so obvious semantics (automatic expansion of program modules). Indeed, automatic expansion of program modules in ASPIDE allows to automatically extend a block under test with the rules from the original program up to the point that a modularity condition is satisfied, such as the splitting condition [33] or the more precise conditions of [30]. In our experience this feature augments the program under test in a way that is not obvious to the programmer, thus we decided to discard this feature. Alternative ways of verifying the correctness of programs with input and output have been recently proposed [17], that could be considered for integration in our framework.

Finally, we observe that our unit testing language has been conceived for ASP-Core-2, nonetheless, it can be applied -almost as it is- to any extension of ASP, such as the richer languages supported by Clingo [22] and DLV 2.0 [1], DLVHEX [14], ASPMT [5,38], CASP [3,4,35], and SPARC [2]. Indeed, annotations (in comments) do not interfere with the specifications.

6   Conclusion

The development of AI applications can be accelerated by resorting to unit testing frameworks. In this paper we revisit unit testing in ASP by proposing a new unit test language that unifies the strengths of previous approaches. The new language allows the development of test cases inline with ASP code, keeps the style of expressing test case conditions from ASPIDE, and is annotation-based as LANA. Moreover it features a refreshed syntax that is nearer to the JUnit framework, and should look more familiar to developers that are accustomed to XUnit style languages. Importantly, the new unit testing language is implemented in a novel web-based development environment for ASP, which supports test driven development of ASP programs.

As future work, we are improving ASP-WIDE with additional editing features and a debugger [10,13,18]; moreover we are evaluating the possibility of using an answer set counting system [20] for test case conditions that require counting answer sets.

References

1. Alviano, M., et al.: The ASP system DLV2. In: Balduccini, M., Janhunen, T. (eds.) LPNMR 2017. LNCS (LNAI), vol. 10377, pp. 215–221. Springer, Cham (2017). https://doi.org/10.1007/978-3-319-61660-5_19
2. Balai, E., Gelfond, M., Zhang, Y.: Towards answer set programming with sorts. In: Cabalar, P., Son, T.C. (eds.) LPNMR 2013. LNCS (LNAI), vol. 8148, pp. 135–147. Springer, Heidelberg (2013). https://doi.org/10.1007/978-3-642-40564-8_14
3. Balduccini, M., Lierler, Y.: Constraint answer set solver EZCSP and why integration schemas matter. Theory Pract. Log. Program. **17**(4), 462–515 (2017)
4. Banbara, M., Kaufmann, B., Ostrowski, M., Schaub, T.: Clingcon: the next generation. TPLP **17**(4), 408–461 (2017)
5. Bartholomew, M., Lee, J.: First-order stable model semantics with intensional functions. Artif. Intell. **273**, 56–93 (2019)
6. Beck: Test Driven Development: By Example. Addison-Wesley Longman Publishing Co., Inc., Boston (2002)
7. Bezerra, C., Freitas, F.: Verifying description logic ontologies based on competency questions and unit testing. In: ONTOBRAS, CEUR 1908, pp. 159–164 (2017)
8. Brewka, G., Eiter, T., Truszczynski, M.: Answer set programming at a glance. Com. ACM **54**(12), 92–103 (2011)
9. Buccafurri, F., Leone, N., Rullo, P.: Enhancing disjunctive datalog by constraints. TKDE **12**(5), 845–860 (2000)
10. Busoniu, P., Oetsch, J., Pührer, J., Skocovsky, P., Tompits, H.: SeaLion: an eclipse-based IDE for answer-set programming with advanced debugging support. TPLP **13**(4–5), 657–673 (2013)
11. Calimeri, F., et al.: Asp-core-2 input language format. Theory Pract. Logic Program. **20**(2), 294–309 (2020). https://doi.org/10.1017/S1471068419000450
12. Calimeri, F., Gebser, M., Maratea, M., Ricca, F.: Design and results of the fifth answer set programming competition. Artif. Intell. **231**, 151–181 (2016)
13. Dodaro, C., Gasteiger, P., Reale, K., Ricca, F., Schekotihin, K.: Debugging non-ground ASP programs: technique and graphical tools. Theory Pract. Log. Program. **19**(2), 290–316 (2019). https://doi.org/10.1017/S1471068418000492
14. Eiter, T., et al.: The DLVHEX system. KI **32**(2–3), 187–189 (2018)
15. Erdem, E., Gelfond, M., Leone, N.: Applications of answer set programming. AI Mag. **37**(3), 53–68 (2016)
16. Erdogmus, H., Morisio, M., Torchiano, M.: On the effectiveness of the test-first approach to programming. IEEE Trans. Software Eng. **31**(3), 226–237 (2005)
17. Fandinno, J., Lifschitz, V., Lühne, P., Schaub, T.: Verifying tight logic programs with anthem and vampire. Theory Pract. Log. Program. **20**(5), 735–750 (2020). https://doi.org/10.1017/S1471068420000344
18. Febbraro, O., Leone, N., Reale, K., Ricca, F.: Unit testing in *ASPIDE*. In: Tompits, H., et al. (eds.) INAP/WLP -2011. LNCS (LNAI), vol. 7773, pp. 345–364. Springer, Heidelberg (2013). https://doi.org/10.1007/978-3-642-41524-1_21

19. Febbraro, O., Reale, K., Ricca, F.: ASPIDE: integrated development environment for answer set programming. In: Delgrande, J.P., Faber, W. (eds.) LPNMR 2011. LNCS (LNAI), vol. 6645, pp. 317–330. Springer, Heidelberg (2011). https://doi.org/10.1007/978-3-642-20895-9_37

20. Fichte, J.K., Hecher, M., Morak, M., Woltran, S.: Counting answer sets via dynamic programming. CoRR abs/1612.07601 (2016)

21. Fraser, S., Beck, K., Caputo, B., Mackinnon, T., Newkirk, J., Poole, C.: Test driven development (TDD). In: Marchesi, M., Succi, G. (eds.) XP 2003. LNCS, vol. 2675, pp. 459–462. Springer, Heidelberg (2003). https://doi.org/10.1007/3-540-44870-5_84

22. Gebser, M., Kaminski, R., Kaufmann, B., Schaub, T.: Multi-shot ASP solving with clingo. TPLP **19**(1), 27–82 (2019)

23. Gebser, M., Maratea, M., Ricca, F.: The sixth answer set programming competition. JAIR **60**, 41–95 (2017)

24. Gelfond, M., Lifschitz, V.: Classical negation in logic programs and disjunctive databases. New Generation Comput. **9**(3/4), 365–386 (1991)

25. Gomes, C.P., Hoffmann, J., Sabharwal, A., Selman, B.: Short XORs for model counting: from theory to practice. In: Marques-Silva, J., Sakallah, K.A. (eds.) SAT 2007. LNCS, vol. 4501, pp. 100–106. Springer, Heidelberg (2007). https://doi.org/10.1007/978-3-540-72788-0_13

26. Gomes, C.P., Sabharwal, A., Selman, B.: Near-uniform sampling of combinatorial spaces using XOR constraints. In: NIPS, pp. 481–488. MIT Press (2006)

27. Greßler, A., Oetsch, J., Tompits, H.: Harvey: a system for random testing in ASP. In: Balduccini, M., Janhunen, T. (eds.) LPNMR 2017. LNCS (LNAI), vol. 10377, pp. 229–235. Springer, Cham (2017). https://doi.org/10.1007/978-3-319-61660-5_21

28. Janhunen, T., Niemelä, I., Oetsch, J., Pührer, J., Tompits, H.: On testing answer-set programs. In: ECAI, pp. 951–956 (2010)

29. Janhunen, T., Niemelä, I., Oetsch, J., Pührer, J., Tompits, H.: Random vs. structure-based testing of answer-set programs: an experimental comparison. In: Delgrande, J.P., Faber, W. (eds.) LPNMR 2011. LNCS (LNAI), vol. 6645, pp. 242–247. Springer, Heidelberg (2011). https://doi.org/10.1007/978-3-642-20895-9_26

30. Janhunen, T., Oikarinen, E., Tompits, H., Woltran, S.: Modularity aspects of disjunctive stable models. J. Artif. Intell. Res. **35**, 813–857 (2009)

31. Lazaar, N., Gotlieb, A., Lebbah, Y.: On testing constraint programs. In: Cohen, D. (ed.) CP 2010. LNCS, vol. 6308, pp. 330–344. Springer, Heidelberg (2010). https://doi.org/10.1007/978-3-642-15396-9_28

32. Lierler, Y., Maratea, M., Ricca, F.: Systems, engineering environments, and competitions. AI Mag. **37**(3), 45–52 (2016)

33. Lifschitz, V., Turner, H.: Splitting a logic program. In: ICLP, pp. 23–37. MIT Press (1994)

34. Madeyski, L.: Test-driven development - an empirical evaluation of agile practice (2010). https://doi.org/10.1007/978-3-642-04288-1

35. Mellarkod, V.S., Gelfond, M., Zhang, Y.: Integrating answer set programming and constraint logic programming. Ann. Math. Artif. Intell. **53**(1–4), 251–287 (2008)

36. Oetsch, J., Prischink, M., Pührer, J., Schwengerer, M., Tompits, H.: On the small-scope hypothesis for testing answer-set programs. In: KR. AAAI Press (2012)

37. Ricca, F.: A Java wrapper for DLV. In: Answer Set Programming. CEUR, vol. 78 (2003)
38. Shen, D., Lierler, Y.: SMT-based constraint answer set solver EZSMT+ for non-tight programs. In: KR, pp. 67–71 (2018)
39. Vos, M.D., Kisa, D.G., Oetsch, J., Pührer, J., Tompits, H.: Annotating answer-set programs in LANA. TPLP **12**(4–5), 619–637 (2012)

An Abstract View on Optimizations in SAT and ASP

Yuliya Lierler[(✉)]

University of Nebraska Omaha, Omaha, USA
ylierler@unomaha.edu

Abstract. Search-optimization problems are plentiful in scientific and engineering domains. MaxSAT and answer set programming with weak constraints (ASP-WC) are popular frameworks for modeling and solving search problems with optimization criteria. There is a solid understanding on how SAT relates to ASP. Yet, the question on how MaxSAT relates to ASP-WC is not trivial. The answer to this question provides us with the means for cross fertilization between distinct subareas of automated reasoning. In this paper, we propose a weighted abstract modular framework that allows us to (i) capture MaxSAT and ASP-WC and (ii) state the exact link between these distinct paradigms. These findings translate, for instance, into the immediate possibility of utilizing MaxSAT solvers for finding solutions to ASP-WC programs.

1 Introduction

We target the advancement of automated reasoning that concerns itself with finding solutions to difficult search-optimization problems occurring in scientific and engineering domains. Specifically, we utilize the realms of propositional satisfiability with optimizations (MaxSAT family) [22] and answer set programming with weak constraints (ASP-WC) [1] to showcase our findings. We propose a "weighted abstract modular system" framework that can capture these logics and their relatives. MaxSAT and ASP-WC are instances exemplifying the utility of this framework. This work is a continuation of a tradition advocated, for example, in [6,16,17,24], where the authors abstract away the syntactic details of studied logics and focus on their semantic properties.

In practice, when search problems are formulated there is *often* an interest not only in identifying a solution, but also in pointing at the one that is optimal with respect to some criteria. Another way to perceive this setting is by having interplay of "hard" and "soft" modules (drawing a parallel to terminology used in formulating partial weighted MaxSAT). Hard modules formulate immutable constraints of a problem, i.e., requirements that solutions to a problem *must* satisfy in order to deserve being called a solution. Soft modules express conditions that are closer to preferences.

The work was partially supported by NSF grant 1707371.

W. Faber et al. (Eds.): JELIA 2021, LNAI 12678, pp. 377–392, 2021.
https://doi.org/10.1007/978-3-030-75775-5_25

Supporting various kinds of optimizations on an encoding and solving level is a holy grail of ASP-WC. Yet, some approaches to answer set solving that rely on translations to related automated reasoning (AR) paradigms – "translational" solvers such as CMODELS [12] and LP2SAT [13], which translate logic programs into propositional satisfiability (SAT) problem [20] – do not provide any support for weak constraints. One reason is that SAT itself has no support for formulating soft requirements. MaxSAT and its variants are extensions to SAT supporting optimizations. The formulations of these extensions significantly differ syntactically and semantically from those used in ASP-WC so that the *exact* link, between ASP-WC and MaxSAT formalisms, required in implementing translational approaches is not obvious. In general, optimizations in different areas of AR (see, for instance, [1,2,5,9,21]) are studied in separation with no clear articulation of the exact links between the languages expressing optimization criteria and their implementations. This paper takes modularity and abstraction as key tools for building a thorough understanding between related and yet disperse advances pertaining to optimizations or soft modules within different AR communities. Lierler and Truszczynski [16] proposed an abstract modular framework that allows us to bypass the syntactic details of a particular logic and study advances in AR from a bird's eye view. That framework is appropriate for capturing varieties of logics within hard modules. We extend the framework in a way that soft modules can be formulated and studied under one roof. We illustrate how a family of SAT based optimization formalisms such as MaxSAT, weighted MaxSAT, and partial weighted MaxSAT (pw-MaxSAT) can be embedded into the proposed framework. We also illustrate how ASP-WC fits into the same framework. We study the abstract framework illustrating a number of its formal properties that then immediately translate into its instances such as MaxSAT or ASP-WC. The paper culminates in a result illustrating how ASP-WC programs can be processed by means of MaxSAT solvers. The opposite link also becomes apparent, but it is left out of the paper to remain succinct. To summarize, we propose to utilize abstract view on logics and modularity as tools for constructing overarching view for distinct criteria used for optimization within different AR communities.

2   Review: Abstract Logics and Modular Systems

We start with the review of an abstract logic by Brewka and Eiter [6]. We then illustrate how it captures SAT and logic programs under answer set semantics. We then review model-based abstract modular systems advocated by Lierler and Truszczynski [16].

A *language* is a set L of *formulas*. A *theory* is a subset of L. Thus the set of theories is closed under union and has the least and the greatest elements: $\emptyset$ and L. We call a theory a *singleton* if it is an element/a formula in L (or a singleton subset, in other words). This definition ignores any syntactic details behind the concepts of a formula and a theory. A *vocabulary* is possibly an infinite countable set of *atoms*. Subsets of a vocabulary σ represent (classical propositional) *interpretations* of σ. We write $Int(\sigma)$ for the family of all interpretations of a vocabulary σ.

Definition 1. *A logic is a triple* $\mathcal{L} = (L_{\mathcal{L}}, \sigma_{\mathcal{L}}, sem_{\mathcal{L}})$, *where*

1. $L_{\mathcal{L}}$ *is a language (*language of $\mathcal{L}$*)*
2. $\sigma_{\mathcal{L}}$ *is a vocabulary (*vocabulary of $\mathcal{L}$*)*
3. $sem_{\mathcal{L}} : 2^{L_{\mathcal{L}}} \rightarrow 2^{Int(\sigma_{\mathcal{L}})}$ *is a function from theories in* $L_{\mathcal{L}}$ *to collections of interpretations (*semantics of $\mathcal{L}$*)*

If a logic $\mathcal{L}$ is clear from the context, we omit the subscript $\mathcal{L}$ from the notation of the language, the vocabulary and the semantics of the logic.

Brewka and Eiter [6] showed that this abstract notion of a logic captures default logic, propositional logic, and logic programs under the answer set semantics. For example, the logic $\mathcal{L} = (L, \sigma, sem)$, where

1. L is the set of propositional formulas over σ,
2. $sem(F)$, for a theory $F \subseteq L$, is the set of propositional models of theory F (where we understand an interpretation to be a model of theory F if it is a model of each element/propositional formula in F) over σ,

captures propositional logic. We call this logic a *pl-logic*. A *clause* is a propositional formula of the form

$$\neg a_1 \vee \ldots \vee \neg a_\ell \vee a_{\ell+1} \vee \ldots \vee a_m \tag{1}$$

where a_i is an atom. If we restrict elements of L to be clauses, then we call $\mathcal{L}$ a *sat-logic*. Intuitively, the finite theories in sat-logic can be identified with CNF formulas. Say, sat-logic theory $\{(a \vee b), (\neg a \vee \neg b)\}$ stands for the formula

$$(a \vee b) \wedge (\neg a \vee \neg b). \tag{2}$$

We now review logic programs. A *logic program* over σ is a finite set of *rules* of the form

$$a_0 \leftarrow a_1, \ldots, a_\ell, \ not \ a_{\ell+1}, \ldots, \ not \ a_m, \tag{3}$$

where a_0 is an atom in σ or $\bot$ (empty), and each a_i $(1 \leq i \leq m)$ is an atom in σ.

It is customary for a given vocabulary σ, to identify a set X of atoms over σ with (i) a complete and consistent set of literals over σ constructed as $X \cup \{\neg a \mid a \in \sigma \setminus X\}$, and respectively with (ii) an assignment function or interpretation that assigns the truth value *true* to every atom in X and *false* to every atom in $\sigma \setminus X$. In the sequel, we may refer to sets of atoms as interpretations and the other way around following this convention. We say that a set X of atoms *satisfies* rule (3), if X satisfies the propositional formula $a_1 \wedge \ldots \wedge a_\ell \wedge \neg a_{\ell+1} \wedge \ldots \wedge \neg a_m \rightarrow a_0$. The *reduct* Π^X of a program Π relative to a set X of atoms is obtained by first removing all rules (3) such that X does not satisfy the propositional formula corresponding to the negative part of the body $\neg a_{\ell+1} \wedge \ldots \wedge \neg a_m$, and replacing all remaining rules with $a \leftarrow a_1, \ldots, a_\ell$. A set X of atoms is an *answer set*, if it is the minimal set that satisfies all rules of Π^X [18]. For example, program

$$
\begin{aligned}
a &\leftarrow not\ b \\
b &\leftarrow not\ a.
\end{aligned}
\tag{4}
$$

has two answer sets $\{a\}$ and $\{b\}$.

Abstract logics of Brewka and Eiter subsume the formalism of logic programs under the answer set semantics. Indeed, let us consider a logic $\mathcal{L} = (L, \sigma, sem)$, where

1. L is the set of logic program rules over σ,
2. $sem(\Pi)$, for a program $\Pi \subseteq L$, is the set of answer sets of Π over σ,

We call this logic the *lp-logic*.

Lierler and Truszczynski [16] propose (model-based) abstract modular systems that allow us to construct heterogeneous systems based of "modules" stemming from a variety of logics. We now review their framework.

Definition 2. *Let $\mathcal{L} = (L_{\mathcal{L}}, \sigma_{\mathcal{L}}, sem_{\mathcal{L}})$ be a logic. A theory of $\mathcal{L}$, that is, a subset of the language $L_{\mathcal{L}}$ is called a* (model-based) *$\mathcal{L}$-module (or a module, if the explicit reference to its logic is not necessary). An interpretation $I \in Int(\sigma_{\mathcal{L}})$ is a model of an $\mathcal{L}$-module B if $I \in sem_{\mathcal{L}}(B)$.*

We use words theory and modules interchangeably at times. Furthermore, for a theory/module in pl- or sat-logics we often refer to these as propositional or SAT formulas (sets of clauses). For a theory/module in lp-logic we refer to it as a logic program.

For an interpretation I, by $I_{|\sigma}$ we denote an interpretation over vocabulary σ constructed from I by dropping all its members not in σ. For example, let σ_1 be a vocabulary such that $a \in \sigma_1$ and $b \notin \sigma_1$, then $\{a, b\}_{|\sigma_1} = \{a\}$. We now extend the notion of a model to vocabularies that go beyond the one of a considered module in a straight forward manner. For an $\mathcal{L}$-module B and an interpretation I whose vocabulary is a superset of the vocabulary $\sigma_{\mathcal{L}}$ of B, we say that I is a *model* of B, denoted $I \models B$, if $I_{|\sigma_{\mathcal{L}}} \in sem_{\mathcal{L}}(B)$. This extension is in spirit of a convention used in classical logic (for example, given a propositional formula $p \wedge q$ over vocabulary $\{p, q\}$ we can speak of interpretation assigning true to propositional variables $\{p, q, r\}$ as a model to this formula).

Definition 3. *A set of modules, possibly in different logics and over different vocabularies is a* (model-based) *abstract modular system (AMS). For an abstract modular system $\mathcal{H}$, the union of the vocabularies of the logics of the modules in $\mathcal{H}$ forms the vocabulary of $\mathcal{H}$, denoted by $\sigma_{\mathcal{H}}$. An interpretation $I \in Int(\sigma_{\mathcal{H}})$ is a model of $\mathcal{H}$ when for every module $B \in \mathcal{H}$, I is a model of B. (It is easy to see that we can extend the notion of a model to interpretations whose vocabulary goes beyond $\sigma_{\mathcal{H}}$ in a straight forward manner.)*

When an AMS consist of a single module $\{F\}$ we identify it with module F itself.

3   Weighted Abstract Modular Systems

In practice, we are frequently interested not only in identifying models of a given logical formulation of a problem (hard fragment) but identifying models that are deemed optimal according to some criteria (soft fragment). Frequently, multi-level optimizations are of interest. An AMS framework is geared towards capturing heterogeneous solutions for formulating hard constraints. Here we extend it to enable the formulation of soft constraints. We start by introducing a "w-condition" – a module accommodating notions of a level and a weight. We then introduce w-systems – a generalization of AMS that accommodates new kinds of modules. In conclusion, we embed multiple popular AR optimization formalisms into this framework.

Definition 4. *Let* $\mathcal{L} = (L_{\mathcal{L}}, \sigma_{\mathcal{L}}, sem_{\mathcal{L}})$ *be a logic. A pair* $(T_{\mathcal{L}}, w@l)$ – *consisting of a theory* $T_{\mathcal{L}}$ *of logic* $\mathcal{L}$ *and an expression* $w@l$, *where* w *is an integer and* l *is a positive integer* – *is called an* $\mathcal{L}$ *-w(eighted)-condition (or a w-condition, if the explicit reference to its logic is not necessary). We refer to integers* l *and* w *as* levels *and* weights, *respectively. An interpretation* $I \in Int(\sigma_{\mathcal{L}})$ *is a model of a* $\mathcal{L}$-w-condition $B = (T_{\mathcal{L}}, w@l)$, *denoted* $I \models B$ *if* $I \in sem_{\mathcal{L}}(T_{\mathcal{L}})$. *A mapping* $[I \models B]$ *is defined as follows*

$$[I \models B] = \begin{cases} 1 & when\, I \models B, \\ 0 & otherwise. \end{cases} \tag{5}$$

By $\lambda(B)$, B_w *we denote level* l *and weight* w *associated with w-condition* B, *respectively.*

We identify w-conditions of the form $(T, w@1)$ with expressions (T, w) (i.e., when the level is missing it is considered to be one).

For a collection $\mathcal{S}$ of w-conditions, the union of the vocabularies of the logics of the w-conditions in $\mathcal{S}$ forms the *vocabulary* of $\mathcal{S}$, denoted by $\sigma_{\mathcal{S}}$.

Definition 5. *A pair* $(\mathcal{H}, \mathcal{S})$ *consisting of an AMS* $\mathcal{H}$ *and a set* $\mathcal{S}$ *of w-conditions (possibly in different logics and over different vocabularies) so that* $\sigma_{\mathcal{S}} \subseteq \sigma_{\mathcal{H}}$ *is called a* w(eighted)-abstract modular system *(or w-system).*

Let $\mathcal{W} = (\mathcal{H}, \mathcal{S})$ be a w-system ($\mathcal{H}$ and $\mathcal{S}$ intuitively stand for *hard* and *soft*). The vocabulary of $\mathcal{H}$ forms the *vocabulary* of $\mathcal{W}$, denoted by $\sigma_{\mathcal{W}}$. For a level l, by $\mathcal{W}_l$ we denote the subset of $\mathcal{S}$ that includes all w-conditions whose level is l. By $\lambda(\mathcal{W})$ we denote the set of all levels associated with w-system $\mathcal{W}$ constructed as $\{\lambda(B) \mid B \in \mathcal{S}\}$.

Definition 6. *Let pair* $\mathcal{W} = (\mathcal{H}, \mathcal{S})$ *be a w-system. An interpretation* $I \in Int(\sigma_{\mathcal{W}})$ *is a* model *of* $\mathcal{W}$ *if it is a model of AMS* $\mathcal{H}$. *A model* I^* *of* $\mathcal{W}$ *is* optimal *if* $\mathcal{S}$ *is empty or there is a level* $l \in \lambda(\mathcal{W})$ *such that the following conditions are satisfied:*

1. *for any level l' that is greater than l and any two models I and I' of $\mathcal{W}$ the following equality holds* $\displaystyle\sum_{B \in \mathcal{W}_{l'}} B_w \cdot [I \models B] = \sum_{B \in \mathcal{W}_{l'}} B_w \cdot [I' \models B]$

2. I^* *satisfies equation* $I^* = \arg\max_I \displaystyle\sum_{B \in \mathcal{W}_l} B_w \cdot [I \models B].$

A model I^* of $\mathcal{W}$ is min-optimal *if it satisfies the conditions of max-optimal model where in the equation of condition 2 we replace max by min.*

This definition has two conditions. The first one identifies the greatest level of w-conditions under which we can "distinguish" models. The second condition is concerned with finding the models that maximize (or minimize in case of min-optimal model) the numeric value associated with the w-conditions of this level (note how w-conditions of any other level do not play a role within these calculations).

MaxSAT Family as W-Systems. We now restate the definitions of *MaxSAT*, *weighted MaxSAT* and *pw-MaxSAT* [22]. We then show how these formalisms are captured in terms of w-systems. In the sections that follow we use w-systems to model logic programs with weak constraints. The uniform language of w-systems allows us to prove properties of theories in these different logics by eliminating the reference to their syntactic form. In the conclusion of the paper we provide translation from logic programs with weak constraints to pw-MaxSAT problems.

To begin we introduce a notion of so called σ-theory. For a vocabulary σ and a logic $\mathcal{L}$ over this vocabulary ($\sigma_{\mathcal{L}} = \sigma$), we call theory $T_{\mathcal{L}}$ a σ-theory/σ-module when it satisfies property $sem(T_{\mathcal{L}}) = Int(\sigma)$. For example, in case of pl-logic or sat-logic a conjunction of clauses of the form $a \vee \neg a$ for every atom $a \in \sigma$ forms a σ-theory. For a σ-theory a logic of the theory becomes immaterial so we allow ourselves to denote an arbitrary σ-theory by T_{σ} disregarding the reference to its logic.

As customary in propositional logic given an interpretation I and a propositional formula F, we write $I \models F$ when I satisfies F (i.e., I is a model of F). A mapping $[I \models F]$ is defined as in (5) with B replaced by F. An interpretation I^* over vocabulary σ is a *solution* to MaxSAT problem F, where F is a CNF formula over σ, when it satisfies the equation $I^* = \arg\max_I \sum_{C \in F}[I \models C]$.

The following result illustrates how w-systems can be used to capture MaxSAT problem.

Proposition 1. *Let F be a MaxSAT problem over σ. The optimal models of w-system $(T_{\sigma}, \{(C, 1) \mid C \in F\})$ – where pairs of the form $(C, 1)$ are sat-logic w-conditions – form the set of solutions for MaxSAT problem F.*

Proposition 1 allows us to identify w-systems of particular form with MaxSAT problem. For example, any w-system of the form $(T_{\sigma}, \{(C_1, 1), \ldots (C_n, 1)\})$ – where C_i ($1 \le i \le n$) is a singleton sat-logic theory – can be seen as a MaxSAT problem composed of clauses $\{C_1, \ldots, C_n\}$.

A weighted MaxSAT problem [3] is defined as a set (C, w) of pairs, where C is a clause and w is a positive integer. An interpretation I^* over vocabulary σ is a *solution* to weighted MaxSAT problem P over σ, when it satisfies the equation

$$I^* = arg \max_{I} \sum_{(C,w) \in P} w \cdot [I \models C]. \tag{6}$$

Proposition 2. *Let P be a weighted MaxSAT problem over σ. The optimal models of w-system (T_σ, P) – where each element in P is understood as a sat-logic w-condition – form the set of solutions for weighted MaxSAT problem P.*

A *pw-MaxSAT problem* [11] is defined as a pair (F, P) over vocabulary σ, where F is a CNF formula over σ and P is a weighted MaxSAT problem over σ. Formula F is referred to as *hard* problem fragment, whereas clauses in P form *soft* problem fragment.

Let (F, P) be a pw-MaxSAT problem over vocabulary σ. An interpretation I over σ is a *model* of (F, P), when I is a model of F. A model I^* of (F, P) is optimal when it satisfies Eq. (6), where I ranges over models of F. The following proposition allows us to identify w-systems of particular form with pw-MaxSAT problems.

Proposition 3. *Let (F, P) be a pw-MaxSAT problem over vocabulary σ. The models and optimal models of w-system (F, P) – where F is a sat-logic module and each element in P is understood as a sat-logic w-condition – coincide with the models and optimal models of pw-MaxSAT problem (F, P), respectively.*

We now present sample pw-MaxSAT problem to illustrate some definitions at work. Take F_1 to denote sat-theory module (2). The pair

$$(F_1, \{(a, 1), (b, 1), (a \vee \neg b, 2), (\neg a \vee b, 0)\}) \tag{7}$$

forms a pw-MaxSAT problem, whose models are $\{a\}$ and $\{b\}$ and $\{a\}$ is an optimal model. If we consider this pw-MaxSAT problem as a respective w-system then the notion of min-optimal model is defined. Model $\{b\}$ is a min-optimal model for this w-system.

Embedding family of MaxSAT problems into w-systems realm provides us with immediate means to generalize their definitions to allow (i) min-optimal models; (ii) negative weights; (iii) distinct levels accompanying weight requirement on its clauses; (iv) removing restriction from its basic syntactic object being a clause and allowing, for example, arbitrary propositional formulas, as a logic for its module and w-conditions. Consider the definition of MaxPL Problem (meant to be a counterpart of pw-MaxSAT defined for arbitrary propositional formulas and incorporating enumerated items). We call a w-system (F, S) a *MaxPL problem*, when F is a pl-logic module and each w-condition in S is in pl-logic. It is easy to see that any pw-MaxSAT problem is a special case instance of MaxPL problem. The pair

$$(F_1, \{(a, 1), (b, 1@3), (a \vee \neg b, 2), (\neg a \vee b, 0)\}) \tag{8}$$

forms a sample MaxPL problem that differs from (7) in boosting the level of one of its w-conditions. The optimal model of this system is $\{b\}$. In the sequel we illustrate that presence of levels and negative weights in w-systems can often be considered as syntactic sugar. Also, the concept of min-optimal model can be expressed in terms of optimal models of a closely related w-system. Yet, from the perspective of knowledge representation, convenience of modeling, algorithm design for search procedures such features are certainly of interest and deserve an attention and thorough understanding.

Optimizations in Logic Programming. We now review a definition of a logic program with weak constraints following the lines of [7]. A *weak constraint* has the form

$$:\sim a_1, \ldots, a_\ell, \; not \; a_{\ell+1}, \ldots, \; not \; a_m[w@l], \tag{9}$$

where $m > 0$ and $a_1, \ldots, a_m$ are atoms, w (weight) is an integer, and l (level) is a positive integer. In the sequel, we abbreviate expression

$$:\sim a_1, \ldots, a_\ell, \; not \; a_{\ell+1}, \ldots, \; not \; a_m \tag{10}$$

occurring in (9) as D and identify it with the propositional formula

$$a_1 \wedge \ldots \wedge a_\ell \wedge \neg a_{\ell+1} \wedge \ldots \wedge \neg a_m. \tag{11}$$

An *optimization program* (or *o-program*) over vocabulary σ is a pair (Π, W), where Π is a logic program over σ and W is a finite set of weak constraints over σ.

Let $\mathcal{P} = (\Pi, W)$ be an optimization program over vocabulary σ (intuitively, Π and W forms *hard* and *soft* fragments, respectively). By $\lambda(\mathcal{P})$ we denote the set of all levels associated with optimization program $\mathcal{P}$ constructed as $\{l \mid D[w@l] \in W\}$. Set X of atoms over σ is an *answer set* of $\mathcal{P}$ when it is an answer set of Π. Let X and X' be answer sets of $\mathcal{P}$. Answer set X' *dominates* X if there exists a level $l \in \lambda(\mathcal{P})$ such that following conditions are satisfied:

1. for any level l' that is greater than l the following equality holds

$$\sum_{D[w@l'] \in W} w \cdot [X \models D] = \sum_{D[w@l'] \in W} w \cdot [X' \models D]$$

2. the following inequality holds for level l

$$\sum_{D[w@l] \in W} w \cdot [X' \models D] < \sum_{D[w@l] \in W} w \cdot [X \models D]$$

An answer set X^* of $\mathcal{P}$ is *optimal* if there is no answer set X' of $\mathcal{P}$ that dominates X^*.

Consider a logic whose language is a strict subset of that of propositional logic: a language that allows only for formulas of the form (11), whereas its semantics is that of propositional logic. We call this logic a *wc-logic*.

Proposition 4. *Let (Π, W) be an optimization logic program over vocabulary σ. The models and min-optimal models of w-system $\left(\Pi, \{(D, w@l) \mid D[w@l] \in W\}\right)$ – where Π is an lp-logic module and pairs of the form $(D, w@l)$ are wc-logic w-conditions – coincide with the answer sets and optimal answer sets of (Π, W), respectively.*

Propositions 1, 2, 3, and 4 allow us to identify MaxSAT, weighted MaxSAT, pw-MaxSAT, and o-programs with respective w-systems. In the following, we often use the terminology stemming from w-systems, when we talk of these distinct frameworks. For instance, we allow ourselves to identify a weak constraint (9) with a wc-logic w-condition

$$(a_1 \wedge \ldots \wedge a_\ell \wedge \neg a_{\ell+1} \wedge \ldots \wedge \neg a_m, w@l). \tag{12}$$

We now exemplify the definition of an optimization program. Let Π_1 be logic program (4). An optimal answer set of optimization program

$$(\Pi_1, \{:\sim a, not\ b. - 2@1\}) \tag{13}$$

is $\{a\}$. We note that the answer sets and the optimal answer set of (13) coincide with the models and the optimal model of pw-MaxSAT problem (7). The formal results of this paper will show that this is not by chance and that these two w-systems in different logics have more in common than meets the eye upon immediate inspection.

4 Formal Properties of W-Systems

We now state some interesting properties and results about w-systems. Word *Property* denotes the results that follow immediately from the model/optimal model definitions.

Property 1. Any two w-systems with the same hard theory have the same models.

Due to this proposition when stating the results for w-systems that share the same hard theory, we only focus on optimal and min-optimal models.

Property 2. Any model of w-system of the form $(\mathcal{H}, \emptyset)$ is optimal/min-optimal.

Property 3. Optimal/min-optimal models of the following w-systems coincide

– w-system $\mathcal{W}$ and
– w-system resulting from $\mathcal{W}$ by dropping all of its w-conditions whose weight is 0.

Thus, the w-conditions, whose weight is 0 are immaterial and can be removed. For instance, we can safely simplify sample pw-MaxSAT problem (7) and MaxPL problem (8) by dropping their w-conditions $(\neg a \vee b, 0)$.

We call a w-system $\mathcal{W}$ *level-normal*, when we can construct the sequence of numbers $1, 2, \ldots, |\lambda(\mathcal{W})|$ from the elements in $\lambda(\mathcal{W})$. It is easy to see that we can always adjust levels of w-conditions in $\mathcal{W}$ to respect such a sequence preserving optimal models of original w-system $\mathcal{W}$.

Proposition 5. *Optimal/min-optimal models of the following w-systems coincide*

- *w-system W and*
- *the level-normal w-system constructed from W by replacing each level l_i occurring in its w-conditions with its ascending sequence order number i, where we arrange elements in $\lambda(W)$ in a sequence in ascending order $l_1, l_2, \ldots l_{|\lambda(W)|}$.*

Sample MaxPL problem (8) is not level normal. Yet, this proposition suggests that it is safe to consider the level-normal w-system $(F_1, \{(a, 1), (b, 1@2), (a \vee \neg b, 2), (\neg a \vee b, 0)\})$ in its place. In the sequel we often assume level-normal w-systems without loss of generality.

Proposition 6. *For a w-system $W = (\mathcal{H}, \mathcal{S})$, if every level $l \in \lambda(W)$ is such that for any distinct models I and I' of W*

$$\sum_{B \in W_l} B_w \cdot [I \models B] = \sum_{B \in W_l} B_w \cdot [I' \models B]$$

then optimal/min-optimal models of w-systems W and $(\mathcal{H}, \emptyset)$ coincide. Or, in other words, any model of W is also optimal and min-optimal model.

By this proposition, for instance, it follows that optimal models of pw-MaxSAT problem $(F_1, \{(a, 1), (b, 1)\})$ coincide with its models $\{a\}$ and $\{b\}$ or, in other words, the problem can be simplified to $(F_1, \emptyset)$.

Let $W = (\mathcal{H}, \mathcal{S})$ be a w-system. For a set S of w-conditions, by $W[\backslash S]$ we denote the w-system $(\mathcal{H}, \mathcal{S} \backslash S)$.

Proposition 7. *For a w-system $W = (\mathcal{H}, \mathcal{S})$, if there is a set $S \subseteq \mathcal{S}$ of w-conditions all sharing the same level such that for any distinct models I and I' of W*

$$\sum_{B \in S} B_w \cdot [I \models B] = \sum_{B \in S} B_w \cdot [I' \models B]$$

then W has the same optimal/min-optimal models as $W[\backslash S]$.

This result provides us with the semantic condition on when it is "safe" to drop some w-conditions from the w-system. By this proposition, for instance, it follows that the optimal models of pw-MaxSAT problem (7) coincide with the optimal models of w-system constructed from (7) by dropping its w-conditions $(a, 1)$ and $(b, 1)$. To summarize, all listed results account to the fact that the optimal models of pw-MaxSAT problem (7) and the following pw-MaxSAT problem coincide

$$(F_1, \{(a \vee \neg b, 2)\}). \tag{14}$$

Let $(\mathcal{H}, \{(T_1, w_1@l_1), \ldots, (T_n, w_n@l_n)\})^{-1\cdot}$ map a w-system into the following w-system $(\mathcal{H}, \{(T_1, (-1 \cdot w_1)@l_1), \ldots, (T_n, (-1 \cdot w_n)@l_n)\})$. The next proposition tells us that min-optimal models and optimal models are close relatives:

Proposition 8. *For a w-system W, the optimal models (min-optimal models) of W coincide with the min-optimal models (optimal models) of $W^{-1\cdot}$.*

Eliminating Negative (or Positive) Weights. We call logics $\mathcal{L}$ and $\mathcal{L}'$ *compatible* when their vocabularies coincide, i.e., $\sigma_{\mathcal{L}} = \sigma'_{\mathcal{L}}$. Let $\mathcal{L}$ and $\mathcal{L}'$ be compatible logics, and T and T' be theories in these logics, respectively. We call a theory T (and a w-condition $(T, w@l)$) *equivalent to* a theory T' (and a w-condition $(T', w@l)$, respectively), when $sem(T) = sem(T')$. For example, sat-logic theory (2) over vocabulary $\{a, b\}$ is equivalent to lp-logic theory (4) over $\{a, b\}$

The following proposition captures an apparent property of w-systems that equivalent modules and w-conditions may be substituted by each other without changing the overall semantics of the system.

Proposition 9. *Models and optimal/min-optimal models of w-systems*

$$(\{T_1, \ldots, T_n\}, \{B_1, \ldots, B_m\}) \ and \ (\{T'_1, \ldots, T'_n\}, \{B'_1, \ldots, B'_m\})$$

coincide when (i) T_i and T'_i ($1 \le i \le n$) are equivalent theories, and (ii) B_i and B'_i ($1 \le i \le m$) are equivalent w-conditions.

For a theory T of logic $\mathcal{L}$, we call a theory $\overline{T}$ in logic $\mathcal{L}'$, compatible to $\mathcal{L}$, *complementary* when (i) $sem(T) \cap sem(\overline{T}) = \emptyset$, and (ii) $sem(T) \cup sem(\overline{T}) = Int(\sigma_{\mathcal{L}})$. For example, in case of pl-logic, theories F and $\neg F$ are complementary. Similarly, a theory $(\neg a \wedge \neg b) \vee (a \wedge b)$ in pl-logic over vocabulary $\{a, b\}$ is complementary to theory (4) in lp-logic over $\{a, b\}$. It is easy to see that given a theory in any logic we can always find, for instance, a pl-logic or sat-logic theory complementary to it. Yet, given a theory in some arbitrary logic we may not always find a theory complementary to it in the same logic. For example, consider vocabulary $\{a, b\}$ and a wc-theory $a \wedge b$. There is no complementary wc-theory to it over vocabulary $\{a, b\}$.

Let $(T, w@l)$ be an $\mathcal{L}$-w-condition. By $(T, w@l)^+$ we denote $(T, w@l)$ itself when $w \ge 0$ and any w-condition in a compatible logic that has the form $(\overline{T}, -1 \cdot w@l)$ (i.e., $\overline{T}$ is some theory complementary to T) when $w < 0$. By $(T, w@l)^-$ we denote $(T, w@l)$ itself when $w \le 0$ and any w-condition in a compatible logic that has the form $(\overline{T}, -1 \cdot w@l)$ (i.e., $\overline{T}$ is some theory complementary to T) when $w > 0$. It is easy to see that $^+$ and $^-$ forms a family of mappings satisfying stated conditions. Applying a member in this family to a w-condition always results in a w-condition with nonnegative and nonpositive weights respectively. For a w-system $\mathcal{W} = (\mathcal{H}, \{B_1, \ldots, B_m\})$, by $\mathcal{W}^+$ we denote the w-system of the form $(\mathcal{H}, \{B_1^+, \ldots, B_m^+\})$, whereas by $\mathcal{W}^-$ we denote the w-system of the form $(\mathcal{H}, \{B_1^-, \ldots, B_m^-\})$. The following proposition tells us that negative/positive weights within w-systems may be eliminated in favour of the opposite sign when theories complementary to theories of w-conditions are found.

Proposition 10. *Optimal/min-optimal models of w-systems $\mathcal{W}, \mathcal{W}^+, \mathcal{W}^-$ coincide.*

The result above can be seen as a consequence of the following proposition:

Proposition 11. *Optimal/min-optimal models of w-systems* $(\mathcal{H}, \{(T, w@l)\} \cup \mathcal{S})$ *and* $(\mathcal{H}, \{(\overline{T}, -1 \cdot w@l)\} \cup \mathcal{S})$ *coincide.*

This proposition suggests that in case of significantly expressive logic the presence of both negative and positive weights in w-conditions is nearly a syntactic sugar. Let us illustrate the applicability of this result in the realm of optimization programs. First, we say that a weak constraint (9) is *singular* if either its weight $w \geq 0$ or $m = 1$. Given a singular weak constraint/wc-logic w-condition $B = (T, w@l)$, it is easy to see that a mapping

$$
B^\uparrow = \begin{cases} B & \text{when } w \geq 0 \text{, otherwise} \\ (\neg a, -1 \cdot w@l) & \text{when } T \text{ has the form } a \\ (a, -1 \cdot w@l) & \text{when } T \text{ has the form } \neg a \end{cases}
$$

is in the B^+ family. We call optimization program *singular* when all of its w-conditions are *singular*. Similarly, given a singular weak constraint/w-condition B of the form (12), it is easy to see that a mapping

$$
B^{sat} = \begin{cases} \left((1), -1 \cdot w@l \right) & \text{when } w \geq 0 \text{, otherwise} \\ B & \text{when } w < 0 \end{cases}
$$

is in the B^- family. Note that the resulting w-condition of this mapping is in sat-logic. For a singular optimization program $(\Pi, \{B_1, \ldots, B_n\})$,

$$
\begin{aligned}
(\Pi, \{B_1, \ldots, B_n\})^\uparrow &= (\Pi, \{B_1^\uparrow, \ldots, B_n^\uparrow\}), \\
(\Pi, \{B_1, \ldots, B_n\})^{sat} &= (\Pi, \{B_1^{sat}, \ldots, B_n^{sat}\}).
\end{aligned}
$$

Proposition 10 tells us that optimal answer sets of singular o-program $\mathcal{P}$ and positive o-program $\mathcal{P}^\uparrow$ coincide. Also, it tells us that optimal answer sets of singular o-program $\mathcal{P}$ coincide with min-optimal models of w-system $\mathcal{P}^{sat}$.

We note that the restriction on an optimization program to be singular is not essential. In particular, given a non-singular program for every weak constraint C of the form (9), whose weight is negative (i) adding to its hard fragment a rule of the form $a^C \leftarrow a_1, \ldots, a_\ell, \text{ not } a_{\ell+1}, \ldots, \text{ not } a_m$, where a_C is a freshly introduced atom and (ii) replacing weak constraint C with $:\sim a^C[w@l]$ produces a singular optimization program. The answer sets of these two programs are in one to one correspondence. Dropping freshly introduced atoms a^C from a newly constructed program results in the answer sets of the original program. This fact is easy to see given the theorem on explicit definitions [10]. Alviano [1] describes a normalization procedure in this spirit.

Eliminating Levels. We call a w-system $\mathcal{W}$ *(strictly) positive* when all of its w-conditions have *(positive) nonnegative* weights. Similarly, we call a w-system $\mathcal{W}$ *(strictly) negative* when all of its w-conditions have *(negative) nonpositive* weights. As we showed earlier the w-conditions with 0 weights may safely be dropped so as such the difference between, for example, strictly positive and positive programs is inessential.

We now show that the notion of level in the definition of w-conditions is immaterial from the expressivity point of view, i.e., they can be considered as syntactic sugar. Yet, they are convenient mechanism for representing what is called hierarchical optimization constraints. It was also shown in practice that it is often of value to maintain hierarchy of optimization requirements in devising algorithmic solutions to search problems with optimization criteria [4]. Here we illustrate that given an arbitrary w-system we can rewrite it using w-conditions of the form (T, w). This change simplifies the definition of an optimal model by reducing it to a single condition. We can adjust weights w across the w-conditions in a way that mimics their distinct levels. A procedure in style was reported by Alviano [1] for the case of o-programs. In this work, we generalize that result to arbitrary w-systems.

Let pair $\mathcal{W} = (\mathcal{H}, \mathcal{S})$ be strictly positive level-normal w-system (as illustrated earlier restricting w-systems to being positive is inessential restriction; recall Proposition 10). Let n denote the number of distinct levels occurring in $\mathcal{S}$, i.e., $|\lambda(\mathcal{W})|$. Let M_l be the number associated with each level integer l in $\lambda(\mathcal{W})$ that is computed as $M_l = 1 + \sum_{(T,w@l)\in\mathcal{S}} w$. Intuitively, this number gives us the upper bound (incremented by 1) for the sum of the weights of the w-conditions of level l. We identify M_0 with 1. We now define the number that serves the role of the factor for adjusting each weight associated with some level. For level i ($1 \leq i \leq n$), let f_i be the number computed as $f_i = \prod_{0\leq j<i} M_j$. By $\mathcal{S}^1$ we denote the set of w-conditions constructed from $\mathcal{S}$ as follows

$$\{(T, f_i \cdot w) \mid (T, w@i) \in \mathcal{S}\} \tag{15}$$

By $\mathcal{W}^1$ we denote the w-system resulting from replacing $\mathcal{S}$ with $\mathcal{S}^1$.

Proposition 12. *Optimal/min-optimal models of strictly positive level-normal w-systems $\mathcal{W} = (\mathcal{H}, \mathcal{S})$ and $\mathcal{W}^1 = (\mathcal{H}, \mathcal{S}^1)$ coincide.*

Optimization Programs as Pw-MaxSAT Problems. It is well known that logic programs under answer set semantic and propositional formulas are closely related (see, for instance, [15] for an overview of translations). For example, for so called "tight" programs a well known completion procedure [8] transforms a logic program into a propositional formula so that the answer sets of the former coincide with the models of the later. Once this formula is clausified the problem becomes a SAT problem. For nontight programs extensions of completion procedure are available [13,19]. Some of those extensions introduce auxiliary atoms. Yet, the appearance of these atoms are inessential as models of resulting formulas are in one to one correspondence with original answer sets. The later can be computed from the former by dropping the auxiliary atoms. The bottom line is that a number of known translations from logic programs to SAT exist. Numerous answer set solvers, including but not limited to CMODELS [12] and LP2SAT [13], rely on this fact by translating logic program in a SAT formula. For a logic program Π over vocabulary σ (that we identify with a module in lp-logic), by F_Π we denote a SAT formula, whose models coincide with these of Π. For example, recall that F_1 and Π_1 denote sat-formula (2) and logic program (4). Formula F_1 forms one of the possible formulas F_{Π_1}. In fact, F_1 corresponds to the clausified completion of program Π_1 (which has the form $(a \leftrightarrow \neg b) \wedge (b \leftrightarrow \neg a)$).

In previous sections we illustrated how multiple levels and negative weights in w-systems/singular optimization programs can be eliminated in favor of a single level and positive weights. Thus, without loss of generality we consider here singular optimization programs with a single level. The following result is a consequence of several propositions stated earlier.

Proposition 13. *Optimal answer sets of singular o-program* $(\Pi, \{B_1, \ldots, B_m\})$ *coincide with optimal models of pw-MaxSAT problem* $((F_\Pi, \{B_1^{sat}, \ldots, B_n^{sat}\})^{-1})$.

This result tells us, for example, that optimal answer sets of optimization program (13) coincide with optimal models of pw-MaxSAT problem (14). Earlier, we illustrated that optimal models of pw-MaxSAT problem (14) coincide with these of pw-MaxSAT problem (7). Proposition 13 provides us with a formal result that tells us how to utilize MaxSAT solvers for finding optimal answer sets of a program in similar ways as SAT solvers are currently utilized for finding answer sets of logic programs as exemplified by such answer set solvers as CMODELS or LP2SAT.

5   Conclusions

We proposed the extension of abstract modular systems to weighted systems in a way that modern approaches to optimizations stemming from a variety of different logic based formalisms can be studied in unified terminological ways so that their differences and similarities become clear not only on intuitive but also formal level. We trust that establishing clear link between optimization statements, criteria, and solving in distinct AR subfields is a truly fruitful endeavor allowing a streamlined cross-fertilization between the fields. In particular, an immediate and an intuitive future work direction is extending a translational based answer set solver CMODELS with capabilities to process optimization statements by enabling it to interface with a MaxSAT solver in place of a SAT solver. In addition, a generalization of results presented here is of interest in the scope of what is called constraint answer set programming [14]. The EZSMT [23] system is a translational constraint answer set solver that translates its programs into satisfiability modulo theories (SMT) formulas. We trust that results obtained here lay the groundwork for obtaining a link between constraint answer set programs with weak constraints and what is called O(ptimization)MT formulas – a formalism extending SMT with optimizations.

References

1. Alviano, M.: Algorithms for solving optimization problems in answer set programming. Intelligenza Artificiale **12**, 1–14 (2018). https://doi.org/10.3233/IA-180119
2. Andres, B., Kaufmann, B., Matheis, O., Schaub, T.: Unsatisfiability-based optimization in clasp. In: Dovier, A., Costa, V.S. (eds.) Technical Communications of the 28th International Conference on Logic Programming (ICLP'12). Leibniz International Proceedings in Informatics (LIPIcs), Dagstuhl, Germany, vol. 17, pp. 211–221. Schloss Dagstuhl-Leibniz-Zentrum fuer Informatik (2012). https://doi.org/10.4230/LIPIcs.ICLP.2012.211, http://drops.dagstuhl.de/opus/volltexte/2012/3623
3. Argelich, J., Li, C.M., Manyà, F., Planes, J.: The first and second max-sat evaluations. J. Satisf. Boolean Model. Comput. **4**, 251–278 (2008)
4. Argelich, J., Lynce, I., Marques-Silva, J.: On solving boolean multilevel optimization problems. In: Proceedings of the 21st International Joint Conference on Artificial Intelligence, pp. 393–398. IJCAI 2009, Morgan Kaufmann Publishers Inc., San Francisco, CA, USA (2009)
5. Brewka, G., Delgrande, J.P., Romero, J., Schaub, T.: asprin: Customizing answer set preferences without a headache. In: Proceedings of the Twenty-Ninth AAAI Conference on Artificial Intelligence, Austin, Texas, USA. pp. 1467–1474 (2015). http://www.aaai.org/ocs/index.php/AAAI/AAAI15/paper/view/9535
6. Brewka, G., Eiter, T.: Equilibria in heterogeneous nonmonotonic multi-context systems. In: Proceedings of National Conference on Artificial Intelligence, vol. 2007, pp. 385–390. AAAI (2007)
7. Calimeri, F., et al.: Asp-core-2 input language format (2013). https://www.mat.unical.it/aspcomp2013/files/ASP-CORE-2.03c.
8. Clark, K.: Negation as failure. In: Gallaire, H., Minker, J. (eds.) Logic and Data Bases, pp. 293–322. Plenum Press, New York (1978)
9. Di Rosa, E., Giunchiglia, E.: Combining approaches for solving satisfiability problems with qualitative preferences. AI Commun. **26**(4), 395–408 (2013). http://dl.acm.org/citation.cfm?id=2594602.2594606
10. Ferraris, P.: Answer sets for propositional theories. In: Proceedings of International Conference on Logic Programming and Nonmonotonic Reasoning (LPNMR), pp. 119–131 (2005)
11. Fu, Z., Malik, S.: On solving the partial MAX-SAT problem. In: Biere, A., Gomes, C.P. (eds.) SAT 2006. LNCS, vol. 4121, pp. 252–265. Springer, Heidelberg (2006). https://doi.org/10.1007/11814948_25
12. Giunchiglia, E., Lierler, Y., Maratea, M.: Answer set programming based on propositional satisfiability. J. Autom. Reas. **36**, 345–377 (2006)
13. Janhunen, T.: Some (in)translatability results for normal logic programs and propositional theories. J. Appl. Non-Classical Logics 35–86 (2006)
14. Lierler, Y.: Relating constraint answer set programming languages and algorithms. Artif. Intell. **207C**, 1–22 (2014)
15. Lierler, Y.: What is answer set programming to propositional satisfiability. Constraints **22**, 307–337 (2017)
16. Lierler, Y., Truszczyński, M.: An abstract view on modularity in knowledge representation. In: Proceedings of the AAAI Conference on Artificial Intelligence (2015)
17. Lierler, Y., Truszczyński, M.: Abstract modular inference systems and solvers. Artif. Intell. **236**, 65–89 (2016)
18. Lifschitz, V., Tang, L.R., Turner, H.: Nested expressions in logic programs. Ann. Math. Artif. Intell. **25**, 369–389 (1999)

19. Lin, F., Zhao, Y.: ASSAT: Computing answer sets of a logic program by SAT solvers. In: Proceedings of National Conference on Artificial Intelligence (AAAI), pp. 112–117. MIT Press (2002)
20. Mitchell, D.G.: A SAT solver primer. EATCS Bull. (Logic Comput. Sci. Column). **85**, 112–133 (2005)
21. Nieuwenhuis, R., Oliveras, A.: On SAT modulo theories and optimization problems. In: Biere, A., Gomes, C.P. (eds.) SAT 2006. LNCS, vol. 4121, pp. 156–169. Springer, Heidelberg (2006). https://doi.org/10.1007/11814948_18
22. Robinson, N., Gretton, C., Pham, D.N., Sattar, A.: Cost-optimal planning using weighted maxsat. In: ICAPS 2010 Workshop on Constraint Satisfaction Techniques for Planning and Scheduling (COPLAS10) (2010)
23. Shen, D., Lierler, Y.: SMT-based constraint answer set solver EZSMT+ for non-tight programs. In: Proceedings of the 16th International Conference on Principles of Knowledge Representation and Reasoning (KR) (2018)
24. Tasharrofi, S., Ternovska, E.: A semantic account for modularity in multi-language modelling of search problems. In: Tinelli, C., Sofronie-Stokkermans, V. (eds.) FroCoS 2011. LNCS (LNAI), vol. 6989, pp. 259–274. Springer, Heidelberg (2011). https://doi.org/10.1007/978-3-642-24364-6_18

Model Reconciliation in Logic Programs

Tran Cao Son[1][(✉)], Van Nguyen[1], Stylianos Loukas Vasileiou[2],
and William Yeoh[2]

[1] New Mexico State University, Las Cruces, NM 88003, USA
{tson,vnguyen}@cs.nmsu.edu
[2] Washington University in St. Louis, St. Louis, MO 63130, USA
{v.stylianos,wyeoh}@wustl.edu

Abstract. Inspired by recent research in explainable planning, we investigate the *model reconciliation* problem between two logic programs π_a and π_h, which represent the knowledge bases of an agent and a human, respectively. Given π_a, π_h, and a query q such that π_a entails q and π_h does not entail q (or π_a does not entail q and π_h entails q), the model reconciliation problem focuses on the question of how to modify π_h, by adding $\epsilon^+ \subseteq \pi_a$ to π_h and removing $\epsilon^- \subseteq \pi_h$ from π_h such that the resulting program $\hat{\pi}_h = (\pi_h \backslash \epsilon^-) \cup \epsilon^+$ has an answer set containing q (or has no answer set containing q). The pair (ϵ^+, ϵ^-) is referred to as a *solution* for the model reconciliation problem (π_a, π_h, q) (or $(\pi_a, \pi_h, \neg q)$). We prove that, for a reasonable selected set of rules $\epsilon^+ \subseteq \pi_a$ there exists a way to modify π_h such that $\hat{\pi}_h$ is guaranteed to credulously entail q (or skeptically entail $\neg q$). Given that there are potentially several solutions, we discuss different characterizations of solutions and algorithms for computing solutions for model reconciliation problems.

Keywords: Model reconciliation · Explainable planning · Answer set programming

1 Introduction

In several problems involving two (or more) agents[1] with different knowledge bases, the agents often discuss about the truth value of an atom. Frequently, the question about the truth value of q—an atom appearing in the knowledge bases of both agents—is raised by an agent, say A, to another one, say B. Facing this question, agent B could potentially inform agent A the reason, constructed using her knowledge, for the truth value of q. This method is reasonable if agents A and B share a knowledge base. When they have different knowledge bases, this method might no longer suitable. For example, in human-aware planning

---

This research is partially supported by NSF grants 1757207, 1812619, 1812628, and 1914635.

[1] We discuss problems involving only two agents in this paper, but our approach could be generalized to multiple agents.

© Springer Nature Switzerland AG 2021
W. Faber et al. (Eds.): JELIA 2021, LNAI 12678, pp. 393–406, 2021.
https://doi.org/10.1007/978-3-030-75775-5_26

problems [3,5,12,13], a planning agent may inform a human user that it has a plan α for achieving a given goal. However, α may not be a feasible plan from the human's perspective. To address this issue, research in explainable planning proposes the *model reconciliation problem*, where the goal is to reconcile some of the differences in the models of the agent and the human (i.e., informs the human what needs to be changed in her model) such that α is an optimal plan, often the minimal length plan, in the reconciled model of the human.

In this paper, we propose a generalization of the model reconciliation problem, introduced in [1], as follows: Given a logic program π_a of a robot and a logic program π_h of a human user such that π_a entails[2] an atom q (resp. does not entail q), the goal is to identify a pair of sub-programs $\epsilon^+ \subseteq \pi_a$ and $\epsilon^- \subseteq \pi_h$ such that $\hat{\pi}_h = \pi_h \backslash \epsilon^- \cup \epsilon^+$ will also entail q (resp. will also not entail q). We refer to this problem as the *model reconciliation in logic programs* (MRLP) problem.

We note that MRLP might appear similar to *strong equivalent program transformation* (e.g., [6]) and *logic program update* (e.g., [11]), both research topics that have been extensively studied by the logic programming community. It is worth pointing out that MRLP's goal is not to make π_a and π_h equivalent. For example, if x is an atom in the languages of both π_a and π_h, π_a entails x, π_h does not entail x, and $\epsilon = (\epsilon^+, \epsilon^-)$ satisfying $\hat{\pi}_h = \pi_h \backslash \epsilon^- \cup \epsilon^+$ entails q then ϵ is an explanation for the problem (π_a, π_h, q) even when $\hat{\pi}_h$ does not entail x, i.e., $\hat{\pi}_h$ is not equivalent to π_a. Comparing to logic programming update, MRLP first needs to identify ϵ and then modifies the human program π_h by deleting or adding rules; it does not change the remaining rules of π_h. We will discuss in more detail the differences between MRLP and logic program update later. In summary, the main contributions of this paper are:

- a generalization of the model reconciliation problem in explainable planning to define the MRLP and a method for solving MRLP problems;
- different characterization of solutions of a MRLP problem that can be used to comparing solutions; and
- an algorithm for computing solutions of a MRLP problem.

The paper is organized as follows. The next section includes a short review of logic programming under answer set semantics and the notion of a justification for an atom with respect to an answer set that will be useful for later discussion. We then propose a general method for solving MRLP problems and discuss different ways to characterize a solution of a MRLP problem. Afterwards, we present algorithms for computing solutions of a given MRLP.

2   Background: Answer Set Programming

Answer set programming (ASP) [7,9] is a declarative programming paradigm based on logic programming under the answer set semantics. A logic program

---

[2] In this paper, whenever we say a program entails a literal, we refer to the *credulous entailment* relationship between a program a literal. Precise definition will be provided in the next section.

Π is a set of rules of the form $a_0 \leftarrow a_1, \ldots, a_m, \; not \; a_{m+1}, \ldots, \; not \; a_n$ where $0 \leq m \leq n$, each a_i is an atom of a propositional language and not represents (default) negation. Intuitively, a rule states that if all positive literals a_i are believed to be true and no negative literal $not \; a_i$ is believed to be true, then a_0 must be true. If a_0 is omitted, the rule is called a *constraint*. If $n = 0$, it is called a *fact*. For a rule r, $head(r)$ denotes a_0; $pos(r)$ and $neg(r)$, referred to as the *positive* and *negative* body, respectively, denotes the set $\{a_1, \ldots, a_m\}$ and $\{a_{m+1}, \ldots, a_n\}$, respectively. Also, $atoms(r)$ denotes the set of all atoms in r, viz. $\{head(r)\} \cup pos(r) \cup neg(r)$; and, $atoms(\Pi)$ denotes the set of all atoms of Π. $heads(\Pi)$ (resp. $negs(\Pi)$) denotes the set of atoms occurring in the head of rules of Π (resp. negative literals of Π).

Let Π be a program. $I \subseteq atoms(\Pi)$ is called an interpretation of Π. For an atom a, a is satisfied by I, denoted by $I \models a$, if $a \in I$. A set of atoms S is satisfied by I if $S \subseteq I$. For a rule r, $I \models body(r)$ if $pos(r) \subseteq I$ and $neg(r) \cap I = \emptyset$. A rule r is satisfied by I if $I \not\models body(r)$ or $I \models head(r)$. I is a *model* of a program if it satisfies all its rules. An atom a is *supported* by I in Π if there exists $r \in P$ such that $head(r) = a$ and $I \models body(r)$.

For an interpretation I and a program Π, the *reduct* of Π w.r.t. I (denoted by Π^I) is the program obtained from Π by deleting *(i)* each rule r such that $neg(r) \cap I \neq \emptyset$, and *(ii)* all negative literals in the bodies of the remaining rules. Formally, $P^I = \{head(r) \leftarrow pos(r) \mid r \in \Pi, \; neg(r) \cap I = \emptyset\}$. Given an interpretation I, observe that the program Π^I is a definite program (a program with no occurrence of negative literals). An interpretation I is an *answer set* [4] of Π if I is the least model of Π^I [2], which is the least fixpoint of the operator T_Π defined by $T_\Pi(I) = \{a \mid \exists r \in \Pi, head(r) = a, I \models body(r)\}$ and is denoted by $lfp(T_\Pi)$.

Given an answer set I of Π and an atom q, a justification for q w.r.t. I is a set of rules $S \subseteq \Pi$ such that $head(r) \in I$ and $I \models body(r)$ for $r \in S$ and $q \in lfp(T_{S^I})$. A justification S for q w.r.t. I is minimal if there exists no proper subset $S' \subset S$ such that S' is also a justification for q w.r.t. I. It is easy to see that if S is a minimal justification for q w.r.t. I then $negs(S) \cap heads(S) = \emptyset$ and $heads(S)$ is an answer set of S.

Given a logic program Π, an atom a. We write $\Pi \mid\!\sim a$ to indicate that a belongs to at least one answer set of Π or a is credulously entailed by Π. Furthermore, we use $\Pi \mid\!\not\sim a$ to indicate that a does not belong to any answer set of Π or $\neg a$ is cautiously entailed by Π.

3   Model Reconciliation in Logic Programs

The model reconciliation problem in logic programs (MRLP) is divided into two sub-problems, one aims at changing the human program so that it entails an atom (e-MRLP) and another focuses on achieving that the updated program does not entail an atom (n-MRLP). Inspired by the problem in explainable planning, we define three different types of MLRP.

Definition 1 (MRLP). *Let π_a and π_h be two logic programs and q be an atom in the language of π_a.*

- *The problem of* model reconciliation for entailment in logic programs *(e-MRLP) is defined by a triple (π_a, π_h, q). A pair of programs (ϵ^+, ϵ^-) such that $\epsilon^+ \subseteq \pi_a$ and $\epsilon^- \subseteq \pi_h$ is a* solution *of (π_a, π_h, q) if $\hat{\pi}_h \mathrel{\vdash\!\!\!\sim} q$ where $\hat{\pi}_h = \pi_h \backslash \epsilon^- \cup \epsilon^+$.*
- *The problem of* model reconciliation for non-entailment in logic programs *(n-MRLP) is defined by a triple $(\pi_a, \pi_h, \neg q)$. A pair of programs (ϵ^+, ϵ^-) such that $\epsilon^+ \subseteq \pi_a$ and $\epsilon^- \subseteq \pi_h$ is a* solution *of $(\pi_a, \pi_h, \neg q)$ if $\hat{\pi}_h \mathrel{\not\vdash\!\!\!\sim} q$ where $\hat{\pi}_h = \pi_h \backslash \epsilon^- \cup \epsilon^+$.*
- *The general problem of* model reconciliation in logic programs *(MRLP) is defined by a triple (π_a, π_h, ω) where $\omega = \omega^+ \wedge \neg \omega^-$ and ω^+ (resp. ω^-) is a conjunction of atoms in π_a. (ϵ^+, ϵ^-) is a solution for the MRLP problem if it is a solution for (π_a, π_h, q) for each conjunct q in ω^+ and solution for $(\pi_a, \pi_h, \neg r)$ for each conjunct r in ω^-.*

We note that e-MRLP focuses on credulous entailment of atoms while n-MRLP on skeptical entailment of negation of atoms. This is because we are interested in applying the framework in situations utilizing answer set programming for problem solving. In this context, it is often the case that the existence (resp. non-existence) of an answer set, that contains a designated atom, indicating that the problem is solvable (resp. not solvable). The combination of e-MRLP and n-MRLP, as in the general MRLP, provides us way to express various types of problems. For example, the shortest plan model reconciliation problem in explainable planning can be expressed by the triple (π_a, π_h, G) where π_a and π_h are the logic programs encoding the planning problem of the agent and the human[3], respectively, and $G = goal(n) \wedge \neg goal(n-1) \wedge \ldots \wedge \neg goal(0)$ representing that the goal of the planning problem must be satisfied after the execution of n actions but it is unsatisfied after the execution of any arbitrary $k < n$ actions.

Observe that e-MRLP implicitly requires that $\hat{\pi}_h$ is consistent. On the other hand, this requirement is missing in n-MRLP. As we are often interested in the general MRLP problem, we will therefore interested in solutions of MRLP problems that guarantee the consistency of $\hat{\pi}_h$. To simplify the presentation, we will assume that given for a MRLP problem (π_a, π_h, ω), $\pi_a \mathrel{\vdash\!\!\!\sim} \omega^+$ and $\pi_a \mathrel{\not\vdash\!\!\!\sim} \omega^-$; for a e-MRLP problem $(\pi_a, \pi_h, q_1 \wedge \ldots \wedge q_k)$, $\pi_a \mathrel{\vdash\!\!\!\sim} q_i$ for $i = 1, \ldots, q_k$; and for a n-MRLP problem $(\pi_a, \pi_h, \neg q_1 \wedge \ldots \wedge \neg q_k)$, $\pi_a \mathrel{\vdash\!\!\!\sim} \neg q_i$ for $i = 1, \ldots, q_k$. Furthermore, we will discuss the solutions of e-MRLP or n-MRLP problems with a single atom q as the solutions for more complex formulas can be computed in the same manner.

We will first discuss how to solve n-MRLP problems. Obviously, if $\pi_h \mathrel{\not\vdash\!\!\!\sim} q$ then $(\emptyset, \emptyset)$ is a solution for $(\pi_a, \pi_h, \neg q)$. Now, assume that $\pi_h \mathrel{\vdash\!\!\!\sim} q$. By definition of answer sets, we can just remove rules from π_h to achieve $\hat{\pi}_h \mathrel{\not\vdash\!\!\!\sim} q$. Let $\pi_h(q) = \{r \mid r \in \pi_h, head(r) = q\}$. It is easy to see that $P \mathrel{\not\vdash\!\!\!\sim} q$ for every $P \subseteq \pi_h \backslash \pi_h(q)$.

---

[3] Strictly speaking, π_a also encodes the shortest plan in explainable planning.

As such, a solution $(\emptyset, \epsilon^-)$ for the n-MRLP problem $(\pi_a, \pi_h, \neg q)$ that guarantees the consistency of $\hat{\pi}_h$ could be determined with $\pi_h(q) \subseteq \epsilon^- \subseteq \pi_h$. Observe that taking π_a into consideration provide alternative solutions as well. For example, given the two programs:

$$\pi_a = \{a \leftarrow\} \quad \pi_h = \{q \leftarrow \ not\ c; c \leftarrow \ not\ q; a \leftarrow \ not\ a,\ not\ q\}$$

It is easy to see that π_h has a unique answer set $\{q\}$ and thus $\pi_h \mathrel{|\!\sim} q$ and $\pi_h \backslash \pi_h(q)$ is inconsistent. On the other hand, either $(\pi_a, \pi_h(q))$ or $(\emptyset, \{q \leftarrow not\ c; a \leftarrow \ not\ a,\ not\ q\})$ is a solution for the n-MRLP problem $(\pi_a, \pi_h, \neg q)$. In either case, $\hat{\pi}_h$ is consistent. The former adds a rule from π_a and removes $\pi_h(q)$ from π_h while the latter only removes rules from π_h.

It should be noted that sometimes, there is no need to remove rules whose head is q to achieve that $\hat{\pi}_h \mathrel{|\!\not\sim} q$. For example, for the program $\pi_h = \{q \leftarrow not\ c; c \leftarrow \ not\ d; d \leftarrow\}$ we have that $\pi_h \backslash \{d \leftarrow\} \mathrel{|\!\not\sim} q$. The two examples show that there are several explanations for a n-MRLP problem. As we will see later, the same holds for e-MRLP problems. In our view, which explanation should be used is application dependent.

We now discuss a method for solving e-MRLP problems (π_a, π_h, q). By definition of answer sets, $\hat{\pi}_h \mathrel{|\!\sim} q$ means that there exists an answer set of $\hat{\pi}_h$ which contains a justification for q. In all likelihood, this justification must come from π_a if $\pi_h \mathrel{|\!\not\sim} q$. In other words, the justification for q in $\hat{\pi}_h$ should be a part of ϵ^+. For this reason, we will focus on how to choose ϵ^+. This can be done by identifying an answer set I supporting q and selecting a justification for q w.r.t. I as ϵ^+. A solution can then determined by identifying $\epsilon^- \subseteq \pi_h$ so that (ϵ^+, ϵ^-) is a solution to the problem (π_a, π_h, q). Assume that I and ϵ^+ have been selected, we motivate the selection of ϵ^- using a series of e-MRLP problems (π_a, π_h, b), i.e., the robot wants to explain to the human that b is entailed by his program.

Example 1. Let $\pi_a = \{a \leftarrow; b \leftarrow a\}$ $\pi_h = \{a \leftarrow\}$ Clearly, π_a has a unique answer set $I_0 = \{a, b\}$ and $\epsilon^+ = \pi_a$ is a justification for b. To explain b to the human, the robot needs to inform the human that the rule $b \leftarrow a$ exists. Furthermore, there is no need to remove anything from π_h, i.e., $\epsilon^- = \emptyset$ *since the rule $a \leftarrow$ is satisfied by I_0.*

The example above discusses a situation in which one needs to add rules to the human's program as part of the explanation process. The next examples discuss different situations in which one needs to also remove rules from the human's program.

Example 2. Let $\pi_a = \{a \leftarrow \ not\ b; b \leftarrow \ not\ a\}$ and $\pi_h = \{a \leftarrow\}$. π_a has two answer sets $I_1 = \{a\}$ and $I_2 = \{b\}$. Only I_2 supports b and $\epsilon^+ = \{b \leftarrow \ not\ a\}$ is the justification of b w.r.t. I_2. It is easy to see that simply adding ϵ^+ to π_h will result in a program with the unique answer set $\{a\}$ which does not support b. It means that the rule $a \leftarrow$ should be removed, i.e., $\epsilon^- = \{a \leftarrow\}$. This suggests that ϵ^- should contain any rule whose head does not belong to I_2.

Example 3. Let $\pi_a = \{b \leftarrow \textit{not } a\}$ $\pi_h = \{c \leftarrow \textit{not } c\}$.
π_a has a unique answer set $I_3 = \{b\}$ and the unique justification for b is $\epsilon^+ = \pi_a$.
The program $\pi_h \cup \pi_a$ is also inconsistent because of the rule $c \leftarrow \textit{not } c$. So, we
need to have $\epsilon^- = \{c \leftarrow \textit{not } c\}$. Observe that in this case, the rule $r =$
"$c \leftarrow \textit{not } c$" satisfies $head(r) \notin I_3$ but $neg(r) \cap I_3 = \emptyset$.

Example 4. Let $\pi_a = \{b \leftarrow \textit{not } a\}$ $\pi_h = \{\leftarrow b\}$.
π_a has a unique answer set $I_4 = \{b\}$ and the unique justification for b is $\epsilon^+ = \pi_a$.
The program $\pi_h \cup \pi_a$ is also inconsistent because of the constraint $\leftarrow b$. So, we
should set $\epsilon^- = \pi_h$. In this case, the constraint $r =$ "$\leftarrow b$" satisfies $head(r) \notin I_4$
but $pos(r) \subseteq I_4$.

Observe that in Example 1, the rule $a \leftarrow$ needs not to be removed since its
body and head are both satisfied by the answer set $\{a, b\}$ which happens to be
the answer set of the justification ϵ^+. In Example 2, the rule $a \leftarrow$ is removed
because of its body is satisfied but its head is not satisfied by the answer set
$\{b\}$. Although it appears differently, Examples 3–4 are similar to Example 2:
The head of the rule is not satisfied and the body of the rule is satisfied by
the answer set of the program ϵ^+. So, one might wonder whether there is any
reasonable situation in which a rule, whose head is not satisfied by the answer
set I, should be kept. Indeed, consider an example similar to Example 4, except
that $\pi_h = \{\leftarrow c\}$. In this case, it would make sense not to remove the constraint
$\leftarrow c$ because it is not falsified by the answer set I_4. The discussion above leads to
the following notion that is useful for the computation of solutions of e-MRLP
problems.

**Definition 2 (Residual of a program w.r.t. a set of rules and a set of
atoms).** *Let π_a and π_h be two programs. Further, let I be a set of atoms of π_a
and $\epsilon^+ \subseteq \pi_a$. The residual of π_h with respect to ϵ^+ and I, denoted by $\otimes(\pi_h, \epsilon^+, I)$,
is the collection of rules from $\pi_h \backslash \epsilon^+$ such that for each rule $r \in \otimes(\pi_h, \epsilon^+, I)$:*

(i) $head(r) \in I$ and $neg(r) \cap I = \emptyset$; or
(ii) $neg(r) \cap heads(\epsilon^+) \neq \emptyset$; or
(iii) $pos(r) \backslash I \neq \emptyset$.

We use $\epsilon^-[\epsilon^+, I, \pi_h]$ to denote the set of rules $\pi_h \backslash \otimes (\pi_h, \epsilon^+, I)$.

It is easy to verify that if we use I and ϵ^+ as in Examples 1–4, then
$(\epsilon^+, \epsilon^-[\epsilon^+, I, \pi_h])$ is a solution for the problem (π_a, π_h, b) in these examples.

Observe that Examples 1–4 are somewhat unique in that, for each answer
set, there exists only one possible justification for the atom b. It is easy to see
that there are situations in which multiple justifications for an atom are present.
For example, consider

$$\pi_a = \{a \leftarrow; b \leftarrow a; b \leftarrow\} \quad \pi_h = \{a \leftarrow\}$$

In this case, π_a also has a unique answer set $I = \{a, b\}$. However, there are
two possible ways for justifying the presence of b in the answer set: (1) $\epsilon_1^+ =$

$\{a \leftarrow; b \leftarrow a\}$ and (2) $\epsilon_2^+ = \{b \leftarrow\}$. It is easy to see that for $i = \{1,2\}$, $(\epsilon_i^+, \epsilon_i^-[\epsilon_i^+, I, \pi_h])$ is a solution for (π_a, π_h, b). A natural question is then which solution should be used? We believe that choosing which solution to present to the human is application dependent; for example, if b represents a fact in the initial state of a planning problem, using ϵ_2^+ is reasonable; on the other hand, if b is a derived fact and is dependent on a, using ϵ_1^+ would be more reasonable as it informs the human of the dependency between a and b, which could potentially be useful for the human.

The above discussion shows that solutions of the e-MRLP problem (π_a, π_h, q) can be computed by identifying I, ϵ^+, and then set $\epsilon^- = \epsilon^-[\epsilon^+, I, \pi_h]$. An appropriate choice of I and ϵ^+ is specified in the next theorem.

Theorem 1. *Let (π_a, π_h, q) be an e-MRLP problem. Further, let I be an answer set of π_a supporting q and $\epsilon^+ \subseteq \pi_a$ be a minimal justification of q w.r.t. I. Then, $(\epsilon^+, \epsilon^-[\epsilon^+, I, \pi_h])$ is a solution of (π_a, π_h, q).*

Proof. Let $P = \pi_h \backslash \epsilon^-[\epsilon^+, I, \pi_h] \cup \epsilon^+$. Let $K = heads(P) \cap I$. Let $P_1 = \{r \in P \mid head(r) \in I, neg(r) \cap K = \emptyset\}$. Clearly, $\epsilon^+ \subseteq P_1$. Furthermore, for each rule $r \in P_1$, $neg(r) \cap heads(P_1) = \emptyset$ since $heads(P_1) \subseteq K$. Therefore, P_1 is consistent and has a unique answer set J containing $heads(\epsilon^+)$ and $J \subseteq I$.

Consider $r \in P \backslash P_1$. We have that $head(r) \notin I$ or $neg(r) \cap K \neq \emptyset$. From Definition 2, we can conclude that $neg(r) \cap heads(\epsilon^+) \neq \emptyset$ or $pos(r) \backslash I \neq \emptyset$. This allows us to show that $P^J = P_1^J \cup R$ and, for every $r \in R$, $pos(r) \backslash J \neq \emptyset$. This implies that J is an answer set of P^J, i.e., $(\epsilon^+, \epsilon^-[\epsilon^+, I, \pi_h])$ is a solution of (π_a, π_h, q). $\square$

It is easy to see that the following holds:

Corollary 1. *For an e-MRLP problem (π_a, π_h, q), if there exists a non-trivial justification $\epsilon^+ \subset \pi_a$ w.r.t. an answer set I of π_a, then it has a non-trivial solution.*

3.1 Computing Solutions of MRLP Problems Using ASP

We will conclude the section with a discussion on how a solution for a general MRLP problem can be constructed. Without loss of generality, assume that we have the problem $(\pi_a, \pi_h, q \wedge \neg r)$ where q and r are atoms of π_a. Recall that we assume that $\pi_a \mathrel{\mid\sim} q$ and $\pi_a \mathrel{\not\mid\sim} r$ in this problem. A solution (ϵ^+, ϵ^-) for $(\pi_a, \pi_h, q \wedge \neg r)$ can be computed by the following steps: (i) compute an answer set I of π_a that supports q and identify a minimal justification ϵ^+ of q w.r.t. I; (ii) compute $\epsilon^- = \epsilon^-[\epsilon^+, I, \pi_h]$; (iii) identify a set of rules λ from $\pi' = \pi_h \backslash \epsilon \cup \epsilon^+$ so that $\pi' \backslash \lambda \mathrel{\not\mid\sim} r$. The final solution for $(\pi_a, \pi_h, q \wedge \neg r)$ is then $(\epsilon^+, \epsilon^- \cup \lambda)$. Note that because ϵ^+ is a justification for q, $\epsilon^+ \mathrel{\not\mid\sim} r$ holds. Therefore, λ always exists and Theorem 1 shows that the problem $(\pi_a, \pi_b, q \wedge \neg r)$ always has some solution.

Given a program π_a and an answer set I supporting ω^+ of π_a, let $\Pi(\pi_a, I)$ be the program such that:

Algorithm 1: solve(π_a, π_h, ω)

Input: Programs π_a, π_h, conjunction ω
Output: a solution (ϵ^+, ϵ^-) for (π_a, π_h, ω)
1 Let I be an answer set of $\pi_a \cup \{\leftarrow not\ q \mid q \in \omega^+\}$
2 Compute $\Pi(\pi_a, I)$
3 Compute an answer set J of $\Pi(\pi_a, I)$
4 Compute $\epsilon^+ = \{head(r) \leftarrow pos(r), neg(r) \mid head(r) \leftarrow pos(r), neg(r), ok(r) \in \Pi(\pi_a, I)$ and $ok(r) \in J\}$
5 Let $\lambda_0 = \{r \mid r \in \pi_h \backslash \epsilon^-[\epsilon^+, I, \pi_h]$ and $head(r) \in \omega^-\}$
6 Identify a set $\lambda_0 \subseteq \lambda \subseteq \pi_h \backslash \epsilon^-[\epsilon^+, I, \pi_h]$ such that $\pi_h \backslash (\epsilon^-[\epsilon^+, I, \pi_h] \cup \lambda) \cup \epsilon^+$ is consistent
7 **return** $(\epsilon^+ \backslash \pi_h, \epsilon^-[\epsilon^+, I, \pi_h] \cup \lambda)$

- $\Pi(\pi_a, I)$ contains the constraint $\leftarrow not\ q$, for each $q \in \omega^+$.
- For each $x \in \pi_a$ s.t. $head(x) \in I$ and $I \models body(x)$:
  - $head(x) \leftarrow pos(x), neg(x), ok(x)$ is a rule in $\Pi(\pi_a, I)$.
  - $\{ok(x)\} \leftarrow$ is a rule of $\Pi(\pi_a, I)$.
  - #mimimize$\{1, X : ok(X)\}$ is a rule of $\Pi(\pi_a, I)$.
- No other rule is in $\Pi(\pi_a, I)$.

We next present an algorithm which uses $\Pi(\pi_a, I)$ for generating solutions of a MRLP problem (π_a, π_h, ω).

Recall that we assume that $\pi_a \hspace{1pt}\vdash\hspace{-9pt}\sim \omega^+$ and $\pi_a \hspace{1pt}\not\vdash\hspace{-9pt}\sim \omega^-$ in this paper. Otherwise, the algorithm needs to check for the two conditions (i) $\pi_a \hspace{1pt}\vdash\hspace{-9pt}\sim \omega^+$, i.e., whether π_a has answer set satisfying ω^+; and (ii) $\pi_a \hspace{1pt}\not\vdash\hspace{-9pt}\sim \omega^-$, i.e., whether π_a has any answer set satisfying any atom occurring in ω^- before continues with the first line. The correctness of the algorithm is proved in Proposition 1 (below) and the fact that all rules whose head occurring in ω^- are removed (Line 4–5).

Proposition 1. *Given a MRLP problem (π_a, π_h, ω) and I is an answer set of π_a supporting ω^+. Let J be an answer set of $\Pi(\pi_a, I)$ and ϵ^+ be the collection of rules:*

$$\left\{ head(r) \leftarrow pos(r), neg(r) \middle| \begin{array}{l} head(r) \leftarrow pos(r), neg(r), ok(r) \in \Pi(\pi_a, I) \wedge \\ ok(r) \in J \end{array} \right\}$$

Then, $J \backslash \{ok(x) \mid x$ is a rule in $\pi_a\} \subseteq I$ and $(\epsilon^+, \epsilon^-[\epsilon^+, I, \pi_h])$ is a solution for (π_a, π_h, ω^+).

Proof (Sketch). The proof of this proposition relies on the following observation: (i) $J \backslash \{ok(x) \mid x$ is a rule in $\pi_a\} \subseteq I$ follows immediately from the definition of $\Pi(\pi_a, I)$; (ii) J must contain q, for $q \in \omega^+$, due to the constraint "$\leftarrow not\ q$"; (iii) the minimization statement ensures that J is a set with minimal number of rules satisfying ω^+; and the fact that $q \in J$ for $q \in \omega^+$ implies that ϵ^+ is indeed a minimal justification for ω^+ w.r.t. I and, hence, $(\epsilon^+, \epsilon^-[\epsilon^+, I, \pi_h])$ is a solution for (π_a, π_h, ω^+). □

4   Characterizing Solutions

As we have discussed earlier, a MRLP might have several solutions and choosing a suitable solution is application dependent. We now discuss some characteristics of solutions that could influence the choice.

Definition 3. *Let* (π_a, π_h, ω) *be an MRLP problem and* (ϵ^+, ϵ^-) *be a solution of* (π_a, π_h, ω). *We say:*

- (ϵ^+, ϵ^-) *is* optimal *if there exists no solution* (λ^+, λ^-) *such that* $\lambda^+ \cup \lambda^- \subset \epsilon^+ \cup \epsilon^-$.
- (ϵ^+, ϵ^-) *is* π-restrictive *for* $\pi \subseteq \pi_a$ *if* $\epsilon^+ \subseteq \pi$; *it is* minimally-restrictive *if there exists no solution* (λ^+, λ^-) *such that* $\lambda^+ \subset \epsilon^+$.
- (ϵ^+, ϵ^-) *is* π-preserving *for* $\pi \subseteq \pi_h$ *if* $\pi \cap \epsilon^- = \emptyset$; *it is* maximally-preserving *if there exists no solution* (λ^+, λ^-) *such that* $\lambda^- \subset \epsilon^-$.
- (ϵ^+, ϵ^-) *is* assertive *if every answer set of* $\pi_h \backslash \epsilon^- \cup \epsilon^+$ *satisfies* ω^+.
- (ϵ^+, ϵ^-) *is* a solution with justification *(or* j-solution*) if* ϵ^+ *contains a justification for* ω^+ *w.r.t. some answer set* I *of* π_a.

Each class of solutions has its own merits and could be useful in different situations. Optimal solutions could be useful when solutions are associated with some costs. Minimally-restrictive solutions focus on minimizing the amount of information that the robot needs to introduce to the human. They will be useful when explaining a new rule is expensive. On the other hand, maximally-preserving solutions is appropriate when one seeks to minimize the amount of information that needs to be removed from the human knowledge. Solutions with justifications are those that come with their own support. Assertive solutions do not leave the human any reason for questioning the atom in discussion. In Examples 1–4, we can see that the solution in Example 1 is not optimal but all others are optimal, minimally-restrictive and maximally-preserving, and solutions with justification. We make the following observations:

Observation 1. • *A minimal solution always exists. Similarly, a minimally-restrictive (resp. maximally-preserving) solution always exists.*
- *If a solution is minimally-restrictive and maximally-preserving, then it is optimal.*
- *For some* π, *there exists no* π-preserving solution. For example, in Example 2, *a* π-preserving solution does not exist for $\pi = \{a \leftarrow\}$. Likewise, for some π *(e.g.,* $\pi = \emptyset$*), there exists no* π-restrictive solution.
- *Not every solution of an MRLP problem is a* j-solution. For example, $(\{b \leftarrow a\}, \emptyset)$ *is not a* j-solution *for the problem* $(\{a \leftarrow; b \leftarrow a; b \leftarrow\}, \{a \leftarrow\}, b)$.
- *Not every solution of an MRLP is assertive. For example,* $(\{b \leftarrow not\ a\}, \emptyset)$ *is not an assertive solution for the problem* $(\{a \leftarrow not\ b; b \leftarrow not\ a\}, \{a \leftarrow not\ b\}, b)$.

While it is natural to think of optimal solutions, there exists subprogram π of π_h such that π-preserving solutions are reasonable. For example, it is reasonable to consider solutions that is $(\pi_a \cap \pi_h)$-preserving since $\pi_a \cap \pi_h$ represents the *common knowledge* between the robot and the human. Examples 2–4 show that, for some π, there might not exists a π-preserving solution (i.e., for $\pi = \{a \leftarrow\}$ in Example 2, a π-preserving solution does not exist). Theorem 1 shows that j-solutions can be constructed from an answer set I of π_a that supports q. It is easy to see that not every solution of the problem must be a j-solution. For example, $(\{b \leftarrow a\}, \emptyset)$ is not a j-solution for the problem $(\{a \leftarrow; b \leftarrow a; b \leftarrow\}, \{a \leftarrow\}, b)$.

4.1   Cost-Based Characterization

An alternative for characterizing solutions is to associate a cost to a solution (ϵ^+, ϵ^-) and use it as a means to compare solutions. In this paper, we are interested in the following cost functions.

Definition 4 (Cost Function and Cost-Optimal Solutions). *A cost function of an MRLP problem (π_a, π_h, ω) is a function $\mathcal{C}$ that maps each rule of $\pi_a \cup \pi_h$ to a non-negative number: $\mathcal{C} : \pi_a \cup \pi_h \to \mathcal{R}^{\geq 0}$.*

The cost of a solution (ϵ^+, ϵ^-) w.r.t. $\mathcal{C}$, denoted by $\mathcal{C}(\epsilon^+, \epsilon^-)$, is then defined as $\Sigma_{r \in \epsilon^+ \cup \epsilon^-} \mathcal{C}(r)$.

Given a cost function $\mathcal{C}$, a solution (ϵ^+, ϵ^-) is cost optimal w.r.t. $\mathcal{C}$ if $\mathcal{C}(\epsilon^+, \epsilon^-)$ is minimal among all solutions.

We define some special cost functions as follows. $\mathcal{C}$ of (π_a, π_h, q) is:

1. *uniform* if $\mathcal{C}(r) = c$ for each rule $r \in \pi_a \cup \pi_h$, where $c > 0$ is a constant.
2. *agent-biased* if $\mathcal{C}(r) = c$ for each rule $r \in \pi_a$, where $c > 0$ is a constant, and $\mathcal{C}(r) = 0$ for each rule $r \in \pi_h$.
3. *human-biased* if $\mathcal{C}(r) = 0$ for each rule $r \in \pi_a$ and $\mathcal{C}(r) = c$, where $c > 0$ is a constant, for each rule $r \in \pi_h$.

Because minimality in cardinality of a set implies minimality with respect to the subset relation, we can easily prove the following.

Proposition 2. *Given a cost function $\mathcal{C}$:*

- *If it is uniform, then a cost-optimal solution w.r.t. $\mathcal{C}$ is optimal (as in Definition 3).*
- *If it is agent-biased, then a cost-optimal solution w.r.t. $\mathcal{C}$ is minimally-restrictive.*
- *If it is human-biased, then a cost-optimal solution w.r.t. $\mathcal{C}$ is maximally-preserving.*

Observe that more general or specific cost functions could be defined and used to compare solutions. More specifically, a cost function discussed above is rule-based. A more specific one could be an atom-level cost function that assigns each atom some cost. A more general one is a solution-level cost function that assigns each solution a cost. While all are theoretically reasonable, we believe that a rule-based cost function is more appropriate because each rule is supposed to encode a piece of knowledge from each agent (robot or human). Alternatively, preferences among atoms that could be added or should be removed can be defined and used in determining most preferred solutions. We will leave this for the future work.

4.2 Assertiveness Characterization

We now propose an alternative perspective that is orthogonal to the characterization defined above. Given an MRLP problem (π_a, π_h, ω), the goal of the robot in providing a solution ϵ is to convince the human that ω is true given its knowledge base. Thus, the success of this process depends on *how much the human believes the solution presented by the robot.* Following this line of thought, we define the notion of an *assertive score* for solutions:

Definition 5 (Assertive Score). *The* assertive score *of a solution* (ϵ^+, ϵ^-) *of an MRLP problem* (π_a, π_h, ω) *is:*

$$S(\epsilon^+, \epsilon^-) = \frac{\#answer\ sets\ of\ \pi_h \backslash \epsilon^- \cup \epsilon^+\ where\ \omega^+\ is\ true}{\#answer\ sets\ of\ \pi_h \backslash \epsilon^- \cup \epsilon^+}$$

A solution (ϵ^+, ϵ^-) *is* assertive-score-maximal *if* $S_{(\pi_h, q)}(\epsilon)$ *is maximal among all solutions.*

Intuitively, $S(\epsilon^+, \epsilon^-)$ represents the probability of the human believing the solution. As we have remarked earlier, $S(\epsilon^+, \epsilon^-)$ is always positive (cf. Theorem 1). The last bullet in Observation 1 shows that can be less than 1. We can prove the following proposition that certain solutions are assertive.

Proposition 3. *For a MRLP problem* (π_a, π_h, ω). *Assume that* I *is an answer set of* π_a *and* ϵ^+ *is a minimal justification of* ω^+ *w.r.t.* I. *If the residual of* π_h *w.r.t.* ϵ^+ *and* I *contains only definite rules then there exists a solution* (ϵ^+, ϵ^-) *for* (π_a, π_h, ω) *with* $\epsilon^-[\epsilon^+, I, \pi_h] \subseteq \epsilon^-$ *such that* $S(\epsilon^+, \epsilon^-) = 1$.

Proof. Let $P = \pi_h \backslash \epsilon^-[\epsilon^+, I, \pi_h] \cup \epsilon^+$. Because $P \backslash \epsilon^+$ is a positive program, we have that $negs(P) = negs(\epsilon^+)$. As such $negs(P) \cap heads(P) = \emptyset$. Hence, any answer set X of P would satisfy that $X \cap negs(P) = \emptyset$. This implies that P has a unique answer set satisfying ω^+. To obtain a solution for (π_a, π_h, ω), we can remove the set λ of rules whose heads occur in ω^- from P. The remaining program $P \backslash \lambda$ is a positive program and entails ω^+. This shows that $S(\epsilon^+, \epsilon^-[\epsilon^+, I, \pi_h] \cup \lambda) = 1$. □

5 Related Work and Discussions

The paper takes inspiration from the discussion in explainable planning (XAIP) [1,12,13] and generalizes it to define MRLP problems. Solutions to a MRLP problem could be viewed as explanations defined in XAIP. It is therefore closely related to the recent paper [8]. Both [8] and this paper employ ASP as the underlying representation language. However, [8] focuses on the development of an ASP-based system for solving XAIP problems while the present work emphasizes the knowledge representation aspects of a generalization of XAIP. This difference in focus leads to the fact that the algorithms proposed in this paper are general in that they are applicable in different classes of problems representable by logic programs and are not as specific as the ones developed in [8]. Furthermore, [8] does not include any characterizations of the solutions of MRLP problems as discussed in this paper.

It is worth noticing that Definition 2 appears to define an update operator to a program π_h with a set of rules ϵ^+ and a set of atoms I. This operator, however, differs from *all* update operators defined in the vast literature on logic programming updates (see, e.g., the survey by [11]). In earlier operators, the inputs are two programs π_h and ϵ^+, and the resulting program $\pi_h \oplus \epsilon^+$ should include ϵ^+ and *retain as much as possible from* π_h or satisfy certain postulates related to belief revision (e.g., the AGM postulates). This is because update models are defined for revising the beliefs of an agent π_h when some new information ϵ^+ arrives. There is no consideration of the third parameter I and there is no requirement that $\pi_h \oplus \epsilon^+ \hspace{0.3em}\vdash\hspace{-0.9em}\sim\hspace{0.3em} \omega^+$ even if ϵ^+ satisfies the conditions in Theorem 1. We note that the idea of eliminating rules in π_h that are "conflicting" with the new rules ϵ^+, presented by [15] and later by [14], could potentially be useful. However, the operator in this work adds rules that are not in $\pi_h \cup \epsilon^+$ to the resulting program.

Last but not least, we observe that Algorithm 1 only computes j-solutions for an MRLP problem. It is easy to see that an arbitrary solution (ϵ^+, ϵ^-) for (π_a, π_h, ω) could be computed by randomly selecting $\epsilon^+ \subseteq \pi_a$ and $\epsilon^- \subseteq \pi_h$ and testing whether (ϵ^+, ϵ^-) is a solution for the problem, i.e., verifying $\pi_h \backslash \epsilon^- \cup \epsilon^+ \mid\hspace{0.3em}\vdash\hspace{-0.9em}\sim\hspace{0.3em} \omega^+$ and $\pi_h \backslash \epsilon^- \cup \epsilon^+ \hspace{0.3em}\not\vdash\hspace{-0.9em}\sim\hspace{0.3em} \omega^-$. This idea is similar to the proposed method of computing explanations of abductive logic programs discussed by [10]. Although this idea is simple and generic, we observe that it can only be applied whenever the symmetric difference between π_a and π_h is small and thus is not practically useful.

It is worth noting that different methods proposed in the literature for computing a justification (sometimes referred to as explanation) for an atom (set of atoms) given a logic program could be used to replace the steps 1–4 in Algorithm 1. The present work does not intend to provide a method for computing such a justification.

6   Conclusions and Future Work

In this paper, we investigate MRLP problems between logic programs, represented by a tuple (π_a, π_h, ω), that focus on identifying a solution (ϵ^+, ϵ^-) where $\epsilon^+ \subseteq \pi_a$ and $\epsilon^- \subseteq \pi_h$ such that $\hat{\pi}_h = \pi_h \backslash \epsilon^- \cup \epsilon^+$ satisfying $\hat{\pi}_h \hspace{0.3em}\vdash\hspace{-0.9em}\sim\hspace{0.3em} \omega^+$ and $\hat{\pi}_h \hspace{0.3em}\not\vdash\hspace{-0.9em}\sim\hspace{0.3em} \omega^-$, i.e., $\hat{\pi}_h \hspace{0.3em}\vdash\hspace{-0.9em}\sim\hspace{0.3em} q$ for every $q \in \omega^+$ and $\hat{\pi}_h \hspace{0.3em}\not\vdash\hspace{-0.9em}\sim\hspace{0.3em} r$ for every $r \in \omega^-$.

We show that if $\pi_a \hspace{0.5mm}\not\hspace{-1.5mm}\sim \omega^+$ and $\pi_a \hspace{0.5mm}\not\hspace{-2mm}\sim \omega^-$ and there exists a justification $\epsilon^+ \subset \pi_a$ for ω^+ then there exists a non-trivial solution (ϵ^+, ϵ^-) for the problem. We discuss different types of solutions of a MRLP problem and algorithms for computing a solution. We also present the notion of a cost-based and assessertive characterization of solutions.

In this paper, we focus on the development of the theoretical foundation of the MRLP problems. One of our immediate future work is to develop a system for computing solutions of MRLP problems. The next goal is to experimentally comparing this system with the system described in [8].

For future work, we note that our work assumes that the robot, who needs to computes solutions, has the knowledge of both programs π_a and π_h, which is the assumption in early work in explainable planning. In practice, this assumption is likely invalid and the robot might also needs to change its program through communication or dialogue with the human. For example, if the robot explains to the human that its plan for going from location a to location c through location b is feasible and the human informs the robot that the path from location a to location b is currently blocked, then the robot should eliminate the action of going from location a to location b from its action description and replan a new path to get to location c. Therefore, we plan to take such dialogue into account and to formalize the process of reaching a consensus between the robot and the human in the near future.

References

1. Chakraborti, T., Sreedharan, S., Zhang, Y., Kambhampati, S.: Plan explanations as model reconciliation: moving beyond explanation as soliloquy. In: IJCAI, pp. 156–163 (2017)
2. van Emden, M., Kowalski, R.: The semantics of predicate logic as a programming language. J. ACM **23**(4), 733–742 (1976)
3. Fox, M., Long, D., Magazzeni, D.: Explainable planning. CoRR abs/1709.10256 (2017). http://arxiv.org/abs/1709.10256
4. Gelfond, M., Lifschitz, V.: Logic programs with classical negation. In: LP, pp. 579–597 (1990)
5. Kambhampati, S.: Synthesizing explainable behavior for human-AI collaboration. In: AAMAS, pp. 1–2 (2019)
6. Lifschitz, V., Pearce, D., Valverde, A.: Strongly equivalent logic programs. ACM Trans. Comput. Log. **2**(4), 526–541 (2001)
7. Marek, V., Truszczyński, M.: Stable models and an alternative logic programming paradigm. In: Apt, K.R., Marek, V.W., Truszczynski, M., Warren, D.S. (eds.) The Logic Programming Paradigm: A 25-Year Perspective. AI, pp. 375–398. Springer, Heidelberg (1999). https://doi.org/10.1007/978-3-642-60085-2_17
8. Nguyen, V., Vasileiou, S.L., Son, T.C., Yeoh, W.: Explainable planning using answer set programming. In: KRR, pp. 662–666 (2020)
9. Niemelä, I.: Logic programming with stable model semantics as a constraint programming paradigm. Ann. Math. Artif. Intell. **25**(3–4), 241–273 (1999)

10. Sakama, C., Inoue, K.: Updating extended logic programs through abduction. In: Gelfond, M., Leone, N., Pfeifer, G. (eds.) LPNMR 1999. LNCS (LNAI), vol. 1730, pp. 147–161. Springer, Heidelberg (1999). https://doi.org/10.1007/3-540-46767-X_11

11. Slota, M., Leite, J.: Exception-based knowledge updates. CoRR abs/1706.00585 (2017). http://arxiv.org/abs/1706.00585

12. Sreedharan, S., Chakraborti, T., Kambhampati, S.: Handling model uncertainty and multiplicity in explanations via model reconciliation. In: ICAPS, pp. 518–526 (2018)

13. Vasileiou, S.L., Previti, A., Yeoh, W.: On exploiting hitting sets for model reconciliation. In: AAAI (2021)

14. Zhang, Y.: Logic program-based updates. ACM Trans. Comput. Log. **7**(3), 421–472 (2006)

15. Zhang, Y., Foo, N.Y.: Updating logic programs. In: ECAI, pp. 403–407 (1998)

Lazy Stream Manipulation in Prolog via Backtracking: The Case of 2P-KT

Giovanni Ciatto[1]([☒])[ID], Roberta Calegari[2][ID], and Andrea Omicini[1][ID]

[1] Department of Computer Science and Engineering (DISI), Cesena, Italy
{giovanni.ciatto,andrea.omicini}@unibo.it
[2] Alma Mater Research Institute for Human-Centered Artificial Intelligence,
Alma Mater Studiorum—Univerisità di Bologna, Bologna, Italy
roberta.calegari@unibo.it

Abstract. The ability to *lazily* manipulate long or infinite *streams* of data is an essential feature in the era of data-driven artificial intelligence. Yet, logic programming technologies currently fall short when it comes to handling long or infinite streams of data. In this paper, we discuss *how* Prolog can be reinterpreted as a stream processing tool, and re-designed around an abstract state-machine capable of lazily manipulating streams of data via backtracking.

Keywords: Prolog · Stream processing · 2P-KT · State machine

1 Introduction

Streams are a powerful abstraction in computer science as they enable the processing of huge amounts of data, especially when keeping all data in memory would be impractical or infeasible. In the era of the Internet of Things (IoT) and data-driven artificial intelligence (AI), the ability to manipulate possibly unlimited streams of data is a must-have for all programming paradigms and languages. Indeed, a growing amount of application scenarios are characterised by the pervasive exploitation of smart devices generating/capturing huge amounts of data, as well as of the software infrastructures aimed at processing them.

A stream is an *ordered sequence* of data that may or may not be limited in length. Depending on how they are *generated*, streams are either *cold* (a.k.a. *pull*) or *hot* (a.k.a. *push*). Each item of a cold stream is generated on the fly, as soon as a consumer *pulls* it from the stream. In the case of hot streams, instead, an external entity is supposed to be in charge of generating items and *pushing* them to the stream, so that consumers can retrieve them in a FIFO way.

Cold streams are the simplest ones. A cold stream can be naturally attained via functional programming and higher-order functions (e.g. map, filter, reduce): this is why mainstream programming languages such as Java, C#, Python, JavaScript, Scala, Kotlin, etc., are being extended to blend functional features and constructs for dealing with streams. Conversely, hot streams

W. Faber et al. (Eds.): JELIA 2021, LNAI 12678, pp. 407–420, 2021.
https://doi.org/10.1007/978-3-030-75775-5_27

are more complex, as they require data to be buffered while waiting for consumption—making them ideal for *temporally* decoupling data consumers and producers. In particular, hot streams are key enablers of advanced stream processing techniques, such as sliding windows, or complex event processing (CEP)—which are deeply entangled with the *time*-related aspects of data production.

In this scenario, logic programming (LP), as well, has its role to play, both in data-driven AI – in particular in relation to explainable systems [6] – or in the IoT [5]. For instance, LP and rule-based frameworks are generally recognised as well-suited to support CEP [1,2], as they are expressive enough to capture complex events from hot streams. Similarly, answer-set programming (ASP) has been extensively exploited as a means for reasoning over hot streams of data [3,4,11].

In this paper, we focus on the Prolog [10] programming language—arguably, the most popular LP language. Currently, Prolog can hardly be considered as a suitable stream-processing technology [15], as it provides minimal support for consuming both cold and hot streams. However, we believe that this should be reconsidered because Prolog already supports the lazy exploration of possibly infinite search spaces via *backtracking*. Thus, the problem with Prolog is not to discuss *whether* it supports stream processing or not, but rather *how*.

Existing solutions extend Prolog with syntactical, semantical, or library enhancements aimed at supporting cold streams explicitly. Conversely, in this paper, we discuss how Prolog can be reinterpreted as a *stream processing tool*, capable of manipulating both cold and hot streams of data. In particular, our solution does not affect the syntax (nor the operation) of the Prolog language. More precisely, we show how Prolog predicates may be interpreted as *generators* of streams to be lazily consumed via backtracking. Along this line, we present an abstract design for Prolog solvers based on finite-state machines, aimed at supporting our notion of generators. Finally, a practical demonstration based on the 2P-KT technology [7] is discussed showing how generators may let a Prolog solver consume events from the external world in a transparent way.

2   Logic Solvers as Streams Prosumers

2.1   Logic Solvers as Stream Producers

Logic solvers *à la Prolog* are typically queried *interactively* by LP users in different *modes*, which are naturally captured by the message passing perspective adopted in Fig. 1. The most common mode of interaction among users and logic solvers is summarised in Fig. 1a: users submit *queries* (a.k.a. *goals*) to a logic solver – e.g. a Prolog interpreter – via some *ad-hoc* operation—e.g., solve. Assuming that one or more *solutions* exist, the solver computes and returns one of them—typically in terms of a *unifying substitution*, assigning values to the query variables of interest for the user. However, the user may be interested in solutions other than the first one: so, the solver should expose one further operation – e.g., next – letting users asking for further solutions to some previously-submitted query. Finally, when no (more) solutions are available for a query, the solver can return one (last) answer carrying the *failed* substitution (represented by ⊥ in Fig. 1) instead of a unifier.

This mode of interaction is very effective since it enables the *lazy* enumeration of a possibly infinite amount of solutions. However, it comes with a few drawbacks. First, despite logic solvers are actually capable of generating streams of solutions, the notion of stream is somewhat *implicit* in the solver machinery—therefore, not explicitly exploitable. Second, solvers are *stateful*, in that they are responsible to keep track of the status of the interaction with each querying user.

To overcome these issues we suggest a shift of perspective, as depicted in Fig. 1b. There, users and solvers interact in a *stream-oriented* mode, where the stream of solutions is *explicit* and the interaction between solvers and users is *stateless*. Thus, solvers expose just one operation – i.e., `solve` – accepting a user's query and returning a reference to the related *cold* stream of solutions. Users just need solvers to create solution streams that users can then lazily consume on demand. Of course, solutions can still be produced lazily behind the scenes: whenever a user tries to consume a new solution, it can be computed on the fly.

Thus, even though interaction does not change from the operational viewpoint, our approach overcomes the limits of traditional logic solvers: solution streams here are *explicitly* represented, and can therefore be *manipulated* as such.

2.2   Logic Solvers as Stream Consumers

By adopting a message passing perspective, logic solvers do not interact with users only. Indeed, logic solvers typically act on a *knowledge base* (KB). In the general case, KBs are containers of the specific knowledge required by solvers to compute solutions to users' queries. For instance, KB for Prolog solvers contains both rules and facts as Horn clauses, and are either static or dynamic.

From an interaction perspective, however, a KB is just a component exploited by solvers as part of their resolution process. More precisely, solvers may need KB to retrieve some clauses, selected via unification, or, to retract or store some knowledge possibly learned/acquired during the resolution.

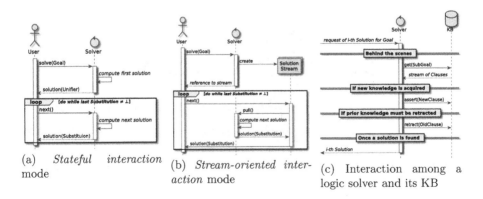

(a) *Stateful interaction* mode

(b) *Stream-oriented interaction* mode

(c) Interaction among a logic solver and its KB

Fig. 1. Interaction modes between logic solvers and users or KB.

In particular, clause retrieval highlights how the interaction between solver and KB can be described in terms of streams as well. As depicted in Fig. 1c, clause retrieval from KB can be modelled as an operation – e.g., `get` – accepting a clause template C and returning the *stream* of clauses unifying with C currently stored into the KB. The solver can then consume the stream as needed, e.g. either lazily or not, depending on the search strategy adopted.

Finally, storing a clause in the KB can be modelled as an `assert` accepting a clause C and adding it to the KB, whereas clause retraction can be modelled as a `retract` accepting a clause template C and removing a clause C' unifying with C. Both operations could be exploited either by the solver or by some *external* entity willing to affect the solver's knowledge.

2.3   Solvers vs. the World

Yet, how can logic solvers deal with event streams coming from the external world? Once KBs are recognised as individual entities, a trivial answer could be: *via KB*. External events may indeed be *reified* into actual knowledge to be stored into some solver's KB. In this scenario, external event streams should be translated into a sequence of `assert`ions aimed at injecting events into the KB, as facts. The solver could then lazily consume the events by `get`ting or `retract`ing the corresponding facts from the KB.

There are, however, two major drawbacks to this approach. First, the reification of events into KB requires space. Second, solvers do not necessarily have to process or *consume* reified events—thus a lot of space is wasted. Accordingly, a different approach is required to let solvers consume event streams from the external world without reifying them unnecessarily.

In this work, we propose *generators* as the basic means to let solvers interact with the external world. A generator is a special Prolog primitive capable of affecting and inspecting the external world via some I/O facility (Fig. 2). It is invoked by a solver and produces a *stream of facts* to be consumed by the same solver. However, from the solvers perspective, generators are ordinary built-in predicates denoted by *signatures*—i.e., name/arity couples of the form p/n.

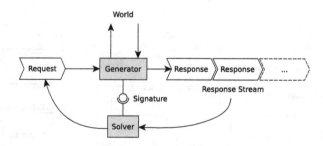

Fig. 2. Dataflow and component view of *generators*, i.e. solvers' gates towards the external world

More precisely, whenever the solver needs to compute the assignment of variables T_i satisfying relation $p(T_1, \ldots, T_n)$, it can trigger the generator denoted by p/n (if it exists), by sending the p/n generator a *request* providing a snapshot of the current resolution context and possibly an initial assignment of some T_i. The generator answers by providing a stream of *responses* – each one with some possible complete assignment of T_i – that the solver can consume accordingly to its resolution strategy—i.e., possibly later. To produce responses, generators may take into account several information sources – e.g., the resolution context, the external world – as a part of the request. They may also attempt to *affect* the external world via some I/O *action*—e.g., triggering a sensor.

Depending on the number of responses a generator provides, it can either be classified as either *functional* or *relational*. Functional generators produce just one response and their execution is therefore analogous to the execution of a function, as they consume an input and return a single result. Conversely, relational generators produce two or more responses.

2.4   Example: TSP in Prolog

Let us consider for instance the case of a user exploiting a standard Prolog system to solve arbitrary instances of the Traveling Salesman Problem (TSP).

Let us assume the system requires maps to be represented as facts in the form `path(+Src, +Dst, +Cst)` – each one representing an undirected path between two locations, and the estimated cost –, like e.g.:

```
path(bucarest, giorgiu, 90).
path(bucarest, pitesti, 101).
path(pitesti, 'rimnicu vilcea', 97).
path(pitesti, craiova, 138).
path('rimnicu vilcea', craiova, 146).
...
```

Under this assumption, Prolog exposes a predicate `tsp(?Cities, ?Circuit, ?Cost)` aimed at computing the best `Circuit` for some set of `Cities`, and the corresponding `Cost`—where, `Cities` is a set of cities, `Circuit` is a list of cities to be visited in a row, and `Cost` is an integer. Following a purely-logical interpretation, the predicate represents a ternary relation $\text{tsp} \subseteq 2^{\mathcal{C}} \times \mathcal{C}^* \times \mathbb{N}$ grouping subsets of cities, lists of cities, and non-negative integers, where $\mathcal{C}$ is the set of all cities mentioned in the KB as either the first or second argument of a `path/3` fact, and $\mathcal{C}^*$ is the Kleene-closure of $\mathcal{C}$. Thus, an assignment of the `Cities`, `Circuit`, and `Cost` variables satisfies the predicate if

- `Circuit` $\equiv [c_0, \ldots, c_{n-1}, c_0]$, and
- `Cities` $\equiv \bigcup_{i=0}^{n-1} \{c_i\}$, and
- $\forall i \in \{1, \ldots, n\}$ `path`$(c_{i-1}, c_{i \bmod n}, x_i) \in$ KB, and
- `Cost` $\equiv \sum_{i=1}^{n} x_i$, and
- `Cost` is *minimal*.

Accordingly, because of Prolog backtracking, a query of the form:

```
?- tsp(Cities, Circuit, Cost).
```

would enumerate all minimally-costly circuits of all possible subsets of cities in C, and their costs—one for each solution. Users may partially instantiate some variable in order to contextualise their queries: for instance, a query of the form:

```
?- tsp({pitesti, craiova, 'rimnicu vilcea'}, [pitesti | Others], Cost).
```

would enumerate all minimally-costly circuits starting in Pitesti, and involving the cities Craiova, and Rimnicu Vilcea.

The predicate tsp/3 could be implemented declaratively in Prolog. In its simplest formulation, the predicate may leverage Prolog's depth-first strategy, and its backtracking mechanism to lazily generate all the possible circuits and select the less costly one: not likely the best possible strategy, yet a working one. However, better strategies have been proposed in the literature for solving the TSP, with efficient implementations built upon them—rarely based on pure Prolog. Here, instead, generators make it possible to exploit external libraries for solving the TSP in Prolog as if they were implemented via LP.

For instance, we assume that an "ACME TSP" C library exists that solves TSP efficiently, which can be wrapped within a relational generator tsp/3 to be exploited by a Prolog solver. Generator tsp/3 should work as follows:

1. whenever the Prolog solver encounters a tsp(Cities, Circuit, Cost) sub-goal, it triggers the generator via a *request* containing a snapshot of the current KB and the *actual* values of Cities, Circuit, and Cost;
2. the generator reads *(i)* the map graph from the KB snapshot, and *(ii)* the cities from the actual value of Cities;
3. the generator generates the stream of all the possible subsets of C and selects the ones unifying with the actual value of Cities, thus: if Cities is bound to a particular sub-set of cities, then the stream has just one element, otherwise it may have several ones;
4. for each sub-set of cities in the stream, the generator triggers ACME TSP and computes the corresponding TSP solution, if any;
5. every time it is triggered, ACME TSP computes zero or more solutions for the TSP and returns them to the generator;
6. for each TSP solution of each selected instantiation of Cities, the generator yields a response to the solver;
7. each response may either contain a unifier – assigning Cities to the selected list of cities, Circuit to the minimally-costly circuit for those cities, and Cost to the cost of that circuit – or a failed substitution—informing the solver the tsp/3 predicate should fail;
8. the solver can consume the response stream lazily via backtracking.

In other words, generators can be exploited as a means to wrap external data producers and let the solver consume the data they produce via streams. In Prolog, streams of this sort are lazily consumed via ordinary backtracking: the solver lazily generates a new choice point for each element in the stream and handles them as usual. Solvers of different sorts may consume the stream differently—e.g. buffering (some slice of) it, or, handling each datum concurrently.

3   Solvers as Streams Prosumers via State Machine

In order to design a Prolog solver supporting our notion of generator, we enhance the Prolog state machine proposed in [13] with the capability of lazily consuming streams of data coming from either a generator or the KB (Fig. 3). In particular, we change how the state machine manages the resolution of (sub-)goals, by supporting the selection of a generator as a means to provide one or more solutions for (sub-)goals, other than the ordinary selection of rules from the KB.

The state machine in Fig. 3 stems from the acknowledgement that a Prolog solver may solve a (sub-)goal by either selecting a generator or a number of logic rules from the KB. In both cases, a stream of data must be lazily consumed by the solver—either carrying generator responses or clauses from the KB.

Whenever a stream of data needs to be processed, there are essentially two major phases: the *opening* of the stream – where a channel between the stream producer and its consumer is created –, and the *consumption* of the stream— where items from the stream are sequentially processed. To support both phases, two more locations are included – namely Generator Selection and Generator Execution – respectively aimed at triggering a generator and consuming the response stream it provides. Furthermore, to support a stream-oriented interaction among the solver and its KB, we model rule management as well through two locations, namely Generator Selection and Generator Execution, respectively aimed at querying the KB, and consuming the rule stream it provides.

All the other aspects are handled in the same way as in [13]. Thus, state machine execution is triggered whenever a user submits a query to the solver: when this is the case, execution starts from the Goal Selection location. Then, it

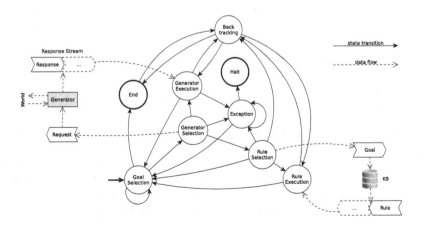

Fig. 3. Handling generators with enhanced Prolog state machine

may go through any location until it eventually reaches some *final* one (End or Halt), where a new solution is yielded—which the user can eventually consume. Once a solution is consumed, the user can either submit a new query or ask for the next solution. In the former case, the automaton is reset to the Goal Selection location. Conversely, the latter case is only possible if the last solution was provided by the End location. In that case, the automaton backtracks and looks for the next solution. This may involve stepping through Backtracking, then moving back into the Generator (resp. Rule) Execution, in order to consume one more element from some previously-opened response (resp. clause) stream.

Overall, our state machine affects the operation of a Prolog solver as follows:

1. [Generator Selection] whenever a new sub-goal is selected, the solver looks for a generator whose signature matches the sub-goal one;
2. [Generator Execution] if some are found, the solver considers the first response in the stream as a solution to the goal, and generates choice points for subsequent responses;
3. [Rule Selection] otherwise, if no generator is selected for the current sub-goal, some rule is looked for instead, whose head unifies with the sub-goal;
4. [Rule Execution] if any such rule is found, resolution can proceed by addressing the rule's body as the next goal to be proved;
5. [Backtracking] otherwise, if no rule is found, the sub-goal is considered failed and resolution must backtrack.

Location Exception completes the picture by intercepting exceptions – possibly thrown by generators as part of some response of theirs –, via the standard catch/3 predicate.

Ordinary Prolog built-in primitives naturally fit the picture as they are re-interpreted as generators by solvers. For instance, the is/2 predicate can be considered a functional generator accepting a variable and an expression and returning a single response assigning the variable to the value attained by reducing the expression – if possible –, or an exception—in case the expression cannot be reduced. Conversely, the member/2 predicate can be considered as a relational generator, enumerating all the possible items in a list. Accordingly, the aforementioned Generator Selection location is where built-in primitives are selected for execution in place of rules from the KB.

4   Backatrackable Predicates as Streams in 2P-KT

In order to demonstrate the feasibility of our approach, we propose a case study based on 2P-KT. 2P-KT [7] is a Kotlin-based ecosystem for LP, including general API for stream-oriented logic solvers of any sort. Regardless of the particular logic, inference rule, or search strategy of choice, a logic solver is modelled in 2P-KT as a prosumer of streams: it produces output streams of solutions and consumes input streams generated by generators. A Prolog solver implementation is available as well, leveraging the state-machine-based design presented in

Sect. 3. Furthermore, 2P-KT involves an API for writing generators in Kotlin, by blending an imperative, object-oriented, and functional programming style.

In this section, we first illustrate briefly the portion of the 2P-KT API involving solvers and generators, then we discuss an example generator implementing the TSP example from Sect. 2.4.

4.1   2P-KT Solvers and Generators API

Figure 4 provides an overview of the 2P-KT API. Here we focus on the resolution-related portion of this API (cf. [9] for further details). There, logic solvers are modelled as instances of the `Solver` type defined as follows:

```
interface Solver {
    val staticKb: Theory
    val dynamicKb: Theory
    val libraries: Libraries
    fun solve(goal: Struct): Sequence<Solution>
}
```

Essentially, a logic solver is any entity exposing a method `solve` which accepts a logic `Structure` – i.e., a particular case of logic `Term` in the 2P-KT type system – as the input goal, and produces a `Sequence` – i.e., a *lazy* stream in the Kotlin type system – of logic `Solutions` as output. Furthermore, 2P-KT requires each logic solver to be composed of at least three more entities, namely: *(i)* a `staticKb` and *(ii)* a `dynamicKb`, both of type `Theory` – that is, an ordered and indexed container of logic clauses, retrievable via unification –, and *(iii)* a `libraries` container of type `Libraries`—which, within the scope of this section, is essentially an implementation of the structure indexing generators.

Each `Solution` in 2P-KT may be of any of three sorts, namely `Yes`, `No`, and `Halt`, representing the positive, negative, and exceptional case, respectively. All solutions carry the original query they are answering to, other than the `Substitution` they are answering through. So for instance, objects of type `Solution.Yes` always contain an object of type `Substitution.Unifier`, whereas other sorts of solutions always contain an object of type `Substitution .Fail`. Similarly, objects of type `Solution.Halt` carry the uncaught exception which interrupted the resolution process.

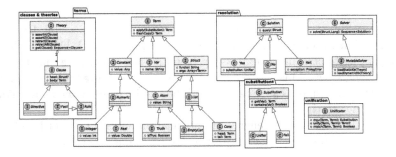

Fig. 4. Overview on the public API of 2P-KT

Generators are modelled in 2P-KT as functions of the type:

```
typealias Generator = (Request) -> Sequence<Response>
```

i.e., functions accepting a Request as input and returning a Sequence of Responses as output. There, Request is a container of all the information needed at runtime to produce a sequence of Responses:

```
class Request(
    val context: ExecutionContext,
    val signature: Signature,
    val arguments: List<Term>
) {
    fun solve(subQuery: Struct): Sequence<Solution>
    fun replySuccess(): Response
    fun replyFail(): Response
    fun replyWith(substition: Substitution): Response
    fun replyException(exception: TuPrologRuntimeException): Response
}
```

These include: *(i)* a snapshot of ExecutionContext at invocation time – in turn including a snapshot of the solver's staticKb and dynamicKb –, *(ii)* the Signature of the invoked generator, and *(iii)* the List of Terms storing actual arguments provided to the generator upon invocation.

Furthermore, each instance of Request exposes a bunch of methods – namely, the many reply*() ones –, aimed at generating a new Response for that particular Request. As Responses are mere containers of Solutions, there are many variants of the reply*() methods, each one aimed at generating a given sort of responses – e.g. responses carrying positive/negative/exceptional solutions – for the sub-goal that triggered the generator. Finally, each request supports the spawning of an inner resolution process via its solve(...) method. This method creates a novel sub-solver through which generator implementors can resolve sub-queries as part of some generator execution.

Thanks to this design, any Kotlin method of the form:

```
fun method(request: Request): Sequence<Response> = sequence {
    request.arguments[i] // read the i-th actual argument
    request.context.staticKb[h] // read clauses in KB whose head matches h
    solve(goal) // perform sub-queries

    val substitution = (arg0 mguWith value0) + (arg1 mguWith value1) + ...

    yield(request.replyWith(substitution))
    // or
    yield(request.replyFail())
    // or
    yield(request.reply*(...))
}
```

can be considered a generator in the eyes of a logic solver. This leverages a particular feature of Kotlin, namely the *sequence* { ... } blocks, which let developers write stream *generators* by blending the imperative and functional programming styles. This is possible because of the *yield*(value) method which users may call inside *sequence* { ... } blocks in place of return value to provide values to the stream.

So, for instance, to implement the predicate natural/1 – which holds true for all natural numbers –, one may write the following generator:

```
fun natural(request: Request): Sequence<Response> = sequence {
    var n = 1
    while (true) {
        yield(Integer.of(n))
        n++
    }
}.map {
    request.replyWith(request.arguments[0] mguWith it)
}
```

A Prolog solver would then treat such a generator as a backtrackable predicate. Thus, in Prolog, one may use the goal `natural(X)` to enumerate all the natural numbers.

Summarising, 2P-KT generators API supports the creation of backtrackable Prolog predicates out of lazy data streams.

4.2 Travelling Salesman Problem in 2P-KT

The real potential of generators is revealed when they are exploited by solvers to manage input data streams from the external world. There, the external world may be any source of data, there including other solvers, possibly of different nature. For example, generators may be exploited to let a Prolog solver call a TSP solver to efficiently compute solutions for TSP instances, as discussed in Sect. 2.4. Accordingly, here we demonstrate how a generator of such a sort may be realised through 2P-KT.

In [8] we provide a GitHub repository hosting the source code of a 2P-KT generator leveraging Google OR-Tools [12] to efficiently solve TSP instances. Google OR-Tools is a C++ library proving many constraint programming and operative research tools – there including routing-related facilities –, and some JVM bindings which let us exploit such tools in Kotlin.

Accordingly, our repository includes some scripts aimed at automating the compilation and execution of a simple demo involving a command-line TSP-enabled Prolog interpreter. Following the discussion from Sect. 2.4, such a Prolog interpreter exposes a `tsp/3` predicate aimed at enumerating the minimally-costly circuits for any given set of cities, provided that the interpreter's KB contains several `path/3` facts describing the connections among those cities. As an ordinary Prolog interpreter, such facts may be either consulted from a .pl file or dynamically asserted via `assert/1`.

The actual operational behaviour of predicate `tsp/3` is governed by the `Tsp` generator whose source code (stub) is shown in Fig. 5 (cf. [8] for full source code). The `Tsp` generator is a singleton object of type `TernaryRelation` – i.e., a particular sort of `Generator`, tailored on ternary predicates –, whose main behaviour is encapsulated within the `computeAll` method.

The `Tsp` object is also endowed with a method – namely, `tsp` – which returns a sequence of circuits and costs for any given list of cities provided as input. Such method assumes each input city to be represented by a logic term – in particular, a constant –, and outputs circuits represented as logic lists of cities represented in the same way. Behind the scenes, the `tsp` interacts with both the Prolog interpreter's KB to read distances among cities, and a Google OR-Tool solver for computing all possible solutions to a particular TSP instance.

The `computeAll` handles the situation where the Prolog interpreter meets a (sub-)goal of the form `tsp(Cities, Circuit, Cost)`—where all variables may be partially or totally uninstantiated. The method operation can then be described as a pipeline of *lazy* operations applied to the actual arguments of `tsp/3`, which we refer as `fst`, `snd`, and `trd` within the method. Accordingly, the method firstly performs a sub-query aimed at computing the set of all cities currently contained into the KB (cf. variable `allCities` in Fig. 5). The sub-query is a Prolog goal of the form `path(_, _, _)`, whose solutions are all eagerly consumed and their first and second arguments – which are assumed to be city names – are merged into a set, to remove duplicates. Then, all possible permutations of all possible subsets of `allCities` are lazily generated. However, only the subsets of cities that unify with `fst` are actually selected (this may be just one set of cities if `fst` refers to a fully instantiated set of cities) for the next steps of the computation. Then, for all selected sets of cities, all possible solutions to the corresponding TSP instance are computed. Finally, each possible circuit (resp. cost) computed for each TSP instance is unified with `snd` (resp. `trd`). Failed unifications are of course dropped, while the successful ones are converted into responses of the `tsp/3` generator.

It is worth to highlight that the whole pipeline is *lazy*. This implies that even once the first TSP solution has been presented to the user, the other ones are still to be computed.

```
import it.unibo.tuprolog.core.List as LogicList

object Tsp : TernaryRelation<ExecutionContext>("tsp") {
  init { com.google.ortools.Loader.loadNativeLibraries() }

  private fun Request<ExecutionContext>.tsp(cities: List<Term>): Sequence<Pair<LogicList, Integer>> { ... }

  // other utility methods

  override fun Request<ExecutionContext>.computeAll(fst: Term, snd: Term, trd: Term): Sequence<Response> {
    val allCities = solve(Struct.template("path", 3))
      .filterIsInstance<Solution.Yes>()
      .map { it.solvedQuery }
      .flatMap { sequenceOf(it[0], it[1]) }
      .toSet()

    return allCities
      .subsets()
      .flatMap { it.permutations() }
      .map { it to (Set.of(it) mguWith fst) }
      .filter { (cities, substitution) -> cities.isNotEmpty() && substitution is Unifier }
      .flatMap { (cities, substitution) -> tsp(cities).map { it.addLeft(substitution) } }
      .map { (substitution, circuit, cost) -> substitution + (snd mguWith circuit) + (trd mguWith cost) }
      .filterIsInstance<Unifier>()
      .map { replySuccess(it) }
  }
}
```

Fig. 5. 2P-KT generator implementing the `tsp/3` predicate

5 Conclusion and Future Work

In this paper we address the issue of stream processing in logic programming.

In particular, we discuss how logic solvers can be naturally conceived as lazy prosumers of data streams as they *(i)* lazily *produce* data streams thanks to their interactive nature, *(ii)* lazily *consume* data streams as part of their resolution process—e.g. when they access knowledge bases.

Furthermore, we show how logic solvers can support the processing of input data stream via the notion of predicates as *generators*, which we introduce in this paper. Summarising, generators are reactive computational units which logic solvers may trigger so as to receive data streams from the external world. This may be useful, for instance, to let a solver delegate some part of its resolution process to some external entity—assuming that it is optimised to the purpose.

To demonstrate the feasibility of our approach in the specific (and technically most relevant) case of Prolog, we propose a generator-enabled modelling of Prolog solvers as state machines, formalising the lazy consumption of streams via backtracking. The proposed formalisation preserves the standard operation of Prolog and requires no modification to the language, while enabling Prolog solvers to process data streams.

Finally, we discuss the use case of 2P-KT [7], a Kotlin-based technology for LP including an implementation of Prolog solvers relying on our state-machine-based formalisation. We then exploit 2P-KT to show how generators can be used to bridge different sorts of solvers together via a few lines of Kotlin code.

In our perspective, this work represents one further step towards the *practical* exploitation of LP – and, in particular, Prolog – as a general means for stream processing. Notably, our contribution presents some similarities with other works [14,15]. In particular, similarly to [15], we focus on letting Prolog manipulate streams of data; while, similarly to [14], we provide a mechanism to let logic solvers delegate computations to external entities. However, differently from [15], we require no variation to the syntax, functioning, or libraries of Prolog; while, unlike [14], we focus on Prolog rather than ASP.

A number of issues remain uncovered in this work, and will be the subject of our future research. Among the many, the most relevant issues concern *time* and *side effects*. In particular we plan to explore the temporal dimension in LP-based stream processing, by providing for instance some means to support time-dependent or time-limited data streams. Similarly, we would like to explore the intricacies related to the processing of data streams which may affect the internal state of a logic solver – e.g. by affecting the KB – in a predictable way.

Acknowledgment. Andrea Omicini has been supported by the H2020 Project "AI4EU" (G.A. 825619). R. Calegari has been supported by the H2020 ERC Project "ompuLaw" (G.A. 833647).

References

1. Anicic, D., Fodor, P., Rudolph, S., Stühmer, R., Stojanovic, N., Studer, R.: A rule-based language for complex event processing and reasoning. In: Hitzler, P., Lukasiewicz, T. (eds.) RR 2010. LNCS, vol. 6333, pp. 42–57. Springer, Heidelberg (2010). https://doi.org/10.1007/978-3-642-15918-3_5
2. Anicic, D., Rudolph, S., Fodor, P., Stojanovic, N.: Real-time complex event recognition and reasoning-a logic programming approach. Appl. Artifi. Intell. **26**(1–2), 6–57 (2012). https://doi.org/10.1080/08839514.2012.636616

3. Beck, H., Dao-Tran, M., Eiter, T.: LARS: a logic-based framework for analytic reasoning over streams. Artif. Intell. **261**, 16–70 (2018). https://doi.org/10.1016/j.artint.2018.04.003

4. Beck, H., Eiter, T., Folie, C.: Ticker: a system for incremental ASP-based stream reasoning. Theory Pract. Logic Program. **17**(5–6), 744–763 (2017). https://doi.org/10.1017/S1471068417000370

5. Calegari, R., Ciatto, G., Mariani, S., Denti, E., Omicini, A.: LPaaS as micro-intelligence: Enhancing IoT with symbolic reasoning. Big Data Cogn. Comput. **2**(3), 23 (2018). https://doi.org/10.3390/bdcc2030023

6. Calegari, R., Ciatto, G., Omicini, A.: On the integration of symbolic and sub-symbolic techniques for XAI: a survey. Intell. Artifi. **14**(1), 7–32 (2020). https://doi.org/10.3233/IA-190036

7. Ciatto, G.: 2P-Kt. https://github.com/tuProlog/2p-kt

8. Ciatto, G.: Travelling salesman problem (TSP) in 2P-KT. https://github.com/tuProlog/ortools-tsp-example

9. Ciatto, G., Calegari, R., Siboni, E., Denti, E., Omicini, A.: 2P-KT: logic programming with objects & functions in Kotlin. In: Calegari, R., Ciatto, G., Denti, E., Omicini, A., Sartor, G. (eds.) WOA 2020–21th Workshop "From Objects to Agents". CEUR Workshop Proceedings, vol. 2706, pp. 219–236. Sun SITE Central Europe, RWTH Aachen University, Aachen, Germany, October 2020. http://ceur-ws.org/Vol-2706/paper14.pdf

10. Colmerauer, A., Roussel, P.: The birth of prolog. In: Lee, J.A.N., Sammet, J.E. (eds.) History of Programming Languages Conference (HOPL-II). pp. 37–52. ACM, April 1993. https://doi.org/10.1145/154766.155362

11. Eiter, T., Ianni, G., Schindlauer, R., Tompits, H.: A uniform integration of higher-order reasoning and external evaluations in answer-set programming. In: Kaelbling, L.P., Saffiotti, A. (eds.) IJCAI-05, Proceedings of the Nineteenth International Joint Conference on Artificial Intelligence, Edinburgh, Scotland, UK, 30 July–5 August 2005, pp. 90–96. Professional Book Center (2005). http://ijcai.org/Proceedings/05/Papers/1353.pdf

12. Perron, L., Furnon, V.: OR-tools. https://developers.google.com/optimization/

13. Piancastelli, G., Benini, A., Omicini, A., Ricci, A.: The architecture and design of a malleable object-oriented Prolog engine. In: Wainwright, R.L., Haddad, H.M., Menezes, R., Viroli, M. (eds.) 23rd ACM Symposium on Applied Computing (SAC 2008), Fortaleza, Ceará, Brazil, 16–20 March 2008, vol. 1, pp. 191–197. ACM (2008). https://doi.org/10.1145/1363686.1363739

14. Redl, C.: The DLVHEX system for knowledge representation: recent advances (system description). Theory Pract. Logic Program. **16**(5–6), 866–883 (2016). https://doi.org/10.1017/S1471068416000211

15. Tarau, P., Wielemaker, J., Schrijvers, T.: Lazy stream programming in Prolog. Electron. Proc. Theory Comput. Sci. **306**, 224–237 (2019). https://doi.org/10.4204/eptcs.306.26

Transforming Gringo Rules into Formulas in a Natural Way

Vladimir Lifschitz$^{(\boxtimes)}$

University of Texas at Austin, Austin, TX, USA

Abstract. Research on the input language of the ASP grounder GRINGO uses a translation that converts rules in that language into first-order formulas. That translation often transforms short rules into formulas that are syntactically complex. In this note we identify a class of rules that can be transformed into formulas in a simpler, more natural way. The new translation contributes to our understanding of the relationship between the language of GRINGO and first-order languages.

1 Introduction

The semantics of some rules in the input language of the ASP grounder GRINGO [1,2] can be characterized in terms of a translation into the language of first-order logic [3, Section 6]. The transformation τ^*, defined in that paper, produces formulas with two sorts—with "program variables" for arbitrary precomputed terms and "integer variables" for numerals. This transformation can be used, for instance, to characterize strong equivalence between GRINGO programs in terms of a similar condition on first-order formulas [3, Proposition 4]. It is used also in the design of the proof assistant ANTHEM [5].

The formulas produced by τ^* may be quite complicated, even in application to short rules, which makes it difficult to use them for reasoning about programs. For example, the result of applying τ^* to the rule

$$q(X + \overline{1}) \leftarrow p(X) \tag{1}$$

is

$$\forall X (\exists Z (Z = X \wedge p(Z)) \rightarrow \forall Z_1 (\exists I J (Z_1 = I + J \wedge I = X \wedge J = \overline{1}) \rightarrow q(Z_1))). \tag{2}$$

(In formulas, we use X, Y, Z as program variables, and I, J, K, L, M, N as integer variables; $\overline{1}$ is the numeral representing the number 1.)

Fortunately, complicated formulas produced by τ^* are often equivalent to much simpler formulas. In this note, equivalence of formulas is understood as equivalence in intuitionistic logic (see Sect. 3 for details). The use of intuitionistically acceptable simplifications in this context is essential because such simplifications do not affect the class of stable models [4]. For example, formula (2) is equivalent to

$$\forall X (p(X) \rightarrow \forall Z_1 I J (Z_1 = I + J \wedge I = X \wedge J = \overline{1} \rightarrow q(Z_1))).$$

© Springer Nature Switzerland AG 2021
W. Faber et al. (Eds.): JELIA 2021, LNAI 12678, pp. 421–434, 2021.
https://doi.org/10.1007/978-3-030-75775-5_28

It can be further rewritten as

$$\forall X(p(X) \rightarrow \forall IJ(I = X \wedge J = \overline{1} \rightarrow q(I + J)))$$

and then as

$$\forall I(p(I) \rightarrow q(I + \overline{1})). \tag{3}$$

Formula (3) is not only short but also natural as a representation of rule (1), in the sense that its syntactic form is similar to the syntactic form of the rule. If our intention is to study properties of a program containing rule (1) using a representation of this rule in a first-order language, then representing it by a simple formula, such as (3), instead of (2) will make our work easier. This is particularly important if we plan to reason "manually," without the assistance of automated reasoning tools.

The goal of this paper is to identify a subset of the domain of τ^* for which transforming a rule into a formula can be performed "in a natural way." The new translation ν produces, whenever it is defined, a sentence equivalent to the result of applying τ^*. For example, in application to rule (1) the translation ν gives formula (3).

In the next section we describe a class of rules that can be transformed into formulas in a natural way. After a review of the syntax of formulas in Sect. 3, the translation ν is defined in Sects. 4 and 5, and its equivalence to τ^* is proved in Sects. 6 and 7. The note is concluded by a discussion of the analogy between regular rules and first-order formulas.

2   Regular Rules

The translation ν is defined on the class of rules that we call "regular."

Recall that in the definition of the syntax of rules, *program terms*, or *p-terms* for short, are defined as expressions formed from numerals, symbolic constants, program variables, and the symbols *inf* and *sup* using the binary function symbols

$$+ \quad - \quad \times \quad / \quad \backslash \quad ..$$

[3, Section 2]. (We call them p-terms to distinguish them from "f-terms" that are allowed in formulas; see Section 3 below.) About a p-term we say that it is *a regular term of the first kind* if

- it contains no function symbols other than $+$, $-$, $\times$, and
- symbolic constants and the symbols *inf*, *sup* do not occur in it in the scope of function symbols.

A regular term of the second kind is a p-term of the form $t_1 .. t_2$, where t_1 and t_2 are regular terms of the first kind that contain neither symbolic constants nor the symbols *inf*, *sup*.

Rules are defined as expressions of the form

$$H \leftarrow B_1 \wedge \cdots \wedge B_n \tag{4}$$

$(n \geq 0)$, where

– the head H is either an atom (then (4) is a *basic rule*), or an atom in braces (then (4) is a *choice rule*), or empty (then (4) is a *constraint*), and
– each member B_i of the body is a literal or a comparison

[3, Section 2]; see that paper for a complete definition of the syntax of rules. We say that a rule (4) is *regular* if it satisfies the following conditions:

1. Every p-term occurring in it is regular (of the first or second kind).
2. If B_i is a literal then it does not contain terms of the second kind.
3. If B_i is a comparison that contains a term of the second kind then B_i has the form $t_1 = t_2 \, .. \, t_3$, where t_1 is a term of the first kind different from symbolic constants and from the symbols *inf*, *sup*.

Condition 1 eliminates, for instance, rules containing any of the terms

$$X/Y, \ \overline{5} \times (X \, .. \, Y), \ london + \overline{5}, \ london \, .. \, \overline{5}.$$

Condition 2 eliminates, for instance, rules containing the atom $p(\overline{1} \, .. \, \overline{5})$ in the body. Condition 3 eliminates, for instance, rules containing any of the comparisons

$$X < \overline{1} \, .. \, \overline{5}, \ X \, .. \, Y = \overline{1} \, .. \, \overline{5}, \ london = \overline{1} \, .. \, X.$$

Some of these "irregular" constructs exemplify differences between the language of GRINGO and conventional mathematical notation. In a mathematical formula, for instance, the arguments of $+$ are expected to represent objects for which addition has been defined. But including $london + \overline{5}$ in a GRINGO program is not considered an error (although the output of GRINGO will include the informational message `info: operation undefined`). The expression $X \, .. \, Y = \overline{1} \, .. \, \overline{5}$ in the body of a GRINGO rule expresses that the interval $\{X, \ldots, Y\}$ contains at least one number between 1 and 5; a mathematician would not use the equal sign to say that two sets have a common element.

The comparison $X = \overline{1} \, .. \, \overline{5}$, which is allowed in the body a regular rule, expresses that the value of X is one of the numbers $1, \ldots, 5$, and this use of the equal sign does not look natural either. We will return to this example in Sect. 8.

3 F-Terms and Formulas

The language of f-terms and formulas is a two-sorted first-order language, with program variables (the same that occur in rules, see Sect. 2) and integer variables [5, Section 3]. The second sort is a subsort of the first. The signature of the language consists of

– numerals, symbolic constants and the symbols *inf*, *sup* as object constants; an object constant is assigned the sort *integer* iff it is a numeral;
– the symbols $+$, $-$ and $\times$ as binary function constants; their arguments and values have the sort *integer*;
– pairs p/n, where p is a symbolic constant and n is a nonnegative integer, as n-ary predicate constants, and the comparison symbols (the same that occur in comparisons) as predicate binary predicate constants.

An atomic formula $(p/n)(t_1,\ldots,t_n)$ can be abbreviated as $p(t_1,\ldots,t_n)$. An atomic formula $\prec (t_1,t_2)$, where $\prec$ is a comparison symbol, can be written as $t_1 \prec t_2$. *Formulas* are formed from atomic formulas using the propositional connectives

$$\perp (\text{``false''}), \wedge, \vee, \rightarrow$$

and the quantifiers $\forall$, $\exists$ as usual in first-order languages.

We use $\top$ as shorthand for $\perp \rightarrow \perp$, $\neg F$ as shorthand for $F \rightarrow \perp$, and $F \leftrightarrow G$ as shorthand for $(F \rightarrow G) \wedge (G \rightarrow F)$.

By *Int* we denote the formal system of intuitionistic logic with equality for the language described above. The natural deduction version of *Int* can be obtained from the standard natural deduction formulation of classical first-order logic [6, Sections 1.2.1, 1.2.2] by removing the law of the excluded middle from the list of axioms. The $\forall$-elimination rule of *Int* sanctions eliminating a universal quantifier that binds a program variable by substituting an f-term of either sort. When a quantifier binding an integer variable is eliminated, the f-term substituted for it is required to be of the sort *integer*. The $\exists$-introduction rule is similar. For instance, the formula $\exists X(I = X)$ can be proved in *Int* by applying $\exists$-introduction to $I = I$, but the formula $\exists I(I = X)$ is not provable. (This formula expresses that the value of X is a numeral.)

We say that formulas F and G are *equivalent* to each other if the formula $F \leftrightarrow G$ is provable in *Int*.

4   Natural Translation, Part 1

According to Condition 3 in the definition of a regular rule (Sect. 2), the left-hand side of a comparison in such a rule is a regular term of the first kind. If the right-hand side is of the first kind as well then we say that the comparison is *of the first kind*; otherwise it has the form $t_1 = t_2 \mathbin{..} t_3$, and we call it a comparison *of the second kind*.

Applying the translation ν to a regular rule (4) involves substituting integer variables for the variables that occur in that rule at least once in the scope of a function symbol or in a comparison of the second kind. Make the list $X_1,\ldots,X_m$ of all such variables, and choose m distinct integer variables $I_1,\ldots,I_m$. For any tuple $\mathbf{t}$ of regular terms of the first kind that occur in (4), the result of substituting $I_1,\ldots,I_m$ for $X_1,\ldots,X_m$ in $\mathbf{t}$ is a tuple of f-terms. The operator that performs this substitution will be denoted by p2f ("p-terms to f-terms"). For instance, in the case of rule (1), p2f$(X + \overline{1})$ is $I + \overline{1}$.

Prior to defining the translation ν we will define the auxiliary transformation ν', which will be used to translate the head H and the members $B_1,\ldots,B_n$ of the body of the rule. The definition of ν' is particularly simple if we restrict attention to the case when the head of the rule does not contain terms of the second kind:

– If **t** is a tuple of regular terms of the first kind then
  - $\nu'(p(\mathbf{t}))$ is $p(\mathrm{p2f}(\mathbf{t}))$,
  - $\nu'(not\ p(\mathbf{t}))$ is $\neg p(\mathrm{p2f}(\mathbf{t}))$,
  - $\nu'(not\ not\ p(\mathbf{t}))$ is $\neg\neg p(\mathrm{p2f}(\mathbf{t}))$,
  - $\nu'(\{p(\mathbf{t})\})$ is $p(\mathrm{p2f}(\mathbf{t})) \vee \neg p(\mathrm{p2f}(\mathbf{t}))$.
– The result of applying ν' to the empty string is $\bot$.
– If $t_1 \prec t_2$ is a comparison of the first kind then $\nu'(t_1 \prec t_2)$ is $\mathrm{p2f}(t_1) \prec \mathrm{p2f}(t_2)$.
– $\nu'(t_1 = t_2 .. t_3)$ is $\mathrm{p2f}(t_2) \leq \mathrm{p2f}(t_1) \leq \mathrm{p2f}(t_3)$.

(We use $t_1 \leq t_2 \leq t_3$ as shorthand for $t_1 \leq t_2 \wedge t_2 \leq t_3$.) This definition is extended to the general case in the next section.

The result of applying the translation ν to rule (4) is defined as the sentence

$$\widehat{\forall}(\nu'(B_1) \wedge \cdots \wedge \nu'(B_n) \to \nu'(H)). \tag{5}$$

(We write $\widehat{\forall}F$ for the universal closure of a formula F.)

One example of applying ν is given in the introduction: ν turns rule (1) into formula (3). If (4) is the rule

$$\leftarrow p(X,Y,Z) \wedge X < Y \wedge Y = \overline{1}..Z$$

then the substitution p2f replaces Y, Z by I_1, I_2; the result of applying ν is

$$\forall X I_1 I_2 \neg(p(X,I_1,I_2) \wedge X < I_1 \wedge \overline{1} \leq I_1 \leq I_2).$$

5   Natural Translation, Part 2

Now we turn to the general case, when the head of rule (4) can contain terms of the second kind. As in the previous section, we start by making the list $X_1, \ldots, X_m$ of variables that occur in the rule at least once in the scope of a function symbol or in a comparison of the second kind, and choose distinct integer variables $I_1, \ldots, I_m$. The result of applying ν' to an atom of the form

$$p(t_1 .. t_1',\ t_2 .. t_2',\ \ldots)$$

is the formula

$$\forall N_1 N_2 \cdots (\mathrm{p2f}(t_1) \leq N_1 \leq \mathrm{p2f}(t_1') \wedge \mathrm{p2f}(t_2) \leq N_2 \leq \mathrm{p2f}(t_2') \wedge \cdots \to \\ p(N_1, N_2, \ldots)),$$

where $N_1, N_2, \ldots$ are distinct integer variables different from $I_1, \ldots, I_m$. For example, the translation ν turns the rule

$$q(\overline{1} .. X, \overline{1} .. Y) \leftarrow p(X,Y,Z)$$

into the formula

$$\forall I_1 I_2 Z (p(I_1, I_2, Z) \to \forall N_1 N_2 (\overline{1} \leq N_1 \leq I_1 \wedge \overline{1} \leq N_2 \leq I_2 \to q(N_1, N_2))).$$

To make ν' applicable to arbitrary atoms allowed in the head of a regular rule we should take into account the fact that such an atom can include arguments of both kinds, in any order. If $\mathbf{t}$ is the tuple

$$\mathbf{t}_1,\ t_1..t_1',\ \mathbf{t}_2,\ \ldots,\ \mathbf{t}_{k-1},\ t_{k-1}..t_{k-1}',\ \mathbf{t}_k,$$

where $k > 1$ and $\mathbf{t}_1,\ldots,\mathbf{t}_k$ are tuples of regular terms of the first kind, then we define:

- $\nu'(p(\mathbf{t}))$ is

$$\forall N_1 \cdots N_{k-1}(\textstyle\bigwedge_{i=1}^{k-1}(\mathrm{p2f}(t_i) \leq N_i \leq \mathrm{p2f}(t_i')) \to \qquad\qquad (6)$$
$$p(\mathrm{p2f}(\mathbf{t}_1), N_1, \mathrm{p2f}(\mathbf{t}_2), \ldots, \mathrm{p2f}(\mathbf{t}_{k-1}), N_{k-1}, \mathrm{p2f}(\mathbf{t}_k))),$$

- $\nu'(\{p(\mathbf{t})\})$ is

$$\forall N_1 \cdots N_{k-1}(\textstyle\bigwedge_{i=1}^{k-1}(\mathrm{p2f}(t_i) \leq N_i \leq \mathrm{p2f}(t_i')) \to$$
$$p(\mathrm{p2f}(\mathbf{t}_1), N_1, \mathrm{p2f}(\mathbf{t}_2), \ldots, \mathrm{p2f}(\mathbf{t}_{k-1}), N_{k-1}, \mathrm{p2f}(\mathbf{t}_k))) \vee \qquad (7)$$
$$\neg p(\mathrm{p2f}(\mathbf{t}_1), N_1, \mathrm{p2f}(\mathbf{t}_2), \ldots, \mathrm{p2f}(\mathbf{t}_{k-1}), N_{k-1}, \mathrm{p2f}(\mathbf{t}_k))).$$

For example, if (4) is the rule

$$\{q(\overline{1}..X,Y)\} \leftarrow p(X,Y)$$

then the result of applying ν is

$$\forall IY(p(I,Y) \to \forall N(\overline{1} \leq N \leq I \to q(N,Y) \vee \neg q(N,Y))).$$

It is clear that every variable occurring in sentence (5) corresponding to rule (4) is either a program variable from (4) different from $X_1,\ldots,X_m$, or one of the integer variables $I_1,\ldots,I_m$, or one of the integer variables N_i in the consequent $\nu'(H)$ of (5).

Theorem. *For any regular rule R the formula $\nu(R)$ is equivalent to $\tau^*(R)$.*

6 Review: Definition of τ^*

We reproduce here the definition of τ^* [3, Section 6] referenced in the proof of the theorem in the next section. The definition makes use of the formulas $val_t(Z)$, where t is a term and Z is a variable that does not occur in t. The definition of $val_t(Z)$ is recursive and includes the following clauses:

- if t is a numeral, a symbolic constant, a program variable, *inf*, or *sup* then $val_t(Z)$ is $Z = t$;
- if t is $t_1 + t_2$ then $val_t(Z)$ is

$$\exists IJ(Z = I + J \wedge val_{t_1}(I) \wedge val_{t_2}(J)),$$

and similarly for $t_1 - t_2$ and $t_1 \times t_2$;

– if t is $t_1 .. t_2$ then $val_t(Z)$ is

$$\exists IJK(val_{t_1}(I) \wedge val_{t_2}(J) \wedge I \leq K \leq J \wedge Z = K).$$

(The other clauses are not required for calculating $val_t(Z)$ when t is regular.) A conjunction of the form

$$val_{t_1}(Z_1) \wedge \cdots \wedge val_{t_k}(Z_k)$$

can be written as

$$val_{t_1,\ldots,t_k}(Z_1,\ldots,Z_k).$$

The auxiliary translation τ^B is defined as follows:

– $\tau^B(p(\mathbf{t}))$ is $\exists \mathbf{Z}(val_{\mathbf{t}}(\mathbf{Z}) \wedge p(\mathbf{Z}))$, where $\mathbf{Z}$ is a tuple of distinct program variables that do not occur in $\mathbf{t}$;
– $\tau^B(not\ p(\mathbf{t}))$ is $\exists \mathbf{Z}(val_{\mathbf{t}}(\mathbf{Z}) \wedge \neg p(\mathbf{Z}))$;
– $\tau^B(not\ not\ p(\mathbf{t}))$ is $\exists \mathbf{Z}(val_{\mathbf{t}}(\mathbf{Z}) \wedge \neg\neg p(\mathbf{Z}))$;
– $\tau^B(t_1 \prec t_2)$ is $\exists Z_1 Z_2(val_{t_1,t_2}(Z_1,Z_2) \wedge Z_1 \prec Z_2)$.

Then the result of applying τ^* to rule (4) is defined as the formula

$$\widehat{\forall}(\tau^B(B_1) \wedge \cdots \wedge \tau^B(B_n) \rightarrow H^*), \tag{8}$$

where H^* stands for

$$\forall \mathbf{Z}(val_{\mathbf{t}}(\mathbf{Z}) \rightarrow p(\mathbf{Z})), \text{ if } H \text{ is } p(\mathbf{t});$$
$$\forall \mathbf{Z}(val_{\mathbf{t}}(\mathbf{Z}) \rightarrow p(\mathbf{Z}) \vee \neg p(\mathbf{Z})), \text{ if } H \text{ is } \{p(\mathbf{t})\};$$
$$\bot, \text{ if } H \text{ is empty.}$$

7   Proof of the Theorem

Consider a regular rule (4), and let C be the conjunction

$$I_1 = X_1 \wedge \cdots \wedge I_m = X_m,$$

where $X_1, \ldots, X_m, I_1, \ldots, I_m$ are as in the definition of p2f (Sect. 5). A conjunction of the form $t_1 = t_1' \wedge \cdots \wedge t_m = t_m'$ can be also written as $(t_1, \ldots, t_m) = (t_1', \ldots, t_m')$.

Lemma 1. *For any tuple $\mathbf{t}$ of regular terms of the first kind that occur in rule (4), the formulas*

(i) $C \rightarrow \forall \mathbf{Z}(val_{\mathbf{t}}(\mathbf{Z}) \leftrightarrow \mathbf{Z} = \mathrm{p2f}(\mathbf{t}))$,
(ii) $C \rightarrow (\nu'(p(\mathbf{t})) \leftrightarrow \forall \mathbf{Z}(val_{\mathbf{t}}(\mathbf{Z}) \rightarrow p(\mathbf{Z})))$,
(iii) $C \rightarrow (\nu'(p(\mathbf{t})) \leftrightarrow \tau^B(p(\mathbf{t})))$,
(iv) $C \rightarrow (\nu'(not\ p(\mathbf{t})) \leftrightarrow \tau^B(not\ p(\mathbf{t})))$,
(v) $C \rightarrow (\nu'(not\ not\ p(\mathbf{t})) \leftrightarrow \tau^B(not\ not\ p(\mathbf{t})))$

are provable in Int.

Proof. (i) It is sufficient to consider the case when **t** is a single term t, so that the formula to be proved is

$$C \to \forall Z(val_t(Z) \leftrightarrow Z = \text{p2f}(t)). \tag{9}$$

The proof is by induction on t. *Case 1:* t is one of the variables X_k $(1 \leq k \leq m)$. Then the consequent of (9) is $\forall Z(Z = X_k \leftrightarrow Z = I_k)$, and the antecedent C contains the conjunctive term $X_k = I_k$. *Case 2:* t is a variable different from $X_1, \ldots, X_m$, or a numeral, or a symbolic constant, or one of the symbols *inf*, *sup*. Then the consequent is $\forall Z(Z = t \leftrightarrow Z = t)$. *Case 3:* t contains a function symbol. Assume, for instance, that t is $t_1 + t_2$. Then p2f(t) is p2f(t_1)+p2f(t_2); this term and its subterms p2f(t_1), p2f(t_2) are of the sort *integer*. By the induction hypothesis, under the assumption C,

$$\begin{aligned}
val_{t_1+t_2}(Z) &= \exists IJ(Z = I + J \wedge val_{t_1}(I) \wedge val_{t_2}(J)) \\
&\leftrightarrow \exists IJ(Z = I + J \wedge I = \text{p2f}(t_1) \wedge J = \text{p2f}(t_2)) \\
&\leftrightarrow \exists IJ(Z = \text{p2f}(t_1) + \text{p2f}(t_2) \wedge I = \text{p2f}(t_1) \wedge J = \text{p2f}(t_2)) \\
&\leftrightarrow Z = \text{p2f}(t) \wedge \exists I(I = \text{p2f}(t_1)) \wedge \exists J(J = \text{p2f}(t_2)).
\end{aligned}$$

Since p2f(t_1) and p2f(t_2) are of the sort *integer*, the last two conjunctive terms are provable in *Int* and can be dropped.

(ii) By (i), under the assumption C,

$$\forall \mathbf{Z}(val_{\mathbf{t}}(\mathbf{Z}) \to p(\mathbf{Z})) \leftrightarrow \forall \mathbf{Z}(\mathbf{Z} = \text{p2f}(\mathbf{t}) \to p(\mathbf{Z})) \leftrightarrow p(\text{p2f}(\mathbf{t})) = \nu'(p(\mathbf{t})).$$

(iii) By (i), under the assumption C,

$$\tau^B(p(\mathbf{t})) = \exists \mathbf{Z}(val_{\mathbf{t}}(\mathbf{Z}) \wedge p(\mathbf{Z})) \leftrightarrow \exists \mathbf{Z}(\mathbf{Z} = \text{p2f}(\mathbf{t}) \wedge p(\mathbf{Z})) \leftrightarrow p(\text{p2f}(\mathbf{t})) = \nu'(p(\mathbf{t})).$$

(iv), (v): Similar to (iii).

Lemma 2. *For any regular terms* t_1, t_2, *of the first kind that occur in rule (4), the formula*

$$C \to (\nu'(t_1 \prec t_2) \leftrightarrow \tau^B(t_1 \prec t_2))$$

is provable in Int.

Proof. By Lemma 1(i), under the assumption C,

$$\begin{aligned}
\tau^B(t_1 \prec t_2) &= \exists Z_1 Z_2(val_{t_1,t_2}(Z_1, Z_2) \wedge Z_1 \prec Z_2) \\
&\leftrightarrow \exists Z_1 Z_2(Z_1 = \text{p2f}(t_1) \wedge Z_2 = \text{p2f}(t_2) \wedge Z_1 \prec Z_2) \\
&\leftrightarrow \text{p2f}(t_1) \prec \text{p2f}(t_2) \\
&= \nu'(t_1 \prec t_2).
\end{aligned}$$

Lemma 3. *For any regular term* $t_1 \mathbin{..} t_2$ *that occurs in rule (4), the formula*

$$C \to (val_{t_1 \mathbin{..} t_2}(Z) \leftrightarrow \exists K(\text{p2f}(t_1) \leq K \leq \text{p2f}(t_2) \wedge Z = K))$$

is provable in Int.

Proof. Since $t_1 .. t_2$ is regular, t_1 and t_2 contain neither symbolic constants nor the symbols inf, sup. Since $t_1 .. t_2$ occurs in rule (4), all variables occurring in t_1, t_2 belong to the list $X_1, \ldots, X_m$. It follows that the f-terms $\mathrm{p2f}(t_1)$ and $\mathrm{p2f}(t_2)$ are of the sort *integer*. By Lemma 1(i), under the assumption C,

$$
\begin{aligned}
val_{t_1 .. t_2}(Z) &= \exists IJK(val_{t_1}(I) \wedge val_{t_2}(J) \wedge I \leq K \leq J \wedge Z = K) \\
&\leftrightarrow \exists IJK(I = \mathrm{p2f}(t_1) \wedge J = \mathrm{p2f}(t_2) \wedge I \leq K \leq J \wedge Z = K) \\
&\leftrightarrow \exists IJK(I = \mathrm{p2f}(t_1) \wedge J = \mathrm{p2f}(t_2) \wedge \\
&\qquad \mathrm{p2f}(t_1) \leq K \leq \mathrm{p2f}(t_2) \wedge Z = K) \\
&\leftrightarrow \exists I(I = \mathrm{p2f}(t_1)) \wedge \exists J(J = \mathrm{p2f}(t_2)) \wedge \\
&\qquad \exists K(\mathrm{p2f}(t_1) \leq K \leq \mathrm{p2f}(t_2) \wedge Z = K).
\end{aligned}
$$

Since $\mathrm{p2f}(t_1)$ and $\mathrm{p2f}(t_2)$ are of the sort *integer*, the first two conjunctive terms are provable in *Int* and can be dropped.

Lemma 4. *If a comparison $t_1 = t_2 .. t_3$ occurs in rule (4) then the formula*

$$
C \rightarrow (\nu'(t_1 = t_2 .. t_3) \leftrightarrow \tau^B(t_1 = t_2 .. t_3))
$$

is provable in Int.

Proof. By Lemma 1(i) and Lemma 3, under the assumption C,

$$
\begin{aligned}
\tau^B(t_1 = t_2 .. t_3) &= \exists Z_1 Z_2 (val_{t_1, t_2 .. t_3}(Z_1, Z_2) \wedge Z_1 = Z_2) \\
&\leftrightarrow \exists Z_1 Z_2 (Z_1 = \mathrm{p2f}(t_1) \wedge val_{t_2 .. t_3}(Z_2) \wedge Z_1 = Z_2) \\
&\leftrightarrow val_{t_2 .. t_3}(\mathrm{p2f}(t_1)) \\
&\leftrightarrow \exists K(\mathrm{p2f}(t_2) \leq K \leq \mathrm{p2f}(t_3) \wedge \mathrm{p2f}(t_1) = K) \\
&\leftrightarrow \mathrm{p2f}(t_2) \leq \mathrm{p2f}(t_1) \leq \mathrm{p2f}(t_3) \\
&= \nu'(t_1 = t_2 .. t_3).
\end{aligned}
$$

Lemma 5. *For any tuple $\mathbf{t}$ of regular terms that occur in rule (4), the formulas*

(i) $C \rightarrow (\nu'(p(\mathbf{t})) \leftrightarrow \forall \mathbf{Z}(val_\mathbf{t}(\mathbf{Z}) \rightarrow p(\mathbf{Z})))$,
(ii) $C \rightarrow (\nu'(\{p(\mathbf{t})\}) \leftrightarrow \forall \mathbf{Z}(val_\mathbf{t}(\mathbf{Z}) \rightarrow p(\mathbf{Z}) \vee \neg p(\mathbf{Z}))$

are provable in Int.

Proof. (i) If all members of the tuple $\mathbf{t}$ are of the first kind then the assertion holds by Lemma 1(ii). Otherwise, $\mathbf{t}$ can be represented in the form

$$
\mathbf{t}_1, \; t_1 .. t_1', \; \mathbf{t}_2, \; \ldots, \; \mathbf{t}_{k-1}, \; t_{k-1} .. t_{k-1}', \; \mathbf{t}_k,
$$

where $k > 1$ and $\mathbf{t}_1, \ldots, \mathbf{t}_k$ are tuples of terms of the first kind. Assume C; we need to derive the equivalence between $\nu'(p(\mathbf{t}))$ and

$$
\forall \mathbf{Z}(val_\mathbf{t}(\mathbf{Z}) \rightarrow p(\mathbf{Z})).
$$

The last formula can be written as

$$
\begin{aligned}
\forall \mathbf{Z}_1 Z_1 \mathbf{Z}_2 \cdots \mathbf{Z}_{k-1} Z_{k-1} \mathbf{Z}_k (val_{\mathbf{t}_1}(\mathbf{Z}_1) \wedge val_{t_1 .. t_1'}(Z_1) \wedge \\
val_{\mathbf{t}_2}(\mathbf{Z}_2) \wedge \cdots \wedge val_{\mathbf{t}_{k-1}}(\mathbf{Z}_{k-1}) \wedge \\
val_{t_{k-1} .. t_{k-1}'}(Z_{k-1}) \wedge val_{\mathbf{t}_k}(\mathbf{Z}_k) \\
\rightarrow p(\mathbf{Z}_1, Z_1, \mathbf{Z}_2, \ldots, \mathbf{Z}_{k-1}, Z_{k-1}, \mathbf{Z}_k)).
\end{aligned}
$$

By Lemma 1(i), under the assumption C it is equivalent to

$$\forall \mathbf{Z}_1 Z_1 \mathbf{Z}_2 \cdots \mathbf{Z}_{k-1} Z_{k-1} \mathbf{Z}_k (\mathbf{Z}_1 = \mathrm{p2f}(\mathbf{t}_1) \wedge val_{t_1 .. t_1'}(Z_1) \wedge$$
$$\mathbf{Z}_2 = \mathrm{p2f}(\mathbf{t}_2) \wedge \cdots \wedge \mathbf{Z}_{k-1} = \mathrm{p2f}(\mathbf{t}_{k-1}) \wedge$$
$$val_{t_{k-1} .. t_{k-1}'}(Z_{k-1}) \wedge \mathbf{Z}_k = \mathrm{p2f}(\mathbf{t}_k)$$
$$\rightarrow p(\mathbf{Z}_1, Z_1, \mathbf{Z}_2, \ldots, \mathbf{Z}_{k-1}, Z_{k-1}, \mathbf{Z}_k))$$

and can be further rewritten as

$$\forall Z_1 \cdots Z_{k-1} (val_{t_1 .. t_1'}(Z_1) \wedge \cdots \wedge val_{t_{k-1} .. t_{k-1}'}(Z_{k-1})$$
$$\rightarrow p(\mathrm{p2f}(\mathbf{t}_1), Z_1, \mathrm{p2f}(\mathbf{t}_2), \ldots, \mathrm{p2f}(\mathbf{t}_{k-1}), Z_{k-1}, \mathrm{p2f}(\mathbf{t}_k))).$$

By Lemma 4, under the assumption C this formula is equivalent to

$$\forall Z_1 \cdots Z_{k-1} (\exists K (\mathrm{p2f}(t_1) \le K \le \mathrm{p2f}(t_1') \wedge Z_1 = K) \wedge \cdots \wedge$$
$$\exists K (\mathrm{p2f}(t_{k-1}) \le K \le \mathrm{p2f}(t_{k-1}') \wedge Z_{k-1} = K)$$
$$\rightarrow p(\mathrm{p2f}(\mathbf{t}_1), Z_1, \mathrm{p2f}(\mathbf{t}_2), \ldots, \mathrm{p2f}(\mathbf{t}_{k-1}), Z_{k-1}, \mathrm{p2f}(\mathbf{t}_k)))$$

and can be further rewritten as

$$\forall Z_1 \cdots Z_{k-1} N_1 \cdots N_{k-1} (\mathrm{p2f}(t_1) \le N_1 \le \mathrm{p2f}(t_1') \wedge Z_1 = N_1 \wedge \cdots \wedge$$
$$\mathrm{p2f}(t_{k-1}) \le N_{k-1} \le \mathrm{p2f}(t_{k-1}') \wedge Z_{k-1} = N_{k-1}$$
$$\rightarrow p(\mathrm{p2f}(\mathbf{t}_1), Z_1, \mathrm{p2f}(\mathbf{t}_2), \ldots, \mathrm{p2f}(\mathbf{t}_{k-1}), Z_{k-1}, \mathrm{p2f}(\mathbf{t}_k))).$$

This formula is equivalent to (6).

The proof of part (ii) is similar.

Lemma 6. *If a regular term t contains a function symbol then, for every variable X occurring in t, the formula*

$$\forall X (\exists Z \, val_t(Z) \rightarrow \exists I (I = X))$$

is provable in Int.

Proof. By induction on t. Consider, for instance, the case when t has the form $t_1 + t_2$. Then the antecedent of the implication to be proved is

$$\exists ZIJ (Z = I + J \wedge val_{t_1}(I) \wedge val_{t_2}(J)).$$

Assume, for instance, that the part of t containing X is t_1. The formula above implies $\exists I \, val_{t_1}(I)$. If t_1 is X then the last formula is $\exists I (I = X)$, which is the consequent of the formula to be proved. Otherwise t_1 contains a function symbol, and $\exists I (I = X)$ follows by the induction hypothesis. If t is $t_1 - t_2$ $t_1 \times t_2$ or $t_1 .. t_2$ then reasoning is similar.

Lemma 7. *If a conjunctive term B_i of the body of rule (4) is a literal or a comparison of the first kind then, for every variable X that occurs in B_i at least once in the scope of a function symbol, the formula $\tau^B(B_i) \rightarrow \exists I (I = X)$ is provable in Int.*

Proof. *Case 1:* B_i is an atom $p(\mathbf{t})$. Then $\tau^B(B_i)$ is $\exists \mathbf{Z}(val_{\mathbf{t}}(\mathbf{Z}) \wedge p(\mathbf{Z}))$, which implies $\exists \mathbf{Z}\, val_{\mathbf{t}}(\mathbf{Z})$ and further $\exists Z\, val_t(Z)$, where t is the component of the tuple $\mathbf{t}$ that contains X in the scope of a function symbol; $\exists I(I = X)$ follows by Lemma 6. *Case 2:* B_i is a literal of the form *not* $p(\mathbf{t})$ or *not not* $p(\mathbf{t})$. Similar to Case 1. *Case 3:* B_i is a comparison $t_1 \prec t_2$. Then $\tau^B(B_i)$ is

$$\exists Z_1 Z_2 (val_{t_1,t_2}(Z_1, Z_2) \wedge Z_1 \prec Z_2),$$

which implies $\exists Z_j\, val_{t_j}(Z_j)$, where t_j is the part of the comparison that contains X in the scope of a function symbol; $\exists I(I = X)$ follows by Lemma 6.

Lemma 8. *For any regular term t and any variable X occurring in t, the formula*

$$\forall X (\exists N\, val_t(N) \rightarrow \exists I(I = X))$$

is provable in Int.

Proof. By induction on t. *Case 1:* t is X. Then the antecedent $\exists N\, val_t(N)$ of the implication to be proved is $\exists N(N = X)$, which is equivalent to its consequent $\exists I(I = X)$. *Case 2:* t has the form $t_1 + t_2$, so that the antecedent is

$$\exists NIJ(N = I + J \wedge val_{t_1}(I) \wedge val_{t_2}(J)).$$

Assume, for instance, that the part of t containing X is t_1. The formula above implies $\exists I\, val_{t_1}(I)$. By the induction hypothesis, $\exists I(I = X)$ follows. *Case 3:* t has the form $t_1 - t_2$, $t_1 \times t_2$ or $t_1 .. t_2$. Similar to Case 2.

Lemma 9. *If a conjunctive term B_i of the body of rule (4) is a comparison of the second kind then, for every variable X that occurs in B_i, the formula $\tau^B(B_i) \rightarrow \exists I(I = X)$ is provable in Int.*

Proof. The antecedent $\tau^B(B_i)$ of the formula to be proved is

$$\exists Z_1 Z_2 (val_{t_1,t_2 .. t_3}(Z_1, Z_2) \wedge Z_1 = Z_2),$$

which is equivalent to

$$\exists Z\, val_{t_1,t_2 .. t_3}(Z, Z). \tag{10}$$

Case 1: X occurs in t_1. Formula (10) can be rewritten as

$$\exists Z(val_{t_1}(Z) \wedge \exists IJK(val_{t_2}(I) \wedge val_{t_3}(J) \wedge I \leq K \leq J \wedge Z = K)).$$

Consequently it implies $\exists K\, val_{t_1}(K)$, and $\exists I(I = X)$ follows by Lemma 8. *Case 2:* X occurs in $t_2 .. t_3$. Formula (10) implies $\exists Z\, val_{t_2 .. t_3}(Z)$, and $\exists I(I = X)$ follows by Lemma 6.

Proof of the Theorem. We need to show that formulas (5) and (8) are equivalent to each other. Consider all variables from the set $\{X_1, \ldots, X_m\}$ that occur in the head H of rule (4) in the scope of a function symbol. Let these variables be $X_1, \ldots, X_k$; then each of the remaining variables $X_{k+1}, \ldots, X_m$ occurs in the body of the rule in the scope of a function symbol or in a comparison of the second kind.

We will show first that the consequent H^* of (8) is equivalent to

$$\exists I(I = X_i) \to H^* \qquad (1 \le i \le k). \tag{11}$$

If H is an atom $p(\mathbf{t})$ then formula (11) is

$$\exists I(I = X_i) \to \forall \mathbf{Z}(val_{\mathbf{t}}(\mathbf{Z}) \to p(\mathbf{Z})),$$

and it is equivalent to

$$\forall \mathbf{Z}(\exists I(I = X_i) \wedge val_{\mathbf{t}}(\mathbf{Z}) \to p(\mathbf{Z}))). \tag{12}$$

Lemma 6 shows that the conjunction in the antecedent is equivalent to its second conjunctive term $val_{\mathbf{t}}(\mathbf{Z})$, so that formula (12) is equivalent to H^*. If H is $\{p(\mathbf{t})\}$ then reasoning is similar. If H is empty then $k = 0$, and there is nothing to prove.

It follows that H^* is equivalent to

$$\exists I(I = X_1) \to (\exists I(I = X_2) \to \dots (\exists I(I = X_k) \to H^*) \dots)$$

and consequently to

$$\bigwedge_{i=1}^{k} \exists I(I = X_i) \to H^*. \tag{13}$$

On the other hand, Lemmas 7 and 9 show that the formulas

$$\tau^B(B_1) \wedge \dots \wedge \tau^B(B_n) \to \exists I(I = X_i) \qquad (k + 1 \le i \le m)$$

are provable in *Int*. It follows that the antecedent

$$\tau^B(B_1) \wedge \dots \wedge \tau^B(B_n)$$

of (8) is equivalent to

$$\bigwedge_{i=k+1}^{m} \exists I(I = X_i) \wedge \tau^B(B_1) \wedge \dots \wedge \tau^B(B_n). \tag{14}$$

From these observations about formulas (13) and (14) we can conclude that the result (8) of applying τ^* to rule (4) is equivalent to the formula

$$\widehat{\forall} \left(\bigwedge_{i=1}^{m} \exists I(I = X_i) \wedge \tau^B(B_1) \wedge \dots \wedge \tau^B(B_n) \to H^* \right),$$

which can be further rewritten as

$$\widehat{\forall}(C \to (\tau^B(B_1) \wedge \dots \wedge \tau^B(B_n) \to H^*)). \tag{15}$$

From Lemmas 1(iii, iv, v), 2, 4, 5 we can conclude that formula (15) is equivalent to

$$\widehat{\forall}(C \to (\nu'(B_1) \land \cdots \land \nu'(B_n) \to \nu'(H))).$$

The only part of the last formula that contains any of the variables X_i is C. Consequently that formula is equivalent to

$$\widehat{\forall}\left(\bigwedge_i \exists X_i(I_i = X_i) \to (\nu'(B_1) \land \cdots \land \nu'(B_n) \to \nu'(H))\right).$$

Since the antecedent $\bigwedge_i \exists X_i(I_i = X_i)$ is provable in *Int*, it can be dropped, which leads us to formula (5).

8   Discussion

It was observed long ago that the head and body of a rule are similar to the consequent and antecedent of an implication, and that choice expressions are similar to excluded middle formulas. For instance, the rule

$$\{q(X)\} \leftarrow p(X)$$

is similar to the formula

$$p(X) \to q(X) \lor \neg q(X).$$

The definition of the translation ν allows us to extend this analogy to regular rules containing arithmetic operations and comparisons:

1. A variable in a regular rule is similar to a variable for integers if it occurs at least once in the scope of a function symbol or in a comparison of the second kind. Otherwise it is similar to a variable for arbitrary precomputed terms.
2. The equal sign in a comparison of the second kind, such as $X = \overline{1}..\overline{5}$, is similar to the membership symbol: it expresses that the integer denoted by the left-hand side is an element of the set denoted by the right-hand side.
3. The atom in the head of a regular rule that contains the interval symbol, such as $q(\overline{1}..X, \overline{1}..Y)$, is similar to a universally quantified formula.

Acknowledgements. Thanks to Jorge Fandinno, Michael Gelfond, Yuliya Lierler, Torsten Schaub, and the anonymous referees for useful comments.

References

1. Gebser, M., et al.: Potassco User Guide, Version 2.0. https://potassco.org (2015)
2. Gebser, M., Harrison, A., Kaminski, R., Lifschitz, V., Schaub, T.: Abstract Gringo. Theory Pract. Logic Program **15**, 449–463 (2015)
3. Lifschitz, V., Lühne, P., Schaub, T.: Verifying strong equivalence of programs in the input language of Gringo. In: Proceedings of the 15th International Conference on Logic Programming and Non-monotonic Reasoning (2019)

4. Lifschitz, V., Pearce, D., Valverde, A.: A characterization of strong equivalence for logic programs with variables. In: Proceedings of International Conference on Logic Programming and Nonmonotonic Reasoning (LPNMR), pp. 188–200 (2007)
5. Fandinno, J., Lifschitz, V., Lühne, P., Schaub, T.: Verifying tight programs with Anthem and Vampire. Theory Pract. Logic Program. **20**, 735–750 (2020)
6. Lifschitz, V., Morgenstern, L., Plaisted, D.: Knowledge representation and classical logic. In: van Harmelen, F., Lifschitz, V., Porter, B. (eds.) Handbook of Knowledge Representation, pp. 3–88. Elsevier, Amsterdam (2008)

DualGrounder: Lazy Instantiation via Clingo Multi-shot Framework

Yuliya Lierler and Justin Robbins$^{(\boxtimes)}$

University of Nebraska at Omaha, Omaha, NE 68182, USA
{ylierler,justinrobbins}@unomaha.edu

Abstract. Answer set programming (ASP) is a declarative programming paradigm that is geared towards difficult combinatorial search problems. Sometimes, run times of ASP systems suffer due to so called grounding bottleneck. Lazy grounding solvers aim to mitigate this issue. In this paper we describe a new lazy grounding solver called DUAL-GROUNDER. The DUALGROUNDER system leverages multi-shot capabilities of the advanced ASP platform CLINGO. This paper also includes experimental data to explore the performance of DUALGROUNDER compared to similar ASP grounding and solving systems.

Keywords: ASP · Lazy grounding · Multishot solving

1 Introduction

Answer Set Programming (ASP) [3] is a prominent declarative programming paradigm that aims to solve difficult search problems by describing problem's specifications by means of a logic program and solving the resulting program. The process of solving ASP programs – logic programs under answer set semantics – typically involves two stages depicted in Fig. 1. To describe these stages let us recall that a logic program consists of rules. When a program contains variables we call it a non-ground program, and ground otherwise. During the first stage of program's processing each rule of a logic program is converted into respective ground rules (rules without variables) in a process called *grounding*. This process involves substituting variables with all possible constant values that variables of given rules could have. The second stage is concerned with the search of so called *answer sets* (sets of ground atoms representing solutions) of the constructed ground program. The basic way of performing this process is to (i) utilize a grounder, for instance, the GRINGO system [10] to ground an ASP program, and then (ii) pipe the output to a solving system such as CLASP [11] or WASP [2]. However, grounding some programs may prove to be a bottleneck in applying ASP technology. Converting a rule with variables into rules with respective constants may require, in the worst case scenario, a substitution of every possible combination of program's constants into the rule. *"Lazy ASP"* methods such as implemented in systems ASPERIX [12], GASP [7], and OMIGA

© Springer Nature Switzerland AG 2021
W. Faber et al. (Eds.): JELIA 2021, LNAI 12678, pp. 435–441, 2021.
https://doi.org/10.1007/978-3-030-75775-5_29

[8] combat this issue by altering the typical ground-solve architecture of ASP systems described here. Lazy ASP architectures delay grounding of some parts of a program until it is determined to be necessary. At times grounding these parts is never necessary. In this work, we design a lazy ASP architecture and implement it within system DUALGROUNDER, or DG, for short. It's a close relative of the WASP-based lazy ASP systems proposed and advocated in [5,6]. The novelty of the DG tool is its reliance on the CLINGO multi-shot framework [9]. This way in place of implementing in house procedures for grounding and solving in various stages of lazy approach we rely on existing instances of GRINGO and CLASP withing the CLINGO multi-shot architecture. Here we describe the exact architecture of the DG system and provide the experimental analysis of the approach comparing it to its close relatives.

Fig. 1. Typical ASP system architecture.

2   Preliminaries

A *logic/ASP program* is a finite set of rules of the form

$$h_1 \mid \cdots \mid h_n \leftarrow a_1, \ldots a_l, \; not \; a_{l+1}, \ldots, \; not \; a_m, \qquad (1)$$

where $m, n \geq 0$, h_i ($1 \leq i \leq n$) and $a_1, \ldots a_m$ are atoms. Expressions to the left hand side of an arrow and the right hand side of an arrow are called *head* and *body* of a rule, respectively. An atom, literal, or rule is *ground* if it has no variables within terms occurring in it. We call a rule a *fact* if its body is empty ($m = 0$). A rule is a *constraint* if its head is empty ($n = 0$); in this case we can identify it with the symbol $\perp$. We say that a rule is *disjunctive* if its head has multiple atoms ($n > 1$). Intuitively, constraints are meant to capture a condition – by means of a set of literals – that should *not* take place in a valid solution to the problem. We assume that a reader is familiar with the definition of an answer set of a (ground) logic program and refer to the paper by Lifschitz et al. [13] for details. One crucial result that constitutes a theoretical basis for this work is the following theorem by Lifschitz et al. [13]:

Theorem 1 (Theorem on Constraints). *For a ground program P and a set C of constraints so that $C \subseteq P$, a set X of atoms is an answer set of P iff X is an answer set of program $P \setminus C$ and X satisfies every constraint in C.*

It tells us that when a program contains constraints we may split a task of computing its answer sets into two subtasks. In the first subtask, we are concerned with finding answer sets of a program resulting from the original program some of whose constraints are removed. In the second subtask, we are concerned with checking that these constraints are satisfied. Grounding a logic program with variables replaces each rule with all its instances obtained by substituting the object constants occurring in the program, for all variables. For a program P, by $ground(P)$ we denote the result of its grounding. *Answer sets* of a logic program P with variables are the answer sets of ground program $ground(P)$. It is easy to see how the theorem on constraints generalizes to the case of programs with variables.

In the introduction we presented a common architecture for processing logic programs. Yet, modern answer set solvers are complex software systems that are designed to accommodate a number of potential uses that go beyond their typical utilization. For example, such answer set solvers as CLASP and WASP allow for something that we will denote *incremental solving*. Incremental ASP-solving allows the user to solve several ground logic programs $P_1, P_2, \ldots, P_n$ one after another (possibly in an "online" mode when an instance of a solver is never terminated but rather is put "on-hold" while preserving its internal search state), if P_{i+1} results from P_i by adding ground constraints. In this case the search for a solution to P_{i+1} may benefit from the knowledge obtained during solving $P_1, \ldots, P_i$ sequence.

3   System DG

Lazy Instantiation by Cuteri et al. [5,6]. Here we review a lazy instantiation method for finding answer sets of a program, studied by Cuteri et al. [5]. The method separates a program P into a program composed of a predetermined subset of its constraints C, and a program composed of the remaining rules $P_{nc} = P \setminus C$. Program P_{nc} is processed using the typical ground and solve process depicted in Fig. 1, except on the onset of solving an instance of an ASP solver capable of incremental solving is considered. As a result an answer set M of P_{nc} is computed. This answer set M is then checked against the constraints in C. If all of the ground instances of the constraints in C are satisfied by M, then M is returned by the method as an answer set of P. Otherwise, ground instances of constraints that are violated by the candidate model are provided to an incremental ASP solver to proceed with the search. The process is repeated up to the point when we are able to either claim that a found M is indeed an answer set of P or establish that P has no answer sets. It is easy to see that at any point of computation an incremental solver is dealing with some subset of $ground(P)$. There are two interesting peculiarities of the approach studied by Cuteri et al. [5]. First, the process of checking current answer set M of some subset of $ground(P)$ against the appropriate set of constraints stemming from C is a custom program produced automatically for each unique problem. In particular, the authors illustrated the case study on three benchmarks. The authors implemented such a check individually for each benchmark via a specialized propagator interface provided by such answer set solvers as CLASP and WASP.

Second, the process of computing ground instances of constraints at hand to extend incrementally solved program was once more implemented by a custom program designed for each problem. Cuteri et al. [5] demonstrated positive results for their case study. Cuteri et al. [6] make the approach described above problem/benchmark independent. They developed an answer set solver based on lazy instantiation method described here that is problem agnostic. In other words, their method is able to utilize constraints of C to implement "a propagator" and then "a grounder" for these constraints to communicate with an incremental solver at hand. C++ is used to implement procedures of above mentioned propagator and grounder based on the information provided by constraints in C.

DG *Specifics*. The DG system mimics the efforts by Cuteri et al. [6]. The key difference in our undertaking is the utilization of the available off the shelf tools for the task of grounding (in particular, GRINGO) rather than implementing a custom solution for this purpose. Implementation of system DG relies on the CLINGO multi-shot framework [9] in a way that the key computational tasks are executed by instances of grounding and solving routines available via this framework. Thus, the role of DG is to orchestrate these routines. First, system DG separates given program P into two parts: a program composed of a specified subset of its constraints C, and a program composed of the remaining rules $P_{nc} = P \setminus C$. Second, system DG rewrites constraints in C procedurally. We use an example to illustrate this rewriting. Assume a sample constraint :- p1(X), p2(Y), not p3(X,Y). Rule p1'1_p2'2_not'p3'12'(X,Y):- p1(X), p2(Y), not p3(X,Y). is used in place of this constraint. Constraints in C rewritten in this way result in program C'. Third, DG orchestrates the back-and-forth communication of two major subroutines that we call MAIN-GS and AUX-G (program C' plays a crucial role in the workings of the AUX-G component).

MAIN-GS: A grounder-solver pair MAIN-GS is responsible for incremental solving procedure of DG. It is first applied to P_{nc} to compute one answer set M; this answer set is then used within the second subroutine AUX-G to either (i) establish that this set M of atoms is indeed an answer set of P or (ii) compute ground constraints due to C that are violated by M; these constraints are then added incrementally to the logic program of MAIN-GS and a solver of MAIN-GS is instructed to find a new answer set to repeat the described process.

AUX-G: The AUX-G routine is responsible for supplying ground instances of constraints in C violated by the "candidate" answer set M given by MAIN-GS. Each time AUX-G subroutine is called it uses a new instance of a grounder GRINGO supplying it with a new program to ground. Component AUX-G calls grounder GRINGO on program $C' \cup M$ (here we identify set M of atoms with the set of facts constructed from its elements). Due to the inner workings of GRINGO and structure of program $C' \cup M$, GRINGO's output consists of M together with the facts such as p1'1_p2'2_not'p3'12'(4,5) (following our earlier example). Facts of the form p1'1_p2'2_not'p3'12'(4,5) are translated procedurally by system DG into constraints of the form :- p1(4), p2(5), not p3(4,5). Such constraints are added incrementally to the MAIN-GS grounder-solver pair of DG.

If given some candidate answer set M, GRINGO invoked on $C' \cup M$ returns M itself, the DG system returns M to the user as it is indeed the answer set to the given program P as no constraints in C are violated.

4 Experimental Evaluation

Our experiments were run on a Linux machine, where each instance's runtime was limited to 10 min and given 16 GB of memory to work with. The benchmark called *Packing* was given an extended 30 min cutoff. Table 1 summarizes the outcomes of our experimental analysis. The dualgrounder implementation used for the experiments can be found at https://www.unomaha.edu/college-of-information-science-and-technology/natural-language-processing-and-knowl edge-representation-lab/software/dualgrunder.php. We now provide the details on considered systems and benchmarks. In parenthesis we give abbreviations used in Table 1. We tested two variants of DG, one with default CLINGO settings (*DG-Clingo*) and another with settings/flags that emulate the heuristics of the WASP solver (*DG-Wasp*) This was done to enable better comparison with other systems used in our experiments. We provide run times of systems CLINGO, WASP, CLINGO with a lazy propagator (*Clingo-Lazy*) [5], WASP with a lazy propagator (*Wasp-Lazy*) [5], and the partial compilation system (*Partial-Comp*) [6]. We used three benchmarks to assess performance of the DG system: *Stable Marriage*, *Natural Language Understanding*, and *Packing*. These benchmarks come from the experimental analysis by Cuteri et al. [5,6]. We refer the reader to these papers for exhaustive details about these benchmarks; the constraints selected for lazy grounding mirror those chosen in these papers. Here we only include few remarks on these problems.

Stable Marriage (SM). Our experiments utilize the 2013 encoding of Stable Marriage from the fourth ASP competition [1]. The lazily grounded constraint for SM checks to see if a couple would rather be with someone else than each other:

```
:- match(M,W1), manAssignsScore(M,W,Smw), W1 != W, , Smw > Smw1,
   manAssignsScore(M,W1,Smw1) match(M1,W),Swm >= Swm1,
   womanAssignsScore(W,M,Swm), womanAssignsScore(W,M1,Swm1).
```

Natural Language Understanding (NLU). First introduced by Schüller [14], the NLU benchmark determines the solution to first order horn clause abduction problems under a variety of cost functions. These cost functions are the cardinality minimality (*card*), cohesion (*coh*), and weight abduction (*wa*) functions. The lazily grounded constraint for these problems ensures transitivity between equation atoms: `:- eq(A,B), eq(B,C), not eq(A,C).`

Packing. The third benchmark in the DG experiments is the packing problem, in which the goal of the problem is to pack a number of different squares into a rectangular area such that none of their areas overlap. This problem is the same as the packing problem in the third ASP competition [4]. The constraints

that check for overlap between each defined square and those that check square
positions are difficult to ground, so they are lazily evaluated:

```
:- pos(I,X,Y), pos(I,X1,Y1), X1 != X.
:- pos(I,X,Y), pos(I,X1,Y1), Y1 != Y.
:- pos(I1,X1,Y1), square(I1,D1), pos(I2,X2,Y2), square(I2,D2),
   I1!=I2, W1=X1+D1, H1=Y1+D1, X2>=X1, X2<W1, Y2>=Y1, Y2<H1.
```

Table 1. Experimental test results; the average execution time is displayed along with
the number of timed out instances for each system and benchmark.

	SM(210)	card(50)	coh(50)	wa(50)	Packing(50)
Clingo	**229.307 (26)**	74.613 (5)	67.303 (7)	78.069 (7)	1521.853 (49)
Clingo-Lazy	142.992 (91)	5.761 (0)	6.211 (0)	6.472 (0)	556.457 (31)
DG-Clingo	93.168 (80)	**2.197 (0)**	2.718 (0)	3.193 (0)	415.834 (38)
DG-Wasp	94.814 (116)	2.374 (0)	**2.598 (0)**	**2.785 (0)**	417.251 (38)
Wasp	186.613 (55)	111.309 (3)	112.397 (3)	135.637 (2)	1550.349 (46)
Partial-Comp	27.613 (64)	5.049 (0)	15.311 (2)	51.757 (1)	**447.513 (28)**
Wasp-Lazy	11.606 (68)	3.078 (0)	23.292 (1)	37.657 (1)	306.962 (38)

Results Discussion. The goal of our experimentation was to evaluate the performance of the DG system. Table 1 presents the experimental outcomes. The
number following the benchmark names is the total number of the instances
considered. The numbers in columns are average run times of the systems on
instances that did not timeout. The number in parenthesis specifies number of
timed out instances.

For the NLU tests (columns card, coh, wa), DG tends to perform slightly
better than other lazy grounding systems, while systems that did not utilize lazy
grounding fell behind by a large margin. The NLU benchmark seems to benefit
greatly from the removal of its "problem" rules. DG's slightly higher performance
when compared to other lazy grounding systems seems to mostly stem from the
lack of overhead in DG when a solution is produced on the first cycle; if a solution
is found, no constraints are constructed and the program ends. In contrast to
the NLU benchmark, DG's performance on the Stable Marriage and Packing
benchmarks drops significantly compared to the other tested systems, especially
on SM. We believe this is due to the string processing done by the system during
constraint construction, and by the increased overhead caused by using Python
over the C++ code used by, for example, the Part-Comp approach. For Stable
Marriage, this is compounded by the fact that the problem is not a good fit
for the lazy grounding approach, as all of the lazy grounding systems hit slower
execution times than the base CLINGO or WASP systems. The Packing problem
presents a problem that is very difficult for both the base systems and the lazy
grounding systems; none of the tested systems were able to solve all of the
tested instances. The performance of DG seems comparable to that of its lazy
grounding peers that overall outperform CLINGO and WASP.

Conclusions and Acknowledgements. We trust that the DG system is a valuable representative among the class of lazy grounding systems. We also see its great value in showcasing how CLINGO multi-shot framework can be used in apparently "unintended" and meaningful ways. The work was partially supported by NSF grant 1707371.

References

1. Alviano, M., et al.: The fourth answer set programming competition: preliminary report. In: Cabalar, P., Son, T.C. (eds.) Logic Programming and Nonmonotonic Reasoning, pp. 42–53. Springer, Heidelberg (2013). https://doi.org/10.1007/978-3-642-40564-8_5

2. Alviano, M., Dodaro, C., Faber, W., Leone, N., Ricca, F.: WASP: a native ASP solver based on constraint learning. In: Cabalar, P., Son, T.C. (eds.) LPNMR 2013. LNCS (LNAI), vol. 8148, pp. 54–66. Springer, Heidelberg (2013). https://doi.org/10.1007/978-3-642-40564-8_6

3. Brewka, G., Eiter, T., Truszczyński, M.: Answer set programming at a glance. Commun. ACM **54**(12), 92–103 (2011)

4. Calimeri, F., Ianni, G., Ricca, F.: The third open answer set programming competition. Theory Pract. Logic Program. **14**(1), 117–135 (2014). https://doi.org/10.1017/S1471068412000105

5. Cuteri, B., Dodaro, C., Ricca, F., Schüller, P.: Constraints, lazy constraints, or propagators in ASP solving: an empirical analysis. Theory Pract. Logic Program. **17**(5–6), 780–799 (2017)

6. Cuteri, B., Dodaro, C., Ricca, F., Schüller, P.: Partial compilation of ASP programs. Theory Pract. Logic Program. **19**(5–6), 857–873 (2019). https://doi.org/10.1017/S1471068419000231

7. Dal Palù, A., Dovier, A., Pontelli, E., Rossi, G.: GASP: answer set programming with lazy grounding. Fundam. Inform. (2009). https://doi.org/10.3233/FI-2009-180

8. Dao-Tran, M., Eiter, T., Fink, M., Weidinger, G., Weinzierl, A.: OMiGA : an open minded grounding on-the-fly answer set solver. In: del Cerro, L.F., Herzig, A., Mengin, J. (eds.) JELIA 2012. LNCS (LNAI), vol. 7519, pp. 480–483. Springer, Heidelberg (2012). https://doi.org/10.1007/978-3-642-33353-8_38

9. Gebser, M., Kaminski, R., Kaufmann, B., Schaub, T.: Multi-shot ASP solving with cingo. Theory Pract. Logic Program. **19**(1), 27–82 (2019). https://doi.org/10.1017/S1471068418000054

10. Gebser, M., Kaminski, R., König, A., Schaub, T.: Advances in *gringo* series 3. In: Delgrande, J.P., Faber, W. (eds.) LPNMR 2011. LNCS (LNAI), vol. 6645, pp. 345–351. Springer, Heidelberg (2011). https://doi.org/10.1007/978-3-642-20895-9_39

11. Gebser, M., Kaufmann, B., Schaub, T.: Conflict-driven answer set solving: from theory to practice. Artif. Intell. **187**, 52–89 (2012)

12. Lefèvre, C., Nicolas, P.: The first version of a new ASP solver: ASPeRiX (2009). https://doi.org/10.1007/978-3-642-04238-6_52

13. Lifschitz, V., Tang, L.R., Turner, H.: Nested expressions in logic programs. Ann. Math. Artif. Intell. **25**, 369–389 (1999)

14. Schüller, P.: Modeling variations of first-order horn abduction in answer set programming. Fundam. Inform. **149**(1–2), 159–207 (2016). https://doi.org/10.3233/FI-2016-1446

A Multi-shot ASP Encoding for the Aircraft Routing and Maintenance Planning Problem

Pierre Tassel[1]([⊠]) and Mohamed Rbaia[2]

[1] University of Klagenfurt, Klagenfurt, Austria
pierre.tassel@aau.at
[2] Amadeus IT Group, Villeneuve-Loubet, France
mohamed.rbaia@amadeus.com

Abstract. The Aircraft Routing and Maintenance Planning problems are integral parts of the airline scheduling process. We study these relevant combinatorial optimization problems from the perspective of Answer Set Programming (ASP) modeling and solving. In particular, we contrast traditional single-shot ASP solving methods to a novel multi-shot solving approach geared to discover near-optimal solutions to sub-problems of increasing granularity rapidly. As it turns out, our multi-shot solving techniques can heavily speed up the optimization process without deteriorating the solution quality compared to single-shot solving. We also provide a customizable instance generator and a solution viewer to facilitate intensive investigation of Aircraft Routing and Maintenance Planning as a benchmark problem. However, our multi-shot solving techniques are not limited to this benchmark alone, and the underlying ideas can be naturally applied to a variety of scheduling problems.

1 Introduction

Combinatorial optimization problems are usually solved in a single shot. Still, we can sometimes decompose them into sub-problems (for example, with a time-window approach [17]) that are then solved with local search. In this paper, we present an approach to solve the Aircraft Routing and Maintenance Planning problem in Answer Set Programming (ASP) [4,9] by decomposing it with a time-window approach using a paradigm called multi-shot solving [10]. Multi-shot ASP solving methods have already been successfully applied in areas like automated planning [7], automated theorem proving [11], human-robot interaction [6], multi-robot (co)operation [19], and stream reasoning [15]. Presumably closest to our work, proposing multi-shot solving techniques to increase the granularity of hard combinatorial optimization problems successively, is the *Asprin* system [3] that implements complex user preferences by sequences of queries, yet without decomposing the underlying problem representation.

An airline operator scheduling process is divided into six major steps [13], sometimes seen as independent sub-problems, sometimes with or without communication between the sub-problems.

This paper also appeared at the 13th Workshop on Answer Set Programming and Other Computing Paradigms (ASPOCP 2020).

© Springer Nature Switzerland AG 2021
W. Faber et al. (Eds.): JELIA 2021, LNAI 12678, pp. 442–457, 2021.
https://doi.org/10.1007/978-3-030-75775-5_30

1. **Flight Schedule Preparation**: The airline designs a set of flights to perform, choosing which airports to serve, at which frequencies to maximize the profit.
2. **Fleet Assignment**: Define the type of aircraft that should perform each specific flight. Each type of aircraft has different characteristics: total number of seats, fuel consumption, number of first-class seats, number of crew members needed to perform the flight, etc.
3. **Aircraft Routing**: Each flight gets a specific aircraft assigned to it, and a sequence of flights assigned to the same plane forms a route. We need to respect some constraints like airport turnaround time (called **TAT**): This is the minimum time on ground between two consecutive flights required to perform operations preparing the aircraft for the next flight. Another condition is **airport continuity**: The start airport of an aircraft's next flight is the same as the end airport of the previous flight.
4. **Maintenance Planning**: We assign **maintenance slots** to each aircraft to respect limits defined by a certain number of cycles (i.e., flights), the number of hours from the last maintenance, or hours of flight. Maintenance can only be performed at specific airports (with required equipment and skill-set), they have a minimum duration, and they need to be performed before the aircraft has reached the limit. A good solution usually maximizes the usage of the aircraft.
5. **Crew Scheduling**: Assign a crew to cover each flight while respecting all legal restrictions. A good solution also tries to fulfill all crew members' preferences.
6. **Disruption Recovery**: Manage the disruption events happening on the day of operation due to unforeseen events such as bad weather conditions, crew strikes, aircraft mechanical failures, airport closure, etc. minimize the impact of different actions like cancellations, delays, diversions, etc. on passenger services.

We aim to solve the Aircraft Routing and Maintenance Planning in the third and fourth item together, considering one type of maintenance to perform every seven days on each aircraft. It is possible to add other types of maintenances that deal with different due limits (e.g., cycles and hours of flight) without too much overhead, but it is out of this paper's scope. Our encoding can find a solution when there is no perfect route that respects all **TAT** constraints. We show how to address this problem with ASP using multi-shot solving, and we implement our approach with *Clingo* [8].

This paper is organized as follows. In Sect. 2, we begin with brief introductions of solving techniques for Aircraft Routing and Maintenance Planning from the literature and of ASP. Section 3 presents our customizable instance generator along with a solution viewer enabling comprehensive benchmarking. In Sect. 4, we develop and experimentally evaluate a variety of multi-shot ASP solving techniques for near-optimal Aircraft Routing and Maintenance Planning. Finally, Sect. 5 concludes the paper.

2 Background

In this section, we first introduce the works previously done in Aircraft Routing and Maintenance Planning, and then we give a brief introduction on ASP.

2.1 Aircraft Routing and Maintenance Planning

Aircraft Routing is usually considered as a feasibility problem, which is NP-hard and can be reduced to a multi-commodity flow problem [18]. Its combination with Maintenance Planning can be viewed as an Euler tour problem with side constraints [14].

Either kind of problem is usually solved using mixed-integer programming, formulated as a multi-commodity flow problem with one commodity per aircraft and side constraints related to maintenance allocation [12, 16]. There are two principal models (where maintenance slots can be understood as flights from and to the same airport):

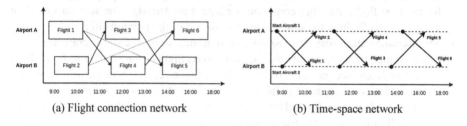

(a) Flight connection network   (b) Time-space network

Fig. 1. Two principal models used for aircraft routing and maintenance planning

1. **Flight connection network** (Fig. 1a): In abscissa the time, in ordinate the airport, each flight is a node, and there is an arc between two flights if they are compatible, i.e., the end airport of flight A is the same as the start airport of flight B, and flight A ends before the departure of flight B [12].
2. **Time-space network** (Fig. 1b): In abscissa the time, in ordinate the airport, each node is an airport at a given time, i.e., flight start or end. Also, there is an arc between two nodes if there is a corresponding flight from one airport to another [20].

2.2 Answer Set Programming

Answer Set Programming (ASP) is a declarative paradigm oriented towards solving combinatorial problems [4, 9]. We represent a problem as a logic program, and the solutions are given by models called answer sets. ASP systems like *Clingo* [8] and *DLV* [5] use a grounder to replace variables with constants and a solver to search for answer sets.

A logic program consists of atoms, literals, and rules. An atom is a proposition, literals are atoms with or without default negation in front of them, and a *rule* is an implication

$$a_1 \mid ... \mid a_n \leftarrow b_1, ..., b_m, not\ c_1, ..., not\ c_o.$$

where $a_1 \mid ... \mid a_n$ is a disjunction of literals called *head*, and $b_1, ..., b_m, not c_1, ..., not c_o$ is the *body*. From the body, we can derive that the head must be true. A special case of disjunctive rules with head $a_1 \mid not\ a_1$ are *choice* rules written as

$$\{a_1\} \leftarrow b_1, ..., b_m, not\ c_1, ..., not\ c_o.$$

This means that a_1 can but need not be derived from the body of the rule. A rule with an empty head is called a *constraint*, and it forbids the body to be true:

$$\leftarrow b_1, \ldots, b_m, \text{ not } c_1, \ldots, \text{ not } c_o.$$

Multi-shot ASP solving is an iterative approach geared for problems where the logic program is continuously changing [10]. In this paper, we use multi-shot solving to decompose the optimization process into a sequence of queries of increasing complexity.

3   Instance Generator

The following subsections discuss how instances for our benchmarks are generated, using the generator provided at [1]. We start by introducing the parameters of the instance generator, then explain the allocation of maintenance slots to obtain a draft solution, further, describe how a cost indicating the draft solution's quality is calculated, and finally, we present a visual solution format.

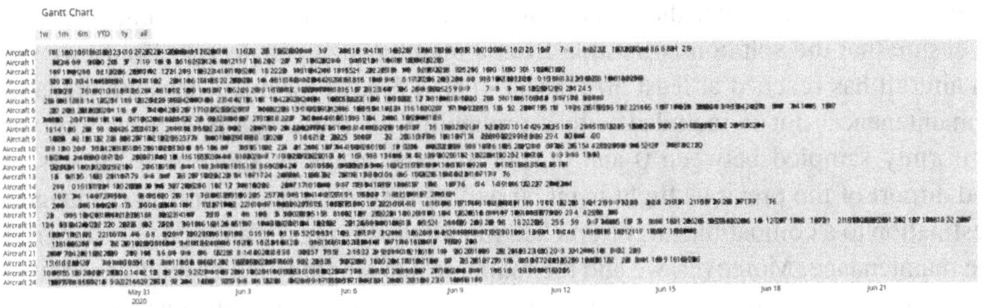

Fig. 2. Gantt chart giving an impression of the draft solution used to generate an instance

3.1   Parametric Generation

We have developed an instance generator that can create random instances along with draft solutions. To make the problem difficult enough to be interesting, we generate quite big instances configured with the following parameters:

Parameter	Value
Number of aircrafts	25
Number of airports	30
Maintenance due limit	7 days
Airports able to perform maintenance	5
Length of maintenance	4 h
Number of flights per aircraft	$20 \leq X \sim \mathcal{N}(50, 10) \leq 80^a$
Length of flights	$80 \leq X \sim \mathcal{N}(140, 120) \leq 600$ min
Length of flights' **TAT**	$30 \leq X \sim \mathcal{N}(45, 10) \leq 60$ min
Ground time between two flights	$0 \leq X \sim \mathcal{N}(240, 120) \leq 1000$ min

$^a \mathcal{N}(\mu, \sigma^2)$ denotes a normal probability distribution of mean μ and standard deviation σ.

We prevent the creation of flights with the same origin and destination but different flight lengths or **TAT** so that the length and **TAT** will be the same for all flights between the same airports. Our benchmark suite comprises 20 random instances. Such instances are quite large in order to make optimal Aircraft Routing and Maintenance Planning challenging. While detailed inspection of a draft solution like the one displayed in Fig. 2 would be intricate, we can still observe that the numbers of flights and resulting time spans of aircrafts' routes vary significantly. As a consequence, we obtain a planning period stretching almost over one month, which necessitates the allocation of a high number of maintenance slots.

3.2   Maintenance Allocation

Initial maintenance counters, expressing the time left before performing maintenance at the start of a route, are generated following a truncated normal distribution with a mean of 3.5 days, a standard deviation of 1 day, a minimum of 0, and a maximum of 6 days. While the generator builds the flight routes of a solution, it also places maintenance slots to ensure that the solution is feasible from a maintenance perspective. To do so, when an aircraft has reached at least 50% usage (i.e., 3.5 days for our 7 days maintenance), a maintenance slot is included with a probability of the usage plus a random value uniformly sampled between 0 and 0.5, or 1 if the usage is above 90%. In case the end airport of the previous flight is incompatible with the maintenance, we change the destination to a compatible airport, picked randomly among the airports able to perform the maintenance. Moreover, we add the maintenance length to the ground time between consecutive flights (meaning that we can have more ground time than needed).

The draft solution generated along with an instance witnesses that all flights can be routed and maintenance due limits are respected. Instead of the entire routes, the generated instance fixes the first flight for each aircraft and dates of remaining flights only, accompanied by information about initial maintenance counters, airports at which maintenance can be performed, the maintenance length, and due limit. That is, allocating aircraft to all but the first flights of routes and incorporating maintenance slots is subject to Aircraft Routing and Maintenance Planning.

3.3   Solution Cost

Along with the actual instance, our generator reports its draft solution together with a cost indicating the solution quality. The latter is calculated as the sum of cost 500 for each **TAT** violation (i.e., too short turnaround time) and 101 for each maintenance slot, where the ratio reflects a higher priority of avoiding **TAT** violations and the odd cost of 101 is taken to facilitate the reading of the number of maintenance slots contained in the draft solution. This information can be used for analysis, considering that the draft solution does not include **TAT** violations and is thus optimal from a flight routing perspective, yet potentially sub-optimal from a maintenance perspective. However, the quality of the draft solution can be assumed to be rather good, given that the usage of each aircraft is at more than 50% before maintenance is performed.

3.4 Solution Viewer

To inspect a solution, we support exporting a graphical representation of it as a Gantt chart (Fig. 2a and Fig. 3). Every flight is represented by a bar, using a unique color for each pair of origin and destination airport, and maintenance slots after flights are indicated similarly. The tail at the right of each (non-maintenance) bar represents the **TAT** of a flight, and a next flight covering part of this tail would point out a **TAT** violation. Each row gives the route of a separate aircraft, with the first flight on the very left and further flights and maintenance slots to the right.

4 ASP-Based Aircraft Routing and Maintenance Planning

In this section, we present our multi-shot ASP encoding for Aircraft Routing and Maintenance Planning. We then introduce a variety of hyper-parameters for multi-shot ASP solving and experimentally evaluate their impact on the solution quality and convergence of the optimization process.

4.1 Problem Encoding

As customary in ASP, we model Aircraft Routing and Maintenance Planning by facts describing a problem instance along with a general first-order encoding specifying (optimal) solutions. Our modeling approach follows the idea of flight connection networks,[1] where two flights can be connected if they are compatible (i.e., flight A arrives before flight B departs from the destination airport of flight A). In the following, we present a simplified yet logically similar version of the full encoding provided at [1].

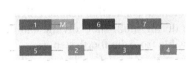

(a) Gantt chart for a small instance

```
flight(1, 1, 366701, 3, 379361).  tat(1, 4520).
flight(2, 3, 385901, 1, 392321).  tat(2, 3300).
flight(3, 1, 401861, 3, 414521).  tat(3, 4520).
flight(4, 3, 421961, 1, 428381).  tat(4, 3300).
flight(5, 1, 366417, 3, 379077).  tat(5, 4520).
flight(6, 3, 391617, 2, 404517).  tat(6, 2640).
flight(7, 2, 409497, 1, 422517).  tat(7, 3300).
first(1, 1).  first(5, 2).
maintenance(seven_day).
airport_maintenance(seven_day, 3).
length_maintenance(seven_day, 9000).
start_counter(seven_day, 366701, 416288, 1).
start_counter(seven_day, 366417, 470841, 2).
limit_counter(seven_day, 604800).
```

(b) ASP facts for the instance shown in Fig. 3a

Fig. 3. Chart and facts for an Aircraft Routing and Maintenance Planning instance

Figure 3a sketches (the optimal solution to) the small Aircraft Routing and Maintenance Planning instance described by the facts in Fig. 3b. We have the flights 1 to 7,

---

[1] We have also devised prototype encodings based on time-space networks and observed drastically increased difficulty of finding feasible routings that incorporate all flights. Hence we chose flight connection networks as basic principle of problem encodings to elaborate further.

declared by facts of the flight/5 predicate whose first argument is the flight identifier, the second stands for the start airport, the third for the start time, the fourth for the destination airport and the fifth for the arrival time. For each of the seven flights, a fact of the tat/2 predicate provides the **TAT** required before the next flight on the route of some aircraft, e.g., 4520 time units (resembling about 75 min) for flight 1. Two facts of the first/2 predicate indicate that flight 1 is the first on the route of aircraft 1, and similarly flight 5 for aircraft 2. The remaining facts address conditions for a maintenance kind labeled seven_day, declared by a fact of maintenance/1. Such maintenance can be performed at airport 3 and requires at least 9000 units of ground time (amounting to 2.5 h), as expressed by facts of the predicates airport_maintenance/2 and length_maintenance/2. The two facts of start_counter/4 denote initial time periods in which the seven_day maintenance is (still) covered: This period stretches from time 366701 to 416288 for aircraft 1, and from 366417 to 470841 for aircraft 2. Finally, the fact of the limit_counter/2 predicate expresses that 604800 time units (7 days) get covered when seven_day maintenance is performed for an aircraft. The (optimal) routing, depicted in Fig. 3a, happens to be such that aircraft 1 takes the flights 1, 6 and 7 with a maintenance slot after flight 1, while aircraft 2 does the remaining flights in the order 5, 2, 3 and 4.

Our multi-shot ASP encoding in Fig. 4 starts by defining constants for levels and weights to penalize **TAT** violations and maintenance slots along the routes of aircrafts. In addition, the constant time_window is crucial for when to consider compatible flight connections in a routing, and the value 3600 expresses that the gap admitted between the arrival and departure of connected flights shall be successively increased by windows of one hour. This gap is reflected by the TIME_G and WINDOW arguments in atoms of the compatible/6 predicate (line 6–11). E.g., we derive the atoms compatible(1,3,379361,2,6540,2) and compatible(1,3,379361,6, 12256,4), indicating a ground time of 6540 time units between the arrival of flight 1 at time 379361 and the departure of flight 2 from airport 3, while this ground time amounts to 12256 time units for flight 6. Given the window size of 3600 time units, the last argument in both atoms expresses that the potential connection between flight 1 and 2 shall be considered from the second step on during multi-shot solving, and the connection continuing with flight 6 becomes admissible from the fourth step on.

The second kind of auxiliary atoms derived from the facts of an instance, those of the maintainable/5 predicate (line 13–18), provide flights FLIGHT1 with their arrival TIME such that performing MAINTENANCE after them covers (later) flights whose arrival and departure times lie in the interval from TIME_M to TIME_N. For our instance in Fig. 3b, we obtain maintainable(seven_day,1,379361,388361,984161) and maintainable(seven_day,5,379077,388077,983877), signaling the possibility of seven_day maintenance after flight 1 and 5, both of which arrive at airport 3 and admit connections to later flights with more than the maintenance length of 9000 time units in-between. Unlike that, performing seven_day maintenance after flight 3, which also arrives at airport 3, would be meaningless because its single available connection with flight 4 does not include sufficient ground time, i.e., 7440 time units only, so that no maintainable/5 atom is derived for flight 3.

```
1   % constants for levels and weights of costs, and time window for connections
2   #const level_tat = 2.              #const weight_tat = 1.
3   #const level_maintenance = 1.  #const weight_maintenance = 1.
4   #const time_window = 3600.
5   % compatible flights with number of time window
6   compatible(FLIGHT1, AIRPORT_E1, TIME_E1, FLIGHT2, TIME_G, WINDOW) :-
7       flight(FLIGHT1, AIRPORT_S1, TIME_S1, AIRPORT_E1, TIME_E1),
8       flight(FLIGHT2, AIRPORT_E1, TIME_S2, AIRPORT_E2, TIME_E2),
9       not first(FLIGHT2, _),
10      TIME_G = TIME_S2 - TIME_E1, 0 <= TIME_G,
11      WINDOW = TIME_G / time_window + 1.
12  % feasible maintenance slots after flights
13  maintainable(MAINTENANCE, FLIGHT1, TIME, TIME_M, TIME_N) :-
14      compatible(FLIGHT1, AIRPORT, TIME, FLIGHT2, TIME_G, WINDOW),
15      airport_maintenance(MAINTENANCE, AIRPORT),
16      length_maintenance(MAINTENANCE, LENGTH), LENGTH <= TIME_G,
17      limit_counter(MAINTENANCE, LIMIT),
18      TIME_M = TIME + LENGTH, TIME_N = TIME + LIMIT.

20  % declare incrementally generated routing as external
21  #external route(FLIGHT1, FLIGHT2, TIME_G, WINDOW) :
22      compatible(FLIGHT1, AIRPORT, TIME, FLIGHT2, TIME_G, WINDOW).
23  % enforce routing sequences that include all flights
24  :- flight(FLIGHT1, AIRPORT_S, TIME_S, AIRPORT_E, TIME_E),
25      #count{FLIGHT2 : route(FLIGHT1, FLIGHT2, TIME_G, WINDOW)} > 1.
26  :- flight(FLIGHT2, AIRPORT_S, TIME_S, AIRPORT_E, TIME_E),
27      not first(FLIGHT2, _),
28      #count{FLIGHT1 : route(FLIGHT1, FLIGHT2, TIME_G, WINDOW)} != 1.
29  % propagate assigned planes along routing
30  assign(FLIGHT1, PLANE) :-
31      first(FLIGHT1, PLANE).
32  assign(FLIGHT2, PLANE) :-
33      assign(FLIGHT1, PLANE), route(FLIGHT1, FLIGHT2, TIME_G, WINDOW).

35  % generate maintenance slots for planes
36  {maintain(MAINTENANCE, TIME, TIME_M, TIME_N, PLANE)} :-
37      maintainable(MAINTENANCE, FLIGHT, TIME, TIME_M, TIME_N),
38      assign(FLIGHT, PLANE).
39  % get covered flights from initial and dynamic maintenance slots
40  covered(MAINTENANCE, FLIGHT, PLANE) :-
41      start_counter(MAINTENANCE, TIME_M, TIME_N, PLANE),
42      flight(FLIGHT, AIRPORT_S, TIME_S, AIRPORT_E, TIME_E),
43      TIME_M <= TIME_S, TIME_E <= TIME_N.
44  covered(MAINTENANCE, FLIGHT, PLANE) :-
45      maintain(MAINTENANCE, TIME, TIME_M, TIME_N, PLANE),
46      flight(FLIGHT, AIRPORT_S, TIME_S, AIRPORT_E, TIME_E),
47      TIME_M <= TIME_S, TIME_E <= TIME_N.
48  % enforce coverage of all flights
49  :- maintenance(MAINTENANCE), assign(FLIGHT, PLANE),
50      not covered(MAINTENANCE, FLIGHT, PLANE).
51  % associate costs with dynamic maintenance slots
52  :~ maintain(MAINTENANCE, TIME, TIME_M, TIME_N, PLANE).
53      [weight_maintenance@level_maintenance, TIME, PLANE]

55  #program step(t).   % incremental program to generate routing
56  % generate new flight connections for current time window
57  {route(FLIGHT1, FLIGHT2, TIME_G, t)} :-
58      compatible(FLIGHT1, AIRPORT, TIME, FLIGHT2, TIME_G, t).
59  % enforce sufficient ground time for dynamic maintenance slots
60  :- compatible(FLIGHT1, AIRPORT, TIME, FLIGHT2, TIME_G, t),
61      maintainable(MAINTENANCE, FLIGHT1, TIME, TIME_M, TIME_N),
62      length_maintenance(MAINTENANCE, LENGTH), TIME_G < LENGTH,
63      maintain(MAINTENANCE, TIME, TIME_M, TIME_N, PLANE),
64      assign(FLIGHT2, PLANE).
65  % associate costs with TAT violations
66  :~ route(FLIGHT1, FLIGHT2, TIME_G, t), tat(FLIGHT1, TAT), TIME_G < TAT.
67      [weight_tat@level_tat, FLIGHT1]
```

Fig. 4. Multi-shot ASP encoding for aircraft routing and maintenance planning

While flight connections are to be made available step-wise during multi-shot solving, an **#external** declaration introduces respective atoms of the `route/4` predicate (line 21–22) right at the beginning. This avoids need for re-instantiating conditions expressed by **#count** aggregates (line 24–28), enforcing a routing with at most one (direct) successor per flight and exactly one predecessor for flights that are not the first on the route of any aircraft, in case new compatible connections become admissible in a step. The same applies to rules for the `assign/2` predicate (line 30–33), which trace connections given by atoms of `route/4` and associate each flight with its corresponding aircraft. Maintenance slots can then be scheduled for aircrafts assigned to flights indicated by the `maintainable/5` predicate, and the arguments TIME_M and TIME_N in `maintain/5` atoms provide the respective time period covered (line 36–38). The flights included in the initial interval or by performing maintenance for an aircraft are signaled by atoms of the predicate `covered/3` (line 40–47), where a subsequent constraint makes sure that each assigned flight is indeed covered (line 49–50). Reconsidering the instance in Fig. 3b, the initial seven_day maintenance period for aircraft 2 includes all flights that can belong to its route, while the flights 4 and 7 exceed the initial interval for aircraft 1. Hence, aircraft 1 needs to be maintained after its first flight, as indicated by the atom `maintain(seven_day,379361,388361,984161,1)` in an (optimal) answer set. The allocation of maintenance slots is however penalized by a weak constraint (line 52–53), and the particular instance :   `maintain(seven_day,379361, 388361,984161,1). [1@1,379361,1]` associates the weight 1 at level 1 with the maintenance of aircraft 1 at time 379361.

In contrast to the upper part of the encoding in Fig. 4, the one below the **#program** directive is instantiated in steps during multi-shot solving, where t is replaced by successive integers starting from 1. The choice rule for `route/4` atoms (line 57–58), which were declared external before, then allows for taking the connections newly admitted at the current step or integer for t, respectively. E.g., `route(1,2,6540,2)` is introduced as a potential connection in the second step, and `route(1,6,12256,4)` in the fourth step. The subsequent constraint enforces sufficient ground time when a maintenance slot is allocated in-between two connected flights (line 60–64).[2] This rules out `route(1,2,6540,2)` for an aircraft subject to seven_day maintenance after flight 1, as it is the case for aircraft 1 whose first flight is 1. Hence, the routing given by an (optimal) answer set is such that the flights 1, 6 and 7 are assigned to aircraft 1, and aircraft 2 takes 5, 2, 3 and 4. One can check that this schedule does not involve **TAT** violations, which would otherwise be penalized by a weak constraint according to the corresponding level and weight (line 66–67). As the greatest step associated with some flight connection in the routing happens to be 4 (indicated by the last argument in `route(1,6,12256,4)`), the multi-shot encoding requires four steps to lead to an answer set, which then describes an optimal solution for the instance in Fig. 3b.

Finally, let us note that a traditional single-shot version can be easily derived from the more sophisticated multi-shot encoding in Fig. 4 by simply omitting the WINDOW and t arguments from atoms related to flight connections, as well as dropping the

---

[2] Our full encoding, provided with the Python multi-shot solving script at [1], includes a more general version of this constraint that is also able to deal with multiple maintenance kinds.

`#external` and `#program` declarations. A respective single-shot encoding is also provided at [1].

4.2 Basic Multi-shot Solving Approach

The main bottleneck of flight connection networks is the large number of arcs when flights with long ground times in-between are taken as connection candidates, e.g., linking the first flight arriving at an airport to the last flight in the planning period departing from it. Such connections could be dropped by imposing a hard constraint on the maximum admissible ground time, yet to the risk of ruling out (optimal) solutions up to making Aircraft Routing and Maintenance Planning infeasible for tricky instances where some connection with long ground time has to be taken.

Rather than constraining ground times, our multi-shot ASP solving approach successively increases the maximum ground time of the considered connections over iterations. For guaranteeing the progress to connections with longer ground times (and eventually all connections), we limit the runtime allotted for optimizing the routing and maintenance allocation in each iteration by means of the following intra-iteration stop criterion: An iteration is aborted when the empirically determined timeout of 60 s for finding some better solution is reached, in which case we continue to the next iteration with an increased maximum ground time of connections. This strategy's rationale is to avoid getting stuck on infeasible sub-problems when the admissible ground time is yet too small in the first iterations or on (near-)optimal solutions that can neither be improved nor verified as optimal in a reasonable runtime. Note that the timeout is reset to 60 s whenever the optimization comes up with a better solution, as we do not want to abort iterations in phases where the optimization makes progress. Upon proceeding to the next iteration, either due to timeout or search space exhaustion, we check that new connections become admissible, or increase the maximum ground time further without relaunching the optimization otherwise. Moreover, the cost of the best solution found so far, if any, is passed on as upper bound to admit better solutions only.

Our experiments consider the 20 random instances whose generation has been described in the previous subsection. As time window for increasing the maximum ground time of connections, we use the value `3600` (one hour), corresponding to the default of our encoding in Fig. 4. Unless noted otherwise, we also stick to the level `2` for weight constraints penalizing **TAT** violations, and the smaller level `1` for maintenance slots implies strictly lower priority of minimizing their number, where each maintenance slot or **TAT** violation is counted with the weight `1`. Note that this scheme is different from the weighted sum taken to calculate the cost of a draft solution in Sect. 3.3, and we reuse the latter for comparability when plotting solution costs in the sequel. All experiments were run with *Clingo* version 5.4.0, each run limited to one hour wall clock time, on an Ubuntu 18.04 machine with two 8-Core Intel Xeon E5520 processors and 48 GB RAM.[3]

---

[3] We also took *Acyc2solver* [21] to translate our single-shot encoding to mixed-integer programming and tried IBM's *CPLEX*. Unfortunately, *CPLEX* could not find any solution in one hour.

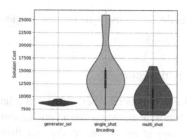

Fig. 5. Solution costs for single-shot and multi-shot solving

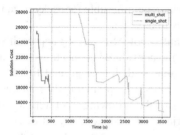
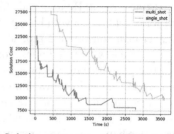

(a) Solution costs per runtime for instance 14   (b) Solution costs per runtime for instance 15

Fig. 6. Instance-wise solution costs per runtime for single-shot and multi-shot solving

Figure 5 plots the costs of best solutions found in one hour with traditional single-shot solving, where the full problem with all flight connections is considered, and with our (basic) multi-shot solving approach in relation to the costs of draft solutions generated together with the instances. Although multi-shot solving with its intra-iteration stop criterion merely probes the search space of sub-problems without guaranteeing that a globally optimal solution will be obtained, it usually finds better solutions than single-shot solving in the time limit, and sometimes its best solution also improves on the draft solution that is of good quality by construction.

Figure 6a and b show the optimization progress in detail for two representative instances, where single-shot solving leads to a better solution for one instance and multi-shot solving for the other.[4] We observe that multi-shot solving finds its solutions much faster and gets then stuck on unsuccessful iterations aborted after 60 s each. Tackling the full problem by single-shot solving makes finding the first feasible routing and then achieving improvements much harder and time-consuming, so that granting non-negligible runtime is a necessity to obtain solutions of good quality. Notably, all runs exhaust the time limit of one hour due to the size and combinatorics of instances.

---

[4] Occasionally rising solution cost over time is due to the weighted sum function used for plotting the solution quality, while the optimization strictly reduces **TAT** violations in such cases and also leads to lower weighted sum values in the long run.

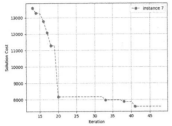
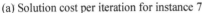

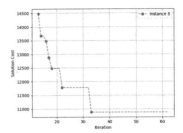

(a) Solution cost per iteration for instance 7   (b) Solution cost per iteration for instance 8

Fig. 7. Instance-wise solution cost per iteration for multi-shot solving

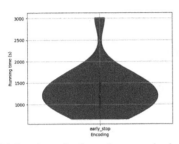
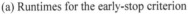

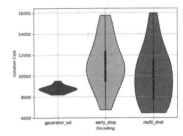

(a) Runtimes for the early-stop criterion   (b) Solution costs for the early-stop criterion

Fig. 8. Runtimes and solution costs for the early-stop criterion

4.3 Early-Stop Multi-shot Solving Approach

Picking two representative instances again, Fig. 7a and b indicate the optimization progress over the iterations of multi-shot solving, where we observe substantial improvements by step-wise increases of the maximum ground time at the beginning, followed by little and then no improvement at all for a substantial number of unsuccessful iterations aborted after 60 s. This suggests the addition of an inter-iteration stop criterion to avoid spending time on unpromising iterations, and our early-stop multi-shot solving approach thus aborts the entire run after timing out without any improvement for three iterations in a row. The deliberate stop of runs constitutes a trade-off between solution quality and computational efforts, and the number of three consecutive timeouts of iterations without improvement is again problem-specific and determined empirically.

The plot in Fig. 8a shows that runtimes are indeed substantially reduced by early-stop multi-shot solving, with the median around 20 min instead of fully exhausting the one hour per instance. Comparing the solution costs in Fig. 8b yields a rather modest quality decline in exchange for runtime savings, which can presumably be tolerated in application scenarios where the time taken for decision making is critical.

4.4 Weighted Sum vs Level Cost Function

The results reported so far rely on distinct priority levels for **TAT** violations and maintenance allocation, and now we compare the performance of optimization relative to the weighted sum function given in Sect. 3.3. Switching to the latter can be easily done by setting the values for the constants `level_tat`, `level_maintenance`, `weight_tat` and `weight_maintenance` used by the encoding in Fig. 4 to 1, 1, 500 and 101.

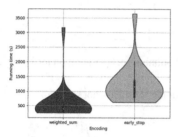
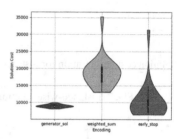

(a) Runtimes for weighted sum and level function

(b) Solution costs for weighted sum and level function

Fig. 9. Runtimes and solution costs for weighted sum and level function

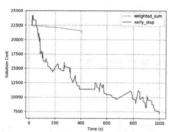
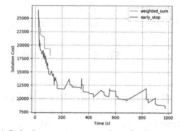

(a) Solution costs per runtime for instance 4

(b) Solution costs per runtime for instance 12

Fig. 10. Instance-wise solution costs per runtime for weighted sum and level function

Figures 9a and b plot runtimes and solution costs for early-stop multi-shot solving with either the weighted sum function or distinct priority levels to penalize **TAT** violations and maintenance slots. Switching to the weighted sum greatly reduces runtimes, yet because optimization turns out to be much harder and the three iterations in a row without improvement are reached way more quickly. Accordingly, the solution quality suffers heavily, even despite the previously considered optimization based on distinct priority levels merely approximates the weighted sum function used for plotting and now in the optimization process as well. The quick outage of improvements after more or less substantial progress in the first iterations becomes also apparent on the detailed inspections of two instances in Fig. 10a and b. We conjecture that higher weighted sum values due to incorporating costs from several sources at the same level complicate recognizing and discarding partial assignments that can eventually not lead to any improvement, so that more search efforts are spent on such fruitless assignments.

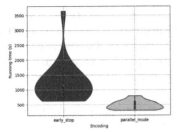

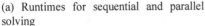

(a) Runtimes for sequential and parallel solving

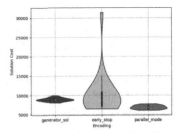

(b) Solution costs for sequential and parallel solving

Fig. 11. Runtimes and solution costs for sequential and parallel solving

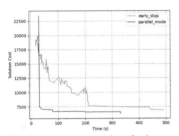

(a) Solution costs per runtime for instance 0

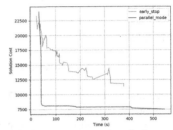

(b) Solution costs per runtime for instance 11

Fig. 12. Instance-wise solution costs per runtime for sequential and parallel solving

4.5 Parallel Solving

While we merely considered single-threaded *Clingo* before, it also allows for running multiple solver threads with complementary search strategies in parallel. The remarkably reduced runtimes and solution costs obtained with eight parallel solver threads are summarized in Fig. 11a and b. Notably, the best solutions found by early-stop multi-shot solving with parallel threads consistently improve on the draft solutions for instances, thus showing that high-quality results can be achieved with reasonable computational efforts. Figure 12a and b additionally plot the much more rapid optimization progress for two representative instances. This robustness is certainly related to the parallel use of complementary search strategies, also considering that the discovery of a better solution by one thread resets the timeout to another 60 s for all threads.

5 Conclusion

The Aircraft Routing and Maintenance Planning problem lends itself to multi-shot ASP solving based on successively increasing ground times of flight connections, given that long ground times are undesirable in practice and should thus be avoided if possible. A direct use of the incremental mode shipped with *Clingo* [10] would be (too) risky though, as it minimizes the number of iterations and can easily get stuck on hard sub-problems. We instead aim at discovering near-optimal solutions in an affordable time, so that approximating solution costs by means of (easier to optimize) priority levels, also found to be advantageous for shift design [2], and interrupting exhaustive iterations, as likewise done in automated planning [7], can be tolerated. The hyper-parameters we used for aborting iterations or entire runs are clearly problem-specific and need re-tuning when switching to another application, where related scheduling problems may benefit from similar techniques as well, so that a general tool supplying them can be valuable. Hence, as future work we plan to generalize our approach and experiment with additional optimization problems.

Acknowledgments. This work was partially funded by KWF project 28472, cms electronics GmbH, FunderMax GmbH, Hirsch Armbänder GmbH, incubed IT GmbH, Infineon Technologies Austria AG, Isovolta AG, Kostwein Holding GmbH, and Privatstiftung Kärntner Sparkasse. We thank the anonymous reviewers for helpful comments.

References

1. https://github.com/prosysscience/Aircraft_Scheduling
2. Abseher, M., Gebser, M., Musliu, N., Schaub, T., Woltran, S.: Shift design with answer set programming. Fundam. Inform. **147**(1), 1–25 (2016)
3. Brewka, G., Delgrande, J., Romero, J., Schaub, T.: asprin: customizing answer set preferences without a headache. In: Proceedings of the AAAI Conference on Artificial Intelligence, pp. 1467–1474. AAAI Press (2015)
4. Brewka, G., Eiter, T., Truszczyński, M.: Answer set programming at a glance. Commun. ACM **54**(12), 92–103 (2011)
5. Calimeri, F., Dodaro, C., Fuscà, D., Perri, S., Zangari, J.: Efficiently coupling the I-DLV grounder with ASP solvers. Theory Pract. Logic Program. **20**(2), 205–224 (2020)
6. Chen, K., Lu, D., Chen, Y., Tang, K., Wang, N., Chen, X.: The intelligent techniques in robot *KeJia*–the champion of RoboCup@Home 2014. In: Bianchi, R.A.C., Akin, H.L., Ramamoorthy, S., Sugiura, K. (eds.) RoboCup 2014. LNCS (LNAI), vol. 8992, pp. 130–141. Springer, Cham (2015). https://doi.org/10.1007/978-3-319-18615-3_11
7. Dimopoulos, Y., Gebser, M., Lühne, P., Romero, J., Schaub, T.: Pasp 3: towards effective ASP planning. Theory Pract. Logic Program. **19**(3), 477–504 (2019)
8. Gebser, M., et al.: Potassco User Guide. University of Potsdam (2019). https://potassco.org
9. Gebser, M., Kaminski, R., Kaufmann, B., Schaub, T.: Answer Set Solving in Practice. Morgan & Claypool Publishers (2012). https://www.cs.uni-potsdam.de/wv/publications/DBLP_series/synthesis/2012Gebser.html
10. Gebser, M., Kaminski, R., Kaufmann, B., Schaub, T.: Multi-shot ASP solving with clingo. Theory Pract. Logic Program. **19**(1), 27–82 (2019)
11. Gebser, M., Sabuncu, O., Schaub, T.: An incremental answer set programming based system for finite model computation. AI Commun. **24**(2), 195–212 (2011)
12. Grönkvist, M.: The tail assignment problem. Ph.D. thesis, Chalmers University of Technology (2005)
13. Jamili, A.: A robust mathematical model and heuristic algorithms for integrated aircraft routing and scheduling, with consideration of fleet assignment problem. J. Air Transp. Manage. **58**, 21–30 (2017)
14. Liang, Z., Chaovalitwongse, W.: The aircraft maintenance routing problem. In: Chaovalitwongse, W., Furman, K., Pardalos, P. (eds.) Optimization and Logistics Challenges in the Enterprise, vol. 30, pp. 327–348. Springer, Boston (2009). https://doi.org/10.1007/978-0-387-88617-6_12

15. Obermeier, P., Romero, J., Schaub, T.: Multi-shot stream reasoning in answer set programming: a preliminary report. Open J. Databases **6**(1), 33–38 (2019)
16. Orhan, İ., Kapanoğlu, M., Karakoç, T.: Concurrent aircraft routing and maintenance scheduling. J. Aeronaut. Space Technol. **5**(1), 73–79 (2011)
17. Ovacik, I., Uzsoy, R.: Decomposition Methods for Complex Factory Scheduling Problems. Springer, New York (2012). https://doi.org/10.1007/978-1-4615-6329-7
18. Roy, K., Tomlin, C.: Solving the aircraft routing problem using network flow algorithms. In: Proceedings of the American Control Conference, pp. 3330–3335. IEEE (2007)
19. Schäpers, B., Niemueller, T., Lakemeyer, G., Gebser, M., Schaub, T.: ASP-based time-bounded planning for logistics robots. In: Proceedings of the International Conference on Automated Planning and Scheduling, pp. 509–517. AAAI Press (2018)
20. Vaaben, B., Larsen, J.: Mitigation of airspace congestion impact on airline networks. J. Air Transp. Manage. **47**, 54–65 (2015)
21. Gebser, M., Janhunen, T., Rintanen, J.: Answer set programming as SAT modulo acyclicity. In: Proceedings of the Twenty-First European Conference on Artificial Intelligence, ECAI'14, pp. 351–356. IOS Press, Prague (2014)

Author Index

Printed in the United States
by Baker & Taylor Publisher Services